Introduction to Finance

Markets, Investments, and Financial Management

14th Edition

Ronald W. Melicher • Edgar A. Norton

For Indian River State College

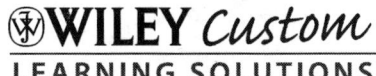

Copyright © 2012 by John Wiley & Sons, Inc.

All rights reserved.

No part of this publication may be reproduced, stored in a retrieval system or transmitted in any form or by any means, electronic, mechanical, photocopying, recording, scanning or otherwise, except as permitted under Sections 107 or 108 of the 1976 United States Copyright Act, without either the prior written permission of the Publisher, or authorization through payment of the appropriate per-copy fee to the Copyright Clearance Center, Inc., 222 Rosewood Drive, Danvers, MA 01923, website www.copyright.com. Requests to the Publisher for permission should be addressed to the Permissions Department, John Wiley & Sons, Inc., 111 River Street, Hoboken, NJ 07030-5774, (201)748-6011, fax (201)748-6008, website http://www.wiley.com/go/permissions.

To order books or for customer service, please call 1(800)-CALL-WILEY (225-5945).

Printed in the United States of America.

ISBN 978-1-118-11192-5
Printed and bound by Strategic Content Imaging.
10 9 8 7 6 5 4 3

INTRODUCTION TO FINANCE

Markets, Investments, and Financial Management

FOURTEENTH EDITION

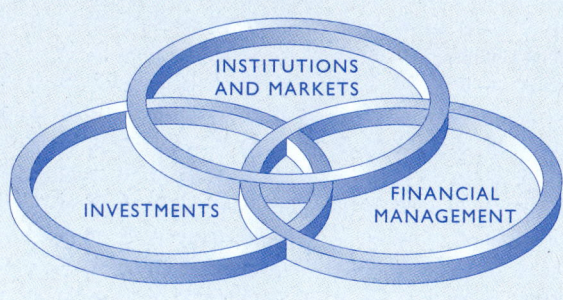

Ronald W. Melicher
Professor of Finance
University of Colorado at Boulder

Edgar A. Norton
Professor of Finance
Illinois State University

John Wiley & Sons, Inc.

*To my parents, William and Lorraine, and
to my wife, Sharon, and our children,
Michelle, Sean, and Thor*

Ronald W. Melicher

*To my best friend and wife, Becky,
and our gifts from God, Matthew and Amy*

Edgar A. Norton

VICE PRESIDENT AND PUBLISHER George Hoffman
ACQUISITIONS EDITOR Lacey Vitetta
PROJECT EDITOR Jennifer Manias
SENIOR ASSISTANT Emily McGee
MARKETING MANAGER Diane Mars
EXECUTIVE MEDIA EDITOR Allison Morris
MEDIA EDITOR Greg Chaput
CREATIVE DIRECTOR Harold Nolan
DESIGNER Kevin Murphy
PRODUCTION MANAGER Dorothy Sinclair
SENIOR PRODUCTION EDITOR Trish McFadden
PRODUCTION MANAGEMENT SERVICES Aptara®, Inc.
COVER DESIGN Michael Boland
COVER PHOTO ©Marcus Lyon/Getty Images, Inc.

This book was set in 10/12 Minion by Aptara Corp. and printed and bound by RRD/JC. The cover was printed by RRD/JC.

This book is printed on acid free paper. ∞

Copyright © 2011 John Wiley & Sons, Inc. All rights reserved. No part of this publication may be reproduced, stored in a retrieval system or transmitted in any form or by any means, electronic, mechanical, photocopying, recording, scanning, or otherwise, except as permitted under Sections 107 or 108 of the 1976 United States Copyright Act, without either the prior written permission of the Publisher, or authorization through payment of the appropriate per-copy fee to the Copyright Clearance Center, Inc., 222 Rosewood Drive, Danvers, MA 01923, (978)750-8400, fax (978)750-4470 or on the web at www.copyright.com. Requests to the Publisher for permission should be addressed to the Permissions Department, John Wiley & Sons, Inc., 111 River Street, Hoboken, NJ 07030-5774, (201)748-6011, fax (201)748-6008, or online at http://www.wiley.com/go/permissions.

Evaluation copies are provided to qualified academics and professionals for review purposes only, for use in their courses during the next academic year. These copies are licensed and may not be sold or transferred to a third party. Upon completion of the review period, please return the evaluation copy to Wiley. Return instructions and a free of charge return shipping label are available at www.wiley.com/go/returnlabel. Outside of the United States, please contact your local representative.

Library of Congress Cataloging-in-Publication Data

Melicher, Ronald W.
    Introduction to finance : markets, investments, and financial management / Ronald W. Melicher, Edgar A. Norton.—14th ed.
        p. cm.
    Includes bibliographical references and index.
    ISBN 978-0-470-56107-2 (hardback)
    1. Finance. 2. Finance—United States. I. Norton, Edgar, 1957- II. Title.
    HG173.M398 2010
    332—dc22
                                                        2010036820

ISBN-13 978-0470-56107-2
ISBN-10 0470-56107-6

Printed in the United States of America

10 9 8 7 6 5 4 3

· PREFACE ·

The fourteenth edition of *Introduction to Finance: Markets, Investments, and Financial Management* builds upon the successes of its earlier editions while maintaining a fresh and up-to-date coverage of the field of finance. Our text is designed to present a more "balanced" first course in finance—one that offers students perspectives on financial markets, investing, and financial management. After making some changes to the previous edition, on the basis of user feedback we have returned to the highly successful pedagogy that reviews markets and institutions, then the world of investments, and, finally, the concepts and applications of business financial management.

A movement has been growing to offer a more balanced first course in finance. Previous editions were developed for such an "overview" first course, and this new edition continues in that vein. Eighteen chapters cover the three major financial areas involving the financial system, investments, and business finance. For the student who does not plan to take additional courses in finance, the book provides a valuable overview of the major concepts of the discipline. For the student who wants to take additional courses in finance, the overview presented provides a solid foundation upon which future courses can build.

Introduction to Finance is meant to be used in a course whose purpose is to survey the foundations of the finance discipline. As such, it is designed to meet the needs of students in a variety of programs. Specifically, *Introduction to Finance* can be used in any of the following ways:

1. As the first course in finance at a college or university where the department wants to expose students to a broad foundational survey of the discipline.

2. As the first and only course in finance for nonfinance business students.

3. As an appropriate text to use at a school that seeks to provide liberal arts majors with a business minor or business concentration. The writing level is appropriate to provide students with a good foundation in the basics of our discipline.

4. As a "lower division" service course whose goal is to attract freshmen and sophomores to business and to even attract them to become finance majors.

The philosophy behind the book is threefold. First, we believe that a basic understanding of the complex world of finance should begin with a survey course that covers an introduction to financial markets, investments, and financial management or business finance. Students can immediately gain an integrated perspective of the interrelationships among these three areas. They will appreciate how both businesses and individuals are affected by markets and institutions, as well as how markets and institutions can be used to help meet the goals of individuals or firms. Given the events in the financial markets and the economy in 2007–2010, this integrated perspective adds value to student learning and student understanding of the field.

Second, we wrote the book as an introductory survey to the field of finance with a readable and "user-friendly" focus in mind. We seek to convey basic knowledge, concepts, and terms that will serve the nonfinance major well into the future and that will form a foundation upon which the finance major can build. Some finer points, discussions of theory, and complicated topics are reserved for "Learning Extensions" in selected chapters. We aim to make students using our text financially literate and cognizant of the richness of the field of finance. The book provides a good foundation for students to build upon in later courses in financial management, investments, or financial markets.

Third, we focus on the practice of finance in the settings of markets, investments, and financial management. We focus on the descriptive in each of these fields. We don't want students to be unable to see the forest of finance because the trees of quantitative methods obscure their view or scare them away. When we do introduce equations and mathematical concepts that are applicable to finance, we show step-by-step solutions.

By learning about markets (including gaining some knowledge about institutions), investments, and management as the three major strands of finance, students will finish their course with a greater understanding of how these three fields interrelate. Financial markets will be seen as the arena to which businesses and financial institutions go to raise funds and as the mechanism through which individuals can invest their savings to meet their future goals. The topic of investments is important in facilitating the savings-investment process. Understanding the trade-off of risk and return, as well as the valuation of bonds and stocks, is essential to both investors and businesses trying to raise financial capital. Understanding how securities markets work is equally important. Financial management uses information it obtains from securities and other financial markets to efficiently and profitably manage assets and to raise needed funds in a cost-efficient manner.

A broad exposure to the discipline of finance will meet the needs of the nonmajor who should know the basics of finance so that he or she can read the *Wall Street Journal*, visit business-related Internet sites, and analyze other business information sources intelligently. It will also help the nonfinance major work effectively as a member of a cross-functional work team—a team that will include finance professionals. In addition, this overview of the field of finance will start the finance major off on the right foot. Rather than receiving a compartmentalized idea of finance—often viewed through the corporate finance lens that many texts use—the finance major will receive a practical introduction to the different disciplines of finance and will better appreciate their relationships to one another.

Part 1 of the book contains six chapters on the financial system, with primary emphasis on financial markets and the tools and skills necessary to better understand how such markets work. We begin with an overview of the three main subfields of finance, identify the "six principles of finance," and discuss career opportunities. The principles of finance are that (1) money has a time value, (2) higher returns are expected for taking on more risk, (3) diversifying one's investments can reduce risk, (4) financial markets are efficient in pricing securities, (5) the objectives of managers and stockholders may differ, and, finally, (6) reputation matters. We discuss the topic of finance and the role and functions of the financial system to a nation's economy. The role of banks, other financial intermediaries, and the Federal Reserve are reviewed, as are their functions in the financial system. Part 1 also introduces the international role of finance and how modern economies are affected by exchange rates, trade, and the flow of global funds.

Following this introduction to the financial system, Part 2 focuses on investments. We review the role of savings in an economy and the ways in which funds flow to and from different sectors. Interest rates are introduced, and the discussion centers on making the student aware of the different influences on the level of interest rates and why the rates change over time. Because interest rates measure the cost of moving money across time, this section reviews basic time-value-of-money concepts with many worked-out examples, including the keystrokes that students can use with financial calculators. Next, after reviewing the characteristics of bonds and stocks, students learn to apply time-value-of-money concepts to find the prices of these securities. Continuing our overview of investments, we discuss the basics of investment banking and the operations of securities markets, as well as the fundamentals of investment risks and returns to conclude Part 2. Advanced classes may want to review the basics of financial derivatives, which are explained in a learning extension to Chapter 11's discussion of securities markets.

The raising of funds by businesses in the institutional and market environments is covered in Parts 1 and 2. Next, in Part 3, the final six chapters of the text introduce students to financial management. The discussion begins with the different ways in which to organize a business and the financial implications of each organizational form. We introduce accounting concepts such as the balance sheet, income statement, and statement of cash flows with simple examples. Financial ratios, which assist in the process of analyzing a firm's strengths and weaknesses, are also discussed. We review their use as a means to help managers plan ahead for future asset and financing needs. Strategies for managing a firm's current assets and current liabilities are examined, as are the funding sources firms use to tap the financial markets for short-term financing. Finally, we introduce students to the basics of capital budgeting and to capital structure concepts.

New and Improved. . . .

The content of *Introduction to Finance* has been updated to incorporate many of the economic and financial events of the past few years. The financial crisis of 2007–2009 and the subsequent recession provide a means to highlight causes, effects, and the integration of finance into our everyday lives as well as the implications for markets, investments, and business finance. A *financial crisis* margin icon is placed next to relevant text material.

We continue our innovation from previous editions by featuring a real firm—Walgreens, the retail drugstore chain—in many of the chapters on investments and financial management as a means of presenting and analyzing data.

In addition to these broad improvements, all of the chapters have been updated and revised; specific notable changes in this fourteenth edition include the following:

Chapter 1, The Financial Environment, has been rewritten to incorporate the history and implications of the 2007–2009 financial crisis. Due to the role played by the real estate market in some aspects of the crisis, the chapter features a new section on mortgage markets.

Chapter 2, Money and the Monetary System, has been updated and now includes materials on money market securities.

Chapter 3, Banks and Other Financial Institutions, features new material on the 2007–2009 financial crisis and a new discussion of bank management.

Chapter 4, Federal Reserve System, describes the current structure and operations of the Fed. Reorganized chapter material improves the clarity of the presentation. Discussion is provided on the roles of past and current chairs of the Fed Board of Governors in establishing monetary policy and leading the Federal Reserve System.

Chapter 5, Policy Makers and the Money Supply, incorporates the recent financial crisis and recession and fiscal and monetary responses to the crisis.

Chapter 6, International Finance and Trade, updates information on the European Union and the euro and on how the international monetary system evolved. Ethics is integrated into this chapter by highlighting differences across cultures and countries.

Chapter 7, Savings and Investment Process, continues to incorporate the causes and consequences of the financial crisis, especially the increased use of debt by consumers to financing their spending.

Chapter 8, Interest Rates, discusses the factors that explain differences in interest rates at a point in time as well as over time. We review default risk and default risk premiums and their role in affecting the interest rates and issuance of "junk" or high-yield bonds.

Chapter 9, Time Value of Money, conveys the importance of compounding (earning interest on interest) in building wealth over time. We present numerous examples showing how to do the calculations with formulas, with interest factor tables, step-by-step financial calculator keystrokes, and Excel spreadsheets, both with formulas keyed in by the user and with Excel's preprogrammed financial functions. The financial crisis is incorporated into this chapter in a discussion of real estate mortgage loans with monthly payments.

Chapter 10, Bond and Stocks: Characteristics and Valuations, contains updated data and improved discussions of bonds and stocks. We also have revised the discussion of bond characteristics, including TIPS (Treasury Inflation Protected Securities). Spreadsheet examples show how to apply time value concepts to calculate bond prices and stock prices.

Chapter 11, Securities Markets, incorporates changes in securities trading, including changes in NYSE–Euronext operations with the replacement of "specialists" with "designated market makers."

Chapter 12, Financial Return and Risk Concepts, is one of the more mathematical chapters; it shows how to do calculations with step-by-step calculator keystrokes and spreadsheet functions.

Chapter 13, Business Organization and Financial Data, features data from Walgreens' financial statements. In response to the financial crisis, we review problems with using stock options as an incentive mechanism for managers.

Chapter 14, Financial Analysis and Long-term Financial Planning, now uses Walgreens and the retail drugstore industry in a practical example of financial ratio analysis.

Chapter 15, Managing Working Capital, expands the discussion of managing cash in a difficult business environment and inappropriate tools to make a firm's working capital look larger than it is on the balance sheet date.

Chapter 16, Short-term Business Financing, was revised to improve pedagogy and to update the material. It contains information on real firms' working capital financing strategies and on the implications of the financial crisis on a firm's ability to obtain short-term financing.

Chapter 17, Capital Budgeting Analysis, combines two chapters from the previous edition into one chapter dealing with capital budgeting issues. The difficulty of estimating cash flows is emphasized in light of recent economic events. We relate the cash flow estimation process for a project to the firm's statement of cash flows from Chapter 13.

Chapter 18, Capital Structure and the Cost of Capital, contains updated discussions of trends in the use of debt by corporations and of the practical difficulties of estimating financing costs in volatile economic environments.

LEARNING AND TEACHING AIDS

The fourteenth edition of *Introduction to Finance* offers the following aids for students and instructors:

CHAPTER OPENERS: Each chapter begins with:

- Chapter Learning Objectives, which students can use to review the chapter's main points and which instructors can use as a basis for in-class lecture or discussion;
- Where We Have Been statements that remind students of what was covered in the previous chapters;
- Where We Are Going previews coverage of chapters to come;
- How Does This Chapter Apply To Me? explains how the content of the chapter, no matter how technical or business specific, has applications to the individual student.

APPLYING FINANCE TO. . . : Boxes show how the topic of each chapter relates to the finance fields of institutions and markets, investments, and financial management.

INTERNET MARGIN NOTES: We direct the student to relevant Web sites at different points in each chapter.

MARGIN DEFINITIONS: Margin definitions of key terms are provided to assist students in learning the language of finance.

CONCEPT CHECKS: These features appear in the margins near the end of every section to quiz students on what they have just learned and how well they've learned it. Concept Checks reinforce the topical material and help students determine what they need to review.

MARGIN ICONS: These are placed in the margin to indicate discussions of finance principles, implications of the recent financial crisis, financial or business ethical issues, and global or international discussions.

SPREADSHEET ILLUSTRATIONS: We show how to use spreadsheets to solve problems and to teach students about the power of spreadsheet functions and analysis.

BOXED FEATURES: Throughout the book, boxes are used to focus on current topics or applications of interest. They are designed to illustrate concepts and practices in the dynamic field of finance.

- Small Business Practice boxes highlight aspects of the chapter topics relating directly to small businesses and entrepreneurship.
- Career Opportunities in Finance boxes provide information about various careers in finance and appear in many chapters.
- Personal Financial Planning boxes provide insight into how the chapter's content can be applied to an individual's finances.

CAREER PROFILES: These items feature individuals who, in an interview format, discuss their jobs and the skills needed to obtain positions in different areas of finance. Some of the positions reviewed are trust officer, business valuation analyst, money manager, collections manager, treasurer, and venture capitalist. Our hope is that the Career Profiles will stimulate discussion and interest so that students will consider pursuing a career in the finance area.

LEARNING EXTENSIONS: Chapter appendixes, called Learning Extensions, are included in many chapters. Learning Extensions provide additional in-depth coverage of topics related to their respective chapters, and many challenge students to use their mathematical skills.

END-OF-CHAPTER MATERIALS: Each chapter provides:

- end-of-chapter Discussion Questions that review chapter material;
- problems for students to solve and exercise their mathematical skills; and
- special challenge problems that are more difficult and that should be solved by using spreadsheets.

COMPANION WEB SITE: The text's Web site at www.wiley.com/college/melicher contains a myriad of resources and links, to aid both learning and teaching.

INSTRUCTOR'S MANUAL AND TEST BANK: The Instructor's Manual is available to adopters of this text. It features detailed chapter outlines, lecture tips, and answers to end-of-chapter questions and problems. The manual also includes an extensive test bank of over 1,500 true–false and multiple-choice examination questions with answers, newly revised and expanded for this edition by Daniel Borgia of Florida Gulf Coast University.

COMPUTERIZED TEST BANK: This program is for use on a PC running Windows. The Computerized Test Bank contains content from the test bank provided within a Test Generating Program that allows instructors to customize their exams.

POWERPOINT PRESENTATIONS: Created by the authors, a PowerPoint presentation is provided for each chapter of the text. Slides include outline notes on the chapter, additional presentation topics, and figures and tables from the text.

STUDENT PRACTICE QUIZZES: New for this edition, Lisa Johnson of Centura College, has created a set of quizzes for students to practice their knowledge and understanding of each chapter. These multiple-choice quizzes are auto-graded to provide students with instant feedback on their work.

SPREADSHEET SOFTWARE: A set of Lotus- and Excel-compatible templates, developed by Robert Ritchey of Texas Tech University, are available on the text Web site. Students can use the templates to help solve some of the end-of-chapter problems and challenge problems.

ACKNOWLEDGMENTS

We would like to thank the Wiley Publishing team of Acquisitions Editor Lacey Vitetta, Project Editor Jennifer Manias, and Editorial Assistant Emily McGee for their role in preparing and publishing the fourteenth edition of *Introduction to Finance*.

In addition, we are especially grateful to the reviewers of this and previous editions for their comments and constructive criticisms:

Saul W. Adelman, *Miami University, Ohio*
Linda K. Brown, *St. Ambrose University*
Lisa Johnson, *Centura College*
Barbara L. Purvis, *Centura College*

Tim Alzheimer, *Montana State University*
Allan Blair, *Palm Beach Atlantic College*
Stewart Bonem, *Cincinnati State Technical and Community College*
Joseph M. Byers, *Community College of Allegheny County, South Campus*
Robert L. Chapman, *Orlando College*
William Chittenden, *Texas State University*
Will Crittendon, *Bronx Community College*
David R. Durst, *University of Akron*
Sharon H. Garrison, *Florida Atlantic University*
Asim Ghosh, *Saint Joseph's University*
Lester Hadsell, *University of Albany*
Irene M. Hammerbacher, *Iona College*
Kim Hansen, *Mid-State Technical College*
Jeff Hines, *Davenport College*
Jeff Jewell, *Lipscomb University*
Ed Krohn, *Miami Dade Community College*
P. John Limberopoulos, *University of Colorado–Boulder*
John K. Mullen, *Clarkson University*
Michael Murray, *Winona State University*
Michael Owen, *Montana State University*
Alan Questell, *Richmond Community College*
Ernest Scarbrough, *Arizona State University*
Amir Tavakkol, *Kansas State University*
Jim Washam, *Arkansas State University*
Howard Whitney, *Franklin University*
David Zalewski, *Providence College*

Likewise, comments from students and teachers who have used previous editions of the book are greatly appreciated, as is the assistance from the dozens of reviewers who have commented about the early editions of *Introduction to Finance*. Special recognition goes to Carl Dauten, who coauthored the first four editions, and Merle Welshans, who was a coauthor on the first nine editions of the book. Finally, and perhaps most importantly, we wish to thank our families for their understanding and support during the writing of the fourteenth edition.

Ronald W. Melicher, *Boulder, Colorado*
Edgar A. Norton, *Normal, Illinois*

• AUTHOR BIOS •

Ron Melicher is a professor of finance and previously served three different terms as chair of the Finance Division, Leeds School of Business, University of Colorado at Boulder. He earned undergraduate, M.B.A., and doctoral degrees from Washington University in St. Louis, Missouri. While at the University of Colorado, he has received several distinguished teaching awards and was designated a university-wide President's Teaching Scholar. Ron teaches corporate finance and financial strategy in the M.B.A. and Executive M.B.A. programs, in addition to entrepreneurial finance and investment banking to undergraduate students. His research has been published in major finance journals, including the *Journal of Finance, Journal of Financial and Quantitative Analysis*, and *Financial Management*. He is also the coauthor of *Entrepreneurial Finance*, third edition (South-Western/Cengage Learning).

Edgar A. Norton is professor of finance in the College of Business at Illinois State University. He holds a double major in computer science and economics from Rensselaer Polytechnic Institute and received his M.S. and Ph.D. from the University of Illinois at Urbana–Champaign. A Chartered Financial Analyst (CFA), he regularly receives certificates of achievement in the field of investments. He has consulted with COUNTRY Financial, Maersk, and the CFA Institute; does pro bono financial planning; and is a past president of the Midwest Finance Association. His research has appeared in numerous journals, such as *Financial Review, Journal of Business Venturing*, and *Journal of Business Ethics*. He has coauthored four textbooks, including *Introduction to Finance*.

• BRIEF CONTENTS •

Preface   iii

PART 1: INSTITUTIONS AND MARKETS   2

Chapter 1: The Financial Environment   4

Chapter 2: Money and the Monetary System   25

Chapter 3: Banks and Other Financial Institutions   49

Chapter 4: Federal Reserve System   79

Chapter 5: Policy Makers and the Money Supply   103

Chapter 6: International Finance and Trade   129

PART 2: INVESTMENTS   156

Chapter 7: Savings and Investment Process   158

Chapter 8: Interest Rates   179

Chapter 9: Time Value of Money   205

Chapter 10: Bonds and Stocks: Characteristics and Valuations   237

Chapter 11: Securities Markets   281

Chapter 12: Financial Return and Risk Concepts   317

PART 3: FINANCIAL MANAGEMENT   350

Chapter 13: Business Organization and Financial Data   352

Chapter 14: Financial Analysis and Long-Term Financial Planning   387

Chapter 15: Managing Working Capital   417

Chapter 16: Short-Term Business Financing   451

Chapter 17: Capital Budgeting Analysis   479

Chapter 18: Capital Structure and the Cost of Capital   521

Appendix   553

Glossary   562

Index   575

• CONTENTS •

PART 1
INSTITUTIONS AND MARKETS 2

CHAPTER 1
THE FINANCIAL ENVIRONMENT 4
WHAT IS FINANCE? 5
  TWO THEMES 6
WHY STUDY FINANCE? 6
SIX PRINCIPLES OF FINANCE 7
  TIME VALUE OF MONEY 8
  RISK VERSUS RETURN 8
  DIVERSIFICATION OF RISK 8
  FINANCIAL MARKETS ARE EFFICIENT 9
  MANAGEMENT VERSUS OWNER OBJECTIVES 9
  REPUTATION MATTERS 10
OVERVIEW OF THE FINANCIAL SYSTEM 11
  CHARACTERISTICS AND REQUIREMENTS 11
  FINANCIAL SYSTEM COMPONENTS AND FINANCIAL FUNCTIONS 12
FINANCIAL MARKETS CHARACTERISTICS 14
  MONEY AND CAPITAL MARKETS 14
  PRIMARY AND SECONDARY MARKETS 14
MAJOR TYPES OF FINANCIAL MARKETS 14
MORTGAGE MARKETS 15
  TYPES OF MORTGAGES AND MORTGAGE-BACKED SECURITIES 15
  CREDIT RATINGS AND SCORES 16
  MAJOR PARTICIPANTS IN THE SECONDARY MORTGAGE MARKETS 17
THE 2007–09 FINANCIAL CRISIS 17
CAREERS IN FINANCE 19
THE PLAN OF STUDY 21

  SUMMARY 23
  KEY TERMS 23
  DISCUSSION QUESTIONS 23
  EXERCISES 24

CHAPTER 2
MONEY AND THE MONETARY SYSTEM 25
PROCESS OF MOVING SAVINGS INTO INVESTMENTS 26
OVERVIEW OF THE MONETARY SYSTEM 27
IMPORTANCE AND FUNCTIONS OF MONEY 29
DEVELOPMENT OF MONEY IN THE UNITED STATES 30
  PHYSICAL MONEY (COIN AND PAPER CURRENCY) 30
  DEPOSIT MONEY 35
MONEY MARKET SECURITIES 36
MEASURES OF THE U.S. MONEY SUPPLY 37
  M1 MONEY SUPPLY 37
  M2 MONEY SUPPLY 39
  M3 MONEY SUPPLY 39
  EXCLUSIONS FROM THE MONEY SUPPLY 40
MONEY SUPPLY AND ECONOMIC ACTIVITY 40
INTERNATIONAL MONETARY SYSTEM 43
  SUMMARY 44
  KEY TERMS 45
  DISCUSSION QUESTIONS 45
  EXERCISES 46
  PROBLEMS 46

CHAPTER 3
BANKS AND OTHER FINANCIAL INSTITUTIONS 49
TYPES AND ROLES OF FINANCIAL INSTITUTIONS 50

xii CONTENTS

- DEPOSITORY INSTITUTIONS 51
- CONTRACTUAL SAVINGS ORGANIZATIONS 52
- SECURITIES FIRMS 53
- FINANCE FIRMS 53

OVERVIEW OF THE BANKING SYSTEM 53
- COMMERCIAL, INVESTMENT, AND UNIVERSAL BANKING 54
- FUNCTIONS OF BANKS AND THE BANKING SYSTEM 55

HISTORICAL DEVELOPMENT OF THE U.S. BANKING SYSTEM 57
- BEFORE THE CIVIL WAR 57
- ENTRY OF THRIFT INSTITUTIONS 58

REGULATION OF THE BANKING SYSTEM 58
- GENERAL BANKING LEGISLATION 58
- THE SAVINGS AND LOAN CRISIS 60
- PROTECTION OF DEPOSITORS' FUNDS 61

STRUCTURE OF BANKS 62
- BANK CHARTERS 62
- DEGREE OF BRANCH BANKING 63
- BANK HOLDING COMPANIES 63

THE BANK BALANCE SHEET 64
- ASSETS 65
- LIABILITIES AND OWNERS' CAPITAL 68

BANK MANAGEMENT 68
- LIQUIDITY MANAGEMENT 69
- CAPITAL MANAGEMENT 70
- 2007–09 FINANCIAL CRISIS 72

INTERNATIONAL BANKING AND FOREIGN SYSTEMS 73
- SUMMARY 75
- KEY TERMS 75
- DISCUSSION QUESTIONS 76
- EXERCISES 76
- PROBLEMS 77

CHAPTER 4
FEDERAL RESERVE SYSTEM 79

THE U.S. BANKING SYSTEM PRIOR TO THE FED 80
- WEAKNESSES OF THE NATIONAL BANKING SYSTEM 80
- THE MOVEMENT TO CENTRAL BANKING 81

STRUCTURE OF THE FEDERAL RESERVE SYSTEM 82
- MEMBER BANKS 82
- FEDERAL RESERVE DISTRICT BANKS 84
- BOARD OF GOVERNORS 85
- FEDERAL OPEN MARKET COMMITTEE 85
- ADVISORY COMMITTEES 86
- ROLE OF THE CHAIR OF THE FED BOARD OF GOVERNORS 86

MONETARY POLICY FUNCTIONS AND INSTRUMENTS 87
- OVERVIEW OF RESPONSIBILITIES 87
- RESERVE REQUIREMENTS 88
- DISCOUNT RATE POLICY 90
- OPEN-MARKET OPERATIONS 92
- IMPLEMENTATION OF MONETARY POLICY 93

FED SUPERVISORY AND REGULATORY FUNCTIONS 93
- SPECIFIC SUPERVISORY RESPONSIBILITIES 93
- SPECIFIC REGULATORY RESPONSIBILITIES 94

FED SERVICE FUNCTIONS 94
- THE PAYMENTS MECHANISM 94
- TRANSFER OF CREDIT 99
- OTHER SERVICE ACTIVITIES 99

CENTRAL BANKS IN OTHER COUNTRIES 99
- SUMMARY 100
- KEY TERMS 100
- DISCUSSION QUESTIONS 100
- EXERCISES 101
- PROBLEMS 101

CHAPTER 5
POLICY MAKERS AND THE MONEY SUPPLY 103

NATIONAL ECONOMIC POLICY OBJECTIVES 104
- ECONOMIC GROWTH 104
- HIGH EMPLOYMENT 105
- PRICE STABILITY 105
- BALANCE IN INTERNATIONAL TRANSACTIONS 105
- THE PERFECT FINANCIAL STORM 106

FOUR POLICY MAKER GROUPS 106
- ETHICAL BEHAVIOR IN GOVERNMENT 107
- POLICY MAKERS IN THE EUROPEAN ECONOMIC UNION 108

GOVERNMENT INFLUENCE ON THE ECONOMY 108

POLICY INSTRUMENTS OF THE U.S. TREASURY 109
- MANAGING THE TREASURY'S CASH BALANCES 109
- POWERS RELATING TO THE FEDERAL BUDGET AND TO SURPLUSES OR DEFICITS 110

CONTENTS xiii

RECENT FINANCIAL CRISIS-RELATED ACTIVITIES   112
DEBT MANAGEMENT   112
CHANGING THE MONEY SUPPLY   113
CHECKABLE DEPOSIT EXPANSION   114
OFFSETTING OR LIMITING FACTORS   118
CONTRACTION OF DEPOSITS   118
FACTORS AFFECTING BANK RESERVES   119
CHANGES IN THE DEMAND FOR CURRENCY   119
FEDERAL RESERVE SYSTEM TRANSACTIONS   120
THE MONETARY BASE AND THE MONEY MULTIPLIER   122
SUMMARY   125
KEY TERMS   125
DISCUSSION QUESTIONS   126
EXERCISES   126
PROBLEMS   126

CHAPTER 6
INTERNATIONAL FINANCE AND TRADE   129

GLOBAL OR INTERNATIONAL MONETARY SYSTEM   130
DEVELOPMENT OF INTERNATIONAL FINANCE   130
HOW THE INTERNATIONAL MONETARY SYSTEM EVOLVED   130
EUROPEAN UNIFICATION   132
EUROPEAN UNION   132
EUROPEAN MONETARY UNION   132
THE EURO   132
CURRENCY EXCHANGE MARKETS AND RATES   133
CURRENCY EXCHANGE MARKETS   133
EXCHANGE RATE QUOTATIONS   133
FACTORS THAT AFFECT CURRENCY EXCHANGE RATES   135
CURRENCY EXCHANGE RATE APPRECIATION AND DEPRECIATION   137
ARBITRAGE   138
EXCHANGE RATE DEVELOPMENTS FOR THE U.S. DOLLAR   139
CONDUCTING BUSINESS INTERNATIONALLY   140
MANAGING FOREIGN EXCHANGE RISK   140
ETHICAL CONSIDERATIONS   141
FINANCING INTERNATIONAL TRADE   141
FINANCING BY THE EXPORTER   141
FINANCING BY THE IMPORTER   144
BANKERS' ACCEPTANCES   146
OTHER AIDS TO INTERNATIONAL TRADE   146
BALANCE IN INTERNATIONAL TRANSACTIONS GOAL   147
NATURE OF THE PROBLEM   148
BALANCE-OF-PAYMENTS ACCOUNTS   148
SUMMARY   151
KEY TERMS   152
DISCUSSION QUESTIONS   152
EXERCISES   152
PROBLEMS   153

PART 2
INVESTMENT   156

CHAPTER 7
SAVINGS AND INVESTMENT PROCESS   158

GROSS DOMESTIC PRODUCT AND CAPITAL FORMATION   159
GDP COMPONENTS   159
IMPLICATIONS OF INTERNATIONAL PAYMENT IMBALANCES   161
LINK BETWEEN SAVING AND INVESTMENT   161
FEDERAL GOVERNMENT RECEIPTS AND EXPENDITURES   163
THE BUDGET   163
FISCAL POLICY MAKERS   164
DEBT FINANCING   165
HISTORICAL ROLE AND CREATION OF SAVINGS   166
FOREIGN SOURCES OF SAVINGS   166
DOMESTIC SUPPLY OF SAVINGS   166
CREATION OF SAVINGS   166
MAJOR SOURCES OF SAVINGS   167
PERSONAL SAVINGS   167
CORPORATE SAVINGS   168
FACTORS AFFECTING SAVINGS   169
LEVELS OF INCOME   169
ECONOMIC EXPECTATIONS   170
ECONOMIC CYCLES   170
LIFE STAGES OF THE INDIVIDUAL SAVER   171
LIFE STAGES OF THE CORPORATION   171
CAPITAL MARKET SECURITIES   172
A FURTHER LOOK AT THE 2007–09 FINANCIAL CRISIS   173
EARLY FACTORS   173
A BORROWING-RELATED CULTURAL SHIFT   175

SUMMARY 176
KEY TERMS 176
DISCUSSION QUESTIONS 176
EXERCISES 177
PROBLEMS 177

CHAPTER 8
INTEREST RATES 179

SUPPLY AND DEMAND FOR LOANABLE FUNDS 180

HISTORICAL CHANGES IN U.S. INTEREST RATE LEVELS 181

LOANABLE FUNDS THEORY 182

DETERMINANTS OF MARKET INTEREST RATES 185

RISK-FREE SECURITIES: U.S. TREASURY DEBT OBLIGATIONS 186

MARKETABLE OBLIGATIONS 187
DEALER SYSTEM 188
TAX STATUS OF FEDERAL OBLIGATIONS 189
OWNERSHIP OF PUBLIC DEBT SECURITIES 189
MATURITY DISTRIBUTION OF MARKETABLE DEBT SECURITIES 190

TERM OR MATURITY STRUCTURE OF INTEREST RATES 190

RELATIONSHIP BETWEEN YIELD CURVES AND THE ECONOMY 191
TERM STRUCTURE THEORIES 192

INFLATION PREMIUMS AND PRICE MOVEMENTS 193

HISTORICAL INTERNATIONAL PRICE MOVEMENTS 194
INFLATION IN THE UNITED STATES 194
TYPES OF INFLATION 196

DEFAULT RISK PREMIUMS 198

SUMMARY 202
KEY TERMS 202
DISCUSSION QUESTIONS 202
EXERCISES 202
PROBLEMS 203

CHAPTER 9
TIME VALUE OF MONEY 205

BASIC CONCEPTS 206

COMPOUNDING TO DETERMINE FUTURE VALUES 207

INFLATION OR PURCHASING POWER IMPLICATIONS 211

DISCOUNTING TO DETERMINE PRESENT VALUES 211

EQUATING PRESENT VALUES AND FUTURE VALUES 214

FINDING INTEREST RATES AND TIME REQUIREMENTS 215

SOLVING FOR INTEREST RATES 215
SOLVING FOR TIME PERIODS 216
RULE OF 72 217

FUTURE VALUE OF AN ANNUITY 217

PRESENT VALUE OF AN ANNUITY 220

INTEREST RATES AND TIME REQUIREMENTS FOR ANNUITIES 221

SOLVING FOR INTEREST RATES 222
SOLVING FOR TIME PERIODS 223

DETERMINING PERIODIC ANNUITY PAYMENTS 223

EXAMPLES INVOLVING ANNUAL PAYMENTS 223
REAL ESTATE MORTGAGE LOANS WITH MONTHLY PAYMENTS 225

MORE FREQUENT COMPOUNDING OR DISCOUNTING INTERVALS 226

COST OF CONSUMER CREDIT 227

UNETHICAL LENDERS 227
APR VERSUS EAR 227

SUMMARY 229
KEY TERMS 230
DISCUSSION QUESTIONS 230
EXERCISES 230
PROBLEMS 231

LEARNING EXTENSION 9
ANNUITY DUE PROBLEMS 233

FUTURE VALUE OF AN ANNUITY DUE 233

PRESENT VALUE OF AN ANNUITY DUE 234

INTEREST RATES AND TIME REQUIREMENTS FOR ANNUITY DUE PROBLEMS 235

QUESTIONS AND PROBLEMS 236

CHAPTER 10
BONDS AND STOCKS: CHARACTERISTICS AND VALUATIONS 237

LONG-TERM EXTERNAL FINANCING SOURCES FOR BUSINESSES 238

DEBT CAPITAL 240

WHO BUYS BONDS? 241
BOND COVENANTS 242
BOND RATINGS 243
BONDHOLDER SECURITY 244
TIME TO MATURITY 246

INCOME FROM BONDS 247
GLOBAL BOND MARKET 248
READING BOND QUOTES 248

CORPORATE EQUITY CAPITAL 250
COMMON STOCK 251
PREFERRED STOCK 252
READING STOCK QUOTES 253

DIVIDENDS AND STOCK REPURCHASES 254
HOW DO FIRMS DECIDE ON THE DOLLAR AMOUNT OF DIVIDENDS? 255
STOCK DIVIDENDS AND STOCK SPLITS 256
SHARE REPURCHASES 257

VALUATION PRINCIPLES 258

VALUATION OF BONDS 260
DETERMINING A BOND'S PRESENT VALUE 260
CALCULATING THE YIELD TO MATURITY 263
RISK IN BOND VALUATION 264

VALUATION OF STOCKS 267
VALUING STOCKS WITH CONSTANT DIVIDENDS 268
VALUING STOCKS WITH CONSTANT DIVIDEND GROWTH RATES 268
RISK IN STOCK VALUATION 269

VALUATION AND THE FINANCIAL ENVIRONMENT 270
GLOBAL ECONOMIC INFLUENCES 270
DOMESTIC ECONOMIC INFLUENCES 271
INDUSTRY AND COMPETITION 271
SUMMARY 273
KEY TERMS 273
DISCUSSION QUESTIONS 274
PROBLEMS 275

LEARNING EXTENSION 10
ANNUALIZING RATES OF RETURN 278

HOLDING PERIOD RETURNS 278
ANNUALIZED RATES OF RETURN 278
PROBLEMS 280

CHAPTER 11
SECURITIES MARKETS 281

ISSUING SECURITIES: PRIMARY SECURITIES MARKETS 282
PRIMARY MARKET FUNCTIONS OF INVESTMENT BANKERS 282
COST OF GOING PUBLIC 287
OTHER FUNCTIONS OF INVESTMENT BANKING FIRMS 289

INVESTMENT BANKING REGULATION 291

TRADING SECURITIES—SECONDARY SECURITIES MARKETS 292
ORGANIZED SECURITY EXCHANGES 292
STRUCTURE OF THE NEW YORK STOCK EXCHANGE 292
SECURITY TRANSACTIONS 294

WHAT MAKES A GOOD MARKET? 298
A WORD ON COMMISSIONS 299
SECURITY MARKET INDEXES 300
FOREIGN SECURITIES 301
INSIDE INFORMATION AND OTHER ETHICAL ISSUES 302
CHANGES IN THE STRUCTURE OF THE STOCK MARKET 303
SUMMARY 305
KEY TERMS 306
DISCUSSION QUESTIONS 306
PROBLEMS 307

LEARNING EXTENSION 11
INTRODUCTION TO FUTURES AND OPTIONS 309

WHY DO DERIVATIVES EXIST? 309
FUTURES CONTRACTS 310
OPTIONS 311
OPTION PAYOFF DIAGRAMS 312
SUMMARY 314
KEY TERMS 314
DISCUSSION QUESTIONS 315
PROBLEMS 315

CHAPTER 12
FINANCIAL RETURN AND RISK CONCEPTS 317

HISTORICAL RETURN AND RISK FOR A SINGLE FINANCIAL ASSET 318
ARITHMETIC AVERAGE ANNUAL RATES OF RETURN 319
VARIANCE AS A MEASURE OF RISK 320
STANDARD DEVIATION AS A MEASURE OF RISK 320

WHERE DOES RISK COME FROM? 323
EXPECTED MEASURES OF RETURN AND RISK 324
HISTORICAL RETURNS AND RISK OF DIFFERENT ASSETS 327
EFFICIENT CAPITAL MARKETS 328
PORTFOLIO RETURNS AND RISK 331

xvi CONTENTS

EXPECTED RETURN ON A PORTFOLIO 331
VARIANCE AND STANDARD DEVIATION
  OF RETURN ON A PORTFOLIO 332
TO DIVERSIFY OR NOT TO DIVERSIFY? 333
PORTFOLIO RISK AND THE NUMBER
  OF INVESTMENTS IN THE PORTFOLIO 334
SYSTEMATIC AND UNSYSTEMATIC RISK 335

CAPITAL ASSET PRICING MODEL 336

ETHICS AND JOB OPPORTUNITIES IN INVESTMENTS 339

SUMMARY 342
KEY TERMS 342
DISCUSSION QUESTIONS 342
PROBLEMS 343

LEARNING EXTENSION 12
ESTIMATING BETA 346

SECURITY MARKET LINE 347

QUESTIONS AND PROBLEMS 349

PART 3
FINANCIAL MANAGEMENT 350

CHAPTER 13
BUSINESS ORGANIZATION AND FINANCIAL DATA 352

STARTING A BUSINESS 353

STRATEGIC PLAN WITH A VISION OR MISSION 353
BUSINESS AND FINANCIAL GOALS 354

FORMS OF BUSINESS ORGANIZATION IN THE UNITED STATES 354

PROPRIETORSHIP 355

THE ANNUAL REPORT 359

ACCOUNTING PRINCIPLES 359

INCOME STATEMENT 361

THE BALANCE SHEET 362

ASSETS 363
LIABILITIES 364
OWNERS' EQUITY 365

STATEMENT OF CASH FLOWS 365

FINANCIAL STATEMENTS OF DIFFERENT COMPANIES 367

GOAL OF A FIRM 368

MEASURING SHAREHOLDER WEALTH 368
LINKING STRATEGY AND FINANCIAL
  PLANS 370
CRITERION FOR NONPUBLIC FIRMS 370
WHAT ABOUT ETHICS? 370

CORPORATE GOVERNANCE 371

PRINCIPAL-AGENT PROBLEM 371
REDUCING AGENCY PROBLEMS 372

FINANCE IN THE ORGANIZATION CHART 374

SUMMARY 377
KEY TERMS 378
DISCUSSION QUESTIONS 378
PROBLEMS 378

LEARNING EXTENSION 13
FEDERAL INCOME TAXATION 382

DEPRECIATION BASICS 384

A FEW WORDS ON DEPRECIATION METHODS 385

QUESTIONS AND PROBLEMS 385

CHAPTER 14
FINANCIAL ANALYSIS AND LONG-TERM FINANCIAL PLANNING 387

FINANCIAL STATEMENT ANALYSIS 388

RATIO ANALYSIS OF BALANCE SHEET AND INCOME STATEMENT 388

TYPES OF FINANCIAL RATIOS 389

LIQUIDITY RATIOS AND ANALYSIS 390
ASSET MANAGEMENT RATIOS AND
  ANALYSIS 392
FINANCIAL LEVERAGE RATIOS AND ANALYSIS 394
PROFITABILITY RATIOS AND ANALYSIS 398
MARKET VALUE RATIOS AND ANALYSIS 399

SUMMARY OF RATIO ANALYSIS FOR WALGREENS 402

DU PONT METHOD OF RATIO ANALYSIS 402

LONG-TERM FINANCIAL PLANNING 404

PERCENTAGE OF SALES TECHNIQUE 405
COST-VOLUME-PROFIT ANALYSIS 407
DEGREE OF OPERATING LEVERAGE 409

SUMMARY 412
KEY TERMS 412
DISCUSSION QUESTIONS 412
PROBLEMS 413

CHAPTER 15
MANAGING WORKING CAPITAL 417

OPERATING AND CASH CONVERSION CYCLES 419

OPERATING CYCLE 419
CASH CONVERSION CYCLE 419

DETERMINING THE LENGTH OF THE OPERATING CYCLE AND CASH CONVERSION CYCLE 421
WORKING CAPITAL REQUIREMENTS 422

CASH BUDGETS 425
MINIMUM DESIRED CASH BALANCE 425
CASH INFLOWS 425
CASH OUTFLOWS 426
CONSTRUCTING THE CASH BUDGET 427
SEASONAL VERSUS LEVEL PRODUCTION 428

MANAGEMENT OF CURRENT ASSETS 430
CASH AND MARKETABLE SECURITIES MANAGEMENT 430
GETTING—AND KEEPING—THE CASH 436

ACCOUNTS RECEIVABLE MANAGEMENT 439
CREDIT ANALYSIS 439
CREDIT-REPORTING AGENCIES 439
CREDIT TERMS AND COLLECTION EFFORTS 440

INVENTORY MANAGEMENT 442

TECHNOLOGY AND WORKING CAPITAL MANAGEMENT 443
CASH MANAGEMENT 443
PROCESSING INVOICES AND FLOAT 443
TRACKING INVENTORY 445
SUMMARY 446
KEY TERMS 446
DISCUSSION QUESTIONS 446
PROBLEMS 447

CHAPTER 16
SHORT-TERM BUSINESS FINANCING 451

STRATEGIES FOR FINANCING WORKING CAPITAL 452
MATURITY-MATCHING APPROACH 453
AGGRESSIVE APPROACH 455
CONSERVATIVE APPROACH 455

FACTORS AFFECTING SHORT-TERM FINANCING 456
OPERATING CHARACTERISTICS 456
OTHER INFLUENCES IN SHORT-TERM FINANCING 458

PROVIDERS OF SHORT-TERM FINANCING 460
COMMERCIAL BANK LENDING 460
TRADE CREDIT FROM SUPPLIERS 463
COMMERCIAL FINANCE COMPANIES 465
COMMERCIAL PAPER 466

ADDITIONAL VARIETIES OF SHORT-TERM FINANCING 468
ACCOUNTS RECEIVABLE FINANCING 468
INVENTORY LOANS 471
LOANS SECURED BY STOCKS AND BONDS 472
OTHER FORMS OF SECURITY FOR BANK LOANS 472

THE COST OF SHORT-TERM FINANCING 473
SUMMARY 475
KEY TERMS 475
DISCUSSION QUESTIONS 476
PROBLEMS 476

CHAPTER 17
CAPITAL BUDGETING ANALYSIS 479

MANAGEMENT OF FIXED ASSETS 480

IDENTIFYING POTENTIAL CAPITAL BUDGET PROJECTS 480

CAPITAL BUDGETING PROCESS 482

CAPITAL BUDGETING TECHNIQUES 485
NET PRESENT VALUE 485
INTERNAL RATE OF RETURN 488
NPV AND IRR 491

MODIFIED INTERNAL RATE OF RETURN 492

PROFITABILITY INDEX 494

CONFLICTS BETWEEN DISCOUNTED CASH FLOW TECHNIQUES 494
DIFFERENT CASH FLOW PATTERNS 494
DIFFERENT TIME HORIZONS 495
DIFFERENT SIZES 495

PAYBACK PERIOD 495

DIFFERENCE BETWEEN THEORY AND PRACTICE 496
SAFETY MARGIN 497
MANAGERIAL FLEXIBILITY AND OPTIONS 497

ESTIMATING PROJECT CASH FLOWS 497
ISOLATING PROJECT CASH FLOWS 498

APPROACHES TO ESTIMATING PROJECT CASH FLOWS 499
CASH FLOW FROM OPERATIONS 499
CASH FLOW FROM INVESTMENT ACTIVITIES 501
CASH FLOW FROM FINANCING ACTIVITIES 501
AN EXAMPLE 501
DEPRECIATION AS A TAX SHIELD 502

KEEPING MANAGERS HONEST 503

RISK-RELATED CONSIDERATIONS 505

SUMMARY 506
KEY TERMS 507
DISCUSSION QUESTIONS 507
PROBLEMS 508

LEARNING EXTENSION 17 511
ESTIMATING PROJECT CASH FLOWS

PROJECT STAGES AND CASH FLOW ESTIMATION 511
INITIAL OUTLAY 511
CASH FLOWS DURING THE PROJECT'S OPERATING LIFE 512
SALVAGE VALUE AND NWC RECOVERY AT PROJECT TERMINATION 512

APPLICATIONS 513
CASH FLOW ESTIMATION FOR A REVENUE EXPANDING PROJECT 513
CASH FLOW ESTIMATION FOR A COST-SAVING PROJECT 515
SETTING A BID PRICE 517
SUMMARY 519
DISCUSSION QUESTIONS 519
PROBLEMS 519

CHAPTER 18
CAPITAL STRUCTURE AND THE COST OF CAPITAL 521

WHY CHOOSE A CAPITAL STRUCTURE? 522
TRENDS IN CORPORATE USE OF DEBT 523

REQUIRED RATE OF RETURN AND THE COST OF CAPITAL 524

COST OF CAPITAL 525
COST OF DEBT 526
COST OF PREFERRED STOCK 526
COST OF COMMON EQUITY 527
COST OF NEW COMMON STOCK 528

WEIGHTED AVERAGE COST OF CAPITAL 528
CAPITAL STRUCTURE WEIGHTS 529
MEASURING THE TARGET WEIGHTS 529

WHAT DO BUSINESSES USE AS THEIR COST OF CAPITAL? 530

DIFFICULTY OF MAKING CAPITAL STRUCTURE DECISIONS 532

PLANNING GROWTH RATES 533
INTERNAL GROWTH RATE 534
SUSTAINABLE GROWTH RATE 534
EFFECTS OF UNEXPECTEDLY HIGHER (OR LOWER) GROWTH 535

EBIT/EPS ANALYSIS 536
INDIFFERENCE LEVEL 536

COMBINED OPERATING AND FINANCIAL LEVERAGE EFFECTS 539
UNIT VOLUME VARIABILITY 539
PRICE-VARIABLE COST MARGIN 539
FIXED COSTS 539
DEGREE OF FINANCIAL LEVERAGE 540
TOTAL RISK 540

INSIGHTS FROM THEORY AND PRACTICE 542
TAXES AND NONDEBT TAX SHIELDS 542
BANKRUPTCY COSTS 542
AGENCY COSTS 544
A FIRM'S ASSETS AND ITS FINANCING POLICY 545
THE PECKING ORDER HYPOTHESIS 545
MARKET TIMING 545
BEYOND DEBT AND EQUITY 546

GUIDELINES FOR FINANCING STRATEGY 546
SUMMARY 549
KEY TERMS 549
DISCUSSION QUESTIONS 549
PROBLEMS 550

APPENDIX 553–561
GLOSSARY 562–574
INDEX 575–590

INTRODUCTION TO FINANCE

Markets, Investments, and Financial Management

PART I
INSTITUTIONS AND MARKETS

INTRODUCTION

Ask someone what he or she thinks "finance" is about. You'll probably get a variety of responses: "It deals with money." "It is what my bank does." "The New York Stock Exchange has something to do with it." "It's how businesses and people get the money they need—you know, borrowing and stuff like that." And they'll all be correct!

Finance is a broad field. It involves national and international systems of banking and financing business. It also deals with the process you go through to get a car loan and what a business does when planning for its future needs.

It is important to understand that while the U.S. financial system is quite complex, it generally operates very efficiently. However, on occasion imbalances can result in economic, real estate, and stock market "bubbles," which when burst cause havoc on the workings of the financial system. The decade of the 2000s began with the bursting of the "tech" or technology bubble and the "dot.com" bubble. Then in mid-2006, the real estate bubble in the form of excessive housing prices burst. This was followed by the peaking of stock prices in 2007 followed by a steep decline that continued into early 2009. Economic activity began slowing in 2007 and progressed into an economic recession beginning in mid-2008, which was accompanied by double-digit unemployment rates. The result was the 2007–09 financial crisis that produced the most financial distress on the U.S. financial system since the depression years of the 1930s.

Within the general field of finance, there are three areas of study–financial institutions and markets, investments, and financial management. These areas are illustrated in the accompanying diagram. Financial institutions collect funds from savers and lend them to or invest them in businesses or people that need cash. Examples of financial institutions are commercial banks, investment banks, insurance companies, and mutual funds. Financial institutions operate as part of the financial system. The financial system is the environment of finance. It includes the laws and regulations that affect financial transactions. The financial system encompasses the Federal Reserve System, which controls the supply of money in the U.S. economy. It also consists of the mechanisms that have been constructed to facilitate the flow of money and financial securities among countries. Financial markets represent ways for bringing together those that have money to invest with those that need funds. Financial markets, which include markets for mortgages, securities, and currencies, are necessary for a financial system to operate efficiently. Part 1 of this book examines the financial system and the role of financial institutions and financial markets in it.

Securities markets play important roles in helping businesses and governments raise new funds. Securities markets also facilitate the transfer of securities between investors. A securities market can be a central location for the trading of financial claims, such as the New York Stock Exchange. It may also take the form of a communications network, as with the over-the-counter market, which is another means by which stocks and bonds can be traded. When people invest funds, lend or borrow money, or buy or sell shares of a company's stock, they are participating in the financial markets. Part 2 of this book examines the role of securities markets and the process of investing in bonds and stocks.

The third area of the field of finance is financial management. Financial management studies how a business should manage its assets, liabilities, and equity to produce a good or service.

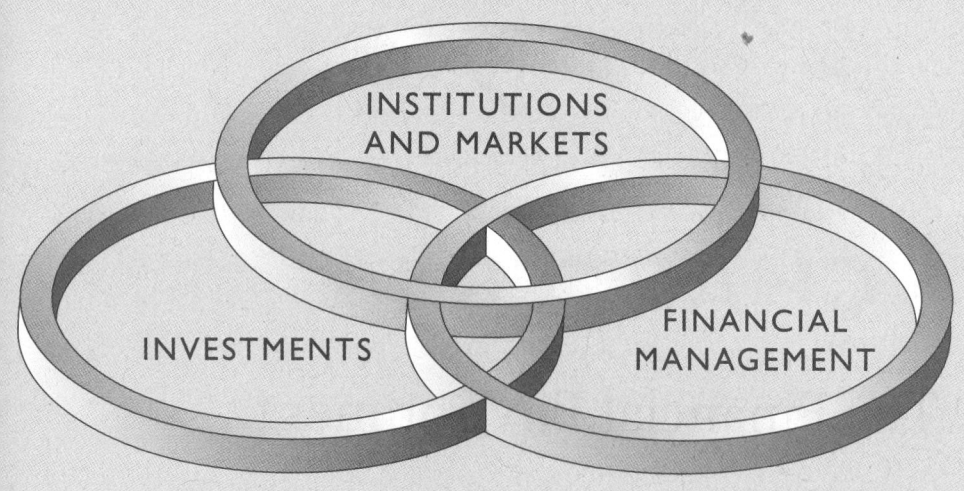

Whether or not a firm offers a new product or expands production, or how it invests excess cash, are examples of decisions that financial managers are involved with. Financial managers are constantly working with financial institutions and watching financial market trends as they make investment and financing decisions. Part 3 discusses how financial concepts can help managers better manage their firms.

It is important to recognize that there are few clear distinctions or separations between the three areas of finance. The diagram intentionally shows institutions and markets, investments, and financial management overlapping one another. Financial institutions operate in the environment of the financial markets and work to meet the financial needs of individuals and businesses. Financial managers do analyses and make decisions based on information they obtain from the financial markets. They also work with financial institutions when they need to raise funds and when they have excess funds to invest. Participants investing in the financial markets use information from financial institutions and firms to evaluate different investments in securities such as stocks, bonds, and certificates of deposit. A person working in one field must be knowledgeable about all three. Thus this book is designed to provide you with a survey of all three areas of finance.

Part 1, Institutions and Markets, presents an overview of the financial system and its important components of policy makers, a monetary system, financial institutions, and financial markets. Financial institutions operate within the financial system to facilitate the work of the financial markets. For example, you can put your savings in a bank and earn interest. But your money doesn't just sit in the bank: The bank takes your deposit and the money from other depositors and lends it to Kathy, who needs a short-term loan for her business; to Ron for a college loan; and to Roger and Maria, who borrow the money to help buy a house. Banks bring together savers and those who need money, such as Kathy, Ron, Roger, and Maria. The interest rate the depositors earn and the interest rate that borrowers pay are determined by national and even international economic forces. Just what the bank does with depositors' money and how it reviews loan applications is determined to some extent by bank regulators and financial market participants, such as the Federal Reserve Board. Decisions by the president and Congress relating to fiscal policies and regulatory laws may also directly influence financial institutions and markets and alter the financial system.

Chapter 2 presents an overview of the role of money in the operation of the U.S. monetary and financial systems, including discussion of how funds are transferred among individuals, firms, and countries. Depository institutions, such as banks and savings and loans, as well as other financial institutions, involved in the financial intermediation process are the topic of Chapter 3. The Federal Reserve System, the U.S. central bank that controls the money supply, is discussed in Chapter 4. Chapter 5 places the previous chapters in perspective, discussing the role of the Federal Reserve and the banking system in helping meet national economic goals for the United States, such as economic growth, low inflation, and stable exchange rates. Part 1 concludes with an explanation of international trade and the topic of international finance in Chapter 6.

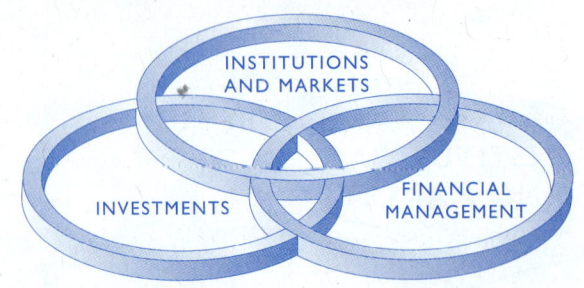

• CHAPTER 1 •

The Financial Environment

Chapter Learning Objectives:

AFTER STUDYING THIS CHAPTER, YOU SHOULD BE ABLE TO:

- Define *finance* and explain why finance should be studied.
- Identify and describe the six principles of finance.
- Identify characteristics and components of an effective financial system.
- Describe the financial functions performed in an effective financial system.
- Briefly describe the four types of financial markets.
- Describe characteristics of the mortgage markets.
- Discuss the developments that led to the recent financial crisis.
- Identify several major career opportunities in finance.

Where We Have Been...

As we progress through this book, we will start each chapter with a brief review of previously covered materials. This will provide you with a reference base for understanding the transition from topic to topic. After completing the text, you will be at the beginning of what we hope is a successful business career.

Where We Are Going...

The financial environment within which we live and work is composed of a financial system, institutions, and markets. Part 1 of this text focuses on developing an understanding of the financial institutions and markets that operate to make the financial system work efficiently. Chapter 2 describes the U.S. monetary system, including how it is intertwined with the capital formation process and how it has evolved. Current types of money are described, and we discuss why it is important to control the growth of the money supply. In following chapters, we turn our attention to understanding how financial institutions, policy makers, and international developments influence how the financial system functions.

How This Chapter Applies to Me...

While it is impossible to predict what life has in store for each of us in terms of health, family, and career, everyone can be a productive member of society. Nearly all of us will take part in making social, political, and economic decisions. A basic understanding of the financial environment that encompasses economic and financial systems will help you in making informed economic choices.

Let us begin with the following quote by George Santayana, a U.S. philosopher and poet:

> *Those who cannot remember the past are condemned to repeat it.*

While this quotation refers to the need to know something about history so that individuals can avoid repeating bad social, political, and economic decisions, it is equally important to the field of finance. It is the responsibility of all individuals to be able to make informed public choices involving the financial environment. By understanding the financial environment and studying the financial system, institutions and markets, investments, and financial management, individuals will be able to make informed economic and financial choices that will lead to better financial health and success. After studying the materials

finance
study of how individuals, institutions, governments, and businesses acquire, spend, and manage financial resources

financial environment
financial system, institutions, markets, businesses, individuals, and global interactions that help the economy operate efficiently

financial institutions
intermediaries that help the financial system operate efficiently and transfer funds from savers to individuals, businesses, and governments that seek to spend or invest the funds

financial markets
locations or electronic forums that facilitate the flow of funds among investors, businesses, and governments

in this book, you will be better informed in making choices that affect the economy and the financial system, as well as be better prepared for a business career—possibly even one in the field of finance.

WHAT IS FINANCE?

Finance is the study of how individuals, institutions, governments, and businesses acquire, spend, and manage money and other financial assets. Understanding finance is important to all students regardless of the discipline or area of study because nearly all business and economic decisions have financial implications. The decision to spend or consume now (for new clothes or dinner at a fancy restaurant) rather than save or invest (for spending or consuming more in the future) is an everyday decision that we all face.

The *financial environment* encompasses the financial system, institutions or intermediaries (we will use these terms interchangeably throughout this text), financial markets, business firms, individuals, and global interactions that contribute to an efficiently operating economy. Figure 1.1 depicts the three areas of finance—institutions and markets, investments, and financial management—within the financial environment. Note that while we identify three distinct finance areas, these areas do not operate in isolation but rather interact or intersect with each other. Our focus in this book is to provide the reader with exposure to all three areas, as well as to show how they are integrated. Of course, students pursuing a major or area of emphasis in finance will take multiple courses in one or more of these areas.

Financial institutions are organizations or intermediaries that help the financial system operate efficiently and transfer funds from savers and investors to individuals, businesses, and governments that seek to spend or invest the funds in physical assets (inventories, buildings, and equipment). *Financial markets* are physical locations or electronic forums that facilitate

FIGURE 1.1
Graphic Illustration of the Financial Environment

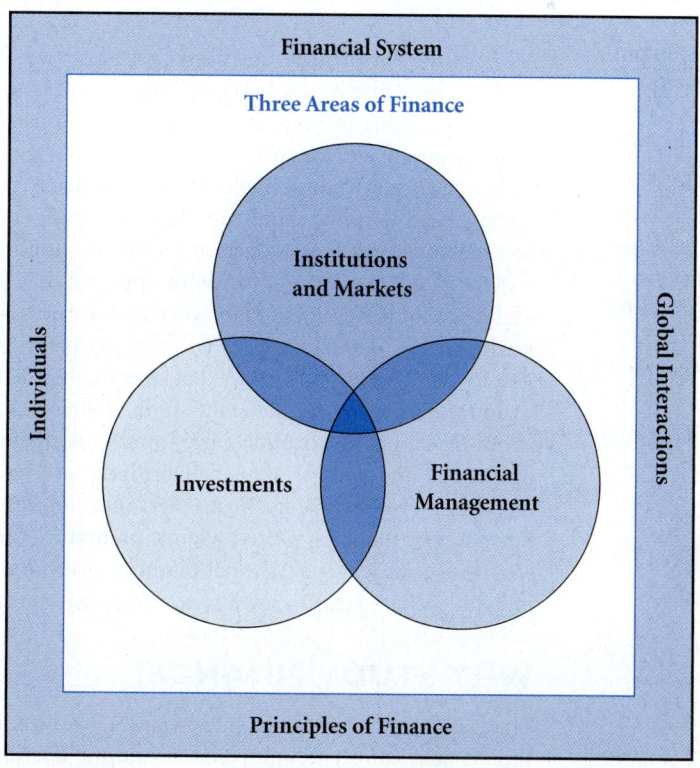

6 PART ONE ○ Institutions and Markets

investments
involves sale or marketing of securities, the analysis of securities, and the management of investment risk through portfolio diversification

financial management
involves financial planning, asset management, and fund-raising decisions to enhance the value of businesses

the flow of funds among investors, businesses, and governments. The **investments** area involves the sale or marketing of securities, the analysis of securities, and the management of investment risk through portfolio diversification. **Financial management** involves financial planning, asset management, and fund-raising decisions to enhance the value of businesses.

Finance has its origins in economics and accounting. Economists use a supply-and-demand framework to explain how the prices and quantities of goods and services are determined in a free-market economic system. Accountants provide the record-keeping mechanism for showing ownership of the financial instruments used in the flow of financial funds between savers and borrowers. Accountants also record revenues, expenses, and profitability of organizations that produce and exchange goods and services.

Efficient methods of production and specialization of labor can exist only if there is an effective means of paying for raw materials and final products. Businesses can obtain the money needed to buy capital goods such as machinery and equipment only if a mechanism has been established for making savings available for investment. Similarly, federal and other governmental units, such as state and local governments and tax districts, can carry out their wide range of activities only if efficient means exist for raising money, for making payments, and for borrowing.

Financial institutions, financial markets, and investment and financial management are crucial elements of the financial environment and well-developed financial systems. Financial institutions are intermediaries, such as banks, insurance companies, and investment companies that engage in financial activities to aid the flow of funds from savers to borrowers or investors. Financial markets provide the mechanism for allocating financial resources or funds from savers to borrowers. Individuals make decisions as investors and financial managers. Investors include savers and lenders as well as equity investors. While we focus on financial managers in this book, we recognize that individuals also must be continuously involved in managing their personal finances. Investment management involves making decisions relating to issuing and investing in stocks and bonds. Financial management in business involves making decisions relating to the efficient use of financial resources in the production and sale of goods and services. The goal of the financial manager in a profit-seeking organization is to maximize the owners' wealth. This is accomplished through effective financial planning and analysis, asset management, and the acquisition of financial capital. Financial managers in not-for-profit organizations aim to provide a desired level of services at acceptable costs and perform the same financial management functions as their for-profit counterparts.

TWO THEMES

As we progress through this book, we offer two themes within the financial institutions and markets, investments, and financial management topic areas. In each chapter we provide boxed materials relating to *small business practice* and *personal financial planning*. Successful businesses typically progress through a series of life-cycle stages—from the idea stage to exiting the business. More specifically, the successful business typically moves through five stages: development stage, startup stage, survival stage, rapid growth stage, and maturity stage. Individuals who choose to become small business owners do so for a number of different reasons. Some small business owners focus on salary-replacement opportunities where they seek income levels comparable to what they could have earned by working for much larger firms. Other individuals pursue lifestyle small business opportunities where they get paid for doing things they like to do. Entrepreneurs seek to own and run businesses that stress high growth rates in sales, profits, and cash flows.

entrepreneurial finance
study of how growth-driven, performance-focused, early-stage firms raise financial capital and manage operations and assets

personal finance
study of how individuals prepare for financial emergencies, protect against premature death and property losses, and accumulate wealth

Entrepreneurial finance is the study of how growth-driven, performance-focused, early-stage (from development through early rapid growth) firms raise financial capital and manage their operations and assets. Our small business practice boxes focus on operational and financial issues faced by early-stage firms. **Personal finance** is the study of how individuals prepare for financial emergencies, protect against premature death and the loss of property, and accumulate wealth over time. Our personal financial planning boxes focus on planning decisions made by individuals in regards to saving and investing their financial resources.

CONCEPT CHECK
What are the three areas of finance?

What two finance themes are carried throughout this book?

WHY STUDY FINANCE?

There are several reasons to study finance. Knowledge of the basics of finance covered in this text should help you make informed: economic decisions, personal and business investment decisions, and career decisions.

SMALL BUSINESS PRACTICE
Importance of Small Firms in the U.S. Economy

As the U.S. economy moved from the industrial age to the information age, dramatic changes occurred in the importance of small businesses. While large firms with five hundred or more employees continued to downsize and restructure throughout the 1990s and into the twenty-first century, small firms provided the impetus for economic growth.

Between the mid-1970s and the beginning of the 1990s firms with fewer than five hundred employees provided over half of total employment and nearly two-thirds of the net new jobs in the United States. Since the decade of the 1990s began, small firms have provided most of the net new jobs.

Why have small firms been so successful in creating new jobs? A Small Business Administration white paper suggests two reasons.

First, small firms provide a crucial role in technological change and productivity growth. Market economies change rapidly, and small firms are able to adjust quickly. Second, small firms provide the mechanism and incentive for millions of individuals to pursue the opportunity for economic success.

Others may argue that it is the entrepreneurial spirit and activity that account for the importance of small firms in the U.S. economy. Whatever the reasons, the ongoing growth of small businesses continues to be an important stimulus to the economy in the early years of the twenty-first century.

For current statistics, visit the Small Business Administration, Office of Advocacy Web site at http://www.sba.gov/advo.

INTERNET ACTIVITY
Go to the Small Business Administration Web site, http://www.sba.gov, and explore what is involved in deciding whether to start a new business.

1. **To make informed economic decisions.**
   As we will see, the operation of the financial system and the performance of the economy are influenced by policy makers. Individuals elect many of these policy makers in the United States, such as the president and members of Congress. Since these elected officials have the power to alter the financial system by creating laws, and since their decisions can influence economic activity, it is important that individuals be informed when making political and economic choices. Do you want a balanced budget, lower taxes, free international trade, low inflation, and full employment? Whatever your financial and economic goals may be, you need to be an informed participant if you wish to make a difference. Every individual should attain a basic understanding of finance as it applies to the financial system. Part 1 of this book focuses on understanding the roles of financial institutions and markets and how the financial system works.

2. **To make informed personal and business investment decisions.**
   An understanding of finance should help you better understand how the institution, government unit, or business that you work for finances its operations. At a personal level, the understanding of investments will enable you to better manage your financial resources and provide the basis for making sound decisions for accumulating wealth over time. Thus, in addition to understanding finance basics relating to the financial system and the economy, you also need to develop an understanding of the factors that influence interest rates and security prices. Part 2 of this book focuses on understanding the characteristics of stocks and bonds and how they are valued, securities markets, and how to make risk-versus-return investment decisions.

3. **To make informed career decisions based on a basic understanding of business finance.**
   Even if your business interest is in a nonfinance career or professional activity, you likely will need to interact with finance professionals both within and outside your firm or organization. Doing so will require a basic knowledge of the concepts, tools, and applications of financial management. Part 3 of this book focuses on providing you with an understanding of how finance is applied within a firm by focusing on decision making by financial managers.

CONCEPT CHECK
Give three reasons for studying finance.

Of course, you may be interested in pursuing a career in finance or at least want to know what people who work in finance actually do. Throughout this text, you will find discussions of career opportunities in finance, as well as a boxed feature entitled Career Opportunities in Finance.

FINANCE PRINCIPLE

SIX PRINCIPLES OF FINANCE

Finance is founded on six important principles. The first five relate to the economic behavior of individuals, and the sixth one focuses on ethical behavior. Knowing about these principles will help us understand how managers, investors, and others incorporate time and risk into their decisions, as well as why the desire to earn excess returns leads to information-efficient financial markets in which prices reflect available information. Unfortunately, sometimes greed associated with the desire to earn excess returns causes individuals to risk losing their reputations by engaging in questionable ethical behavior and even unethical behavior in the form of fraud or other illegal activities. The bottom line is "Reputation matters!" The following are the six principles that serve as the foundation of finance:

- Money has a time value.
- Higher returns are expected for taking on more risk.
- Diversification of investments can reduce risk.
- Financial markets are efficient in pricing securities.
- Manager and stockholder objectives may differ.
- Reputation matters.

TIME VALUE OF MONEY

Let's look at these principles one by one. Money in hand today is worth more than the promise of receiving the same amount in the future. The "time value" of money exists because a sum of money today could be invested and grow over time. For example, assume that you have $1,000 today and that it could earn $60 (6 percent) interest over the next year. Thus, $1,000 today would be worth $1,060 at the end of one year (i.e., $1,000 plus $60). As a result, a dollar today is worth more than a dollar received a year from now. The time value of money principle helps us understand the economic behavior of individuals and the economic decisions of the institutions and businesses that they run. This finance principle pillar is apparent in many of our day-to-day activities, and knowledge of it will help us better understand the implications of time-varying money decisions. We explore the details of the time value of money in Chapter 9, but this first principle of finance will be apparent throughout this book.

RISK VERSUS RETURN

A trade-off exists between risk and expected return in all types of investments—both assets and securities. Risk is the uncertainty about the outcome or payoff of an investment in the future. For example, you might invest $1,000 in a business venture today. After one year, the firm might be bankrupt and you would lose your total investment. On the other hand, after one year your investment might be worth $2,400. This variability in possible outcomes is your risk. Instead, you might invest your $1,000 in a U.S. government security, where after one year the value may be $950 or $1,100. Rational investors would consider the business venture investment to be riskier and would choose this investment only if they feel the expected return is high enough to justify the greater risk. Investors make these trade-off decisions every day.

Business managers make similar trade-off decisions when they choose between different projects in which they could invest. Understanding the risk/return trade-off principle also helps us understand how individuals make economic decisions. While we specifically explore the trade-off between risk and expected return in greater detail in Part 2, this second principle of finance is involved in many financial decisions throughout this text.

DIVERSIFICATION OF RISK

While higher returns are expected for taking on more risk, all investment risk is not the same. In fact, some risk can be removed or *diversified* by investing in several different assets or securities. Let's return to the example involving a $1,000 investment in a business venture where after one year the investment we could provide a return of either zero dollars or $2,400. Now let's assume that there also is an opportunity to invest $1,000 in a second unrelated business venture in which the outcomes would be zero dollars or $2,400. Let's further assume that we will put one-half of our $1,000 investment funds in each investment opportunity such that the individual outcomes for each $500 investment would be zero dollars or $1,200.

While it is possible that both investments could lose everything (i.e., return zero dollars) or return $1,200 each (a total of $2,400), it is also possible that one investment would go broke and the other would return $1,200. So, four outcomes are now possible:

POSSIBLE OUTCOMES	COMBINED INVESTMENT	POSSIBLE RETURNS		COMBINED RETURN
Outcome 1:	$500 + $500	$0 + $0	=	$0
Outcome 2:	$500 + $500	$0 + $1,200	=	$1,200
Outcome 3:	$500 + $500	$1,200 + $0	=	$1,200
Outcome 4:	$500 + $500	$1,200 + $1,200	=	$2,400

If each outcome has an equal one-fourth (25 percent) chance of occurring, most of us would prefer this diversified investment. While it is true that our combined investment of $1,000 ($500 in each investment) at the extremes could still return zero dollars or $2,400, it is also true that we have a 50 percent chance of getting $1,200 back for our $1,000 investment. As a result, most of us would prefer investing in the combined or diversified investment rather than in either of the two investments separately. We will explore the benefits of investment diversification in Part 2 of this text.

FINANCIAL MARKETS ARE EFFICIENT

A fourth finance-related aspect of economic behavior is that individuals seek to find undervalued and overvalued investment opportunities involving both real and financial assets. It is human nature, economically speaking, to search for investment opportunities that will provide returns higher than those expected for undertaking a specified level of risk. This attempt by many to earn excess returns or to "beat the market" leads to financial markets being information efficient. However, at the same time it becomes almost impossible to consistently earn returns higher than those expected in a risk–return trade-off framework. Rather than looking at this third pillar of finance as a negative consequence of human economic behavior, we prefer to couch it positively in that it leads to information-efficient financial markets.

A financial market is said to be information efficient if at any point the prices of securities reflect all information available to the public. When new information becomes available, prices quickly change to reflect that information. For example, let's assume that a firm's stock is currently trading at $20 per share. If the market is efficient, both potential buyers and sellers of the stock know that $20 per share is a fair price. Trades should be at $20, or near to it, if the demand (potential buyers) and supply (potential sellers) are in reasonable balance. Now, let's assume that the firm announces the production of a new product that is expected to substantially increase sales and profits. Investors might react by bidding up the price to, say, $25 per share to reflect this new information. Assuming this new information is assessed properly, the new fair price becomes $25 per share. This informational efficiency of financial markets exists because a large number of professionals are continually searching for mispriced securities. Of course, as soon as new information is discovered, it becomes immediately reflected in the price of the associated security. Information-efficient financial markets play an important role in the marketing and transferring of financial assets between investors by providing liquidity and fair prices. The importance of information efficient financial markets is examined throughout this text and specifically in Chapter 11.

MANAGEMENT VERSUS OWNER OBJECTIVES

A fifth principle of finance relates to the fact that management objectives may differ from owner objectives. Owners or equity investors want to maximize the returns on their investments but often hire professional managers to run their firms. However, managers may seek to emphasize the size of firm sales or assets, have company jets or helicopters available for their travel, and receive company-paid country club memberships. Owner returns may suffer as a result of manager objectives. To bring manager objectives in line with owner objectives, it often is necessary to tie manager compensation to measures of performance beneficial to owners. Managers are often given a portion of the ownership positions in privately held firms and are provided stock options and bonuses tied to stock price performance in publicly traded firms.

The possible conflict between managers and owners is sometimes called the *principal-agent problem*. We will explore this problem in greater detail and describe how owners provide incentives to managers to manage in the best interests of equity investors or owners in Chapter 13.

ETHICAL ISSUES

ethical behavior
how an individual or organization treats others legally, fairly, and honestly

REPUTATION MATTERS

The sixth principle of finance is "Reputation matters!" An individual's reputation reflects his or her ethical standards or behavior. **Ethical behavior** is how an individual or organization treats others legally, fairly, and honestly. Of course, the ethical behavior of organizations reflects the ethical behaviors of their directors, officers, and managers. For institutions or businesses to be successful, they must have the trust and confidence of their customers, employees, and owners, as well as the community and society within which they operate. All would agree that firms have an ethical responsibility to provide safe products and services, to have safe working conditions for employees, and to not pollute or destroy the environment. Laws and regulations exist to ensure minimum levels of protection and the difference between unethical and ethical behavior. Examples of high ethical behavior include when firms establish product-safety and working-condition standards well above the legal or regulatory standards.

Unfortunately, and possibly due in part to the greed for excess returns (such as higher salaries, bonuses, more valuable stock options, personal perquisites, etc.), directors, officers, managers, and other individuals sometimes are guilty of unethical behavior for engaging in fraudulent or other illegal activities. Reputations are destroyed, criminal activities are prosecuted, and involved individuals may receive jail sentences. The unethical behavior of directors, officers, and managers also may lead to a loss of reputation and even destruction of the institutions and businesses for which they work.

Many examples of fraudulent and illegal unethical behavior have been cited in the financial press over the past few decades, and most seem to be tied to greed for personal gain. In such cases, confidential information was used for personal benefit, illegal payments were made to gain business, accounting fraud was committed, business assets were converted to personal use, and so forth. In the early 1980s, a number of savings and loan association managers were found to have engaged in fraudulent and unethical practices, and some managers were prosecuted and sent to prison while their institutions were dissolved or merged with other institutions.

In the late 1980s and early 1990s, fraudulent activities and unethical behavior by investment banking firms resulted in several high-profile financial wheeler-dealers going to prison. This resulted in the collapse of Drexel, Burnham, Lambert and the near collapse of Salomon Brothers. By the early part of the twenty-first century, such major firms as Enron, its auditor Arthur Andersen, and WorldCom ceased to exist because of fraudulent and unethical behavior on the part of their managers and officers. In addition, key officials of Tyco and Adelphia were charged with illegal actions and fraud. In 2009, Bernie Madoff was convicted and sent to prison for operating a "Ponzi scheme" that resulted in investors losing billions of dollars. Returns in a Ponzi scheme are fictitious and not earned. Early investors receive their "returns" from the contributions of subsequent investors. Ultimately such a scheme collapses when there are not substantial new investors and when existing investors want to sell their investments.

While the financial press chooses to highlight examples of unethical behavior, most individuals exhibit sound ethical behavior in their personal and business dealings and practices. In fact, the sixth principle of finance depends on most individuals practicing high-quality ethical behavior and believing that reputation matters. To be successful, an organization or business must have the trust and confidence of its various constituencies, including customers, employees, owners, and the community. High-quality ethical behavior involves treating others fairly and honestly and goes beyond just meeting legal and regulatory requirements. High reputation value reflects high-quality ethical behavior, so employing high ethical standards is the right thing to do. Many organizations and businesses have developed and follow their own code of ethics. The importance of practicing sound ethical behavior is discussed throughout this text.

CONCEPT CHECK

What are the six principles of finance?

FIGURE 1.2
Graphic View of the U.S. Financial System

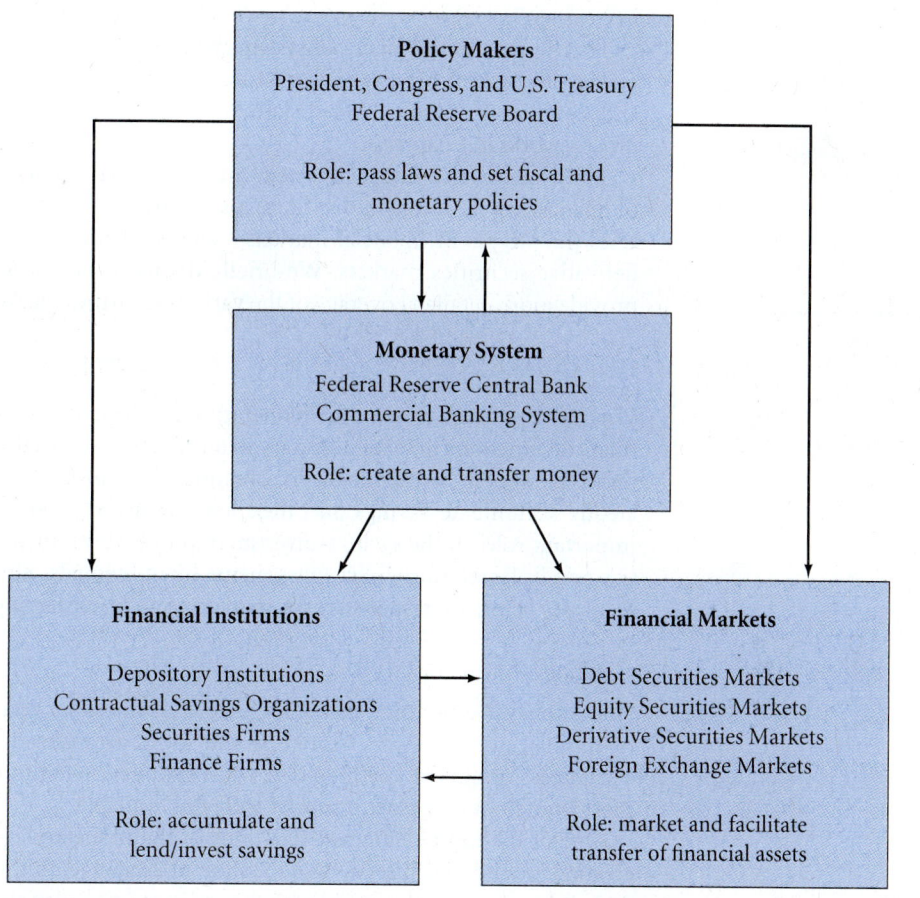

OVERVIEW OF THE FINANCIAL SYSTEM

financial system
interaction of intermediaries, markets, instruments, policy makers, and regulations to aid the flow from savings to investments

The **financial system** is a complex mix of financial intermediaries, markets, instruments, policy makers, and regulations that interact to expedite the flow of financial capital from savings into investment. We present a brief overview of the financial system in Chapter 1 and then follow with more detailed coverage in the remaining chapters of Part 1.

CHARACTERISTICS AND REQUIREMENTS

Figure 1.2 provides a graphic review of the U.S. financial system. First, an effective financial system must have several sets of *policy makers* who pass laws and make decisions relating to fiscal and monetary policies. These policy makers include the president, Congress, and the U.S. Treasury, plus the Federal Reserve Board. Since the United States operates within a global economy, political and economic actions of foreign policy makers influence, although indirectly, the U.S. financial system and its operations. Major economic goals are identified and policy maker actions designed to achieve those goals are discussed in Chapter 5.

Second, an effective financial system needs an efficient *monetary system* that is composed of a central bank and a banking system that is able to create and transfer a stable medium of exchange called money. In the United States, the dollar is the medium of exchange, the central bank is the Federal Reserve System, and the banking system is commonly referred to as the commercial banking system. Characteristics of money and the monetary system are discussed in Chapter 2, and the Federal Reserve System is covered in Chapter 4.

Third, an effective financial system also must have *financial institutions* or intermediaries that support capital formation either by channeling savings into investment in physical assets or by fostering direct financial investments by individuals in financial institutions and businesses. The

INTERNET ACTIVITY
Go to the Business Week Web site, http://www.businessweek.com, and identify a major business development relating to the financial environment.

process of accumulating and then lending and investing savings is referred to as the savings-investment process. Four types of financial intermediaries are listed in Figure 1.2. Depository institutions, contractual savings organizations, securities firms, and finance firms are discussed in Chapter 3.

Fourth, an effective financial system requires financial assets or instruments necessary for the savings-investment process to work efficiently. We cover the types of financial asset instruments and securities used in the United States throughout the text and cover how the savings-investment process works in Chapter 7.

Fifth, an effective financial system must also have *financial markets* that facilitate the transfer of financial assets among individuals, institutions, businesses, and governments. Figure 1.2 identifies three types of financial markets—debt securities markets, equity securities markets, and derivative securities markets. We briefly discuss these markets later in this chapter and then provide more detailed coverage of the various securities markets throughout the text.

FINANCIAL SYSTEM COMPONENTS AND FINANCIAL FUNCTIONS

We can express the roles of the monetary system, financial institutions, and financial markets as financial functions that are necessary in an effective financial system. Figure 1.3 indicates that the monetary system is responsible for creating and transferring money. Financial institutions efficiently accumulate savings and then lend or invest these savings. Financial institutions play important roles in the savings-investment process both through financial intermediation activities and in facilitating direct investments by individuals. Financial markets, along with certain securities firms, are responsible for marketing and transferring financial assets or claims.

Creating Money

Since money is something that is accepted as payment for goods, services, and debts, its value lies in its purchasing power. Money is the most generalized claim to wealth, since it can be exchanged for almost anything else. Most transactions in today's economy involve money, and most would not take place if money were not available.

One of the most significant functions of the monetary system within the financial system is creating money, which serves as a medium of exchange. In the United States, the Federal Reserve System is primarily responsible for the amount of money that is created, although most of the money is actually created by depository institutions. A sufficient amount of money is essential if economic activity is to take place at an efficient rate. Having too little money constrains economic growth. Having too much money often results in increases in the prices of goods and services.

CONCEPT CHECK

What five requirements are necessary for a financial system to be effective?

FIGURE 1.3
Three Financial System Components and Their Financial Functions

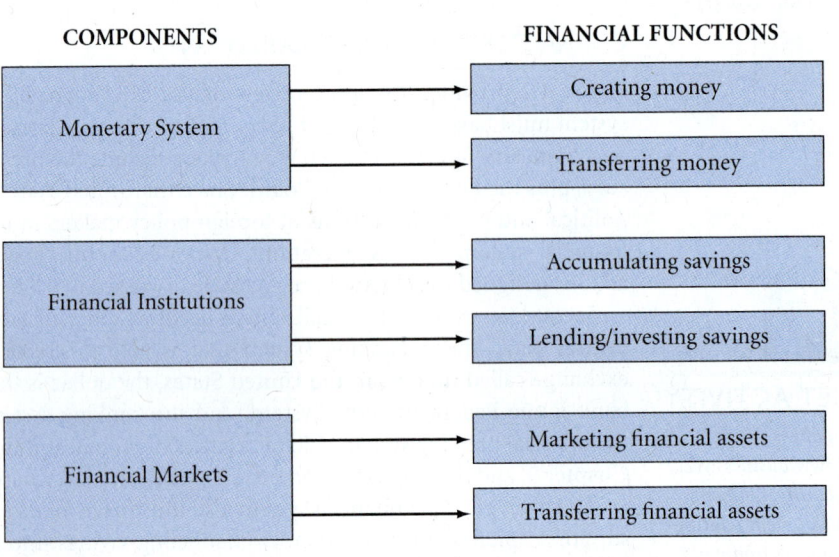

PERSONAL FINANCIAL PLANNING
People Are the Financial System

The main participant in the financial system is not the large institution or corporation . . . it's you and others like you. Households, families, and individuals provide up to 80 percent of the savings flows in the U.S. economy in any year. There are three main sources of savings: personal savings, business savings (that is, retained earnings), and government surpluses. Personal savings far outweigh the other two sources combined as a source of savings flows in the United States.

Another way to look at this is: Where do financial institutions get the funds they invest and loan? Banks get their funds mainly from individuals' checking and savings accounts and certificates of deposit (CDs). Pension funds obtain their cash from the savings of working people. Insurance firms accumulate funds to invest from policyholders' payments of premiums for their life, health, car, and home insurance. Mutual funds obtain investable cash by selling their shares to investors like you who want to accumulate savings and returns on savings to fund a future goal such as retirement, a new car, a house down payment, or children's college expenses.

Transferring Money

Individuals and businesses hold money for purchases or payments they expect to make in the near future. One way to hold money is in checkable deposits at depository institutions. When money is held in this form, payments can be made easily by check. The check is an order to the depository institution to transfer money to the party who received the check. This is a great convenience, since checks can be written for the exact amount of payments, can be safely sent in the mail, and provide a record of payment. Institutions can also transfer funds between accounts electronically, making payments without paper checks. Funds transfers can be made by telephone, at automated teller machines (ATMs) connected to a bank's computer, and via the Internet.

Accumulating Savings

A function performed by financial institutions is the accumulation or gathering of individual savings. Most individuals, businesses, and organizations do not want to take the risks involved in having cash on hand. Even if relatively small, cash amounts are put into a depository institution for safekeeping. When all the deposits are accumulated in one place, they can be used for loans and investments in amounts much larger than any individual depositor could supply. Depository institutions regularly conduct advertising campaigns and other promotional activities to attract deposits.

Lending and Investing Savings

Another basic function of financial institutions is lending and investing. The money that has been put into these intermediaries may be lent to businesses, farmers, consumers, institutions, and governmental units. It may be lent for varying periods and for different purposes, such as to buy equipment or to pay current bills. Some financial institutions make loans of almost all types. Others specialize in only one or two types of lending. Still other financial institutions invest all or part of their accumulated savings in the stock of a business or in debt obligations of businesses or other institutions.

Marketing Financial Assets

New financial instruments and securities are created and sold in the primary securities market. For example, a business may want to sell shares of ownership, called stock, to the general public. It can do so directly, but the process of finding individuals interested in investing funds in that business is likely to be difficult, costly, and time consuming. One particular financial intermediary—an investment banking firm—can handle the sale of shares of ownership. The function of the investment banking firm is essentially one of merchandising. Brokerage firms market existing, or "seasoned," instruments and securities.

CONCEPT CHECK
What are the financial functions that take place in the financial system?

Transferring Financial Assets

Several types of financial institutions facilitate or assist the processes of lending and selling securities. Brokerage firms market and facilitate the transferring of existing or seasoned instruments and securities. Also, if shares of stock are to be sold to the general public, it is desirable to have a ready market in which such stocks can be resold when the investor desires. Organized stock exchanges and the over-the-counter market provide active secondary markets for existing securities. The ability to buy and sell securities both quickly and at fair-market values is important in an efficient financial system.

FINANCIAL MARKETS CHARACTERISTICS

Financial markets facilitate the raising of financial capital by government entities and business firms. Government entities can issue or sell debt securities to finance the building of roads and bridges or to provide added services to the people. Business firms can issue debt securities, and corporations can sell equity securities or stocks to raise funds to invest in and grow their businesses. Financial markets also facilitate the transferring of previously issued debt and equity securities from existing to new investors.

MONEY AND CAPITAL MARKETS

money markets
where debt securities of one year or less are issued or traded

Money markets are where debt securities with maturities of one year or less are issued and traded. These markets are generally characterized by high liquidity whereby *money market securities* can be easily sold or traded with little loss of value. These short-lived securities generally have low returns and low risk. Money market securities will be discussed in Chapter 2.

capital markets
where debt securities with maturities longer than one year and corporate stocks are issued or traded

Capital markets are where debt instruments or securities with maturities longer than one year and corporate stocks or equity securities are issued and traded. *Capital market securities* are generally issued to finance the purchase of homes by individuals, buildings and equipment by businesses, and the providing of infrastructure (roads, bridges, buildings, etc.) by governments. Business firms and governments issue long-term debt securities, called bonds, to finance their assets and operations. *Mortgages* are issued to finance homes and buildings. Corporations also issue stocks to meet their financing needs. We will cover capital market securities in Part 2.

PRIMARY AND SECONDARY MARKETS

primary markets
where the initial offering or origination of debt and equity securities takes place

There are primary and secondary markets for debt (bonds and mortgages) and equity securities. The initial offering or origination of debt and equity securities takes place in **primary markets**. Proceeds from the sale of new securities after issuing costs go to the issuing business or government issuer. The primary market is the only "market" where the security issuer directly benefits (receives funds) from the sale of its securities. Mortgage loans provide financing for the purchase of homes and other real property.

secondary markets
where the transfer of existing debt (bonds and mortgages) and equity securities between investors occurs

Secondary markets are physical locations or electronic forums where debt (bonds and mortgages) and equity securities are traded. Secondary markets for securities facilitate the transfer of previously issued securities from existing investors to new investors. Security transactions or transfers typically take place on organized security exchanges or in the electronic over-the-counter market. Individuals and other investors can actively buy and sell existing securities in the secondary market. While these secondary market investors may make gains or losses on their securities investments, the issuer of the securities does not benefit (nor does it lose) from these activities. The secondary market for securities is typically divided into short-term (money) and long-term (capital) market categories. We discuss primary and secondary securities markets in detail in Chapter 11. There also is an active secondary market for real estate mortgages. We will discuss the basics of secondary markets for mortgages later in this chapter.

CONCEPT CHECK
How do money markets and capital markets differ?
How do primary markets differ from secondary markets?

debt securities markets
where money market securities, bonds, and mortgages are sold and traded

MAJOR TYPES OF FINANCIAL MARKETS

There are four main types of financial markets—debt securities markets, equity securities markets, derivative securities markets, and foreign exchange markets. *Debt securities* are obligations to repay borrowed funds. **Debt securities markets** are markets where money market securities, bonds (corporate, financial institution, and government), and mortgages are originated and traded. *Bond markets* are where debt securities with longer-term maturities are originated and traded. Government entities (federal, state, and local), financial institutions, and business firms can issue bonds. While bonds and bond markets are discussed throughout this text, there is a specific focus in Chapter 10. *Mortgage markets* are where loans to purchase real estate (buildings and houses) are originated and traded. Mortgage markets are initially discussed in the next section because of the major role real estate mortgages and mortgage markets played in the recent financial crisis.

Equity securities markets are markets where ownership rights in the form of *common stocks* are initially sold and traded. Corporations can raise funds either through a *private placement*, which involves issuing new securities directly to specific investors, or through a *public offering*, which involves selling new securities to the general public. Financial institutions can also raise equity capital by selling stocks in their firms. Equity securities and markets are discussed in detail in Chapter 11.

In addition to money and capital markets, there are also **derivative securities markets**, which are markets for financial contracts or instruments that derive their values from underlying debt and equity securities. A familiar form of *derivative security* is the opportunity to buy or sell a corporation's equity securities for a specified price and within a certain amount of time. Derivative securities may be used to speculate on the future price direction of the underlying financial assets or to reduce price risk associated with holding the underlying financial assets. Organized exchanges handle standardized derivative security contracts, while negotiated contracts are handled in electronic markets often involving commercial banks or other financial institutions. We discuss derivative securities in the Learning Extension to Chapter 11.

Foreign exchange markets (also called FOREX markets) are electronic markets in which banks and institutional traders buy and sell various currencies on behalf of businesses and other clients. In the global economy, consumers may want to purchase goods produced, or services provided, in other countries. Likewise, an investor residing in one country may wish to hold securities issued in another country. For example, a U.S. consumer may wish to purchase a product in a foreign country. If the product is priced in the foreign country's currency, it may be necessary to exchange U.S. dollars for the foreign currency in order to complete the transaction. Businesses that sell their products in foreign countries usually receive payment in the foreign currencies. However, because the relative values of currencies may change, firms often use the currency exchange markets to reduce the risk of holding too much of certain currencies. We discuss currency exchange rates and foreign exchange markets in Chapter 6.

MORTGAGE MARKETS

A *mortgage* is a loan backed by real property in the form of buildings and houses. *Mortgage markets* are markets in which mortgage loans are created to purchase buildings and houses and are originated in primary markets and traded in secondary markets. Mortgage debt is typically divided into farm loans, nonfarm, nonresidential loans that include commercial property, and residential property loans. Mortgage loans on residential property also are typically divided into multifamily loans and one- to four-family loans. Residential mortgages account for the largest portion of outstanding mortgage debt and thus receive emphasis in this text. Furthermore, because residential mortgage-related developments contributed to the recent financial crisis, we discuss mortgage markets fundamentals now.

Mortgage loans are either federally insured or conventional mortgages. In the event a borrower defaults on a mortgage, federal insurance guarantees the loan repayment to the bank making the mortgage loan. The Federal Housing Administration (FHA) and the Veterans Administration (VA) provide insurance on FHA and VA mortgage loans. Lenders making conventional mortgage loans may assume the risk that the borrower may default or purchase private insurance to protect against borrower default.

TYPES OF MORTGAGES AND MORTGAGE-BACKED SECURITIES

The purchase of houses in the United States traditionally has been financed with fixed interest rate, long-term loans. A *fixed-rate mortgage* typically has a fixed interest rate and constant monthly payments over the life of the loan, which is typically 15 or 30 years. A loan that is repaid in equal payments over a specified time period is referred to as an *amortized* loan. We discuss amortized loans in Chapter 9. The traditional fixed-rate residential mortgage loan also required a sizeable down payment, typically 20 percent of the house purchase price, at the time the loan was made.

Holders of fixed-rate mortgages benefited by knowing that their monthly mortgage payment would not change over the loan's life, and thus they could plan and budget for the contractual monthly payment amounts. As a result, the *default rate,* or failure to make timely periodic payments, was low on fixed-rate mortgage loans. However, the benefits of fixed-rate mortgages were offset, in part, by the fact that only a portion of the U.S. population could qualify to purchase their own houses.

During the past couple of decades, a period of generally high fixed-rate mortgage loan interest rates and a time in which it was desired to extend housing ownership to more individuals in the United States, the use of adjustable-rate mortgages grew. An **adjustable-rate mortgage (ARM)** has an interest rate that changes or varies over time with market-determined interest rates on a U.S. Treasury bill or other debt security. The interest rate on an ARM is often adjusted annually to reflect changes in U.S. Treasury bill rates (or other interest rate benchmark). Also lenders typically offer ARMs with variable interest rates for one to five years with a provision to switch to a fixed rate over the remaining life of the ARM.

Because ARMs typically offer lower initial interest rates and lower monthly payments, more individuals can qualify for home ownership. However, because of possible changing market-determined interest rates and potential changeovers to fixed interest rates, individuals who were able to make initially low monthly mortgage payments may find themselves unable to meet their mortgage payments if interest rates are adjusted upwards.

Mortgage loans are originated in the primary mortgage markets by mortgage brokers, mortgage companies, and depository financial institutions, which include banks, savings and loans, savings banks, and credit unions. Mortgage brokers and mortgage companies typically sell the mortgage loans they originated in the secondary mortgage markets. Commercial banks, which are the dominant type of depository institution that originate mortgage loans, either hold and collect the periodic payments by borrowers on the loans they originated or sell the loans in the secondary mortgage markets.

In some instances, banks and other mortgage lenders "pool" together loans they originated into securities. Other financial intermediaries "repackage" mortgage loans into securities. **Securitization** is the process of pooling and packaging mortgage loans into debt securities. A **mortgage-backed security** is a debt security created by pooling together a group of mortgage loans whose periodic payments belong to the holders of the security. Some mortgage-backed securities "pass through" the interest and principal payments to the owners of the securities. Payments on the underlying mortgages are made to the financial institution that created the mortgage-backed security. The institution, in turn, pays or passes through the payments to the investors or owners of the securities. In some mortgage-backed securities, the issuer separates or "strips" the interest and principal payment streams into separate securities. Cash flows from interest and principal payments are dependent on continued mortgage payments by the borrowers on the underlying mortgage loans. The uncertainty of mortgage payments is further increased when mortgages are prepaid during periods of declining interest rates.

CREDIT RATINGS AND SCORES

A **credit rating** indicates the expected likelihood that a borrower will miss interest or principal payments and possibly default on the debt obligation in the form of a loan, mortgage, or bond. Credit ratings are prepared by private organizations on individuals, financial institutions, business firms, and government entities.

A credit rating for an individual is typically expressed in terms of a **credit score**, which is a number that indicates an individual's creditworthiness or likelihood that a debt will be paid according to the terms that were initially agreed to. Creditworthiness reflects an individual borrower's capacity to pay, collateral or security to the lender, and character. Some borrowers have the capacity to pay but may not be sufficiently trustworthy that they will pay. Credit scores

---

adjustable-rate mortgage (ARM)
interest rate and periodic payments that vary with market interest rates over the real estate loan's life

securitization
Process of pooling or packaging mortgage loans into debt securities

mortgage-backed security
debt security created by pooling together a group of mortgage loans

CONCEPT CHECK
What is a mortgage loan?
What are the primary types of mortgages?
What are mortgage-backed securities?

credit rating
indicates the expected likelihood that a borrower will pay a debt according to the terms agreed to

credit score
a number that indicates the creditworthiness or likelihood that a borrower will make loan payments when due

prime mortgage *home loan made to a borrower with a relatively high credit score indicating the likelihood that loan payments will be made as agreed to*

subprime mortgage *home loan made to a borrower with a relatively low credit score indicating the likelihood that loan payments might be missed when due*

are based on an individual's credit history as reflected in credit report information (e.g., payments on credit cards, auto loans, mortgages) and public records (e.g., bankruptcies, tax liens).

While there are many different credit score systems in use, they each attempt to differentiate among high quality, moderate quality, and low quality borrowers. For example, a credit scoring system may range from 500 to 1,000 in 100-point increments. Mortgage loans issued to borrowers with credit scores above 700 might be viewed as prime mortgage loans. A **prime mortgage** is a home loan to a borrower with relatively high credit worthiness indicating a relatively high likelihood that mortgage payments will be made when due. Of course, the higher the credit score, the higher the borrower's credit quality with scores above 900 reflecting the highest credit quality classification.

Mortgage loan borrowers with credit scores of 700 or below, for example, might be considered to be subprime borrowers. A **subprime mortgage** is a home loan to a borrower with a relatively poor credit score indicating a higher likelihood the borrower will miss mortgage payments when due. Making mortgage loans to subprime borrowers is a risky business in that an event such as an economic downturn in the form of a recession could result in a large percentage of subprime mortgage borrowers missing their mortgage payments and even defaulting on their home loans.

MAJOR PARTICIPANTS IN THE SECONDARY MORTGAGE MARKETS

Mortgage companies originate mortgage loans and then sell them in secondary markets. Banks and other depository institutions (savings and loans, savings banks, and credit unions) also originate mortgage loans. While these financial institutions hold and "service" (i.e., collect interest and principal payments) some of the loans they originated, other mortgage loans are also sold in the secondary mortgage markets. Some banks pool the loans they originated and package them in mortgage-backed securities for sale in the secondary mortgage markets.

The federal government has played an active role in the development of secondary mortgage markets. In 1938, the president and Congress created the Federal National Mortgage Association (Fannie Mae) to support the financial markets by purchasing home mortgages from banks and thus freeing-up funds that could be lent to other borrowers. Fannie Mae was converted to a government-sponsored enterprise (GSE), or "privatized," in 1968 by making it a public, investor-owned company. The Government National Mortgage Association (Ginnie Mae) was created in 1968 as a government-owned corporation. Ginnie Mae issues its own debt securities to obtain funds that are invested in mortgages made to low-to-moderate income home purchasers. The Federal Home Loan Mortgage Corporation (Freddie Mac) was formed in 1970 as a government-owned corporation. In 1989, Freddie Mac also became a GSE when it became a public, investor-owned company.

Ginnie Mae and Fannie Mae issue mortgage-backed securities to fund their mortgage purchases and holdings. Ginnie Mae purchases FHA and VA federally insured mortgages and packages them into mortgage-backed securities, which are sold to investors. Ginnie Mae guarantees the payment of interest and principal on the mortgages held in the pool. Fannie Mae purchases individual mortgages or mortgage pools from financial institutions and packages or repackages them into mortgage-backed securities. The securitization of mortgage loans by pooling and packaging the loans into mortgage-backed securities by Ginnie Mae and Fannie Mae aided in the development of the secondary mortgage markets.

CONCEPT CHECK
What is a credit rating and what is a credit score?

How do prime and subprime mortgages differ?

CONCEPT CHECK
Who are some of the major participants in the secondary mortgage markets?

FINANCIAL CRISIS

THE 2007–09 FINANCIAL CRISIS

A number of negative economic and financial trends and events all came together to contribute to the financial crisis of 2007–09. Housing and stock prices declined sharply, and the U.S. economy entered a severe and prolonged recession at a time when individuals, financial institutions, and business firms were heavily in debt. The result was a "perfect financial storm."[1]

---

1. This discussion, as well as other discussions involving the 2007–2009 financial crisis throughout this text, draws heavily from Edgar A. Norton, Jr., "The Financial Crisis: 2007–2009," Wiley Custom Learning Solutions, 2009.

Housing prices peaked in 2006 and then started to decline sharply and still had not begun to recover by the end of 2009. Stock market prices peaked in 2007 and declined sharply before reaching a bottom in March 2009. Economic activity slowed during 2007, and the United States entered into one of its deepest economic downturns that lasted for four quarters beginning during the second half of 2008 and continuing through the first half of 2009.

The availability of very low interest rates was accompanied by the willingness of individuals, businesses, and institutions to take on large amounts of debt. Individuals in the United States were not saving and had borrowed large amounts on their credit cards and their homes in the form of mortgages and home equity loans. Lenders were offering large numbers of subprime mortgages to home purchasers with low credit scores. The deregulation of financial institutions and lax oversight by government regulatory agencies and private debt rating agencies contributed to the severity of the financial crisis. Financial institutions and business firms borrowed large amounts of debt in an attempt to reach out for a little higher return for their investors. Individuals, financial institutions, and business firms failed to "balance" the financial principle relating to "risk versus return" with the result being the taking on of excessive risk.

By the second half of 2008, the "perfect financial storm" had been created and the U.S. economy was on the verge of collapse. This financial crisis was not limited to the United States, and most major economies throughout the world also were worried by a possible global financial system meltdown. Individuals in the United States were missing their mortgage payments as housing prices continued to decline with some borrowers finding the size of their mortgages exceeding the value of their homes. The result was increasing numbers of mortgage foreclosures. Business corporations and financial institutions, which had borrowed too heavily, were being forced into bankruptcy. The value of securities backed by home mortgages collapsed as the real estate bubble burst, and by early 2008 the "perfect financial storm" had been created.

In March 2008, Bear Sterns, a major financial institution, was on the verge of failing due to the collapse of the values of mortgage-backed securities and had to be acquired by the JPMorgan Chase & Co. with the help of the Federal Reserve and the U.S. Treasury.

The Federal National Mortgage Association (Fannie Mae) had purchased and packaged large amounts of residential mortgages, many of which were subprime loans, into mortgage-backed securities. Fannie Mae either held these securities or sold them to other investors. The Federal Home Mortgage Association (Freddie Mac) purchased and held mortgage loans, including subprime loans. As default rates on these mortgage loans increased, both Fannie Mae and Freddie Mac suffered cash and liquidity crises. To avoid a meltdown, the Federal Reserve provided rescue funds in July 2008, and the U.S. government assumed control of both firms in September. Large banks that also had created mortgage-backed securities, as well as financial institutions that had purchased mortgage-back securities created by Fannie Mae and others, found themselves holding "troubled" or "toxic" mortgage securities.

By September 2008, the financial crisis was at its peak. Lehman Brothers, a major investment bank, was allowed to fail, and Merrill Lynch was sold to Bank of America. Shortly after the Lehman bankruptcy and the Merrill sale, American International Group (AIG), the largest insurance firm in the United States, was "bailed out" by the Federal Reserve with the U.S. government receiving an ownership interest in AIG. Like Merrill, Fannie Mae, and Freddie Mac, AIG was considered "too large to fail" due to its potential impact on the global financial markets.

In late September 2008, Washington Mutual, the largest savings and loan in the United States, failed with most of its assets being purchased by JPMorgan Chase. Wachovia Bank, then the fourth largest commercial bank in the United States, was also on the brink of bankruptcy before finally agreeing to be purchased by Wells Fargo Bank. Citigroup and the Bank of America, the first and second largest U.S. banks, respectively, also were suffering financial difficulties.[2]

---

2. For some of the many other views concerning the recent financial crisis, see Dave Kansas, *The Wall Street Journal Guide to the End of Wall Street As We Know It* (New York: Collins Business, HarperCollins Publishers, 2009); David Faber, *And Then the Roof Caved In* (Hoboken, NJ: John Wiley & Sons, Inc., 2009); and John Bellamy Foster and Fred Magdoff, *The Great Financial Crisis* (New York: Monthly Review Press, 2009).

CONCEPT CHECK

What were some of major developments that led to the "perfect financial storm" in 2008?

How did the U.S. government react to solve the recent financial crisis?

The U.S. government responded with the passage of the Economic Stabilization Act of 2008 in early October 2008. A primary focus of the legislation was to provide the U.S. Treasury to purchase up to $700 billion of "troubled" or "toxic" assets held by financial institutions. This became known as the Troubled Asset Relief Program (TARP). However, much of the TARP funds were actually used to invest capital in banks with little equity in their balance sheets, as well as to rescue large nonfinancial business firms, specifically General Motors and Chrysler, who were on the verge of failing. In an effort to stimulate economic activity, the U.S. government also passed the $787 billion American Recovery and Reinvestment Act of 2009 in February 2009. Funds were to be used to provide tax relief, appropriations, and direct spending. We will discuss the legislative and other actions by the U.S. government and the Federal Reserve to counter the perfect financial storm in Chapter 5.

By the end of 2009, unemployment was in excess of 10 percent, many mortgages were underwater in that borrowers owed more money on their mortgage loans than the their homes were worth. Home mortgage foreclosure rates were continuing to increase, personal and business bankruptcies also were increasing, and over 100 banks in the United States had already failed with over 500 more being considered financially weak. While there was evidence that the U.S. economy was improving by late 2009, it would likely take several more years for the United States to fully recover from the 2007–09 financial crisis.

CAREERS IN FINANCE

INTERNET ACTIVITY

Go to the Wall Street Journal Web site section at http://www.careerjournal.com, and find information relating to job hunting.

Career opportunities in finance are available in financial management, depository financial institutions, contractual savings and real property organizations, and securities markets and investment firms. While you may aspire to own your own business or to be a chief executive officer (CEO) or chief financial officer (CFO) in a major corporation, most of us must begin our careers in an entry-level position. Following are some of the ways to get started in a finance career.

1. *Financial management*

   Larger businesses or corporations divide their finance activities into treasury and control functions, whereas smaller firms often combine these functions. The treasurer is responsible for managing the firm's cash, acquiring and managing the firm's assets, and selling stocks and bonds to raise the financial capital necessary to conduct business. The controller is responsible for cost accounting, financial accounting, and tax record-keeping activities. Entry-level career opportunities include the following:

   - *Cash management analyst*: involves monitoring and managing the firm's day-to-day cash inflows and outflows
   - *Capital expenditures analyst*: involves estimating cash flows and evaluating asset investment opportunities
   - *Credit analyst*: involves evaluating credit applications and collecting amounts owed by credit customers
   - *Financial analyst*: involves evaluating financial performance and preparing financial plans
   - *Cost analyst*: involves comparing actual operations against budgeted operations
   - *Tax analyst*: involves preparing financial statements for tax purposes

2. *Depository financial institutions*

   Banks and other depository institutions offer the opportunity to start a finance career in consumer or commercial lending. Banks also hold and manage trust funds for individuals and other organizations. Entry-level career opportunities include the following:

   - *Loan analyst*: involves evaluating consumer and/or commercial loan applications
   - *Bank teller*: involves assisting customers with their day-to-day checking and banking transactions
   - *Investments research analyst*: involves conducting research on investment opportunities for a bank trust department

3. **Contractual savings and real property organizations**

   Insurance companies, pension funds, and real estate firms also provide opportunities for starting a career in finance. These institutions need a variety of employees willing to blend marketing or selling efforts with financial expertise. Entry-level career opportunities include the following:

   - *Insurance agent (broker)*: involves selling insurance to individuals and businesses and participating in the processing of claims
   - *Research analyst*: involves analyzing the investment potential of real property and securities for pension fund holdings
   - *Real estate agent (broker)*: involves marketing and selling or leasing residential or commercial property
   - *Mortgage analyst*: involves analyzing real estate loan applications and assisting in the arranging of mortgage financing

4. **Securities markets and investment firms**

   Securities firms and various investment-related businesses provide opportunities to start a finance career in the investments area. Opportunities include buying and selling seasoned securities, analyzing securities for investment potential, marketing new securities issues, and even helping individuals plan and manage their personal financial resources. Entry-level career opportunities include the following:

   - *Stockbroker (account executive)*: involves assisting clients in purchasing stocks and bonds and building investment wealth
   - *Security analyst*: involves analyzing and making recommendations on the investment potential of specific securities
   - *Investment banking analyst*: involves conducting financial analysis and valuation of new securities being issued
   - *Financial planner assistant*: involves analyzing individual client insurance needs and investment plans to meet retirement goals

While we have focused on entry-level careers in profit-motivated businesses and financial organizations, careers in finance are also available in government or not-for-profit organizations. Finance opportunities at the federal or state government levels include managing cash funds, making asset expenditure decisions, and issuing debt securities to raise funds. Hospitals and other not-for-profit organizations also need expert financial managers to manage assets, control costs, and obtain funds. Financial and other analysts are hired both by government units and not-for-profit organizations to perform these tasks.

All of these entry-level finance job opportunities also can be found in the international setting. For example, many businesses engaged in producing and marketing products and services in foreign markets often offer employees opportunities for international job assignments. Large U.S.

CAREER OPPORTUNITIES IN FINANCE
You Are Likely to Have More than One Business Career

Students are advised today to prepare for several business careers during their working lifetimes. Corporate America continues to restructure and reinvent itself. At the same time, new industries associated with the information age are developing, and old industries are dropping by the wayside. These developments make it even more likely that each of you will have the opportunity for multiple business careers.

Graduates of Harvard University are periodically surveyed concerning their work experiences and careers. Responses to one survey of individuals twenty-five years after graduation found that over half had worked for four or more employers while one-fourth had been fired (or, in kinder terms, "involuntarily terminated"). Over half of the men and women respondents had had at least two substantially different careers, and in many instances significant retraining was required.

Remember as you read this book that even if you don't currently plan on a career in finance, learning about finance might become very important to you later in your working lifetime. And, no matter where your business career takes you, you will always need to know and understand your personal finances.

CONCEPT CHECK
What are the major areas for possible careers in finance?

banks also offer international job experiences through their foreign banking operations. Furthermore, since worldwide securities markets exist, securities analysts and financial planners often must analyze and visit foreign-based firms.

At the end of each chapter, you will find a Career Profile feature about a real person. In addition, several more detailed Career Opportunities in Finance boxes are presented in selected chapters. We hope these materials provide a better understanding of some of the many career opportunities that exist in the finance field. We are also sure that new finance job opportunities will occur in the future as the field continues to develop and change. It is now time to begin learning about finance!

THE PLAN OF STUDY

The subject matter of this book includes the entire scope of the financial environment from the perspective of the financial system and the three areas of finance—institutions and markets, investments, and financial management. You will learn about the markets in which funds are traded and the institutions that participate in and assist these flows of funds. You will learn about the investments area of finance, including the characteristics of debt and equity securities that are issued, the markets where securities are traded, and investment risk-return concepts. You will study the financial management principles and concepts that guide financial managers to make sound financial planning, asset acquisition, and financing decisions. International finance applications also are integrated throughout the text.

INTERNET ACTIVITY
The Monster.com Web site, http://www.monster.com, provides information on current finance jobs that are available. Click on "Select Category" and then "Finance/Economics" and list some of the entry-level finance positions available.

Part 1 focuses on the financial institutions, markets, and other participants that make the U.S. financial system operate effectively both domestically and within the global economy. Chapter 2 introduces the role of money within the overall financial system and its monetary system component. Chapter 3 focuses on the financial intermediation roles of depository and other financial institutions, as well as how they operate within the financial system. Chapter 4 discusses the Federal Reserve System. Chapter 5 discusses economic objectives, the role and actions of policy makers, and how money and credit are provided to meet the needs of the economy. We conclude Part 1 with a chapter on international finance and trade because of its importance in understanding market economies worldwide.

Part 2 is concerned with the investments area of finance. Chapter 7 discusses the savings and investment process and its major role in the U.S. market economy. This is followed by Chapter 8, which describes the structure of interest rates. Time value of money concepts are covered in Chapter 9, and the characteristics and valuations of bonds and stocks are presented in Chapter 10. Chapter 11 discusses the characteristics and workings of the securities market. Part 2 concludes with Chapter 12, which describes financial return and risk concepts for a single asset or security, and for portfolios of securities.

Part 3 focuses on the financial management of businesses. We begin Chapter 13 with an introduction and overview of the types of business organizations and follow with a review of basic financial statements and financial data important to the financial manager. Chapter 14 discusses the need for, and the way in which to conduct, financial analysis of past performance and concludes with a section on financial planning for the future. Chapter 15 covers the management of working capital, while Chapter 16 focuses on sources of short-term business financing. We then turn our attention in Chapter 17 to the process and methods for conducting capital budgeting analysis. We conclude Part 3 with Chapter 18, which provides a discussion of capital structure and cost of capital concepts.

CONCEPT CHECK
What do the three parts of this book cover?

Of course, as we illustrated in Figure 1.1, the three areas of finance are not independent but rather are continually interacting or overlapping. For example, financial institutions provide an important financial intermediation role by getting individual savings into the hands of businesses so that financial managers can efficiently use and invest those funds. Financial managers also rely heavily on the investments area of finance when carrying out their financial management activities. Corporations often need to raise funds in the primary securities markets, and secondary securities markets, in turn, provide investors with the liquidity of being able to buy and sell previously issued securities. Our approach in this book is to provide survey exposure to all three areas of finance.

CAREER PROFILES

DON PARSONS
Partner, Centennial Funds

BS Electrical Engineering, Northwestern
MBA Finance, University of Michigan

"We'll lose our entire investment in almost half of the companies we fund."

Q: *You work in the venture capital industry. Please explain what that means.*
A: Our firm looks for entrepreneurial companies, especially in the high-tech field, where we can make an equity investment and hopefully produce a high return on our investment over a five-to-nine-year period. We also take an active role with the entrepreneurs to help them succeed.

Q: *What kind of help do entrepreneurs need?*
A: Most entrepreneurs are experts in their specific fields—computers, electronics, whatever—but they're not experts in starting a business and making it profitable. We provide experience that can help a small company avoid common mistakes and improve its chance of survival.

Q: *But success is not guaranteed.*
A: Not at all. According to industry averages, we'll lose our entire investment in almost half of the companies we fund. And only a handful turn into huge successes like Microsoft or Intel, which started very small. In the case of a big success, we might make fifty times our original investment. But these few big successes must make up for the many that don't survive.

Q: *Describe an entry-level position in venture capital.*
A: I started as an investment analyst, which is really an apprentice kind of position. I was assigned to a different partner every six months, and I helped those partners evaluate potential investment in new companies. There's a lot of research involved—in the industry, the technology, the product, the management team of the company—and the investment analyst does a lot of that research. Then we compile our findings into a very comprehensive report that is used to make the investment recommendation.

Q: *How were you qualified to evaluate these start-up companies?*
A: I have an electrical engineering degree and worked with IBM during and after college. At IBM I was involved with the design of several of its early personal computers, so I learned a lot about the development process of new technology products. Not everyone brings a technology background into this business, but many do. It has helped me a lot. After IBM I got my MBA, which enabled me to gain the financial skills necessary to evaluate investment opportunities.

Q: *What skills help you most in your job?*
A: There are many aspects to building a successful company, so the job requires a broad set of skills. You have to understand the technology, the finances, tax considerations, the legal and securities aspects, negotiation, and whatever other issues arise. You must be able to successfully interact with many different people. And parallel thinking is also an absolute requirement. If you can't juggle multiple issues and multiple projects, you would find this a very frustrating business.

Q: *What's the toughest part of this job?*
A: It's difficult to evaluate your results. It may be four, seven, ten years before we can tell if a new company is going to survive, much less succeed. It keeps you humble.

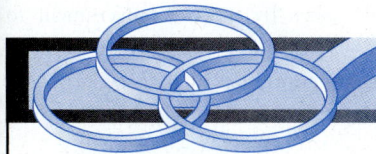

APPLYING FINANCE TO...

INSTITUTIONS AND MARKETS

Financial institutions and financial markets are necessary components of an efficient financial system. Institutions perform an important financial intermediation role by gathering the savings of individuals and then lending the pooled savings to businesses that want to make investments.

INVESTMENTS

Securities markets are also important components of an efficient financial system. The primary securities market facilitates raising funds by issuing new debt and equity securities. The secondary market for securities facilitates the transfer of ownership of existing securities among investors. Mortgage markets help individuals finance the purchase of homes.

FINANCIAL MANAGEMENT

Business firms continually interact with financial institutions as they carry out their day-to-day operations. Businesses also often seek to raise additional funds to finance investment in inventories, equipment, and buildings needed to support growth in sales. Bank loans and mortgage loans are important financing sources, along with the proceeds from the issuance of new debt and equity securities.

SUMMARY

Finance is the study of how businesses and others acquire, spend, and manage money and other financial resources. More specifically, finance is composed of three areas—financial institutions and markets, investments, and financial management. However, these three areas are not independent of one another but rather intersect or overlap. A survey approach to the study of finance thus covers all three areas.

An effective financial system requires policy makers, a monetary system, and financial institutions and financial markets to facilitate the flow of financial capital from savings into investments. Policy makers pass laws and set fiscal and monetary policies designed to manage the economy. A monetary system creates and transfers money. Financial institutions accumulate and lend/invest individual savings. Financial markets facilitate the transfer of securities and other financial assets. All these activities operate together to create a smooth running and efficient financial system.

There are four types of financial markets—debt securities markets, equity securities markets, derivative securities markets, and foreign exchange markets. Characteristics of the mortgage markets were introduced in this chapter because of the role mortgages and mortgage markets played in the recent financial crisis.

KEY TERMS

adjustable-rate mortgage (ARM)
capital markets
credit rating
credit score
debt securities markets
derivative securities markets
entrepreneurial finance
equity securities markets
ethical behavior
finance

financial environment
financial institutions
financial management
financial markets
financial system
fixed-rate mortgage
foreign exchange markets
investments
money markets
mortgage

mortgage-backed security
mortgage markets
personal finance
primary markets
prime mortgage
secondary markets
securitization
subprime mortgage

DISCUSSION QUESTIONS

1. What is finance?
2. What is meant by the term *financial environment*?
3. What are the three areas of finance?
4. Briefly describe the terms *entrepreneurial finance* and *personal finance*.
5. Identify and briefly describe several reasons for studying finance.
6. What are the six principles of finance?
7. Describe what is meant by *ethical behavior*.
8. What are the basic requirements of an effective financial system?
9. Identify and briefly describe the financial functions in the financial system.
10. Briefly describe the differences between money and capital markets.
11. What are the differences between primary and secondary markets?
12. Identify the four types of major financial markets.
13. What is a mortgage? What is meant by the term *mortgage markets*?
14. Identify and briefly describe the two major types of residential real estate mortgages.
15. What is meant by the term *securitization*? What is a mortgage-backed security?

16. Briefly describe credit ratings and credit scores.

17. Identify and describe the roles of several major participants in the secondary mortgage markets.

18. How did the 2007–09 financial crisis evolve?

19. What initial actions were taken by the U.S. government to respond to the 2007–09 financial crisis?

20. Indicate some of the career opportunities in finance available to business graduates today.

EXERCISES

1. The U.S. financial system is composed of: (1) policy makers, (2) a monetary system, (3) financial institutions, and (4) financial markets. Indicate which of these components is associated with each of the following roles:
    a. accumulate and lend/invest savings
    b. create and transfer money
    c. pass laws and set fiscal and monetary policies
    d. market and facilitate transfer of financial assets

2. Financial markets may be categorized as: (1) debt securities markets, (2) equity securities markets, (3) derivative securities markets, and (4) foreign exchange markets. Indicate in which of these markets the following securities trade:
    a. residential mortgages
    b. corporate bonds
    c. corporate stocks
    d. currencies

3. In business, ethical dilemmas or situations occur frequently. Laws and regulations exist to define what unethical behavior is. However, the practicing of high-quality ethical behavior often goes beyond just meeting laws and regulations. Indicate how you would respond to the following situations.
    a. Your boss has just told you that tomorrow the Federal Drug Administration will announce its approval of your firm's marketing of a new breakthrough drug. As a result of this information, you are considering purchasing shares of stock in your firm this afternoon. What would you do?
    b. In the past, your firm has been in compliance with regulatory standards relating to product safety. However, you have heard through the company grapevine that recently some of your firm's products have failed resulting in injuries to customers. You are considering quitting your job due to personal moral concerns. What would you do?

4. Obtain several recent issues of *Business Week*. Identify, read, and be prepared to discuss at least one article relating to one of the six principles of finance.

5. Obtain several recent issues of *Business Week*. Identify, read, and be prepared to discuss at least one article relating to one of the four types of financial markets identified in Chapter 1.

6. Obtain several recent issues of the *Wall Street Journal*. Identify, read, and be prepared to discuss at least one article relating specifically to the mortgage markets.

7. Obtain several recent issues of the *Wall Street Journal*. Identify, read, and be prepared to discuss at least one article relating to the 2007–09 financial crisis.

8. Go to the U.S. Small Business Administration (SBA) Web site, http://www.sba.gov, and search for sources of information on starting a new business. Identify and prepare a written summary of the *startup basics* described on the SBA site.

CHAPTER 2

Money and the Monetary System

Chapter Learning Objectives:

AFTER STUDYING THIS CHAPTER, YOU SHOULD BE ABLE TO:

- Describe the three ways in which money is transferred from savers to businesses.
- Identify the major components of the monetary system.
- Describe the functions of money.
- Give a brief review of the development of money in the United States.
- Describe major types of money market securities.
- Briefly explain the M1, M2, and M3 definitions of the money supply.
- Explain possible relationships between money supply and economic activity.
- Comment on developments in the international monetary system.

Where We Have Been...

In Chapter 1, we provided a general overview of the financial environment. We also hope that we provided you with a convincing argument as to why you should study finance. You should also know what is required for a financial system to be effective, know the types of financial markets that are available to aid the transferring of financial assets, and have a basic understanding of some of the factors that contributed to the 2007–09 financial crisis. Finally, you should now have some idea of the career opportunities that are available in finance.

Where We Are Going...

As we progress through Part 1, we build on our understanding of the U.S. financial system. Chapter 3 focuses on understanding the importance of depository and other institutions in the financial system. We discuss how your savings are pooled with the savings of other individuals in financial institutions and then are made available to businesses, governments, and other individuals who may want to invest in inventories, invest in highways, or purchase homes. The remaining chapters in Part 1 focus on the Federal Reserve System, the role of policy makers, and how international developments influence the financial system.

How This Chapter Applies to Me...

Each of us needs money. While you may feel you need more or less money than your friend, money is necessary for each of us to conduct day-to-day activities. You may have to buy gas for your car or pay for public transportation to school or work. Your may need money for lunch or supplies. You may even want to borrow money to purchase a house someday. After reading this chapter you should have a clearer understanding of the functions and types of money available to you.

John Kenneth Galbraith, a U.S. economist, said the following about money:

> Money is a singular thing. It ranks with love as man's greatest source of joy. And with death as his greatest source of anxiety. Over all history it has oppressed nearly all people in one of two ways: either it has been abundant and very unreliable, or reliable and very scarce.

Why should any "one thing" be so important? Money is what makes the financial system work. Money is a measure of wealth. Money can be used to purchase goods and services. Money is acceptable to repay debts. Creating and transferring money are integral parts of the capital formation process. However, too much money in an economy is associated with unsustainable economic growth and rapidly rising prices. On the other hand, too little money in an economy is associated with poor economic performance and sometimes recession.

PROCESS OF MOVING SAVINGS INTO INVESTMENTS

Financial institutions and markets move or transfer money from individuals and institutions with excess money to business firms and others who have needs for more money. We usually look at individuals in total or in the aggregate as an economic unit. Financial institutions, business firms, and governments (federal, state, and local) also are viewed as economic units. A *surplus economic unit* generates more money than it spends, and thus it has excess money to save or invest. A *deficit economic unit* spends more money than it brings in and must balance its money receipts with money expenditures by obtaining money from surplus units.

Individuals taken as a group have generally been a surplus economic unit in the past. Of course, while some individuals are saving, others are borrowing to cover the purchase of goods and services. Individuals desiring to purchase homes also borrow by taking out mortgage loans. Some business firms are savers when their revenues exceed their costs of operation and reinvestment back in the businesses. Other businesses choose to borrow or sell stock to finance their operations and grow their businesses with the intent of providing higher returns to their investors. Private-sector financial institutions also have responsibilities to provide returns to their investor-owners and sometimes borrow heavily to grow their institutions and hopefully provide higher returns. Sometimes, government entities (federal, state, and local) have tax revenues that exceed expenditures and thus are surplus economic units. However, when government entities spend more than they receive from tax revenues, they must borrow the money shortfall and thus are deficit economic units.

For the U.S. financial system to operate effectively over time depends on each of the three overall economic units (individuals, business firms, and government entities) to achieve a reasonable balance between their aggregate revenues and expenditures. When expenditures exceed revenues for extended periods of time, deficit economic units must build up large amounts of debts. A major factor in the severity of the 2007–09 financial crisis was the massive amounts of debt taken on by individuals, business firms, financial institutions, and government entities during the decade leading up to the crisis. In an effort to alleviate the financial crisis, government entities, through increased expenditures in the form of stimulus programs, have increased their deficits and, in the case of the U.S. government, dramatically increased the size of the national debt.

Our primary focus is on the *savings-investment process* that involves the direct or indirect transfer of individual savings to business firms in exchange for their debt and stock securities. Figure 2.1 shows three ways whereby money is transferred from savers to a business firm. As illustrated in the top part, savers can directly purchase the securities (stocks or debt instruments) of a business firm by exchanging money for the firm's securities. No financial institution is used in this type of savings-investment transaction since it involves only a saver and the business firm.

The use of indirect transfers is the more common way by which money is transferred from savers to investors. The middle part of Figure 2.1 shows how the transfer process usually takes place when savers purchase new securities issued by a business. From Chapter 1 you should recall that this indirect transfer involves use of the primary securities market. In this process, financial institutions operate to bring savers and security issuers together. Savers provide money to purchase the business firm's securities. However, rather than a direct transfer taking place, financial institutions, such as investment banks, may facilitate the savings-investment process by first purchasing the securities being issued by a corporation and then reselling the securities to savers. No additional securities are created in this type of indirect transfer.

The bottom part of Figure 2.1 illustrates the typical capital formation process involving a financial institution. Savers deposit or invest money with a financial institution such as a bank, insurance company, or mutual fund. The financial institution issues its own securities to the

FIGURE 2.1
Savings-Investment Process: From Individual Savers to a Business Firm

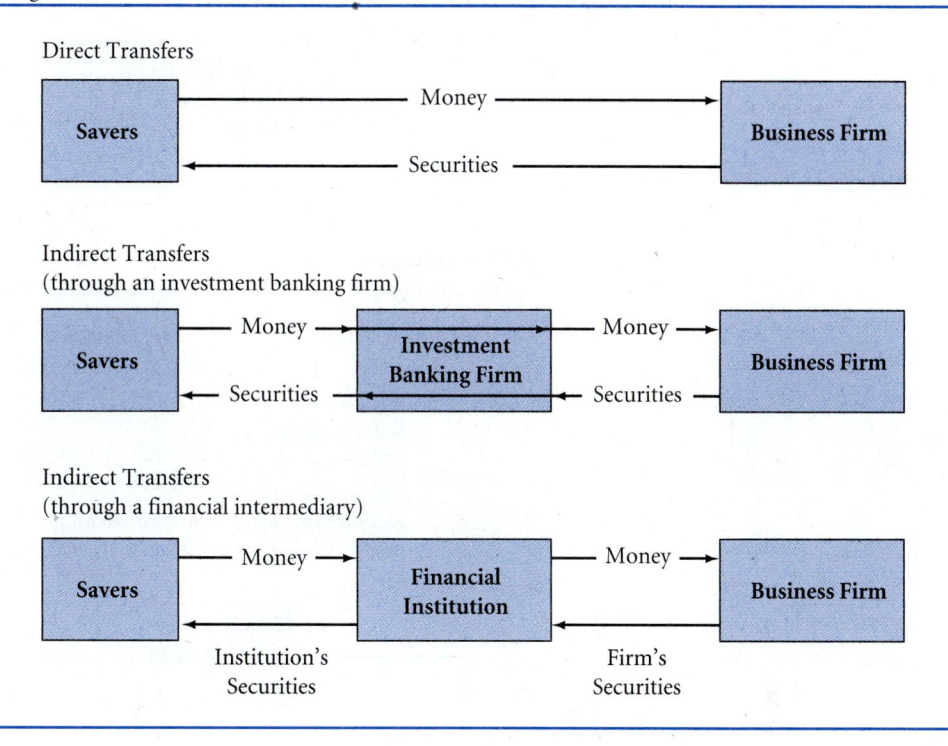

Direct Transfers

Savers → Money → Business Firm
Savers ← Securities ← Business Firm

Indirect Transfers
(through an investment banking firm)

Savers → Money → Investment Banking Firm → Money → Business Firm
Savers ← Securities ← Investment Banking Firm ← Securities ← Business Firm

Indirect Transfers
(through a financial intermediary)

Savers → Money → Financial Institution → Money → Business Firm
Savers ← Institution's Securities ← Financial Institution ← Firm's Securities ← Business Firm

---

saver. For example, a saver may give money in the form of currency to a bank in exchange for the bank's savings or time-deposit obligation. The bank, in turn, may lend money to a business firm in exchange for that firm's "I owe you" (IOU) in the form of a loan. As money passes from savers through a financial institution to a business firm, a debt instrument or security is created by the financial institution and by the business firm. This is the process of financial intermediation that we will discuss further in Chapter 3.

Of course, the savings-investment process could alternatively focus on the flow of money from savers to government entities that are operating at deficits caused by expenditures greater than tax revenues. The U.S. government and state and local governments can sell their debt securities directly to savers who might be individuals, business firms, or financial institutions. Indirect transfers also could take place with the aid of financial institutions to facilitate the movement of government entity debt securities to savers. A financial institution may operate as a conduit in the primary securities market. Alternatively, the financial institution may purchase the government entity's debt securities and, in turn, issue its own debt securities to individuals and other savers.

The savings-investment process could also focus on moving the savings of individuals and other savers to those individuals, businesses, institutions, and governments that want to finance real-estate investments. Many individuals want to own their own homes and can do so only by taking on mortgage debt or home loans. Other organizations also may wish to invest in real property in the form of offices, manufacturing facilities, or other buildings. To do so, often requires the need to finance a part of the purchase price with a mortgage loan on the real property being purchased. While our focus in this text is primarily on the savings-investment process involving the raising of money or financial capital by business firms, the process for financing deficits by government entities will be discussed in Chapter 5, and the financing of residential and commercial property will be addressed in Chapter 7.

OVERVIEW OF THE MONETARY SYSTEM

The monetary system is responsible for carrying out the financial functions of creating and transferring money. Money is needed to conduct day-to-day activities, facilitate the capital investment process, and support economic growth. Businesses need money to invest in inventories,

---

CONCEPT CHECK

What are surplus economic units and deficit economic units?

How does the savings-investment process take place when financial institutions are involved?

Which economic units, in addition to business firms, might need money from savers to invest?

FIGURE 2.2
The U.S. Monetary System

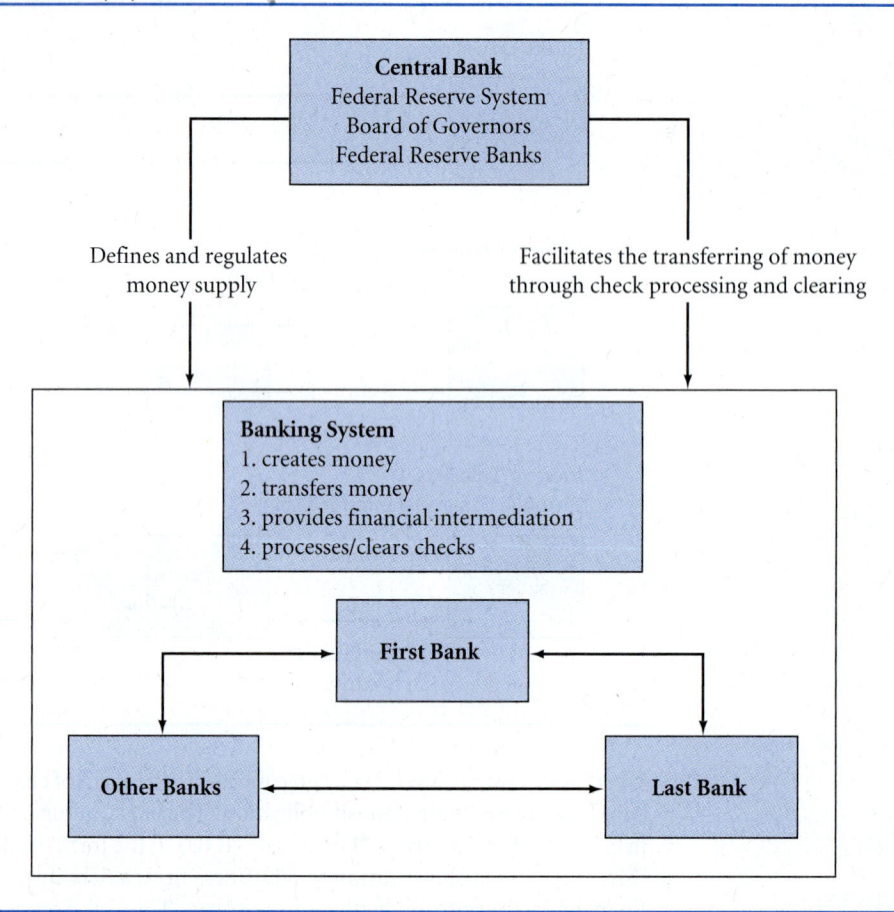

```
                    Central Bank
                 Federal Reserve System
                  Board of Governors
                  Federal Reserve Banks
                 /                    \
   Defines and regulates      Facilitates the transferring of money
     money supply             through check processing and clearing
                 \                    /
        ┌──────────────────────────────────────────┐
        │      Banking System                      │
        │      1. creates money                    │
        │      2. transfers money                  │
        │      3. provides financial intermediation│
        │      4. processes/clears checks          │
        │                                          │
        │              First Bank                  │
        │             /        \                   │
        │    Other Banks  ←→  Last Bank            │
        └──────────────────────────────────────────┘
```

equipment, and buildings. Governments need money to construct roads, buildings, parks, and other infrastructure for the people. Individuals need money to purchase goods, services, and homes

Figure 2.2 indicates the major participants in the U.S. monetary system. A central bank is needed to define and regulate the amount of the money supply in the financial system. A central bank also facilitates the transferring of money by processing and clearing checks, a form of money called deposit money. The central bank in the United States is called the Federal Reserve System (or Fed for short). We will discuss the characteristics and operation of the Fed in Chapter 4 and cover its policy-making activities in Chapter 5.

An efficient banking system also is needed. Not all types of financial institutions are the same. For example, while insurance companies and investment companies can provide a financial intermediation function between savers and investors, only depository institutions as a group can create money. Depository institutions include commercial banks, S&Ls, savings banks, and credit unions. For purposes of presentation, it is common practice to refer to all depository institutions as "banks," and they all are part of the banking system. We discuss the characteristics of depository and other major financial institutions in Chapter 3.

The banking system, as depicted in Figure 2.2 is composed of all the banks in the system. For illustration purposes, there is a first bank and a last bank. The banking system creates money (technically deposit money) and, along with the Fed, clears checks and transfers money within the overall financial system. Checks can be cleared either through other banks in the banking system or with the aid of the Fed. We will examine the check-clearing process in Chapters 3 and 4.

While an individual bank, such as First Bank, cannot create money, the banking system can. Let's assume that First Bank receives $1,000 from the ABC business firm and sets up a checking account (demand deposit) for the firm. The $1,000 received by First Bank is called "reserves" and represents money held by First Bank so that it can pay off checks written by ABC against its checking account balance. However, rather than holding the full $1,000 in reserves, First Bank

CONCEPT CHECK
Who are the major participants in the U.S. monetary system?

will only hold a fraction (e.g., 20 percent, or $200) in reserves and will lend out the remaining $800 to the XYZ firm. As long as XYZ places the $800 loan proceeds in its checking account at a bank (e.g., Last Bank) somewhere in the banking system, the initial $1,000 demand deposit established for ABC has increased to $1,800 (the $1,000 for ABC plus the $800 for XYZ). As long as deposit money keeps coming back into the banking system, more deposit money is created.[1] We will explore the deposit money creation process in greater detail in Chapter 5 when we discuss the Fed's monetary policy-making activities.

IMPORTANCE AND FUNCTIONS OF MONEY

real assets
include the direct ownership of land, buildings or homes, equipment, inventories, durable goods, and precious metals

financial assets
money, debt securities and financial contracts, and equity securities that are backed by real assets and the earning power of the issuers

money
anything that is generally accepted as payment for goods, services, and debts

medium of exchange
the basic function of money

barter
exchange of goods or services without using money

store of value
money held for some period of time before it is spent

Real assets include the direct ownership of land, buildings or homes, equipment, inventories, durable goods, and even precious metals. **Financial assets** are money, debt instruments, equity securities, and other financial contracts that are backed by real assets and the earning abilities of issuers. A loan to you to purchase an automobile usually provides for the lender to hold the auto title (ownership) until the loan is repaid. Long-term debt issued by a corporation may represent a claim against specific assets, such as buildings and equipment, or the general assets of the issuer. A mortgage loan to you will be backed by the house against which the loan is being made.

Money is anything generally accepted as a means of paying for goods and services and for paying off debts. For something to serve successfully as money, it must be easily divisible so that exchanges can take place in small or large quantities, relatively inexpensive to store and transfer, and reasonably stable in value over time. Money must perform three basic functions, serving as a medium of exchange, a store of value, and a standard of value.

Money was first developed to serve as a **medium of exchange** to facilitate transactions. Primitive economies consisted largely of self-sufficient units or groups that lived by means of hunting, fishing, and simple agriculture. There was little need or occasion to exchange goods or services. As economies developed, however, the process of exchange became important. Some individuals specialized, to a degree at least, in herding sheep, raising grain, or shaping gold as metalsmiths. To aid in the exchanging of goods for goods, called **barter**, tables of relative values were developed from experience. For example, a table might show the number of furs, measures of grain, or amount of cloth agreed to equal one cow. This arrangement eased exchanges, but the process still had many serious drawbacks. For example, if a person had a cow and wanted to trade it for some nuts and furs, he or she would need to find someone who had an excess of both these items to trade. The need for a simpler means of exchange led to the development of money, with its relatively low storage and transfer costs, to be used as a medium of exchange.

Money also may be held as a **store of value**. That is, money may be spent immediately after it is received or after it has been held for some time. While money is held, it is a liquid asset and provides its owner with flexibility, but the owner pays for this flexibility by giving up the potential return that could be earned through investment or the satisfaction that could be gained from spending it for goods and services. Money can perform its function as a store of value only if its "purchasing power" is relatively stable over time. Under this condition, the spending decision is separated from the income decision. Once income is received, the holder of the income can

SMALL BUSINESS PRACTICE
Starting Your Small Business

Today, with modern telecommunication facilities and the Internet, many small businesses can be located wherever their owners want to live and work. At the same time, certain cities and geographical areas in the United States may be more conducive to helping small businesses succeed.

The Dun & Bradstreet Company (D&B) provides a wealth of information relating to the starting of a new business. D&B provides information on how to establish, manage, and grow your small business. When considering whether to establish or start a business, it is important to ask: "Are you really ready to start?" It is also important to "plan your business," as well as "understand legal and tax issues." And, before "opening your doors," you might want to review the D&B article titled "Why Do Many Small Businesses Fail?" Access the D&B Web site at: http://www.dnb.com.

---

1. As we will see, deposit money can theoretically continue to increase until the total "held" reserves equal the initial deposit. In practice, the Fed establishes the percentage of reserves that must be held against demand deposits.

liquidity
how easily and with little loss of value an asset can be exchanged for money

standard of value
a function of money that occurs when prices and debts are stated in terms of the monetary unit

individual net worth
sum of an individual's money, real assets, and financial assets less the individual's debt obligations

CONCEPT CHECK
How do real assets and financial assets differ?

What is money?

What are the three functions performed by money?

choose to spend it or save it. If the decision is to save, then that money can be made available through the savings-investment process to those who may want to invest now.

Any asset other than money can also serve as a store of value as long as that asset can be converted into money quickly and without significant loss of value. We refer to this quality—the ease with which an asset can be exchanged for money or other assets—as **liquidity**. Money is perfectly liquid since it is a generally accepted medium of exchange. Other assets, such as savings deposits held at depository institutions, approach the liquidity of money. The existence of such liquid assets reduces the need for holding money itself as a store of value.

Money also serves as a **standard of value,** which means that prices and contracts for deferred payments are expressed in terms of the monetary unit. For example, in the United States, prices and debts are usually expressed in terms of dollars without stating whether the purchase will be cash or credit. Of course, if money is to perform its function as a standard of value, it is essential that the value of the monetary unit be relatively stable over time. For example, if one dollar can be used to purchase two ballpoint pens today but only one tomorrow, such money would not be very effective as either a store of value or a standard of value.

While money is the fundamental measure of wealth, an individual's net worth usually consists of more than just money. **Individual net worth** is the sum of an individual's money, real assets, and financial assets or claims against others less the individual's debt obligations. Recall that real assets include the automobile that you own, your house (if you have one) and its contents, clothes, and even jewelry or precious stones. You may also own shares of stock in a mutual fund. While this is a financial asset, it is still part of your net worth. However, you may have borrowed from a bank to purchase your automobile, and you probably have a mortgage loan on the house you purchased. These are financial claims held by others against some of your real property. You must subtract debt obligations or financial claims against you or your real property in order to determine your individual net worth. It is estimated that there are about 7.7 million millionaires in the world with about 2.3 million of them being in the United States.[2] If you wish to join this group some day, you will have to accumulate a net worth in excess of $1 million. Good luck!

DEVELOPMENT OF MONEY IN THE UNITED STATES

The two basic components of money supply in the United States are physical (coin and currency) money and deposit money. A review of the development of money in the United States will help us understand the characteristics of money today, as well as how well U.S. money performs the three functions of money listed.

PHYSICAL MONEY (COIN AND PAPER CURRENCY)

The first function of "successful" money is that it serves as a medium of exchange. Physical money is the coin and paper currency used to purchase goods and services and to settle debts. We will first examine how U.S. coins have changed in terms of their precious metal (gold and silver) content over time. Then, we will examine how U.S. paper currency has changed in terms of both its physical characteristics and "backing" with precious metals.

U.S. Coins

While barter was undoubtedly important in early American history, the government moved swiftly toward a monetary system based on precious metals that would serve as an efficient medium of exchange. During much of the seventeenth and eighteenth centuries, the American colonies relied primarily on the Spanish dollar to conduct business transactions.[3] In 1785 the word *dollar* was adopted by the U.S. Congress as the standard monetary unit or standard of value. The first monetary act in the United States, passed in 1792, provided for a **bimetallic standard**

bimetallic standard
monetary standard based on two metals, usually silver and gold

---

2. "Return of the Millionaires," http://money.cnn.com/2004/06/15/pf/millionaires/index.htm. To learn more about how people become wealthy and some of their characteristics, see Thomas J. Stanley and William D. Danko, *The Millionaire Next Door* (New York: Pocket Books, 1996) and Thomas J. Stanley, *The Millionaire Mind* (Kansas City, MO: Andrews McMeel Publishing, 2001).

3. The Spanish dollar often was cut into eight pieces or "bits" to make change. If you have heard the U.S. quarter-dollar referred to as "two bits," you now know that this term originated from cutting the Spanish dollar into "pieces of eight."

full-bodied money
coins that contain the same value in metal as their face value

based on both gold and silver. The dollar was defined in both grains of pure silver and grains of pure gold. All gold and silver coins were to be **full-bodied money** because their metal content was worth the same as their face values. For example, one silver dollar was to contain one dollar's worth of silver, a ten-dollar gold coin was to contain ten dollars' worth of gold, and so on.

A law enacted in 1837 modified the weight for the silver dollar to 412.5 grains of silver with .900 fineness. Copper of .100 fineness was used to make the coins last longer. The result was that each dollar contained .77344 ounce of pure silver. Since the value of the silver content was to be $1, silver was valued at $1.29 per ounce ($1/.77344).

Figure 2.3 shows examples of full-bodied and token U.S. coins. The top portion shows the front side (obverse) of the peace-type dollar and the Franklin half-dollar. The peace-type dollar was produced from 1921 to 1935. The Franklin half-dollar, produced from 1948 to 1963, contained .36169 ounce of pure silver. Since silver prices had been gradually rising, the Franklin half-dollar was full-bodied money at a silver price of $1.38 ($.50/.36169). Depending on the prevailing market price of silver, a silver coin such as the half-dollar could be less than, greater than, or exactly full-bodied.

For full-bodied money, its store of value was reflected in the then-current value of its precious metal content, and as long as the price of precious metals moved in unison with the prices of goods and services, this money's store of value reflected the store of purchasing power.

FIGURE 2.3
Examples of Full-Bodied and Token (Copper-Nickel-Clad) U.S. Coins

Two Full-Bodied Coins
[Face value and silver metal content were equal when coin was issued]

Peace Type Dollar
(issued 1921–35)
[contains .77344
ounces of silver]

Franklin Half Dollar
(issued 1948–63)
[contains .36169
ounces of silver]

Two Token Coins
[Face value much greater than metal (no silver) content]

Eisenhower Dollar
(issued 1971–78)
[contains only
copper and nickel]

Kennedy Half Dollar
(issued 1971–present)
[contains only
copper and nickel]

token coins
coins containing metal of less value than their stated value

Rapidly rising silver prices in the 1960s, however, made silver coins worth more as melted-down bullion than their face values. As a result, the U.S. government "debased" its full-bodied money by replacing silver content with copper and nickel. Coins with face values higher than the value of their metal content are called **token coins.** The bottom portion of Figure 2.3 shows two copper-nickel–clad (token) U.S. coins. The Eisenhower dollar was minted from 1971 to 1978. Kennedy half-dollars were full-bodied coins in 1964, were changed to silver-clad (reduced silver content) coins from 1965 to 1970, and have been copper-nickel–clad coins since 1971.

The production of gold coins began in 1795 with the $5 and $10 coins. The issuance of full-bodied gold dollars was authorized in 1849, and production continued through 1889. For several decades, the value of a U.S. dollar was expressed both in terms of silver and gold. All gold coin production was stopped in 1933, and in 1934 U.S. citizens were prohibited from holding monetary gold in the United States. This restriction was extended to gold held abroad by U.S. citizens in 1961. All restrictions on holding gold in money form were removed in 1975.

Paper Currency

The evolution and use of paper currency in the United States have been characterized by a very erratic history. While some paper money was issued by individual colonies, the first effort of a government to issue paper money occurred when the Continental Congress authorized the issuance of notes called Continentals to finance the Revolutionary War. While these notes were denominated in dollars, they had no backing in either silver or gold. Rather, they were backed only by possible future tax revenues to be gathered when the colonies became independent. As you might guess, the Continentals soon became worthless. This led to a long period of distrust of paper money. After a brief experience with two national banks, American banking went through a period of no federal regulation and nonuniformity in operating laws. State-chartered banks issued their own paper currency almost at will and in many cases with no or little backing of their notes with gold or silver deposits.[4]

INTERNET ACTIVITY
Go to the U.S. Treasury Web site, http://www.treas.gov. Go to "Coins and Currency" and then to "Bureau of Engraving and Printing." Find recent information on redesigned currency.

representative full-bodied money
paper money fully backed by a precious metal

Paper money may be either representative full-bodied money or fiat money. **Representative full-bodied money** is paper money that is backed by an amount of precious metal equal in value to the face amount of the paper money. The U.S. government has issued two types of representative full-bodied money. Gold certificates were issued from 1865 through 1928. Since they could be redeemed for gold with a value equal to the paper currency's face amount, they were "as good as gold." However, since most gold certificates were issued in large denominations, they were not intended to be used in general circulation but rather to settle institutional gold accounts. The issuance of silver certificates was authorized beginning in 1878. A switch to "small-size" silver certificates occurred in 1929, and they continued to be issued and used through 1963.

Figure 2.4 shows examples of full-bodied and fiat U.S. paper currency. The top portion shows a silver certificate. These certificates could be exchanged for silver dollars or silver bullion when presented to the U.S. Treasury. Of course, like full-bodied silver coins, these silver certificates became worth more in terms of the bullion value of silver relative to their face values as silver prices began climbing in the 1960s. As a result, redemption of silver certificates in silver dollars was halted in 1964 by the U.S. government, and in 1968 redemption in silver bullion also was stopped.

fiat money
legal tender proclaimed to be money by law

Today, almost all paper money in circulation is in the form of Federal Reserve Notes, which were authorized under the *Federal Reserve Act of 1913*. The bottom portion of Figure 2.4 shows a Federal Reserve Note. These notes, which are not backed by either gold or silver, are called **fiat money** because the government decreed the notes to be "legal tender" for purposes of making payments and discharging public and private debts. Of course, the copper-nickel–clad, or token, coins of today are also fiat money because their metal content values are less than their face values.

The reliance on the use of fiat money can be problematic. First, fiat money generally becomes worthless if the issuing government fails. As an example, Confederate currency was issued during the U.S. Civil War. However, when the Confederacy lost the war, this fiat money became worthless. Second, since there is no required backing in gold or silver, it is relatively easy to issue more and more fiat money. Issuing too much money can, in turn, lead to rising prices and a lack

---

4. By 1865, it was estimated that about one-third of the circulating paper currency was counterfeit. As a result, the U.S. Treasury established the U.S. Secret Service to control counterfeiting activities.

FIGURE 2.4
Examples of Representative Full-Bodied and Fiat U.S. Paper Currency

Representative Full-Bodied Paper Currency
[Face value and silver metal "backing" were equal when the bill was issued]

Silver Certificate (small size issued 1929–63)
[exchangeable for silver dollars or silver bullion equal to face amount]

Fiat Paper Currency
[No "backing" with silver (or other precious metal) deposits]

Federal Reserve Note (small size issued 1929–present)
[U.S. government states on each note: "This note is legal tender for all debts, public and private"]

of confidence in the government. An effective monetary system with a strong central bank and prudent policy makers are needed when a financial system relies on fiat money to carry out its transactions.

Several major changes in Federal Reserve Notes have taken place over time. In 1929, the size of the notes was reduced about 30 percent from large notes (7.42 inches by 3.13 inches) to small notes (6.14 inches by 2.61 inches). This change made production less expensive and made it easier to handle and less costly to store and transfer paper money. Figure 2.5 shows the old and current design of the $20 U.S. Federal Reserve Note. The "small portrait" $20 note is shown in the top portion of the figure.

ETHICAL ISSUES

When it comes to money, how individuals "behave" ranges from exhibiting high ethical standards down to deceit, fraud, and counterfeiting. How you acquire and deal with money affects your reputation. Individuals who work hard, follow the law, and treat other individuals they are involved with in money transactions fairly and honestly are able to find success, accumulate wealth, and build high-quality reputations. However, probably almost from the origins of money creation, there have been individuals driven by greed who have engaged in counterfeiting activities to illegally get money rather than work for it. It is difficult for most of us to understand such extreme unethical behavior, which typically results in getting caught, serving prison time, and destroying reputations of those involved.

FIGURE 2.5
Old and Current Designs of the $20 U.S. Federal Reserve Note

Old Design $20 Bill
[Relatively easy to copy and counterfeit]

Old Design $20 Federal Reserve Note (small size issued 1929–97)

Current Design $20 Bill
[More difficult to copy and counterfeit]

Current Design $20 Federal Reserve Note (issued beginning in 2003)

Unfortunately, attempts to counterfeit U.S. currencies represent a big illegal business for some individuals and organizations. Furthermore, the ability to counterfeit currency has been aided in recent years by the introduction of high-quality color copiers. To thwart counterfeiting efforts, the U.S. Treasury Department's Bureau of Engraving and Printing has developed new currency designs in recent years. A new series of notes that made use of microprinting and an embedded security strip was introduced in 1990 to improve security and to make counterfeiting more difficult. A more complete design change began with the $100 "large-portrait" bill in 1996. Large-portrait $50 bills were introduced in 1997, and $20 bills were placed in circulation in 1998. New $5 and $10 bills were introduced in 2000 so that today only the $1 bill continues to use the small-portrait format.

Further currency design changes were implemented in 2003. The bottom portion of Figure 2.5 shows the most recent "large-portrait" $20 bill, which still features Andrew Jackson. In the 1998 version, the larger portrait was placed off-center to allow the inclusion of a watermark that is visible from both sides when held up against a light. The bill contains a vertically embedded security thread, which glows red when exposed to ultraviolet light, at the far left of the portrait. Color-shifting ink, fine line printing, and microprinting were added. In the 2003 version, U.S. currency began taking on added colors. Peach and light blue hues were added to the previous green-and-black bills. Other changes included removing the circle around Andrew Jackson's head and adding a faded bald eagle to the left of the portrait and the words "Twenty USA" and "USA Twenty" to the right of the portrait.

PERSONAL FINANCIAL PLANNING
Local Currency: Another Form of Savings and Spending Power

The monetary system has evolved from barter of goods and services to today's credit money. Money is a means to facilitate exchange. Rather than carpenter Jim trading a chair for new shirts sewn by seamstress Jane, Jim and Jane use Federal Reserve Notes to buy chairs and shirts from each other.

Some areas of the United States have two monetary systems. About 30 cities and towns print their own versions of money used for transactions within a locality. One reason communities do so is to keep money in the community. For example, local currency circulates in Ithaca, New York; Madison, Wisconsin; Takoma Park, Maryland; Detroit, Michigan; Austin, Texas; and Waldo County, Maine. Such currency is legal, but it must be printed in a size smaller than the U.S. $1 bill and issued in denominations of at least $1.

Ithaca's local currency is denominated in Ithaca Hours; each Hour is worth about $10, the area's average hourly wage. Denominations range from one-eighth of an Hour up to two Hours. Since it started in 1991, Hours have been earned and spent by 1,500 people and are accepted by 300 businesses. Most stores accept them only as partial payment for goods; they require the balance to be paid in U.S. currency. An advisory board oversees the supply of Hours.

The idea of local currency in the United States is not new; it has a long history. You may have experience with traveler's checks; they also are a form of private currency. One purchases traveler's checks with cash; the checks can then be used as currency because they represent this cash. The recognizable name and good credit of the issuer (e.g., American Express or Thomas Cook), rather than that of the individual making the payment, guarantees the value of the checks. Since lost or stolen traveler's checks can be reported, payment stopped, and new checks issued in their place, they provide users with a level of safety not available with cash.

CONCEPT CHECK
What is meant by full-bodied money?

What is meant by fiat money?

These anti-counterfeiting efforts, while very costly, are essential to maintaining the public's trust and confidence in fiat money. Of course, it is important to remember that even though the appearance of U.S. paper money may be changing, the government honors all previously issued U.S. paper currency at full face value. There is no requirement or time limit for exchanging old notes for new ones. Old notes continue to remain in circulation until depository institutions return them to the Fed to be retired.

DEPOSIT MONEY

The use of physical (coin and currency) money to complete transactions can be costly and inefficient if large amounts and/or long distances are involved. As a result of these constraints on the use of physical money, along with confidence in the banking system, a special type of credit money called *deposit money* has grown readily in importance in the U.S. monetary system. **Credit money** is money backed by the creditworthiness of the issuer.[5] Deposit money is backed by the creditworthiness of the depository institution that issued the deposit.

credit money
money worth more than what it is made of

Deposit money takes the form of demand deposits held at commercial banks or other checkable deposits held at S&Ls, savings banks, and credit unions. A demand deposit gets its name from the fact that the owner of a deposit account "demands" that all or a portion of the amount in his or her demand deposit account be transferred to another individual or organization. Checks or drafts have traditionally been used to transfer demand deposit or other checkable deposit amounts. Let's return to our example where the ABC business firm deposits $1,000 at First Bank to set up a $1,000 demand deposit account in ABC's name. ABC then writes a $1,000 check against its deposit account and sends the check to an equipment manufacturer as payment for purchase of equipment. The equipment manufacturer deposits the check in its own demand deposit account in a bank (e.g., Last Bank). The check then must be processed and cleared through the banking system, either with or without the assistance of the Fed. That is, it must be returned to First Bank, which will pay the check amount to Last Bank and deduct $1,000 from the business firm's demand deposit account at First Bank.

automatic transfer service (ATS) accounts
provide for direct deposits to, and payments from, checkable deposit accounts

The processing of paper checks is time consuming and costly. An alternative is to electronically transfer funds held in demand and other checkable deposit accounts. For example, **automatic transfer service (ATS) accounts** are increasingly used to make direct deposits to, and payments from, checkable deposit accounts. Employers can have their employees' wages deposited directly in their checking accounts, rather than issuing payroll checks. Individuals can have regular payments such as mortgage payments or insurance premiums automatically

---

5. Fiat money is a form of credit money. However, while the government declares fiat money to be "legal tender," other forms of credit money such as deposit money do not have governmental support or backing.

debit cards
provide for immediate direct transfer of deposit amounts

CONCEPT CHECK
Why is deposit money said to be credit money?

money market securities
debt securities with maturities of one year or less

Treasury bill
short-term debt obligation issued by the U.S. federal government

negotiable certificate of deposit (negotiable CD)
short-term debt instrument issued by depository institutions that can be traded in the secondary money markets

deducted from their accounts. Electronic funds transfers by telephone—for payment of utility bills, credit card balances, and so forth—are increasingly common. **Debit cards** provide for the immediate direct transfer of deposit amounts. For example, when a debit card is used to purchase merchandise at a retailer's point-of-sale cash register, the card holder's bank transfers the designated amount from the purchaser's demand account to the retailer's account. In a similar fashion, debit cards can be used to pay for purchases made using the Internet. Debit cards also can be used to make cash withdrawals from automated teller machines (ATMs). When cash is dispersed, the user's demand deposit account's balance is immediately reduced by the amount of cash withdrawn.

MONEY MARKET SECURITIES

As noted in Chapter 1, *Money markets* are the markets where debt securities with maturities of one year or less are originated (primary markets) or traded (secondary markets). **Money market securities** are debt instruments or securities with maturities of one year or less. In general, money markets securities have low default risk and high liquidity. That is, issuers are expected to meet their debt obligations when due and short maturities and secondary markets for many of these securities allow them to be sold with little loss of value.

Figure 2.6 identifies and provides characteristics of major money market securities. A **Treasury bill** is a short-term debt obligation issued by the U.S. federal government to meet its short-term borrowing needs when imbalances exist between tax revenues and government expenditures. Treasury bills are generally issued with maturities between four weeks and one year. Investors buy Treasury bills for safety and liquidity reasons. First, it is extremely unlikely that the federal government will default on its debt obligations. Second, there is an active secondary money market for Treasury bills, so investors can easily sell them at any time before maturity if cash needs arise.

A **negotiable certificate of deposit (negotiable CD)** is a short-term debt instrument issued by depository institutions to individual or institutional depositors. Negotiable certificates of deposit are issued by commercial banks in denominations of $100,000 or more with typical maturities ranging from one month to one year. Negotiable CDs are money market securities with an active secondary market that allows short-term investors to easily match their cash or liquidity needs when they arise. It is important, of course, to recognize that negotiable CDs differ from smaller-denomination CD time deposits offered by depository institutions to individual depositors. Small-deposit CDs are nonnegotiable and must be redeemed with the issuer, and thus no secondary securities market exists for them. In fact, owners of nonnegotiable CDs redeemed before maturity usually are charged an interest deduction penalty.

FIGURE 2.6
Major Money Market Securities

TYPE	TYPICAL MATURITIES	ISSUERS	INVESTORS	SECONDARY MARKET
Treasury bills	4 weeks to 1 year	U.S. government	Individuals, business firms, and institutions	High activity
Commercial paper	1 day to 9 months	Business firms and institutions	Business firms and institutions	Moderate activity
Negotiable certificates of deposit (Negotiable CDs)	Up to 1 year	Depository institutions	Business firms	Low activity
Banker's acceptances	Up to 6 months	Banks	Business firms	High activity
Repurchase agreements	Up to 1 year	Business firms and institutions	Business firms and institutions	No market
Federal funds	1 day to 1 week	Depository institutions	Depository institutions	No market

at historically high levels. Since then, prime rates have been in a generally consistent decline with secondary peaks in 1990, 2000, and 2006, with the 2006 rate peaking at 8.25 percent. During the 2007–09 financial crisis, the prime rate declined to about 7 percent at the end of 2007 and down to 3.25 percent at the end of 2008. The prime rate remained at the 3.25 percent level throughout 2009.

A loan customarily includes a specified rate of interest such as the prevailing prime rate or prime plus some percentage point amount. For short-term loans, the interest often is paid along with the principal amount of the loan when the loan contract matures. In some instances, a discount loan or note is offered. With a discount loan, the interest is deducted from the stated amount of the note at the time the money is lent. The borrower receives less than the face value of the note, but repays the full amount of the note when it matures.

A given discount rate results in a higher cost of borrowing than an interest loan made for the same rate. This is true because under the discount arrangement actual money received by the borrower is less, although the amount paid for its use is the same. For example, if $5,000 is borrowed on a loan basis at an interest rate of 10 percent for one year, at maturity $5,000 plus $500 interest must be repaid. In general terms, the annual percent cost of borrowing for a one-year loan with interest paid annually is determined as:

Standard Loan:

$$\text{Percent Annual Rate} = \frac{\text{Interest Paid}}{\text{Amount Borrowed}} \times 100 \quad (3.1)$$

For our example, we have:

$$\text{Percent Annual Rate} = \frac{\$500}{\$5,000} \times 100 = .10 \times 100 = 10.0\%$$

In contrast, if the $5,000 is borrowed on a discount basis and the rate is 10 percent, a deduction of $500 from the face value of the note is made and the borrower receives only $4,500. At the end of the year, the borrower repays the face amount of the note, $5,000. In general terms, the percent annual rate on a one-year discount loan is calculated as follows:

Discount Loan:

$$\text{Percent Annual Rate} = \frac{\text{Discount Amount}}{\text{Amount Borrowed} - \text{Discount Amount}} \times 100 \quad (3.2)$$

For our example, we have:

$$\text{Percent Annual Rate} = \frac{\$500}{\$5,000 - \$500} \times 100 = \frac{\$500}{\$4,500} \times 100 = .111 \times 100 = 11.1\%$$

In the first case, the borrower has paid $500 for the use of $5,000; in the second case, $500 has been paid for the use of only $4,500. The effective rate of interest, therefore, on the discount basis is approximately 11.1 percent compared with the even 10 percent paid when the $5,000 was borrowed on a loan basis.

Loans to individuals also are an important category for commercial bank lending. Loans to individuals constitute about one-fifth of all bank loans. Credit cards and related loan plans comprise a little less than half of all bank loans to individuals.

Other Bank Assets

Other bank assets represent about 16 percent of total bank assets. They include bank premises and fixed assets, assets held in trading accounts, and all other assets, including other real estate owned and intangible assets.

As noted, about three-fifths of the assets of commercial banks are in the form of loans, with about one-fourth of assets being held in the form of real estate loans. In contrast, S&Ls and savings banks have about three-quarters of their assets in the form of real estate mortgages and mortgage-backed securities. The assets of credit unions are largely consumer loans with a small percentage in government securities. Some credit unions also make home mortgage loans, although such mortgage financing typically constitutes a small percentage of their total assets.

LIABILITIES AND OWNERS' CAPITAL

There are two major sources from which banks and other depository institutions acquire their capital funds and liabilities. Owners' capital or equity represents the initial investment and retained earnings of the owners of the institutions. Liabilities represent the funds owed to depositors and others from whom the bank has borrowed. The most important liability of a depository institution consists of its deposits of various kinds, but the other liabilities should be understood also.

Deposits

As can be seen in Figure 3.5, deposits represent about two-thirds of FDIC-insured commercial bank liabilities and owners' capital. Deposits are separated into transactional accounts, which include demand (checking account) deposits and NOW accounts, and nontransactional accounts. Transactional accounts constitute about one-fifth of total deposits, and demand deposits represent over three-fourths of transactional account deposits. Nontransactional accounts comprise three-fifths of total deposits. The remaining components are nondomestic or foreign deposits. Nontransactional accounts are in the form of time and savings deposits, each being about one-half of the total. Money market deposit accounts (MMDAs) represent the largest component of savings accounts.

Most time deposits are **certificates of deposit (CDs)** that have a stated maturity and either pay a fixed rate of interest or are sold at a discount. Although records reveal that commercial banks issued certificates of deposit as early as 1900, a major innovation in the early 1960s resulted in a tremendous growth in their importance. Large-denomination CDs for deposits of $100,000 or more were issued in negotiable form, which meant they could be bought and sold. *Negotiable certificates of deposit (negotiable CDs)* were discussed in Chapter 2. The vastly increased use of negotiable CDs in the 1960s caused a secondary market for them to develop. Today, CDs issued by banks and other depository institutions are purchased and sold in the money markets as readily as most forms of debt obligations.

certificates of deposit (CDs) time deposits with a stated maturity

Other Liabilities

The second category of liabilities is represented by items that when combined have smaller dollar significance than that of deposits. Included are federal funds purchased or borrowed from other banks. As discussed in Chapter 2, *federal funds* are very short-term (usually overnight) loans from banks with excess reserves to banks that need to borrow funds to meet minimum reserve requirements. Other borrowed money and liabilities include longer-term notes and debt issues, as well as taxes, interest, and wages owed.

Owners' Capital

The owners' equity capital includes stock, surplus, and undivided profits or retained earnings. At the time a bank is formed, stock is purchased by the owners of the bank or by the public. In the case of credit unions, the members buy shares. From time to time additional stock may be sold to accommodate bank expansion. A bank's common stock account reflects the number of shares of stock outstanding times a "par" or stated value per share. The surplus account is used to record separately the difference between the sales price of the stock and the stock's par value.

CONCEPT CHECK

Which is the largest category of bank assets, and what are some of the components of that category?

Which is the largest category of bank liabilities, and what are some of the components of that category?

bank liquidity reflects ability to meet depositor withdrawals and to pay off other liabilities when due

bank solvency reflects ability to keep the value of a bank's assets greater than its liabilities

BANK MANAGEMENT

Banks are managed to make profits and increase the wealth of their owners. However, bank management must also consider the interests of depositors and bank regulators. Profitability often can be increased when bank managers take on more risk at the expense of bank safety. The lower the level of bank safety, the greater the likelihood of bank failure. Bank managers must trade off higher profitability objectives against the desire of depositors to maintain the safety of their deposits. Bank regulators try to ensure that bank managers are prudent in their trade-off decisions between profitability and risk or safety.

Banks can fail either because of inadequate liquidity or by becoming insolvent. **Bank liquidity** reflects the ability to meet depositor withdrawals and to pay off other liabilities when they come due. The inability to meet withdrawal and debt repayments results in bank failure. **Bank solvency** reflects the ability to keep the value of a bank's assets greater than its liabilities. When the value of

FIGURE 3.7
Trade-Off of Profitability Objective Against Bank Liquidity and Bank Solvency

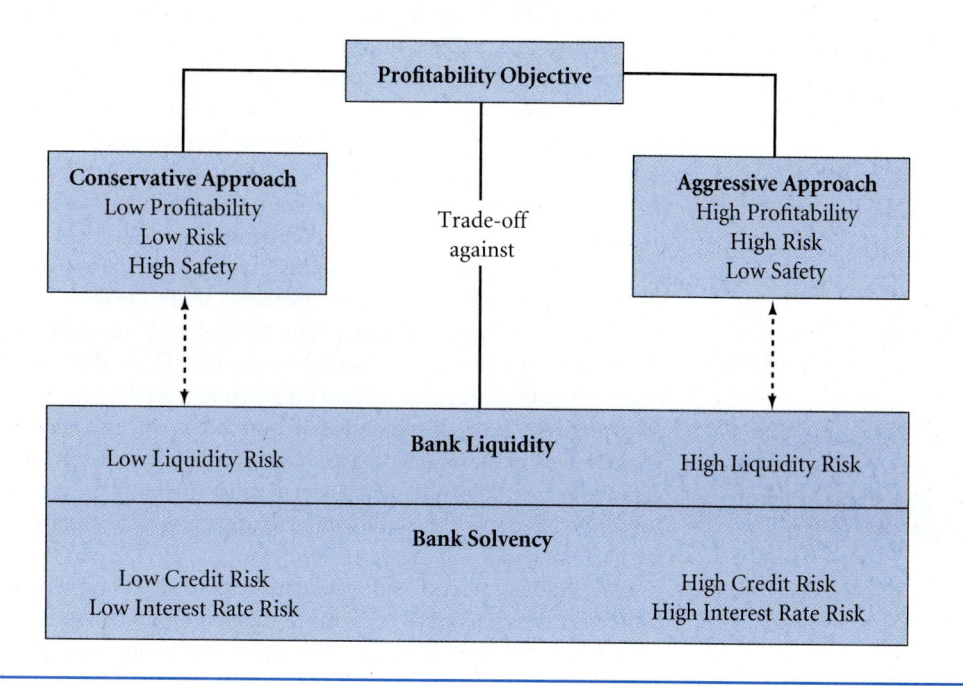

```
                         Profitability Objective
                        /                       \
        Conservative Approach                    Aggressive Approach
        Low Profitability         Trade-off      High Profitability
        Low Risk                  against        High Risk
        High Safety                              Low Safety
               ⇅                                        ⇅
        ┌─────────────────────────────────────────────────────┐
        │                    Bank Liquidity                    │
        │  Low Liquidity Risk              High Liquidity Risk │
        ├─────────────────────────────────────────────────────┤
        │                    Bank Solvency                     │
        │  Low Credit Risk                  High Credit Risk   │
        │  Low Interest Rate Risk           High Interest Rate Risk │
        └─────────────────────────────────────────────────────┘
```

a bank's liabilities exceeds its assets, the bank is insolvent and thus has "failed." However, from a technical standpoint failure does not take place until depositors or creditors are not paid and consequently take legal action. Figure 3.7 illustrates the trade-off involving profitability and bank safety or risk. Bank managers manage their bank's riskiness in terms of bank liquidity and bank solvency. We will first discuss bank liquidity management and then cover the issue of bank solvency in terms of capital adequacy management.

LIQUIDITY MANAGEMENT

liquidity risk
likelihood that a bank will be unable to meet depositor withdrawal demands and other liabilities when due

Liquidity management is the management of a bank's **liquidity risk,** which is the likelihood that the bank will be unable to meet its depositor withdrawal demands and/or other liabilities when they are due. Figure 3.7 shows that lower liquidity risk is associated with higher bank safety and generally lower bank profits. The opposite is the case when bank managers choose to take on greater liquidity risk to improve profits. In deciding on how much liquidity risk is appropriate, bank managers make asset management and liability management decisions.

Asset Management

A bank needs cash assets to meet depositor withdrawal requests when demanded. However, cash assets do not earn interest for the bank. Thus, the more cash assets are held, the lower the profitability and vice versa. In contrast, banks earn higher interest on loans and on longer-maturity securities investments. However, these types of assets are not easily converted into cash assets, and if converted the conversion costs can be quite high. For example, if a loan is sold to another investor, the loan may have to be heavily discounted, sold well below its face value.

primary reserves
vault cash and deposits held at other depository institutions and at Federal Reserve Banks

Let's now return to the aggregate bank balance sheet depicted in Figure 3.5. The cash assets of the firm included under the heading "cash and balances due from depository institutions" are considered to be the bank's **primary reserves** to meet liquidity requirements. Vault cash and deposits held at other depository institutions and at Federal Reserve Banks are immediately available. Cash items in process of collection, while not immediate cash, are being converted into cash on an ongoing basis. However, primary reserves do not earn interest, and thus bank managers want to minimize the amount of primary reserves they hold. Notice that FDIC-insured commercial banks hold primary reserves that amount to about 7 percent of total bank assets.

secondary reserves
short-term securities held by banks that can be quickly converted into cash at little cost

To supplement their primary reserves, banks also hold secondary reserves to help meet depositor withdrawal demands and other liabilities as they come due. **Secondary reserves** are short-term securities held by banks that are quickly converted into cash at little cost to the banks. For example, the holding of U.S. Treasury bills is an important source of secondary reserves for most banks. Banks would prefer to hold secondary reserves over primary reserves because interest is earned on secondary reserves. On the other hand, secondary reserves are less liquid than cash assets and thus provide a little more liquidity risk than do primary reserves. In Figure 3.5, both short-term and long-term securities are grouped together under the heading "securities." As a consequence, we cannot readily estimate the average amount of secondary reserves held by banks.

Let's not lose sight of the fact that banks are in business to make profits for the bank owners. Banks accept deposits from savers and, in turn, make loans to businesses and individuals. Figure 3.5 shows that nearly three-fifths of bank assets are in the form of loans. Bank loans are generally less liquid and have higher risks of default than other bank assets. As a consequence, bank loans offer higher potential profit than do other securities. Thus, after setting primary reserve and secondary reserve targets, banks concentrate on meeting loan demand by individuals and businesses. **Credit (default) risk** is the likelihood that borrowers will not make interest and principal payments. Higher interest rates can be charged to riskier borrowers, but such customers also are more likely to default on their loans. Bank managers must trade off the size of their loan portfolios against the amount of credit risk they are willing to assume. The acceptance of higher credit risk also increases the likelihood of insolvency.

credit (default) risk
the chance of nonpayment or delayed payment of interest or principal

After primary reserve and secondary reserve targets have been set, loan demand met, and bank fixed asset decisions have been made, remaining funds are invested in longer-maturity securities. Included would be U.S. government notes and bonds, state and local government debt securities, and other securities. These are riskier than the short-term securities held as secondary reserves and thus offer higher potential profitability that is second only to the potential profitability of bank loans.

Liability Management

A bank's liabilities can be managed to help the bank maintain a desired level of liquidity. This is possible because certain types of bank liabilities are very sensitive to changes in interest rates. Included would be negotiable certificates of deposit (CDs), commercial paper, and federal funds. For example, if a bank needs cash to meet unexpected depositor withdrawals, it could immediately attract more liabilities by raising short-term interest rates it will pay on negotiable CDs or by issuing commercial paper at acceptable interest rates being demanded in the marketplace. Likewise the bank could borrow federal funds from other banks that have excess reserves as long as it is willing to pay that day's interest rate. You should recall that federal funds are overnight loans, and thus the bank may have to reborrow each day for several days to offset liquidity pressures.

Time and savings deposits generally are less sensitive to immediate changes in interest rates and thus receive less focus from a liability management standpoint. Longer-term debt and bank capital do not work well in terms of liquidity management because of the time it takes for debt and equity securities to be issued or sold.

CONCEPT CHECK
What is meant by asset management by a bank?

How does a bank conduct liability management?

Liability management is meant to supplement asset management in managing bank liquidity. In banks incurring severe liquidity problems, bank managers may find that they are unable to even sell their negotiable CDs or commercial paper. Furthermore, if banks pay higher and higher interest rates to sell negotiable CDs, they must find assets to invest in that will provide returns higher than the cost of funds. Otherwise, profitability will suffer.

CAPITAL MANAGEMENT

Adequate capital is necessary to ensure that banks remain solvent, meet depositor demands, and pay their debts as they come due. A bank is considered solvent as long as its assets are worth more than its liabilities. Let's return to Figure 3.5. Since we know that total assets must equal total liabilities plus owners' capital, the difference between total assets and total liabilities is owners' capital, which reflects the degree of solvency.

What can cause a bank to become insolvent? One reason is that excessive credit risk could result in nonrepayment of loans. For example, if businesses default on the loans they owe to a bank, that bank's assets will decline by the amount of the defaults. If a bank's assets decline enough relative to its liabilities, the bank could become insolvent. In addition to credit risk reasons, a bank may become insolvent because of **interest-rate risk,** which is the risk associated with changing market interest rates on the value of underlying debt instruments.[4] For example, let's assume that a bank purchases $100 million of long-term U.S. government bonds when interest rates are 6 percent. If interest rates rise, the value of the bonds held as assets will decline. If the decline in the bond value causes the bank's assets to be less than its liabilities, the bank would be insolvent.

Adequate bank capital represents an important cushion against both credit risk and interest-rate risk as they affect bank solvency. Bank regulators set minimum capital ratio requirements for the banks and other depository institutions that they regulate. A basic equity capital ratio could be defined as owners' or equity capital divided by total assets.

interest-rate risk
possible price fluctuations in fixed-rate debt instruments associated with changes in market interest rates

$$\text{Equity Capital Ratio} = \frac{\text{Equity Capital}}{\text{Total Assets}} \times 100 \tag{3.3}$$

The Equity Capital Ratio for a bank with owners' equity of $3 million and total assets of $50 million would be:

$$\text{Equity Capital Ratio} = \$3 \text{ million} / \$50 \text{ million} = 6\%$$

Other capital ratios are now in use by bank regulators. Adjustments often are made to exclude intangible assets such as goodwill, which is created in mergers and acquisitions. A broader view of capital also is often used. Banks sometimes hold securities that count as equity capital called trust-preferred securities and provide for loan-loss reserves in the event that loans have to be written off. Tier 1 capital is composed of common equity plus trust-preferred securities minus intangible assets. Tier 2 capital is a bank's loan-loss reserve amount plus other qualifying securities (e.g., subordinated debt, preferred stock) plus net unrealized gains on marketable securities. Total capital is the sum of Tier 1 and Tier 2 capital.

The central banks and other national supervisory authorities of major industrialized countries met in Basel, Switzerland, in mid-1988 (*Basel I Accord*) and again in 2003 (*Basel II Accord*). The objectives were to improve risk measurement and management of large internationally involved banks, and to improve the transparency of bank riskiness to customers and other constituencies. As a result, the Bank for International Settlements (BIS) established capital adequacy requirements for banks with international operations based on the use of risk-weighted assets. The weightings were established as follows:

BANK ASSETS	RISK-WEIGHT (%)
Cash and equivalents	0%
Government securities	0
Interbank loans	20
Mortgage loans	50
Ordinary loans	100
Standby letters of credit	100

Two capital ratios (Tier 1 and Total Capital) are calculated using risk-adjusted assets. They are defined as:

$$\text{Tier 1 Ratio} = \frac{\text{Tier 1 Capital}}{\text{Risk-Adjusted Assets}} \times 100 \tag{3.4}$$

INTERNET ACTIVITY

Go to the Federal Reserve Board of Governors' Web site, http://www.federalreserve.gov, and find information on regulation and operations of the banking system.

$$\text{Total Capital Ratio} = \frac{\text{Tier 1 + Tier 2 Capital}}{\text{Risk-Adjusted Assets}} \times 100 \tag{3.5}$$

Let's assume that a bank has owners' capital of $3.0 million, trust-preferred securities of $.5 million, and a $2 million loan-loss reserve account. Intangible assets (goodwill) amount to $2 million. In terms of other assets: cash and equivalents = $1 million; government securities = $2

---

[4]. There is an inverse relationship between the price or value of debt instruments and interest rates. When market interest rates increase, debt instruments go down in value, and vice versa.

INTERNET ACTIVITY

Go to the Small Business Administration's Web site, http://www.sba.gov. Find information about small business lending in the United States and write a brief summary.

million; interbank loans = $5 million; mortgage loans = $20 million; ordinary loans = $18 million; and standby letters of credit = $2 million.

Tier 1 capital = $3 million in owners' equity + $.5 million in trust-preferred securities − $2 million in intangible assets, or $1.5 million. Total capital = Tier 1 capital of $1.5 million + $1.0 million in loan-loss reserves, or $2.5 million. Risk-adjusted assets are:

Cash and equivalents	=	$1 million	×	0.00	=	$0 million
Government securities	=	$2 million	×	0.00	=	$0 million
Interbank loans	=	$5 million	×	0.20	=	$1 million
Mortgage loans	=	$20 million	×	0.50	=	$10 million
Ordinary loans	=	$18 million	×	1.00	=	$18 million
Standby letters of credit	=	$2 million	×	1.00	=	$2 million
Risk-adjusted assets	=					$31 million

The Tier 1 and Total Capital ratios are calculated as follows:

$$\text{Tier 1 Ratio} = \frac{\$1.5 \text{ million}}{\$31 \text{ million}} \times 100 = .0484 \times 100 = 4.84\%$$

$$\text{Total Capital Ratio} = \frac{\$2.5 \text{ million}}{\$31 \text{ million}} \times 100 = .0806 \times 100 = 8.06\%$$

CONCEPT CHECK

How are the primary capital and the total capital ratios calculated?

What is the Basel Capital Accord?

How does the FDIC use risk-based capital ratios?

To be considered to be "adequately capitalized," a bank needs to have a 4 percent Tier 1 capital ratio and an 8 percent Total Capital (Tier 1 plus Tier 2) ratio. U.S. bank regulatory authorities adopted these ratio requirements.

There is a strong incentive for bank managers to meet minimum capital ratio requirements. Banks that are classified as being undercapitalized by the FDIC must submit plans to the FDIC indicating how they intend to become adequately capitalized. Significantly undercapitalized banks may be required to replace their managers and even their board of directors, as well as restructure their balance sheets. Critically undercapitalized banks must restructure and may even be seized by the FDIC

FINANCIAL CRISIS

2007–09 FINANCIAL CRISIS

During the decade of the 2000s, many banks aggressively originated, held, and packaged questionable home mortgage loans and made risky loans on commercial property. Recall from our discussion of mortgage markets in Chapter 1 that lenders turned to emphasizing adjustable-rate mortgages (ARMs) and often engaged in subprime lending. A *subprime mortgage* is a home loan made to a borrower with a relatively low credit score indicating the likelihood that loan payments might be missed when due.

Many banks also engaged in *securitization*, which is the process of pooling and packaging mortgage loans into debt securities. The result was the creating and holding of mortgage-backed securities. A *mortgage-backed security* is a debt security created by pooling together a group of mortgage loans whose periodic payments belong to the holders of the security. Financial engineering led to new derivative securities, which were difficult to assess in terms of their degree of riskiness. One example of these securities is a *collateralized debt obligation* (CDO), which is a security backed by mortgage-backed securities. CDOs could be "sliced and diced" into different "tranches"—parts that would appeal to different investors.

However, after the home real estate price bubble burst in 2006, housing prices began a steep and prolonged decline. Homeowners holding subprime mortgages were first to miss mortgage payments, and many had their homes foreclosed on. To make matters worse, many homeowners found that their lower home values were below the amount of their mortgages resulting in terms like having "underwater loans" or "negative-equity" ownership positions. Banks and other lenders quickly found that they were holding large amounts of high-risk under-performing individual mortgage loans, mortgage-backed securities, and collateralized debt obligations.

Underperforming mortgage and related securities soon became referred to as "troubled" or "toxic assets." Banks and other holders of these securities were forced to "write down" the values of these assets to reflect their new market values. This, in turn, reduced their bank capital ratios to unacceptable levels. By late 2008, Washington Mutual, the largest savings and loan association in the United States failed. Wachovia Bank, the fourth largest commercial bank at the time in the United States, was on the brink of bankruptcy and finally was purchased by Wells Fargo Bank. Citigroup and the Bank of America, then the two largest U.S. banks, were suffering financial difficulties and needed assistance from the U.S. government as provided in the Economic Stabilization Act of 2008. By the end of 2009, more than 100 U.S. banks had failed.

INTERNATIONAL BANKING AND FOREIGN SYSTEMS

ETHICAL ISSUES

international banking when banks operate in more than one country

Banks with headquarters in one country may open offices or branches in other countries. When banks operate in more than one country, we call this **international banking.** European banks dominated international banking until the 1960s, when world trade began expanding rapidly and multinational corporations increased in number and size. As a response to these and other developments involving international trade, American banks began opening offices in foreign countries and establishing correspondent banking arrangements with foreign banks. In essence, as U.S. corporations began expanding their operations in other countries, the American banks with which they were working followed them. Likewise, the growing importance of the U.S. dollar in international transactions and the movement by foreign corporations to invest in the United States resulted in foreign banks opening offices in the United States. Today, U.S. banks are actively involved throughout the world with major operations in Europe, Asia, and Latin America, and foreign banks have opened hundreds of offices in the United States.

Banking in the United States has traditionally been highly regulated to protect depositor funds and to maintain citizen confidence in the U.S. banking system. European and most other countries generally have adopted less restrictive approaches to bank regulation. This led to a competitive disadvantage for U.S. domestic banks relative to foreign-owned banks. The result was the passage of the *International Banking Act (IBA)* of 1978, which was intended to provide a "level playing field" for all banks. Some of the provisions included restricting foreign banks in terms of their U.S. interstate banking activities and giving authority to the Fed to impose reserve requirements on foreign banks. Rules against nonbanking operations for U.S. banks were extended to foreign banks operating in the United States. Congress strengthened regulations relating to foreign banks by enacting the *Foreign Bank Supervision Enhancement Act* in 1991. This act requires that the Fed give its approval before foreign banks can open offices in the United States and that the Fed examine U.S. offices of foreign banks each year.

While most countries have central banking systems that operate much like the U.S. Federal Reserve System, some countries allow their banks to engage in both commercial banking and investment banking. This is called *universal banking*. As noted earlier in the chapter, Germany is a universal banking country. Its largest banks participate in both types of banking. The United Kingdom does not restrict its banks from engaging in both commercial banking and investment banking. However, British banks traditionally have been either "clearing banks," which are similar to U.S. commercial banks, or "merchant banks," which are similar to U.S. investment banks. In recent years, some British clearing banks have formed subsidiaries to perform a wide range of investment banking activities. Likewise, merchant banks are expanding beyond investment banking. As a result, banking consolidations are taking place and the United Kingdom is moving more toward universal banking. Commercial banking and investment banking are separated in Japan much as in the United States.

CONCEPT CHECK

What is international banking and why has it grown in importance?

What is universal banking and which country has important universal banks?

German banks are allowed to own shares of stock in German firms and also are permitted to vote those shares. Japanese banks also are allowed to own common stock in their business customer firms, as well as to engage in various cross holdings of stock involving other Japanese firms and banks. United Kingdom banks are not actively involved with the firms that they conduct business with. While stock ownership in business firms by banks is not restricted in the United Kingdom, British banks are generally risk averse to ownership of common stock.

CAREER PROFILES

MOKEY SHEA
Private Banking Relationship Manager
Key Trust Company of Florida

BA, Political Science
University of Maine

"The whole basis for this service is that I become very familiar with the personal finances of the client."

Q: *What is private banking?*
A: Private banking means providing very personalized and specialized services to high-net-worth individuals and families.

Q: *What kind of services are involved?*
A: We use a team approach to meet the needs of these clients. I supply the checking, savings, and mortgage instruments, the normal retail banking pieces. There is a brokerage officer on the team who provides investment services. Then we have a trust officer who deals with issues such as estate planning. It's not unusual for a bank or other financial services company to provide all of these functions. What's new about private banking is that we all work as a team rather than independently.

Q: *How high does a client's net worth need to be to qualify?*
A: There are several criteria we look for, but in general we look for investable assets of $250,000. This would be above and beyond whatever they have invested in real estate. We're located in Naples, Florida, which has an unusual number of wealthy retirees that fit the profile we look for. There are other banks in town that require even higher net worth to qualify for their private banking services.

Q: *You're a "relationship manager." What is that?*
A: The whole basis for this service is that I become very familiar with and involved in the personal finances of the client. The more I know about a client's financial situation and needs, the better our team can meet those needs. It really is a relationship. I get to know their families, learn about their lifestyles, discuss their futures, including what happens after they die. So the term *relationship manager* is very accurate.

Q: *You were a branch manager for Key Bank before you took your current position. How would you describe that experience?*
A: I ran a branch in Maine with about a dozen employees. In that setting you need to be a true jack-of-all-trades. At nine o'clock I might open a savings account for a 12-year-old who has a paper route. At ten o'clock I might discuss a $100,000 business loan. At eleven o'clock I might open a checking account for a small business. So I was dealing with every imaginable kind of client. Plus I had the management and operations responsibilities. I was essentially running a small bank. I had profitability targets I needed to meet and other requirements set at our main office.

Q: *Do you miss anything about that job?*
A: It was a tough job because it combined the sales and management roles. Either one of those roles is plenty of work. Doing both demands a lot. The thing I miss the most is working with new businesses and watching them grow from ideas into successes. Most of my private banking clients are past the point of starting a new business. But what I like about my current job is that I get so involved with my clients. I can be much more focused on them and spend more time with them than in the branch environment where it's a continuous stream of different people all day long.

APPLYING FINANCE TO...

INSTITUTIONS AND MARKETS

Commercial banks, insurance companies, pension funds, and mutual funds play important roles in getting the savings of individuals into the hands of business firms so that investments can be made to maintain and grow the businesses. Thrift institutions (savings and loans, savings banks, and credit unions) along with commercial banks comprise the banking system and help with the financial functions of creating money and transferring money, which is conducted largely through a highly efficient check processing or clearing system. In contrast with commercial banks, while thrift institutions also accept the savings of individuals, they focus on lending to individuals, who want to purchase durable goods and homes.

INVESTMENTS

Bank loans to businesses and other debt obligations such as small certificates of deposit originate in the primary debt obligations market. However, since they are specific arrangements with business borrowers and depositors, these debt obligations do not trade in a secondary debt obligations market. Rather, business loans and small CDs are usually held to maturity, and loans are repaid and depositors redeem their CDs. Investment banking firms and brokerage houses help businesses market their new debt and equity securities issues so funds can be raised in addition to those provided by banks.

FINANCIAL MANAGEMENT

Financial managers borrow from commercial banks and depend on the banking system to help support day-to-day operating activities involving producing and selling their products and services. Materials must be purchased from suppliers and are usually paid for by writing checks. Sales made to consumers also are often paid by check. Business firms depend on the banking system having a highly efficient check clearing system so that cash outflows and inflows can be reasonably balanced. Financial managers also rely on mutual funds, insurance companies, and pension funds to buy their new security issues.

SUMMARY

This chapter began with a review of the financial institutions that currently play major roles in the financial system. We provided an overview of the banking system followed by a comparison of commercial banking, investment banking, and universal banking. We then discussed the five current functions of banks and the banking system: (1) accepting deposits, (2) granting loans, (3) issuing checkable deposit accounts, (4) clearing checks, and (5) creating deposit money. A sixth function, investment banking, has been added as the United States moves to universal banking.

We next presented a review of the historical development of the U.S. banking system. Banking prior to the Civil War was described first, followed by how and when thrift institutions entered the banking system. Legislation passed to govern the banking system and to protect depositors' funds was then covered.

Our attention turned to the structure and operation of U.S. banks. Banks may obtain either state or federal charters, which makes the United States a dual banking system. Individual states have the authority to decide whether banks can operate branches in their states. Today, most states permit statewide branching, although a few states still have limited branch banking laws that restrict branching to a specified geographical area such as a county. Banks may be independently owned or owned by either a one-bank holding company (OBHC) or a multibank holding company (MBHC).

A bank's balance sheet is composed of assets that equal its liabilities and owners' capital. Bank assets are primarily in the form of cash and balances due from depository institutions, securities, loans, and fixed assets. Most assets are held in the form of loans. A bank's liabilities are primarily in the form of deposits that may take the form of transaction accounts such as demand deposits or nontransactional accounts, which are time and savings deposits. Owners' capital is provided through the purchase of common stock or by retaining profits in the bank.

Bank management involves the trade-off of potential profitability against bank safety. Banks can fail because of inadequate bank liquidity or because of bank insolvency. Bank liquidity is the ability to meet depositor withdrawals and to pay debts as they come due. Bank solvency reflects the ability to maintain the value of the bank's assets above the value of its liabilities. Liquidity management is practiced in terms of both asset management and liability management. Capital management focuses on maintaining adequate bank capital relative to assets to protect the bank against insolvency and liquidity risk.

The development of international banking and some examples of foreign banking systems compared to the U.S. banking system were described in the last section of the chapter.

KEY TERMS

bank liquidity
bank solvency
banking system
brokerage firms
certificates of deposit (CDs)
commercial banks
contractual savings organizations

credit (default) risk
credit unions
depository institutions
dual banking system
finance companies
finance firms
financial intermediations

Glass-Steagall Act of 1933
Gramm-Leach-Bliley Act of 1999
insurance companies
interest-rate risk
international banking
investment bank
investment banking firms

investment companies
limited branch banking
liquidity risk
mortgage banking firms
multibank holding companies (MBHCs)
mutual funds
one-bank holding companies (OBHCs)
pension funds
primary reserves
prime rate
savings bank
savings and loan associations
secondary reserves
secured loan
securities firms
statewide branch banking
thrift institutions
unit banking
universal bank
unsecured loan

DISCUSSION QUESTIONS

1. Describe the major financial institutions engaged in getting the savings of individuals into business firms that want to make investments to maintain and grow their firms.

2. Compare commercial banking with investment banking. What is universal banking?

3. Describe the functions of banks and the banking system.

4. Describe the three basic ways for processing or collecting a check in the United States.

5. How did the First Bank of the United States serve the nation? Also briefly describe why the Second Bank of the United States was chartered.

6. Briefly describe why and when thrift institutions were founded.

7. Why was it considered necessary to create the Federal Reserve System when we already had the benefits of the National Banking Act?

8. Comment on the objectives of the Depository Institutions Deregulation and Monetary Control Act of 1980.

9. Why was the Garn–St. Germain Depository Institutions Act thought to be necessary?

10. Describe the reasons for the savings and loan crisis that occurred during the 1980s.

11. Briefly describe the purpose of the Financial Institutions Reform, Recovery, and Enforcement Act (FIRREA) of 1989. Also, indicate the purpose of the Resolution Trust Corporation (RTC).

12. How are depositors' funds protected today in the United States?

13. Describe the structure of banks in terms of bank charters, branch banking, and bank holding companies.

14. What are the major asset categories for banks? Identify the most important category. What are a bank's major liabilities and which category is the largest in size?

15. What is meant by bank liquidity and bank solvency?

16. Describe how assets are managed in terms of a bank's liquidity risk. Also briefly describe how liquidity management is used to help manage liquidity risk.

17. Describe what is meant by liquidity risk, credit risk, and interest-rate risk.

18. Define and describe the following terms: primary capital ratio, total capital ratio, risk-based capital ratio. How are these used by bank regulators?

19. What were the Basel Accords, and what was their purpose?

20. Define international banking. Describe how some foreign banking systems differ from the U.S. banking system.

EXERCISES

1. Go to http://www.stlouisfed.org and identify sources and uses of funds for commercial banks.

2. You are the treasurer of a midsize industrial manufacturer. Your firm's cash balances vary between $300,000 and $1,000,000. During the last three board meetings a board member has asked how you protect this cash while it is being lodged in banks or other temporary facilities. Your problem is to satisfy the board member, obtain some income from the cash or cash equivalent balances, and have funds available for immediate payout if required. What course of action do you follow?

3. You and three other staff members of the U.S. Office of Comptroller of the Currency have been assigned identical projects. You are to review the articles that have been written, the speeches made, and in general the suggestions that have been offered to revamp the structure of the FDIC to render it more stable and financially able to withstand adverse events. Based on the few suggestions offered in this chapter and your own ideas, what is your conclusion?

4. You are the mayor of a community of 12,000 people. You are active in virtually all of the civic activities of the town and as such your opinion is solicited on political, economic, sociological, and other factors. You have been asked by one of the civic groups to comment on the implications for the community of a prospective purchase of the largest local commercial bank by an out-of-state bank holding company. What is your response?

5. Banks provide checking account services, accept savings deposits, and lend to borrowers. In other words, they are in the money business. We all have heard stories of banks or their partner firms "misplacing" or "losing" bags of money. Lending rates are also subject to change periodically. Both of these situations can produce ethical dilemmas or decisions. How would you react to the following scenarios?

   a. You are walking down the street and see a large money bag with "First National Bank" printed on it. The bag is sitting on the sidewalk in front of a local office of First National Bank. You are considering whether to pick up the bag, check its contents, and then try to find the owner. Alternatively, you could pick up the money bag and take it to the local police station or return it directly to the bank itself. What would you do?

   b. You are a loan officer of First National Bank. The owner of a small business has come into the bank today and is requesting an immediate $100,000 loan for which she has appropriate collateral. You also know that the bank is going to reduce its lending interest rate to small businesses next week. You could make the loan now or inform the small business owner that she could get a lower rate if the loan request is delayed. What would you do?

PROBLEMS

1. The following three one-year "discount" loans are available to you:

   Loan A: $120,000 at a 7 percent discount rate
   Loan B: $110,000 at a 6 percent discount rate
   Loan C: $130,000 at a 6.5 percent discount rate

   a. Determine the dollar amount of interest you would pay on each loan and indicate the amount of net proceeds each loan would provide. Which loan would provide you with the most upfront money when the loan takes place?
   b. Calculate the percent interest rate or effective cost of each loan. Which one has the lowest cost?

2. Assume that you can borrow $175,000 for one year from a local commercial bank.

   a. The bank loan officer offers you the loan if you agree to pay $16,000 in interest plus repay the $175,000 at the end of one year. What is the percent interest rate or effective cost?
   b. As an alternative you could get a one-year, $175,000 discount loan at 9 percent interest. What is the percent interest rate or effective cost?
   c. Which one of the two loans would you prefer?
   d. At what discount loan interest rate would you be indifferent between the two loans?

3. ABE Banc has the following asset categories:

Cash	$1 million
Securities	$4 million
Loans	?
Other assets	$2 million
Total assets	?

   a. What would be the bank's total assets if loans were twice the size of the amount of securities?
   b. If total assets were $12 million, what would be the amount of the loans?
   c. If total assets were $11 million, and $1 million of securities were sold with the proceeds placed in the cash account, what would be the amount of the loans?

4. ATM Banc has the following liabilities and equity categories:

Deposits	$9 million
Other liabilities	$4 million
Owners' capital	?
Total liabilities and capital	?

   a. What would be the bank's total liabilities and capital if owners' capital were half the size of other liabilities?
   b. If total liabilities and capital were $15.5 million, what would be the amount of the owners' capital?
   c. If total liabilities and capital were $14 million, and $1 million of deposits were withdrawn from the bank, what would be the amount of the owners' capital?

5. Following are selected balance sheet accounts for Third State Bank: vault cash = $2 million; U.S. government securities = $5 million; demand deposits = $13 million; nontransactional accounts = $20 million; cash items in process of collection = $4 million; loans to individuals = $7 million; loans secured by real estate = $9 million; federal funds purchased = $4 million; and bank premises = $11 million.

   a. From these accounts, select only the asset accounts and calculate the bank's total assets.
   b. Calculate the total liabilities for Third State Bank.
   c. Based on the totals for assets and liabilities, determine the amount in the owners' capital account.

6. A bank's assets consist of:

Cash:	$1.5 million
Loans:	$10.0 million
Securities:	$4.5 million
Fixed assets:	$2.0 million

   In addition, the bank's owners' capital is $1.5 million.

   a. Calculate the equity capital ratio.
   b. If $2 million in bad loans were removed from the bank's assets, show how the equity capital ratio would change.

7. Rearrange the following accounts to construct a bank balance sheet for Second National Bank. What are the total amounts that make the bank's balance sheet balance?

   Demand deposits: $20 million
   Cash assets: $5 million
   Loans secured by real estate: $30 million
   Commercial and industrial loans: $18 million
   Owners' capital: $6 million
   Government securities owned: $7 million
   Bank fixed assets: $14 million
   Time and savings deposits: $40 million
   Federal funds purchased: $6 million
   Other long-term liabilities: $2 million

8. Use the data from Problem 7 for Second National Bank and calculate the equity capital ratio.

9. Tenth National Bank has common stock of $2 million, retained earnings of $5 million, loan loss reserves of $3 million, and subordinated notes outstanding in the amount of $4 million. Total bank assets are $105 million. Calculate the equity capital ratio.

10. Let's assume that you have been asked to calculate risk-based capital ratios for a bank with the following accounts:

    Cash = $5 million
    Government securities = $7 million
    Mortgage loans = $30 million
    Other loans = $50 million
    Fixed assets = $10 million
    Intangible assets = $4 million
    Loan-loss reserves = $5 million
    Owners' equity = $5 million
    Trust-preferred securities = $3 million

    Cash assets and government securities are not considered risky. Loans secured by real estate have a 50 percent weighting factor. All other loans have a 100 percent weighting factor in terms of riskiness.

    a. Calculate the equity capital ratio.
    b. Calculate the Tier 1 Ratio using risk-adjusted assets.
    c. Calculate the Total Capital (Tier 1 plus Tier 2) Ratio using risk-adjusted assets.

11. **Challenge Problem** This problem focuses on bank capital management and various capital ratio measures. Following are recent balance sheet accounts for Prime First National Bank.

Cash assets	$17 million	Demand deposits	$50 million
Loans secured by real estate	40	Time & savings deposits	66
Commercial loans	45	Federal funds purchased	15
Government securities owned	16	Trust-preferred securities	2
Goodwill	5		
Bank fixed assets	15	Owners' capital	5
Total assets	$138 million	Total liabilities and owners' capital	$138 million

All amounts are in millions of dollars.

Note: The bank has loan-loss reserves of $10 million. The real estate and commercial loans shown on the balance sheet are net of the loan-loss reserves.

a. Calculate the equity capital ratio. How could the bank increase its equity capital ratio?

b. Risk-adjusted assets are estimated using the following weightings process: cash and government securities $=.00$; real estate loans $=.50$; commercial and other loans $= 1.00$.
   Calculate the risk-adjusted assets amount for the bank.

c. Calculate the Tier 1 Ratio based on the information provided and the risk-adjusted assets estimate from Part b.

d. Calculate the Total Capital (Tier 1 plus Tier 2) Ratio based on the information provided and the risk-adjusted assets estimate from Part b.

e. What actions could the bank management team take to improve the bank's Tier 1 and Total Capital ratios?

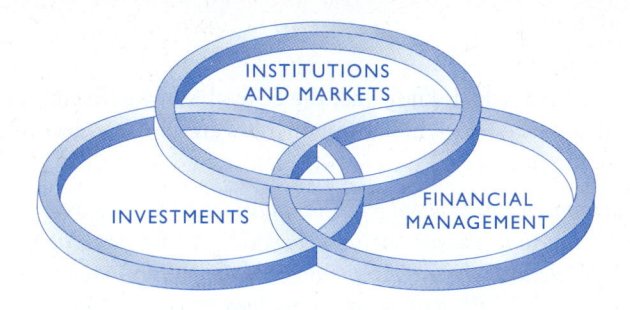

CHAPTER 4

Federal Reserve System

Chapter Learning Objectives:

AFTER STUDYING THIS CHAPTER, YOU SHOULD BE ABLE TO:
- Identify three weaknesses of the national banking system that existed before the Federal Reserve System.
- Describe Federal Reserve membership in terms of who must join and who may join.
- Describe the composition of the Fed Board of Governors.
- Discuss how the Fed uses reserve requirements to carry out monetary policy.
- Discuss how discount rate policy is employed by the Fed.
- Describe the Fed's use of open-market operations to alter bank reserves.
- Describe the ways in which the Reserve Banks accommodate the clearance and collection of checks.
- Discuss structural characteristics of central banks located in selected foreign countries.

Where We Have Been...

In Chapter 3 we discussed the types and roles of financial institutions that have evolved in the United States to meet the needs of individuals and businesses and help the financial system operate efficiently. We also described the traditional differences between commercial banking and investment banking followed by coverage of the functions of banks (all depository institutions) and the banking system. By now you also should have an understanding of the structure and chartering of commercial banks, the availability of branch banking, and the use of bank holding companies. You also should now have a basic understanding of the bank balance sheet and how the bank management process is carried out in terms of liquidity and capital management. Selected information also was provided on international banking and several foreign banking systems.

Where We Are Going...

The last two chapters in Part 1 address the role of policy makers in the financial system and how international finance and trade influence the U.S. financial system. In Chapter 5 you will have the opportunity to review economic objectives that direct policy-making activities. We then briefly review fiscal policy and how it is administered through taxation and expenditure plans. This is followed by a discussion of the policy instruments employed by the U.S. Treasury and how the Treasury carries out its debt management activities. You will then see how the money supply is changed by the banking system, as well as develop an understanding of the factors that affect bank reserves. The monetary base and the money multiplier also will be described and discussed. Chapter 6 focuses on how currency exchange rates are determined and how international trade is financed.

How This Chapter Applies to Me...

Actions taken by the Fed impact your ability to borrow money and the cost or interest rate on that money. When the Fed is taking an easy monetary stance, the availability of money and its cost will be lower. Such an action, in turn, will likely result in lower interest rates on your credit card, your new automobile loan, and possibly your interest rate on a new mortgage loan. Actions by the Fed also influence economic activity and the type and kind of job opportunities that may be available to you. For example, a tightening of monetary policy in an effort to control inflation may lead to an economic slowdown.

While many individuals know that the Federal Reserve System is the central bank of the United States, what the Fed does and how it operates are a lot less clear. William Greider had the following to say about the Fed:

> *The community of elected politicians acquiesced to its power. The private economy responded to its direction. Private capital depended on it for protection. The governors of the Federal Reserve decided the largest questions of the political economy, including who shall prosper and who shall fail, yet their role remained opaque and mysterious. The Federal Reserve was shielded from scrutiny partly by its own official secrecy, but also by the curious ignorance of the American public.*[1]

Of course, others don't view the Fed as being secretive. Stephen H. Axilrod comments:

> *There must be almost as many images of the Fed as an institution and of the wellsprings of its actions as there are viewers. Mine, born of a particular experience, is a generally benign one. It is of an unbiased, honest, straightforward institution that quite seriously and carefully carries out its congressionally given mandates. . . . It is of course through the window of monetary policy that the public chiefly sees and judges the Fed.*[2]

Whether the Fed operates "secretively" or "openly" is open for opinion. With this said, this chapter focuses on understanding the structure and functions of the Fed. Chapter 5 describes how the Fed administers monetary policy in cooperation with fiscal policy and Treasury operations to carry out the nation's economic objectives. After completing the next two chapters, the "veil of secrecy" surrounding the Fed should be lessened.

THE U.S. BANKING SYSTEM PRIOR TO THE FED

In Chapter 1, when we discussed the characteristics of an effective financial system, we said that one basic requirement was the need for a monetary system that efficiently carried out the financial functions of creating and transferring money. While we have an efficient monetary system today, this was not always the case. To understand the importance of the Federal Reserve System, it is useful to review briefly the weaknesses of the banking system that gave rise to the establishment of the Fed. National banking acts passed in 1863 and 1864 provided for a national banking system. Banks could receive national charters, capital and reserve requirements on deposits and banknotes were established, and banknotes could be issued only against U.S. government securities owned by the banks but held with the U.S. Treasury Department. These banknotes, backed by government securities, were supposed to provide citizens with a safe and stable national currency. Improved bank supervision also was provided for with the establishment of the Office of the Comptroller of the Currency under the control of the U.S. Treasury.

WEAKNESSES OF THE NATIONAL BANKING SYSTEM

Although the national banking system overcame many of the weaknesses of the prior systems involving state banks, it lacked the ability to carry out other central banking system activities that are essential to a well-operating financial system. Three essential needs or requirements include: (1) an efficient national payments system, (2) an elastic or flexible money supply that can respond to changes in the demand for money, and (3) a lending/borrowing mechanism to help alleviate liquidity problems when they arise. The first two requirements relate directly to the transferring and creating money functions. The third requirement relates to the need to maintain adequate bank liquidity. Recall from Chapter 3 that we referred to bank liquidity as the ability to meet depositor withdrawals and to pay other liabilities as they come due. All three of these needs were deficient until the Federal Reserve System was established.

The payments system under the National Banking Acts was based on an extensive network of banks with correspondent banking relationships. It was costly to transfer funds from region to region, and the check-clearing and collection process sometimes was quite long. Checks written

---

1. William Greider, *Secrets of the Temple: How the Federal Reserve Runs the Country,* New York: Simon and Schuster, 1987, p. 12.
2. Stephen H. Axilrōd, *Inside the Fed,* Cambridge: The MIT Press, 2009, p. 159.

on little-known banks located in out-of-the-way places often were discounted or were redeemed at less than face value. For example, let's assume that a check written on an account at a little-known bank in the western region of the United States was sent to pay a bill owed to a firm in the eastern region. When the firm presented the check to its local bank, the bank might record an amount less than the check's face value in the firm's checking account. The amount of the discount was to cover the cost of getting the check cleared and presented for collection to the bank located in the western region. Today, checks are processed or cleared quickly and with little cost throughout the U.S. banking system. Recall from Chapter 3 that the current U.S. payments system allows checks to be processed either directly or indirectly. The indirect clearing process can involve the use of bank clearinghouses as discussed in Chapter 3 or a Federal Reserve Bank. The role of the Fed in processing checks is discussed in this chapter.

INTERNET ACTIVITY
Go to the Federal Reserve Board of Governors' Web site, http://www.federalreserve.gov, and access "statistical releases." Identify the amount of bank reserves and note any recent changes.

A second weakness of the banking system under the National Banking Acts was that the money supply could not be easily expanded or contracted to meet changing seasonal needs and/or changes in economic activity. As noted, banknotes could be issued only to the extent that they were backed by U.S. government securities. Note issues were limited to 90 percent of the par value, as stated on the face of the bond, or the market value of the bonds, whichever was lower. When bonds sold at prices considerably above their par value, the advantage of purchasing bonds as a basis to issue notes was eliminated.[3]

For example, if a $1,000 par value bond was available for purchase at a price of $1,100, the banks would not be inclined to make such a purchase since a maximum of $900 in notes could be issued against the bond, in this case 90 percent of par value. The interest that the bank could earn from the use of the $900 in notes would not be great enough to offset the high price of the bond. When government bonds sold at par or at a discount, on the other hand, the potential earning power of the note issues would be quite attractive and banks would be encouraged to purchase bonds for note issue purposes. The volume of national bank notes, and thus the money supply, therefore depended on the government bond market rather than the seasonal or cyclical needs of the nation for currency.

A third weakness of the national banking system involved the arrangement for holding reserves and the lack of a central authority that could lend to banks when they had temporary liquidity problems. A large part of the reserve balances of banks was held as deposits with large city banks, in particular with large New York City banks. Banks outside of the large cities were permitted to keep part of their reserves with their large city bank correspondents. Certain percentages of deposits had to be retained in their own vaults. These were the only alternatives for holding reserve balances. During periods of economic stress, the position of these large city banks was precarious because they had to meet the demand for deposit withdrawals by their own customers as well as by the smaller banks. The frequent inability of the large banks to meet such deposit withdrawal demands resulted in extreme hardship for the smaller banks whose reserves they held. A mechanism for providing loans to banks to help them weather short-term liquidity problems is crucial to a well-functioning banking system.

THE MOVEMENT TO CENTRAL BANKING

central bank
federal government agency that facilitates the operation of the financial system and regulates money supply growth

A **central bank** is a government-established organization responsible for supervising and regulating the banking system and for creating and regulating the money supply. While central bank activities may differ somewhat from country to country, central banks typically play an important role in a country's payments system. It is also common for a central bank to lend money to its member banks, hold its own reserves, and be responsible for creating money.

Even though the shortcomings of the national banking system in terms of the payments system, inflexible money supply, and illiquidity were known, opposition to a strong central banking system still existed in the United States during the late 1800s. The vast western frontiers and the local independence of the southern areas during this period created distrust of centralized financial control. This distrust deepened when many of the predatory practices of large corporate combinations were being made public by legislative commissions and investigations around the turn of the century.

---

3. A bond's price will differ from its stated or face value if the interest rate required in the marketplace is different from the interest rate stated on the bond certificate. Bond valuation calculations are discussed in Chapter 10.

CONCEPT CHECK

What were the three main deficiencies associated with the national banking system prior to the establishment of the Fed?

What types of functions and activities do central banks usually perform?

Federal Reserve System (Fed)
U.S. central bank that sets monetary policy and regulates banking system

The United States was one of the last major industrial nations to adopt a permanent system of central banking. However, many financial and political leaders had long recognized the advantages of such a system. These supporters of central banking were given a big boost by the financial panic of 1907. The central banking system adopted by the United States under the Federal Reserve Act of 1913 was, in fact, a compromise between the system of independently owned banks in this country and the single central bank systems of such countries as Canada, Great Britain, and Germany. This compromise took the form of a series of central banks, each representing a specific region of the United States. The assumption was that each central bank would be more responsive to the particular financial problems of its region.

STRUCTURE OF THE FEDERAL RESERVE SYSTEM

The **Federal Reserve System (Fed)** is the central bank of the United States and is responsible for setting monetary policy and regulating the banking system. William Greider made the following observations:

> The Federal Reserve System was an odd arrangement, a unique marriage of public supervision and private interests, deliberately set apart from the elected government, though still part of it. The Fed enjoyed privileges extended to no other agency in Washington—it raised its own revenue, drafted its own operating budget and submitted neither to Congress for approval.[4]

As we progress through this chapter and the next one, the basis for some of Greider's observations should become clearer.

However, before we start it is important to understand that the Fed did not replace the system that existed under the National Banking Acts of 1863 and 1864 but rather was superimposed on the national banking system created by these acts. Certain provisions of the National Banking acts, however, were modified to permit greater flexibility of operations.

The Fed system consists of five components:

- Member banks
- Federal Reserve District Banks
- Board of Governors
- Federal Open Market Committee
- Advisory committees

These five components are depicted in Figure 4.1.

MEMBER BANKS

The Federal Reserve Act provided that all national banks were to become members of the Fed. In addition, state-chartered banks were permitted to join the system if they could show evidence of a satisfactory financial condition. The Federal Reserve Act also required that all member banks purchase capital stock of the Reserve Bank of their district up to a maximum of 6 percent of their paid-in capital and surplus. In practice, however, member banks have had to pay only 3 percent; the remainder is subject to call at the discretion of the Fed. Member banks are limited to a maximum of 6 percent dividends on the stock of the Reserve Bank that they hold. The Reserve Banks, therefore, are private institutions owned by the many member banks of the Fed.

State-chartered banks are permitted to withdraw from membership with the Fed six months after written notice has been submitted to the Reserve Bank of their district. In such cases, the stock originally purchased by the withdrawing member is canceled and a refund is made for all money paid in.

Approximately 3,500, or about one-third, of the nation's commercial banks are members of the Fed. This includes all commercial banks with national charters plus roughly one-fifth of the state-chartered banks. These member banks hold approximately three-fourths of the deposits

---

4. William Greider, *Secrets of the Temple: How the Federal Reserve Runs the Country,* New York: Simon and Schuster, 1987, p. 50.

FIGURE 4.1
Organization of the Federal Reserve System

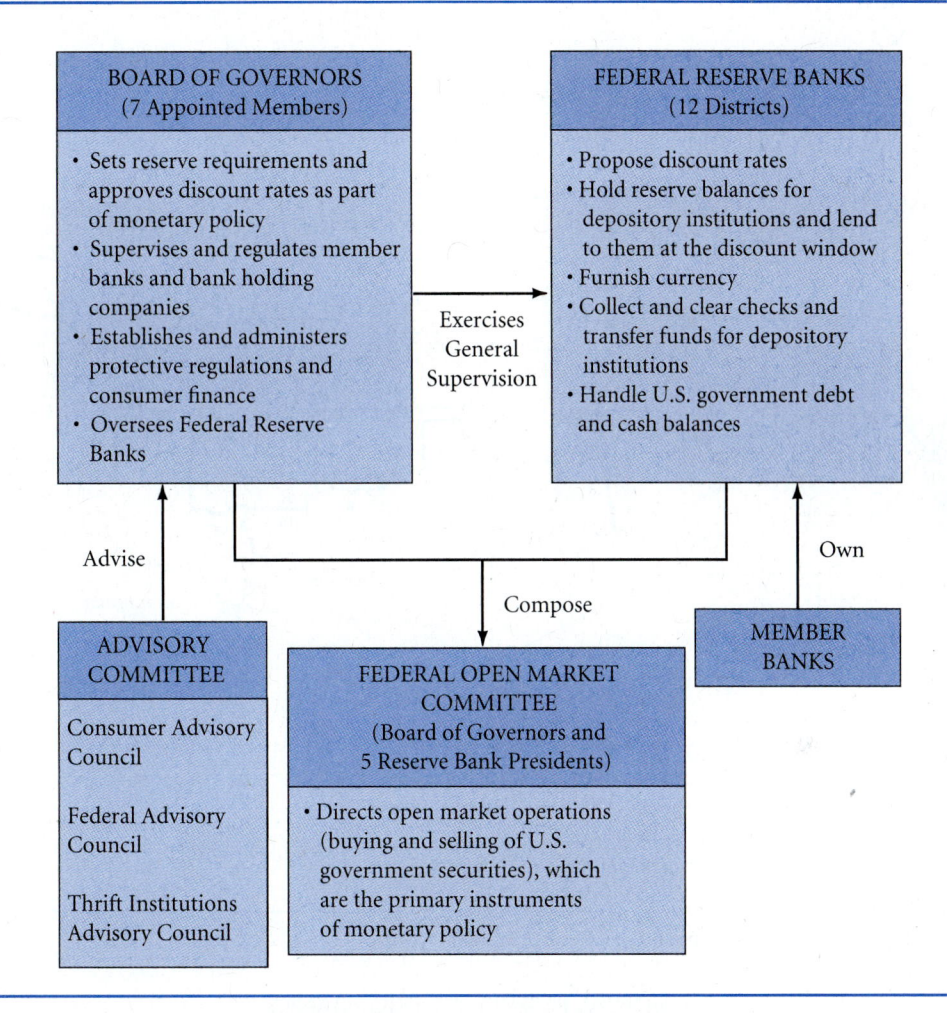

```
┌─────────────────────────────────────┐         ┌─────────────────────────────────────┐
│      BOARD OF GOVERNORS             │         │      FEDERAL RESERVE BANKS          │
│      (7 Appointed Members)          │         │           (12 Districts)            │
│                                     │         │                                     │
│ • Sets reserve requirements and     │         │ • Propose discount rates            │
│   approves discount rates as part   │         │ • Hold reserve balances for         │
│   of monetary policy                │         │   depository institutions and lend  │
│ • Supervises and regulates member   │         │   to them at the discount window    │
│   banks and bank holding            │ Exercises│ • Furnish currency                 │
│   companies                         │ General │ • Collect and clear checks and      │
│ • Establishes and administers       │Supervision│  transfer funds for depository    │
│   protective regulations and        │   ──→   │   institutions                      │
│   consumer finance                  │         │ • Handle U.S. government debt       │
│ • Oversees Federal Reserve          │         │   and cash balances                 │
│   Banks                             │         │                                     │
└─────────────────────────────────────┘         └─────────────────────────────────────┘
              ▲                                                      ▲
              │ Advise                                         Own   │
              │                  │ Compose                           │
┌──────────────────┐  ┌──────────▼───────────────┐         ┌──────────────────┐
│    ADVISORY      │  │  FEDERAL OPEN MARKET     │         │      MEMBER      │
│    COMMITTEE     │  │       COMMITTEE          │         │       BANKS      │
│                  │  │  (Board of Governors and │         │                  │
│ Consumer Advisory│  │  5 Reserve Bank Presidents)│       └──────────────────┘
│ Council          │  │                          │
│                  │  │ • Directs open market    │
│ Federal Advisory │  │   operations             │
│ Council          │  │   (buying and selling of U.S.│
│                  │  │   government securities), which│
│ Thrift Institutions│ │   are the primary instruments│
│ Advisory Council │  │   of monetary policy     │
└──────────────────┘  └──────────────────────────┘
```

of all commercial banks. National banks control about three-fifths of the total assets of all FDIC-insured commercial banks, and the state-chartered banks that belong to the Fed control another one-fourth of total assets. Even these figures understate the importance of the Federal Reserve in the nation's financial system. As indicated in Chapter 3, the Monetary Control Act of 1980 generally eliminated distinctions between banks that are members of the Fed and other depository institutions by applying comparable reserve and reporting requirements to all these institutions.

SMALL BUSINESS PRACTICE
Commercial Banks as Providers of Small Business Credit

The 1980s and 1990s were difficult for the banking industry in the United States. Many savings and loan associations failed, and there were many mergers involving S&Ls and commercial banks. Furthermore, many of the consolidations involved small commercial banks that traditionally tended to specialize in small business lending. As a result, concern has been expressed about where, or even whether, small businesses are able to obtain loans and other forms of business credit.

In contrast, the first part of the decade of the 2000s was characterized by Fed monetary policy that emphasized liquidity and low interest rates in an effort to stimulate economic recovery after the dot.com and the tech bubbles burst at the beginning of the decade and in reaction to the September 11, 2001, terrorist attack. Even after the U.S. economy began recovering, the Fed maintained an easy monetary policy. Then came the real estate housing price bubble burst, followed by the 2007–09 financial crisis. During the crisis, the availability of bank loans for small businesses virtually dried up. There now is an ongoing effort to encourage banks to increase the availability of loan funds to small businesses.

FIGURE 4.2
The Federal Reserve System

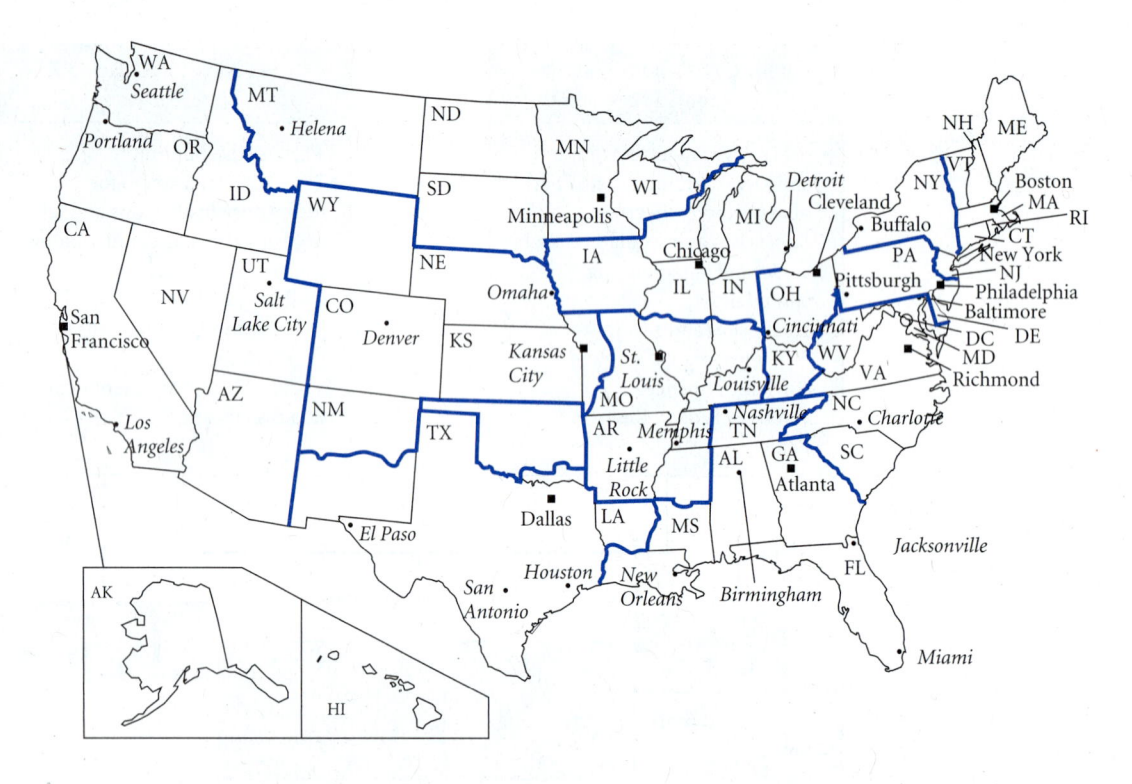

- ○ Board of Governors of the Federal Reserve System
- ■ Federal Reserve Bank cities
- • Federal Reserve Branch cities

Source: Board of Governors of the Federal Reserve System.

FEDERAL RESERVE DISTRICT BANKS

The Federal Reserve Act of 1913 provided for the establishment of twelve Federal Reserve districts. Each district is served by a Federal Reserve Bank. Figure 4.1 indicates that district banks have a wide range of responsibilities, including holding reserve balances for depository institutions and lending to them at the prevailing discount (interest) rate. The district banks also issue new currency and withdraw damaged currency from circulation, as well as collect and clear checks and transfer funds for depository institutions. The boundaries of the districts and the cities where district banks are located are shown in Figure 4.2.

Directors and Officers

Each Reserve Bank has corporate officers and a board of directors. The selection of officers and directors is unlike that of other corporations. Each Reserve Bank has on its board nine directors, who must be residents of the district in which they serve. The directors serve terms of three years, with appointments staggered so that three directors are appointed each year. To ensure that the various economic elements of the Federal Reserve districts are represented, the nine members of the board of directors are divided into three groups: *Class A*, *Class B*, and *Class C*.

Both Class A and Class B directors are elected by the member banks of the Federal Reserve district. The Class A directors represent member banks of the district, and the Class B directors represent nonbanking interests. These nonbanking interests are commerce, agriculture, and industry. The Class C directors are appointed by the Board of Governors of the Federal Reserve System. These persons may not be stockholders, directors, or employees of existing banks.

The majority of the directors of the Reserve Banks are elected by the member banks of each district. However, the three nonbanking members of each board appointed by the Board of Governors of the Federal Reserve System are in a more strategic position than the other board members. One member appointed by the Board of Governors is designated chairperson of the board of directors and Federal Reserve agent, and a second member is appointed deputy chairperson. The Federal Reserve agent is the Board of Governors' representative at each Reserve Bank. He or she is responsible for maintaining the collateral that backs the Federal Reserve notes issued by each Reserve Bank.

Each Reserve Bank also has a president and first vice president, who are appointed by its board of directors and approved by the Board of Governors. A Reserve Bank may have several additional vice presidents. The president is responsible for executing policies established by the board of directors and for the general administration of Reserve Bank affairs. All other officers and personnel of the Reserve Bank are subject to the authority of the president.

Federal Reserve Branch Banks

In addition to the twelve Reserve Banks, twenty-five branch banks have been established. These branch banks are for the most part in geographical areas not conveniently served by the Reserve Banks themselves. For this reason, the geographically large western Federal Reserve districts have most of the Reserve Branch Banks. The San Francisco district has four, the Dallas district has three, and the Atlanta district has five branch banks. The New York Federal Reserve district, on the other hand, has only one branch bank, while the Boston district has no branches. The cities in which Reserve Banks and their branches are located are also shown in Figure 4.2.

BOARD OF GOVERNORS

Fed Board of Governors seven-member board of the Federal Reserve that sets monetary policy

The **Fed Board of Governors,** or formally the Board of Governors (BOG) of the Federal Reserve System, is composed of seven members and is responsible for setting monetary policy. Each member is appointed for a term of fourteen years. The purpose of the fourteen-year term undoubtedly was to reduce political pressure on the board. Board members can be of any political party, and there is no specific provision concerning the qualifications a member must have. All members are appointed by the president of the United States with the advice and consent of the Senate. One member is designated as the chairperson and another as the vice chairperson.

The appointive power of the president and the ability of Congress to alter its structure make the Board of Governors a dependent political structure. However, it enjoys much independence in its operations. The Board of Governors of the Federal Reserve System is, in fact, one of the most powerful monetary organizations in the world. The chair of the board plays an especially influential role in policy formulation. Because the board attempts to achieve its goals without political considerations, disagreement between the administration in power and the board is common. From time to time pressures from Congress or the president have undoubtedly influenced the board's decisions, but its semi-independence generally prevails.

Figure 4.1 illustrates how the Board of Governors establishes monetary policy. The Fed BOG sets reserve requirements and reviews and approves the discount rate actions of the twelve district banks. The Fed BOG also operates through the Federal Open Market Committee to control the money supply as a means of meetings monetary policy objectives. We will explore these monetary policy instruments in more detail later in the chapter.

INTERNET ACTIVITY

Go to the Federal Reserve Board of Governors' Web site, http://www.federalreserve.gov, and find the Fed's list of regulations. Write a brief summary about the materials on Regulation Z.

In addition to setting the nation's monetary policy, the board directs and coordinates the activities of the twelve Reserve Banks under its jurisdiction. The board is responsible for approving the applications of state-chartered banks applying for membership in the system and for recommending the removal of officers and directors of member banks when they break rules established by the Fed and other regulatory authorities. In addition, the board implements many of the credit control devices that have come into existence since the mid-1960s, such as the *Truth-in-Lending Act,* the *Equal Credit Opportunity Act,* and the *Home Mortgage Disclosure Act.*

The Board of Governors also publishes the *Federal Reserve Bulletin,* which carries articles of current interest and offers a convenient source of the statistics compiled by the Fed. The Board and all twelve of the Reserve Banks engage in intensive research in monetary matters.

FEDERAL OPEN MARKET COMMITTEE

As early as 1922, efforts were made to coordinate the timing of purchases and sales of securities by the Federal Reserve Banks to achieve desirable national monetary policy objectives. The Federal Open Market Committee (FOMC), with the additional powers granted to it by the *Banking*

CONCEPT CHECK

Which type of commercial bank must belong to the Federal Reserve System, and which type can choose to join?

What is the number of Federal Reserve Banks, and how many branch banks operate in the Federal Reserve System?

How many individuals serve on the Fed Board of Governors, and what is the Board responsible for?

ETHICAL ISSUES

Act of 1935, has full control over all open-market operations of the Reserve Banks. As noted in Figure 4.1, this committee consists of the seven members of the Board of Governors of the Fed plus five presidents (one of whom must be from New York) of Reserve Banks. The FMOC conducts open-market operations through the process of buying and selling U.S. government securities. These activities represent the primary method for carrying out monetary policies.

ADVISORY COMMITTEES

Figure 4.1 indicates that the Federal Reserve System has three major advisory committees. The Federal Advisory Council provides advice and general information on banking-related issues to the Board of Governors. Each of the twelve Federal Reserve Districts elects one member to serve on the council. The membership of the Consumer Advisory Council is composed of representatives from depository institutions and their customers and, as the committee title suggests, provides advice relating to consumer issues. The Thrift Institutions Advisory Council consists of members from savings and loans associations, savings banks, and credit unions and provides advice on issues that directly affect thrift institutions.

ROLE OF THE CHAIR OF THE FED BOARD OF GOVERNORS

Special authority attaches to the chairperson of any board. The chair of the Board of Governors (BOG) of the Federal Reserve System is no exception. The holder of that position is generally recognized as the most powerful influence on monetary policy in the nation. As for any chairperson, the chair's power derives in large measure from the personality, experience, and leadership of the individual.

High moral and ethical standards are a must for the chair of the Fed BOG. A successful chair must have the confidence and trust of the president and Congress, bank officers, business leaders, foreign officials, and the general public. While the Fed has tried in recent years to make its activities and intentions more transparent, the impact of Fed actions are not often felt for many months afterward. Constituents must trust the chair will do what is right for the economy and society. Unethical behavior on the part of a Fed BOG chair would not be tolerated. High-quality reputation matters!

Since the early l950s there have been six Fed chairs. The chairs, along with the period served, are:

- William McChesney Martin Jr. (1951–1970)
- Arthur Burns (1970–1978)
- G. William Miller (1978–1979)
- Paul Volcker (1979–1987)
- Alan Greenspan (1987–2006)
- Ben Bernanke (2006–present)

William Martin's tenure as chair has been the longest in Fed history. He focused on maintaining the Fed's independence from Congress and the president. The 1970s were a particularly difficult decade from an economic standpoint in the United States. Inflation was increasing at a rapid rate. Oil price shocks occurred in 1973–1974 and again in 1978–1979. Wage and price controls were tried with no success. Arthur Burns served as chair throughout most the 1970s until his term expired in 1978. President Jimmy Carter nominated William Miller as chair, but he served only one year. By 1979, public confidence in Carter was very low. Reactions in the financial markets in New York City also suggested concern over whether the president could control inflation.

In July 1979, Paul Volcker's name had surfaced as a possible chair of the Fed who could ably fight inflation in the United States. Volcker was an economist who had served as president of the New York Federal Reserve Bank and was well known on Wall Street. Volcker also had served in government positions in the Kennedy, Johnson, and Nixon administrations, as well as in commercial banking with Chase Manhattan.

While Volcker had impressive credentials, some of the comments gathered by the Carter administration included: "rigidly conservative . . . very right-wing . . . arbitrary and arrogant . . . not a team player."[5] While the Fed is legally independent from the White House, it is normal for the

---

5. William Greider, *Secrets of the Temple: How the Federal Reserve Runs the Country,* New York: Simon and Schuster, 1987, p. 35.

Fed chair to work with a president's economic advisors in a joint effort to reach certain economic objectives. Of course, there are times when it might be in the best interest of the people if the Fed pursues its own direction in applying monetary policy to achieve objectives such as lower inflation.

History shows that under the guidance of Paul Volcker, a restrictive Fed policy brought down the double-digit inflation of the 1970s and the early 1980s. Volcker dominated the Board during his tenure, and the Federal Open Market Committee consistently responded to his leadership. When Volcker resigned as chairman in June 1987, the financial markets reacted negatively. The U.S. dollar fell relative to other currencies, and U.S. government and corporate bond prices fell. Why? In a word, uncertainty—that is, uncertainty about the future direction of monetary policy. Volcker was a known inflation fighter. In contrast, the policies of the incoming Fed chair, Alan Greenspan, were unknown.

Greenspan was viewed as a conservative economist. He served as an economics advisor to President Gerald Ford and as a business consultant. Greenspan's first big test was the stock market crash of October 1987. He responded by immediately pumping liquidity into the banking system. The result was avoidance of monetary contraction and asset devaluation of the kind that followed the stock market crash of 1929. A reversal of policy occurred in mid-1988 when interest rates were raised to fight increasing inflation. A relatively mild recession occurred during 1990–1991. However, inflation has been kept below the 3 percent level since then. During Greenspan's service as chair of the Fed Board, there was real economic growth in the U.S. economy, interest rates declined to historic lows, and stock prices reached all-time highs. A 1996 survey of more than two hundred chief executive officers of the largest U.S. corporations gave overwhelming support for the "good job" that Greenspan was doing Since then, the business and financial sectors of the United States have maintained their strong support of Greenspan's Fed leadership. In 2004, Greenspan was nominated by President George W. Bush and confirmed by the U.S. Senate for a fifth and final four-year term as chair of the Fed. A Fed policy of high monetary liquidity and low interest rates was established during the early part of the decade of the 2000s in response to an economic downturn that was exacerbated by the September 11, 2001, terrorist attack. This easy money policy was continued through Greenspan's tenure, which lasted through January 2006.

Ben Bernanke became chair of the Fed Board in February 2006. It was only a few months before the housing price bubble burst and the economy started slowing down. Bernanke was responsible for establishing monetary policy that helped guide the U.S. through the "perfect storm" 2007–09 financial crisis, which had placed the U.S. economic system on the verge of collapse.[6]

CONCEPT CHECK
Who have been the three chairs of the Fed Board of Governors since the beginning of the 1980s?

MONETARY POLICY FUNCTIONS AND INSTRUMENTS

OVERVIEW OF RESPONSIBILITIES

The primary responsibility of the Fed is to formulate **monetary policy,** which involves regulating the growth of the supply of money, and therefore regulating its cost and availability. By exercising its influence on the monetary system of the United States, the Fed performs a unique and important function: promoting economic stability. It is notable that the system's broad powers to affect economic stabilization and monetary control were not present when the Fed came into existence in 1913. At that time, the system was meant to: help the money supply contract and expand as dictated by economic conditions, serve as bankers' banks in times of economic crisis, provide a more effective check clearance system, and establish a more effective regulatory system. Much of these responsibilities initially fell to the twelve Reserve Banks, but as the scope of responsibility for the monetary system was broadened, power was concentrated with the Board of Governors. Today the responsibilities of the Fed may be described as those relating to monetary policy, to supervision and regulation, and to services provided for depository institutions and the government.

monetary policy
formulated by the Fed to regulate money supply growth

Public discussions of Fed operations are almost always directed toward **dynamic actions** that stimulate or repress the level of prices or economic activity. However, we should recognize that this area is but a minor part of the continuous operation of the Federal Reserve System. Far more

dynamic actions
Fed actions that stimulate or repress the level of prices or economic activity

---

6. For an interesting personal experience perspective of working with the Fed chairs, see: Stephen H. Axilrod, *Inside the Fed*, Cambridge: The MIT Press, 2009.

significant in terms of time and effort are the defensive and accommodative responsibilities. **Defensive activities** are those that contribute to the smooth everyday functioning of the economy. Unexpected developments and shocks occur continually in the economy; unless these events are countered by appropriate monetary actions, disturbances may develop. Large unexpected shifts of capital out of or into the country and very large financing efforts by big corporations may significantly alter the reserve positions of the banks. Similarly, buyouts and acquisitions of one corporation by another, supported by bank financing, also affect reserve positions. In our competitive market system, unexpected developments contribute to the vitality of our economy. Monetary policy, however, has a special responsibility to absorb these events smoothly and prevent many of their traumatic short-term effects. The **accommodative function** of the nation's monetary system is the one with which we are the most familiar. Meeting the credit needs of individuals and institutions, clearing checks, and supporting depository institutions represent accommodative activities.

> *defensive activities*
> Fed activities that offset unexpected monetary developments and contribute to the smooth everyday functioning of the economy

> *accommodative function*
> Fed efforts to meet credit needs of individuals and institutions, clearing checks, and supporting depository institutions

The basic policy instruments of the Fed that allow it to increase or decrease the money supply are:

- Changing reserve requirements
- Changing the discount rate
- Conducting open-market operations

The Fed sets reserve requirements for depository institutions (i.e., banks), sets the interest rate at which to lend to banks, and executes open-market operations. By setting reserve requirements, the Fed establishes the maximum amount of deposits the banking system can support with a given level of reserves. The amount of reserves can be affected directly through open-market operations, thereby causing a contraction or expansion of deposits by the banking system. Discount or interest rate policy on loans to banks also affects the availability of reserves to banks and influences the way they adjust to changes in their reserve positions. Thus the Fed has a set of tools that together enable it to influence the size of the money supply to attain the Fed's broader economic objectives.

RESERVE REQUIREMENTS

The banking system of the United States is a **fractional reserve system** because banks are required by the Fed to hold reserves equal to a specified percentage of their deposits. **Bank reserves** are defined as vault cash and deposits held at the Reserve Banks. **Required reserves** are the minimum amount of bank reserves that must be held by banks. The **required reserves ratio** is the percentage of deposits that must be held as reserves. If a depository institution has reserves in excess of the required amount, it may lend them out. This is how institutions earn a return, and it is also a way in which the money supply is expanded. In our system of fractional reserves, control of the volume of checkable deposits depends primarily on reserve management. In Chapter 5 the mechanics of money supply expansion and contraction are explained in detail.

> *fractional reserve system*
> reserves must be held equal to a certain percentage of bank deposits

> *bank reserves*
> vault cash and deposits held at Federal Reserve Banks

> *required reserves*
> the minimum amount of total reserves that a depository institution must hold

> *required reserves ratio*
> percentage of deposits that must be held as reserves

> *excess reserves*
> the amount by which total reserves are greater than required reserves

The banking system has **excess reserves** when bank reserves are greater than required reserves. The closer to the required minimum the banking system maintains its reserves, the tighter the control the Fed has over the money creation process through its other instruments. If the banking system has close to the minimum of reserves (that is, if excess reserves are near zero), then a reduction of reserves forces the system to tighten credit to reduce deposits. If substantial excess reserves exist, the pressure of reduced reserves is not felt so strongly. When reserves are added to the banking system, depositories may expand their lending but are not forced to do so. However, since depositories earn no interest on reserves, profit maximizing motivates them to lend out excess reserves to the fullest extent consistent with their liquidity requirements. When interest rates are high, this motivation is especially strong.

The ability to change reserve requirements is a powerful tool the Fed uses infrequently. For a number of reasons, the Fed prefers to use open-market operations to change reserves rather than change reserve requirements. If reserve requirements are changed, the maximum amount of deposits that can be supported by a given level of reserves changes. It is possible to contract total deposits and the money supply by raising reserve requirements while holding the dollar amount of reserves constant. Lowering reserve requirements provides the basis for expanding money and credit.

It has been argued that "changing reserve requirements" is too powerful a tool and that its use as a policy instrument would destabilize the banking system. The institutional arrangements through which the banking system adjusts to changing levels of reserves might not respond as efficiently to changing reserve requirements. Another advantage of open-market operations is that they can be conducted quietly, while changing reserve requirements requires a public announcement. The Fed feels that some of its actions would be opposed if public attention were directed toward them.

Changing reserve requirements has been used as a policy instrument on occasion. In the late 1930s the nation's banks were in an overly liquid position because of excessive reserves. Banks had large amounts of loanable funds that businesses did not wish, or could not qualify, to borrow because of the continuing depression. The reserves were so huge that the Fed could no longer resolve the situation through its other policy instruments. Therefore it increased reserve requirements substantially to absorb excess reserves in the banking system.

Reserve requirements were lowered during World War II in order to ensure adequate credit to finance the war effort. But they were raised again in the postwar period to absorb excess reserves. In the 1950s and early 1960s, reserve requirements were lowered on several occasions during recessions. In each case, the lowering made available excess reserves to encourage bank lending, ease credit, and stimulate the economy. By using this policy tool, the Fed was publicly announcing its intention to ease credit, in hopes of instilling confidence in the economy.

In the late 1960s and 1970s, reserve requirements were selectively altered to restrain credit because the banking system was experimenting with new ways to get around Fed controls. Banks were using more negotiable certificates of deposit, Eurodollar borrowings, and other sources of reserve funds. This prompted the Fed to impose restraint on the banks by manipulating the reserve requirements on specific liabilities.

The evolution of the banking system eventually led Congress to pass the *Depository Institutions Deregulation and Monetary Control Act (DIDMCA) of 1980*, which made significant changes in reserve requirements throughout the financial system. Up to this time the Fed had control over the reserve requirements of its members only. Nonmember banks were subject to reserve requirements established by their own states, and there was considerable variation among states. As checks written on member banks were deposited in nonmember banks and vice versa, funds moved among banks whose deposits were subject to different reserve requirements. This reduced the Fed's control over the money supply.

The 1980 act applies uniform reserve requirements to all banks with certain types of accounts. For banks that were members of the Fed, these requirements are, in general, lower now than they were prior to the act. In general, for approximately the first $50 million of transaction account deposits at a depository institution, the reserve requirement is 3 percent. For deposits over approximately $50 million, the reserve requirement is 10 percent, which was reduced from 12 percent in April 1992. The "break point" between the 3 percent and the 10 percent rates is subject to change each year based on the percentage change in transaction accounts held by all depository institutions. In general, transaction accounts include deposits against which the account holder is permitted to make withdrawals to make payments to third parties or others. Accounts that restrict the amount of withdrawals per month are considered to be savings accounts rather than transaction accounts.

Banks and other depository institutions with large transaction account balances thus are required to hold a proportionately higher percentage of reserves. Let's illustrate this point under the assumption that the reserve requirement will be 3 percent on the first $50 million of transaction account balances and 10 percent on amounts over $50 million. Assume that First Bank has $50 million in transaction accounts while Second Bank has $100 million. What are the dollar amounts of required reserves for each bank? What percentage of required reserves to total transaction deposits must be held by each bank? Following are the calculations:

BANK	ACCOUNT AMOUNT	RESERVE PERCENTAGE	RESERVE REQUIREMENT AMOUNT
First Bank	$50 million	3%	$1.5 million
	0	10%	0
Total	**$50 million**		**$1.5 million**
Percent	($1.5 million/$50 million) =		3.0%
Second Bank	$50 million	3%	$1.5 million
	50	10%	5.0
Total	**$100 million**		**$6.5 million**
Percent	($6.5 million/$100 million) =		6.5%

CONCEPT CHECK

What is meant by the terms required reserves and excess reserves?

Which bank assets are counted as bank reserves for the purpose of meeting reserve requirements?

Notice that while First Bank was required to hold reserves of only 3 percent against its $50 million in transaction account balances, Second Bank had to hold reserves of 6.5 percent of its $100 million in transaction accounts. Depository institutions with even larger transaction account balances will have to hold proportionately higher reserves. As a result, their percentage of reserves to total transactions accounts will be closer to 10 percent.

A change in reserve requirement percentages on large transaction account balances has the most impact. For example, if the reserve requirement for transaction balances greater than $50 million is increased from 10 percent to 12 percent, Second Bank would have reserve requirements of $7.5 million—or 7.5 percent of its $100 million in transaction accounts. The required reserves on the second $50 million increase to $6 million, which is the result of multiplying $50 million times 12 percent. Adding the $1.5 million on the first $50 million in transaction accounts and the $6 million on the second $50 million results in total required reserves of $7.5 million, which is 7.5 percent of the total transaction accounts of $100 million. Thus, it should be evident that even a small change in reserve requirements is likely to have a major impact on the money supply and economic activity.

DISCOUNT RATE POLICY

The Fed serves as a lender to depository institutions. Banks can go to the Fed's "discount window" and borrow funds to meet reserve requirements, depositor withdrawal demands, and even business loan demands. The **Fed discount rate** is the interest rate that a bank must pay to borrow from its regional Federal Reserve Bank. While each Fed Bank sets its own discount rate, the rates have been similar across all twelve Reserve Banks in recent years. The Fed sets the interest rate on these loans to banks and thus can influence the money supply by raising or lowering the cost of borrowing from the Fed. Higher interest rates will discourage banks from borrowing, while lower rates will encourage borrowing. Increased borrowing will allow banks to expand their assets and deposit holdings and vice versa.

Fed discount rate
interest rate that a bank must pay to borrow from its regional Federal Reserve Bank

Loans to depository institutions by the Reserve Banks may take two forms. One option allows the borrowing institution to receive an advance, or loan, secured by its own promissory note together with "eligible paper" it owns. In the second option, the borrower may discount—or sell to the Reserve Bank—its eligible paper, which includes securities of the U.S. government and federal agencies, promissory notes, mortgages of acceptable quality, and bankers' acceptances. This discounting process underlies the use of the terms "discount window" and "discount rate policy."

Discount rate policy was originally intended to work in the following fashion. If the Fed wanted to cool an inflationary boom, it would raise the discount rate. An increase in the discount rate would lead to a general increase in interest rates for loans, decreasing the demand for short-term borrowing for additions to inventory and accounts receivable. This in turn would lead to postponing the building of new production facilities and, therefore, to a decreased demand for capital goods. As a consequence, the rate of increase in income would slow down. In time, income would decrease and with it the demand for consumer goods. Holders of inventories financed by borrowed funds would liquidate their stocks in an already weak market. The resulting drop in prices would tend to stimulate the demand for, and reduce the supply of, goods. Thus economic balance would be restored. A reduction in the discount rate was expected to have the opposite effect.

PERSONAL FINANCIAL PLANNING
The Fed and the Consumer

The Fed affects personal finance in several ways. First, the Fed controls the money supply. Actions that severely restrict the supply of money may lead to an economic recession. Too rapid a growth in the money supply may result in inflation and a decrease in purchasing power. Should the Fed act to slow down or reduce the growth rate of the money supply, there will be growing constraints on the ability of banks to lend as their excess reserves decline. This may result in higher loan rates, as loanable funds become scarcer. This could help bank savers, however, as banks and other depository institutions may raise the interest they pay on saving accounts and CDs to attract more funds that they will later lend to others.

The Fed acts in other ways to maintain people's trust and confidence in the banking system. As this chapter discusses, the Fed has supervisory power over many banks to ensure they have adequate capital and reserves and are following regulations. The Fed's Regulation Z requires lenders to tell borrowers the annual percentage rate on the loans they receive. The Fed clears checks by transporting them between banking centers and by debiting and crediting bank balances with the Fed.

FIGURE 4.3
Fed Lending Rate Versus Bank Prime Rate Changes, 1980–2009

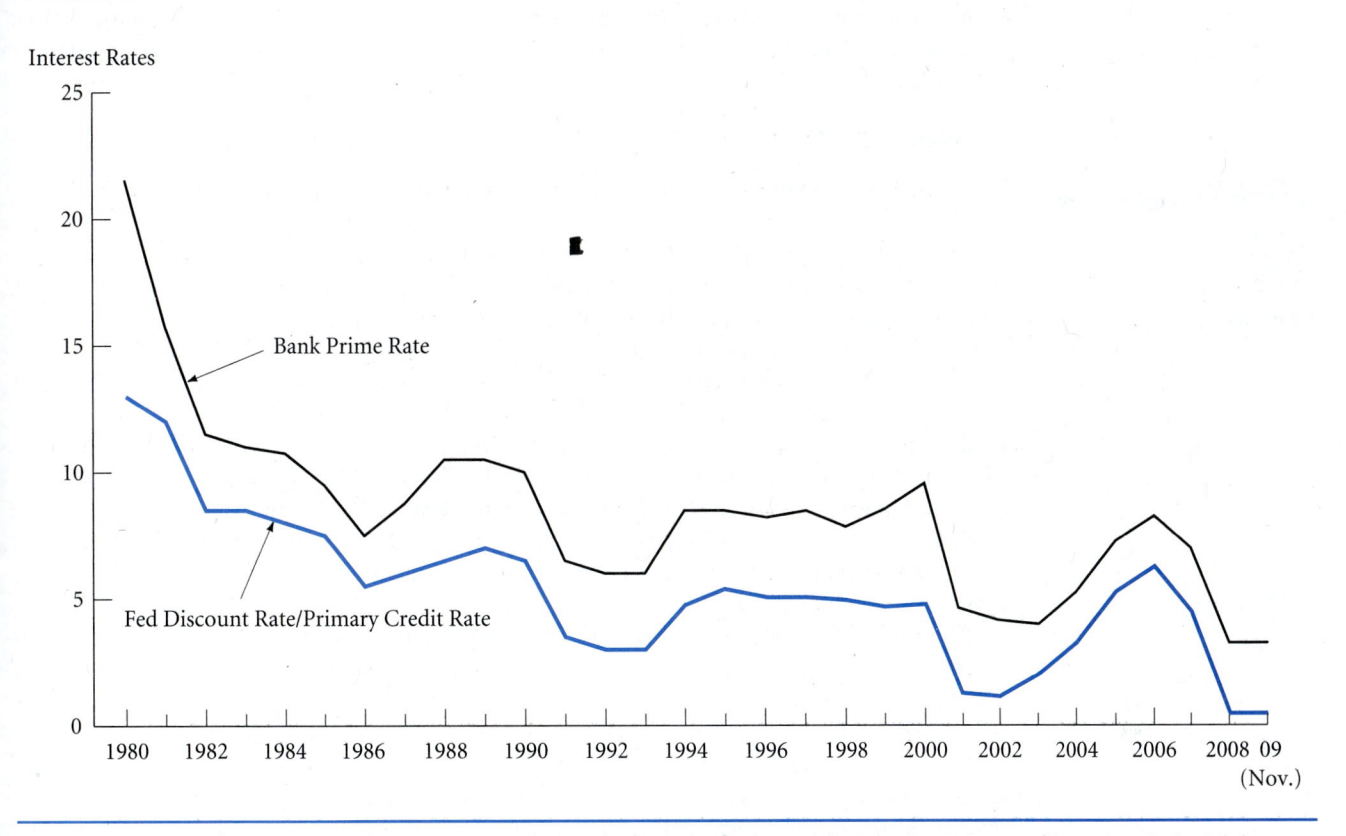

Source: *Statistical Supplements to the Federal Reserve Bulletin*, various issues, and http://www.stlouisfed.org.

INTERNET ACTIVITY

Go to the St. Louis Federal Reserve Bank's Web site, http://www.stlouisfed.org, and find the current discount rate charged by Federal Reserve Banks on loans to depository institutions. Describe recent changes or trends in discount rates.

CONCEPT CHECK

What is meant by the term discount rate, and how does the Fed use it?

Discount policy is no longer a major instrument of monetary policy and, in fact, is now regarded more as an adjustment or fine-tuning mechanism. As an adjustment mechanism, the discount arrangement does provide some protection to depository institutions in that other aggressive control actions may be temporarily moderated by the ability of banks to borrow. For example, the Fed may take a strong restrictive position through open-market operations. Individual banks may counter the pressure by borrowing from their Reserve Banks. The Reserve Banks are willing to tolerate what appears to be an avoidance of their efforts while banks are adjusting to the pressure being exerted. Failure to reduce their level of borrowing can always be countered by additional Fed open-market actions.

Figure 4.3 shows year-end interest rates charged by the Federal Reserve Bank of New York for "discount window borrowing" or *adjustment credit* over the 1980–2009 period. Interest rates for *adjustment credit* are plotted through 2002 and reflect the rate on short-term loans made available to depository institutions that had temporary needs for funds not available through "reasonable" alternative sources. Beginning in 2003 the discount window interest rate reflects the rate for *primary credit*, which replaced the prior adjustment credit designation. Primary credit is available ordinarily for overnight loans to depository institutions in generally sound financial condition.

For comparative purposes, year-end bank prime rates presented in Chapter 3 are also plotted in Figure 4.3. The Fed lending rate and the bank prime rate generally "track" each other over time. Both interest rate series peaked at the end of 1980 and remained high during 1981, when inflation rates were also very high in the United States. In 2003 the Fed changed from a single discount rate to a prime credit rate and a secondary credit rate. Figure 4.3 plots the prime credit rate beginning in 2003. In response to the 2007–09 financial crisis, both the bank prime rate and the Fed prime credit rate were sharply reduced. The bank prime rate, which was 8.25 percent at the end of 2006, was decreased to 3.25 percent by the end of 2008 and continued at that level throughout 2009. The Fed's prime credit rate, which was 6.25 percent at the end of 2006, was lowered to 0.50 percent by the end of 2008 and was maintained at that level through 2009.

Notice that the Fed's lending rate to depository institutions was consistently lower than the bank prime lending rate throughout the 1980–2009 period. Of course, in order to make profits banks must be able to borrow from depositors, and sometimes from the Fed, at rates lower than the rates the banks lend at. The determinants of interest rates will be discussed in detail in Chapter 8.

OPEN-MARKET OPERATIONS

open-market operations
buying and selling of securities by the Federal Reserve to alter the supply of money

The most used instrument of monetary policy is **open-market operations,** the buying and selling of securities in the "open market" by the Fed through its Federal Open Market Committee (FOMC) to alter bank reserves. The Fed can purchase securities to put additional reserves at the disposal of the banking system or sell securities to reduce bank reserves. You might ask, "Where does the Fed get securities to sell?" A brief look at the Fed's balance sheet will help provide an answer.

The Fed's assets are primarily held in the form of government and government agency securities, which generally represent over 85 percent of total assets. Coins and cash in the process of collection are about 2 percent of total assets. The remainder is assets that include gold certificates and Fed premises. Federal reserve notes (recall our discussion of fiat money in Chapter 2) represent nearly 90 percent of the Fed's total liabilities and capital. Deposits in the form of depository institution reserves held at the Reserve Banks are about 7 percent of the total. Other liabilities, particularly U.S. Treasury deposits and capital in the form of stock purchased by member banks and surplus earned from operations, make up the remaining total liabilities and capital.

The original Federal Reserve Act did not provide for open-market operations. However, to maintain stability in the money supply, this policy instrument developed out of Reserve Bank experiences during the early years of Fed operations. Unfortunately, these early efforts were not well coordinated. Reserve Banks bought government securities with funds at their disposal to earn money for meeting expenses and to make a profit and pay dividends on the stock held by member banks. All twelve Reserve Banks usually bought and sold the securities in the New York market. At times, their combined sales were so large that they upset the market. Furthermore, the funds used to buy the bonds ended up in New York member banks and enabled them to reduce their borrowing at the Reserve Bank of New York. This made it difficult for the Reserve Bank of New York to maintain effective credit control in its area. As a result, an open-market committee was set up to coordinate buying and selling of government bonds. The Federal Open Market Committee was legally established in 1933. In 1935 its present composition was established: the Federal Reserve Board of Governors plus five of the presidents of the twelve Reserve Banks, who serve on a rotating basis.

Open-market operations have become the most important and effective means of monetary and credit control. These operations can take funds out of the market and thus raise short-term interest rates and help restrain inflationary pressures, or they can provide for easy money conditions and lowered short-term interest rates. Of course, such monetary ease will not necessarily start business on the recovery road after a recession. When used with discount rate policy, open-market operations are basically an effective way of restricting credit or making it more easily available.

Open-market operations differ from discount operations in that they increase or decrease bank reserves at the initiative of the Fed, not of individual banking institutions. The process in simplified form works as follows. If the Federal Open Market Committee wants to buy government securities, it contacts dealers to ask for offers and then accepts the best offers that meet its needs. The dealers receive wire transfers of credit for the securities from the Reserve Banks. These credits are deposited with member banks. The member banks, in turn, receive credit for these deposits with their Reserve Banks, thus adding new bank reserves that form the basis for additional credit expansion. It is important to note that the Fed restricts its purchases to U.S. government securities primarily because of their liquidity and safety.

If the Fed wants to reduce bank reserves, it sells government securities to the dealers. The dealers pay for them by a wire transfer from a depository to a Reserve Bank. The Reserve Bank then deducts the amount from the reserves of the depository institution.

CONCEPT CHECK
What is meant by open-market operations?

Open-market operations do not always lead to an immediate change in the volume of deposits. This is especially true when bonds are sold to restrict deposit growth. As bonds are sold by the Reserve Banks, some banks lose reserves and are forced to borrow from their Reserve

Bank. Since they are under pressure from the Fed to repay the loans, they use funds from maturing loans to repay the Reserve Bank. Thus, credit can be gradually restricted as a result of the adjustments banks must make to open-market operations.

IMPLEMENTATION OF MONETARY POLICY

Monetary policy can focus either on trying to control the rate of change or growth in the money supply (such as M1) or on targeting a level for a specific type of interest rate. In fact the Fed in practice targets the ***federal funds rate,*** which is the rate on overnight loans from banks with excess reserves to banks that have deficit reserves. Open-market purchases of securities add to bank reserves and increase the money supply. Sales of securities lower reserves and the money supply. However, when the target is the money supply, interest rates may fluctuate widely because the demand for money may change relative to a specific money supply target. Furthermore, a focus on the money supply might not produce the desired impact on gross domestic product because of changes in the velocity of money, as we saw in Chapter 2.

In recent years, the Fed has chosen to focus on the level of the federal funds rate as the primary means of carrying out monetary policy. Recall that the federal funds rate is the overnight borrowing rate between banks. Banks with excess reserves lend to banks that need to borrow funds to meet reserve requirements. Interest rates such as the federal funds rate reflect the intersection of the demand for reserves and the supply of reserves. Open-market purchases of securities causes the federal funds rate to fall, whereas sales of securities cause the rate to rise.

The Fed uses its open-market operations to provide liquidity to the banking system in times of emergency and distress. For example, the stock market crash on October 19, 1987, caused concern of a possible economic collapse. The Fed, through open-market purchases, moved quickly to increase the money supply. The terrorist attacks on September 11, 2001, caused widespread concern about the near-term ability of stock and other financial markets to function properly with a related possibility of economic collapse. The FOMC moved quickly to provide liquidity to the banking system and to encourage renewed confidence in the financial system by reducing the federal funds rate on September 17, 2001, from 3.5 percent to 3.0 percent.

In 2001 the Fed further lowered the federal funds rate to 2.5 percent on October 2, to 2.0 percent on November 2, and finally to 1.75 percent on December 11. The next rate reduction, to 1.25 percent, occurred on November 6, 2002; that was followed by a reduction to 1.0 percent on June 25, 2003. As the U.S. economy began growing, concern shifted to the possibility of renewed inflation, causing the Fed to begin increasing the federal funds rate in 2004. In reaction to the 2007–09 financial crisis, the federal funds rate was decreased to historical lows. From 5.25 percent at the end of 2006, the federal funds rate was reduced to 0.15 percent by the end of 2008 and stayed well below 0.25 percent throughout 2009.

FED SUPERVISORY AND REGULATORY FUNCTIONS

A strong and stable banking system is vital to the growth and the stability of the entire economy. The supervision of commercial banks and other depository institutions is primarily concerned with the safety and soundness of individual institutions. It involves oversight to ensure that depository institutions are operated carefully. Depository institution regulation relates to the issuance of specific rules or regulations that govern the structure and conduct of operations.

SPECIFIC SUPERVISORY RESPONSIBILITIES

On-site examination of commercial banks is one of the Fed's most important responsibilities. This function is shared with the federal Office of the Comptroller of the Currency (OCC), the Federal Deposit Insurance Corporation (FDIC), and state regulatory agencies. Although the Federal Reserve is authorized to examine all member banks, in practice it limits itself to state-chartered member banks and all bank holding companies. It cooperates with state examining agencies to avoid overlapping examining authority. The OCC directs its attention to nationally chartered banks, and the FDIC supervises insured nonmember commercial banks.

---

federal funds rate
rate on overnight loans from banks with excess reserves to banks who have deficit reserves

CONCEPT CHECK
What are the two targets that the Fed can focus on when formulating monetary policy?

INTERNET ACTIVITY
Each of the twelve Federal Reserve Banks has its own Web site and tries to specialize in specific types of information. Go to the Federal Reserve Bank of San Francisco's Web site, http://www.frbsf.org, and the Federal Reserve Bank of Minneapolis's Web site, http://www.minneapolisfed.org/, and identify the types of consumer and economic information they provide.

CONCEPT CHECK

What federal agencies are responsible for conducting on-site examinations of commercial banks?

What federal agencies are responsible for regulating depository agencies that are not commercial banks?

In addition to these three federal banking supervisory agencies, two federal agencies are primarily responsible for supervising and regulating depository institutions that are not commercial banks. The National Credit Union Administration (NCUA) supervises and regulates credit unions, and the Office of Thrift Supervision (OTS) oversees S&Ls and other savings institutions. The examination generally entails (1) an appraisal of the soundness of the institution's assets; (2) an evaluation of internal operations, policies, and management; (3) an analysis of key financial factors, such as capital and earnings; (4) a review for compliance with all banking laws and regulations; and (5) an overall determination of the institution's financial condition.

The Federal Reserve conducts on-site inspections of parent bank holding companies and their nonbank subsidiaries. These inspections include a review of nonbank assets and funding activities to ensure compliance with the Bank Holding Company Act.

The Federal Reserve has broad powers to regulate the overseas activities of member banks and bank holding companies. Its aim is to allow U.S. banks to be fully competitive with institutions of host countries in financing U.S. trade and investment overseas. Along with the OCC and the FDIC, the Federal Reserve also has broad oversight authority to supervise all federal and state-licensed branches and agencies of foreign banks operating in the United States.

SPECIFIC REGULATORY RESPONSIBILITIES

The Federal Reserve has legal responsibility for the administration of the Bank Holding Company Act of 1956, the Bank Merger Act of 1960, and the Change in Bank Control Act of 1978. Under these acts, the Fed approves or denies the acquisitions of banks and other closely related nonbanking activities by bank holding companies. Furthermore, it permits or rejects changes of control and mergers of banks and bank holding companies.

The Federal Reserve is responsible for writing rules or enforcing a number of major laws that offer consumers protection in their financial dealings. In 1968 Congress passed the **Consumer Credit Protection Act**, which requires the clear explanation of consumer credit costs and garnishment procedures (taking wages or property by legal means) and prohibits overly high-priced credit transactions. **Regulation Z**, which was drafted by a Federal Reserve task force, enacts the Truth in Lending section of the act. The purpose of the law and Regulation Z is to make consumers aware of, and able to compare, the costs of alternate forms of credit. Regulation Z applies to consumer finance companies, credit unions, sales finance companies, banks, S&Ls, residential mortgage brokers, credit card issuers, department stores, automobile dealers, hospitals, doctors, dentists, and any other individuals or organizations that extend or arrange credit for consumers.

Consumer Credit Protection Act
1968 act requiring clear explanation of consumer credit costs and prohibiting overly high-priced credit transactions

Regulation Z
enacts Truth in Lending section of the Consumer Credit Protection Act with intent to make consumers able to compare costs of alternate forms of credit

The law requires a breakdown of the total finance charge and the annual percentage rate of charge. The finance charge includes all loan costs, including not only interest or discount but service charges, loan fees, finder fees, insurance premiums, and points (an additional loan charge). Fees for such items as taxes not included in the purchase price, licenses, certificates of title, and the like may be excluded from the finance charge if they are itemized and explained separately. Figure 4.4 lists the Truth in Lending and other consumer protection acts that fall under Fed jurisdiction.

In addition to consumer protection laws, the Federal Reserve, through the Community Reinvestment Act of 1977, encourages depository institutions to help meet the credit needs of their communities for housing and other purposes while maintaining safe and sound operations. This is particularly true in neighborhoods of families with low or moderate income.

CONCEPT CHECK

What is Regulation Z?

FED SERVICE FUNCTIONS

The Reserve Banks provide a wide range of important services to depository institutions and to the U.S. government. The most important of these services is the payments mechanism, a system whereby billions of dollars are transferred each day. Other services include electronic fund transfers, net settlement facilities, safekeeping and transfer of securities, and serving as fiscal agent for the United States.

THE PAYMENTS MECHANISM

An efficient payments mechanism is necessary for the monetary system to carry out the financial function of transferring money, which in turn is a requirement for an effective financial system. Figure 4.5 provides a review of how checks have traditionally been processed through the banking system. Recall from Chapter 3 that banks can clear checks either directly with one

FIGURE 4.4
Consumer Protection Responsibilities of the Federal Reserve System

- The *Truth in Lending* section of the *Consumer Credit Protection Act* requires disclosure of the finance charge and the annual percentage rate of credit along with certain other costs and terms to permit consumers to compare the prices of credit from different sources. This act also limits liability on lost or stolen credit cards.

- The *Fair Credit Billing Act* sets up a procedure for the prompt correction of errors on a revolving charge account and prevents damage to credit ratings while a dispute is being settled.

- The *Equal Credit Opportunity Act* prohibits discrimination in the granting of credit on the basis of sex, marital status, race, color, religion, national origin, age, or receipt of public assistance.

- The *Fair Credit Reporting Act* sets up a procedure for correcting mistakes on credit records and requires that records be used only for legitimate business purposes.

- The *Consumer Leasing Act* requires disclosure of information to help consumers compare the cost and terms of one lease of consumer goods with another and to compare the cost of leasing versus buying on credit or for cash.

- The *Real Estate Settlement Procedures Act* requires disclosure of information about the services and costs involved at the time of settlement when property is transferred from seller to buyer.

- The *Electronic Fund Transfer Act* provides a basic framework regarding the rights, liabilities, and responsibilities of consumers who use electronic transfer services and of the financial institutions that offer them.

- The *Federal Trade Commission Improvement Act* authorizes the Federal Reserve Board to identify unfair or deceptive acts or practices on the part of banks and to issue regulations to prohibit them.

Source: *The Federal Reserve System Purposes & Functions,* Board of Governors of the Federal Reserve System, Washington, D.C.

another or indirectly through bank clearinghouses. Checks also can be processed or cleared through the Federal Reserve Banks. The payments mechanism administered by the Fed also includes providing currency and coin and electronic funds transfers.

Electronic forms of payment are replacing the check, as a payment method. Included alternatives are credit cards, debit cards, and online account transfers. Furthermore, instead of transporting and sorting paper checks, more and more banks process the checks they receive electronically.

Coin and Currency

Even though the movement toward a cashless society continues, the United States remains highly dependent on currency and coin to conduct transactions. The Fed is responsible for ensuring that the economy has an adequate supply of cash to meet the public's demand. Currency and coin are put into or retired from circulation by the Reserve Banks, which use depository institutions for this purpose. Virtually all currency in circulation is in the form of Federal Reserve notes. These notes are printed by the Bureau of Engraving and Printing of the U.S. Treasury.

Check Clearance and Collection

One of the Fed's important contributions to the smooth flow of financial interchange is to facilitate the clearance and collection of checks of the depository institutions of the nation (see Figure 4.5). Each Reserve Bank serves as a clearinghouse for all depository institutions in its district, provided that they agree to pay the face value on checks forwarded to them for payment. Today, nearly all the checks processed for collection by Federal Reserve Banks are received as electronic check images.

Let's illustrate how the check-clearing process traditionally took place through Reserve Banks. Assume that the owner of a business in Sacramento, California, places an order for merchandise with a distributor in San Francisco. The order is accompanied by a check drawn on the owner's bank in Sacramento. The distributor deposits the check with its bank in San Francisco, at which

FIGURE 4.5
Traditional Method for Processing Checks Through the Banking System

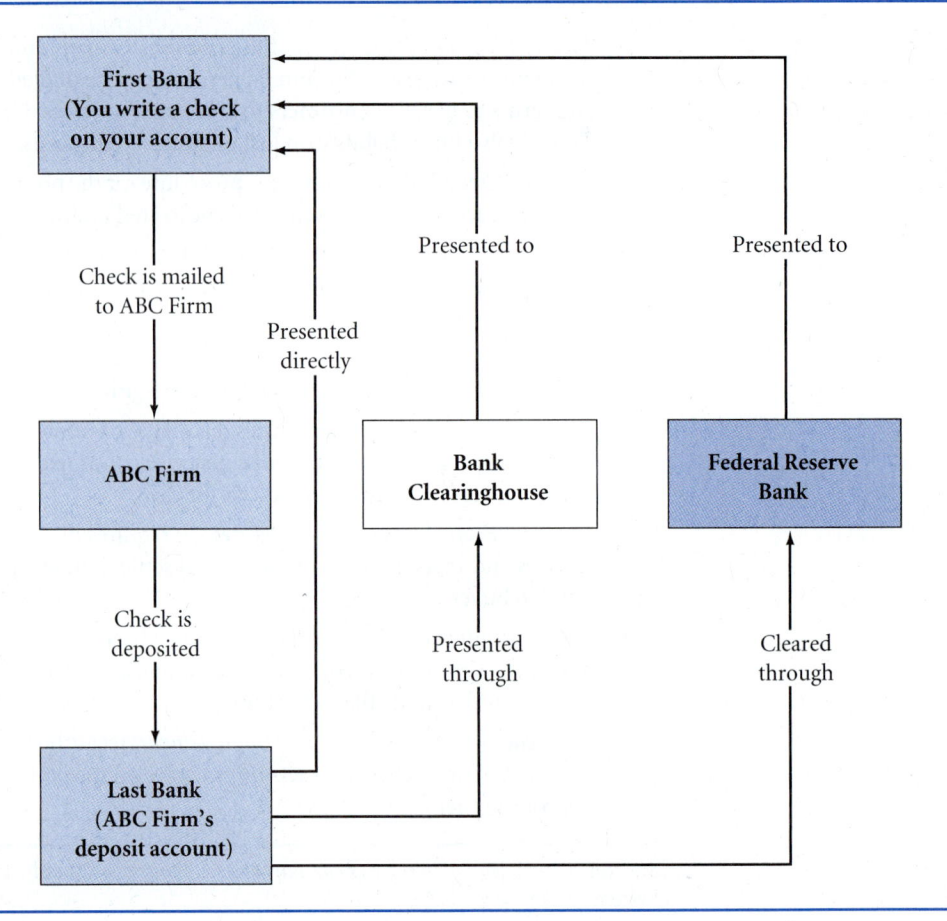

time the distributor receives a corresponding credit to its account with the bank. The distributor's bank will send the check to the Reserve Bank of its district, also located in San Francisco. The Reserve Bank will forward the check to the bank in Sacramento on which the check was drawn. The adjustment of accounts is accomplished at the Reserve Bank through an alternate debit and credit to the account of each bank involved in the transaction. The San Francisco bank, which has honored the check of its customer, will receive an increase in its reserves with the Reserve Bank, while the bank in Sacramento will have its reserves decreased by a corresponding amount. The bank in Sacramento will then reduce the account of the business on which the check was written. Notice that the exchange takes place without any transfer of currency.

Check Clearance among Federal Reserve Districts

If an order was also placed by the Sacramento firm with a distributor of goods in Chicago, the check would be subject to an additional step in being cleared through the Fed. The Chicago distributor, like the San Francisco distributor, deposits the check with the bank of its choice and in turn receives an increase in its account. The Chicago bank deposits the check for collection with the Reserve Bank of Chicago, which forwards the check to the Reserve Bank of San Francisco. The Reserve Bank of San Francisco, of course, then presents the check for payment to the bank on which it was drawn. Thus there are two routes of check clearance: the *intradistrict settlement*, in which the transaction takes place entirely within a single Federal Reserve district, and the *interdistrict settlement*, in which there are relationships between banks of two Federal Reserve districts.

As described, Reserve Banks are able to minimize the actual flow of funds by increasing or decreasing reserves of the participating depository institutions. In the same way, the Interdistrict Settlement Fund eliminates the flow of funds between the Reserve Banks needed to make interdistrict settlements. The Interdistrict Settlement Fund in Washington, D.C., has a substantial deposit from each of the Reserve Banks. These deposit credits are alternately increased or decreased, depending on the clearance balance of the day's activities on the part of each Reserve Bank. At a certain hour each day, each Reserve Bank informs the Interdistrict Settlement Fund by direct wire of the amount of checks it received the previous day that were drawn upon depository institutions in other Federal Reserve districts. The deposit of each Reserve Bank with the Interdistrict Settlement Fund is increased or decreased according to the balance of the day's check-clearance activities.

Check Clearance through Federal Reserve Branch Banks

Branch banks of the Reserve Banks enter into the clearance process in a very important way. If a check is deposited with a depository located closer to a Reserve Branch Bank than to a Reserve Bank, the branch bank, in effect, takes the place of the Reserve Bank. The Federal Reserve facilitates the check-clearing services of the reserve banks and their branches by maintaining a small group of regional check-processing centers.

Check Routing

In the past, a many employees at the twelve Reserve Banks were engaged in check clearing. Fundamental to the clearance process was the need to read the system of symbols and numerals shown in Figure 4.6. Although these symbols are slightly different from conventional numbers, they are easily read and are referred to as the magnetic ink character recognition (MICR) line.

FIGURE 4.6
Traditional use of Check Routing Symbols

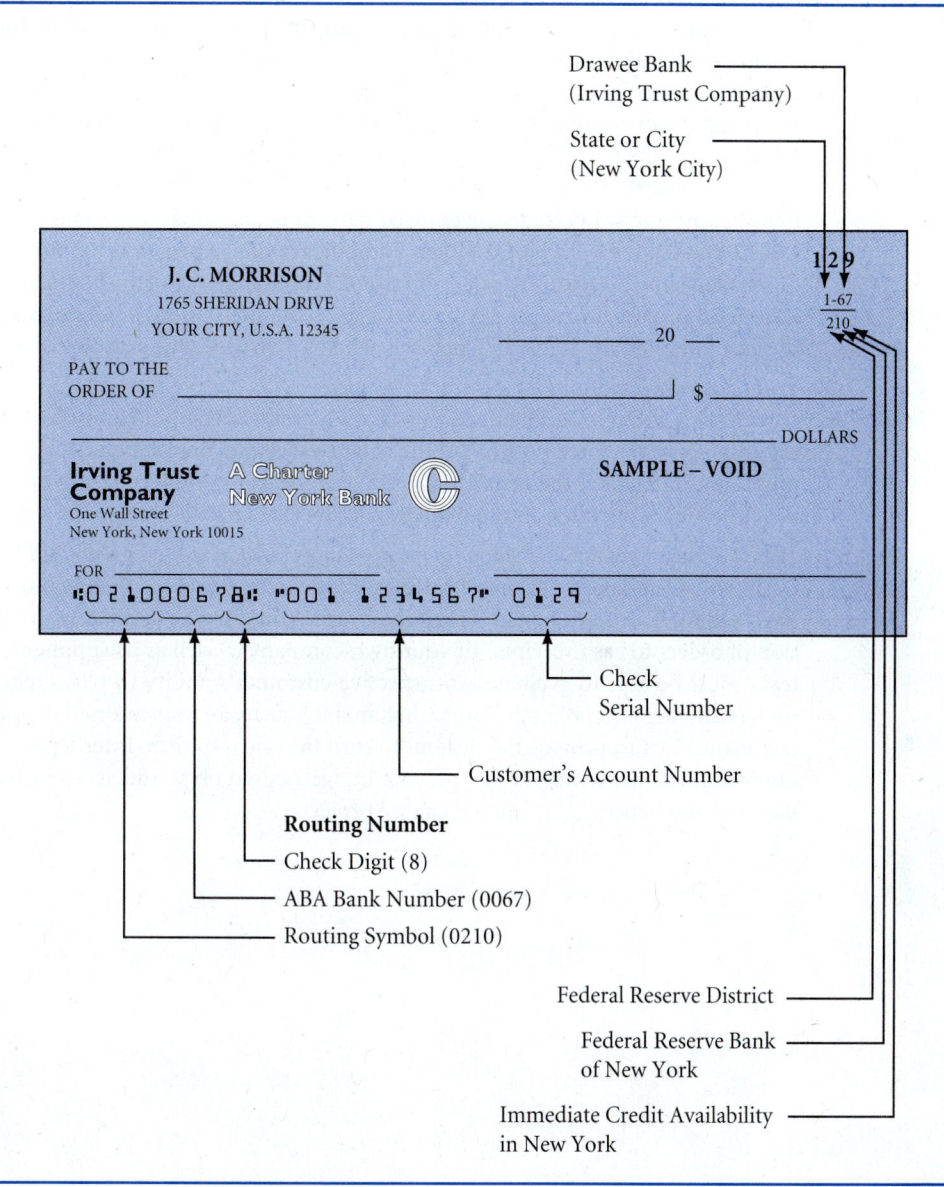

CAREER PROFILES

LESLIE L. ROGERS
President, Telecapital Solutions, Inc.

BA, Psychology
University of Michigan

"Lending combines the knowledge of credit, industry characteristics, and financial products."

Q: *Why did you become a consultant after twenty years in banking and corporate finance?*

A: My role as a corporate finance consultant gives me the opportunity to use everything that I learned in my banking and corporate finance positions. I enjoy the flexibility of working with different companies and managing my own schedule. I can focus on the larger economic picture and provide unbiased advice about finance as well as the impact of business decisions on operations, marketing, and sales. Other positives include the freedom to be creative and personally impact the success of my clients.

Q: *What were some of the highlights of your career?*

A: I started at Dun & Bradstreet as a credit analyst, where I learned the fundamentals of credit and the importance of paying bills on time to establish a record of responsibility. My job involved the research and preparation of credit reports about companies. Then I began what turned into a twenty-year career in banking, which is a dynamic way to become acquainted with the interrelationship of finance, economics, and credit. I started as an internal bank credit-auditor for a major New York City bank, reviewing the credit of companies that had already received loans and assessing the company's ongoing ability to repay the loan. I was promoted from credit to lending, eventually becoming a vice president and department head. Lending combines the knowledge of credit, industry characteristics, and financial products. I particularly enjoyed becoming an industry specialist. Lending also requires sales skills, to match the right types of loans and other financial products to the customer.

As managing director, treasury, of Lucent Technologies' North America Customer Finance Group, I arranged project financing. My market and credit analysis skills were especially valuable in assessing the customer's ability to pay, particularly when we financed the sale ourselves.

Q: *What skills are important for a career in finance?*

A: Obviously, a firm grounding in accounting is a must. You should know how each journal entry affects the company and its relationship to the balance sheet, income statement and cash flow statement. You must also understand the firm's business environment—the economics of its industry and the countries in which it operates. Interpersonal skills are extremely important as well.

Q: *Why is it important to understand financial management, even if you work in IT, marketing, or operations?*

A: Cash is the foundation of a viable business model. Personnel in all areas must understand their role in the creation, distribution, and retention of cash. You must be familiar with the cash cycle (the conversion of orders to cash receipts) of your own company as well as its suppliers and customers. The sales team must be able to evaluate a prospective customer's ability to pay. Operations personnel should understand the effect of each purchasing, maintenance, and inventory decision on the cash cycle of the company. IT must provide the systems to turn the sale into cash. Interdepartmental communication is essential. Each department must prepare budgets based on sound assumptions and be able to analyze the costs and benefits of proposed capital projects.

Information about the clearance process is printed on the lower part of the check. In addition to the clearance symbol, banks include a symbol for each customer's account. Banks also continue to include the older check routing symbol in the upper right-hand corner of their checks. Today, banks can keep an image of a check and process payment electronically through automated clearinghouses (ACHs). Banks now also have several ways to clear checks.

TRANSFER OF CREDIT

The Fed provides for the transfer of hundreds of millions of dollars in depository balances around the country daily. The communication system called Fedwire may be used by depository institutions to transfer funds for their own accounts, to move balances at correspondent banks, and to send funds to another institution on behalf of customers.

OTHER SERVICE ACTIVITIES

A large portion of Fed employees hold jobs directly related to the Fed's role as *fiscal agent* for the U.S. government. The services include holding the Treasury's checking accounts; assisting in the collection of taxes; transferring money from one region to another; and selling, redeeming, and paying interest on federal securities. The federal government makes most of its payments to the public from funds on deposit at the Reserve Banks. The Fed also acts as fiscal agent for foreign central banks and international organizations such as the International Monetary Fund.

CENTRAL BANKS IN OTHER COUNTRIES

Central banks in other developed countries, like the U.S. Fed, are responsible for regulating the country's money supply, safeguarding the country's currency, and carrying out the country's monetary policy. Most other countries have a single central bank with branches that differ from the Fed's twelve Reserve Banks. Of course, the Fed Board of Governors has effectively centralized control of U.S. monetary policy.

Empirical evidence shows a link between central bank independence from government intervention and inflation and economic growth rates. In countries where central banks are relatively independent from their governments, there have generally been lower inflation rates and higher economic growth rates than in countries where central banks are closely tied to their governments.

Three economically important foreign central banks are those from the United Kingdom, Japan, and the European Monetary Union. The central bank in the United Kingdom is the *Bank of England (BOE)*. It was created well before the formation of the Federal Reserve System in 1913. The BOE is managed by a governor and five additional officers, all of whom are appointed for five-year terms. The BOE governor reports to the chancellor, who has final responsibility for setting monetary policy. In contrast with the United States, commercial banks in Great Britain are not required to hold reserves at the Bank of England. Also recall from Chapter 3 that Great Britain does not legally separate commercial banking and investment banking activities.

The central bank of Japan, called the *Bank of Japan (BOJ)*, was created in 1947. The top official of the BOJ is the governor, who heads the Policy Board, which is the central decision-making authority. The governor and some members of the board are appointed by the Japanese equivalent of the U.S. Congress, and other board members are appointed by the finance minister. Japanese commercial banks, like their U.S. counterparts, are required to hold reserves on deposit with the BOJ, and banks can borrow at an official discount rate from the BOJ.

The **European Central Bank (ECB)** conducts monetary policy for the twelve European countries that formed the *European Monetary Union* and adopted the euro as their common currency at the beginning of 1999. Euro notes and coins were officially introduced at the beginning of 2002, and all twelve individual national currencies were withdrawn as legal tender by July 1, 2002. The ECB, which is headquartered in Frankfurt, Germany, is responsible for controlling inflation and for managing the value of the euro relative to other currencies. The ECB structure is somewhat similar to the U.S. Fed's in that the twelve national central banks of the euro countries operate much like the twelve Federal Reserve District Banks. Like the Fed BOG, the governing council of the ECB includes governors from some of the national central banks. Each national central bank is responsible for managing payment systems and furnishing currency and credit in its home country.

CONCEPT CHECK
How are checks cleared between Federal Reserve districts?

GLOBAL DISCUSSION

INTERNET ACTIVITY
Go to the European Central Bank's Web site, http://www.ecb.int, and find information on how it is structured and how it operates.

European Central Bank (ECB)
conducts monetary policy for the twelve European countries that adopted the euro as their common currency

CONCEPT CHECK
What are three major central banks in addition to the Fed?

APPLYING FINANCE TO...

INSTITUTIONS AND MARKETS

Depository institutions, commercial banks, savings and loans, savings banks, and credit unions comprise the banking system. The Fed is the U.S. central bank, which supervises and regulates the banking system. The Fed, along with depository institutions, creates and transfers money. Monetary policy actions of the Fed affect the primary financial markets for debt obligations, influencing the availability of bank loans and the interest rates that must be paid on those loans.

INVESTMENTS

Securities markets, both primary and secondary, are also affected by Fed actions. An increase in reserve requirements will restrict the amount of individual savings that would be available to make loans. Other Fed actions may cause banks to raise loan interest rates and cause the economy to slow down and security prices to decline. When the Fed raises the discount rate, banks react to protect their profit margins by raising their lending rates to individuals and businesses.

FINANCIAL MANAGEMENT

Financial management activities are directly affected by Fed monetary policy actions. A tightening of monetary policy makes it more difficult and costly for businesses to borrow funds. To the extent that economic activity also declines, it is more difficult for financial managers to sell new stocks and bonds in the primary securities markets. Of course, an easing of monetary policy will make it easier for financial managers to raise financial capital and they will be able to do so at lower interest rates.

SUMMARY

This chapter began with a discussion of the U.S. banking system prior to the establishment of the Fed. The national banking system suffered from an inflexible money supply, liquidity problems, and payment transfer problems. While the movement to a central banking system in the United States was a slow process, the Federal Reserve Act was finally passed in 1913. Coverage then focused on the organization and structure of the Federal Reserve System in terms of membership, Federal Reserve Banks, the Board of Governors, and the Federal Open Market Committee. National banks must belong to the Federal Reserve System, while state-chartered banks and other depository institutions can elect to join the Fed.

The Fed has dynamic, defensive, and accommodative responsibilities. Dynamic activities attempt to influence economic activity by controlling the money supply. Defensive activities attempt to smooth changes in day-to-day economic operations. Accommodative activities provide credit and checking-related services to individuals and institutions.

The basic policy instruments of the Fed include setting reserve requirements, lending to depository institutions at the discount rate, and conducting open-market operations involving the purchase and sale of U.S. government securities. Open-market operations are the primary method used today for carrying out monetary policy objectives.

The Fed also performs supervisory, regulatory, and service functions. Supervision of commercial banks is shared by the Fed with the Office of the Comptroller of the Currency and the Federal Deposit Insurance Corporation. Service functions performed by the Fed include providing and supporting a national payments mechanism as well as other activities, such as publishing research results. Payments mechanism activities involve providing currency and coin, clearing and collecting checks, and electronic transferring of funds.

The last section of the chapter described some of the characteristics of central banks in the United Kingdom, Japan, and the European Monetary Union.

KEY TERMS

accommodative function
bank reserves
central bank
Consumer Credit Protection Act
defensive activities
dynamic actions
European Central Bank (ECB)
excess reserves
Fed Board of Governors
Fed discount rate
federal funds rate
Federal Reserve System (Fed)
fractional reserve system
monetary policy
open-market operations
Regulation Z
required reserves
required reserves ratio

DISCUSSION QUESTIONS

1. Describe the weaknesses of the national banking system that was in place prior to passage of the Federal Reserve Act of 1913.

2. What functions and activities do central banks usually perform?

3. Describe the organizational structure of the Federal Reserve System in terms of its five major components.

4. Explain how the banking interests of large, medium, and small businesses are represented on the board of directors of each Reserve Bank.

5. What is a Reserve Branch Bank? How many such branches exist, and where are most of them located?

6. How are members of the Board of Governors of the Federal Reserve System appointed? To what extent are they subject to political pressures?

7. Discuss the structure, the functions, and the importance of the Federal Open Market Committee.

8. Identify the six individuals who served as chairs of the Fed Board of Governors since the early 1950s. Indicate each individual's approximate time and length of service as chair.

9. Distinguish among the dynamic, defensive, and accommodative responsibilities of the Fed.

10. Identify and briefly describe the three instruments that may be used by the Fed to set monetary policy.

11. Reserve Banks have at times been described as bankers' banks because of their lending powers. What is meant by this statement?

12. Describe the two "targets" that the Fed can use when establishing monetary policy. Which target has the Fed focused on in recent years?

13. Explain the usual procedures for examining national banks. How does this process differ from the examination of member banks of the Federal Reserve System holding state charters?

14. What federal agencies are responsible for supervising and regulating depository institutions that are not commercial banks?

15. Describe the objectives of the Consumer Credit Protection Act of 1968. What is the Truth in Lending section of the act? What is Regulation Z?

16. Explain the process by which the Federal Reserve Banks provide the economy with currency and coin.

17. Describe how a check drawn on a commercial bank but deposited for collection in another bank in a distant city might be cleared through the facilities of the Federal Reserve System.

18. What is the special role of the Federal Reserve Interdistrict Settlement Fund in the check-clearance process?

19. In what way do the Reserve Banks serve as fiscal agents for the U.S. government?

20. Briefly describe and compare the central banks in the United Kingdom, Japan, and European Monetary Union.

EXERCISES

1. You are a resident of Seattle, Washington, and maintain a checking account with a bank in that city. You have just written a check on that bank to pay your tuition. Describe the process by which the banking system enables your college to collect the funds from your bank.

2. As the executive of a bank or thrift institution you are faced with an intense seasonal demand for loans. Assuming that your loanable funds are inadequate to take care of the demand, how might your Reserve Bank help you with this problem?

3. The Federal Reserve Board of Governors has decided to ease monetary conditions to counter early signs of an economic downturn. Because price inflation has been a burden in recent years, the Board is eager to avoid any action that the public might interpret as a return to inflationary conditions. How might the Board use its various powers to accomplish the objective of monetary ease without drawing unfavorable publicity to its actions?

4. An economic contraction (recession) is now well under way, and the Fed plans to use all facilities at its command to halt the decline. Describe the measures that it may take.

5. You have recently retired and are intent on extensive travel to many of the exotic lands you have only read about. You will be receiving not only a pension check and Social Security check but also dividends and interest from several corporations. You are concerned about the deposit of these checks during your several months of absence, and you have asked your banker if there is an arrangement available to solve this problem. What alternative might the banker suggest?

6. The prime rate, and other interest rates, offered by banks often change in the same direction as a change in the Fed's target for the federal funds rate. As an employee of a Federal Reserve District Bank you have been told that your District Bank will be increasing its discount rate early next week. Expectations are that an increase in the discount rate will lead to an increase in the federal funds rate, which will lead to an increase in the prime rate and other bank lending rates. You have been thinking about buying a new automobile for the past couple of months. Given this information of a planned discount rate increase, you are considering buying your new automobile before the end of the week. What are the ethical issues, if any, involved in this scenario? What would you do?

PROBLEMS

1. A new bank has vault cash of $1 million and $5 million in deposits held at its Federal Reserve District Bank.
   a. If the required reserves ratio is 8 percent, what dollar amount of deposits can the bank have?
   b. If the bank holds $65 million in deposits and currently holds bank reserves such that excess reserves are zero, what required reserves ratio is implied?

2. Assume a bank has $5 million in deposits and $1 million in vault cash. If the bank holds $1 million in excess reserves and the required reserves ratio is 8 percent, what level of deposits are being held?

3. A bank has $110 million in deposits and holds $10 million in vault cash.
   a. If the required reserves ratio is 10 percent, what dollar amount of reserves must be held at the Federal Reserve Bank?
   b. How would your answer in Part (a) change if the required reserves ratio was increased to 12 percent?

4. A bank has $10 million in vault cash and $110 million in deposits. If total bank reserves were $15 million with $2 million considered to be excess reserves, what required reserves ratio is implied?

5. The Friendly National Bank holds $50 million in reserves at its Federal Reserve District Bank. The required reserves ratio is 12 percent.
   a. If the bank has $600 million in deposits, what amount of vault cash would be needed for the bank to be in compliance with the required reserves ratio?
   b. If the bank holds $10 million in vault cash, determine the required reserves ratio that would be needed for the bank to avoid a reserves deficit.

c. If the Friendly National Bank experiences a required reserves deficit, what actions can it take to be in compliance with the existing required reserves ratio?

6. Assume that banks must hold a 2 percent reserve percentage against transaction account balances up to and including $40 million. For transaction accounts above $40 million, the required reserve percentage is 8 percent. Also assume that Dell National Bank has transaction account balances of $200 million.

   a. Calculate the dollar amount of required reserves that Dell National Bank must hold.
   b. What percentage of Dell's total transaction account balance must be held in the form of required reserves?

7. Assume that the Fed decides to increase the required reserve percentage on transaction accounts above $40 million from 8 percent to 10 percent. All other information remains the same as given in Problem 6, including the transaction account balances held by Dell National Bank.

   a. What would be the dollar amount of required reserves?
   b. What percentage of total transaction account balances held by Dell would be held as required reserves?

8. Show how your answers in Problem 6 would change if the Fed lowered the cut-off between the 2 percent rate and the 8 percent rate from $40 million in transaction account balances down to $20 million.

9. **Challenge Problem** You have been asked to assess the impact of possible changes in reserve requirement components on the dollar amount of reserves required. Assume the reserve percentages are set at 2 percent on the first $50 million of traction account amounts, 4 percent on the second $50 million, and 10 percent on transaction amounts over $100 million. First National Bank has transaction account balances of $100 million, while Second National Bank's transaction balances are $150 million and Third National Bank's transaction balances are $250 million.

   a. Determine the dollar amounts of required reserves for each of the three banks.
   b. Calculate the percentage of reserves to total transactions accounts for each of the three banks.
   c. The Central Bank wants to slow the economy by raising the reserve requirements for member banks. To do so, the reserve percentages will be increased to 12 percent on transaction balances above $100 million. Simultaneously, the 2 percent rate will apply on the first $25 million. Calculate the reserve requirement amount for each of the three banks after these changes have taken place.
   d. Show the dollar amount of changes in reserve requirement amounts for each bank. Calculate the percentage of reserve requirement amounts to transaction account balances for each bank.
   e. Which of the two reserve requirement changes discussed in (c) causes the greatest impact on the dollar amount of reserves for all three of the banks?
   f. Now assume that you could either (1) lower the transactions account amount for the lowest category from $50 million down to $25 million or (2) increase the reserve percentage from 10 percent to 12 percent on transactions account amounts over $200 million. Which choice would you recommend if you were trying to achieve a moderate slowing of economic activity?

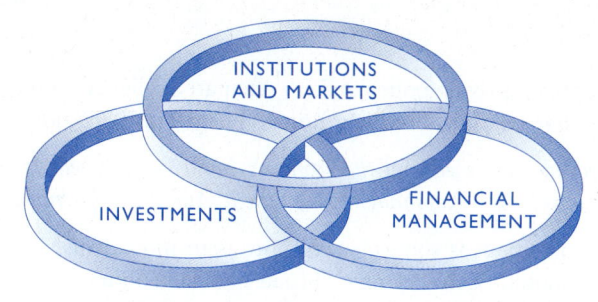

CHAPTER 5

Policy Makers and the Money Supply

Chapter Learning Objectives:

AFTER STUDYING THIS CHAPTER, YOU SHOULD BE ABLE TO:

- Discuss the objectives of national economic policy and the conflicting nature of these objectives.
- Identify the major policy makers and briefly describe their primary responsibilities.
- Identify the policy instruments of the U.S. Treasury and briefly explain how the Treasury manages its activities.
- Describe U.S. Treasury tax policy and debt management responsibilities.
- Discuss how the expansion of the money supply takes place in the U.S. banking system.
- Briefly summarize the factors that affect bank reserves.
- Explain the meaning of the monetary base and money multiplier.
- Explain what is meant by the velocity of money and give reasons why it is important to control the money supply.

Where We Have Been...

In Chapter 4 we discussed the role of the Federal Reserve System as the central bank in the U.S. banking system. Money must be easily transferred, checks must be processed and cleared, banks must be regulated and supervised, and the money supply must be controlled. The Fed either assists or directly performs all of the activities that are necessary for a well-functioning financial system. You also learned about the characteristics and requirements of Federal Reserve membership and the composition of the Fed Board of Governors. You also were introduced to the Fed's monetary policy functions—its open-market operations, the administration of reserve requirements, and the setting of interest rates on loans to depository institutions. Fed supervisory and regulatory functions were also discussed.

Where We Are Going...

The last chapter in Part 1 focuses on how currency exchange rates are determined and how international trade is financed. We begin by discussing what is meant by currency exchange rates and foreign exchange markets. This is followed by a discussion of factors that determine exchange rate relationships and changes in those relationships over time. You will then learn about how the financing of international trade takes place, including how exporters finance with a draft or bill of exchange. Financing by the importer and the use of a commercial letter of credit and a trust receipt are also covered. The last section will introduce you to the importance of balancing international transactions or what is also referred to as international financial equilibrium. In Part 2 our focus will be on investments, including the securities and other financial markets needed to market and transfer financial assets.

How This Chapter Applies to Me...

The opportunity to vote gives you a way of influencing economic and political developments in this country. The president and members of Congress are policy makers elected by the people. After reading this chapter you should have a better understanding of the national economic policy objectives in the United States and how government officials and the Fed influence the economy. You then will be in a more knowledgeable position to make informed economic decisions about activities that may influence your life and career.

Government and private policy makers often are maligned in the press and sometimes even by themselves. For example, President Ronald Reagan in 1986 said:

The government's view of the economy could be summed up in a few short phrases: If it moves, tax it. If it keeps moving, regulate it. And if it stops moving, subsidize it.

While this statement is somewhat humorous to most of us, it also serves to start us thinking about what should be the country's broad-based economic objectives and what mechanisms are needed for achieving these objectives. We need a system of checks and balances to ensure that policy makers will operate in the best interests of the people of the United States. The president and Congress pass laws and set fiscal policy, while the Fed sets monetary policy and attempts to regulate the supply of money and the availability of credit.

NATIONAL ECONOMIC POLICY OBJECTIVES

Ernest Hemingway said:

The first panacea for a mismanaged nation is inflation of the currency; the second is war. Both bring a temporary prosperity; both bring a permanent ruin. Both are the refuge of political and economic opportunists.

Most of us would agree with Hemingway that currency inflation and war are not acceptable economic objectives. While people with differing views debate the proper role of government, there is broad agreement that decisions by government policy makers to levy taxes and make expenditures significantly affect the lives of each of us. In addition to the checks and balances offered by two political parties, the Fed is expected to operate independently of the government but also in the best interests of the country and its people. There is also a strong tradition in the United States that national economic objectives should be pursued with minimum interference to the economic freedom of individuals.

The *Employment Act of 1946* and the *Full Employment and Balanced Growth Act of 1978*, which is typically referred to as the *Humphrey-Hawkins Act*, spell out the role of the U.S. government in carrying out the economic goals of economic growth and stable prices. Most of us also would agree that economic growth is good if it leads to improved living standards for the people. However, for this to occur, economic growth must be accompanied by stable prices and high and stable employment levels. The relationship between the money supply and demand affects the level of prices and economic activity in our market economy. Therefore, the process by which the money supply is increased and decreased is a very important factor to the success of the economy. Since we live in a global environment, our economic well-being also depends on achieving a reasonable balance in international trade and other transactions. To summarize, our country's economic policy actions are directed toward these four general goals:

- Economic growth
- High employment
- Price stability
- Balance in international transactions

Accompanying these economic goals is also a desire for stability in interest rates, financial markets, and foreign exchange markets.

ECONOMIC GROWTH

The standard of living of U.S. citizens has increased dramatically during the history of the United States as a result of the growth of the economy and its productivity. Of course, growth means more than merely increasing total output. It requires that output increase faster than the population so that the average output per person expands. Growth is a function of two components: an increasing stock of productive resources—the labor force and stock of capital—and improved technology and skills.

The output of goods and services in an economy is referred to as the **gross domestic product (GDP)**. The United States began the 1980s with a double-dip recession or economic downturn in "real" terms (i.e., after price changes have been factored out). A mild economic decline

gross domestic product (GDP)
measures the output of goods and services in an economy

occurred in 1980, followed by a deeper decline that lasted from mid-1981 through most of 1982. The GDP then grew in real terms throughout the remainder of the 1980s, before a mild downturn began in mid-1990 and lasted through the first quarter of 1991. Although some industries underwent substantial downsizing and restructuring, the economy continued to grow in real terms throughout the 1990s. As we moved into the twenty-first century, economic growth slowed both domestically and worldwide resulting in a U.S. recession in 2001. Economic recovery began in 2002 and economic growth continued for a number of years until the United States entered into one of its deepest economic downturns beginning in 2008.

HIGH EMPLOYMENT

Unemployment represents a loss of potential output and imposes costs on the entire economy. The economic and psychological costs are especially hard on the unemployed. While there is some disagreement over what we should consider full employment, it is a stated objective of the U.S. government to promote stability of employment and production at levels close to the national potential. This aim seeks to avoid large changes in economic activity, minimizing the hardships that accompany loss of jobs and output.

The U.S. unemployment rate reached double-digit levels during the early 1980s with a peak at about 11 percent near the end of 1982. As the economy began expanding, unemployment levels declined throughout the remainder of the 1980s until the rate fell below 5.5 percent. The recession that began in mid-1990, along with other job dislocations associated with corporate downsizing and restructuring, resulted in an unemployment rate exceeding 7.5 percent in 1992. The remainder of the 1990s was characterized by a steady decline in the unemployment rate to a level below 4.5 percent. As the country entered the twenty-first century, economic activity slowed and the unemployment level began rising. With an economic recovery beginning in 2002 employment opportunities improved for a period of years. However, the economy began slowing in 2007 and entered into a steep decline in 2008, causing the unemployment rate to exceed the 10 percent level. Even with economic recovery beginning during the second-half of 2009, the unemployment rate remained at the 10 percent level as the decade of the 2000s came to a close.

PRICE STABILITY

inflation
occurs when an increase in the price of goods or services is not offset by an increase in quality

In recent decades the importance of stable prices has become well accepted but difficult to achieve. Consistently stable prices help create an environment in which the other economic goals are more easily reached. **Inflation** occurs when a rise or increase in the prices of goods and services is not offset by increases in the quality of those goods and services. Inflation discourages investment by increasing the uncertainty about future returns. Therefore, high inflation rates are no longer considered acceptable as a price to pay for high levels of employment.

Inflation was at double-digit levels during the early 1980s, and this was reflected in record-high interest rates. However, as the economy turned down in the 1981–1982 recession, inflation rates also started down and continued down until inflation fell below 3 percent. After a brief rise at the beginning of the 1990s, inflation steadily declined to 2 percent and continued at very low levels in the early years of the twenty-first century. However, the Fed began expressing concern in 2004 about possible rising inflation and reacted by increasing the federal funds rate. Inflation remained low throughout the remainder of decade of the 2000s even though the Fed reduced its target for the federal funds rate to historically low levels in response to the financial and economic pressures faced in the United States.

BALANCE IN INTERNATIONAL TRANSACTIONS

The increasing importance of international trade and international capital markets has resulted in a new emphasis on worldwide financial affairs. The U.S. economy is so large that the actions taken with respect to the country's own national affairs also influence the economies of other nations. Economic policy makers, therefore, must always maintain a worldview rather than a narrow nationalistic approach.

Nations that produce and sell (export) more than they buy (import) will have a net capital inflow or surplus and vice versa. For example, Japan has used its large surplus of exports over imports with the United States to make investments in the United States. Nations that continually operate with international trade deficits will become increasingly weaker economically, while those with consistent surpluses will become economically stronger. Movement toward international financial equilibrium over time thus is in the best interests of worldwide trade and economic growth.

During the 1980s, 1990s, and the first decade of the 2000s, the United States consistently operated with a large negative trade balance. In other words, its imports of goods and services have consistently exceeded its exports of goods and products. U.S. service exports are generally larger than its service imports. However, the much larger negative merchandise trade or goods balance results in a negative overall trade balance. This negative trade balance remains of great concern to policy makers today. Unfortunately, throughout the first part of the twenty-first century, the negative trade balances, particularly with China, have been increasing in size.

THE PERFECT FINANCIAL STORM

FINANCIAL CRISIS

As initially discussed in Chapter 1, a "perfect financial storm" developed in 2008 and the U.S. economy was on the verge of collapse. The housing price "bubble" burst in 2006 and began a sharp decline. Stock market prices peaked in 2007 and began a sharp decline. The economy began slowing in 2007 and entered into a steep recession in 2008. Individuals were defaulting on their home mortgages in increasing numbers due to falling home prices and increasing unemployment. Business firms and financial institutions, which had borrowed heavily during years of easy money and low interest rates, were faced with their own financial difficulties as economic activity slowed markedly. Many of the mortgage-related debt securities originated by banks and sold to others, or held by banks, were difficult to value during the perfect financial storm and quickly became known as "troubled" or "toxic" assets.

Numerous major financial institutions and business corporations were on the verge of collapse or failure. Some of the very largest financial institutions were deemed as being "too big to fail" because their failure would cause cascading negative repercussions throughout the United States and many foreign economies. The Federal Reserve moved to increase liquidity in the monetary system and reduced its target federal funds rate to a below .25 percent level. The Fed also worked with the U.S. Treasury to help facilitate the merging of financially weak institutions with institutions that were financially stronger. For example, in March 2008, the Fed and Treasury assisted in the acquisition of Bear Sterns by JPMorgan Chase & Co.

The Federal National Mortgage Association (Fannie Mae) and the Federal Home Mortgage Association (Freddie Mac), discussed in Chapter 1 as being major participants in the secondary mortgage markets, were on the verge of financial insolvency and possible collapse in mid-2008. Fannie Mae was actively creating and packaging mortgage-backed securities, many of which became "troubled" assets as home owners began defaulting on the underlying mortgages. Freddie Mac purchased home mortgages, including lower-quality subprime mortgages, attempting to support the mortgage markets and home ownership. In an attempt to avoid a meltdown, the Fed provided rescue funds in July 2008 and the U.S. government assumed control of both Fannie Mae and Freddie Mac in September 2008.

In addition to the efforts of the Fed and the Treasury, the U.S. Congress and the president responded with the passage of the Economic Stabilization Act of 2008 in early October of that year. A primary focus of this legislation, which became know as the Troubled Asset Relief Program (TARP), was to allow the U.S. Treasury purchase up to $700 billion of troubled or toxic assets held by financial institutions. Then, in an effort to stimulate economic activity, Congress and the president passed the $787 billion American Recovery and Reinvestment Act of 2009 in February 2009 with the funds to be used to provide tax relief, appropriations, and direct spending. In part, as a result of these actions, economic activity in the United States began recovering in the second half of 2009. However, as the decade of the 2000s came to a close, the unemployment rate remained at the 10 percent level.

CONCEPT CHECK
What are the four goals or objectives of economic policy?

FOUR POLICY MAKER GROUPS

Four groups of policy makers are actively involved in achieving the nation's economic policy objectives. They are:

- Federal Reserve System
- The president
- Congress
- U.S. Treasury

FIGURE 5.1
Policy Makers and Economic Policy Objectives

Policy Makers
- Federal Reserve System
- The President
- Congress
- U.S. Treasury

Types of Policies or Decisions
- Monetary Policy
- Fiscal Policy
- Debt Management

Economic Objectives
- Economic Growth
- High Employment
- Price Stability
- International Balance

Figure 5.1 illustrates how the four groups use monetary and fiscal policies, supported by debt management practices, to carry out the four economic objectives of economic growth, stable prices, high employment, and balance in international transactions.

As discussed earlier, the Fed establishes monetary policy, and we will see later in this chapter how the money supply is actually changed. **Fiscal policy** reflects government influence on economic activity through taxation and expenditure plans. Fiscal policy is carried out by the president and Congress. The U.S. Treasury supports economic policy objectives through its debt management practices.

fiscal policy
government influence on economic activity through taxation and expenditure plans

ETHICAL BEHAVIOR IN GOVERNMENT

Since World War II, twelve individuals have served as president of the United States. The decade of the 1990s included George H. W. Bush and Bill Clinton. The decade of the 2000s was primarily under the direction of George W. Bush and Barack Obama. One would expect that the leader of the United States should and would exhibit a very high level of moral and ethical behavior. We expect the people of our nation to practice sound ethical behavior by treating others fairly and honestly. Certainly, the president has the opportunity to lead by example.

Two recent presidents, Richard Nixon (who served as president during 1969–1974) and William Clinton (who served as president during 1993–2001), were each accused of unethical behavior while president. Nixon resigned on August 9, 1974, just before he was about to be impeached because of the Watergate scandal involving office break-ins. In 1998, Clinton became the second president to be impeached by the House of Representatives. Clinton's handling of personal indiscretions with a White House intern led to his trial in the Senate. He was found not guilty and completed his second term.[1]

Unethical behavior in government has not been limited to presidents. There also have been numerous accounts of unethical behavior on the part of members of Congress. Some individuals have been impeached and others have been sent to prison. With this said, the vast majority of

SMALL BUSINESS PRACTICE
Government Financing Assistance for Small Businesses

Small businesses can seek financing help from both the federal and state or local levels. The Small Business Administration (SBA) was created in 1953 by the federal government. The SBA provides financial assistance to small firms that are unable to obtain loans from private lenders at reasonable terms and interest costs. We discuss the SBA in greater detail in Chapter 16.

Small business investment companies (SBICs) are chartered and regulated by the SBA. SBICs help finance small businesses by making both equity investments and loans. SBICs get their funds (to be lent or invested in small businesses) from privately invested capital and long-term bonds purchased or guaranteed by the SBA. These bonds typically have ten-year maturities. A small business is currently defined as a firm with less than $6 million in net worth or net income of less than $2 million.

At the state and local level, there also are possible sources of financing help for small businesses. For example, most states have Small Business Development Centers (SBDCs) that can help small businesses find sources of financing. Small businesses also may find sources of financing help by contacting their state's Department of Economic Development or Department of Commerce.

---

[1]. For a further discussion of past U.S. presidents, see Frank Freidel and Hugh S. Sidey, *The Presidents of the United States of America*, Willard, OH: R.R. Donnelley and Sons, 1996.

GLOBAL DISCUSSION

members of Congress and past presidents have practiced high ethical behavior, including treating their constituents fairly and honestly. The other good news is that the U.S. government and society have overcome the isolated unethical behavior of a few leaders.

POLICY MAKERS IN THE EUROPEAN ECONOMIC UNION

As in the United States, European governments use monetary and fiscal policies to try to achieve similar economic goals such as economic growth and price stability. In December 1991, the members of the *European Union (EU)* signed the *Maastricht Treaty* in Maastricht, Netherlands. The objective was to converge their economies, fix member country exchange rates, and introduce the euro as a common currency at the beginning of 1999. Monetary and fiscal policy actions of each country were to focus on maintaining price stability, keeping government budget deficits below 3 percent of gross domestic product (GDP) and total government debt below 60 percent of GDP, and maintaining stability in relative currency exchange rates. Twelve members of the EU ratified the Maastricht Treaty and adopted the euro as their common currency. They are known as the *European Monetary Union (EMU)*.

It is striking that twelve countries with widely different applications of monetary and fiscal policies in the past could agree on similar economic and financial objectives. While each country continues to formulate its own fiscal policies today, the *European Central Bank (ECB)* focuses on maintaining price stability across the twelve euro-member countries. The sheer size of the EMU also means that European policy makers and U.S. policy makers must work closely together in trying to achieve the worldwide goals of economic growth and price stability.

GOVERNMENT INFLUENCE ON THE ECONOMY

The federal government plays a dual role in the economy. In its traditional role, it provides services that cannot be provided as efficiently by the private sector. In this role, it acts like a firm, employing resources and producing a product. The magnitude of this role and its influence on economic activity has led to its more modern role: guiding or regulating the economy. The decisions of a number of policy-making entities must be coordinated to achieve the desired economic objectives.

A government raises funds to pay for its activities in three ways:

- Levies taxes
- Borrows
- Prints money for its own use

Because the last option has tempted some governments, with disastrous results, Congress delegated the power to create money to the Fed. Our federal government collects taxes to pay for most of its spending, and it borrows, competing for funds in the financial system, to finance its deficits.

To illustrate the complex nature of the government's influence on the economy, consider the many effects of a federal deficit. To finance it, the government competes with other borrowers in the financial system. This absorbs savings, and it may raise interest rates. Private investment may be reduced if it becomes more difficult for firms to borrow the funds needed. On the other hand, a deficit stimulates economic activity. The government is either spending more or collecting less in taxes, or both, leaving more income for consumers to spend. The larger the deficit, the more total spending, or aggregate demand, there will be. In some circumstances this stimulation of the economy generates enough extra income and savings to finance both the deficit and additional investment by firms.

Furthermore, the Fed may buy government securities, financing some of the deficit and providing additional reserves to the banking system, thus increasing the money supply. This process is known as **monetizing the debt.** The Fed has at times monetized some of the deficit, especially during World Wars I and II. It does not do so now since that would be counter to current monetary policy. It would also have a significant impact on the financial markets. The competition for funds would make it more difficult for some borrowers to meet their financing needs. The characteristics and maturities of debt sold by the Treasury would determine which sectors were most affected.

monetizing the debt
Fed increases the money supply to help offset the demand for increased funds to finance the deficit

The decisions of policy makers enter this process at a number of points. The president and the Council of Economic Advisors formulate a *fiscal policy:* the relationship of the Treasury's tax plans to its expenditure plans to influence the economy of the nation. Congress must pass legislation authorizing the Treasury's plan or a variation of it. The Treasury is actually responsible for collecting taxes and disbursing funds and for the huge task of debt management, which includes financing current deficits and refinancing the outstanding debt of the government. As discussed in the previous chapter, the Fed contributes to the attainment of the nation's economic goals by formulating monetary policy. It uses its powers to regulate the growth of the money supply and thus influence interest rates and the availability of loans.

The principal responsibilities of these policy makers have not always been the same. When the Fed was established in 1913, most of the power to regulate money and credit was placed in its hands. However, as the public debt grew during World War I, the Great Depression of the 1930s, and World War II, the Treasury became vitally interested in credit conditions. Policies that affect interest rates and the size of the money supply affect the Treasury directly, since it is the largest borrower in the nation. Therefore, the U.S. Treasury took over primary responsibility for managing the federal debt. In managing the large public debt and various trust funds placed under its jurisdiction, the Treasury has the power to influence the money market materially. The Fed came back into its own in the 1950s and is now the chief architect of monetary policy.

When it is felt that the Fed is not being responsive to the needs of the economy, the president will usually exercise pressure. The president also formulates budgetary and fiscal policy, but Congress must pass legislation to implement these policies. Congress regularly exercises its authority to modify presidential proposals before passing legislation. In short, there is much overlap of influence among those who make policy decisions. All three types of policies, however, are directed toward achieving the four objectives: economic growth, high employment, price stability, and a balance in international transactions.

CONCEPT CHECK
What is fiscal policy?
What is monetizing the debt?

It should not be surprising that the policy instruments of the various policy makers at times put them at cross purposes. A long-standing debate continues over the balance between full employment and price stability. A particular policy that leads toward one may make the other more difficult to achieve, yet each objective has its supporters. As with all governmental policy, economic objectives are necessarily subject to compromise and trade-offs.

Recent legislative efforts to stimulate economic activity in the United States have their own cost or price. For example, the $787 billion American Recovery and Reinvestment Act of 2009 provided for tax relief, appropriation expenditures, and direct spending. The bottom line was a short-fall between tax receipts and spending of $1.4 trillion in fiscal 2009. The budget proposal for 2010 calls for a $3.8 trillion budget with a forecasted deficit of $1.6 trillion.

POLICY INSTRUMENTS OF THE U.S. TREASURY

The Treasury has vast power to affect the supply of money and credit. The very magnitude of Treasury operations, however, dictates that it must play as defensive or neutral a role as possible. The power to regulate the money supply has been placed primarily in the hands of the Fed; close cooperation between the Treasury and the Fed must exist if Treasury operations are not to disrupt the money supply.

Consider the impact on monetary affairs of a massive withdrawal of taxes from the banking system without offsetting actions. The decrease in bank deposits would result in a temporary breakdown of the system's ability to serve the credit needs of the public. Yet, the federal government periodically claims taxes without significant impact on lending institutions. In like manner, borrowing by the government or the refunding of maturing obligations could be traumatic in their effect on money and credit, but such is not the case. In short, the Fed efficiently manages these dynamic aspects of money and credit, while the Treasury largely limits its actions to taxing, borrowing, paying bills, and refunding maturing obligations. The Treasury carries out these functions with as little interference with the conduct of monetary affairs as possible. This is no small challenge.

MANAGING THE TREASURY'S CASH BALANCES

Treasury operations involve spending over $1 trillion a year. It is necessary to maintain a large cash balance, since Treasury receipts and payments do not occur on a regular basis throughout the year. This makes it critical for the Treasury to handle its cash balances in such a way that it will not create undesirable periods of credit ease or tightness. To affect bank reserves as little as possible, the Treasury has developed detailed procedures for handling its cash balances.

Treasury Tax and Loan Accounts

The Treasury's primary checkable deposit accounts for day-to-day operations are kept at Reserve Banks. Most cash flows into the Treasury through Treasury Tax and Loan Accounts of banks, S&Ls, and credit unions (referred to here as *banks,* for short). Employers deposit the income taxes, Social Security, and railroad retirement taxes they withheld in their Treasury Tax and Loan Accounts. They have the option of depositing these government receipts with either Reserve Banks or one of the other banks. Most employers make their payments to the latter.

The Treasury may also pay income and eligible profits taxes in Tax and Loan Accounts. Many excise taxes may also be paid either to a Reserve Bank or to a qualified bank with a Tax and Loan Account. The proceeds from a large portion of the sales of new government securities also flow into Tax and Loan Accounts. If the Treasury feels its balances at the Reserve Banks are too large, it can transfer funds to its accounts at the banks.

Treasury Receipts and Outlays

The Treasury tries to handle its cash receipts, outlays, and balances to avoid large changes in bank reserves. To do this, the Treasury tries to keep balances in its accounts at the Reserve Banks relatively stable. Almost all Treasury disbursements are made by checks drawn against its deposits at the Reserve Banks. Most Treasury receipts are deposited in Tax and Loan Accounts at the various banks, but some are deposited directly in the Treasury accounts at the Reserve Banks. The Treasury adjusts its withdrawals to keep its balances at the Reserve Banks as stable as possible. This means that the funds shifted from banks and the funds deposited directly in Reserve Banks must closely correspond to the volume of Treasury checks that are likely to be presented to the Reserve Banks.

If the Treasury accounts at the Reserve Banks are kept at about the same level, bank reserves are not changed. This is possible only if accurate forecasts are made of the daily receipts and spending from the Treasury account so that funds from the Tax and Loan Accounts may be shifted in the right amounts at the right time. If the forecasts were not worked out with a reasonable degree of success, Treasury operations would cause bank reserves to change a great deal over short periods. Despite these precautions, the Treasury's account frequently does fluctuate by as much as several billion dollars from day to day. The Fed closely monitors the Treasury account and takes any changes into consideration in conducting daily open-market operations to minimize the effect on bank reserves.

POWERS RELATING TO THE FEDERAL BUDGET AND TO SURPLUSES OR DEFICITS

The government may also influence monetary and credit conditions indirectly through taxation and expenditure programs, especially by having a significant cash deficit or surplus. Budget-making decisions rest with Congress and are usually based on the needs of the government and on political considerations, without giving much weight to monetary and credit effects. Because of the magnitude of the federal budget, government income and spending may be one of the most important factors in determining credit conditions.

General Economic Effects of Fiscal Policy

Economic activity depends largely on aggregate demand, or total spending in the economy. An increase in aggregate demand will generally cause an increase in production and employment but may also cause prices to rise. If the economy is already close to full employment, increases in aggregate demand will likely increase prices more than output. Similarly, decreases in aggregate demand will result in lower employment and reduced prices.

Fiscal policy significantly affects aggregate demand and economic activity. Not only is government spending itself a large component of aggregate demand, but also any change in government spending has a multiplied effect on aggregate demand. An increase in government spending increases employment and incomes and thus also increases consumer spending. In a downturn, not only does spending decrease, but tax receipts of all types—including those for Social Security—also decrease when fewer people are at work because these taxes are based on payrolls. Changes in taxes also directly affect disposable income and affect aggregate demand through consumer spending.

INTERNET ACTIVITY

Go to the U.S. Treasury's Web site, http://www.treas.gov, and identify the mission and goals of the U.S. Department of the Treasury. Write a brief summary.

CONCEPT CHECK

Where does the Treasury keep its primary checkable deposits?

automatic stabilizers
continuing federal programs that stabilize economic activity

Various federal government programs act to stabilize disposable income and economic activity in general. Some act on a continuing basis as **automatic stabilizers**. Other government fiscal actions, such as actions to continue federal programs that stabilize economic activity, are discretionary and depend on specific congressional actions. Automatic stabilizers include the following:

- Unemployment insurance program
- Welfare payments
- Pay-as-you-go progressive income tax

The unemployment insurance program is funded largely by the states. Under this program, payments are made to workers who lose their jobs, providing part of their former incomes. Another stabilizer is welfare payments under federal and state aid programs. Both unemployment and welfare benefits are examples of **transfer payments,** or income payments for which no current productive service is rendered.

transfer payments
government payments for which no current services are given in return

Another important automatic stabilizer is the pay-as-you-go progressive income tax. Pay-as-you-go refers to the requirement that tax liabilities of individuals and institutions be paid on a continuing basis throughout the year. The progressive nature of our income tax means that as income increases to various levels the tax rate increases. In other words, as incomes increase, taxes increase at a faster rate. The reverse is also true: at certain stages of decreased income, the tax liability decreases more quickly. The result is generally immediate since, for most wages subject to withholding taxes, tax revenues change almost as soon as incomes change.

These programs are a regular part of our economy. In times of severe economic fluctuations, Congress can help stabilize disposable income. Income tax rates have been raised to lower disposable income and to restrain inflationary pressures; they have been lowered during recessions to increase disposable income and spending. Government spending can also be increased during recessions to increase disposable income. Likewise, it could be cut during prosperity to reduce disposable income, but for political reasons attempts to do this have not been successful.

When a recession is so severe that built-in stabilizers or formulas are not adequate to promote recovery, there is seldom a complete agreement on the course of action to take. A decision to change the level of government spending and/or the tax rates must be made. Increased spending or a comparable tax cut would cost the same number of dollars initially, but the economic effects would not be the same. When income taxes are cut, disposable income is increased almost immediately under our system of tax withholding. This provides additional income for all sectors of the economy and an increase in demand for many types of goods.

Congress may decide to increase government spending, but the effects of increased government spending occur more slowly than those of a tax cut, since it takes time to get programs started and put into full operation. The increased income arises first in those sectors of the economy where the money is spent. Thus, the initial effect is on specific areas of the economy rather than on the economy as a whole.

The secondary effects of spending resulting from a tax cut or from increased government spending depend on how and what proportion the recipients spend. To the extent that they spend it on current consumption, aggregate demand is further increased in the short run. The goods on which recipients spend the income determine the sectors of the economy that receive a boost. If they invest the added income and later use it to purchase capital goods, spending is also increased. In this case, however, there is a time lag, and different sectors of the economy are affected. If the money is saved thus added to idle funds available for investment, there is no secondary effect on spending.

The effects must also be considered if economic activity is to be restrained by a decrease in government spending or by a tax increase. A decrease in spending by the government will cut consumer spending by at least that amount; the secondary effects may cut it further. A tax increase may not cut spending by a like amount since some taxpayers may maintain their level of spending by reducing current saving or by using accrued savings. A tax increase could, however, cut total spending more if it should happen to discourage specific types of spending, such as on home building or on credit purchases of consumer durable goods. This could lead to a spending cut that is substantially greater than the amount of money taken by the higher taxes.

CONCEPT CHECK
What are automatic stabilizers?
What are transfer payments?

Effects of Tax Policy

tax policy
setting the level and structure of taxes to affect the economy

The **tax policy** and tax program of the federal government have a direct effect on monetary and credit conditions that may work in several ways. The level of taxes in relation to national income may affect the volume of saving and thus the funds available for investment without credit expansion. The tax structure also determines whether saving is done largely by upper-income groups, middle-income groups, or all groups. This can affect the amount of funds available for different types of investment. Persons in middle-income groups may be more conservative than those with more wealth. They tend to favor bonds or mortgages over equity investments. Persons in high tax brackets, on the other hand, tend to invest in securities of state and local governments because income from these investments is not subject to income taxes. They also may invest for capital gains, since taxes on the gains may be deferred until the asset is sold.

Changes in corporate tax rates also may affect the amount of funds available for short-term investment in government bonds and the balances kept in bank accounts. The larger the tax payments, the less a corporation has available for current spending. Also, if tax rates are raised with little warning, a corporation may be forced to use funds it had been holding for future use. Businesses that are short of funds may be forced to borrow to meet their taxes. In either case, a smaller amount of credit is available for other uses.

Effects of Deficit Financing

deficit financing
how a government finances its needs when spending is greater than revenues

crowding out
lack of funds for private borrowing caused by the sale of government obligations to cover large federal deficits

The government spending program affects not only the overall economy but also monetary and credit conditions. When the spending rate is faster than the collection of taxes and other funds, **deficit financing** will affect the monetary and banking system. The effect will depend on how the deficit is financed. Budgetary deficits result in government competition for private investment funds. When credit demands are great, there may be a threat of **crowding out** private borrowers from the capital markets. When credit demands are slack, the sale of Treasury obligations puts idle bank reserves to use. When deficit financing is so large that the private sector cannot or will not absorb the Treasury obligations offered, the Fed may purchase a significant portion of the issues.

As previously noted, expected deficits for fiscal 2009 ($1.4 trillion) and fiscal 2010 ($1.6 trillion) were adding $3 trillion to the U.S. national debt over a two-year period. This is a significant future price for Americans to pay in an attempt to recover from the 2007–09 financial crisis (perfect financial storm) by stimulating economic activity and hopefully bringing down high unemployment levels. The U.S. national debt now stands well above the $10 trillion level.

RECENT FINANCIAL CRISIS-RELATED ACTIVITIES

FINANCIAL CRISIS

The U.S. Treasury, under the leadership of Treasury Secretary Henry Paulson, played an important role in helping the U.S. survive the 2007–09 financial crisis. The Treasury, sometimes working closely with the Fed, helped in the acquisition of Bear Sterns by JPMorgan Chase & Co. in March 2008. Under the leadership of Henry Paulson, the Treasury was actively involved in trying to help financial institutions on the brink of collapse find help through mergers with financially stronger institutions. In September 2008, Bank of America acquired Merrill Lynch. However, during the same month, Lehman Brothers declared bankruptcy when no viable financial alternatives surfaced. Shortly thereafter, American International Group (AIG) was "bailed out" by the Federal Reserve and Treasury efforts with the U.S. government receiving an ownership interest in AIG.

The Economic Stabilization Act of 2008 provided the Treasury with funds to purchase troubled or toxic assets held by financial institutions. However, much of the Troubled Asset Relief Program (TARP) funds were used to invest capital in banks with little equity in their balance sheets, as well as to rescue large "too big to fail" financial institutions and even large nonfinancial business firms—such as General Motors and Chrysler—who were on the verge of failing.

DEBT MANAGEMENT

debt management
various Treasury decisions connected with refunding debt issues

Debt management includes determining the types of refunding to carry out, the types of securities to sell, the interest rate patterns to use, and decisions to make on callable issues. Since World War II, federal debt management has become an important Treasury function affecting economic conditions in general and money markets in particular. The economy and the money

CONCEPT CHECK
What is deficit financing?

INTERNET ACTIVITY
Go to the U.S. Treasury's Web site, http://www.treas.gov, and find information on the size of the national debt and how the national debt is financed. Write a brief summary.

CONCEPT CHECK
What is debt management?

markets are affected in several ways by the large government debt. First, interest must be paid on government securities that are issued to finance the national debt, which now exceeds $5.5 trillion. The U.S. national debt grew rapidly because annual budget deficits occurred every year since the end of the 1960s until fiscal 1998, when a budget surplus was recorded. However, we returned to large annual deficits during the early part of the twenty-first century.

Interest payments do not transfer resources from the private to the public sector, but they do represent a transfer of funds from taxpayers in general to security holders. When the debt is widely held, there is little or no redistribution of income among groups. However, the taxes levied to pay the interest may decrease taxpayer incentive and so affect economic activity. This could lead to less risk taking and slow down economic growth.

One of the basic objectives of debt management is to handle it in such a way as to help establish an economic climate that encourages orderly growth and stability. To avoid inflation in boom periods, large numbers of individuals have been encouraged to save and to buy bonds. During recessions, the Treasury can borrow in ways that are least likely to compete with private demands for funds. For instance, the Treasury can sell short-term securities to attract idle short-term funds, especially idle bank reserves. Thus, there will be no restriction of credit for business and individuals. Credit will be available in larger amounts to the extent that bank purchases of bonds lead to credit expansion.

Another objective of debt management policy is to hold down Treasury interest costs. The influence of Treasury policies may also tend to reduce all interest rates. Lower interest rates tend to stimulate home building, the construction of business plant and equipment, commercial building, and so forth. This objective of lower interest rates and lower Treasury interest costs, however, may conflict at times with the need for higher interest rates to help restrain inflationary pressures.

A lesser Treasury objective is to maintain satisfactory conditions in the government securities market by maintaining investor confidence. It also tries to discourage wide price swings and maintain orderly buying and selling.

Among the more technical objectives are issuing securities to fit the needs of various investor groups and obtaining an evenly spaced scheduling of debt maturities to ease debt retirement if funds are available, or allowing for refunding when that is necessary. Our heavy dependence on foreign investors to purchase new issues in recent years has added a special dimension to the problem of U.S. debt management. The terms of new issues must be geared to the special needs of foreign investors from all parts of the world, including a particular need to focus on investors from Japan and China.

CHANGING THE MONEY SUPPLY

As we saw in Chapter 2, the M1 definition of the money supply consists of currency (including coins), demand deposits, other checkable deposits, and traveler's checks. Currency is in the form of Federal Reserve notes and is backed by gold certificates, *Special Drawing Rights (SDRs)*, eligible paper, or U.S. government and agency securities. SDRs are a form of reserve asset, or "paper gold," created by the International Monetary Fund. Their purpose is to provide worldwide monetary liquidity and to support international trade. Eligible paper in the form of business notes and drafts provides little collateral today. Instead, Federal Reserve notes have been increasingly backed by government securities. At the end of September 2008, the backing for $801.4 billion in net Federal Reserve notes (total issued of $989.1 billion less $187.7 billion held by Federal Reserve Banks) was $11.0 billion of gold certificates, $2.2 billion of SDRs, $499.0 billion of U.S. Treasury and agency securities, and $289.1 in other assets pledged.[2]

Demand deposits and other checkable deposits at commercial banks, S&Ls, savings banks, and credit unions comprise over 70 percent of the M1 money supply and are collectively termed *checkable deposits*. To simplify further discussion of money supply expansion and contraction, we will refer to checkable deposits simply as *deposits* in the *banking system*, which includes all of the depository institutions. The word *bank* also is used generically to refer to a depository institution.

---

2. *Statistical Supplement to the Federal Reserve Bulletin* (December, 2008), p. 10.

PERSONAL FINANCIAL PLANNING
How Does the Fed Affect Me?

Suppose you hear on the radio that the Fed has moved to cut interest rates. Such a rate cut does not affect just banks or large corporate borrowers; it can have an impact on individuals, too. So how might a rate cut affect you?

If you have savings at a depository institution, the effect may be negative. Attempts to lower interest rates in the economy may lead to lower interest rates on your interest-on-checking account, your savings account, or the next CD you invest in.

Of course, there is a potential benefit on the borrowing side. An attempt to lower rates can lead to lower loan rates for a car loan, student loan, home equity loan, or a home mortgage. If someone has a variable or adjustable rate mortgage, his or her interest payments may fall as rates decline. Some interest rates on credit card balances are linked to a market interest rate, so as market interest rates fall, the interest rates on credit card balances will fall, too.

Lower interest rates can help investors in stocks and bonds too. As we will see in Chapter 10, an economic environment with lower interest rates can lead to increases in stock and bond prices, thus increasing the value of an investor's stock and bond holdings.

---

fractional reserve system
reserves held with the Fed that are equal to a certain percentage of bank deposits

primary deposit
deposit that adds new reserves to a bank

derivative deposit
deposit of funds that were borrowed from the reserves of primary deposits

CONCEPT CHECK
What is a fractional reserve system?

How does a primary deposit differ from a derivative deposit?

The banking system of the United States can change the volume of deposits as the need for funds by individuals, businesses, and governments change. This ability to alter the size of the money supply is based on the use of a **fractional reserve system.** In our fractional reserve system, banks must hold with the Fed reserves equal to a certain percentage of their deposits. To understand the deposit expansion and contraction process, one must study the operations of banks as units in a banking system and the relationship of bank loans to deposits and to bank reserves.

In analyzing deposit expansion, it is helpful to distinguish between primary deposits and derivative deposits. For example, the deposit of a check drawn on the Fed is a **primary deposit** because it adds new reserves to the bank where deposited and to the banking system. A **derivative deposit** occurs when reserves created from a primary deposit are made available to borrowers through bank loans. Borrowers then deposit the loans so they can write checks against the funds. When a check is written and deposited in another bank, there is no change in total reserves of the banking system. The increase in reserves at the bank where the check is deposited is offset by a decrease in reserves at the bank on which the check is drawn. Banks must keep reserves against both primary and derivative deposits.

CHECKABLE DEPOSIT EXPANSION

When reserves were first required by law, the purpose was to assure depositors that banks had the ability to handle withdrawals of cash. This was before the establishment of the Federal Reserve System, which made it possible for a healthy bank to obtain additional funds in time of need. Depositor confidence is now based on deposit insurance and more complete and competent bank examinations by governmental agencies. Today, the basic function of reserve requirements is to provide a means for regulating deposit expansion and contraction.

Deposit creation takes place as a result of the operations of the whole system of banks, but it arises out of the independent transactions of individual banks. To explain the process, therefore, we will consider the loan activities of a single bank. First we will focus on the bank itself; then we will examine its relationship to a system of banks. This approach is somewhat artificial since a bank practically never acts independently of the actions of other banks, but it has been adopted to clarify the process. Furthermore, it helps explain the belief of some bankers that they cannot create deposits, since they only lend funds placed on deposit in their banks by their depositors. This analysis shows how a system of banks, in which each bank is carrying on its local activities, can do what an individual banker cannot do.

For illustration, let us assume that a bank receives a primary deposit of $10,000 and that it must keep reserves of 20 percent against deposits. The $10,000 becomes a cash asset to the bank as well as a $10,000 liability, since it must stand ready to honor a withdrawal of the money. The bank statement, ignoring all other items, would then show the following:

ASSETS		LIABILITIES	
Reserves	$10,000	Deposits	$10,000

Against this new deposit of $10,000 the bank must keep required reserves of 20 percent, or $2,000. Therefore, it has $8,000 of excess reserves available. Excess reserves are reserves above the level of required reserves.

It may appear that the banker could proceed to make loans for $40,000, since all that is needed is a 20 percent reserve against the resulting checkable deposits. If this were attempted, however, the banker would soon be in a difficult situation. Since bank loans are usually obtained just before a demand for funds, checks would very likely be written against the deposit accounts almost at once. Many of these checks would be deposited in other banks, and the bank would be faced with a demand for cash as checks were presented for collection. This demand could reach the full $40,000. Since the bank has only $8,000 to meet it, it could not follow such a course and remain in business.

The amount that the banker can safely lend is the $8,000 of excess reserves. If more is lent, the banker runs the risk of not being able to make payments on checks. After an $8,000 loan, the books show:

ASSETS		LIABILITIES	
Reserves	$10,000	Deposits	$18,000
Loans	$ 8,000		

If a check were written for the full amount of the derivative deposit ($8,000) and sent to a bank in another city for deposit, the lending bank would lose all of its excess reserves. This may be seen from its books, which would appear as follows:

ASSETS		LIABILITIES	
Reserves	$2,000	Deposits	$10,000
Loans	$8,000		

In practice, a bank may be able to lend somewhat more than the $8,000 in this example, because banks frequently require customers to keep an average deposit balance of about 15 to 20 percent of the loan. The whole of the additional $1,500 to $2,000 cannot be lent safely, because an average balance of $1,500 to $2,000 does not prevent the full amount of the loan from being used for a period of time. With an average balance in each derivative deposit account, however, not all accounts will be drawn to zero at the same time. Therefore, some additional funds will be available for loans.

It may be argued that a banker will feel sure that some checks written against the bank will be redeposited in the same bank and that therefore larger sums can be lent. However, because any bank is only one of thousands, the banker cannot usually count on such redepositing of funds. Banks cannot run the risk of being caught short of reserves. Thus, when an individual bank receives a new primary deposit, it cannot lend the full amount of that deposit but only the amount available as excess reserves. From the point of view of an individual bank, therefore, deposit creation appears impossible. Because a part of every new deposit cannot be lent out because of reserve requirements, the volume of additional loans is less than new primary deposits.

It is important to recognize: *What cannot be done by an individual bank can be done by the banking system.* This occurs when many banks are expanding loans and derivative deposits at the same time. To illustrate this point, assume that we have an economy with just two banks, A and B. This example can be realistic if we assume further that Bank A represents one bank in the system and Bank B represents all other banks combined. Bank A, as in our previous example, receives a new primary deposit of $10,000 and is required to keep reserves of 20 percent against deposits. Therefore, its books would appear as follows:

BANK A

ASSETS		LIABILITIES	
Reserves	$10,000	Deposits	$10,000

A loan for $8,000 is made and credited as follows:

BANK A

ASSETS		LIABILITIES	
Reserves	$10,000	Deposits	$18,000
Loans	$ 8,000		

Assume that a check is drawn against this primary deposit almost immediately and deposited in Bank B. The books of the two banks would then show the following:

BANK A

ASSETS		LIABILITIES	
Reserves	$2,000	Deposits	$10,000
Loans	$8,000		

BANK B

ASSETS		LIABILITIES	
Reserves	$8,000	Deposits	$8,000

The derivative deposit arising out of a loan from Bank A has now been transferred by check to Bank B, where it is received as a primary deposit. Bank B must now set aside 20 percent as required reserves and may lend or reinvest the remainder. Its books after such a loan (equal to its excess reserves) would appear as follows:

BANK B

ASSETS		LIABILITIES	
Reserves	$8,000	Deposits	$14,400
Loans	$6,400		

Assume a check is drawn against the derivative deposit of $6,400 that was created due to the loan by Bank B. This reduces its reserves and deposits as follows:

BANK B

ASSETS		LIABILITIES	
Reserves	$1,600	Deposits	$8,000
Loans	$6,400		

The check for $6,400 will most likely be deposited in a bank, in our example in Bank A or Bank B itself, since we have assumed that only two banks exist. In the U.S. banking system, it may be deposited in one of the thousands of banks or other depository institutions.

Deposit expansion as when a bank makes a loan can take place in the same way when it buys securities. Assume, as we did in the case of a bank loan, the following situation:

BANK A

ASSETS		LIABILITIES	
Reserves	$10,000	Deposits	$10,000

Securities costing $8,000 are purchased and the proceeds credited to the account of the seller, giving the following situation:

BANK A

ASSETS		LIABILITIES	
Reserves	$10,000	Deposits	$18,000
Investments	$8,000		

Assume that a check is drawn against the seller's deposit and is deposited in Bank B. The books of the two banks would then show:

BANK A

ASSETS		LIABILITIES	
Reserves	$2,000	Deposits	$10,000
Investments	$8,000		

BANK B			
ASSETS		**LIABILITIES**	
Reserves	$8,000	Deposits	$8,000

As in the case of a loan, the derivative deposit has been transferred to Bank B, where it is received as a primary deposit.

At each stage in the process, 20 percent of the new primary deposit becomes required reserves, and 80 percent becomes excess reserves that can be lent out. In time, the whole of the original $10,000 primary deposit will have become required reserves, and $50,000 of deposits will have been credited to deposit accounts, of which $40,000 will have been lent out.

Table 5.1 further illustrates the deposit expansion process for a 20 percent reserve ratio. A primary deposit of $1,000 is injected into the banking system, making excess reserves of $800 available for loans and investments. Eventually, $5,000 in checkable deposits will be created.

Multiple expansion in the money supply created by the banking system through its expansion of checkable deposits also can be expressed in formula form as follows:

$$\text{Change in checkable deposits} = \frac{\text{Increase in excess reserves}}{\text{Required reserves ratio}} \quad (5.1)$$

We define the terms *excess reserves* and the *required reserves ratio* in the next section. For our purposes, the maximum increase in the amount of checkable deposits is determined by dividing a new inflow of reserves into the banking system by the percentage of checkable deposits that must be held in reserves.

In the example presented in Table 5.1, the maximum expansion in the checkable deposits component of the money supply, which is the same as the final-stage figure shown for checkable deposit liabilities, would be:

$$\text{Change in checkable deposits} = \$1,000 \div .20 = \$5,000$$

The maximum increase in deposits (and money supply) that can result from a specific increase in excess reserves is can be referred to as a *money multiplier*. In our very basic example, the money multiplier (m) is equal to 1 divided by the required reserves ratio, or $m = \div .20 = 5$.

TABLE 5.1
Multiple Expansion of Deposits—20 Percent Reserve Ratio

	ASSETS				LIABILITIES
	RESERVES				
	TOTAL	REQUIRED	EXCESS	LOANS AND INVESTMENTS	CHECKABLE DEPOSITS
Initial Reserves	$1,000	$200	$800	$0	$1,000
Stage 1	1,000	360	640	800	1,800
Stage 2	1,000	488	512	1,440	2,440
Stage 3	1,000	590	410	1,952	2,952
Stage 4	1,000	672	328	2,362	3,362
Stage 5	1,000	738	262	2,690	3,690
Stage 6	1,000	790	210	2,952	3,952
Stage 7	1,000	832	168	3,162	4,162
Stage 8	1,000	866	134	3,330	4,330
Stage 9	1,000	893	107	3,464	4,464
Stage 10	1,000	914	86	3,571	4,571
.	.	.	.	.	.
.	.	.	.	.	.
.	.	.	.	.	.
Final Stage	$1,000	$1,000	$0	$4,000	$5,000

However, in the complex U.S. economy there are several factors or "leakages" that reduce the ability to reach the maximum expansion in the money supply depicted in this simplified example. We will discuss a more realistic money multiplier ratio in the last section of this chapter.

CONCEPT CHECK

How can an increase in excess reserves produce a larger increase in checkable deposits?

OFFSETTING OR LIMITING FACTORS

Deposit creation can go on only to the extent that the activities described actually take place. If for any reason the proceeds of a loan are withdrawn from the banking system, no new deposit arises to continue the process. A new deposit of $10,000 permits loans of $8,000 under a 20 percent required reserve; but if this $8,000 were used in currency transactions without being deposited in a bank, no deposit could be created. The custom of doing business by means of checks makes deposit creation possible.

In the examples above, no allowance was made for either cash leakage or currency withdrawal from the system. In actual practice, as the volume of business in the economy increases, some additional cash is withdrawn for hand-to-hand circulation and to meet the needs of business for petty cash.

Money may also be withdrawn from the banking system to meet the demand for payments to foreign countries, or foreign banks may withdraw some of the money they are holding on deposit in U.S. banks. The U.S. Treasury may withdraw funds it has on deposit in banks. All of these factors reduce the multiplying capacity of primary deposits.

Furthermore, this process can go on only if excess reserves are actually being lent by the banks. This means that banks must be willing to lend the full amount of their excess reserves and that acceptable borrowers who have a demand for loans must be available.

The nonbank public's decisions to switch funds between checkable deposits and time or savings deposits also will influence the ability to expand the money supply and credit. This is explored later in the chapter.

CONTRACTION OF DEPOSITS

When the need for funds by business decreases, deposit expansion can work in reverse. Expansion takes place as long as excess reserves exist and the demand for new bank loans exceeds the repayment of old loans. Deposit contraction takes place when old loans are being repaid faster than new loans are being granted and banks are not immediately investing these excess funds.

Assuming that Bank A has no excess reserves, let us see the effect of a loan being repaid. Before the borrower began to build up deposits to repay the loan, the bank's books showed:

BANK A			
ASSETS		**LIABILITIES**	
Reserves	$2,000	Deposits	$10,000
Loans	$8,000		

The borrower of the $8,000 must build up his or her deposit account by $8,000 to be able to repay the loan. This is reflected on the books as follows:

BANK A			
ASSETS		**LIABILITIES**	
Reserves	$10,000	Deposits	$18,000
Loans	$ 8,000		

After the $8,000 is repaid, the books show the following:

BANK A			
ASSETS		**LIABILITIES**	
Reserves	$10,000	Deposits	$10,000

If no new loan is made from the $10,000 of reserves, deposit contraction will result. This is true because $8,000 of funds have been taken out of the banking system to build up deposits to repay the loan and are now being held idle by Bank A as excess reserves. Furthermore, taking out $8,000 of reserves from the banking system may be cumulative on the contraction side just as it was during expansion.

FACTORS AFFECTING BANK RESERVES

The level of a bank's excess reserves determines the extent to which deposit expansion (or contraction) takes place. This is true for an individual bank and for the banking system as a whole. Therefore, the factors that affect the level of bank reserves are significant in determining the size of the money supply. **Bank reserves** in the banking system consist of reserve balances and vault cash used to meet reserve requirements. Reserve balances are deposits held at the Reserve Banks by commercial banks and other depository institutions. Vault cash is currency, including coin, held on the premises of these institutions.

Total bank reserves can be divided into two parts. The first, **required reserves,** is the minimum amount of total reserves that a depository institution must hold. The percentage of deposits that must be held as reserves is called the **required reserves ratio.** The second part of total reserves is **excess reserves,** the amount by which total reserves exceed required reserves. If required reserves are larger than the total reserves of an institution, the difference is called **deficit reserves.**

Two kinds of factors affect total reserves: those that affect the currency holdings of the banking system and those that affect deposits at the Fed. Currency flows in response to changes in the demand for it by households and businesses. Reserve balances are affected by a variety of transactions involving the Fed and banks that may be initiated by the banking system or the Fed, by the Treasury, or by other factors. Although the Fed does not control all of the factors that affect the level of bank reserves, it does have the ability to offset increases and decreases. Thus it has broad control over the total reserves available to the banking system. Figure 5.2 provides a summary of the transactions that affect bank reserves. Discussion of these transactions follows.

CHANGES IN THE DEMAND FOR CURRENCY

Currency flows into and out of the banking system affect the level of reserves of the banks receiving the currency for deposit. Let's assume that an individual or a business finds they have excess currency of $100 and deposit it in Bank A. Deposit liabilities and the reserves of Bank A are increased by $100. The bank now has excess reserves of $80, assuming a 20 percent level of required reserves. These reserves can be used by the banking system to create $400 in additional deposits. If the bank does not need the currency but sends it to its Reserve Bank, it will receive a $100 credit to its account. The volume of Federal Reserve notes in circulation is decreased by $100. These transactions may be summarized as follows:

1. Deposits in Bank A are increased by $100 ($20 in required reserves and $80 in excess reserves).
2. Bank A's deposit at its Reserve Bank is increased by $100.
3. The amount of Federal Reserve notes is decreased by $100.

FIGURE 5.2
Transactions Affecting Bank Reserves

NONBANK PUBLIC	FEDERAL RESERVE SYSTEM	U.S. TREASURY
Change in the non-bank public's demand for currency to be held outside the banking system	Change in reserve ratio Open-market operations (buying and selling government securities) Change in bank borrowings Change in float Change in foreign deposits held in Reserve Banks Change in other Federal Reserve accounts	Change in Treasury spending out of accounts held at Reserve Banks Change in Treasury cash holdings

---

CONCEPT CHECK

What causes deposit contraction to take place?

bank reserves
reserve balances held at Federal Reserve Banks and vault cash held in the banking system

required reserves
the minimum amount of total reserves that a depository institution must hold

required reserves ratio
the percentage of deposits that must be held as reserves

excess reserves
the amount by which total reserves are greater than required reserves

deficit reserves
the amount by which required reserves are greater than total reserves

CONCEPT CHECK

What is the definition of bank reserves?

What is the difference between required reserves and excess reserves?

What is the required reserves ratio?

INTERNET ACTIVITY

Go to the St. Louis Federal Reserve Bank's Web site, http://www.stlouisfed.org, and access the FRED database. Find monetary base, money supply, and gross domestic product data. Calculate the money multiplier and the velocity of money.

The opposite takes place when the public demands additional currency. Let us assume that a customer of Bank A needs additional currency and cashes a check for $100. The deposits of the bank are reduced by $100, and this reduces required reserves by $20. If the bank has no excess reserves, it must take steps to get an additional $80 of reserves by borrowing from its Reserve Bank, demanding payment for a loan or not renewing one that comes due, or selling securities. When the check is cashed, the reserves of the bank are also reduced by $100. If the bank has to replenish its supply of currency from its Reserve Bank, its reserve deposits are reduced by $100. These transactions may be summarized thus:

1. Deposits in Bank A are reduced by $100 ($20 in required reserves and $80 in excess reserves).
2. Bank A's deposit at its Reserve Bank is reduced by $100.
3. The amount of Federal Reserve notes in circulation is increased by $100.

Changes in the components of the money supply traditionally have occurred during holiday periods, with the most pronounced change taking place during the year-end holiday season. These changes are beyond the immediate control of the Fed, which must anticipate and respond to them to carry out possible money-supply growth targets. Generally, there has been an increase in currency outstanding between November and December and a subsequent partial reversal during January. An increase in circulating currency prior to the Christmas holidays requires adjustment by the Fed to control the money supply. As large amounts of cash are withdrawn from depository institutions, deposit contraction might occur unless the Fed moves to offset it by purchasing government securities in the open market.

Also there traditionally has been an increase in demand deposits between November and December and a subsequent decline in demand deposits during the early part of the next year. This also seems to reflect the public's surge in spending during the Christmas holiday season and the payment for many of the purchases early in the next year by writing checks on demand deposit accounts. The Fed, in its effort to control bank reserves and the money supply, also must take corrective actions to temper the impact of these seasonal swings in currency and checking account balances. Of course, the increasing use of credit cards and debit cards continues to alter the use of currency and the writing of checks.

FEDERAL RESERVE SYSTEM TRANSACTIONS

Transactions of banks with the Fed and changes in reserve requirements by the Fed also affect either the level of total reserves or the degree to which deposits can be expanded with a given volume of reserves. Such transactions are initiated by the Fed when it buys or sells securities, by a depository institution when it borrows from its Reserve Bank, or by a change in Federal Reserve float. These are examined here in turn, and then the effect of a change in reserve requirements is described. Finally, we will look at Treasury transactions, which can also affect reserves in the banking system.

Open-Market Operations

When the Fed, through its open-market operations, purchases securities such as government bonds, it adds to bank reserves. The Fed pays for the bonds with a check. The seller deposits the check in an account and receives a deposit account credit. The bank presents the check to the Reserve Bank for payment and receives a credit to its account. When the Fed buys a $1,000 government bond, the check for which is deposited in Bank A, the transactions may be summarized as follows:

1. Bank A's deposit at its Reserve Bank is increased by $1,000. The Reserve Bank has a new asset—a bond worth $1,000.
2. Deposits in Bank A are increased by $1,000 ($200 in required reserves and $800 in excess reserves).

The opposite takes place when the Fed sells securities in the market.

In contrast to the other actions that affect reserves in the banking system, open-market operations are entirely conducted by the Fed. For this reason they are the most important policy tool the Fed has to control reserves and the money supply. Open-market operations are conducted

CONCEPT CHECK

Why does the demand for currency change around the end of the calendar year?

CONCEPT CHECK

Who is responsible for conducting open-market operations?

CAREER OPPORTUNITIES IN FINANCE
Government or Not-for-Profit Organizations

Opportunities

The federal government is the largest employer in the United States. In addition, state and local governments also hire thousands of workers across the nation. Not-for-profit organizations, such as hospitals, employ numerous workers with backgrounds in business and finance. Many job seekers, however, never consider that government and not-for-profit organizations need the same financial services as businesses do. Therefore, jobs available in this field often go unnoticed. All federal and state jobs are listed at your local state employment services office and online at http://usajobs.opm.gov/. You may also contact your state or regional Federal Employment Information Center for more information on federal jobs (your state or federal representative will know how to get in touch with these offices).

Jobs

Financial manager
Financial analyst
Financial planner

Responsibilities

A *financial manager* manages cash funds, makes asset acquisition decisions, controls costs, and obtains borrowed funds. A financial manager with either a government or a not-for-profit organization must also stay abreast of current legislation and public and private grant opportunities.

A *financial analyst* assesses the short- and long-term financial performance of a government or not-for-profit organization.

A *financial planner* uses financial analysis to develop a financial plan.

Education

Knowledge of economics and finance is necessary for these jobs, and an understanding of the executive and legislative process is helpful. In addition, a primary way in which government and not-for-profit groups obtain funds is by getting grants. Therefore, strong research and writing skills for grant proposals also are essential.

---

virtually every business day, both to smooth out ups and downs caused by other transactions and to implement changes in the money supply called for by the Federal Open Market Committee.

Depository Institution Transactions

When a bank borrows from its Reserve Bank, it is borrowing reserves; so reserves are increased by the amount of the loan. Similarly, when a loan to the Reserve Bank is repaid, reserves are reduced by that amount. The transactions when Bank A borrows $1,000 from its Reserve Bank may be summarized as follows:

1. Bank A's deposit at its Reserve Bank is increased by $1,000. The assets of the Reserve Bank are increased by $1,000 by the note from Bank A.
2. Bank A's excess reserves have been increased by $1,000. It also has a new $1,000 liability, its note to the Reserve Bank.

This process is reversed when a debt to the Reserve Bank is repaid.

Federal Reserve Float

Federal Reserve float
temporary increase in bank reserves from checks credited to one bank's reserves and not yet debited to another's

Changes in Federal Reserve float also affect bank reserves. *Float* arises out of the process of collecting checks handled by Reserve Banks. **Federal Reserve float** is the temporary increase in bank reserves that results when checks are credited to the reserve account of the depositing bank before they are debited from the account of the banks on which they are drawn. Checks drawn on nearby banks are credited almost immediately to the account of the bank in which they were deposited and debited to the account of the bank on which the check was drawn. Under Fed regulations, all checks are credited one or two days later to the account of the bank in which the check was deposited. It may take longer for the check to go through the collection process and be debited to the account of the bank upon which it is drawn. When this happens, bank reserves are increased, and this increase is called *float*. The process by which a $1,000 check drawn on Bank B is deposited in Bank A and credited to its account before it is debited to the account of Bank B may be summarized:

1. Bank A transfers $1,000 from its Cash Items in the Process of Collection to its account at the Reserve Bank. Its reserves are increased by $1,000.
2. The Reserve Bank takes $1,000 from its Deferred Availability Account and transfers it to Bank A's account.

CONCEPT CHECK
What is the meaning of the term Federal Reserve float?

Thus, total reserves of banks are increased temporarily by $1,000. They are reduced when Bank B's account at its Reserve Bank is reduced by $1,000 a day or two later.

Changes in reserve requirements change the amount of deposit expansion that is possible with a given level of reserves. With a reserve ratio of 20 percent, excess reserves of $800 can be expanded to $4,000 of additional loans and deposits. If the reserve ratio is reduced to 10 percent, it is possible to expand $800 of excess reserves to $8,000 of additional loans and deposits. When the reserve ratio is lowered, additional expansion also takes place because part of the required reserves becomes excess reserves. This process is reversed when the reserve ratio is raised.

Bank reserves are also affected by changes in the level of deposits of foreign central banks and governments at the Reserve Banks. These deposits are maintained with the Reserve Banks at times as part of the monetary reserves of a foreign country and may also be used to settle international balances. A decrease in such foreign deposits with the Reserve Banks increases bank reserves; an increase in them decreases bank reserves.

Treasury Transactions

Bank reserves are also affected by the transactions of the Treasury. They are increased by spending and making payments and decreased when the Treasury increases the size of its accounts at the Reserve Banks. The Treasury makes almost all of its payments out of its accounts at the Reserve Banks, and such spending adds to bank reserves. For example, the recipient of a check from the Treasury deposits it in a bank. The bank sends it to the Reserve Bank for collection and receives a credit to its account. The Reserve Bank debits the account of the Treasury. When a Treasury check for $1,000 is deposited in Bank A and required reserves are 20 percent, the transactions may be summarized as follows:

1. The deposits of Bank A are increased by $1,000, its required reserves by $200, and excess reserves by $800.
2. Bank A's reserves at the Reserve Bank are increased by $1,000.
3. The deposit account of the Treasury at the Reserve Bank is reduced by $1,000.

Treasury funds from tax collections or the sale of bonds are generally deposited in its accounts in banks. When the Treasury needs payment funds from its accounts at the Reserve Banks, it transfers funds from commercial banks to its accounts at the Reserve Banks. This process reduces bank reserves. When $1,000 is transferred from the account in Bank A and required reserves are 20 percent, transactions may be summarized as follows:

1. The Treasury deposit in Bank A is reduced by $1,000, required reserves by $200, and excess reserves by $800.
2. The Treasury account at the Reserve Bank is increased by $1,000, and the account of Bank A is reduced by $1,000.

The Treasury is the largest depositor at the Fed. The volume of transfers between the account of the Treasury and the reserve accounts of banks is large enough to cause significant changes in reserves in the banking system. For this reason, the Fed closely monitors the Treasury's account and often uses open-market operations to minimize its effect on bank reserves. This is accomplished by purchasing securities to provide reserves to the banking system when the Treasury's account increases and selling securities when the account of the Treasury falls to a low level.

The effect on bank reserves is the same for changes in Treasury cash holdings as it is for changes in Treasury accounts at the Reserve Banks. Reserves are increased when the Treasury decreases its cash holdings, and reserves are decreased when it increases such holdings.

CONCEPT CHECK
Bank reserves are decreased when the Treasury takes what actions?

THE MONETARY BASE AND THE MONEY MULTIPLIER

Earlier in this chapter we examined the deposit multiplying capacity of the banking system. Recall that, in the example shown in Table 5.1, excess reserves of $1,000 were introduced into a banking system having a 20 percent required reserves ratio, resulting in a deposit expansion of $5,000. This can also be viewed as a money multiplier of 5.

In our complex financial system, the money multiplier is not quite so straightforward. It will be useful to focus on the relationship between the monetary base and the money supply to better understand the complexity of the money multiplier. The **monetary base** is defined as banking system reserves plus currency held by the public. More specifically, the monetary base consists of reserve deposits held in Reserve Banks, vault cash or currency held by depository institutions, and currency held by the nonbank public. The **money multiplier** is the number of times the monetary base can be expanded or magnified to produce a given money supply level. Conceptually, the M1 definition of the money supply is the monetary base (MB) multiplied by the money multiplier (m). In equation form we have:

monetary base
banking system reserves plus currency held by the public

money multiplier
number of times the monetary base can be expanded or magnified to produce a given money supply level

$$M1 = MB \times m \qquad (5.2)$$

The size and stability of the money multiplier are important because the Fed can control the monetary base, but it cannot directly control the size of the money supply. Changes in the money supply are caused by changes in the monetary base, in the money multiplier, or in both. The Fed can change the size of the monetary base through open-market operations or changes in the reserve ratio. The money multiplier is not constant. It can and does fluctuate over time, depending on actions taken by the Fed as well as by the nonbank public and the U.S. Treasury.

In June 2008, the money multiplier was approximately 1.62, as determined by dividing the $1,393.8 billion M1 money stock by the $863.0 billion monetary base.[3] Taking into account the actions of the nonbank public and the Treasury, the formula for the money multiplier in today's financial system can be expressed as:[4]

$$m = \frac{(1 + k)}{[r(1 + t + g) + k]} \qquad (5.3)$$

where
r = the ratio of reserves to total deposits (checkable, noncheckable time and savings, and government)
k = the ratio of currency held by the nonbank public to checkable deposits
t = the ratio of noncheckable deposits to checkable deposits
g = the ratio of government deposits to checkable deposits

Let's illustrate how the size of the money multiplier is determined by returning to our previous example of a 20 percent reserve ratio. Recall that in a more simple financial system, the money multiplier would be determined as $1 \div r$ or $1 \div .20$, which equals 5. However, in our complex system we also need to consider leakages into currency held by the nonbank public, noncheckable time and savings deposits, and government deposits. Let's further assume that the reserve ratio applies to total deposits, a k of 40 percent, a t of 15 percent, and a g of 10 percent. The money multiplier then would be estimated as:

$$m = \frac{(1 + .40)}{[.20(1 + .15 + .10) + .40]} = \frac{1.40}{.65} = 2.15$$

Of course, if a change occurred in any of the components, the money multiplier would adjust accordingly, as would the size of the money supply.

In Chapter 2 we briefly discussed the link between the money supply and economic activity. You should be able to recall that the money supply (M1) is linked to the gross domestic product (GDP) via the velocity or turnover of money. More specifically, the **velocity of money** measures the rate of circulation of the money supply. It is expressed as the average number of times each dollar is spent on purchases of goods and services and is calculated as nominal GDP (GDP in current dollars) divided by M1. Changes in the growth rates for money supply (M1g) and money velocity (M1Vg) affect the growth rate in real economic activity (RGDPg) and the rate of inflation (Ig) and can be expressed in equation form as follows:

velocity of money
the rate of circulation of the money supply

$$M1_g + M1V_g = RGDP_g + I_g \qquad (5.4)$$

---

[3]. Federal Reserve Bank of St. Louis, *Federal Reserve Economic Database* (*FRED*), http://stlouisfed.org. As the 2007–09 financial crisis worsened, the ratio dropped below 1.0 in late 2008 and throughout 2009.

[4]. The reader interested in understanding how the money multiplier is derived will find a discussion in most financial institutions and markets textbooks.

CODY PRESS
Managing Director of Public
Finance—West Coast
Citigroup Global Market, Inc.

BS, Dartmouth College
MBA Finance
University of Pennsylvania

CAREER PROFILES

•

"Common sense and judgment are very important."

•

Q: *What is the purpose of public finance?*
A: The short answer is that we help municipalities and other nonprofit entities solve their financing problems.

Q: *Who are these entities?*
A: Basically, you can use the rule that anyone who is tax-exempt and needs to raise money could be a client: municipalities, museums, counties, states, nonprofit hospitals, and so on. In many cases we will be hired to secure financing for a specific project, such as a bridge or a toll road.

Q: *Let's take a simple example. How would a city finance a bridge?*
A: There could be several options, but in many cases we will help the city issue bonds to generate the money necessary to build the bridge. The city borrows the money by selling bonds and repays it over time, quite possibly through a toll or fee for using the bridge. This is generally a better option than raising taxes because it means that the people who use the bridge pay for it throughout its useful life.

Q: *What role do you play in this transaction?*
A: We work with the municipality on two levels. We work with the elected officials on the higher-level decisions, helping them understand what their options are for raising the funds they need to implement their plans. Then we work with their staff people on the more technical aspects of the bond issue, how it will be structured and so forth. When the bonds are sold, we keep a percentage of the proceeds as our compensation.

Q: *Would you describe your function as sales or management?*
A: It's a combination of both. Several years ago there were twenty people in my group, so I spent more time on management then. Now I have eleven people, so I spend more time on sales. I spend at least two days a week out of the office, meeting mostly with our existing clients.

Q: *Is this a competitive field?*
A: It's very competitive. The size of the market is much smaller now than it was just a few years ago, so we all compete for the available deals.

Q: *What skills do you rely on most?*
A: Common sense and judgment are very important. There are always decisions about where to focus your time and resources, and good judgment is essential in making the right choices. Honesty is an important quality, too.

Q: *What are the career options in this field?*
A: That's an interesting issue. Because public finance is so specialized, it's not easy to move to another field. You really have to be very interested in working with government clients for the long haul, because you may not have a lot of other options.

APPLYING FINANCE TO...

INSTITUTIONS AND MARKETS

Policy makers pass laws and implement fiscal and monetary policies. A recent change in law, as noted in Chapter 3, allows U.S. commercial banks again to engage in both commercial banking and investment banking activities and become universal banks. Policy makers influence and change the types of financial institutions and their operations. The operations of depository institutions are directly influenced by monetary policy decisions relating to reserve requirements and Fed discount rates. The ability of financial institutions to carry out the savings-investment process also is affected by the actions of policy makers.

INVESTMENTS

The prices of securities typically reflect economic activity and the level of interest rates. Real growth in the economy, accompanied by high employment and low interest rates, makes for attractive investment opportunities. Individual and institutional investors usually find the values of their investments rising during periods of economic prosperity. However, there are times when policy makers fear that the loss of purchasing power associated with high inflation outweighs the value of economic expansion. During these times, securities prices suffer.

FINANCIAL MANAGEMENT

The operations of businesses are directly effected by policy makers. Fiscal and monetary policies that constrain economic growth make it difficult for businesses to operate and make profits. Financial managers must periodically raise financial capital in the securities markets. Actions by policy makers to constrain the money supply and to make borrowing more costly will give financial managers many sleepless nights. On the other hand, expansive monetary policy accompanied by low inflation usually is conducive to business growth, lower interest rates, and higher stock prices—making it easier for financial managers to obtain, at reasonable costs, the financial capital needed to grow their businesses.

CONCEPT CHECK
What is the monetary base?
What does the velocity of money measure?

For example, if the velocity of money remains relatively constant, then a link between money supply and the nominal GDP should be observable. Likewise, after nominal GDP is adjusted for inflation, the resulting real GDP growth can be examined relative to M1 growth rates. Changes in money supply have been found to lead to changes in economic activity.

The ability to predict M1 velocity in addition to money supply changes is important in making successful monetary policy. Fed M1 growth targets need to take into consideration expected velocity movements to achieve the desired effects on real GDP and inflation. It would be naive, however, to believe that regulating and controlling the supply of money and credit are all that is needed to manage our complex economy. We also know that economic activity is affected by government actions concerning government spending, taxation, and the management of our public debt.

SUMMARY

This chapter began with a discussion of the four national policy objectives—economic growth, stable prices, high levels of employment, and a balance in international transactions. The Federal Reserve System, the president, Congress, and the U.S. Treasury were identified as major policy makers. The Fed formulates monetary policy, and Congress and the president set fiscal policy. The Treasury helps administer and carry out fiscal policy, and the Treasury is responsible for financing the national debt.

The remainder of the chapter focused on several aspects of the money supply. First, the mechanics of deposit expansion and contraction within the banking system were covered. Deposit expansion (and contraction) can take place in the banking system because only a small fraction of the dollar amount of deposits must be held as reserves. Thus, when an individual bank receives a new deposit, a portion of the deposit must be held as reserves while the remainder can be lent out to businesses or individuals. This was followed by a discussion of the factors that affect bank reserves. For example, changes in the demand for currency, the Fed's open-market operations, and Treasury transactions can affect the level of bank reserves. Finally, the terms *monetary base* and *money multiplier* were defined and the importance of controlling the money supply was discussed.

KEY TERMS

automatic stabilizers
bank reserves
crowding out
debt management
deficit financing
deficit reserves
derivative deposit
excess reserves
Federal Reserve float
fiscal policy
fractional reserve system
gross domestic product (GDP)

inflation
monetary base
monetizing the debt
money multiplier

primary deposit
required reserves
required reserves ratio
tax policy

transfer payments
velocity of money

DISCUSSION QUESTIONS

1. List and describe briefly the economic policy objectives of the nation.

2. Describe the relationship among policy makers, types of policies, and policy objectives.

3. Describe the effects of tax policy on monetary and credit conditions.

4. Federal government deficit financing may have a very great influence on monetary and credit conditions. Explain.

5. Discuss the various objectives of debt management.

6. Explain how Federal Reserve notes are supported or backed in our financial system.

7. Why are the expansion and contraction of deposits by the banking system possible in our financial system?

8. Trace the effect on its accounts of a loan made by a bank that has excess reserves available from new deposits.

9. Explain how deposit expansion takes place in a banking system consisting of two banks.

10. Explain the potential for deposit expansion when required reserves average 10 percent and $2,000 in excess reserves are deposited in the banking system.

11. Trace the effect on bank reserves of a change in the amount of cash held by the public.

12. Describe the effect on bank reserves when the Federal Reserve sells U.S. government securities to a bank.

13. Summarize the factors that can lead to a change in bank reserves.

14. What is the difference between the monetary base and total bank reserves?

15. Briefly describe what is meant by the money multiplier and indicate the factors that affect its magnitude or size.

16. Define the velocity of money, and explain why it is important to anticipate changes in money velocity.

17. Why does it seem to be important to regulate and control the supply of money?

EXERCISES

1. Go to the St. Louis Federal Reserve Bank's website at http://www.stlouisfed.org, and access current economic data.
   a. Find M1 and the monetary base, and then estimate the money multiplier.
   b. Determine the nominal gross national product (GNP in current dollars). Estimate the velocity of money using M1 from (a) and nominal GNP.
   c. Indicate how the money multiplier and the velocity of money have changed between two recent years.

2. Important policy objectives of the federal government include economic growth, high employment, price stability, and a balance in international transactions. The achievement of these objectives is the responsibility of monetary policy, fiscal policy, and debt management carried out by the Federal Reserve System, the president, Congress, and the U.S. Treasury. Describe the responsibilities of the various policy makers in trying to achieve the four economic policy objectives.

3. An economic recession has developed, and the Federal Reserve Board has taken several actions to retard further declines in economic activity. The U.S. Treasury now wishes to take steps to assist the Fed in this effort. Describe the actions the Treasury might take.

4. The president and members of Congress are elected by the people and are expected to behave ethically. Let's assume that you are a recently elected member of Congress. A special-interest lobbying group is offering to contribute funds to your next election campaign in the hope that you will support legislation being proposed by others that will help the group achieve its stated objectives. What would you do?

PROBLEMS

1. Assume that Banc One receives a primary deposit of $1 million. The bank must keep reserves of 20 percent against its deposits. Prepare a simple balance sheet of assets and liabilities for Banc One immediately after the deposit is received.

2. Assume that Bank A receives a primary deposit of $100,000 and that it must keep reserves of 10 percent against deposits.
   a. Prepare a simple balance sheet of assets and liabilities for the bank immediately after the deposit is received.
   b. Assume Bank A makes a loan in the amount that can be "safely lent." Show what the bank's balance sheet of assets and liabilities would look like immediately after the loan.
   c. Now assume that a check in the amount of the "derivative deposit" created in (b) was written and sent to another bank. Show what Bank A's (the lending bank's) balance sheet of assets and liabilities would look like after the check is written.

3. Rework Problem 2 assuming Bank A has reserve requirements that are 15 percent of deposits.

4. Assume that there are two banks, A and Z, in the banking system. Bank A receives a primary deposit of $600,000, and it must keep reserves of 12 percent against deposits. Bank A makes a loan in the amount that can be safely lent.
   a. Show what Bank A's balance sheet of assets and liabilities would look like immediately after the loan.
   b. Assume that a check is drawn against the primary deposit made in Bank A and is deposited in Bank Z. Show what the

balance sheet of assets and liabilities would look like for each of the two banks after the transaction has taken place.

c. Now assume that Bank Z makes a loan in the amount that can be safely lent against the funds deposited in its bank from the transaction described in (b). Show what Bank Z's balance sheet of assets and liabilities would look like after the loan.

5. The SIMPLEX financial system is characterized by a required reserves ratio of 11 percent; initial excess reserves are $1 million, and there are no currency or other leakages.

   a. What would be the maximum amount of checkable deposits after deposit expansion, and what would be the money multiplier?
   b. How would your answer in (a) change if the reserve requirement had been 9 percent?

6. Assume a financial system has a monetary base of $25 million. The required reserves ratio is 10 percent, and there are no leakages in the system.

   a. What is the size of the money multiplier?
   b. What will be the system's money supply?

7. Rework Problem 6 assuming the reserve ratio is 14 percent?

8. The BASIC financial system has a required reserves ratio of 15 percent; initial excess reserves are $5 million, cash held by the public is $1 million and is expected to stay at that level, and there are no other leakages or adjustments in the system.

   a. What would be the money multiplier and the maximum amount of checkable deposits?
   b. What would be the money supply amount in this system after deposit expansion?

9. Rework Problem 8, assuming that the cash held by the public drops to $500,000 with an equal amount becoming excess reserves and the required reserves ratio drops to 12 percent.

10. The COMPLEX financial system has these relationships: the ratio of reserves to total deposits is 12 percent, and the ratio of noncheckable deposits to checkable deposits is 40 percent. In addition, currency held by the nonbank public amounts to 15 percent of checkable deposits. The ratio of government deposits to checkable deposits is 8 percent, and the monetary base is $300 million.

    a. Determine the size of the M1 money multiplier and the size of the money supply.
    b. If the ratio of currency in circulation to checkable deposits were to drop to 13 percent while the other ratios remained the same, what would be the impact on the money supply?
    c. If the ratio of government deposits to checkable deposits increases to 10 percent while the other ratios remained the same, what would be the impact on the money supply?
    d. What would happen to the money supply if the reserve requirement increased to 14 percent while noncheckable deposits to checkable deposits fell to 35 percent? Assume the other ratios remain as originally stated.

11. **Challenge Problem** ABBIX has a complex financial system with the following relationships: The ratio of required reserves to total deposits is 15 percent, and the ratio of noncheckable deposits to checkable deposits is 40 percent. In addition, currency held by the nonbank public amounts to 20 percent of checkable deposits. The ratio of government deposits to checkable deposits is 8 percent. Initial excess reserves are $900 million.

    a. Determine the M1 multiplier and the maximum dollar amount of checkable deposits.
    b. Determine the size of the M1 money supply.
    c. What will happen to ABBIX's money multiplier if the reserve requirement decreases to 10 percent while the ratio of noncheckable deposits to checkable deposits falls to 30 percent? Assume the other ratios remain as originally stated.
    d. Based on the information in (c), estimate the maximum dollar amount of checkable deposits, as well as the size of the M1 money supply.
    e. Assume that ABBIX has a target M1 money supply of $2.8 billion. The only variable that you have direct control over is the required reserves ratio. What would the required reserves ratio have to be to reach the target M1 money supply amount? Assume the other original ratio relationships hold.
    f. Now assume that currency held by the nonbank public drops to 15 percent of checkable deposits and that ABBIX's target money supply is changed to $3.0 billion. What would the required reserves ratio have to be to reach the new target M1 money supply amount? Assume the other original ratio relationships hold.

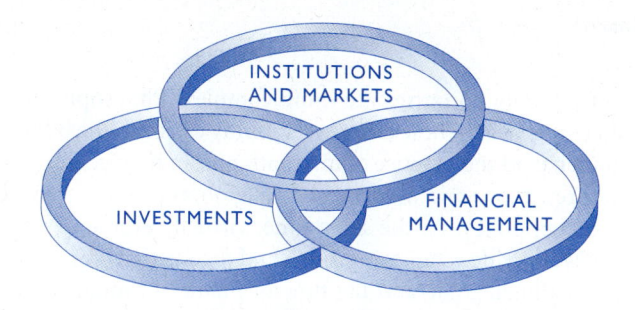

• CHAPTER 6 •

International Finance and Trade

Chapter Learning Objectives:

AFTER STUDYING THIS CHAPTER, YOU SHOULD BE ABLE TO:

- Explain how the international monetary system evolved and how it operates today.
- Describe the efforts undertaken to achieve economic unification of Europe.
- Describe how currency or foreign exchange markets are organized and operate.
- Explain how currency exchange rates are quoted.
- Describe the factors that affect currency exchange rates.
- Describe how the world banking systems facilitate financing of sales by exporters and purchases by importers.
- Identify recent developments in the U.S. balance of payments.

Where We Have Been...

In Chapter 5, you learned how the Fed operates in conjunction with governmental policy makers (the president, Congress, and the U.S. Treasury) in the common effort of trying to achieve the goals of economic growth, high and stable employment levels, price stability, and a balance in international transactions. You now understand policy instruments of the Treasury and how the national debt is managed. You also learned how the money supply is expanded and contracted and the importance of the monetary base and money multiplier in setting monetary policy.

Where We Are Going...

In Part 2, we focus on developing a better understanding of the area of investments including how securities are valued and how securities markets operate. Chapter 7 examines how savings are directed into various investments, and Chapter 8 discusses how interest rates, or the "price" of money, are determined in the financial markets. Chapter 9 introduces "time" as a factor when determining rates of return on investments. In the remaining chapters you will learn about the characteristics of bonds and stocks and how they are priced or valued, how securities markets work, and the need to consider risk versus return trade-offs when investing in securities.

How This Chapter Applies to Me...

You live in a global environment. You likely have already purchased products grown or manufactured in foreign countries and sold in the United States. For example, you may purchase fresh fruit during the winter that was grown in and shipped from South America. Or, you may have purchased a Swiss-made watch from a retail store in the United States. You may also have had to convert U.S. dollars into a foreign currency such as euros for a direct product purchase from a manufacturer in Germany. You may have traveled internationally and needed to exchange your dollars for that country's currency. You may even live and work outside the United States in the future. Thus, a basic understanding of international trade and factors that affect currency exchange rates will be useful knowledge to have.

It is important to have an "open view" of other countries from the perspective of what they do and why they do it. Maria Mitchell, a U.S. astronomer, probably summed it up best when she stated:

I have never been in any country where they did not do something better than we do it, think some thoughts better than we think, catch some inspiration from heights above their own.

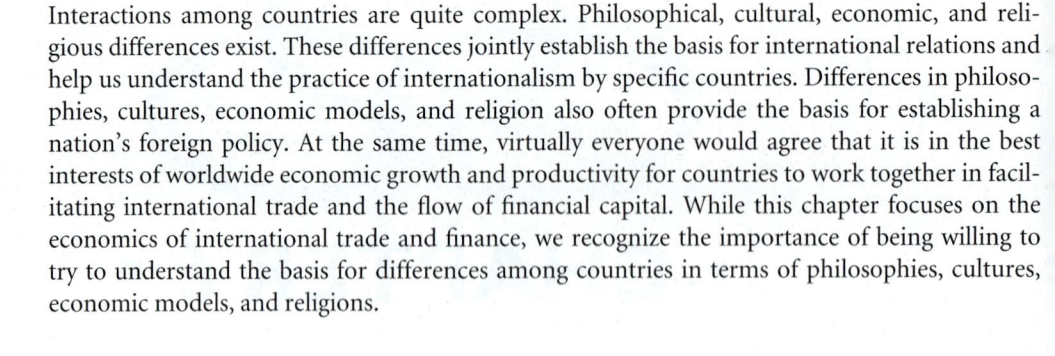

Interactions among countries are quite complex. Philosophical, cultural, economic, and religious differences exist. These differences jointly establish the basis for international relations and help us understand the practice of internationalism by specific countries. Differences in philosophies, cultures, economic models, and religion also often provide the basis for establishing a nation's foreign policy. At the same time, virtually everyone would agree that it is in the best interests of worldwide economic growth and productivity for countries to work together in facilitating international trade and the flow of financial capital. While this chapter focuses on the economics of international trade and finance, we recognize the importance of being willing to try to understand the basis for differences among countries in terms of philosophies, cultures, economic models, and religions.

GLOBAL OR INTERNATIONAL MONETARY SYSTEM

In the first five chapters of Part 1, we focused on covering the role of the U.S. financial system, the monetary system, and monetary policy. When viewed in a global context, responsibilities become more complex. The global or **international monetary system** is a system of institutions and mechanisms to foster world trade, manage the flow of financial capital, and determine currency exchange rates. We first begin with a brief discussion of the historical development of international trade and finance. Then we turn our attention to how the international monetary system has changed or evolved over the past couple of centuries.

international monetary system
institutions and mechanisms to foster international trade, manage the flow of financial capital, and determine currency exchange rates

DEVELOPMENT OF INTERNATIONAL FINANCE

International finance probably began about 5,000 years ago when Babylonian cities rose to importance as centers of trading between the Mediterranean Sea and civilizations in the East. Gold was used for transactions and as a store of value probably beginning around 3000 B.C., when the pharaohs ruled Egypt. Centers of international finance shifted to the Greek city of Athens around 500 B.C. and to the Roman Empire and Rome around 100 B.C.[1] It appears that whenever international trade developed, financial institutions came into existence and international bankers followed.

Instruments and documents similar to those in use today were designed to control movement of cargo, insure against losses, satisfy government requirements, and transfer funds. Financial centers shifted to the northern European cities during the 1500s, and in more recent years to London, New York, and Tokyo. Today, international trade takes place and international claims are settled around the clock. It is no longer necessary to have a physical center, such as a city, in which to carry out international financial operations.

HOW THE INTERNATIONAL MONETARY SYSTEM EVOLVED

Before World War I

Prior to the start of World War I in 1914, the international monetary system operated mostly under a **gold standard** whereby the currencies of major countries were convertible into gold at fixed exchange rates. For example, 1 ounce of gold might be worth 20 U.S. dollars, or $1 would be worth one-twentieth (or .05) of an ounce of gold. At the same time, 1 ounce of gold might be worth 5 French francs (FF), or FF1 would be worth one-fifth (or .20) of an ounce of gold. Since $20 could be converted into 1 ounce of gold that could then be used to purchase 5 FF, or 20 U.S. dollars, the exchange rate between the dollar and franc would be 20 to 5, or 4 to 1. Alternatively, .20 ÷ .05 equals 4 to 1.

Recall from Chapter 1 that the American colonies relied primarily on the Spanish dollar to conduct business transactions prior to the 1800s. In 1792 the first U.S. monetary act was enacted and provided for a *bimetallic standard* based on both gold and silver. A standard based solely on gold was not adopted until 1879. In those days, coins were *full-bodied money* in that their metal content was worth the same as their face values. Paper money then was *representative full-bodied money* because the paper money was backed by an amount of precious metal equal to the money's face value.

gold standard
currencies of countries are convertible into gold at fixed exchange rates

CONCEPT CHECK
When did international finance begin?

What is meant by being on a gold standard?

---

[1]. For a more detailed look at the early development of international finance, see Robert D. Fraser, *International Banking and Finance,* 6th ed., Washington, DC: R&H Publishers, 1984, ch. 2.

INTERNET ACTIVITY

Go to the International Monetary Fund Web site, http://www.imf.org, and find information about "special drawing rights" and how they are used as reserve assets.

During the 1800s most other developed countries also had their own currencies tied to gold, silver, or both. By the end of the 1800s most countries had adopted just the gold standard. However, coinciding with the start of World War I, most countries went off the gold standard. For example, the Federal Reserve Act of 1913 provided for the issuance of Federal Reserve Notes, called *fiat money* because they were not backed by either gold or silver. Recall from Chapter 2 that the government decreed the notes to be "legal tender" for purposes of making payments and discharging public and private debts. Fiat money has value that is based solely on confidence in the U.S. government's being able to achieve economic growth and maintain price stability. Most foreign governments also moved to monetary systems based on fiat money.

A major criticism of the gold standard was that as the volume of world trade increased over the years, the supply of "new" gold would fail to keep pace. Thus, without some form of supplementary international money, the result would be international deflation. A second criticism of the gold standard was a lack of an international organization to monitor and report whether countries were deviating from the standard when it was in their own best interests.

World War I through World War II: 1915–1944

During the interwar period from 1915 through 1944, which encompassed most of World War 1, the period in between, and World War II, an attempt was made to go back onto the gold standard. Many nations returned to the gold standard during the 1920s only to go off it again in the early 1930s because of financial crises associated with the Great Depression. A series of bank failures and continued outflow of gold caused the United States to abandon the gold standard in 1933.

Bretton Woods Fixed Exchange Rate System: 1945–1972

In mid-1944, authorities from all major nations met in Bretton Woods, New Hampshire, to formulate a post–World War II international monetary system. The **International Monetary Fund (IMF)** was created to promote world trade through monitoring and maintaining fixed exchange rates and by making loans to countries facing balance of trade and payments problems. The International Bank for Reconstruction and Development or **World Bank** also was created to help economic growth in developing countries.

The most significant development of the conference was the exchange rate agreement commonly called the **Bretton Woods system,** in which individual currencies would be tied to gold through the U.S. dollar via fixed or pegged exchange rates. One ounce of gold was set equal to $35. Each participating country's currency was then set at a "par" or fixed value in relation to the U.S. dollar. For example, one French franc might be one-seventh of a U.S. dollar or $.1429. Thus, a franc would "indirectly" be worth $5 in gold (i.e., $35 ÷ 7). In essence, one franc could be exchanged for $.1429, which could be exchanged for $5 in gold (.1429 × $35).

Countries adopting the Bretton Woods system could hold their reserves either in gold or U.S. dollars because the dollar was the only currency on the gold standard. This eliminated one of the criticisms associated with all currencies being on a gold standard system in that world economic growth was restricted to the rate of increase in new gold production, since gold was the only monetary reserve. Since the Bretton Woods System allowed for the holding of both gold and U.S. dollars as foreign exchange reserves, this new monetary system allowed for less restrictive world economic growth. The negative side of the Bretton Woods system was that the U.S. government had to produce balance-of-payments deficits so that foreign exchange reserves would grow.

Unfortunately, by the 1960s the value of the U.S. gold stock was less than the amount of foreign holdings of dollars. This, of course, caused concern about the viability of the Bretton Woods system. To help keep the system operating, in 1970 the International Monetary Fund (IMF) created a new reserve asset called *special drawing rights (SDRs)*, a basket or portfolio of currencies that could be used to make international payments. At first the SDR comprised a weighted average of sixteen currencies. At the beginning of the 1980s, the SDR basket was reduced to include only five major currencies. The current SDR basket includes the U.S. dollar (45 percent weight), euro (29 percent weight), Japanese yen (15 percent weight), and British pound (11 percent weight).

Attempts were made to save the Bretton Woods system in 1971 when representatives of major central banks met at the Smithsonian Institution in Washington, D.C., and raised the price of gold to $38 per ounce. In early 1973 the price of gold was further increased to $42 per ounce. However, the end of fixed exchange rates was at hand.

International Monetary Fund (IMF)
created to promote world trade through monitoring and maintaining fixed exchange rates and by making loans to countries with payments problems

World Bank
International Bank for Reconstruction and Development created to help economic growth in developing countries

Bretton Woods system
international monetary system in which the U.S. dollar was valued in gold and other exchange rates were pegged to the dollar

special drawing rights (SDRs)
reserve asset created by the IMF and consisting of a basket of currencies that could be used to make international payments

flexible exchange rates
a system in which currency exchange rates are determined by supply and demand

Flexible Exchange Rate System: 1973–Present

Beginning in March 1973 major currencies were allowed to "float" against one another. By the mid-1970s gold was abandoned as a reserve asset, and IMF members accepted a system of *flexible exchange rates*, in which currency exchange rates are determined by supply and demand. A primary objection to flexible exchange rates is the possibility of wide swings in response to changes in supply and demand, with a resulting uncertainty in world trade. Evidence indicates that exchange rates indeed have been much more volatile since the collapse of the Bretton Woods system compared to when the system was in place.

Today, many countries allow their currencies to float against others, including Australia, Japan, Canada, the United States, and the United Kingdom. The European Monetary Union also allows the euro to float freely. In contrast, India, China, and Russia employ semifloating or managed floating systems involving active government intervention. China, for example, pegs its currency to the dollar, with adjustments being related to monetary targets. Thus, the current exchange rate system is a composite of flexible or floating exchange rates, managed floating exchange rates, and pegged exchange rates.

CONCEPT CHECK

What was the Bretton Woods System of exchange rates?

What exchange rate system is in use today?

GLOBAL DISCUSSION

EUROPEAN UNIFICATION

EUROPEAN UNION

European Union (EU)
organization established to promote trade and economic development among European countries

Efforts to unify the countries of Europe have resulted in a common currency for twelve of the countries and major changes in the international monetary system. The **European Union (EU)** was established to promote trade and economic development among European countries. Economic integration was to be achieved by eliminating barriers that previously restricted the flow of labor, goods, and financial capital among countries. The European Union's history can be traced back to a treaty that established the *European Economic Community (EEC)* in 1957. The EEC became the *European Community (EC)* in 1978, and the EC became the EU in 1994.

In late 1991, members of the European Community met in Maastricht, Netherlands, to prepare, sign, and later ratify the *Maastricht Treaty*, which provided for economic convergence, the fixing of member country exchange rates, and the introduction of the euro as the common currency at the beginning of 1999. By 1995, the fifteen EU members were Austria, Belgium, Denmark, Finland, France, Germany, Greece, Ireland, Italy, Luxembourg, Netherlands, Portugal, Spain, Sweden, and the United Kingdom. In May 2004, the European Union grew to a total of twenty-five members with the addition of Cyprus, Czech Republic, Estonia, Hungary, Latvia, Lithuania, Malta, Poland, Slovakia, and Slovenia. At the beginning of 2007, Bulgaria and Romania were added to the European Union, resulting in a union of twenty-seven independent states.

EUROPEAN MONETARY UNION

European Monetary Union (EMU)
organization of European countries that agreed to have a common overall monetary policy and the euro as common currency

The **European Monetary Union (EMU)** began as a twelve-member subset of the original fifteen members. By ratifying the Maastricht Treaty, the EMU agreed to have overall monetary policy set by the *European Central Bank (ECB)* and adopted the euro as its common currency. Of the original fifteen EU members, Denmark, Sweden, and the United Kingdom chose not to join the EMU. Slovenia was added to the EMU in 2004 when it was allowed to adopt the euro as its currency. None of the other eleven "new" members of the EU that joined in 2004 or 2007 currently qualify for EMU status because they do not comply with the standards for budget deficits and government debt relative to gross domestic product.

euro
official currency of the countries in the European Monetary Union

THE EURO

CONCEPT CHECK

What is the European Union?

What is the European Monetary Union?

What is a euro?

On January 1, 1999, the official currency of the European Monetary Union members became the *euro*, a paper currency consisting of seven denominations from 5 to 500. Coins were designed and minted separately. At the beginning of 2002, individual EMU countries' currencies began being phased out; only the euro coin and currency were legal tender by July 2002.

Designing the euro paper currency was a difficult task. It could not include images (e.g., the Eiffel Tower) that could be associated with a single country. Likewise, portraits of individuals

SMALL BUSINESS PRACTICE
Finding Foreign Customers

To conduct business in a foreign country, a domestic firm must either export to that country or produce goods or offer services in that country. Exporting may take place indirectly or directly. Indirect exporting by U.S. companies involves U.S.-based exporters. These exporters may sell for manufacturers, buy for overseas customers, buy and sell for their own account, and/or buy on behalf of middle-persons or wholesalers.

Exporters that sell for manufacturers usually are manufacturers' export agents or export management companies. A manufacturer's export agent usually represents several noncompeting domestic manufacturers. An export management company acts as an export department for a number of noncompeting domestic firms. Exporters that purchase for overseas customers are called export commission agents since they are paid a commission by foreign purchasers to buy on their behalf.

Small businesses usually find it necessary to use indirect exporting. Direct exporting uses manufacturers' agents, distributors, and retailers located in the countries where they are conducting business. Only large domestic firms are able to engage in direct exporting.

Various forms of government assistance are available to help businesses in their exporting efforts. Many states have government "trade export" departments that assist firms in their export activities. At the federal level, the Export-Import Bank of the United States was founded in 1934 to aid domestic businesses in finding foreign customers and markets for their products. Export credit insurance also is available to help exporters. The Foreign Credit Insurance Association (FCIA) provides credit insurance policies to U.S. exporters to protect against nonpayment by foreign customers.

In some instances, "countertrading" is used to foster sales to foreign customers. Under such an arrangement, a U.S. exporter sells its goods to a foreign producer in exchange for goods produced by that foreign company. Simple kinds of countertrading take the form of a barter arrangement between a domestic firm and a foreign firm.

GLOBAL DISCUSSION

(e.g., royalty, military leaders) could not be used. Ultimately, the euro was designed to include "gates" and "windows" for the front of the bills "to symbolize the future"; "bridges" were chosen for the back of the bills. The paper currency uses multicolored ink, watermarks, and three-dimensional holographic images to thwart counterfeiting efforts.

currency exchange markets
electronic markets where banks and institutional traders buy and sell currencies on behalf of businesses, other clients, and themselves

foreign exchange markets
same as currency exchange markets

currency exchange rate
value of one currency relative to another currency

direct quotation method
indicates the amount of a home country's currency needed to purchase one unit of a foreign currency

indirect quotation method
indicates the number of units of a foreign currency needed to purchase one unit of the home country's currency

CURRENCY EXCHANGE MARKETS AND RATES

CURRENCY EXCHANGE MARKETS

We ordinarily think of a market as a specific place or institution, but this is not always so. **Currency exchange markets,** also called **foreign exchange markets,** are electronic markets where banks and institutional traders buy and sell various currencies on behalf of businesses, other clients, and themselves. The major financial centers of the world are connected electronically so that when an individual or firm engaged in a foreign transaction deals with a local bank, that individual or firm is, in effect, dealing with the exchange markets of the world. Transactions throughout the world may be completed in only a few minutes by virtue of the effective communications network serving the various financial institutions, including central banks of every nation.

EXCHANGE RATE QUOTATIONS

A **currency exchange rate** indicates the value of one currency relative to another currency. Table 6.1 shows the currency exchange rates for a variety of foreign currencies relative to the U.S. dollar on December 11, 2009. Currency exchange rates are stated in two basic ways. The **direct quotation method** indicates the value of one unit of a foreign currency in terms of a home country's currency. For illustration purposes, let's focus on the U.S. dollar as the domestic or home country's currency relative to the European Monetary Union's euro. Notice in Table 6.1 that the "U.S. dollar equivalent" of one euro was $1.4620; or, stated differently, it took $1.4620 to buy one euro. The **indirect quotation method** indicates the number of units of a foreign currency needed to purchase one unit of the home country's currency. By again turning to Table 6.1, we see that it takes .6840 euros to purchase one U.S. dollar.

Table 6.1 also shows the value of other major currencies in U.S. dollar terms on December 11, 2009. An Australia dollar was worth $.9124, a United Kingdom (British) pound had a value $1.6259, a Swiss franc equaled $.9669, and a Japanese yen was worth $.0112. The corresponding indirect quotations in units relative to one U.S. dollar were: Australia dollar = 1.0960, United Kingdom pound = .6150, Swiss franc = 1.0342, and Japanese yen = 89.17. It should be apparent

INTERNET ACTIVITY

Go to the European Central Bank Web site, http://www.ecb.int, and find information about the history of the euro.

CONCEPT CHECK

What are currency exchange markets?

INTERNET ACTIVITY

Go to the CNNMoney Web site, http://money.cnn.com. Access "markets" and then "currencies" and find current currency exchange rates for the U.S. dollar relative to the Australian dollar, British pound, and Canadian dollar. Find either the direct or indirect exchange rate and calculate the other one.

TABLE 6.1
Selected Foreign Exchange Rates, December 11, 2009

COUNTRY	CURRENCY	FOREIGN CURRENCY IN U.S. DOLLARS (DIRECT METHOD)	FOREIGN CURRENCY PER U.S. DOLLAR (INDIRECT METHOD)
Australia	Dollar	0.9124	1.0960
Canada	Dollar	0.9428	1.0607
China	Yuan	0.1465	6.8276
Denmark	Krone	0.1964	5.0907
Hong Kong	Dollar	0.1290	7.7508
India	Rupee	0.0215	46.5116
Japan	Yen	0.0112	89.1700
Mexico	Peso	0.0777	12.8705
Russia	Ruble	.0333	30.0300
Singapore	Dollar	0.7189	1.3910
South Africa	Rand	0.1335	7.4900
Sweden	Krona	0.1404	7.1246
Switzerland	Franc	0.9669	1.0342
United Kingdom	Pound	1.6259	0.6150
European Monetary Union	Euro	1.4620	0.6840

Sources: http://www.Reuters.com, http://www.money.cnn.com, and other sources.

that it is easy to find the other quotation if we know either the direct quotation or the indirect quotation. For example, the indirect quotation can be calculated as follows:

$$\text{Indirect Quotation (foreign currency units)} = \frac{1}{\text{Direct Quotation (home currency value)}} \quad (6.1)$$

For illustration purposes, let's use the euro versus U.S. dollar relationships previously noted. A euro was worth $1.4620 and represents a direct quotation where the United States is the home country. To find the indirect quotation, we would calculate:

$$\text{Indirect Quotation} = \frac{1}{\$1.4620} = .6840 \text{ euros}$$

Of course, if we knew that the indirect quotation for the euro relative to the dollar was .6840 euros per U.S. dollar, we could divide that value into 1 to get the direct quotation value: 1 ÷ .6840 = 1.4620 or $1.4620.

Table 6.2 shows the "crossrates" amongst several major currencies—the U.S. dollar, the British pound, the yen, and the euro. It is possible to calculate the exchange rate between the yen and the euro by first knowing each of their values relative to the U.S. dollar. For example, a yen was worth $.011215 and a euro $1.462 on December 11, 2009. Dividing .011215 by 1.46 gives a value of one yen in euros as 0.007671 euros. Since Table 6.2 shows the crossrates between the yen and the euro, we can read the value of one yen in terms of euros as 0.007671 euros. Of course, if we wanted to know the value of a Brazilian real in euros, we would have to return to Table 6.1 and make the calculation directly. On December 11, 2009, the U.S. dollar value of a Brazilian real was $.5683 and the value of a euro was $1.462. Dividing .5683 by 1.46 indicates that one real was worth .3887 euros.

TABLE 6.2
Selected Foreign Exchange Crossrates, December 11, 2009

CURRENCY	U.S DOLLAR	EURO	YEN	BRITISH POUND
U.S. Dollar	1.0	.6840	89.17	0.6150
Euro	1.4620	1.0	130.367	0.899
Yen	0.011215	0.007671	1.0	0.006897
British Pound	1.626	1.1121	144.98	1.0

Sources: http://www.Reuters.com, http://www.money.cnn.com, and other sources.

CONCEPT CHECK

What is the difference between the direct and indirect quotation methods for stating currency exchange rates?

It is worth noting that electronic and newspaper exchange rate quotes are for large unit transfers within the currency exchange markets. Consequently, individuals buying foreign currencies would not get exactly the same ratio. The currency exchange prices for an individual always favor the seller, who makes a margin of profit.

The balance in the foreign account of a U.S. bank is subject to constant drain as the bank sells foreign currency claims to individuals who import goods or obtain services from other countries. These banks may reestablish a given deposit level in their correspondent banks either through selling dollar claims in the foreign countries concerned or by buying claims from another dealer in the foreign exchange.

FACTORS THAT AFFECT CURRENCY EXCHANGE RATES

Each currency exchange rate shown in Table 6.1 is said to be a ***spot exchange rate,*** or the current rate being quoted for delivery of the currency "on the spot." Actually, it is common practice to have up to two days for delivery after the trade date. It is also possible to enter into a contract for the purchase or sale of a currency when delivery will take place at a future date. In this case, the negotiated exchange rate is referred to as a ***forward exchange rate.***

spot exchange rate
rate being quoted for current delivery of the currency

forward exchange rate
rate for the purchase or sale of a currency where delivery will take place at a future date

Supply and Demand Relationships

The supply and demand relationship involving two currencies is said to be in "balance" or equilibrium at the current or spot exchange rate. Demand for a foreign currency derives from the demand for the goods, services, and financial assets of a country (or group of countries, such as the EMU). For example, U.S. consumers and investors demand a variety of EMU member goods, services, and financial assets, most of which must be paid for in euros. The supply of euros comes from EMU member demand for U.S. goods, services, and financial assets. A change in the relative demand for euros versus U.S. dollars will cause the spot exchange rate to change. Currency exchange rates also depend on relative inflation rates, relative interest rates, and political and economic risks.

Figure 6.1 illustrates how exchange rates are determined in a currency exchange market. Graph A depicts a supply and demand relationship between the U.S. dollar and the European

FIGURE 6.1
Exchange Rate Determination in the Currency Exchange Market

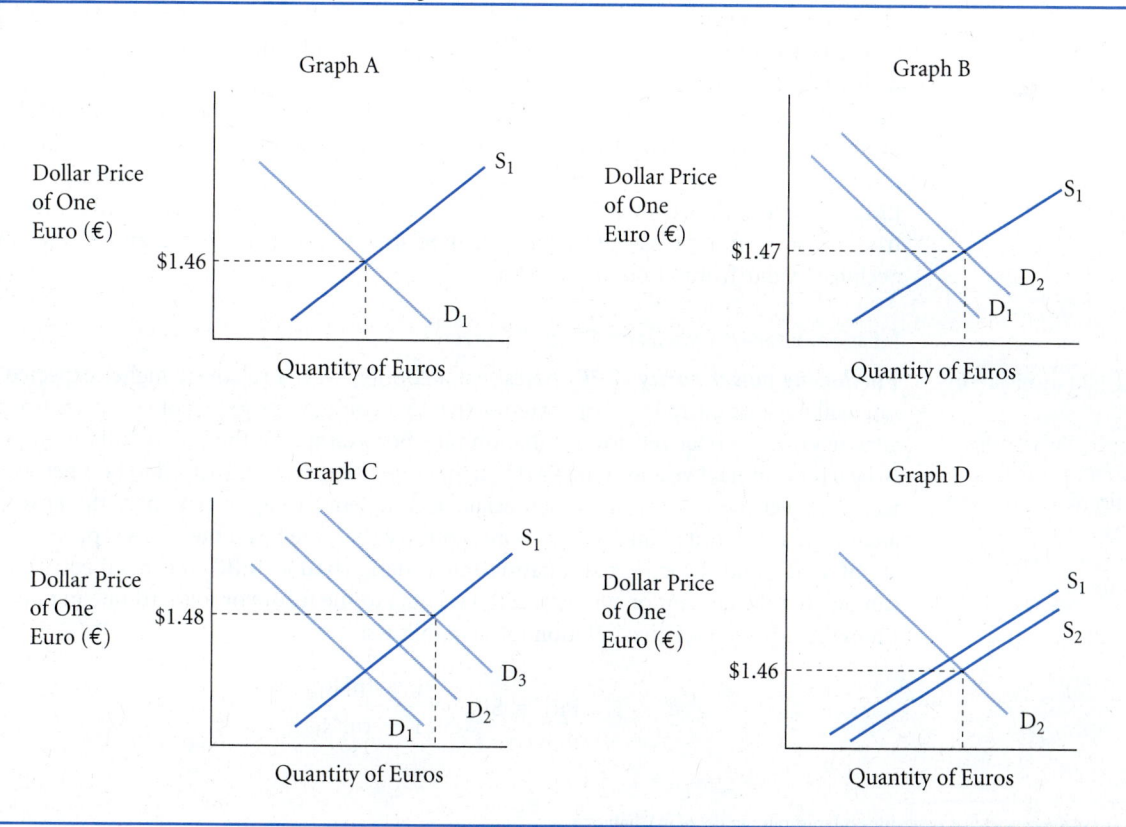

CONCEPT CHECK

What factors determine currency exchange rates?

Monetary Union euro (€). The market, in our example, is in balance when one euro is worth $1.46. This price reflects the market-clearing price that equates the demand (D_1) for euros relative to the supply (S_1) of euros.

Now, assume Americans increase their demand for products and services from EMU member countries such as Germany and France. These products and services would be priced in euros. Americans will need to exchange their dollars for euros to pay for their purchases. The consequence is an increase or shift in demand for euros from D_1 to D_2, as depicted in Graph B of Figure 6.1. The supply of euros reflects demand by EMU member countries for U.S. products and services, and as long as there is no change, S_1 will remain unchanged. As a consequence of this scenario, the increased demand for euros results in a new higher equilibrium price of $1.47.

A further increased demand for the goods and services from EMU member countries could cause the dollar price or value of one euro to increase even more. Graph C in Figure 6.1 depicts such an increase as a shift from D_2 to D_3. Again, with no change in the supply of euros, the new market-clearing price of a euro might be $1.48. Of course, as the euro's dollar value increases, the prices of EMU member products also increase. At some point, as EMU member products become more costly, U.S. demand for these foreign goods will decline. Graph D depicts this cutback in U.S. demand for euros as a shift downward from D_3 in Graph C to D_2. In a similar fashion, the higher dollar value of the euro in Graph C makes U.S. goods and services less costly to EMU members, and thus the supply of euros might increase or shift from S_1 to S_2. The net result could be a new equilibrium exchange rate in which the dollar price of a euro is $1.46.

A change in the demand for one country's financial assets relative to another country's financial assets also will cause the currency exchange rate between the two countries to change to a new equilibrium price. For example, a nation with a relatively strong stock market will attract investors who seek out the highest returns on their investment funds, much as a nation with a higher relative economic growth rate attracts capital investments. For example, if the stock market in the United States is expected to perform poorly relative to the stock markets in EMU member countries, investors will switch or move their debt investments denominated in U.S. dollars into euro-denominated debt investments. This increased demand for euros relative to U.S. dollars will cause the euro's dollar value to increase.

Now let's turn our attention to what happens if changes occur in relative nominal (observed) interest rates and inflation rates between two countries. Recall that the nominal interest rate for government debt securities is composed of a "real rate" plus an inflation expectation.[2] Thus, the higher (lower) the inflation rate, the higher (lower) will be the nominal interest rate. A nation with a relatively lower inflation rate will have a relatively stronger currency. For example, if inflation becomes lower in the United States relative to EMU member countries, EMU member products of comparable quality will become increasingly more expensive. Americans will find it less expensive to buy American products and so will EMU members. The result will be fewer EMU member imports into the United States and greater U.S. exports to EMU member countries, causing an appreciation of the dollar relative to the euro. For example, the euro might decline in value from $1.46 to, say, $1.44.

Inflation, Interest Rates, and Other Factors

Purchasing power parity (PPP) states that a country with a relatively higher expected inflation rate will have its currency depreciate relative to a country (or group of countries using a single currency) with a relatively lower inflation rate. For example, if the U.S. inflation rate is expected to be 6 percent next year and the EMU member inflation rate is expected to be 3 percent, then we would expect the U.S. dollar to depreciate and the euro to appreciate over the next year. Let's assume that the United States is the home country (hc), the EMU members represent the foreign country (fc), and the expected inflation rate is designated as InfR. In general equation form we can say that the current or spot rate (SR_0) is equal to the future or forward rate in one year (FR_1) times the expected relative inflation rates, as follows:

purchasing power parity (PPP)
currency of a country with relatively higher inflation rate will depreciate relative to the currency of a country with a relatively lower inflation rate

$$FR_1 = SR_0 \times \frac{1 + InfR_{hc}}{1 + InfR_{fc}} \qquad (6.2)$$

---

[2]. We will cover the factors that determine interest rates in detail in Chapter 8.

For our example, let's assume that the spot rate for a euro is $1.46. We estimate the forward rate as follows:

$$FR_1 = \$1.46 \times \frac{1.06}{1.03}$$

And,

$$FR_1 = \$1.46 \times 1.0291 = \$1.50$$

Thus, based on relative expected inflation rates, we expect the euro to appreciate from $1.46 to $1.50 over the next year.

Interest rate parity (IRP) states that a country with a relatively higher nominal interest rate will have its currency depreciate relative to a country with a relatively lower nominal interest rate. For example, let's assume that the interest rate (IntR) on a one-year U.S. government debt security is 9 percent while the interest rate on a comparable one-year EMU government debt security is 6 percent. We can use an equation similar to the one for PPP to calculate the forward rate based on IRP:

$$FR_1 = SR_0 \times \frac{1 + IntR_{hc}}{1 + IntR_{fc}} \tag{6.3}$$

interest rate parity (IRP) *currency of a country with a relatively higher interest rate will depreciate relative to the currency of a country with a relatively lower interest rate*

For consistency, let's assume that the spot rate for a euro is $1.46. We estimate the forward rate as follows:

$$FR_1 = \$1.46 \times \frac{1.09}{1.06}$$

And,

$$FR_1 = \$1.46 \times 1.0283 = \$1.50$$

Thus, based on relative one-year government interest rates, we expect the euro to appreciate from $1.46 to $1.50 over the next year.[3]

Political risk is the risk associated with the possibility that a national government might confiscate or expropriate assets held by foreigners. A nation with relatively lower political risk will generally have a relatively stronger currency. **Economic risk** is the risk associated with the possibility of slow or negative economic growth, as well as variability in economic growth. A nation that has a relatively higher economic growth rate, along with growth stability, will generally have a stronger currency. Furthermore, a nation with a relatively stronger economic growth rate will attract more capital inflows relative to a nation growing more slowly. For example, a stronger U.S. economy relative to the British economy will cause investors in both countries to switch from pound investments to dollar investments.

political risk *actions by a sovereign nation to interrupt or change the value of cash flows accruing to foreign investors*

economic risk *risk associated with possible slow or negative economic growth, as well as with the likelihood of variability*

CURRENCY EXCHANGE RATE APPRECIATION AND DEPRECIATION

The change (appreciation or depreciation) of a foreign currency (FC) relative to a domestic or home currency is typically expressed on a percentage basis:

$$\% \text{ FC Change} = \frac{\text{FC's New Value} - \text{FC's Old Value}}{\text{FC's Old Value}} \tag{6.4}$$

Let's use an example where the demand for EMU member financial assets increases relative to the demand for U.S. financial assets, causing the U.S. dollar value of the euro to increase from $1.46 to $1.49. The associated percent euro change would be:

$$\% \text{ Euro Change} = \frac{\$1.49 - \$1.46}{\$1.46} = \frac{\$0.03}{\$1.46} = 2.1\%$$

In other words, the euro would have appreciated by 2.1 percent relative to the dollar.

---

[3]. The PPP and IRP will provide slightly different estimates of the one-year forward rate if we extend the decimal places beyond two. This is due to the fact that the ratios of 1.06/1.03 and 1.09/1.06 are slightly different.

PERSONAL FINANCIAL PLANNING
Investing Overseas

People living in the United States are affected by international finance at least two ways. First, the growth or recession of overseas economies affects jobs in the United States. If foreign economies go into recession (as the Japanese and other Asian economies did in the mid- to late 1990s) there will be less export demand for U.S. goods and services. Thus, a worker's personal financial status can be imperiled by a layoff or reduced working hours.

The second effect on individuals is perhaps less clear to see—the effect of foreign investors on U.S. financial markets and interest rates. Stock and bond prices are affected, as is any other price, by supply and demand. Foreign inflows of capital into U.S. financial markets can help raise U.S. stock and bond prices, giving U.S. investors better returns on their own investment. Of course, money can flow out, too. If foreign investors sell their U.S. security holdings, this can lead to lower security prices and lower, even negative, returns to U.S. investors.

Pessimism about the strength of the U.S. dollar can even lead to higher U.S. interest rates on everything from Treasury bills to home mortgages. Here's how this can happen, using a Japanese investor as an example. A Japanese investor will compare U.S. and Japanese interest rates before deciding to, say, buy Japanese government debt or U.S. Treasury bonds. But, in addition to looking at U.S. interest rates, the Japanese investor will also consider the expected change in the U.S. dollar exchange rate with the Japanese yen. If the U.S. dollar is expected to weaken against the yen, that means the Japanese investor's U.S. dollar investment may lose value by the time it is converted back to yen at maturity. To be attractive, U.S. interest rates will have to be higher to compensate the Japanese investor for the falling dollar.

Suppose interest rates in Japan are 4 percent and economists predict the U.S. dollar will fall in value against the yen by 3 percent in the next year. That means Japanese investors will not find U.S. bonds attractive unless their interest rate is at least 4 percent (the Japanese interest rate) + 3 percent (the expected loss in the value of the U.S. dollar) or 7 percent. If the dollar is expected to fall by 5 percent, U.S. interest rates will have to be 9 percent (4 percent + 5 percent) to attract Japanese investors. A falling or weaker dollar puts upward pressure on interest rates throughout the U.S. economy.

Previously we discussed the possibility that the value of an EMU euro might drop from $1.46 to $1.44 if the inflation rate in the United States is lower than the inflation rate for the EMU member countries. The percent change in the euro would be calculated as:

$$\% \text{ Euro Change} = \frac{\$1.44 - \$1.46}{\$1.46} = \frac{-\$0.02}{\$1.46} = -1.4\%$$

INTERNET ACTIVITY

Go to the CNNMoney Web site, http://money.cnn.com. Access "markets" and then "currencies" and find current currency exchange rates for the U.S. dollar relative to the Japanese yen, European Monetary Union euro, and the Swiss franc. Find either the direct or indirect exchange rate and calculate the other one.

Thus, the euro has depreciated by 1.4 percent relative to the U.S. dollar because of the new and relatively higher EMU member inflation rate.

The amount of U.S. dollar ($US) appreciation or depreciation also can be easily calculated, since the value of one currency is simply the inverse of the other currency. For example, when the dollar price of a euro is $1.46, one $US is worth €0.6849 (i.e., 1 ÷ $1.46). Similarly, when the dollar price of a euro declines to $1.44, one $US is worth 1 ÷ $1.44, or €0.6944. When the dollar value of the euro increases, one dollar can be exchanged for fewer euros and vice versa.

An appreciation (or depreciation) of a home currency (HC) relative to a foreign currency can be expressed on a percentage basis as follows:

$$\% \text{ HC Change} = \frac{1/\text{FC's New Value} - 1/\text{FC's Old Value}}{1/\text{FC's Old Value}} \tag{6.5}$$

Using the preceding data for the relative interest rate example involving the American dollar and the EMU euro, we have:

$$\% \$US \text{ Change} = \frac{1/\$1.44 - 1/\$1.46}{1/\$1.46} = \frac{€0.6944 - €0.6849}{€0.6849} = \frac{0.0095}{0.6849} = 1.4\%$$

arbitrage
buying commodities, securities, or bills of exchange in one market and immediately selling them in another to make a profit from price differences in the two markets

Thus, the U.S. dollar in this example appreciated by 1.4 percent relative to the euro, which is the mirror opposite of the −1.4 percent decline (depreciation) of the euro from $1.46 to $1.44.

ARBITRAGE

Arbitrage is the simultaneous, or nearly simultaneous, purchasing of commodities, securities, or bills of exchange in one market and selling them in another where the price is higher. In international exchange, variations in quotations among countries at any time are quickly brought into alignment through the arbitrage activities of international financiers. For example, if the exchange rate was reported in New York at €1 = $1.34 and in Brussels, Belgium, at €1 = $1.33, alert international arbitrageurs simultaneously would sell claims to euros in New York at the rate of $1.34 and would have Brussels correspondents sell claims on U.S. dollars in Brussels at the rate of $1.33 for each euro. Such arbitrage would be profitable only when dealing in large sums. Under these circumstances, if an arbitrageur sold a claim on €100 million in New York, $134 million would be received. The corresponding sale of claims on American dollars in Brussels would be at the rate of €100 million for $133 million. Hence, a profit of $1 million would be realized on the transaction. A quotation differential of as little as one-sixteenth of one cent may be sufficient to encourage arbitrage activities.

The ultimate effect of large-scale arbitrage activities on exchange rates is the elimination of the variation between the two markets. The sale of large amounts of claims to American dollars in Brussels would drive up the price for euros, and in New York the sale of claims to euros would force the exchange rate down.

EXCHANGE RATE DEVELOPMENTS FOR THE U.S. DOLLAR

The dollar continues to be an important currency for international commercial and financial transactions. Because of this, both the United States and the rest of the world benefit from a strong and stable U.S. dollar. Its strength and stability depend directly on the ability of the United States to pursue noninflationary economic policies. In the late 1960s and the 1970s, the United States failed to meet this objective. Continuing high inflation led to a dollar crisis in 1978, which threatened the stability of international financial markets.

Figure 6.2 shows the strength of the dollar relative to an index of major currencies that trade widely outside the United States for the years 1980 through 2008. As inflation was brought under control in the early 1980s and economic growth accelerated after the 1981–1982 recession, the dollar rose against other major currencies until it reached record highs in 1985. As discussed, relatively higher economic growth and relatively lower inflation rates lead to a relatively stronger currency. These economic developments, coupled with a favorable political climate, caused the value of the dollar to rise sharply.

However, the renewed strength of the dollar contributed to a worsening of the trade imbalance because import prices were effectively reduced while exported U.S. goods became less cost competitive. Beginning in 1985, United States economic growth slowed relative to economic growth in other developed countries. Also, the belief that the U.S. government wanted the dollar to decline on a relative basis so as to reduce the trade deficit contributed to a decline in the

FIGURE 6.2
U.S. Dollar Value Relative to an Index of Major Currencies

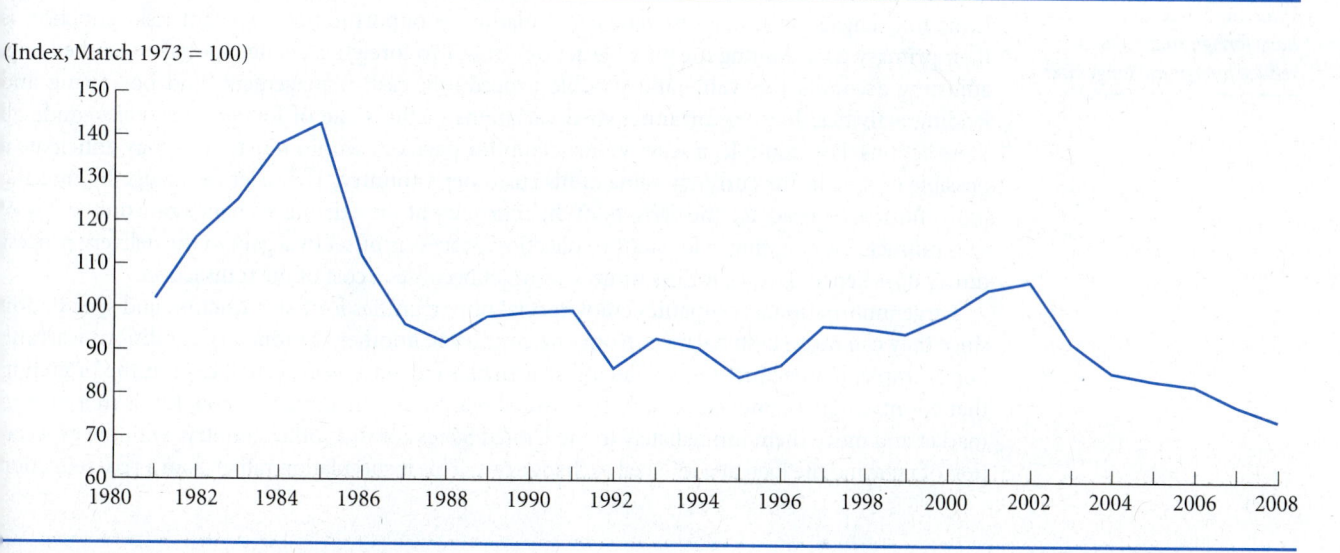

Source: Currency exchange rate data can be accessed at http://www.federalreserve.gov/releases/.

desirability of holding dollars. This resulted in a major shift toward holding more foreign assets and fewer U.S. assets. As a consequence, the dollar's value declined by 1987 to levels below those in place when flexible exchange rates were reestablished in 1973. Between 1987 and 2000, the value of the dollar in international exchange fluctuated within a fairly narrow range compared to the 1980–1987 period.

The U.S. dollar appreciated relative to other currencies in 2000 and 2001. Stock prices peaked in 2000 and then began declining rapidly as the "internet/tech" bubble burst. Declining stock prices were followed by a recession in 2001 and the terrorist attack on September 11, 2001. After first raising interest rates, the Federal Reserve moved quickly to reduce interest rates and to provide liquidity in the financial markets. The Fed then continued its high liquidity, low interest rate environment throughout the remainder of the decade. This financial markets environment was accompanied by large amounts of borrowing by business firms, financial institutions, and individuals. Housing prices peaked in 2006, stock prices peaked in 2007, and the U.S. economy was in recession in 2008. Debt-heavy individuals began defaulting on their home mortgages, financial institutions were finding it difficult to remain solvent, and business firms were failing during this "perfect financial storm." These economic developments were accompanied by the U.S. dollar declining rapidly against an index of major currencies beginning in 2002. Figure 6.2 shows this decline continuing through 2008.

The U.S. dollar continued to decline relative to other major currencies throughout most of 2009. The low value of the U.S. dollar in December 2009 relative to most other individual currencies is shown in Table 6.1. As the end of 2009 neared, the worst of the U.S. financial crisis seemed to be over. However, efforts to stimulate the U.S. economy resulted in large annual budget deficits and a record national debt.

In contrast, a stronger dollar leads to concern about the deficit in the U.S. trade balance, but at the same time it offers hope of lower inflation. A stronger dollar results in more imports of foreign merchandise since it requires fewer dollars for purchase. Just as a U.S. tourist abroad finds it cheaper to travel when the dollar is strong, importers find prices lower when their dollars increase in relative strength. When the dollar weakens, inflation may follow, countered by a reduced balance of trade deficit. We discuss balance of trade and balance of payments implications in the last section of this chapter.

CONDUCTING BUSINESS INTERNATIONALLY

MANAGING FOREIGN EXCHANGE RISK

Firms that have foreign sales must be concerned with the stability of the governments and changing values of currency in the countries in which they do business. They must also pay attention to commodity price changes and other uncertainties related to monetary systems.

Large firms usually have special departments that handle international transactions. These firms may engage in foreign exchange speculation as opportunities arise, but risk reduction is their primary goal. Among the possible actions of skilled foreign exchange specialists are hedging, adjusting accounts receivable and payable procedures, cash management, and borrowing and lending activities. Existing or anticipated variations in the value of foreign currencies guide all these actions. For example, a seller with a claim for payment within ninety days may anticipate a possible decline in the currency value of his customer's country. The seller can hedge by entering into a futures contract for the delivery of that currency at the existing exchange rate on the day of the contract.[4] By so doing, a loss in the collection process is offset by a gain in the delivery process ninety days hence. The fee for the futures contract becomes a cost of the transaction.

Large multinational companies enjoy special opportunities for risk reduction and speculation since they can move cash balances from one country to another as monetary conditions warrant. For example, if a decline in the value of a particular currency is expected, cash in the branch in that country may be moved back to the United States, or a firm may borrow funds in a foreign market and move them immediately to the United States (or to another country) with the expectation of repaying the loan at a reduced exchange rate. This is speculation rather than a risk-reduction

CONCEPT CHECK
What actions can firms that have foreign sales take to reduce foreign exchange risk?

---
[4]. We discuss futures contracts in the Learning Extension at the end of Chapter 11.

activity. An expected decline in a currency may lead to an attempt to accelerate collection of accounts receivable, with funds transferred quickly to another country. Payments on accounts payable may be delayed in the expectation of a decline in exchange rates. If, on the other hand, a foreign currency is expected to increase in relative value, the preceding actions would be reversed.

New career opportunities have developed with the increasing importance of multinational financial management. Some corporations maintain special departments to study foreign business activities and their prospective profitability; to analyze governmental attitudes, tax rates, and duties; and to determine how foreign operations are to be financed. In addition, to protect bank balances and other investments, almost constant attention must be given to day-to-day exchange rate changes.

ETHICAL CONSIDERATIONS

The concept of acceptable ethical behavior differs across cultures and countries. In some primarily developing countries, it seems to be acceptable practice for government officials and others to request "side" payments and even bribes as a means for foreign companies being able to do business in these countries. This is morally wrong. In addition, the Foreign Corrupt Practices Act (FCPA) prohibits U.S. firms from bribing foreign officials. For violators of the FCPA, the U.S. Justice Department may impose monetary penalties and criminal proceedings may be brought against violators. Government actions may result in lost reputations and firm values.

For example, Titan Corporation had its proposed 2004 sale to Lockheed Martin Corporation implode because it could not promptly resolve a bribery investigation brought by the Justice Department.[5] Another example was the 2004 indictment of two former HealthSouth Corporation executives for conspiracy in a bribery scheme involving a Saudi Arabian hospital. An attempt was made to conceal the bribery by setting up a bogus consulting contract for the director general of the Saudi foundation that owned the hospital. The former HealthSouth executives were indicted after a Justice Department investigation alleged that they had violated the *U.S. Travel Act* by using interstate commerce when making the bribes and the FCPA by falsely reflecting the bogus bribe payments as legitimate consulting expenses on HealthSouth's financial statements.[6]

When conducting business activities in certain foreign countries, business executives also are sometimes faced with extortion demands by organized criminals. Most of us would agree that extortion payments are morally wrong. Paying organized criminals is not different from paying corrupt government officials.

FINANCING INTERNATIONAL TRADE

One of the substantial financial burdens of any industrial firm is the process of manufacture itself. When a U.S. manufacturer exports goods to distant places such as India or Australia, funds are tied up not only for the period of manufacture but also for a lengthy period of transportation. To reduce costs, manufacturers may require the foreign importer to pay for the goods as soon as they are on the way to their destination. In this way, a substantial financial burden is transferred to the importer.

FINANCING BY THE EXPORTER

If the exporter has confidence in foreign customers and is in a financial position to sell to them on an open-book account, then sales arrangements should operate very much as in domestic trade, subject, of course, to the complex nature of any international transaction.

Sight and Time Drafts

draft (bill of exchange) an unconditional order for the payment of money from one person to another

As an alternative to shipping merchandise on open-account financing, the exporter may use a collection draft. A ***draft (bill of exchange)*** is an unconditional written order, signed by the party

---

5. Jonathan Karp, "As Titan Mutates to Meet Needs of Pentagon, Risks Become Clear," *The Wall Street Journal* (June 28, 2004), p. A1.
6. "Ex-HealthSouth Execs Indicted," http://money.cnn.com/2004/07/01/news/international/healthsouth.reut/index.htm, accessed July 7, 2004.

FIGURE 6.3
Sight Draft or Bill of Exchange

```
$ 2,500.00            New Orleans, Louisiana, August 15, 20-

   At sight - - - - - - - - - - - - - - - - - - - - - -
                                                              PAY TO THE
              Mervin J. Mansfield
   ORDER OF

   Two thousand five hundred no/100 - - - - - -
                                                                 DOLLARS

VALUE RECEIVED AND CHARGE TO ACCOUNT OF
        Brazilian Import Company              NEW ORLEANS EXPORT COMPANY
   TO
        11678 Rio de Janeiro, Brazil            Theresa M. Jones
   No.
```

sight draft
draft requiring immediate payment

time draft
draft that is payable at a specified future date

documentary draft
draft that is accompanied by an order bill of lading and other documents

order bill of lading
document given by a transportation company that lists goods to be transported and terms of the shipping agreement

clean draft
a draft that is not accompanied by any special documents

CONCEPT CHECK
What is meant by a draft or bill of exchange?

What is an order bill of lading?

drawing it, requiring the party to whom it is addressed to pay a certain sum of money to order or to bearer. A draft may require immediate payment by the importer upon its presentation—on demand—or it may require only acceptance on the part of the importer, providing for payment at a specified future time. An instrument requiring immediate payment is classified as a **sight draft**; one requiring payment later is a **time draft**. A draft may require remittance, or payment, in the currency of the country of the exporter or of the importer, depending on the transaction's terms. An example of a sight draft form is shown in Figure 6.3.

Drafts may be either documentary or clean. A **documentary draft** is accompanied by an order bill of lading along with other papers such as insurance receipts, certificates of sanitation, and consular invoices. The **order bill of lading** (see Figure 6.4) represents the written acceptance of goods for shipment by a transportation company and the terms under which the goods are to be transported to their destination. In addition, the order bill of lading carries title to the merchandise being shipped, and only its holder may claim the merchandise from the transportation company. The documentary sight draft is generally referred to as a D/P draft (documentary payments draft), and the documentary time draft is referred to as a D/A draft (documentary acceptance draft).

A **clean draft** is one that is not accompanied by any special documents and is generally used when the exporter has confidence in the importer's ability to meet the draft when presented. Once the merchandise is shipped to the importer, it is delivered by the transportation company, regardless of any actions by the importer in terms of the draft.

Bank Assistance in the Collection of Drafts

An importer will generally try to avoid paying for a purchase before the goods are actually shipped, because several days or perhaps weeks may elapse before the goods arrive. But the exporter is often unwilling to send the draft and documents directly to the importer. Therefore, the exporter usually works through a commercial bank.

A New York exporter dealing with an importer in Portugal with whom there has been little experience may ship goods on the basis of a documentary draft that has been deposited for collection with the local bank. That bank, following the specific instructions regarding the manner of collection, forwards the draft and the accompanying documents to its correspondent bank in Lisbon. The correspondent bank holds the documents until payment is made in the case of a sight draft or until acceptance is obtained if a time draft is used. When collection is made on a sight draft, it is remitted to the exporter.

Financing Through the Exporter's Bank

It is important to recognize that throughout the preceding transaction the banking system only provided a service to the exporter and in no way financed the transaction itself. The exporter's bank, however, may offer financing assistance by allowing the exporter to borrow against the security of a documentary draft. Such loans have the financial strength of both the exporter and

FIGURE 6.4
Order Bill of Lading

UNITED STATES LINES CO.

(SPACES IMMEDIATELY BELOW FOR SHIPPERS MEMORANDA– NOT PART OF BILL OF LADING)

FORWARDING AGENT – REFERENCES	EXPORT DEC. No.
John Doe Shipping Co., #E6776 F.M.B. #9786	X67-90687

DELIVERING CARRIER TO STEAMER:	CAR NUMBER – REFERENCE
Penn Central Company	876528

BILL OF LADING (SHORT FORM)   (NOT NEGOTIABLE UNLESS CONSIGNED "TO ORDER")

SHIP American Banker	FLAG	PIER 61 N.R.	PORT OF LOADING NEW YORK
PORT OF DISCHARGE FROM SHIP Liverpool	AM.	THROUGH BILL OF LADING	

SHIPPER Midwest Printing Company

CONSIGNED TO: ORDER OF M.T. Wilson & Co.

ADDRESS ARRIVAL NOTICE TO Same at 15 Dock St., Liverpool, E.C. 3

PARTICULARS FURNISHED BY SHIPPER OF GOODS

MARKS AND NUMBERS	NO. OF PKGS.	DESCRIPTION OF PACKAGES AND GOODS	MEASUREMENT	GROSS WEIGHT IN POUNDS
M. T. W. & Co. Liverpool	56	Books		10,145
		SPECIMEN		

FREIGHT PAYABLE IN NEW YORK

(10,145) @ ____ PER 2240 LBS..... $ ____
____ @ ____ PER 100 LBS....... $ ____
____ FT. @ ____ PER 40 CU. FT.... $ ____
545 FT. @ $1.05 PER CU. FT....... $ 572 25
____ $ ____
____ $ ____
____ $ ____
____ $ ____
TOTAL............. $ ____

(TERMS OF THIS BILL OF LADING CONTINUED FROM REVERSE SIDE HEREOF)

IN WITNESS WHEREOF,
THE MASTER OR AGENT OF SAID VESSEL HAS SIGNED........ **3**
BILLS OF LADING, ALL OF THE SAME TENOR AND DATE, ONE OF WHICH
BEING ACCOMPLISHED, THE OTHERS TO STAND VOID.

UNITED STATES LINES COMPANY
BY *JD*
FOR THE MASTER
ISSUED AT NEW YORK, N.Y.

B/L No.
M-105

January 12 20--
MO. DAY YEAR

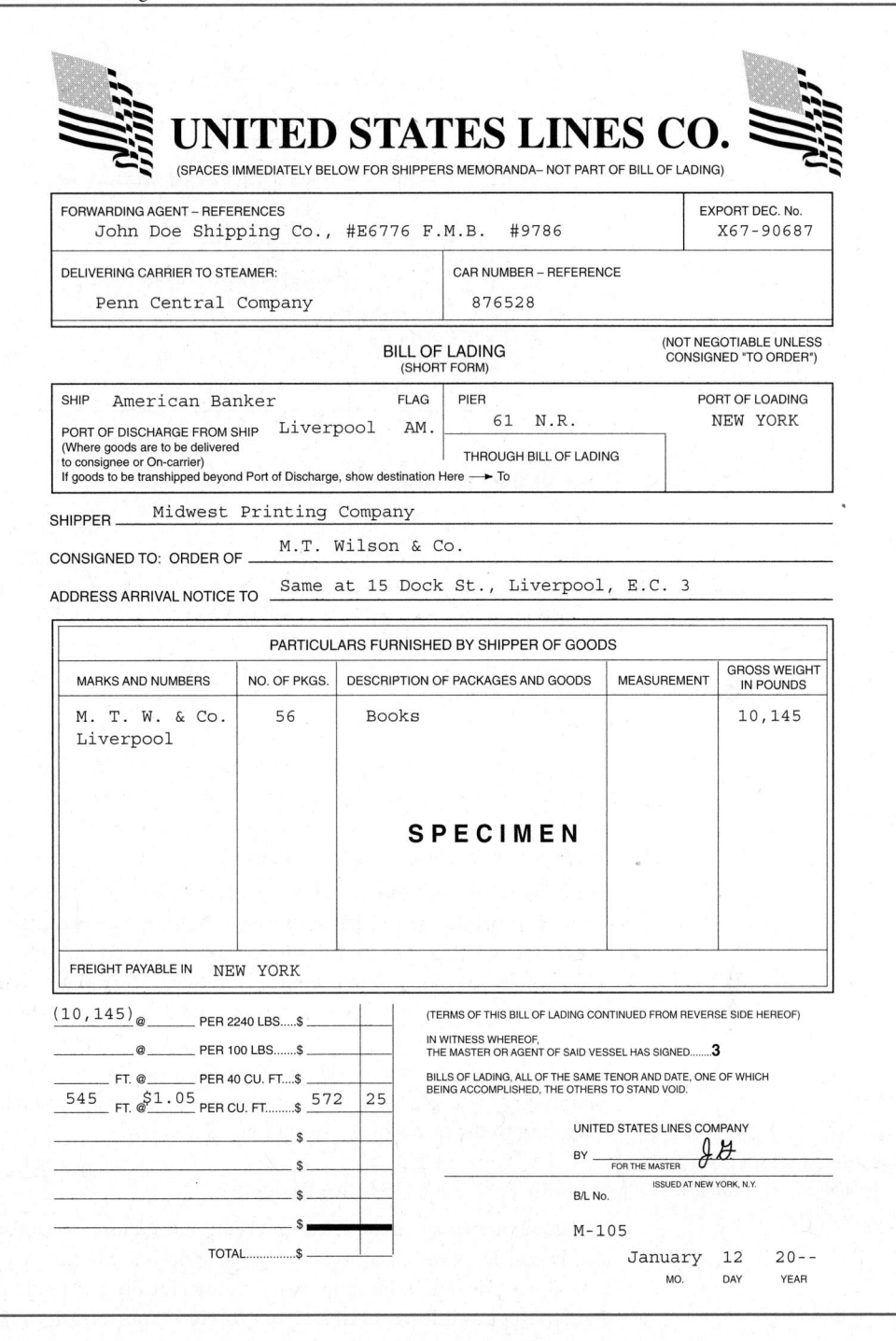

the importer to support them, since documents for taking possession of the merchandise are released only after the importer has accepted the draft.

The amount that the exporter can borrow is less than the face amount of the draft and depends mainly on the credit standing of both the exporter and the importer. When the exporter is financially strong enough to offer suitable protection to the bank, a substantial percentage of the draft may be advanced even though the importer may not be known to the exporter's bank. In other cases, the advance may be based on the importer's financial strength.

The character of the goods shipped also has an important bearing on the amount lent, since the goods offer collateral security for the advance. Goods that are not breakable or perishable are better as collateral; goods for which there is a ready market are preferable to those with a very limited market.

FIGURE 6.5
Banker's Acceptance

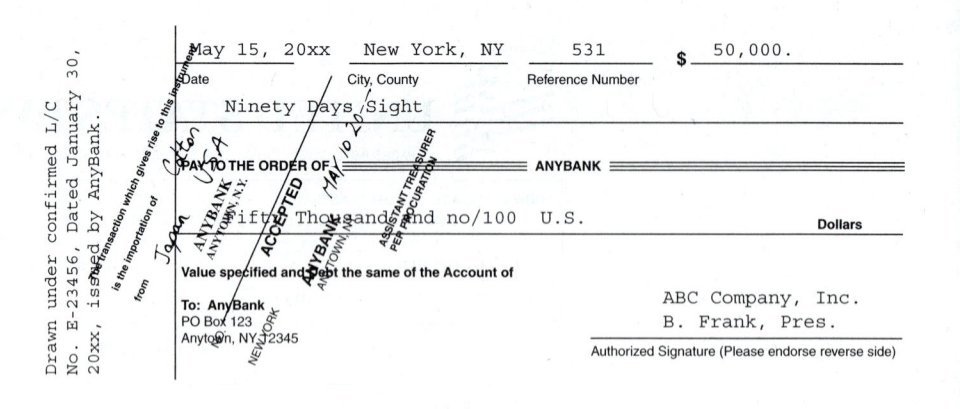

```
May 15, 20xx    New York, NY      531        $  50,000.
Date            City, County      Reference Number

Ninety Days Sight

PAY TO THE ORDER OF ══════════════ ANYBANK ══════════════

Fifty Thousand and no/100   U.S.                   Dollars

Value specified and debt the same of the Account of

To: AnyBank                              ABC Company, Inc.
    PO Box 123                           B. Frank, Pres.
    Anytown, NY 12345                    Authorized Signature (Please endorse reverse side)
```

(Drawn under confirmed L/C No. E-23456, Dated January 30, 20xx, issued by AnyBank. This transaction which gives rise to this instrument is the importation of Japan from USA. ACCEPTED MAY 10 20xx ANYBANK ANYTOWN NY. ASSISTANT TREASURER PER PROCURATION)

FINANCING BY THE IMPORTER

Like the exporter, the importer may also arrange payment for goods without access to bank credit. When an order is placed, payment in full may be made or a partial payment offered. The partial payment gives some protection to both the exporter and the importer. It protects the exporter against rejection of the goods for no reason, and it gives the importer some bargaining power in the event the merchandise is damaged in shipment or does not meet specifications. When the importer is required to make full payment with an order but wants some protection in the transaction, payment is sent to a bank in the exporter's country. The bank is instructed not to release payment until certain documents are presented to the bank to prove shipment of the goods according to the terms of the transaction. The bank, of course, charges a fee for this service.

Financing Through the Importer's Bank

In foreign trade, because of language barriers and the difficulty in obtaining credit information about companies in foreign countries, the use of the banker's acceptance is common. The *banker's acceptance* is a draft drawn on and accepted by a bank rather than the importing firm. An example of a banker's acceptance is shown in Figure 6.5. The importer must, of course, make arrangements with the bank in advance. The exporter, too, must know before shipment is made whether or not the bank in question has agreed to accept the draft. This arrangement is facilitated by the use of a **commercial letter of credit,** a bank's written statement to an individual or firm guaranteeing acceptance and payment of a draft up to a specified sum if the draft is presented according to the terms of the letter (see Figure 6.6).

commercial letter of credit
statement by a bank guaranteeing acceptance and payment of a draft up to a stated amount

Importer Bank Financing—An Example

The issue of a commercial letter of credit and its use in international finance are shown in this example. The owner of a small exclusive shop in Chicago wishes to import expensive perfumes from Paris. Although the shop is well known locally, its financial reputation is not known widely enough to permit it to purchase from foreign exporters on the basis of an open-book account or drafts drawn on the firm. Under these circumstances the firm would substitute the bank's credit for its own through the use of a letter of credit. Upon application by the firm, the bank issues the letter if it is entirely satisfied that its customer is in a satisfactory financial condition.

The letter of credit is addressed to the French exporter of perfumes. The exporter, upon receipt of the commercial letter of credit, would not be concerned about making the shipment. Although the exporter may not have heard of the Chicago firm, the bank issuing the commercial letter of credit may be known to the exporter or to his bank. (International bank directories provide bank credit information.) The French exporter then ships the perfumes and at the same time draws a draft in the appropriate amount on the bank that issued the letter of credit. The draft and the other papers required by the commercial letter of credit are presented to the exporter's bank. The bank sends the draft and the accompanying documents to its New York

FIGURE 6.6
Irrevocable Commercial Letter of Credit

```
Irrevocable Commercial      AnyBank                    AnyBank           Cable Address:   Letter Of Credit
Letter Of Credit            P.O. Box 123                                 AnyBank          Division
                            Anytown, New York 12345

                            May 2, 20--                                      $50,000.

         Drafts drawn hereunder must be marked
         "Drawn under AnyBank Anytown
         L/C Ref.  E-23456       "and indicate the date hereof

              ABC Company, Inc.
              B. Frank, President
                                                SPECIMEN

         Gentlemen:
         We hereby authorize you to draw on  AnyBank, Anytown

         by order of    J. R. Doe & Company, New York, N.Y.

         and for account of   J. R. Doe & Company

         up to an aggregate amount of    Fifty Thousand Dollars U.S. Currency

         available by your drafts at  90 days sight, for full invoice value, in duplicate
         accompanied by   Commercial Invoice in triplicate . . .
                          Consular Invoice in duplicate . . .
                          Full set of onboard Bills of Lading to order of AnyBank,
         Anytown, marked Notify J. R. Doe & Company, New York,N.Y., and bearing
         a separate onboard endorsement signed by the Master and also marked
         freight collect at port of destination . . . .

         Relating to shipment of Cotton.

         . . . Any charges for negotiation of the draft(s) are for your account.
         . . . Marine and war risk insurance covered by buyers.


         Drafts must be drawn and negotiated  not later than   October 2, 20--

         The amounts thereof must be endorsed on this Letter Of Credit.
         We hereby agree with the drawers, endorsers, and bonafide holders of all drafts drawn under and in compliance
         with the terms of this credit, that such drafts will be duly honored upon presentation to the drawee.
         This letter of credit is subject to the Uniform Customs and Practice for Documentary Credits (1974 Revision) Inter-
         national Chamber Of Commerce Publication No. 290.

                                                                    Yours very truly,

                                                                    D.E. Price

                                                                    D. E. Price
                                                                    Vice President
                                                                    Authorized Signature
```

correspondent, who forwards them to the importer's bank in Chicago. The importer's bank thoroughly inspects the papers that accompany the draft to make sure that all provisions of the letter of credit have been met. If the bank is satisfied, the draft is accepted and the appropriate bank officials sign it. The accepted draft, now a banker's acceptance, may be held until maturity by the accepting bank or returned to the exporter on request. If the acceptance is returned to the exporter, it may be held until maturity and sent to the accepting bank for settlement or it may be sold to other investors. An active market for bankers' acceptances exists in the world's money centers.

After having accepted the draft, the Chicago bank notifies its customer that it has the shipping documents and that arrangements should be made to take them over. As the shop sells the perfume, it builds up its bank account with daily deposits until it is sufficient to retire the acceptance. The bank can then meet its obligation on the acceptance without having advanced its own funds at any time.

trust receipt
an instrument through which a bank retains title to goods until they are paid for

In releasing shipping documents to a customer, some banks prefer to establish an agency arrangement between the firm and the bank whereby the bank retains title to the merchandise. The instrument that provides for this is called a ***trust receipt.*** Should the business fail, the bank would not be in the position of an ordinary creditor trying to establish its claim on the business assets. Rather, it could repossess, or take back, the goods and place them with another agent for sale since title had never been transferred to the customer. As the merchandise is sold under a trust receipt arrangement, generally the business must deposit the proceeds with the bank until the total amount of the acceptance is reached.

In summary, the banker's acceptance and the commercial letter of credit involve four principal parties: the importer, the importer's bank, the exporter, and the exporter's bank. Each benefits to a substantial degree through this arrangement. The importer benefits by securing adequate credit. The importer's bank benefits because it receives a fee for issuing the commercial letter of credit and for the other services provided in connection with it. The exporter benefits by being assured that payment will be made for the shipment of merchandise. Thus, a sale is made that might otherwise have been rejected because of lack of guaranteed payment. Finally, the exporter's bank benefits if it discounts the acceptance, since it receives a high-grade credit instrument with a definite, short-term maturity. Acceptances held by commercial banks provide a low, but certain, yield, and banks can liquidate them quickly if funds are needed for other purposes.

CONCEPT CHECK
What is meant by a commercial letter of credit?
What is a trust receipt?

BANKERS' ACCEPTANCES

The Board of Governors of the Federal Reserve System authorizes member banks to accept drafts that arise in the course of certain types of international transactions. These include the import and export of goods, the shipment of goods between foreign countries, and the storage of highly marketable staple goods in any foreign country. A ***banker's acceptance*** is a promise of future payment issued by a firm and guaranteed by a bank. The maturity of a banker's acceptance arising out of international transactions may not exceed six months. This authority to engage in banker's acceptance financing is intended to encourage banks to participate in financing international trade and to strengthen the U.S. dollar abroad.

banker's acceptance
a promise of future payment issued by a firm and guaranteed by a bank

Bankers' acceptances are used to finance international transactions on a wide variety of items, including coffee, wool, rubber, cocoa, metals and ores, crude oil, jute, and automobiles. Because of the growth of international trade in general and the increasing competition in foreign markets, banker's acceptances have become increasingly important. Exporters have had to offer more liberal terms on their sales to compete effectively. The banker's acceptance permits them to do so without undue risk.

The cost of financing an international transaction with the banker's acceptance involves not only the interest cost involved in the exporter's discounting the acceptance but also the commission charge of the importer's accepting bank. Foreign central banks and commercial banks regard banker's acceptances as attractive short-term funds commitments. In recent years, foreign banks have held more than half of all dollar-denominated banker's acceptances, with most of the remainder held by domestic banks. Nonfinancial corporations have played only a small role as investors in acceptances. Relatively few firms deal in banker's acceptances. These dealers arrange nearly simultaneous exchanges of purchases and sales.

CONCEPT CHECK
What are bankers' acceptances and how are they used?

OTHER AIDS TO INTERNATIONAL TRADE

The Export-Import Bank

The ***Export-Import Bank*** was authorized in 1934 and became an independent agency of the government in 1945. The bank's purpose is to help finance and facilitate exports and imports between the United States and other countries. It is the only U.S. agency engaged solely in financing foreign trade.

Export-Import Bank
bank established to aid in financing and facilitating trade between the United States and other countries

The Export-Import Bank is a government-owned corporation with capital of $1 billion in nonvoting stock paid in by the U.S. Treasury. It may borrow from the Treasury on a revolving basis and sell short-term discount promissory notes. It pays interest on these loans and dividends on the capital stock. In performing its function, the bank makes long-term loans to private enterprises and governments abroad to finance the purchase of U.S. equipment, goods, and services. The Export-Import Bank also aids substantially in the economic development of foreign countries by giving emergency credits to assist them in maintaining their level of U.S.

imports during temporary balance-of-payments difficulties. In addition, the bank finances or guarantees the payment of medium-term commercial export credit extended by exporters and, in partnership with private insurance companies, offers short- and medium-term credit insurance. It lends and guarantees only where repayment is reasonably assured and avoids competition with sources of private capital.

Traveler's Letter of Credit

A firm's buyer who is traveling abroad may not know in advance from which individuals or firms purchases will be made—for example, an art buyer touring several countries. The buyer could carry U.S. currency, but this involves possible physical loss of the money and sometimes a substantial discount for its conversion into the local currency. A traveler's letter of credit is a convenient and safer method for travelers who need large amounts of foreign currency.

The **traveler's letter of credit** is issued by a bank in one country and addressed to a list of foreign banks. These banks are usually correspondents of the issuing bank and have agreed to purchase sight drafts presented to them by persons with appropriate letters of credit. When a bank issues a letter of credit, it sends a copy of the signature of the person to whom the letter is issued to each of its foreign correspondent banks. When someone presents a draft for payment in foreign currency to one of these correspondent banks, his or her signature is compared with the signature the bank already has. The bank may also ask the individual for supplementary identification.

As with a commercial letter of credit, a maximum total draft amount is stated in a traveler's letter of credit. So that an individual with such a letter does not exceed authorized withdrawals, each bank to which the letter is presented enters on it the amount of the draft it has honored.

Traveler's Checks

Traveler's checks, which are offered by banks and other financial intermediaries in the United States, are generally issued in denominations of $10, $20, $50, and $100. These checks, generally purchased by an individual before leaving for a foreign country, promise to pay on demand the even amounts indicated on the face of the checks. Each check must be signed by the purchaser twice, once when it is bought and again in the presence of a representative of the business, hotel, or financial institution where it is presented for payment. This allows the person cashing a traveler's check to determine whether the signature is authentic.

The use of traveler's checks is widespread and offers several advantages to the traveler, including protection in the event of loss and almost certain acceptance when they are presented for payment. Traveler's checks are usually sold for their face amount plus a charge of 1 percent. They can now be purchased in the United States in major foreign currency denominations—for example, British pounds. This eliminates a traveler's exposure to varying exchange rates and the extra amount that is often charged (in the form of a less favorable exchange rate than the official rate) when U.S. dollar checks are cashed in a foreign country.

BALANCE IN INTERNATIONAL TRANSACTIONS GOAL

Just as monetary policy plays an important role in the nation's stability, growth, interest rates, and price levels, it also helps keep international financial relationships in balance. Since the dollar is widely held as a medium of international exchange, U.S. monetary policy has especially significant effects on the world economy. No nation is a world unto itself, nor can a nation pursue whatever policies it desires without regard to other nations. Policy makers of all economies must recognize the interdependence of their actions in attempting to maintain a balance in international transactions that is sometimes referred to as international financial equilibrium.

Briefly, the nations of the world attempt to achieve international financial equilibrium by maintaining a balance in their exchange of goods and services. In general, international trade benefits all countries involved. Consumers benefit by getting lower-cost goods, since the goods come from the country where they are produced most efficiently. Producers benefit by expanding their markets. Well over one-tenth of the U.S. national income comes from selling goods to foreigners, and a like amount of our needs are met through imports. However, individuals and firms make the decisions to import and export, and problems arise if they are out of balance over time.

CONCEPT CHECK
What is the Export-Import Bank, and what does it do?

traveler's letter of credit *issued by a bank to banks in other countries authorizing them to cash checks or purchase drafts presented by the bearer*

CONCEPT CHECK
What is a traveler's letter of credit and how is it used internationally?

CONCEPT CHECK
What are the advantages associated with the use of traveler's checks?

GLOBAL DISCUSSION

INTERNET ACTIVITY

Go to the CNNMoney Web site, http://money.cnn.com. Access "markets," then "currencies," and finally "crossrates." Find current currency exchange rates for the European Monetary Union euro relative to the United Kingdom (British) pound, and the Japanese yen. Find both direct and indirect currency exchange quotations.

NATURE OF THE PROBLEM

Exports are sales to foreigners; they are a source of income to domestic producers. Imports divert spending to foreign producers and therefore represent a loss of potential income to domestic producers. When the two are in balance there is no net effect on total income in the economy. However, an increase in exports over imports tends to expand the economy just as an increase in investment or government spending does. An excess of imports tends to contract the economy.

As in the domestic economy, goods and services are not exchanged directly in international trade; payment flows through monetary or financial transactions. Methods of making payments and financing international trade were discussed previously. Other short- and long-term lending and investment are conducted across national boundaries on a large scale. In addition, government grants for both military and civilian purposes and private gifts and grants are sources of international financial flows. These flows can have an important impact on domestic economies and may affect monetary policy.

Since producers, consumers, and investors in different countries use different currencies, the international financial system requires a mechanism for establishing the relative values, or exchange rates, among currencies and for handling their actual exchange. Under the system of *flexible exchange rates* that began in 1973, rates are determined in the actual process of exchange: by supply and demand in the foreign exchange market. This system reduces the impact of international financial transactions on domestic money supplies. Still, changes in exchange rates do affect imports and exports and can thus affect domestic production, incomes, and prices. International financial markets strongly influence domestic interest rates and vice versa, so that domestic monetary policy still involves international considerations.

In short, domestic economies are linked to one another in a worldwide economic and financial system. The United States has played a leading role in the development and growth of that system. Before we take a closer look at that role, we should examine the accounting system used to keep track of international financial transactions.

BALANCE-OF-PAYMENTS ACCOUNTS

The U.S. **balance of payments** involves all of its international transactions, including foreign investment, private and government grants, U.S. military spending overseas, and many other items besides the buying and selling of goods and services. The most important element of the balance of payments is the **balance of trade,** which is the net balance of exports and imports of goods and services. A more narrow view considers only the import and export of goods and is termed the **merchandise trade balance.** The merchandise trade balance was consistently favorable between the 1950s and the beginning of the 1970s. However, imports of goods have exceeded exports since the latter part of the 1970s.

The following are exports, imports, and balance on goods amounts in billions of dollars for selected years at the beginning of each decade beginning with 1980 and for 2005:

balance of payments
a summary of all economic transactions between one country and the rest of the world

balance of trade
the net value of a country's exports of goods and services compared to its imports

merchandise trade balance
the net difference between a country's import and export of goods

YEAR	EXPORTS	IMPORTS	BALANCE ON GOODS
1980	$224.3	−$249.8	−$25.5
1990	387.4	−498.4	−111.0
2000	772.0	−1,224.4	−452.4
2005	894.6	−1,677.4	−782.8

Source: *Economic Report of the President*, February 2007, p. 348.

As recorded in the preceding table, exports increased nearly four times from $224.3 billion in 1980 to $894.6 billion in 2005. However, over the same period, imports increased well over six times, from $249.8 billion in 1980 to $1,677.4 billion in 2005, and the balance on goods grew from −$25.5 billion in 1980 to −$782.8 billion in 2005.

Factors that impact international trade balances include the exchange value of the U.S. dollar relative to other currencies, relative inflation rates, and economic growth. A relatively stronger U.S. economy means that more will be spent on imports, while the weaker foreign economy means that less will be spent on U.S. exports. A relatively weaker real exchange rate, where the nominal exchange rate is adjusted for inflation differences, makes for a weaker U.S. dollar, which lowers the dollar cost of U.S. goods relative to foreign goods.

TABLE 6.3
U.S. Balance of Payments in 2007 ($Billions)

	INCOME (+)	PAYMENTS (−)	NET
Current Account			
Goods and services			
Exports	$1,645.7		
Imports		$2,346.0	
Balance on goods and services			−$700.3
Income, net			81.8
Unilateral current transfers, net			−112.7
Balance on current account			−$731.2
Capital Account			
Changes in U.S. government assets other than official reserve assets		22.3	
Changes in U.S. private assets abroad		1,267.5	
Changes in foreign official assets in U.S.	411.1		
Changes in foreign private assets in U.S.	1,646.6		
Changes in U.S. official reserve assets		.1	
Capital account transactions, net		1.8	
Balance on capital account			$ 766.2
Statistical discrepancy (calculated)			−35.0
Adjusted balance on capital account			$ 731.2

Source: http://www.federalreserve.gov/econresdata/releases/intlsumm/usintltranssum20090131.htm, accessed December 16, 2009.

We can better understand the U.S. balance of payments by examining the current account and capital account balances information shown in Table 6.3. An annual balance of trade (goods and services) deficit of $700.3 billion occurred in 2007 and reflects the net of merchandise trade, service transactions, and military transactions. We find the current account balance by adjusting the goods and services balance for net income flows that come primarily from investments and also from unilateral, or one-way, transfers. These transfers include remittances, pensions, private gifts and grants, and U.S. government grants (excluding military). Thus, the **current account balance** shows the flow of income into and out of the United States during a specified period. For 2007, the current account balance showed a deficit of $731.2 billion.

The **capital account balance** includes all foreign private and government investment in the United States netted against U.S. investments in foreign countries. Deficits or surpluses in the current account must be offset by changes in the capital account. That is, changes in the current account and the capital account must be equal except for statistical discrepancies caused by measurement errors and the inability to keep track of all international transactions. According to Table 6.3, the balance on the capital account for 2007 was a surplus of $766.2 billion. Since this amount was more than the current account deficit of $731.2 billion, the difference reflects a statistical discrepancy of −$35 billion for 2007.

The first item in the capital account section, changes in U.S. government assets other than official reserve assets, represents an outflow of $22.3 billion and includes government ownership of assets in foreign countries, gold, and the reserve position in the International Monetary Fund. The second item, changes in U.S. private assets abroad, reflects private investments abroad and represents an outflow of capital which was $1,267.5 billion in 2007.

The third and fourth items reflect foreign ownership changes, both government and private, in investments in the United States. Among those changes are increases in bank deposits, purchases of government and corporate securities, loans, and direct investment in land and buildings. Both of these items give rise to inflows of capital with $411.1 billion coming from an increase in foreign official assets and $1,646.6 billion from foreign private assets in 2007. The fifth item reflects a decrease in U.S. official reserve assets of $.1 billion in 2007. Capital account transactions (net) reflected payments of $1.8 billion in 2007 for debt forgiveness and the disposition of certain assets.

---

current account balance
the flow of income into and out of the United States during a specified period

capital account balance
foreign government and private investment in the United States netted against similar U.S. investment in foreign countries

CONCEPT CHECK

What is the U.S. balance of payments?

What are the differences between the current account balance and the capital account balance?

CAREER PROFILES

VALERIE R. COLVILLE
Vice President, Project Finance Group, Fluor Corporation

B.A., Geology, Williams College
M.Sc., Petroleum Geology, University of Wisconsin
Executive MBA, University of Michigan

"We hedge our exchange rate positions and manage our cross-currency positions on a daily basis."

Q: *Describe Fluor and its international operations.*
A: Fluor Corporation is one of the largest publicly traded engineering and construction companies in the world. With over 50,000 employees worldwide, we provide engineering, construction, procurement and operations and maintenance services to clients in sixteen industry sectors including energy, chemicals, mining, manufacturing, power/utilities, telecommunications, transportation, operations and maintenance services. About 50 percent of our revenues come from international projects, and we have offices in seventy countries globally. This local presence helps us understand the business environment in which we operate.

Q: *What are your current position and responsibilities?*
A: As vice president, project finance, I am one of only five women in Fluor's 200-person worldwide senior management group. I arrange debt and equity financing from the global financial markets for each of our business units for the following regions: Europe, Africa, the former Soviet Union, the Middle East, and Latin America. Most of our deals are between $200 million and $2 billion. We also provide financial advisory services. I am responsible for the entire process, from creating the appropriate financial structure to closing the transaction.

Q: *Do you use any special financing techniques for international projects?*
A: For projects in emerging markets we often access nontraditional lending institutions such as export credit agencies and multilaterals such as the World Bank. We raise capital from a variety of internationally based financial institutions, using the best financing structure and product for each transaction, whether it is tax-exempt financing for toll roads in the United States, private finance initiative communications projects in the United Kingdom, or export credit agency financing in Indonesia.

Q: *How do exchange rate movements affect your business?*
A: Since approximately 40 to 50 percent of all project costs are for labor and local construction services, we hedge our exchange rate positions and manage our cross-currency positions on a daily basis. We also try to have as much of our contracts paid in U.S. dollars as possible. For each contract we analyze foreign exchange risk and look for ways to reduce our exposure. We consider the credit quality of our clients and their ability to convert their local currency into U.S. dollars to pay us for locally incurred costs. This is particularly important on very large emerging market transactions.

Q: *What skills are important to your position?*
A: Project finance specialists must be well-rounded bankers. I use finance skills including corporate finance, mergers/acquisitions, accounting, and financial modeling. Also critical are general business skills like strategic planning, marketing, and computer literacy, and many "life skills": strong written and verbal communication, leadership, mentoring, and team management and building. Project finance also requires knowledge of global markets (commodities) and geopolitics. We need to understand complex financing techniques, tax treatment, and accounting standards. Project finance also requires a significant amount of legal knowledge, plus conflict resolution and negotiation skills. Success in international markets calls for a keen understanding of—and respect for—cultural diversity. Perhaps the greatest skill of all is patience coupled with a true team orientation: it is impossible to complete a project financing without collaborating with other specialists.

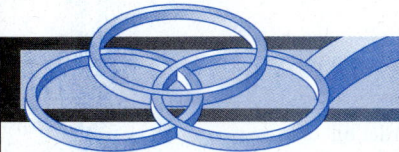

APPLYING FINANCE TO...

INSTITUTIONS AND MARKETS

Commercial banks play an important role in financing international trade. Banks provide commercial letters of credit that guarantee acceptance and payment of drafts. Bankers' acceptances, promises of future payment issued by a firm and guaranteed by a bank, also are important financial instruments that facilitate international trade. Banks throughout the world also are important participants in the electronic currency exchange markets. Traveler's letters of credit and traveler's checks are provided by financial institutions to help travelers purchase products and cover living expenses while in foreign countries.

INVESTMENTS

Individuals and businesses interested in investing in securities issued by foreign corporations may need to use the currency exchange markets to convert U.S. dollars into the currencies of the countries where those corporations are located. Individuals traveling internationally also will need to convert their U.S. dollars into the local currencies through the aid of financial institutions. Investors may also speculate on the relative future movements of currencies through the use of spot and forward markets.

FINANCIAL MANAGEMENT

Financial managers use currency exchange markets to hedge against currency exchange risk associated with possible changes in the exchange rates between currencies. Financial managers may hedge in the forward markets or seek the aid of banks to sell unneeded currencies or to purchase currencies needed to conduct business operations. Financial managers also rely on banks and other financial institutions to aid them in their international transactions both as importers and as exporters.

From an international monetary management point of view, U.S. government ownership of foreign assets is of special interest. Under the current system of flexible exchange rates, a country's central bank does not have to redeem its currency. However, it may try to control its exchange rate by entering the foreign exchange market to buy or sell that currency, thus adding to demand or supply. Intervention by central banks in the flexible exchange rate system is called a *managed float*.

Under a pure flexible system in which central banks do not enter the foreign exchange market at all, there would be no change in the official government ownership of foreign assets. Note, however, that the rest of the accounts would still balance. Any surplus or deficit in current accounts would be balanced by the capital accounts. For example, a trade deficit might be balanced partly by an increase in foreign assets in the United States, including deposits in U.S. banks.

SUMMARY

In this chapter we discussed the development of international finance and the international monetary system as it evolved from a gold standard system to a system of flexible exchange rates. We also covered the developments toward European economic unification through the creation of the European Union (EU) and the European Monetary Union (EMU). The EU is currently composed of twenty-seven country members, while the EMU consists of the thirteen countries that have adopted the euro as their common currency and the European Central Bank as their central monetary policy-making authority. The banking system, along with the arbitrage activities of international financiers, support and facilitate international transactions and activities. Management of foreign exchange is particularly important to multinational corporate financial managers as they attempt to protect their international claims against currency fluctuations.

Foreign exchange markets are electronic communication systems that connect major financial centers throughout the world. Numerous factors determine exchange rates: supply-and-demand relationships, relative interest-rate levels, relative inflation rates, political risk, and economic risk. Alternatives to effect the settlement of purchase and sale claims were explored, along with the instruments available to exporters and importers for financing their international activities.

Nations of the world try to maintain a balance in their exchange of goods and services, as well as in their payments balances. When international financial equilibrium does not exist, exchange rates usually adjust to reflect these imbalances. Furthermore, when the current account shows a surplus or deficit in the flow of income into and out of the United States, changes in the capital account must offset the current account imbalance. This is accomplished by a change in the relationship between foreign private and government investment in the United States relative to U.S. investment in foreign countries.

152 PART ONE • Institutions and Markets

KEY TERMS

- arbitrage
- balance of payments
- balance of trade
- bankers' acceptances
- Bretton Woods system
- capital account balance
- clean draft
- commercial letter of credit
- currency exchange markets
- currency exchange rate
- current account balance
- direct quotation method
- documentary draft
- draft (bill of exchange)
- economic risk
- euro
- European Monetary Union (EMU)
- European Union (EU)
- Export-Import Bank
- flexible exchange rates
- foreign exchange markets
- forward exchange rate
- gold standard
- indirect quotation method
- interest rate parity (IRP)
- International Monetary Fund (IMF)
- international monetary system
- merchandise trade balance
- order bill of lading
- political risk
- purchasing power parity (PPP)
- sight draft
- special drawing rights (SDRs)
- spot exchange rate
- time draft
- traveler's letter of credit
- trust receipt
- World Bank

DISCUSSION QUESTIONS

1. What is the purpose of an international monetary system?

2. What is meant by the statement that the international monetary system has operated mostly under a "gold standard"? What are the major criticisms associated with being on a gold standard?

3. Describe the Bretton Woods system for setting currency exchange rates. What are "special drawing rights" and how are they used to foster world trade?

4. What is an international monetary system based on "flexible exchange rates"?

5. Describe the international monetary system currently in use.

6. What is the European Union (EU)? How did it develop? Who are the current members of the EU?

7. What is the European Monetary Union (EMU)? How does it differ from the EU? Who are the current members of the EMU?

8. What is the euro? Identify some of its distinguishing characteristics.

9. What are currency or foreign exchange markets?

10. Explain the role of supply and demand in establishing exchange rates between countries.

11. Describe the activities and economic role of the arbitrageur in international finance.

12. What is meant by the statement that foreign exchange quotations may be given in terms of sight drafts, cable orders, and time drafts?

13. Describe the various ways by which an exporter may finance an international shipment of goods. How may commercial banks assist the exporter in collecting drafts?

14. How do importers protect themselves against improper delivery of goods when they are required to make payment as they place an order?

15. Describe the process by which an importing firm may substitute the credit of its bank for its own credit in financing international transactions.

16. How may a bank protect itself after having issued a commercial letter of credit on behalf of a customer?

17. Describe the costs involved in connection with financing exports through banker's acceptances.

18. Describe the ultimate sources of funds for export financing with banker's acceptances. How are acceptances acquired for investment by these sources?

19. Explain the role played in international trade by the Export-Import Bank. Do you consider this bank to be in competition with private lending institutions?

20. Commercial letters of credit, traveler's letters of credit, and traveler's checks all play an important role in international finance. Distinguish among these three types of instruments.

21. Briefly indicate the problems facing the United States in its attempt to maintain international financial equilibrium.

22. The U.S. international balance of payments position is measured in terms of the current account balance. Describe the current account balance and indicate its major components.

23. Discuss the meaning of the capital account balance and identify its major components.

EXERCISES

1. You are the owner of a business that has offices and production facilities in several foreign countries. Your product is sold in all these countries, and you maintain bank accounts in the cities in which you have offices. At present, you have short-term notes outstanding at most of the banks with which you maintain deposits. This borrowing is to support seasonal production activity. One of the countries in which you have offices is now strongly rumored to be on the point of devaluation, or lowering, of its currency relative to that of the rest of the world. What actions might this rumor cause you to take?

2. Explain the concept of "balance" as it relates to a nation's balance of payments.

3. As an exporter of relatively expensive electronic equipment you have a substantial investment in the merchandise that you ship. Your foreign importers are typically small- or medium-size firms without

a long history of operations. Although your terms of sales require payment upon receipt of the merchandise, you are concerned about the possible problem of nonpayment and the need to reclaim merchandise that you have shipped. How might the banking system assist and protect you in this situation?

4. As an importer of merchandise you depend on the sale of the merchandise for funds to make payment. Although customary terms of sale are ninety days for this type of merchandise, you are not well-known to foreign suppliers because of your recent entry into business. Furthermore, your suppliers require almost immediate payment to meet their own expenses of operations. How might the banking systems of the exporter and importer accommodate your situation?

5. As a speculator in the financial markets you notice that for the last few minutes Swiss francs are being quoted in New York at a price of $0.5849 and in Frankfurt at $0.5851.

   a. Assuming that you have access to international trading facilities, what action might you take?
   b. What would be the effect of your actions and those of other speculators on these exchange rates?

6. You manage the cash for a large multinational industrial enterprise. As a result of credit sales on ninety-day payment terms, you have a large claim against a customer in Mexico City. You have heard rumors of the possible devaluation of the Mexican peso. What actions, if any, can you take to protect your firm against the consequences of a prospective devaluation?

7. Assume, as the loan officer of a commercial bank, that one of your customers has asked for a commercial letter of credit to enable his firm to import a supply of well-known French wines. This customer has a long record of commercial success, yet has large outstanding debts to other creditors. In what way might you accommodate the customer and at the same time protect your bank?

8. For the entire year, the nation's balance of trade with other nations has been in a substantial deficit position, yet, as always, the overall balance of payments will be in "balance." Describe the various factors that accomplish this overall balance, in spite of the deficit in the balance of trade.

9. Assume you are the international vice president of a small U.S.-based manufacturing corporation. You are trying to expand your business in several developing countries. You are also aware that some business practices are considered to be "acceptable" in these countries but not necessarily in the United States. How would you react to the following situations?

   a. You met yesterday with a government official from one of the countries in which you would like to make sales. He said that he could speed up the process for acquiring the necessary licenses for conducting business in his country if you would pay him for his time and effort. What would you do?
   b. You are trying to make a major sale of your firm's products to the government of a foreign country. You have identified the key decision maker. You are considering offering the official a monetary payment if she would recommend buying your firm's products. What would you do?
   c. Your firm has a local office in a developing country where you are trying to increase business opportunities. Representatives from a local crime syndicate have approached you and have offered to provide "local security" in exchange for a monthly payment to them. What would you do?

PROBLEMS

1. Exchange rate relationships between the U.S. dollar and the euro have been quite volatile. When the euro began trading at the beginning of 1999, it was valued at 1.18 U.S. dollars. By late-2000, a euro was worth only $.82. However, by mid-2008, a value of a euro reached $1.55. Calculate the percentage changes in the value of a euro from its initial value to its late-2000 value and to its high mid-2008 value.

2. In mid-March 2007, the U.S. dollar equivalent of a euro was $1.3310. In mid-July 2009, the U.S. dollar equivalent of a euro was $1.4116. Using the indirect quotation method, determine the currency per U.S. dollar for each of these dates.

3. In mid-March 2007, the U.S. dollar equivalent of a euro was $1.3310. In mid-July 2009, the U.S. dollar equivalent of a euro was $1.4116. Determine the percentage change of the euro between these two dates.

4. Three years ago the U.S. dollar equivalent of a foreign currency was $1.2167. Today, the U.S. dollar equivalent of a foreign currency is $1.3310. Using the indirect quotation method, determine the currency per U.S. dollar for each of these dates.

5. Three years ago the U.S. dollar equivalent of a foreign currency was $1.2167. Today, the U.S. dollar equivalent of a foreign currency is $1.3310. Determine the percentage change of the euro between these two dates.

6. If the U.S dollar value of a British Pound is $1.95 and a euro is $1.55, calculate the implied value of a euro in terms of a British Pound.

7. Assume a U.S. dollar is worth 10.38 Mexican pesos and .64 euros. Calculate the implied value of a Mexican Peso in terms of a euro.

8. Assume that five years ago a euro was trading at a direct method quotation of $.8767. Also assume that this year the indirect method quotation was .8219 euros per U.S. dollar.

   a. Calculate the euro "currency per U.S. dollar" five years ago.
   b. Calculate the "U.S. dollar equivalent" of a euro this year.
   c. Determine the percentage change (appreciation or depreciation) of the U.S. dollar value of one euro between five years ago and this year.
   d. Determine the percentage change (appreciation or depreciation) of the euro currency per U.S. dollar between five years ago and this year.

9. Assume that last year the Australian dollar was trading at $.5527, the Mexican peso at $.1102, and the United Kingdom (British) pound was worth $1.4233. By this year the U.S. dollar value of an Australian dollar was $.7056, the Mexican peso was $.0867, and the British pound was $1.8203. Calculate the percentage appreciation or depreciation of each of these three currencies between last year and this year.

10. Assume that the Danish krone (DK) has a current dollar ($US) value of $0.18.

    a. Determine the number of DK that can be purchased with one $US.

b. Calculate the percentage change (appreciation or depreciation) in the Danish krone if it falls to $0.16.

c. Calculate the percentage change (appreciation or depreciation) in the U.S. dollar if the DK falls to $0.16.

11. Assume the U.S. dollar ($US) value of the Australian dollar is $0.73 while the U.S. dollar value of the Hong Kong dollar is $0.13.

   a. Determine the number of Australian dollars that can be purchased with one $US.

   b. Determine the number of Hong Kong dollars that can be purchased with one $US.

   c. In $US terms, determine how many Hong Kong dollars can be purchased with one Australian dollar.

12. Assume one U.S. dollar ($US) can currently purchase 1.316 Swiss francs. However, it has been predicted that one $US soon will be exchangeable for 1.450 Swiss francs.

   a. Calculate the percentage change in the $US if the exchange rate change occurs.

   b. Determine the dollar value of one Swiss franc at both of the above exchange rates.

   c. Calculate the percentage change in the dollar value of one Swiss franc based on the preceding exchange rates.

13. Assume inflation is expected to be 3 percent in the United States next year compared with 6 percent in Australia. If the U.S. dollar value of an Australian dollar is currently $0.500, what is the expected exchange rate one year from now based on purchasing power parity?

14. Assume inflation is expected to be 8 percent in New Zealand next year compared with 4 percent in France. If the New Zealand dollar value of a euro is $0.400, what is the expected exchange rate one year from now based on purchasing power parity?

15. Assume the interest rate on a one-year U.S. government debt security is currently 9.5 percent compared with a 7.5 percent on a foreign country's comparable maturity debt security. If the U.S. dollar value of the foreign country's currency is $1.50, what is the expected exchange rate one year from now based on interest rate parity?

16. Assume the interest rate in Australia on one-year government debt securities is 10 percent and the interest rate on Japanese one-year debt is 5 percent. Assume the current Australian dollar value of the Japanese yen is $0.0200. Using interest rate parity, estimate the expected value of the Japanese yen in terms of Australian dollars one year from now.

17. **Challenge Problem** Following are currency exchange "crossrates" between pairs of major currencies. Currency crossrates include both direct and indirect methods for expressing relative exchange rates.

	U.S. DOLLAR	U.K. POUND	SWISS FRANC	JAPANESE YEN	EUROPEAN EURO
European Monetary Union	1.1406	?	0.6783	0.0087	—
Japan	130.66	185.98	77.705	—	114.60
Switzerland	1.6817	2.3936	—	0.0129	?
United Kingdom	?	—	0.4178	?	0.6162
United States	—	1.4231	?	0.0077	0.8767

a. Fill in the missing exchange rates in the crossrates table.

b. If the inflation rate is expected to be 3 percent in the European Monetary Union and 4 percent in the United States next year, estimate the forward rate of one euro in U.S. dollars one year from now.

c. If the one-year government interest rate is 6 percent in Japan and 4 percent in the United Kingdom, estimate the amount of yen that will be needed to purchase one British pound one year from now.

d. Based solely on purchasing power parity, calculate the expected one-year inflation rate in the United States if the Swiss inflation rate is expected to be 3.5 percent next year and the one-year forward rate of a Swiss franc is $.6100.

e. Assume the U.S. dollar is expected to depreciate by 15 percent relative to the euro at the end of one year from now and the interest rate on one-year government securities in the European Monetary Union is 5.5 percent. What would be the current U.S. one-year government security interest rate based solely on the use of interest rate parity to forecast forward currency exchange rates?

PART 2
INVESTMENTS

INTRODUCTION

The field of finance is composed of three areas—institutions and markets, investments, and financial management. These areas are illustrated in the accompanying diagram. Part 2 focuses on the investments area of finance. Investments involve the sale or marketing of securities, the analysis and valuation of securities and other financial claims, and the management of investment risk through holding diversified portfolios. Money flows into the financial markets from households' and firms' retained earnings. Funds flow into financial institutions such as banks and life insurance companies, which, in turn, invest the funds in various securities such as stocks and bonds, as well as other financial claims. Financial claims are anything that has a debt or equity claim on income or property, such as a car loan, a mortgage, or an equity investment in a small partnership. Financial institutions facilitate the work of the financial markets by directing funds from savers to those individuals, firms, or governments who need funds to finance current operations or growth.

Part 1 dealt with the operations of the financial markets in general within the context of the financial system. The financial crisis of 2007–09, sometimes referred to as the "perfect financial storm," tested the workings of the U.S. financial system to an extent not seen since the 1930s depression. Although some evidence suggested that the U.S. financial system was on the verge of collapse in late 2008, efforts on the part of policy makers, business leaders, and individuals set the stage for economic recovery and a return to financial stability as the decade of the 2000s came to an end.

Part 2 introduces many of the important concepts and tools that financial institutions and investors use in the financial markets. For example, no one would want to invest (except perhaps altruistically) $100 now and expect to receive only their $100 back after one year. Because they give up the use of their money for some time, investors expect a return on their investments. Thus we say that money has a "time value." Having one dollar today is of greater value to us than the promise of receiving one dollar sometime in the future.

How much can we expect to receive for our $100 investment? The answer is determined in the financial markets. As with any other market, the financial markets consider demand and supply forces to determine the "price" of money, namely the interest rate or the expected return on an investment. The amount of interest received on a certificate of deposit or a bond, or the expected return on a common stock investment, all depends on the workings of the financial markets and the marketplace's evaluation of the investment opportunity.

It is through the investing process that institutions, firms, and individual investors come together. Firms and governments go to the financial markets, seeking investors and institutions to whom they can sell financial securities. Investors and institutions participate in the financial markets, seeking profitable investments to help meet their goals. For an investor, the goal may be a comfortable retirement or accumulating funds to purchase a car or house. For financial institutions, the higher the returns they earn on prudent investments, the greater will be their profits and the stronger their competitive position. A financial institution that prudently earns higher returns in the financial markets will be able to offer current and potential customers higher interest rates on their deposits than a competitor whose financial market returns are lower.

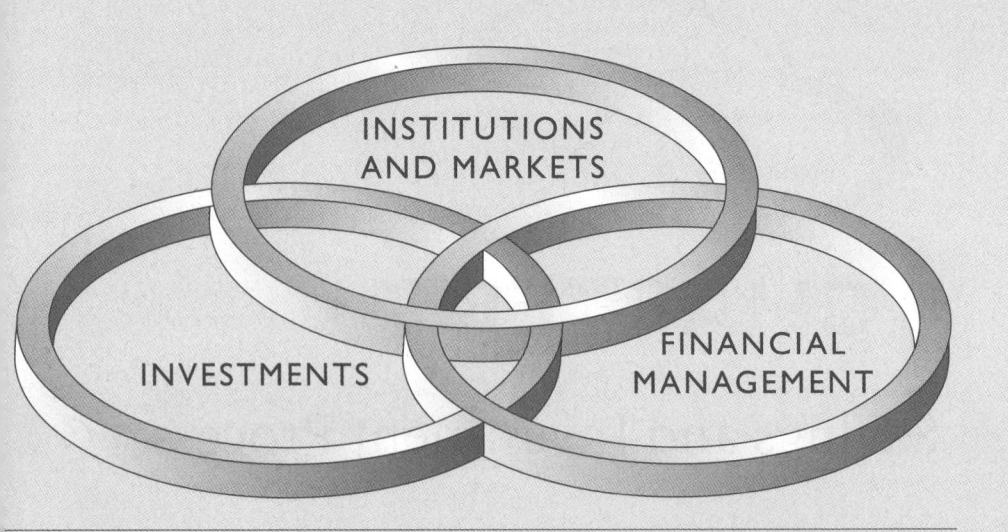

Part 2 introduces us to the process of investing and to the tools that can be used to evaluate financial market securities. Chapter 7 examines the work of financial markets to direct savings into various investments. Chapter 8 discusses influences that affect the financial market's determination of the price of money, or the interest rate or expected return on an investment. Chapter 9 examines the effect of interest rates more closely by introducing the concept of time value of money. This chapter shows us how we can compare different dollar amounts of cash over time to determine whether an investment is attractive or not. Chapter 10 introduces us to bonds and stocks. We review their characteristics, and we use the time value concepts from Chapter 9 in a pragmatic manner to see how we can estimate their value. We also learn in Chapter 10 how to read and interpret information about bonds and stocks from the financial pages of papers such as *The Wall Street Journal*.

Chapter 11 delves deeper into the workings of the securities markets. It focuses on the processes that institutions and firms use to issue securities and the process that investors use when buying or selling securities. Chapter 12 completes our overview of investing in the securities markets by examining the trade-off between risk and expected return: to have an incentive to invest in higher-risk securities, investors must have higher returns. Chapter 12 introduces us to the tools that investors and securities market participants use to evaluate and to control investment risk.

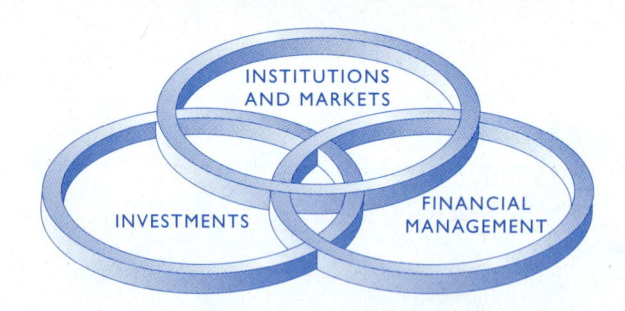

• CHAPTER 7 •

Savings and Investment Process

Chapter Learning Objectives:

AFTER STUDYING THIS CHAPTER, YOU SHOULD BE ABLE TO:

- Identify and briefly describe the major components of the gross domestic product.
- Describe how the balance between exports and imports affects the gross domestic product.
- Describe recent developments in the aggregate level of personal and corporate savings.
- Describe the principal sources of federal government revenues and expenditures.
- Discuss the historical role of savings in the United States and how savings are created.
- Identify the major sources of savings in the United States.
- Identify and describe the factors that affect savings.
- Describe major capital market securities that facilitate the savings and investment process.
- Discuss the role of individuals in the recent financial crisis.

Where We Have Been… Part 1 of this book introduced you to how the U.S. financial system works. In Chapter 1 you learned about the role of finance and were able to answer the question: What is finance? Chapter 2 provided you with information about the development of the U.S. monetary system, and Chapter 3 covered the importance of commercial banks and other financial institutions in helping the financial system operate smoothly. In Chapter 4 you learned about the Federal Reserve System and its monetary policy functions and instruments. After reading Chapter 5, you should have a better understanding of who the U.S. policy makers are and how they carry out monetary policy, fiscal policy, and debt management to achieve the nation's economic objectives. Chapter 6 showed how international trade is conducted and how currency exchange markets support international trade.

Where We Are Going… Part 2 focuses on the area of finance called investments. In Chapter 8 you will be introduced to the structure of interest rates. You will learn about the supply and demand for loanable funds and the determinants of nominal or market interest rates. Characteristics of U.S. Treasury debt obligations, which are considered to be free of default risk, will be discussed. Our attention then turns to the term or maturity structure of interest rates. Next we cover inflation premiums and price movements. The last section of the chapter examines default risk premiums. The remainder of Part 2 includes Chapter 9 on the time value of money, Chapter 10 on the characteristics and valuations of bonds and stocks, Chapter 11 on securities markets, and Chapter 12 on financial return and risk concepts.

How This Chapter Apply to Me… Every day you are faced with deciding whether to "consume more" or to "save." For example, after buying dinner at a restaurant you may still have a few dollars left in the form of extra income, possibly from a part-time job while you are in college. What will you do with the money? You might buy a new CD or take a friend to the movie theater. Alternatively, you might decide to place the money in a savings account at a bank. The process of intermediation then moves your discretionary money from savings into investment. Of course, saving is not costless. Each time you make a decision to save, you are foregoing current consumption. This action on your part not to immediately consume all of your income helps the economy grow.

Our parents and other "experts" have likely provided similar advice to each of us about the importance of saving for a "rainy day." Of course, they were telling us not to consume all of our current income but rather to put some aside for an unexpected financial need—that is, a "rainy day." Such an action of saving not only provides protection against unanticipated future expenditures for the individual, but also allows investment. You are probably not a saver at this stage in your life. We say this because most individuals are spenders of their parents' earnings and savings during their formative years from birth through college. At the time of college graduation, most individuals have little or no savings but possess "earning power." As earnings exceed expenditures, individuals have the opportunity to save in a variety of ways ranging from short-term money market investments (considered to be cash) to long-term real estate investments in the form of home ownership.

As you move through your life cycle, you likely will have the opportunity to invest in stocks and bonds. Likewise, having an understanding of the types of financial assets that are used by businesses to finance and grow their businesses will be of value to those of you who pursue business careers.

GROSS DOMESTIC PRODUCT AND CAPITAL FORMATION

Recall from Chapter 5 our discussion of the national economic policy objectives of economic growth, high employment, price stability, and balance in international transactions. Economic growth and employment are reflected in the output of goods and services by a nation, as well as the nation's ability to build buildings, roads, inventories, and other infrastructure.

All of a nation's output of goods and services may be consumed, or a portion of them may be saved. Individuals consume by making expenditures on durable and nondurable goods and services. Governments consume by purchasing goods and services. If all output is not consumed, savings can be invested to construct residential and commercial structures, manufacture producers' durable equipment, and increase business inventories. This process is termed **capital formation** and results in economic growth.

capital formation
process of constructing real property, manufacturing producers' durable equipment, and increasing business inventories

GDP COMPONENTS

Recall that *gross domestic product (GDP)* is a nation's output of goods and services achieved over a specified period such as one year. Increases in GDP over time measure the extent of economic growth, which is one of the country's national economic policy objectives. In Chapter 2 we focused on the relationship between GDP and monetary policy in terms of the money supply and velocity.

GDP is composed of consumption and investment components, as well as the net export of goods and services. More specifically, GDP consists of four components:

- Personal consumption expenditures
- Government expenditures including gross investment
- Gross private domestic investment
- Net exports of goods and services

personal consumption expenditures (PCE)
expenditures by individuals for durable goods, nondurable goods, and services

Personal consumption expenditures (PCE) indicate expenditures by individuals for durable goods, nondurable goods, and services. We all like to eat, buy clothes, have roofs over our heads, enjoy the comforts of heating and cooling, benefit from interior lighting, own automobiles and televisions, receive education, travel, and get haircuts and other services. The fact is we consume throughout our lives. Depending on where we are in our life cycles, we typically meet our consumption desires by spending our parents' earnings and savings during our formative years from birth through college graduation, generating our own earnings during our working lives, and spending our own savings during our retirement years.

government expenditures (GE)
expenditures for goods and services plus gross investments by federal, state, and local governments

Government expenditures (GE) include expenditures for goods and services plus gross investments by both the federal and the state and local governments. The federal government spends over one-half of its total expenditures on direct payments to individuals in the form of health, Social Security, and income security support. This should not be a surprise, since some would argue that the elected representatives of the people run the U.S. government for the benefit of the people.

160 PART TWO Investments

INTERNET ACTIVITY

Go to the Web site of the Federal Reserve Bank of St. Louis, http://www.stlouisfed.org. Access the Federal Reserve Economic Database (FRED), and find the current size of the U.S. gross domestic product (GDP) and its major components.

TABLE 7.1
Gross Domestic Product Consumption, Investment, and International Components ($ Billions)

	2003	2006	2009
Total gross domestic product	$10,987.9	$13,253.9	$14,258.7
Personal consumption expenditures	7,757.4	9,270.8	10,092.6
Durable goods	941.6	1,071.3	1,034.4
Nondurable goods	2,209.7	2,716.0	2,223.3
Services	4,606.2	5,483.6	6,835.0
Gross private domestic investment	1,670.6	2,218.4	1,622.9
Fixed investment	1,673.0	2,165.0	1,747.9
Nonresidential	1,110.6	1,397.9	1,386.6
Structures	259.2	411.6	480.7
Equipment and software	851.3	986.2	906.0
Residential structures	562.4	767.1	361.3
Change in private inventories	−2.4	53.4	−125.0
Net exports of goods and services	−495.0	−761.8	−390.1
Exports	1,048.9	1,466.2	1,560.0
Imports	1,543.8	2,228.0	1,950.1
Government consumption expenditures and gross investment	2,054.8	2,526.4	2,933.3
Federal	757.2	926.4	1,144.9
State and local	1,297.6	1,600.0	1,788.4

Source: *Survey of Current Business* and http://www.bea.gov.

gross private domestic investment (GPDI)
investment in residential and nonresidential structures, producers' durable equipment, and business inventories

net exports (NE)
exports of goods and services minus imports

Gross private domestic investment **(GPDI)** measures fixed investment in residential and nonresidential structures, producers' durable equipment, and changes in business inventories. The final component of GDP is the *net exports* **(NE)** of goods and services, or exports minus imports.

In equation form, we have:

$$GDP = PCE + GE + GPDI + NE \tag{7.1}$$

Consumption is reflected by the sum of personal consumption expenditures and government purchases of goods and services. Savings used for capital formation produce the gross private domestic investment. In addition, if the exports of goods and services exceed imports, GDP will be higher.

Table 7.1 shows the breakdown in these components for the United States for 2003, 2006, and 2009. For 2009 the gross domestic product was $14.3 trillion. This compares with domestic output of about $11.0 trillion GDP in 2003 and $13.3 trillion for 2006. However, the rate of increase over the decade of the 2000s slowed during the latter part of the decade, which coincided with the 2007–09 financial crisis period.

Personal consumption expenditures of $10.1 trillion in 2009 accounted for about 71 percent of GDP. This percentage relationship has been very stable throughout the decade of the 2000s and shows the importance of the individual in sustaining and improving the standard of living as reflected in GDP growth over time. However, in dollar terms personal consumption expenditures for both durable goods and nondurable goods declined from the 2006 levels as the economy began slowing in 2007 and entered into a recession in 2008. However, the increase in individual expenditures for services from 2006 to 2009 more than offset the decline in expenditures for goods.

Government expenditures, in the form of consumption and gross investment, amounted to $2.9 trillion in 2009. Continued increases occurred in both federal and state and local government expenditures occurred over the three years shown in Table 7.1. Capital formation measured in terms of gross private domestic investment was $1.6 trillion in 2009 down from $2.2 trillion for 2006 and down near the 2003 level. Fixed investment declined between 2006 and 2009 largely due to a dramatic decline in residential structures and reflects the housing price bubble that burst in 2006, resulting in a steep decline in home prices that was still continuing through 2009. The change in private inventories for 2009 was –$125 billion, reflecting the severity of the financial crisis of 2007–09.

IMPLICATIONS OF INTERNATIONAL PAYMENT IMBALANCES

Table 7.1 shows that imports of goods and services exceeded exports by about $495 billion in 2003, nearly $761.8 billion in 2006, and $390 billion in 2009. To place this in perspective, negative net exports were about 5 percent of the U.S. GDP in 2003 and over 6 percent of GDP in 2006 before falling to about 3 percent in 2009. Dollar amounts of exports increased in 2006 over 2003 and in 2009 over 2006. In contrast, while the dollar amount of imports increased dramatically in 2006 over 2003, they actually fell in 2009 relative to the 2006 level. These developments reflect the impact of the 2007–09 financial crisis and the weakening of the U.S. dollar relative to other major currencies as the decade of the 2000s came to a close.

Of course, the consequences of negative balances of goods and services caused by imports exceeding exports were GDPs lower than what would have occurred, other things being equal, if export-import equilibrium had existed.

The importance of achieving a balance in international transactions was discussed in Chapter 6. Recall that when completing the accounting transactions for the U.S. balance of payments, a deficit balance on goods and services in the *current account* is offset in the *capital account* by a net increase in foreign government and private ownership of U.S. assets. When the U.S. operates at a *balance of payments* deficit, the Fed must either reduce its reserve assets or borrow from foreign central banks. *Reserves* are in the form of gold, foreign exchanges (currencies), special drawing rights (SDRs), and reserves credit in the International Monetary Fund (IMF). Foreign exchanges (currencies) accounts represent the vast majority of all international reserve assets with the U.S. dollar comprising over half of these currency assets. Thus the U.S. dollar has been the most important reserve currency for conducting world trade, although in recent years the value of the U.S. dollar relative to the euro has been declining.

While the negative net exports over imports reflects an aggregate of trade with many countries, the United States has been running large trade deficits in goods and services with both Japan and China in recent years. This means that the United States has been buying more from Japan and China than those countries have been buying from the United States. One consequence is that Japan and China could have been investing more in the United States by purchasing U.S. assets (both financial and real) relative to U.S. investments in Japan and China. However, if the Japanese decide to hold relatively fewer claims on U.S. assets, the exchange rate between the yen and the dollar must change. In contrast, the Chinese renminbi (which is the currency foreigners can hold, or yuan, the currency within China) is a much more politically controlled currency that is pegged within a narrow range to the U.S. dollar.

Also recall from Chapter 6 that an equilibrium exchange rate between the currencies of two countries is established by the supply and demand for those currencies. A U.S. trade deficit in goods and services with Japan means that the demand for yen by Americans will be greater than the supply of yen from the Japanese. That is, Americans will demand more yen to pay for their purchases of Japanese goods and services relative to the supply of yen reflected in the demand by Japanese for American goods and services. The result will be a stronger yen and a weaker dollar unless offsetting actions occur, such as a willingness of the Japanese to invest more in U.S. assets or government intervention in the foreign exchange markets to support the dollar.

In 1990, one U.S. dollar could be exchanged for more than 150 yen. By late 1995 the exchange rate was about 100 yen per dollar. In other words, the dollar value of one yen had increased from roughly $0.007 (1/150) to $0.01 (1/100). By late 2009, the exchange rate was about 90 yen per dollar. Of course, in a worldwide market economy, at some point a lower dollar should lead to fewer imports of Japanese goods and services (because of their higher cost in terms of dollars) by Americans. At the same time, the Japanese should find American goods and services to be less costly (because of the stronger yen), and American exports to Japan should increase. The net result of a lower dollar could be to reduce the trade deficit with Japan in the future.

LINK BETWEEN SAVING AND INVESTMENT

Table 7.2 shows the link between saving and investment in the United States. For 2008 (data for 2009 were not yet available) gross saving was slightly more than $1.8 trillion. Gross saving is

TABLE 7.2
Saving and Investment in the United States ($ Billions)

	2003	2006	2008
Gross saving	$1,552.8	$2174.4	$1,824.1
Net saving	198.7	513.7	−23.0
Net private saving	613.9	666.5	659.8
Personal saving	289.8	235.0	286.4
Undistributed corporate profits	234.8	644.7	480.7
Inventory valuation adjustment	−11.3	−38.0	−38.2
Capital consumption adjustment	85.6	−176.4	−64.1
Wage accruals less disbursements	15.0	1.3	−5.0
Net government saving	−415.2	−152.7	−682.7
Federal	−376.4	−203.8	−642.6
State and local	−38.8	51.0	−40.2
Consumption of fixed capital	$1,354.1	1.660.7	1,847.1
Private	1,135.9	1,391.4	1,536.2
Domestic business	935.4	1,123.3	1,252.3
Households and institutions	200.5	268.1	283.9
Government	218.1	269.3	310.9
Federal	90.8	106.6	119.8
State and local	127.3	162.7	191.2
Gross domestic investment	$2,085.5	$2,752.2	$2,632.4
Gross private domestic investment	1,729.7	2,327.2	2,136.1
Gross government investment	355.8	425.1	496.3
Capital account transactions	3.8	4.2	−.4
Net lending or borrowing (−)	−519.9	−802.6	−706.8

Source: *Survey of Current Business* and http://www.bea.gov.

composed of net saving and consumption of fixed capital both private and government. Net saving was –$23 billion in 2008. This is because net private saving of nearly $660 billion was more than offset by net government saving of nearly –$693 billion due largely to a federal government deficit. In comparison, gross saving was nearly $2.2 trillion in 2006 with net saving being about $514 billion. For 2006, net private saving amounted to slightly more that $666 billion while net government saving was –$153 billion. These differing results between 2006 and 2008 reflect the financial crisis that began in 2007.

Personal saving by individuals provided about $286 billion in net savings in 2008, which represented about 43 percent of net private saving. Corporate profits that were not distributed to owners amounted to almost $481 billion in 2008. Total corporate saving is composed of undistributed corporate profits plus adjustments for corporate inventory valuation and capital consumption. Inventory valuation adjustment amounted to −$38 billion in 2008. *Capital consumption adjustment*, also called depreciation, is the estimate of the "using up" of plant and equipment assets for business purposes. These allowances amounted to –$64 billion in 2008. The combined total of the three sources of corporate saving amounted to slightly more than $378 billion in 2008. In comparison, undistributed corporate profits were about $645 billion in 2006 with a net for corporate savings of $430 billion. The slowing economy between 2006 and 2008 are shown in these data.

As Table 7.2 shows, the consumption of fixed capital comes primarily from the private sector. In 2008 consumption of fixed capital was slightly more than $1.8 trillion with the private sector consumption being about $1.5 trillion and the government sector only about $311 billion. Domestic business accounted for about 82 percent of private consumption in 2008 with households and institutions making up the remainder of private consumption.

Gross savings leads to gross investment. Table 7.2 shows that most gross investment is in the form of gross private domestic investment indicating the importance of personal and corporate savings. In contrast, net government savings was negative in 2008 while gross government investment was positive indicating the reliance on government deficits to finance government spending.

CONCEPT CHECK

What are personal consumption expenditures (PCE)?

What is meant by gross private domestic investment (GPDI)?

When the U.S. dollar declines in value relative to the Japanese yen, what is the likely impact of exports and imports between the two countries?

What are capital consumption allowances?

SMALL BUSINESS PRACTICE
Typical Life Cycle Patterns for the Small Venture Firm

A successful entrepreneurial firm will typically progress through several stages of financing. The first stage is called the "seed" or development stage. Here a firm works on an idea, development of a concept, or prototype product and may conduct some preliminary market research. If the firm is successful in producing a product or delivering a service it moves into the start-up stage. Financing will be needed for "working capital" investments in inventories and to extend trade credit to customers. A manufacturing "start-up" also will need to invest in plant and equipment.

A third stage can be viewed as the *breakeven* stage, when the firm is now starting to generate enough revenues to cover its operating costs. A fourth stage represents the *recovery of investment* stage. If the firm continues to be successful, the fifth stage results in the *maximum generation of profits*. This occurs because cash flows from operations far exceed new capital expenditure requirements, as well as additional investment in working capital. A sixth stage may be viewed as *maturity or stability*.

Timmons and Spinelli report that it takes an average of two and a half years for a firm to break even from an operating standpoint and over six years on average to recover initial equity investments.* Of course, some firms will recover initial investment more rapidly, while others will fail or not progress beyond the start-up stage. Ultimately, a plan is needed for how the successful entrepreneur will "exit" or leave the business. For example, the firm could be sold or merged with another firm.

---

* Jeffry A. Timmons and Stephen Spinelli, *New Venture Creation*, 7th Edition (New York: McGraw-Hill/Irwin, 2007), pp. 390–391.

FEDERAL GOVERNMENT RECEIPTS AND EXPENDITURES

THE BUDGET

Beginning in 1970 and continuing until fiscal year 1998, the federal government operated with an annual budget deficit. The government was willing to spend much more than it received in the form of taxes and other revenues for more than twenty-five consecutive fiscal years. Surplus budgets lasted for only four fiscal years, with annual budget deficits again being the norm beginning in fiscal 2002 with forecasts of a $1.4 trillion deficit for fiscal 2009 and a $1.6 trillion deficit for 2010. On the one hand, fiscal policy can use a deficit budget to stimulate economic activity. On the other hand, frequent large deficits resulted in a national debt that grew to over $12 trillion by the end of 2009.

The federal government relies primarily on tax revenues to support its various expenditure programs. In addition, revenues for general expenditures are received for specific services benefiting the persons charged. Examples of these revenues include postal receipts, rental receipts from federal housing projects, and food and housing payments collected from some government employees. The federal government also receives substantial insurance trust revenues from contributions to such programs as Medicare and Social Security. In turn, it makes large disbursements from these revenues. The federal government relies on borrowing to bridge the gap between revenues and expenditures.

Figure 7.1 provides a graphic illustration of the percentage breakdown of revenues (income) and expenditures (outlays) for fiscal year 2008. The major income sources are personal income taxes (39 percent) and social insurance receipts (Social Security, Medicare, and unemployment and other retirement taxes), which accounted for 30 percent of receipts. Corporate taxes accounted for 10 percent of income and excise, customs, estate, gift, and miscellaneous taxes contributed 6 percent of income. The remaining income of 15 percent came from borrowing to cover the deficit.

The primary expenditures for fiscal year 2008 were in the form of Social Security, Medicare, and other retirement outlays and accounted for 37 percent of the total outlays. Outlays for national defense, veterans, and foreign affairs activities amounted to 24 percent of outlays. The third most important outlays category was for social programs (Medicaid, food stamps, temporary assistance for needy families, supplemental security income, etc.) and accounted for 20 percent of fiscal 2008 expenditures. The remaining outlays were for physical, human, and community development (9 percent), net interest on the debt (8 percent), and law enforcement and general government activities (2 percent).

Local governments depend heavily on property taxes for their revenues, while state governments depend largely on sales taxes and special taxes such as those on motor fuel, liquor, and

FIGURE 7.1
The Federal Government Dollar, Fiscal Year 2008

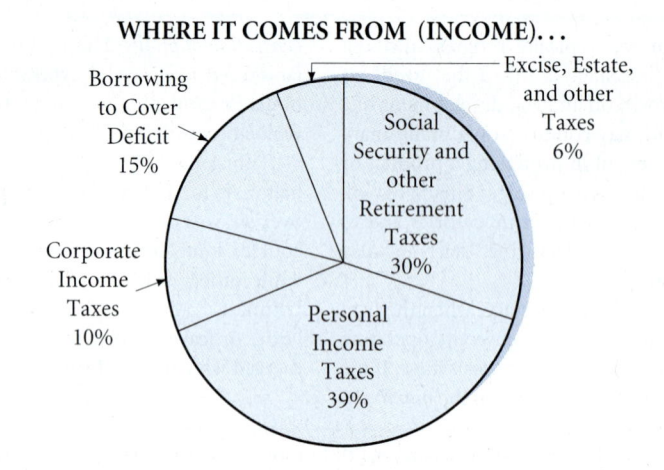

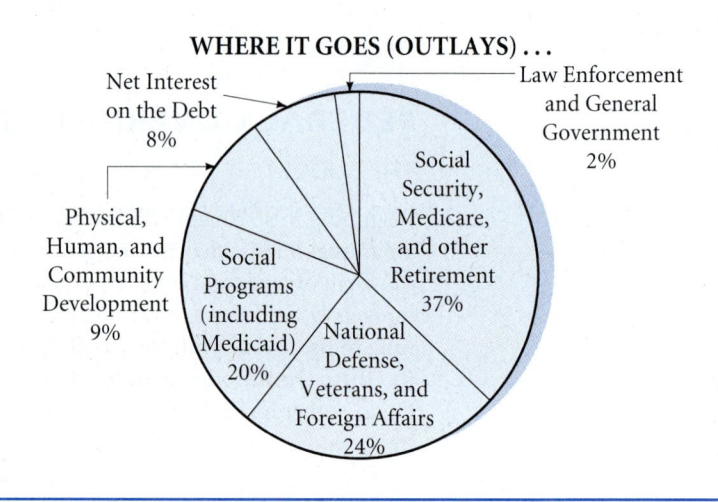

WHERE IT COMES FROM (INCOME)...

- Borrowing to Cover Deficit 15%
- Excise, Estate, and other Taxes 6%
- Social Security and other Retirement Taxes 30%
- Corporate Income Taxes 10%
- Personal Income Taxes 39%

WHERE IT GOES (OUTLAYS)...

- Net Interest on the Debt 8%
- Law Enforcement and General Government 2%
- Physical, Human, and Community Development 9%
- Social Programs (including Medicaid) 20%
- Social Security, Medicare, and other Retirement 37%
- National Defense, Veterans, and Foreign Affairs 24%

Source: Department of the Treasury, Internal Revenue Service, http://www.irs.gov.

ETHICAL ISSUES

tobacco products. In contrast, the federal government relies primarily on individual income taxes, social insurance taxes, and corporate income taxes for its revenues.

FISCAL POLICY MAKERS

In Chapter 5 we noted that Congress and the president determine the nation's fiscal policy. These individuals are elected by the people under the belief that they are to serve the people. Decisions relating to taxing and spending, and the resulting impact on whether federal budgets will be surpluses or deficits, are important to voters. Voters also expect their elected politicians to behave ethically by acting honestly and fairly with their constituencies.

For the most part, our elected federal politicians seemed to have acted ethically and with integrity. However, there have been some examples of unethical and illegal behavior. *Impeachment* is a formal legislative process in which charges of "high crimes and misdemeanors" are brought against high-level officials. The House of Representatives votes on whether to impeach an official; if it does impeach, a trial is held in the Senate. In the United States, only two presidents out of forty-three have been impeached. They were Andrew Johnson, the seventeenth president, and William Clinton, the forty-second president. Both were acquitted. Former President Richard Nixon resigned before being impeached.

Occasionally members of Congress have engaged in illegal activities. Some have been convicted in criminal court. Since the mid-1970s, at least twelve members have received prison sentences for

PERSONAL FINANCIAL PLANNING
Develop a Personal Financial Plan

Developing a personal financial plan is necessary to increase the chances for reaching your financial goals. Goals in business, life, and finances rarely are met by accident. With a bewildering array of investment choices and confusing tax laws, more and more people are turning to an investment professional for help and guidance. An important step in creating a personal financial plan is to develop a policy statement. A policy statement contains basic information to help guide future financial decisions. A policy statement will describe an investor's objective. An objective will have two components: a return goal (capital gain, income, or both) and information about the investor's risk tolerance. Investors who cannot handle the ups and downs of the stock market will not want to place as much of their savings in stocks as someone who is willing to take on the additional risk.

In addition to an objective, the policy statement needs to include information about the five sets of constraints faced by every investor:

1. Liquidity needs. Does the investor need to be able to sell assets and obtain cash quickly?

2. Time horizon. Over what time horizon can be funds be invested? Two years? Ten? Thirty years or more?

3. Taxes. The investor's tax situation is an important consideration as investing goals should focus on after-tax returns. Capital gains and losses, income, IRA accounts, 401(k) retirement plans, and taxable versus nontaxable securities all lead to decision-making complications.

4. Legal and regulatory factors. Investment decisions are affected by rules and regulations. Even something as basic as investing money in a bank CD often carries with it the warning: "substantial interest penalty upon early withdrawal."

5. Unique needs and preferences. This constraint can include wanting to exclude certain investments because of personal preference or social consciousness reasons. For example, an investor may not want to own stock or bonds issued by firms that produce or sell pornography, tobacco, or alcoholic beverages.

---

such activities as accepting bribes, taking part in kickback schemes, extortion, illegal sex offenses, and mail fraud. While the activities of these individuals have tainted Congress, by far most members behave ethically both personally and professionally when representing the people who elected them.

DEBT FINANCING

As we have observed, the federal government obtains funds for expenditures primarily through tax revenues. When these tax and other general revenues fail to meet expenditures, a **budgetary deficit** is incurred. Until recent years these deficits have been of modest size compared to total government expenditures. However, their cumulative impact has created a vast increase in the total federal debt. Although Congress had set **federal statutory debt limits**, it was necessary to raise the limits at frequent intervals when the federal government was running ongoing deficits.

budgetary deficit
occurs when expenditures are greater than revenues

federal statutory debt limits
limits on the federal debt set by Congress

U.S. citizens and financial institutions hold or own a large portion of the U.S. federal debt that is outstanding. Part of our debt is due to our role as a creditor nation from 1918 until 1985. Until World War I the United States depended heavily on foreign investment, and it was not until 1985 that liabilities to foreign creditors again exceeded claims against foreign creditors. Our return to being a debtor nation was due in large measure to relatively high domestic interest rates, relative political stability in the world arena, and the development of an extremely unfavorable balance of trade. The nation's excess of imports relative to exports has continued to be very large since 1964. To the extent that foreign claims resulting from a surplus of imports are invested in federal obligations, foreign ownership of the federal debt increases.

Nowhere in the economy is the significance of a smoothly functioning financial system more apparent than in connection with the federal debt. Not only does the financial system accommodate the federal government by financing its frequent budgetary deficits, but it also provides for the smooth transition from old debt issues that mature to the new issues that replace them. The financial markets face a greater challenge in such refunding of government issues than in absorbing net new debt. Just as the nation's industrial development depended on an equally efficient development of financial institutions, so, too, do many of the financial activities of modern government depend on these same institutions.

CONCEPT CHECK
What are the major revenues and expenditures in the federal budget?

What is meant by a budgetary deficit?

It is notable that public borrowing is a relatively modern development. During the Middle Ages, governments borrowed from wealthy merchants and others on an individual basis. Often crown jewels were offered as collateral for such advances. Large public borrowing by governments, as for businesses, became possible only when monetary systems were refined and efficient financial institutions developed that could facilitate the transfer of monetary savings.

HISTORICAL ROLE AND CREATION OF SAVINGS

As the size of U.S. businesses expanded, the importance of accumulating and converting large amounts of financial capital to business use increased. The corporate form of organization provided a convenient and flexible legal arrangement for bringing together available financial capital. These advantages of the corporation over sole proprietorship, or private ownership, and partnership are described in Chapter 13.

Developments in public transportation were often too costly and speculative for private promoters to undertake. The magnitude of early canal, turnpike, and railroad construction was such that the government undertook much of the financing of these projects. In fact, until the end of the nineteenth century, governmental units contributed more funding to these efforts than did private interests. Since this government financing was accomplished largely through bond issues rather than current revenues, the ultimate source of funds was the savings of individuals who bought the bonds.

FOREIGN SOURCES OF SAVINGS

Foreign investors purchased large amounts of the securities sold by government and private promoters to develop the United States. In particular, foreign capital played a decisive role in the development of the nation's early transportation system.

The huge role that foreign capital played in the economic development of the United States is found in the developing nations of today. These nations now face many of the financial problems that the United States experienced during its early years. Private savings in many of these countries are negligible because almost all current income must be used for immediate consumption. Individual nations and such international organizations as the World Bank supply large amounts of capital to the developing nations of the world to increase their productive capacity.

The flow of development capital not only stimulates economic expansion in these countries but also makes their capital much more efficient. For example, speedier transportation reduces the amount of goods in transit, thus releasing working capital for other purposes. In due time, as internal capital formation increases, it is hoped that the need for foreign capital will be eliminated and that these countries can then enjoy an independent capital formation process.

CONCEPT CHECK
How were the savings of individuals important in the early development of the United States?

DOMESTIC SUPPLY OF SAVINGS

As capital formation began increasing at a faster and faster rate after the Civil War, the demand for funds also increased. Wealthy Americans and foreign investors could no longer provide funds at a rapid enough rate. Britain was investing heavily in India because of political commitments, and the other European countries were not large or wealthy enough to continue supplying funds in quantities adequate to sustain U.S. growth. The American family soon took over the function of providing savings for the capital formation process. Per capita income rose to a level at which American families could afford luxuries well beyond the subsistence level and could save part of what they had earned. Thus, the United States gradually developed to the stage where it could generate sufficient capital to finance its own expansion. Ultimately the result was a change in the country's status from a debtor nation to a creditor nation.

savings
income that is not consumed but held in the form of cash and other financial assets

savings surplus
occurs when current income exceeds investment in real assets

undistributed profits
proportion of after-tax profits retained by corporations

CREATION OF SAVINGS

Today the U.S. financial system is viewed as comprising three basic economic units: individuals, business firms (including financial institutions), and governments (federal, state, and local). **Savings** occur when all of an economic unit's income is not consumed and are represented by the accumulation of cash and other financial assets. **Savings surplus** occurs when an economic unit, such as individuals taken as a group, has current income that exceeds its direct investment in real assets. These surplus savings are made available to savings deficit units. For example, business firms as a group are often unable to meet all their plant and equipment investment needs out of **undistributed profits** or earnings retained in the business, which are profits remaining after taxes and, in the case of corporations, after the cash dividends are paid to stockholders.

savings deficit
occurs when investment in real assets exceeds current income

When expenditures on real assets exceed current income, a *savings deficit* situation exists and it becomes necessary to acquire funds from a savings surplus unit.

MAJOR SOURCES OF SAVINGS

An important savings sector in the economy is the savings of individuals called *personal saving*. In equation form, we have:

$$\text{Personal saving} = \text{personal income} - \text{personal current taxes} - \text{personal outlays} \quad (7.2)$$

CONCEPT CHECK
What is the difference between savings surplus and savings deficit units?

Personal income includes compensation of employees, personal income of persons with capital consumption adjustment, personal interest and dividend income, and net government social benefits to persons. Personal income less personal current taxes equals disposable personal income. Then, subtracting personal outlays (personal consumption expenditures, personal nonmortgage interest payments, and personal current transfer payments made primarily to the government) equals personal saving.

personal saving
savings of individuals equal to personal income less personal current taxes less personal outlays

Voluntary savings are savings in the form of financial assets held or set aside for use in the future. **Contractual savings** are savings accumulated on a regular schedule for a specified length of time by prior agreement. An example is the accumulation of reserves in insurance and pension funds. Contractual savings are not determined by current decisions. They are disciplined by previous commitments that the saver has some incentive to honor.

voluntary savings
savings held or set aside by choice for future use

It is from individuals that most financial intermediaries accumulate capital. Individuals as a group consistently represent a savings surplus unit. Corporations also represent an important source of savings. However, their large demand for investment funds, as is also the case for unincorporated business firms, generally results in a net need for external funds. While financial intermediaries can also save, their primary role in the U.S. financial system is to aid the savings-investment process. The U.S. government, on balance, has operated as a savings-deficit unit in recent years. Thus, the ability to provide adequate funds to meet investment needs primarily depends on the savings of individuals and corporations.

contractual savings
savings accumulated on a regular schedule by prior agreement

PERSONAL SAVINGS

CONCEPT CHECK
What are the differences between voluntary savings and contractual savings?

Table 7.3 shows personal savings in the United States for 2003, 2006, and 2009. Personal income rose from nearly $11.3 trillion in 2006 to about $12.1 trillion in 2009. Personal current taxes decreased, while individuals increased their personal outlays from $9.7 trillion to nearly $10.5 trillion. As a result, personal savings increased from $235.0 billion in 2006 to a $502.7 billion in 2009. Thus, in terms of the personal savings rate in the United States, which is personal savings as a percentage of disposable personal income, the change was a change from 2.4 percent to a 4.6 percent from 2006 to 2009. Possibly, in part due to the financial crisis of 2007–09, individuals chose to save more. The U.S. savings rate continues to lag the personal savings rates in Japan and Western Europe.

INTERNET ACTIVITY
Go to the Web site of the Federal Reserve Bank of St. Louis, http://www.stlouisfed.org. Access the Federal Reserve Economic Database (FRED) and find current information on the size of disposable personal income and personal savings.

TABLE 7.3
Personal Savings in the United States ($ Billions)

	2003	2006	2009
Personal income	$9,208.0	$11,268.1	$12,072.1
Less: personal current taxes	991.5	1,352.4	1,107.6
Disposable personal income	8,216.5	9,915.7	10,964.5
Less: personal outlays	8,043.0	9,680.7	10,461.8
Personal savings	173.5	235.0	502.7
Savings rate (personal savings/disposable personal income)	2.1%	2.4%	4.6%

Sources: *Survey of Current Business* and www.bea.gov.

U.S. personal savings rates were higher in the past. For example, historical savings rates for each five-year interval from 1960 through 2005 were:

YEAR	SAVINGS RATES (%)	YEAR	SAVINGS RATES (%)
1960	5.8	1985	4.5
1965	7.0	1990	4.3
1970	8.1	1995	4.8
1975	9.2	2000	1.0
1980	7.1	2005	1.4

Notice that the savings rate increased from below 6 percent in 1960 to more than 9 percent by 1975. Tax reform in the form of lower personal income tax rates in the mid-1960s and in the 1970s may have contributed to this higher personal savings rate. However, the savings rate declined to less than 5 percent by 1985 and remained below 5 percent in 1990 and 1995 before dropping dramatically to the 1 percent level in 2000 and remained below the 2 percent level in 2005. Of course, we know from the data in Table 7.3 that the personal savings rate in the United States has shown an increase to 2.4 percent in 2006 and to 4.6 percent in 2009.

Individuals maintain savings for a number of reasons. They set aside a part of their current income to make mortgage payments on loans used to purchase homes. They also save to acquire costly durable consumer goods, such as cars and appliances. Savings are set aside by individuals to meet unforeseeable financial needs. These savings are not set aside for specific future consumption; instead, they represent emergency or rainy-day funds. Individuals may also save for such long-term foreseeable spending as children's college education or for retirement. For short periods, people may save a portion of current income simply because desirable goods and services are not available for purchase.

A number of media are available in which to maintain savings, ranging in liquidity from cash balances to stocks and bonds. Three factors usually influence a person's choice of medium: liquidity, degree of safety, and return. Various types of financial instruments and securities that individuals may hold are discussed later in this chapter.

CORPORATE SAVINGS

Table 7.4 shows nonfinancial corporate savings in the United States for 2003, 2006, and 2008 (data for 2009 were not available). Corporate profits before taxes increased from 2003 to 2006, which coincided with growth in U.S. economic activity. However, corporate profits before taxes declined from $923.9 billion in 2006 to $711.6 billion in 2008. Between 2006 and 2008, nonfinancial corporate tax liabilities also decreased from $307.6 billion to $237.8 billion. The net result was a decline in after-tax profits from $616.2 billion in 2006 to $473.8 billion in 2008. This decline coincided with the 2007–09 financial crisis.

Corporations save by producing profits after taxes and then not paying all profits to investors in the form of dividends. The proportion of after-tax profits retained in the organization is referred to as undistributed profits. Corporate profits that were not distributed to owners

TABLE 7.4

Nonfinancial Corporate Savings in the United States ($ Billions)

	2003	2006	2008
Profits before taxes (with IVA and CCAdj)	$486.1	923.9	711.6
Less: tax liabilities	132.9	307.6	237.8
Profits after taxes	352.2	616.2	473.8
Less: dividends	293.4	471.1	409.3
Undistributed profits	59.8	145.1	64.5
Retention rate (undistributed profits/profits after taxes)	17.0%	30.5%	15.8%
Addenda:			
Profits before taxes (without IVA and CCAdj)	$425.9	1,117.9	806.7
Inventory valuation adjustment (IVA)	−11.3	−38.0	−38.2
Capital consumption adjustment (CCAdj)	71.5	−156.0	−56.8

Source: *Survey of Current Business* and http://www.bea.gov.

amounted to $145.1 billion in 2006 and $64.5 billion in 2008 and resulted in retention rates (undistributed profits divided by profits after taxes) of 30.5 percent and 15.8 percent, respectively.

Table 7.4 refers to nonfinancial corporate profits before taxes and includes an inventory valuation adjustment (IVA) and a capital consumption adjustment (CCAdj). Inventory values may increase or decrease in a given year and thus can affect nonfinancial corporate profits before taxes. **Capital consumption adjustment**, also called depreciation, is the estimate of the "using up" of plant and equipment assets for business purposes. By subtracting the IVA and CCAdj) amounts from the profits before taxes (including IVA and CCAdj), the results were adjusted profits before taxes of $1,179.9 billion in 2006 and $806.7 billion in 2008.

capital consumption adjustment — estimates of the "using up," or depreciation, of plant and equipment assets for business purposes

Corporate saving for short-term working capital purposes is by far the most important reason for accumulating financial assets. Seasonal business changes create an uneven demand for corporate operating assets, such as inventories and accounts receivable. Because of these seasonal changes, cash inflow is seldom in just the right amount and at the right time to accommodate the increased levels of operating assets. Quarterly corporate income tax liabilities also impose the necessity of accumulating financial assets.

The short-term accumulation of financial assets on the part of business corporations does not add to the level of long-term savings of the economy as a whole. However, these funds do enter the monetary stream and become available to users of short-term borrowed funds. As such, these short-term savings serve to meet a part of the demand for funds of consumers, government, and other businesses. A corporation typically holds this type of savings in the form of checkable deposits with commercial banks, short-term obligations of the federal government, commercial paper, and certificates of deposit issued by commercial banks. These financial assets meet the requirements of safety and liquidity.

Corporations also engage in the savings process to meet planned spending in the future. Reserves are often set up to provide all or part of the cost of construction, purchase of equipment, or major maintenance and repairs to existing facilities. Savings committed to these purposes are often invested in securities that have longer maturities and higher yields than those held for short-term business purposes. These securities include the debt obligations of both corporations and government and, to a limited extent, corporate stock.

CONCEPT CHECK
What are capital consumption adjustments?
How do corporations save?

FACTORS AFFECTING SAVINGS

Several factors influence the total amount of savings in any given period:

- Levels of income
- Economic expectations
- Cyclical influences
- Life stage of the individual saver or corporation

The precise relationship between savings and consumption is the subject of much debate and continuing study, however, and we limit our observations here to broad generalizations.

LEVELS OF INCOME

For our purposes, savings have been defined as current income minus tax payments and consumption spending. Keeping this definition in mind, let us explore the effect of changes in income on the levels of savings of individuals. As income falls, the individual attempts to maintain his or her present standard of living as long as possible. In so doing, the proportion of his or her consumption spending increases and total savings diminish. As income is further reduced, the individual may be forced to curtail consumption spending, which results in a lower standard of living. Such reduction is reasonably limited, however, since the basic needs of the individual or family unit must be met. Not only will personal savings be eliminated when income is drastically reduced, but the individual may also **dissave,** that is, spend accumulated savings rather than further reduce consumption spending.

dissave — to liquidate savings for consumption uses

As income increases, the individual will again be in a position to save. However, the saving will not necessarily begin immediately, as the individual may desire to buy the things that he or she could not afford during the low-income period. The amount of this need, notably for durable consumer goods, largely determines the rate of increase in savings during periods of income recovery.

On the whole, income levels are closely associated with levels of employment. Changes in business activity, in turn, influence employment levels. Downturns in the economy during 1980, 1981–1982, 1990, 2001, and 2008 resulted in declines in employment levels and correspondingly lowered levels of income. Post–World War II unemployment highs of the early 1980s exceeded 10 percent. During the decade of the 1990s unemployment averaged less than 5 percent, with deviations resulting in higher levels in the 1990 and 2001 recessions. The 2007–09 financial crisis, including the 2008 economic downturn, resulted in unemployment levels at the 10 percent level.

ECONOMIC EXPECTATIONS

The anticipation of future events has a significant effect on savings. If individuals believe that their incomes will decrease in the near future, they may curtail their spending to establish a reserve for the expected period of low income. For example, a worker anticipating a protracted labor dispute may increase current savings as partial protection against the financial impact of a strike.

Expectations of a general increase in price levels may also have a strong influence on the liquidity that savers want to maintain. The prospect of price increases in consumer durable goods may cause an increase in their sales as individuals try to buy before prices increase. Savings are thus quickly converted to consumer spending. Corporate savings, too, may be reduced as a result of price increase expectations. In addition to committing funds to plant and office equipment before price increases take place, corporations typically increase their inventory positions. As for the individual, the prospect of an interruption in the supply of inventory because of a labor strike or other cause often results in a rapid stockpiling of raw materials and merchandise. The prospect of price decreases and of large production capacity has the opposite effect: The liquidity and financial assets of a business increase relative to its operating assets.

Unprecedented price increases during the inflationary 1970s led many individuals to develop a "buy it now because it will cost more later" philosophy. This resulted in a classic example of the impact of price increase expectations on the spend-save decisions of individuals. Inflation peaked at double-digit levels at the beginning of the 1980s. However, after some upward pressure in the form of price increases at the end of the 1980s, inflation during the 1990s and the early years of the twenty-first century has been in the 2 percent to 3 percent range.

ECONOMIC CYCLES

Cyclical movements in the economy are the primary cause of changes in levels of income. Cyclical movements affect not only the amounts but also the types of savings. Economic cycles may be viewed in terms of the two- to four-year traditional business cycle or in terms of much longer cycles that correspond with generations of people.

Let's begin with a discussion that concentrates on the traditional business cycle. In general, interest rates on securities with short maturities are lower than interest rates on long-term maturities.[1] However, when economic activity is peaking, short-term interest rates are higher than long-term interest rates. Generally, interest rates are high because inflation rates are high, and the Fed raises short-term interest rates even further to slow economic activity and reduce inflation. As a recession deepens, short-term interest rates fall faster than long-term interest rates. Finally, when interest rates get low enough, businesses will find it attractive to borrow and grow. The savings rate usually goes down in a recessionary period and savers emphasize liquidity and safety when they do save. When the economy is growing, individuals usually save more and may hold their savings in riskier short-term securities.

Harry Dent Jr. discusses much longer cycles based on *generation waves*, with the largest generation wave in the history of the United States being the baby boom wave.[2] In his view, a generation wave consists of birth wave, innovation wave, spending wave, and organization wave components or stages. These components correspond with birth, coming of age, adulthood, and maturity. For the baby boom generation, the birth wave peaked in the early 1950s. The innovation wave peaked in the 1980s. This was a period of rapid introduction of new technologies, and the country began the movement from a production economy to an information economy.

---

1. We discuss the term or maturity structure of interest rates in detail in Chapter 8.
2. Harry Dent, Jr., *The Great Boom Ahead*, New York: Hyperion, 1993. Also see Harry Dent, Jr., *The Roaring 2000s*, New York: Simon & Schuster, 1998.

CONCEPT CHECK
What are general factors that affect savings?

According to Dent, the spending wave, in turn, which will peak early in this century, has driven the economic successes of the 1990s. The last stage will peak when the baby boomers reach age sixty-five in roughly 2025. While a lot of economists are skeptical about broad-based generalizations made by Harry Dent and others, all will agree that the economic clout of a large number of individuals moving through their life cycles at about the same time can influence the economy and the securities markets.

LIFE STAGES OF THE INDIVIDUAL SAVER

The pattern of savings over an individual's life span follows a somewhat predictable pattern when viewed over the total population. A successful individual life cycle would have the following stages:

- Formative/education developing
- Career starting/family creating
- Wealth building
- Retirement enjoying

Individuals save very little during their formative and education developing stage simply because little income is produced. They typically consume a portion of their parents' earnings and savings, which is substantial if they attend college. As they enter their career starting and family creating stage they possess little savings but have large "earning power" potential. Their income increases. However, expenses also increase during these early family-forming years. Saving and investing typically focus on purchasing a home and accruing life and disability insurance.

By the time an individual reaches his or her wealth building stage, two new factors result in increased savings. First, income is typically much higher than at any previous time; second, the expense of raising and educating children has been reduced or eliminated. Thus it is this group that typically saves the most. At the retirement-enjoying stage, the individual's income is sharply reduced. He or she may now begin the process of *dissaving*. Pension fund payments along with accumulated savings are drawn upon for current living expenses.

The level of savings of individuals is therefore a function of the age composition of the population as a whole. A population shift to a large proportion of individuals in the productive middle-age years would result in a greater savings potential. These views of the life stages of the individual saver are consistent with the generation-wave approach described by Harry Dent Jr. That is, if a large number of individuals are moving through their individual life cycles at approximately the same time, their combined efforts will have a major impact on the overall economy. On a collective basis, they spend at about the same time and are also likely to save at about the same time. Spending has kept the U.S. economy in almost continual growth since the early 1980s, and saving/investing in retirement plans and directly in mutual funds (which in turn buy bonds and stocks) helped the stock market reach historical highs during the 1990s. However, since then a substantial decline in stock prices preceded a downturn in economic activity in 2000–01 and again during the 2007–09 financial crisis.

CONCEPT CHECK
How does the pattern of savings usually differ over an individual's lifetime?

LIFE STAGES OF THE CORPORATION

Just as the financial savings of an individual are governed in part by age, so the financial savings generated by a business firm are a function of its life stage. The following are the life cycle stages of a successful business firm:

- Start-up stage
- Survival stage
- Rapid growth stage
- Maturity stage

It is true, of course, that not all business firms proceed through a fixed life-stage cycle. To the extent, however, that a firm experiences the typical pattern of starting up, surviving, vigorous growth, and ultimate maturity, its flow of financial savings may experience a predictable pattern.

INTERNET ACTIVITY

Go to the Web Site of the Federal Reserve Board of Governors of the Federal Reserve System, http://www.federalreserve.gov, and identify current interest rates on U.S. Treasury bills and bonds.

CONCEPT CHECK

What are some of the stages in a typical corporate life cycle?

During the development of the business idea and starting the business stage, the firm is spending cash rather than building cash. The business firm typically continues to burn cash as it tries to find a successful operating niche. During the early part of the expansion years (rapid growth stage) of a successful business, the volume of physical assets typically increases rapidly. So rapid is this growth that the firm is unable to establish a strong position with respect to its financial assets. Indeed, it is during these years of the corporate life cycle that there is a large need for borrowed capital. At this time the corporation is typically a heavy user of financial assets rather than a provider.

As the firm reaches the second part of its rapid growth stage, it begins building surplus or "free" cash flow and increasing the firm's value. Free cash is money available after funds have been reinvested in the firm to sustain its growth. As the enterprise matures and its growth slows down to a long-run sustainable growth rate, it reaches its peak of savings. Earnings and cash flows are high, and commitment of funds to increased operating assets is reduced. The maturity stage can last almost indefinitely as long as the firm remains competitive in its industry. Of course, sometimes a firm's products or services are no longer competitive or needed by consumers, and the firm again starts consuming more cash than it brings in. Such firms will eventually cease to exist.

CAPITAL MARKET SECURITIES

Financial markets play an important role in the marketing and transferring of financial assets and thus are an integral part of the savings and investment process. In Chapter 1 we defined *money markets* as markets where debt securities of one year or less are issued or traded. In Chapter 2 we discussed *money market securities*—which, as you recall, are debt instruments or securities with maturities of one year or less. The major securities that trade in the money markets are treasury bills, negotiable certificates of deposit, commercial paper, banker's acceptances, repurchase agreements, and federal funds. Treasury bills and negotiable certificates of deposit are short-term investment vehicles available to individuals. These two short-term investments as well as commercial paper, banker's acceptances, and repurchase agreements are investments used by business firms. Federal funds are used by depository institutions with excess funds lending to depository institutions that have a need for funds.

In Chapter 1 we also defined *capital markets* as markets where debt securities with maturities longer than one year and corporate stocks are issued or traded. **Capital market securities** are debt securities with maturities longer than one year and corporate stocks. Capital markets are important to individuals who seek to finance home purchases. Capital markets are very important to corporations who raise funds to finance their operations. Individuals and corporations with excess funds also invest in capital market securities.

Figure 7.2 shows the basic securities that are issued and traded in capital securities markets. In Chapter 1 we initially defined a mortgage. We review the definition here as part of our discussion of capital market securities. A **mortgage** is a loan backed by real property in the form of buildings and houses. In the event the debt is not repaid, the lender can use proceeds from the sale of the real property to extinguish any remaining loan interest or principal balance. Individuals rely heavily on residential mortgages to assist them in owning their own homes. Businesses also often find it worthwhile to borrow against the real property they own.

Bonds are long-term debt instruments issued by government units and business corporations. A **Treasury bond,** sometimes referred to as a *note* for shorter securities, is a debt instrument or security issued by the U.S. federal government with a typical maturity ranging from five to twenty years. Treasury bonds are sold to raise funds needed to reconcile longer-term imbalances between tax receipts and government expenditures. These bonds have very low risks of default, and investors know that they are easily marketable in the secondary securities market. For example, if an investor initially purchases a twenty-year federal government bond and later identifies another investment opportunity, the bond can be easily sold in the secondary capital market. A **municipal bond** is a debt instrument or security issued by a state or local government. Maturities on state and local government bonds, like Treasury bonds, often are in the five-year to twenty-year range. However, municipal bonds issued to build airports or bridges may have their maturities set approximately equal to the expected lives of the assets being financed. Some investors find municipal bonds to be attractive investments because the interest paid on

capital market securities
debt securities with maturities longer than one year and corporate stocks

mortgage
loan backed by real property in the form of buildings and houses

Treasury bond
long-term debt instrument issued by the U.S. federal government

municipal bond
long-term debt instrument issued by a state or local government

FIGURE 7.2

Major Capital Market Securities

SECURITIES	TYPICAL MATURITIES	ISSUERS	INVESTORS	SECONDARY MARKET
Mortgages	Up to 30 years	Financial intermediaries	Individuals, business firms and institutions	High activity
Treasury bonds	Up to 30 years	U.S. government	Individuals, business firms, and institutions	High activity
Municipal bonds	Up to 30 years	State/local governments	Individuals, business firms, and institutions	Moderate activity
Corporate bonds	Up to 30 years	Corporations	Individuals, business firms, and institutions	Moderate activity
Corporate stocks	None	Corporations	Individuals, business firms, and institutions	High activity

corporate bond
debt instrument issued by a corporation to raise long-term funds

common stock
ownership interest in a corporation

derivative security
financial contract that derives its value from a bond, stock, or other asset

CONCEPT CHECK

What financial instruments typically have maturities up to one year?

What financial instruments and securities typically have maturities in excess of one year?

FINANCIAL CRISIS

these securities is exempt from federal income taxes and because these bonds also can be sold in a secondary market.

Corporations issue financial instruments or securities, called debt and equity, to raise funds to acquire real assets to support the operations of their firms. Corporate debt instruments are bonds and equity securities are stocks. A **corporate bond** is a debt instrument issued by a corporation to raise long-term funds. Corporate bonds are typically issued with five- to twenty-year maturities and may be secured by the pledge of real property, plant, or equipment or they may be issued with only the backing of the general credit strength of the corporation.[3] A share of **common stock** represents an ownership interest in a corporation. Corporations often issue new shares of their common stocks to raise funds for capital expenditures and investments in inventories. Active secondary markets exist for trading the common stocks of larger corporations after the stocks are initially issued. Corporations also can issue various classes of common stock, another type of stock called *preferred stock*, and even securities that are convertible into shares of common stock, as will be discussed later.

Corporations also can use derivative securities to insure or hedge against various financial risks. A **derivative security** is a financial contract that derives its value from the value of another asset such as a bond or stock.[4]

A FURTHER LOOK AT THE 2007–09 FINANCIAL CRISIS

EARLY FACTORS

How did the Financial Crisis of 2007–2009 begin?[5] The seeds of the problem were sown in the 2001 recession. Businesses emphasized cost cutting and improved operating efficiencies in the latter part of the 1980s. These efforts, coupled with a nearly decade-long economic growth in the 1990s left the U.S. awash with vast amounts of unused financial capital. The U.S. economy benefited further from large expenditures to hopefully minimize the so-called "Year 2000 (or Y2K)" problem associated with the fact that many computer programs used only two digits to indicate the year. For example, 1901 was coded as 01 and 1999 as 99. No one was sure what would happen when the first year of the new century was designated as 00. As a result, large precautionary expenditures were incurred to hopefully minimize potential problems.

---

3. Various types of corporate bonds and their characteristics are discussed in Chapter 10.
4. The use of derivatives is explored in Chapter 11.
5. As noted in Chapter 1, our discussion of the recent financial crisis draws heavily on the work of Edgar A. Norton Jr., "The Financial Crisis: 2007–2009," Wiley Custom Learning Solutions, 2009.

CAREER PROFILES

JAMIE BREEN
Marketing
Disciplined Investment Advisors

BS, Radio, TV, and Film
Northwestern University
MBA, Marketing/Finance
Northwestern University

"For lack of a more specific title, I'm the marketing guy."

Q: *Describe the firm you work for.*
A: I work for Disciplined Investment Advisors, which is a small money management firm. We manage (invest) money for corporate pension funds.

Q: *You say it's a small firm. How small?*
A: We manage over a billion dollars for our clients. That's a lot of money, but compared to Fidelity with several hundred billion, we're definitely at the lower end. In the industry we'd be called a "boutique" firm.

Q: *And what do you do there?*
A: For lack of a more specific title, I'm the marketing guy. It's my job to spread the word about what we do, generate new clients, and keep existing ones.

Q: *So you call on pension fund managers?*
A: Yes, that's part of it. Our clients all have a person or team in charge of managing the pension fund, trying to invest it profitably and safely. So I call on those people, but there's another group of people that I spend even more time with. They are the outside consultants that help the pension managers decide whom to hire.

Q: *What do you do with these consultants?*
A: Basically, I try to demonstrate to them that we are a good firm to recommend to their clients. I present them with information about our investment strategy and our performance during previous periods. But more important than the numbers is demonstrating to the consultants that we can help them look good, that we can make a professional presentation to their clients, explain our strategy coherently, and so on.

Q: *So if you impress the consultant, the consultant may recommend you to take over the investing of a company's pension fund.*
A: Part of a company's pension fund. To diversify, most funds divide the investment job between a number of companies like ours: four or five for a smaller fund, up to a hundred or more for a very large corporation.

Q: *Is this a competitive business?*
A: It's very competitive because there's so much money involved. There are probably a thousand money managers that we could conceivably compete against. So even if our results are excellent, say in the top quartile, there are another 250 companies that can say the same thing.

Q: *So how do you differentiate yourself from the crowd?*
A: One of the unique aspects of our company is that it was founded by university professors, true experts in the field of finance. So part of our message is based on the amount and quality of research that backs up our investment strategy. We provide both the pension fund managers and the consultants with a great deal of research data and information that helps them do their jobs. In return we hope to be selected to manage their money. And the other piece of the puzzle is simply to establish trust and credibility. Like any other sales job.

The late 1990s saw the internet "bubble" in the stock market—stock prices rose out of proportion from the ability of firms to generate earnings or cash flows. In particular, "high-flying" stocks included internet or "tech" oriented stocks. Some forecast the end of long-standing business models and the genesis of new ways of doing business using the internet and information as tools to gain profits. However, the movement from "brick and mortar" firms to "e-commerce" firms did not pave the way to a "new economic world," and the internet/tech bubble burst.

Stock prices peaked in 2000 and began a rapid decline. The falling stock market, coupled with a slowing post-Y2K economy and recession in 2001, encouraged the Federal Reserve System to lower interest rates to try to stimulate spending, borrowing, and economic growth. The terrorist attacks of September 11, 2001, added concern and uncertainty about the economy. To assist the economy, the Federal Reserve maintained liquidity of the financial sector and continued to lower interest rates. The Federal Reserve System was covered in Chapter 4, and we discussed the role of the Federal Reserve Board as a major policy maker group in Chapter 5.

Fiscal policy also became stimulative, with increased government spending and the passage of tax cuts in 2002. Fiscal policy influences economic activity through taxation and expenditure plans and is carried out by the President and Congress with the support of the U.S. Treasury. We discussed the role of fiscal policy in Chapter 5. Overall, the setting of low interest rates, fiscal policy stimulation, and the resulting growing economy helped to create an environment conducive for excessive spending and borrowing.

A BORROWING-RELATED CULTURAL SHIFT

On the whole, U.S. consumers used to limit their use of debt, but over time the American psyche changed to wanting sooner, if not instant, gratification with respect to buying large-ticket items. Rather than saving and waiting to purchase expensive items, the use of credit cards rose. Borrowing now replaced "save now, buy later" as a spending philosophy. The U.S. savings rate was typically above 8 percent from the late 1950s through the mid-1980s. Since then, the U.S. savings rate fell to around the 1 percent level during the early part of the decade of the 2000s. However, probably as a result of the onset of the 2007–09 financial crisis, individuals increased their savings rate to in excess of 4 percent of their disposable income by 2009.

The cultural shift that allowed the public to "spend now and pay later"—rather than their parents' or grandparents' philosophy of "save now, spend later" also affected household budgets. In addition to carrying a home mortgage and/or car loan or lease payments, the average American household has over $8,000 in unpaid credit card debt. With a growing use of debt, a larger portion of Americans' household budgets go toward debt service—repaying borrowing funds with principal and interest. Americans spent less than 11 percent of their disposable income paying debt interest and principal in the early 1990s but over 14 percent in recent years.

U.S. government officials engaged in efforts to expand home ownership by encouraging lenders to make mortgage loans available to a broader spectrum of individuals during the 1990s and the first few years of the 2000s. The typical, traditional home loan has been a 40-year, fixed interest rate amortized loan involving a constant monthly payment that would result in a zero loan balance at maturity. These traditional home loans also typically required a 20 percent down payment. In order to increase the number of individuals who could qualify for home ownership, alternative mortgage loan instruments were developed and in some instances credit standards were lowered.

As discussed in Chapter 1, the traditional fixed-rate mortgage was often replaced by an adjustable-rate mortgage called an ARM. Mortgage lenders often offered initial below market interest rates on ARMs as well as offered subprime mortgages to borrowers with relatively low credit scores, which suggested that the likelihood that loan payments might be missed when due. Soon after the housing price bubble burst in mid-2006 and the economy began slowing in 2007, poorly qualified borrowers began defaulting on their mortgages. Developments in the mortgage markets were major contributors to the severity of the 2007–09 financial markets. Of course, while individuals were ultimately responsible for entering into very risky home mortgages, they were encouraged to do so by government officials, government-supported agencies, and mortgage originators and financial institution lenders.

CONCEPT CHECK

What early factors contributed to the 2007–09 financial crisis?

What cultural shift occurred on the part of individuals that contributed to the 2007–09 financial crisis?

APPLYING FINANCE TO...

INSTITUTIONS AND MARKETS

Savings of individuals are accumulated in a number of ways by financial institutions that, in turn, make pooled savings available to businesses so that they can maintain and grow their operations. Savings are gathered by commercial banks and other depository institutions. Insurance companies collect premium payments and pension funds, gather contributions, and invest these funds until needed. Mutual funds also play a major role in attracting the savings of individuals and then investing the pooled funds in securities.

INVESTMENTS

Governments issue debt securities to finance their needs and corporations issue both debt and equity securities to maintain and grow their businesses. The savings of individuals are the primary source for raising financial capital by governments and corporations. Financial institutions gather savings and make the savings available to governments and corporations in the primary securities markets. The process of determining interest rates for borrowing financial capital and pricing new stock issues will be covered as we progress through Part 2.

FINANCIAL MANAGEMENT

Financial managers often must raise additional amounts of debt and equity funds to finance the plans for their firms. While they may depend somewhat on loans from banks, they may also need to attract financial capital by selling bonds or stocks either privately or publicly. A decision to raise funds must be accompanied with the willingness to pay the required interest rates established in the marketplace or selling stock at a market-determined price.

SUMMARY

This chapter focused on how savings are created and how they are converted into investments. The major components of gross domestic product were identified and discussed in terms of consumption, investment, and the net exports balance of goods and services.

The three basic economic units were identified as individuals, business firms (including financial intermediaries), and governments. It was shown that the federal government has been primarily a savings deficit unit over the past several decades. This produced many annual budget deficits and a large national debt. Major sources of savings in the United States come from individuals and business firms. These savings may be directly invested and accumulated in financial institutions and then loaned or invested.

Factors that affect the level of savings were then discussed. This was followed by a discussion of capital market securities including long-term debt and stock securities used by issuers and investors that help the savings and investment process work efficiently. Characteristics of the 2007–09 financial crisis involving individuals and their pursuit of home ownership were discussed.

KEY TERMS

budgetary deficit
capital consumption adjustment
capital formation
capital market securities
common stock
contractual savings
corporate bond
derivative security
dissave
federal statutory debt limits
government expenditures (GE)
gross private domestic investment (GPDI)
mortgage
municipal bond
net exports (NE)
personal consumption expenditures (PCE)
personal saving
savings
savings deficit
savings surplus
Treasury bond
voluntary savings
undistributed profits

DISCUSSION QUESTIONS

1. What is capital formation?

2. Describe the major components of gross domestic product.

3. Identify the major components of net saving and describe their relative contributions in recent years.

4. Identify the various sources of revenues in the federal budget.

5. Identify the major expense categories in the federal budget.

6. Describe whether the federal government has been operating with surplus or deficit budgets in recent years.

7. Briefly describe the historical role of savings in the United States.

8. Compare savings surplus and savings deficit units. Indicate which economic units are generally of one type or the other.

9. Define *personal saving*.

10. Also, differentiate between voluntary and contractual savings.

11. Describe the recent levels of savings rates in the United States.

12. How and why do corporations save?

13. Describe the principal factors that influence the level of savings by individuals.

14. How do economic cycle movements affect the media or types of savings by businesses?

15. What are the life cycle stages of individuals?

16. How does each life cycle stage relate to the amount and type of individual savings?

17. What are the life cycle stages of corporations and other business firms?
18. Explain how financial savings generated by a business are a function of its life cycle stage.
19. What are the two types of maturity-related financial markets?
20. Identify and briefly describe the major securities that are originated or traded in capital securities markets.
21. What role did individuals play in the development of the 2007–09 financial crisis?

EXERCISES

1. Go to the U.S. Department of Commerce, Bureau of Economic Analysis website at http://www.bea.gov and determine:
   a. The current personal savings rate in the United States.
   b. The amount of current corporate savings as reflected in the amount of undistributed profits.

2. Assume you are an elected member of Congress. A lobbying group has agreed to provide financial support for your reelection campaign next year. In return for the group's support, you have been asked to champion their self-interests in the form of a spending bill that is being considered by Congress. What would you do?

3. Match the following financial instruments and securities with their issuers.

Instruments/Securities	Issuers
a. corporate stocks	1. commercial banks
b. Treasury bonds	2. corporations
c. municipal bonds	3. U.S. government
d. negotiable certificates of deposit	4. state/local governments

4. Match the following financial instruments and securities with their typical maturities.

Instruments/Securities	Maturities
a. corporate stocks	1. less than one year
b. Treasury bills	2. no maturity
c. mortgages	3. up to about 30 years
d. commercial paper	4. up to one year

PROBLEMS

1. A very small country's gross domestic product is $12 million.
   a. If government expenditures amount to $7.5 million and gross private domestic investment is $5.5 million, what would be the amount of net exports of goods and services?

2. How would your answer change in Problem 1 if the gross domestic product had been $14 million?

3. Personal income amounted to $17 million last year. Personal current taxes amounted to $4 million and personal outlays for consumption expenditures, nonmortgage interest, and so forth were $12 million.
   a. What was the amount of disposable personal income last year?
   b. What was the amount of personal saving last year?
   c. Calculate personal saving as a percentage of disposable personal income.

4. Assume personal income was $28 million last year. Personal outlays were $20 million and personal current taxes were $5 million.
   a. What was the amount of disposable personal income last year?
   b. What was the amount of personal saving last year?
   c. Calculate personal saving as a percentage of disposable personal income.

5. The components that comprise a nation's gross domestic product were identified and discussed in this chapter. Assume the following accounts and amounts were reported by a nation last year. Government expenditures (purchases of goods and services) were $5.5 billion; personal consumption expenditures were $40.5 billion; gross private domestic investment amounted to $20 billion; capital consumption allowances were $4 billion; personal savings were estimated at $2 billion; imports of goods and services amounted to $6.5 billion; and the exports of goods and services were $5 billion.
   a. Determine the nation's gross domestic product.
   b. How would your answer change if the dollar amounts of imports and exports were reversed?

6. Assume that some of the data provided in Problem 1 change next year. Specifically, government expenditures increase by 10 percent; gross private domestic investment declines by 10 percent; and imports of goods and services drop to $6 billion. Assume the other information as given remains the same next year.
   a. Determine the nation's gross domestic product for next year.
   b. How would your answer change in (a) if personal consumption expenditures are only $35 billion next year and capital consumption allowances actually increase by 10 percent?

7. A nation's gross domestic product is $600 million. Its personal consumption expenditures are $350 million, and government expenditures are $100 million. Net exports of goods and services amount to $50 million.
   a. Determine the nation's gross private domestic investment.
   b. If imports exceed exports by $25 million, how would your answer to (a) change?

8. A nation's gross domestic product is stated in U.S. dollars at $40 million. The dollar value of one unit of the nation's currency (FC) is $0.25.
   a. Determine the value of GDP in FCs.
   b. How would your answer change if the dollar value of one FC increases to $0.30?

9. A country in Southeast Asia states its gross domestic product in terms of yen. Assume that last year its GDP was 50 billion yen when one U.S. dollar could be exchanged for 120 yen.

   a. Determine the country's GDP in terms of U.S. dollars for last year.
   b. Assume the GDP increases to 55 billion yen for this year, while the dollar value of one yen is now $0.01. Determine the country's GDP in terms of U.S. dollars for this year.
   c. Show how your answer in (b) would change if one U.S. dollar could be exchanged for 110 yen.

10. **Challenge Problem** (*Note:* This exercise requires knowledge of probabilities and expected values.) Following are data relating to a nation's operations last year.

Capital consumption allowances	$150 million
Undistributed corporate profits	40 million
Personal consumption expenditures	450 million
Personal savings	50 million
Corporate inventory valuation adjustment	25 million
Federal government deficit	230 million
Government expenditures	10 million
State and local governments surplus	1 million
Net exports of goods and services	22 million
Gross private domestic investment	200 million

   a. Determine the nation's gross domestic product (GDP).
   b. How would your answer change in (a) if exports of goods and services were $5 million and imports were 80 percent of exports?
   c. Show how the GDP in (a) would change under the following three scenarios:

   Scenario 1 (probability of .20): the GDP components would be 120 percent of their values in (a).

   Scenario 2 (probability of .50): the GDP component values used in (a) would occur.

   Scenario 3 (probability of .30): the GDP components would be 75 percent of their values in (a).

   d. Determine the nation's gross savings last year.
   e. Show how your answer in (d) would change if each account simultaneously increases by 10 percent.
   f. Show how your answer in (d) would change if each account simultaneously decreases by 10 percent.
   g. Show how your answer in (d) would have changed if capital consumption allowances had been 10 percent less and personal consumption expenditures had been $400 million.

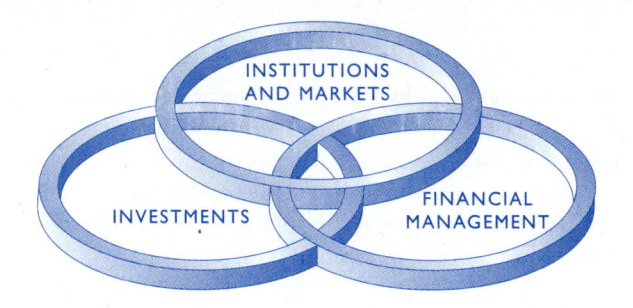

CHAPTER 8

Interest Rates

Chapter Learning Objectives:

AFTER STUDYING THIS CHAPTER, YOU SHOULD BE ABLE TO:

- Describe how interest rates change in response to shifts in the supply and demand for loanable funds.
- Identify major historical movements in interest rates in the United States.
- Describe the loanable funds theory of interest rates.
- Identify the major determinants of market interest rates.
- Describe the types of marketable securities issued by the U.S. Treasury.
- Describe the ownership of Treasury securities and the maturity distribution of the federal debt.
- Explain the term or maturity structure of interest rates.
- Identify and briefly describe the three theories used to explain the term structure of interest rates.
- Identify broad historical price level changes in the United States and other economies and discuss their causes.
- Describe the various types of inflation and their causes.
- Discuss the effect of default risk premiums on the level of long-term interest rates.

Where We Have Been...

In Chapter 7 you learned about the savings and investment process as it takes place in the United States. The gross domestic product (GDP) and capital formation were discussed. GDP is composed of personal consumption expenditures, government purchases, gross private domestic investment, and the net export of goods and services. The historical role of savings and how financial assets and liabilities are created was covered. You should now also have a basic understanding of the federal government's source of receipts and where expenditures are allocated. You should also understand the major sources of savings, how the major financial institutions direct funds from savings into investment, and factors that affect savings.

Where We Are Going...

Chapter 9 focuses on the time value of money. By saving and investing, money can "grow" over time through the compounding of interest. We first cover simple interest and then turn to compounding of current investments (determining future values) and discounting of future cash receipts (finding present values). You will also be introduced to annuities, which are investments that involve constant periodic payments or receipts of cash. Chapter 10 focuses on the characteristics and valuations of bonds and stocks. In Chapter 11 you will learn about the characteristics and operation of primary and secondary securities markets. Part 2 concludes with Chapter 12, which focuses on helping you learn and understand concepts relating to financial returns and risks associated with investing in stocks and bonds.

How This Chapter Applies to Me...

It is nearly impossible to get through the day without seeing some reference to interest rates on saving or borrowing money. You may see interest rates being offered on savings accounts by depository institutions, interest rates on new and used automobiles, and even the rate at which you could borrow for a loan to pay your tuition or to purchase a home. Your cost of borrowing will generally be higher when you are just starting your working career and your credit quality has not yet been established. Understanding the factors that determine the level of interest rates hopefully will help you make more informed decisions concerning when to spend, save, and borrow.

We all have been tempted by the advertisements for goods and services that suggest we should "buy now and pay for it later." These advertisements are hoping that we will decide that the value of "more" current consumption to us is worth the added interest that we will have to pay on the funds that we must borrow to finance this consumption.

Sometimes individuals like to consume more now, even though they don't have the money to pay for this consumption. For example, you may see a pair of shoes in a store window "that you have to have right now." Maybe you don't currently have the money to pay for the shoes. Don't despair; if you have a credit card, the credit card issuer may lend you the money to pay for the shoes. In return, you will have to pay back the amount borrowed plus interest on the loan.

You might also be considering making a current investment in your future by borrowing money to go to college. In this case you hope that your current education will lead to an increase in your future earning power, out of which you will have to repay your student loan. When you purchased your shoes on credit, you decided to consume now and pay later for this current consumption. When you decide to invest in your education, you expect that future earnings will be larger, making it easier to repay the student loan. Businesses also borrow to make investments in inventory, plant, and equipment that will earn profits sufficient to pay interest, repay the amount borrowed, and provide returns to equity investors. In this chapter we focus on the cost or price of borrowing funds. An understanding of interest rates—what causes them to change and how they relate to changes in the economy—is of fundamental importance in the world of finance.

SUPPLY AND DEMAND FOR LOANABLE FUNDS

Lenders are willing to supply funds to borrowers as long as lenders can earn a satisfactory return on their loans (i.e., an amount greater than that which was lent). Borrowers will demand funds from lenders as long as borrowers can invest the funds so as to earn a satisfactory return above the cost of their loans. Actually, the supply and demand for loanable funds will take place as long as both lenders and borrowers have the expectation of satisfactory returns. Of course, returns received may differ from those expected because of inflation, failure to repay loans, and poor investments. Return experiences will, in turn, affect future supply-and-demand relationships for loanable funds.

interest rate
price that equates the demand for and supply of loanable funds

The basic price that equates the demand for and supply of loanable funds in the financial markets is the **interest rate.** Figure 8.1 depicts how interest rates are determined in the financial markets. Graph A shows the interest rate (r) that clears the market by bringing the demand (D_1) by borrowers for funds in equilibrium with the supply (S_1) by lenders of funds. For illustrative purposes, we have arbitrarily chosen a rate of 7 percent as the cost or price that makes savings equal to investment (i.e., where the supply and demand curves intersect).

Interest rates may move from an equilibrium level if an unanticipated change or "shock" causes the demand for, or supply of, loanable funds to change. For example, an increase in the desire to invest in business assets because of an expanding economy might cause the demand for loanable funds to increase or shift upward (i.e., from D_1 to D_2). The result, depicted in Graph B, will be an increase or rise in interest rates to, say, 8 percent—assuming no immediate adjustment in the supply of funds. Of course, as higher interest rates become available to savers, savings may increase, which could cause the supply of loanable funds to increase. A decline in business activity would be expected to have the opposite impact on interest rates.

Graph C depicts an unanticipated increase in inflation, which leads lenders (suppliers) to require a higher rate of interest. This is shown by the shift in supply from S_1 to S_2, which for illustrative purposes shows an increase in the interest rate from 7 percent to 9 percent. At this point, we have not taken into consideration the fact that borrowers also may adjust their demand for loanable funds because of the likelihood of more costly loans. Graph D depicts the situation that borrowers (users) may cut back on their demand for loanable funds from D_1 to D_3 because of the unanticipated increase in inflation. For example, this would occur if borrowers felt that their higher borrowing costs could not be passed on to their customers and thus the returns on their investments would be adversely affected by the higher inflation rates. Instead of the unanticipated increase in inflation shock causing the interest rate to rise to 9 percent, the new equilibrium rate where supply equals demand (investment) might be only 8 percent.

CONCEPT CHECK
How are interest rates determined in the financial markets?

FIGURE 8.1
Interest Rate Determination in the Financial Markets

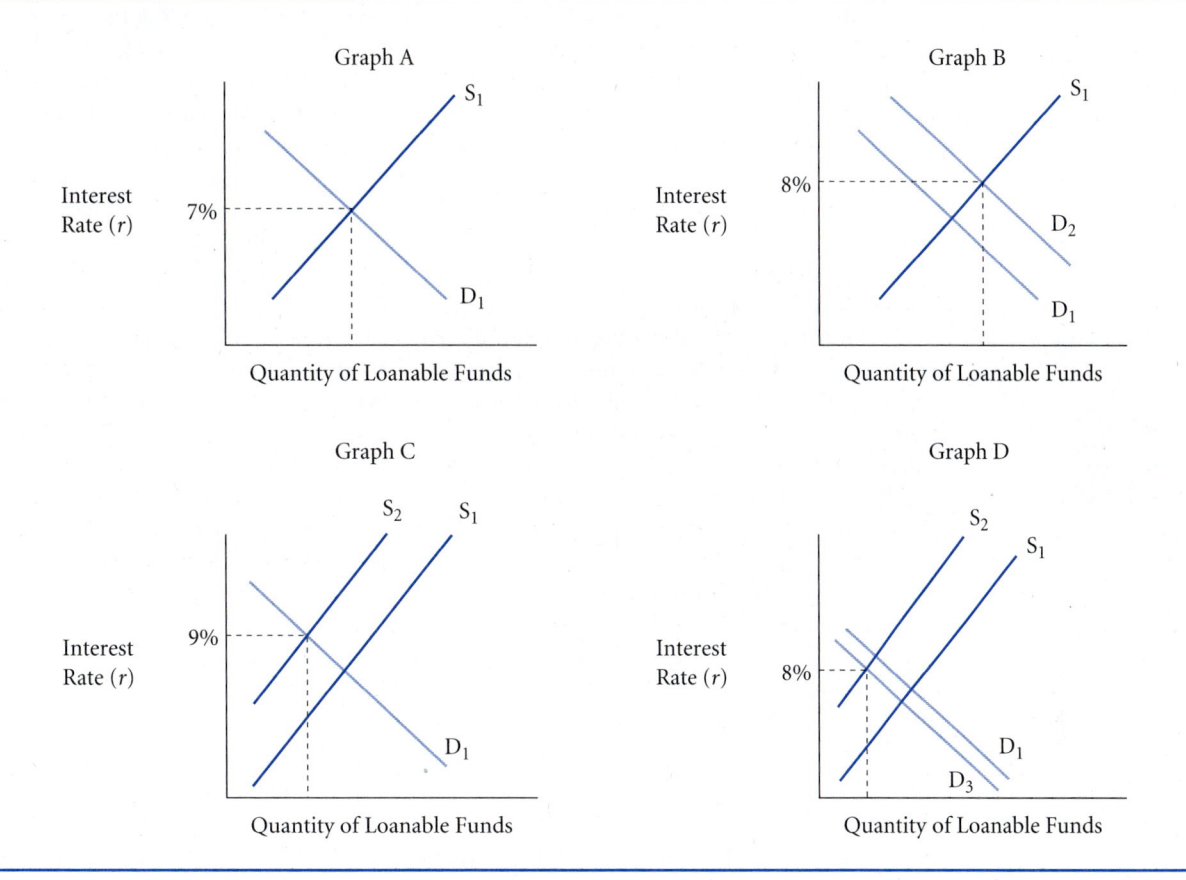

Graph A

Graph B

Graph C

Graph D

HISTORICAL CHANGES IN U.S. INTEREST RATE LEVELS

Interest rates for loanable funds have varied throughout the history of the United States as the result of shifting supply and demand. Since just after the Civil War, there have been four periods of rising or relatively high long-term interest rates and four periods of falling or relatively low interest rates on long-term loans and investments.

Periods of increasing/high long-term interest rates were:

- 1864–1873
- 1905–1920
- 1927–1933
- 1946–1982

The rapid economic expansion after the Civil War caused the first period of rising interest rates from 1864 to 1873. The second period, from 1905 to 1920, was based on both large-scale prewar expansion and the inflation associated with World War I. The third period, from 1927 to 1933, was due to the economic boom from 1927 to 1929 and the unsettled conditions in the securities markets during the early part of the Depression, from 1929 to 1933. The rapid economic expansion following World War II led to the last period, from 1946 to 1982.

Periods of decreasing/low long-term interest rates were:

- 1873–1905
- 1920–1927
- 1933–1946
- 1982–present

The first period of falling interest rates was from 1873 to 1905. As the public debt was paid off and funds became widely available, the supply of funds grew more rapidly than the demand for them. Prices and interest rates fell, even though the economy was moving forward. The same general factors were at work in the second period, 1920 to 1927. The third period of low interest rates, from 1933 to 1946, resulted from the government's actions in fighting the Great Depression and continued during World War II, when interest rates were pegged, or set.

Beginning in 1966, interest rates entered a period of unusual increases, leading to the highest rates in U.S. history. This increase in rates began as a result of the Vietnam War. It continued in the 1970s because of a policy of on-again, off-again price controls and increased demands for capital arising from ecological concerns and the energy crisis. Furthermore, several periods of poor crops coupled with sharp price increases for crude oil caused worldwide inflation. Interest rates peaked at the beginning of the 1980s, with short-term rates above 20 percent and long-term rates in the high teens. In summary, double-digit inflation, a somewhat tight monetary policy, and heavy borrowing demand by business contributed to these record levels.

The fourth period of declining long-term interest rates began in 1982, when rates peaked, and continued through 2009. Inflation rates dropped dramatically from double-digit levels during the beginning of the 1980s and remained around 2 to 3 percent since the early 1990s and continuing through 2009. The decline in inflation rates seems to have been a primary reason long-term interest rates have also trended downward.

Short-term interest rates generally move up and down with the business cycle. Therefore, they show many more periods of expansion and contraction. Both long-term and short-term interest rates tend to rise in prosperity periods during which the economy is expanding rapidly. The only major exception was during World War II, when interest rates were pegged. During this period the money supply increased rapidly, laying the base for postwar inflation.

LOANABLE FUNDS THEORY

The **loanable funds theory** holds that interest rates are a function of the supply of and demand for loanable funds. This is a flow theory, in that it focuses on the relative supply and demand of loanable funds during a specified period. How the supply of and the demand for loanable funds interact determines both the interest rate and the quantity of funds that flows through the financial markets during any period. If the supply of funds increases, holding demand constant, interest rates will tend to fall. Likewise, an increase in the demand for loans will tend to drive up interest rates. This is depicted in Graph B of Figure 8.1.

Sources of Loanable Funds

There are two basic sources of loanable funds:

- Current savings
- Expansion of deposits by depository institutions

The supply of savings comes from all sectors of the economy, and most of it flows through U.S. financial institutions. Individuals may save part of their incomes, either as voluntary savings or through contractual savings programs—such as purchasing whole life or endowment insurance policies or repaying installment or mortgage loans. Governmental units and nonprofit institutions sometimes have funds in excess of current expenditures. Corporations may have savings available because they are not paying out all their earnings as dividends. Depreciation allowances that are not being used currently to buy new capital equipment to replace older equipment may also be available for lending.

Pension funds, both governmental and private, provide another source of saving. These funds, which are building up large reserves to meet future commitments, are available for investment.

Some savings are invested as ownership equity in businesses either directly in single proprietorships or partnerships or by buying stock in corporations. This is, however, only a small part of total savings. The bulk of the total savings each year is available as loanable funds. Funds may be loaned directly: for example, when someone lends money to a friend to enable the friend to expand business operations. However, most savings are loaned through financial institutions, one of whose basic functions is the accumulation of savings.

The other basic source of loanable funds is that created by the banking system. Banks and other depository institutions not only channel savings to borrowers, but also create deposits, which are the most widely used form of money in the U.S. economy. This process was discussed in Chapter 3. Net additions to the money supply are a source of loanable funds; during periods when the money supply contracts, the flow of loanable funds drops below the level of current savings.

CONCEPT CHECK
What do short-term interest rates generally move with?

loanable funds theory
states that interest rates are a function of the supply of and demand for loanable funds

CONCEPT CHECK
What is the loanable funds theory?

SMALL BUSINESS PRACTICE
The Family Business or Venture

Family businesses continue to be very popular in the United States. For publicly held firms, corporate goals may differ in part from the goals of managers. For closely held firms that are not family owned, the business goals and the personal goals of owner/managers are closely aligned. For family-owned or family-controlled firms, a third set of goals—family goals—also must be considered. When family goals are closely aligned with the business and manager goals, the business can benefit from family sharing and closeness. However, when family goals differ from business and/or manager goals, conflict and an argumentative environment may prevail. In such instances, family-controlled businesses often fail or the family is forced to sell.

Jeffry Timmons lists several problems unique to family businesses or ventures.* First, problems of control, fairness, and equity often exist. For example, family members may have different ideas as to how the business should be run. Fairness and equity issues relate to the division of work and relative contributions to running the business. Second is the issue of credibility, whereby founding parents find it difficult to believe that their children can perform in a manner comparable to their own.

The third potential problem relates to family dynamics. Since it often is difficult to separate business operations from family life, tensions in one area often spill over into the other area. Fourth is the problem of deciding succession. If succession is to involve a next-generation family member, the founder must disengage his or her ownership rights and delegate an increased level of responsibility to the new person in control. For succession to succeed, the founder must be willing to assume the role of advisor to the family member who was selected to run the firm in the future.

---

*Jeffry Timmons, *New Venture Creation*, 4th Edition (Boston: Irwin/McGraw-Hill, 1994). Also see Jeffry A. Timmons and Stephen Spineilli, *New Venture Creation*, 7th Edition (New York: McGraw-Hill/Irwin, 2007), Chapter 17.

CONCEPT CHECK
What are the basic sources of loanable funds?

Loanable funds can be grouped in several ways. They may be divided into short-term funds and long-term funds. We can also group funds by (1) use—such as business credit, consumer credit, agricultural credit, and government credit—and (2) the institutions supplying each type.

Factors Affecting the Supply of Loanable Funds

Many factors affect the supply of loanable funds. Both sources of funds have some tendency to increase as interest rates rise. However, this effect is often small compared to other factors that limit or otherwise affect the volume of savings or the ability of the banking system to expand deposits.

Volume of Savings

The major factor that determines the volume of savings, corporate as well as individual, is the level of national income. When income is high, savings are high; when it is low, savings are low. The pattern of income taxes—both the level of the tax and the tax rates in various income brackets—also influences savings volume. Furthermore, the tax treatment of savings itself influences the amount of income saved. For example, the tax deferral on (or postponement of) savings placed in individual retirement accounts (IRAs), increases the volume of savings.

The age of the population has an important effect on the volume of savings. As we discussed in Chapter 7, little saving is done during the formative and education-building stage or during the family-creating stage. Therefore, an economy with a large share of young couples with children will have less total savings than one with more people in the older wealth-building stage.

The volume of savings also depends on the factors that affect indirect savings. The more effectively the life insurance industry promotes the sale of whole life and endowment insurance policies, the larger the volume of savings. The higher the demand for private pension funds (which accumulate contributions during working years to make payments on retirement), the larger the volume of savings. The effect of interest rates on such savings is often just the opposite of the normal effect of price on supply. As interest rates decrease, more money must be paid for insurance for the same amount of coverage, because a smaller amount of interest will be earned from the reinvestment of premiums and earnings. Inversely, as interest rates rise, less money needs to be put into reserves to get the same objectives. The same is true of the amount of money that must be put into annuities and pension funds.

When savings result from the use of consumer credit, the effect of interest rates is delayed. For example, assume a car is bought with a three-year loan. Savings, in the form of repaying the loan, must go on for three years regardless of changes in interest rates. There may even be an opposite effect in the case of a mortgage because, if interest rates drop substantially, the loan can be refinanced. At the lower interest rate the same dollar payments provide a larger amount for repayment of principal, that is, for saving.

Expansion of Deposits by Depository Institutions

The amount of short-term credit available depends largely on the lending policies of commercial banks and other depository institutions and on the policies of the Federal Reserve System. Lenders are influenced by such factors as present business conditions and future prospects. However, the Federal Reserve has great control over the ability of the banking system to create new deposits, as discussed in Chapter 4.

How much long-term credit of different types is available depends on the policies of the different suppliers of credit. Since depository institutions do not play a major role in this field, the money supply is not expanded directly to meet long-term credit demands. Indirectly, however, their policies and those of the Federal Reserve are very important: if the banking system expands the money supply to meet short-term needs, a larger proportion of the supply of loanable funds can be used for long-term credit.

Liquidity Attitudes

How lenders see the future has a significant effect on the supply of loanable funds, both long term and short term. Lenders may feel that the economic outlook is so uncertain that they are reluctant to lend their money. This liquidity preference can be so strong that large amounts of funds lie idle, as they did during the depression in the 1930s. Lenders may also prefer liquidity because they expect either interest rates to go up in the near future or opportunities for direct investment to be more favorable. Thus, liquidity attitudes may result in keeping some funds idle that would normally be available for lending.

CONCEPT CHECK
What are the major factors that affect the supply of loanable funds?

Effect of Interest Rates on the Demand for Loanable Funds

The demand for loanable funds comes from all sectors of the economy. Business borrows to finance current operations and to buy plant and equipment. Farmers borrow to meet short-term and long-term needs. Institutions, such as hospitals and schools, borrow primarily to finance new buildings and equipment. Individuals finance the purchase of homes with long-term loans and purchase durable goods or cover emergencies with intermediate- and short-term loans. Governmental units borrow to finance public buildings, bridge the gap between expenditures and tax receipts, and meet budget deficits. The factors affecting the demand for loanable funds are different for each type of borrower. We have considered such factors in detail when analyzing the various types of credit. Therefore, this discussion covers only how interest rates affect the major types of borrowing.

Historically, one of the biggest borrowers has been the federal government, and Congress generally gives little consideration to interest rates in its spending programs. Minor changes in interest rates do not affect short-term business borrowing. However, historical evidence shows that large increases in short-term interest rates do lead to a decrease in the demand for bank loans and other forms of short-term business borrowing.

Changes in long-term interest rates also affect long-term business borrowing. Most corporations put off long-term borrowing when rates are up if they expect rates to go down in the near future.

Likewise, minor changes in interest rates have little effect on consumer borrowing. For short-term installment loans, the monthly repayments of principal are so large compared to the interest cost that the total effect on the repayment schedule is small. However, larger interest rate changes have strongly influenced consumer borrowing in the past. This happened during periods when home mortgage rates reached historically high levels and new housing starts declined sharply.

CONCEPT CHECK
How do interest rates influence the demand for loanable funds?

Roles of the Banking System and of the Government

While the effect of interest rates on loanable funds varies, both the supply of and the demand for loanable funds are affected by the actions of the banking system and the government. When depository institutions expand credit by increasing the total volume of short-term loans, the supply of loanable funds increases. When credit contracts, the supply of loanable funds decreases. The actions of the Federal Reserve in setting discount rates, buying securities in the open market, and changing reserve requirements also affect the supply of loanable funds. In fact, all actions that affect the level of banking system reserves and creation of checkable deposits affect the supply of loanable funds in the market.

Government borrowing has become a major influence on demand for funds and will remain so for the foreseeable future. Government surpluses or deficits make funds available in the market or take them out of the market in substantial amounts. Treasury debt management policies also affect the supply-and-demand relationships for short-, intermediate-, and long-term funds.

The financial markets are thus under the influence of the Treasury, and the Federal Reserve strongly influences the supply of funds. The Treasury, through tax policies and other government programs, also plays a role on this side of the market. However, the Treasury's major influence is on the demand for funds, as it borrows heavily to finance federal deficits.

International Factors Affecting Interest Rates

Interest rates in the United States are now no longer influenced only by domestic factors. The large trade surpluses with China and Japan, with their accumulation of funds to invest, have had important influences on the rates the federal government pays in issuing new securities. This international influence adds to the critical need to balance the national budget and to avoid the frequency of financing. As production has shifted to many other countries, investment has also shifted. In short, the Treasury and the Federal Reserve must now carefully consider the influence of international movements of funds on domestic interest rates.

DETERMINANTS OF MARKET INTEREST RATES

In addition to supply-and-demand relationships, interest rates are determined by a number of specific factors. First, the interest rate (r) that we observe in the marketplace is called a ***nominal interest rate*** because it includes a premium for expected inflation. Second, a nominal interest rate that is not free from the risk of default by the borrower also will have a default risk premium. Thus, in its simplest form, the nominal interest rate can be expressed as:

$$r = RR + IP + DRP \tag{8.1}$$

where RR is the real rate of interest, IP is an inflation premium, and DRP is the default risk premium.

The ***real rate of interest*** is the interest rate on a risk-free financial debt instrument when no inflation is expected. The ***inflation premium*** is the average inflation rate expected over the life of the instrument.

The ***default risk premium*** indicates compensation for the possibility that the borrower will not pay interest and/or repay principal according to the financial instrument's contractual arrangements. The DRP reflects the application of the risk-return principle of finance presented in Chapter 1. In essence, "higher returns are expected for taking on more risk." This is a higher "expected" return because the issuer may default on some of the contractual returns. Of course, the actual "realized" return on a default risky debt investment could be substantially less than the expected return. At the extreme, the debt security investor could lose all of his or her investment. The DRP is discussed further in the last section of this chapter. The risk-return finance principle to stock investments and to portfolios of securities is further extended in Chapter 12. Instead of a default risk premium, the concentration is on "stock risk premiums" and "market risk premiums."

To cover both short-term and long-term debt instruments, two additional premiums are frequently added to the equation that explains nominal interest rates. This expanded version can be expressed as:

$$r = RR + IP + DRP + MRP + LP \tag{8.2}$$

where MRP is the maturity risk premium and LP is the liquidity premium on a financial instrument.

The ***maturity risk premium*** is the added return expected by lenders or investors because of interest rate risk on instruments with longer maturities. ***Interest rate risk*** reflects the possibility of changes or fluctuations in market values of fixed-rate debt instruments as market interest rates change over time. There is an inverse relationship in the marketplace

---

nominal interest rate
interest rate that is observed in the marketplace

real rate of interest
interest rate on a risk-free debt instrument when no inflation is expected

inflation premium
average inflation rate expected over the life of the security

default risk premium
compensation for the possibility a borrower will fail to pay interest and/or principal when due

maturity risk premium
compensation expected by investors due to interest rate risk on debt instruments with longer maturities

interest rate risk
possible price fluctuations in fixed-rate debt instruments associated with changes in market interest rates

liquidity premium *compensation for securities that cannot easily be converted to cash without major price discounts*

CONCEPT CHECK

What is the nominal interest rate, and what is the real rate of interest?

What are the definitions of the following: default risk premium, maturity risk premium, and liquidity premium?

What is interest rate risk?

between debt instrument values or prices and nominal interest rates. For example, if interest rates rise from, say, 7 percent to 8 percent because of a previously unanticipated inflation rate increase, the values of outstanding debt instruments will decline. Furthermore, the longer the remaining life until maturity, the greater the reductions in a fixed-rate debt instrument's value to a given interest rate increase. These concepts with numerical calculations are explored in Chapter 10.

The **liquidity premium** is the compensation for those financial debt instruments that cannot be easily converted to cash at prices close to their estimated fair market values. For example, a corporation's low-quality bond may be traded very infrequently. As a consequence, a bondholder who wishes to sell tomorrow may find it difficult to sell except at a very large discount in price.

Those factors that influence the nominal interest rate are discussed throughout the remainder of this chapter, beginning with the concept of a risk-free interest rate and a discussion of why U.S. Treasury securities are used as the best estimate of the risk-free rate. Other sections focus on the term or maturity structure of interest rates, inflation expectations and associated premiums, and default risk and liquidity premium considerations.

RISK-FREE SECURITIES: U.S. TREASURY DEBT OBLIGATIONS

risk-free rate of interest *interest rate on a debt instrument with no default, maturity, or liquidity risks (Treasury securities are the closest example)*

By combining the real rate of interest and the inflation premium, we have the **risk-free rate of interest,** which in the United States is represented by U.S. Treasury debt instruments or securities. It is generally believed that even with the large national debt, the U.S. government is not going to renege on its obligations to pay interest and repay principal at maturity on its debt securities. Thus, we view U.S. Treasury securities as being default-risk free. Technically, a truly risk-free financial instrument also has no liquidity risk or maturity risk (as reflected by interest rate risk). Treasury marketable securities are considered to have virtually no liquidity risk and only longer-term Treasury securities have maturity or interest rate risk associated with changes in market-determined interest rates that occur over time.

Economists have estimated that the annual real rate of interest in the United States and other countries has averaged in the 2 to 4 percent range in recent years. One way of looking at the risk-free rate is to say that this is the minimum rate of interest necessary to get individuals and businesses to save. There must be an incentive to invest or save idle cash holdings. One such incentive is the expectation of some real rate of return above expected inflation levels. For illustrative purposes, let's assume 3 percent is the current expectation for a real rate of return. Let's also assume that the nominal interest rate is currently 7 percent for a one-year Treasury security.

Given these assumptions, we can turn to Equation 8.1 to determine the average inflation expectations of holders or investors as follows:

$$7\% = RR + IP + DRP$$
$$7\% = 3\% + IP + 0\%$$
$$IP = 7\% - 3\% = 4\%$$

Thus, investors expect a 4 percent inflation rate over the next year; and if they also want a real rate of return of 3 percent, the nominal interest rate must be 7 percent.

Let's now also use the expanded equation to explain nominal interest rates as expressed in Equation 8.2. However, since this is a Treasury security there is no liquidity premium and no maturity risk premium if we are planning to hold the security until its maturity at the end of one year. Thus, Equation 8.2 would be used as follows to find the average expected inflation rate:

$$7\% = RR + IP + DRP + MRP + LP$$
$$7\% = 3\% + IP + 0\% + 0\% + 0\%$$
$$IP = 7\% - 3\% = 4\%$$

CONCEPT CHECK

What is the risk-free rate of interest?

Of course, the answer has not changed and is still 4 percent, since there were no additional risk premiums. The impact of a maturity risk premium is introduced after discussion of the types of marketable securities issued by the Treasury.

MARKETABLE OBLIGATIONS

Marketable government securities, as the term implies, are those that can be purchased and sold through customary market channels. Large commercial banks and securities dealers maintain markets for these obligations. In addition, nearly all other securities firms and commercial banks, large or small, will help their customers purchase and sell federal obligations by routing orders to institutions that do maintain markets in them. The investments of institutional investors and large personal investors in federal obligations are centered almost exclusively in the marketable issues. These marketable issues are bills, notes, and bonds—the difference between them being their maturity at time of issue. Although the maturity of an obligation is reduced as it remains in effect, the obligation continues to be called by its original descriptive title. Thus, a twenty-year Treasury bond continues to be described in the quotation sheets as a bond throughout its life.

> **marketable government securities**
> *securities that may be bought and sold through the usual market channels*

Treasury Bills

Treasury bills are issued with maturities up to one year and thus are the shortest maturities of federal obligations. They are typically issued for 91 days, with some issues carrying maturities of 182 days. Treasury bills with a maturity of one year are also issued at auction every four weeks. Issues of Treasury bills are offered each week by the Treasury to refund the part of the total volume of bills that matures. In effect, the 91-day Treasury bills mature and are rolled over in thirteen weeks. Each week, approximately one-thirteenth of the total volume of such bills is refunded.

When the flow of cash revenues into the Treasury is too small to meet expenditure requirements, additional bills are issued. During those periods of the year when revenues exceed expenditures, Treasury bills are allowed to mature without being refunded. Treasury bills, therefore, provide the Treasury with a convenient financial mechanism to adjust for the lack of a regular revenue flow into the Treasury. The volume of bills may also be increased or decreased in response to general surpluses or deficits in the federal budget from year to year.

Treasury bills are issued on a discount basis and mature at par. Each week the Treasury bills to be sold are awarded to the highest bidders. Dealers and other investors submit sealed binds. Upon being opened, these bids are arrayed from highest to lowest. Those bidders asking the least discount (offering the highest price) are placed high in the array. The bids are then accepted in the order of their position in the array until all bills are awarded. Bidders seeking a higher discount (offering a lower price) may fail to receive any bills that particular week. Investors interested in purchasing small volumes of Treasury bills ($10,000 to $500,000) may submit their orders on an average competitive price basis. The Treasury deducts these small orders from the total volume of bills to be sold. The remaining bills are allotted on the competitive basis described above. Then these small orders are executed at a discount equal to the average of the successful competitive bids for large orders.

Investors are not limited to purchasing Treasury bills on their original issue. Because Treasury bills are issued weekly, a wide range of maturities in the over-the-counter market is available. The Treasury bonds, notes, and bills section of the *Wall Street Journal* shows available maturities from one week to one year. The bid and ask quotations are shown in terms of annual yield equivalents. The prices of the various issues obtained from a dealer would reflect a discount based on these yields. Because of their short maturities and their absence of risk, Treasury bills provide the lowest yield available on taxable domestic obligations. Although some business corporations and individuals invest in Treasury bills, by far the most important holders of these obligations are commercial banks.

> **Treasury bills**
> *federal obligations issued with maturities up to one year*

Treasury Notes

Treasury notes are issued at specified interest rates usually for maturities ranging from two to ten years. These intermediate-term federal obligations are also held largely by commercial banks.

> **Treasury notes**
> *federal obligations usually issued for maturities of two to ten years*

Treasury Bonds

Treasury bonds typically have original maturities in excess of five years and often are issued for twenty and sometimes even thirty years. These bonds bear interest at stated rates. Many issues of these bonds are callable, or paid off, by the government several years before their maturity. For example, a twenty-year bond issued in 2005 may be described as having a maturity of 2025–2030.

> **Treasury bonds**
> *federal obligations issued with maturities over five years and often for twenty or even thirty years*

This issue may be called for redemption at par as early as 2025 but in no event later than 2030. The longest maturity of Treasury bonds is thirty years. Dealers maintain active markets for the purchase and sale of Treasury bonds and the other marketable securities of the government.

All marketable obligations of the federal government, with the exception of Treasury bills, are offered to the public through the Federal Reserve Banks at prices and yields set in advance. Investors place their orders for new issues, and these orders are filled from the available supply of the new issue. If orders are larger than available supply, investors may be allotted only a part of the amount they requested.

Treasury bonds, because of at least initial long-term maturities, are subject to maturity or interest rate risk. Treasury notes with shorter maturities are affected to a lesser extent. For illustrative purposes, let's assume that the nominal interest rate on ten-year Treasury bonds is currently 9 percent. Let's further assume that investors expect the inflation rate will average 4 percent over the next ten years. By applying Equation 4.2 we can find the maturity risk premium to be:

$$9\% = RR + IP + DRP + MRP + LP$$
$$9\% = 3\% + 4\% + 0\% + MRP + 0\%$$
$$MRP = 9\% - 3\% - 4\% = 2\%$$

Our interpretation is that the holders or investors require a 2 percent maturity risk premium to compensate them for the possibility of volatility in the price of their Treasury bonds over the next ten years. If market-determined interest rates rise and investors are forced to sell before maturity, the bonds will be sold at a loss. Furthermore, even if these investors hold their bonds to maturity and redeem them with the government at the original purchase price, the investors would have lost the opportunity of the higher interest rates being paid in the marketplace. This is what is meant by interest rate risk. Of course, if market-determined interest rates decline after the bonds are purchased, bond prices will rise above the original purchase price.

CONCEPT CHECK
How do Treasury bills, Treasury notes, and Treasury bonds differ?

dealer system
composed of a small group of dealers in government securities with an effective marketing network throughout the United States.

DEALER SYSTEM

The **dealer system** for marketable U.S. government securities occupies a central position in the nation's financial markets. The smooth operation of the money markets depends on a closely linked network of dealers and brokers. Dealers report their daily activity in U.S. government securities to the Federal Reserve Bank of New York. In recent years there have been on average forty to fifty such dealers, with a little less than half being commercial banks and the remainder being nonbank dealers. New dealers are added only when they can demonstrate a satisfactory responsibility and volume of activity. The dealers buy and sell securities for their own account, arrange transactions with both their customers and other dealers, and also purchase debt directly from the Treasury for resale to investors. Dealers do not typically charge commissions on their trades. Rather, they hope to sell securities at prices above the levels at which they were bought. The dealers' capacity to handle large Treasury financing has expanded enough in recent years to handle the substantial growth in the government securities market. In addition to the dealers' markets, new issues of federal government securities may be purchased directly at the Federal Reserve Banks.

CONCEPT CHECK
What is the dealer system for marketable U.S. government securities?

PERSONAL FINANCIAL PLANNING
Home Mortgages

Interest rates on home mortgages are affected by the influences discussed in this chapter. A typical thirty-year fixed rate mortgage incorporates the factors that affect a thirty-year Treasury bond (real rate + inflation expectations + maturity risk premium + liquidity premium) in addition to these other influences, such as default risk premium (since the typical homeowner is a higher risk than the U.S. government) and security premium (this helps lower the mortgage interest rate, since in case of default the lender can take possession of the borrower's house and sell it to recoup the amount lent). Homeowners can play the short end of the term structure, too. Adjustable-rate or variable-rate mortgages rise and fall in line with a specified short-term interest rate, usually a Treasury security. The interest rate paid by the homeowner equals the short-term rate plus a premium, to reflect the homeowner's higher degree of default risk. The danger of buying a home with an adjustable-rate mortgage is that an inflation scare or some other reason may cause a rapid rise in short-term rates, whereas the rate on a fixed-rate loan does not fluctuate. Since short-term rates usually are less than long-term rates, an adjustable-rate mortgage is an attractive financing possibility for those willing to take the risk of fluctuating short-term rates or those who expect to own their home for only three to five years before they move out of it.

TAX STATUS OF FEDERAL OBLIGATIONS

Until March 1941, interest on all obligations of the federal government was exempt from all taxes. The interest on all federal obligations is now subject to ordinary income taxes and tax rates. The Public Debt Act of 1941 terminated the issuance of tax-free federal obligations. Since that time, all issues previously sold to the public have matured or have been called for redemption. Income from the obligations of the federal government is exempt from all state and local taxes. Federal obligations, however, are subject to federal and state inheritance, estate, or gift taxes.

OWNERSHIP OF PUBLIC DEBT SECURITIES

> **nonmarketable government securities** *issues that cannot be transferred between persons or institutions and must be redeemed with the U.S. government*

The U.S. national debt must be financed and refinanced through the issuance of government securities, both marketable and nonmarketable. **Nonmarketable government securities** are those securities that cannot be transferred to other persons or institutions and can be redeemed only by being turned in to the U.S. government. The sheer size of the national debt, over $9.5 trillion in mid-2008, makes the financing process a difficult one. In fact, the United States must rely on the willingness of foreign and international investors to hold a substantial portion of the outstanding interest-bearing public debt securities issued to finance the national debt.

The ownership of public debt securities, by group or category, is shown in Table 8.1. Private investors, who owned approximately 48 percent of the total outstanding federal debt securities in 2003 and 2006, increased their ownership to nearly 51 percent by 2008. The percentage of federal debt held by U.S. government accounts (agencies and trust funds) and Federal Reserve Banks dropped from about 52 percent down to 49 percent in 2008. During the time period depicted in Table 8.1, foreign and international investors increased their holdings of total public debt from about 22 percent in 2003, to 25 percent in 2006, and to about 28 percent in 2008. This shows the continuing importance of foreign and international investors in financing the U.S. national debt. No other category of private investors held more than about 6 percent of the total federal debt outstanding in 2008.

During the last half of the 1980s, the annual increase in foreign ownership was due primarily to the flow of Japanese capital to this country. Japanese investment in real estate and corporate securities has been well publicized. However, as the dollar declined relative to the Japanese yen and other major foreign currencies, investment in U.S. assets became less attractive after interest and other returns were converted back into the foreign currencies. In recent years, interest on the part of Europeans and Chinese has increased. The large trade surpluses China has had with the United States have resulted in the Chinese holding ever-increasing amounts of U.S. financial assets.

CONCEPT CHECK
What are nonmarketable government securities?

TABLE 8.1
Ownership of Public Debt of U.S. Treasury Securities (% of Total Debt)

	2003	2006 (SEPT)	2008 (JUNE)
Federal Reserve and government accounts	51.7%	52.1%	49.4%
Private investors			
Foreign and international investors	21.9	25.1	27.9
State and local governments	5.2	5.5	5.5
U.S. savings bonds	2.9	2.4	2.1
Depository institutions	2.2	1.3	1.2
Insurance companies	2.0	1.9	4.7
Mutual funds	4.0	2.8	4.1
Pension funds	4.5	3.8	3.8
Other miscellaneous groups of investors*	5.6	5.1	1.3
Total private investors	**48.3%**	**47.9%**	**50.6%**
Total U.S. agencies and private investors	**100.0%**	**100.0%**	**100.0%**
Dollar Amount of Public Debt ($ Trillions)	$7.0	$8.5	9.5

*Includes individuals, corporate and other businesses, dealers and brokers, government-sponsored agencies, bank personal trusts and estates, and other investors.

Source: *Economic Report of the President* (selected issues) and http://www.stlouisfed.org.

TABLE 8.2
Average Length and Maturity Distribution of Marketable Interest-Bearing Federal Obligations (% of Total Marketable Debt)

MATURITY CLASS	2003	2006	2008 (NOV)
Within 1 year	37.7%	32.1%	47.8%
1–5 years	34.1	37.3	28.1
5–10 years	12.5	17.8	14.3
10–20 years	8.7	8.0	6.7
20 years and over	7.0	4.8	3.1
Total	100.0%	100.0%	100.0%
Average maturity of all marketable issues:	5 years, 1 month	4 years, 9 months	3 years, 10 months

Source: *Economic Report of the President* (selected issues) and http://www.stlouisfed.org.

MATURITY DISTRIBUTION OF MARKETABLE DEBT SECURITIES

The various types of marketable obligations of the federal government have already been described in this section. However, the terms of bills, notes, and bonds describe the general maturity ranges only at the time of issue. To determine the maturity distribution of all obligations, therefore, it is necessary to observe the remaining life of each issue regardless of its class. The maturity distribution and average length of marketable interest-bearing federal obligations are shown in Table 8.2. Notice that the average maturity decreased from five years and one month in 2003 to three years and ten months in November 2008.

The heavy concentration of debt in the very short maturity range (within one year) has increased from about 38 percent in 2003 to about 48 percent of the total amount outstanding in late-2008. However, this heavy concentration in very short-term maturities poses a special problem for the Treasury. This also is a problem for the securities markets because the government is constantly selling additional securities to replace those that mature. The heavy concentration of short-term maturities will not necessarily change by simply issuing a larger number of long-term obligations. Like all institutions that seek funds in the financial markets, the Treasury has to offer securities that will be readily accepted by the investing public. Furthermore, the magnitude of federal financing is such that radical changes in maturity distributions can upset the financial markets and the economy in general. The management of the federal debt has become an especially challenging financial problem, and much time and energy are spent in meeting the challenge.

If the Treasury refunds maturing issues with new short-term obligations, the average maturity of the total debt is reduced. As time passes, longer-term issues are brought into shorter-dated categories. Net cash borrowing, which results from budgetary deficits, must take the form of maturities that are at least as long as the average of the marketable debt if the average maturity is not to be reduced. The average length of the marketable debt reached a low level of two years and five months in late 1975. Since that time, progress has been made in raising the length of maturities—although the average maturity continues to be under five years—by selling long-term obligations.

One of the new debt-management techniques used to extend the average maturity of the marketable debt without disturbing the financial markets is *advance refunding*. This occurs when the Treasury offers the owners of a given issue the opportunity to exchange their holdings well in advance of the holdings' regular maturity for new securities of longer maturity.

In summary, the Treasury is the largest and most active borrower in the financial markets. The Treasury is continuously in the process of borrowing and refinancing. Its financial actions are tremendous in contrast with all other forms of financing, including those of the largest business corporations. Yet, the financial system of the nation is well adapted to accommodate its needs smoothly. Indeed, the very existence of a public debt of this magnitude is predicated on the existence of a highly refined monetary and credit system.

CONCEPT CHECK
What is the average maturity of U.S. marketable debt securities?

term structure
relationship between interest rates or yields and the time to maturity for debt instruments of comparable quality

yield curve
graphic presentation of the term structure of interest rates at a given point in time

TERM OR MATURITY STRUCTURE OF INTEREST RATES

The **term structure** of interest rates indicates the relationship between interest rates or yields and the maturity of comparable quality debt instruments. This relationship is typically depicted through the graphic presentation of a **yield curve.** A properly constructed yield curve must first

TABLE 8.3
Term Structure of Interest Rates for Treasury Securities at Selected Dates (%)

TERM TO MATURITY	MARCH 1980	MARCH 1982	NOVEMBER 2001	NOVEMBER 2003	OCTOBER 2006	OCTOBER 2008
6 months	15.0%	12.8%	1.9%	1.0%	4.9%	0.2%
1 year	14.0	12.5	2.2	1.3	5.0	0.4
5 years	13.5	14.0	4.0	3.3	4.7	2.3
10 years	12.8	13.9	4.7	4.3	4.7	3.4
20 years	12.5	13.8	5.3	5.2	4.9	4.2
30 years	12.3	13.5	5.1	NA	4.9	4.2

Source: *Statistical Supplement to the Federal Reserve Bulletin*, various issues, and http://www.stlouisfed.org.

INTERNET ACTIVITY

Go to the Web site of the Federal Reserve Bank of St. Louis, http://www.stlouisfed.org, and access the FRED database. Find current interest rates for different maturities of U.S. Treasury securities, and construct the yield curve.

reflect securities of similar default risk. Second, the yield curve must represent a particular point in time, and the interest rates should reflect yields for the remaining time to maturity. That is, the yields should not only include stated interest rates but also consider that instruments and securities could be selling above or below their redemption values. (The process for calculating yields to maturity is shown in Chapter 9.) Third, the yield curve must show yields on a number of securities with differing lengths of time to maturity.

U.S. government securities provide the best basis for constructing yield curves because Treasury securities are considered to be risk free, as previously noted in terms of default risk. Table 8.3 contains interest rates for Treasury securities at selected dates and for various maturities. In early 1980, the annual inflation rate was in double digits. As a result, interest rates were very high, even though the economy was in a mild recession. Longer-term interest rates were even higher in March 1982, even though the economy was in a deep recession. Apparently, investors still were expecting the high levels of inflation to continue. However, by the latter part of the 1980s interest rates had dropped dramatically because of reduced inflation. Interest rates on one-year Treasury bills were at 6 percent in March 1991, compared with 14 percent in March 1980. Interest rates declined further as the economy began expanding from a mild recession at the beginning of the 1990s.

By November 1998, after the Fed first pushed up short-term interest rates in an effort to head off possible renewed inflation and then lowered rates in an effort to avoid a recession during the mid-1990s, interest rates were relatively flat across different maturities. The Fed lowered its discount rate many times during the first years of the twenty-first century due to concern about an economic downturn and the terrorist attack in New York City on September 11, 2001. By November 2001, short-term interest rates had dropped to about 2 percent. Short-term interest rates continued to fall and were at about 1 percent in November 2003. However, in an effort to keep inflation under control, the Fed forced short-term interest rates to higher levels so that short-term rates reached about 5 percent in October 2006. In reaction to the then developing 2007–2009 financial crisis, short-term interest rates declined sharply and were less than .5 percent by October 2008.

Figure 8.2 shows yield curves for March 1980, November 2003, October 2006, and October 2008 reflecting the plotting of the corresponding data in Table 8.3. Because of high inflation rates and monetary policy trying to constrain economic activity, the March 1980 yield curve was both downward sloping and at very high overall interest rate levels. In contrast, the yield curve for November 2003 was upward sloping and much lower overall due to lower expected inflation rates and efforts by monetary policy to stimulate economic activity.

By October 2006, the yield curve was nearly flat across all maturities with a variation only between about 4.7 percent and 5.0 percent. This flattening of the yield curve was attributable primarily to the Fed's effort to raise short-term interest rates as a way of possibly combating the possibility of increases in inflation rates. As the financial crisis of 2007–09 developed, short-term interest rates were forced to historically low levels. In October 2008, the yield curve was again upward sloping but from very low levels.

CONCEPT CHECK

What is meant by term structure of interest rates?

What is the definition of a yield curve?

RELATIONSHIP BETWEEN YIELD CURVES AND THE ECONOMY

Historical evidence suggests that interest rates generally rise during periods of economic expansion and fall during economic contraction. Therefore, the term structure of interest rates as

FIGURE 8.2
Yield Curves for Treasury Securities at Selected Dates

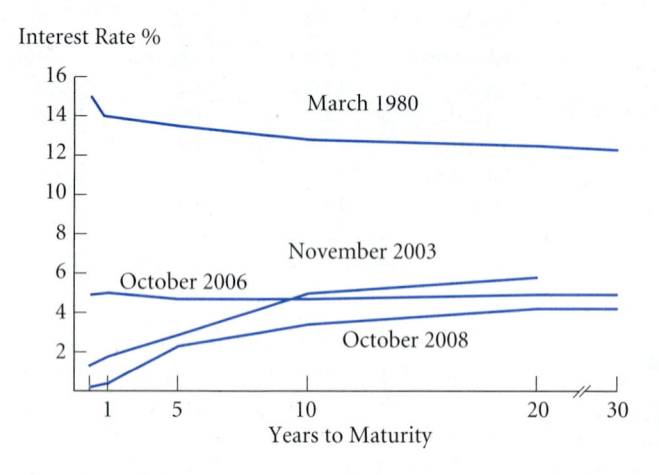

Source: *Statistical Supplement to the Federal Reserve Bulletin,* various issues, and http://www.stlouisfed.org.

depicted by yield curves shifts upward or downward with changes in economic activity. Interest rate levels generally are the lowest at the bottom of a recession and the highest at the top of an expansion period. Furthermore, when the economy is moving out of a recession, the yield curve slopes upward. The curve begins to flatten out during the latter stages of an expansion and typically starts sloping downward when economic activity peaks. As the economy turns downward, interest rates begin falling and the yield curve again goes through a flattening-out phase, to become upward sloping when economic activity again reaches a low point.

TERM STRUCTURE THEORIES

> **expectations theory** states that the shape of the yield curve indicates investor expectations about future inflation rates

Three theories are commonly used to explain the term structure of interest rates. The **expectations theory** contends that the shape of a yield curve reflects investor expectations about future inflation rates. If the yield curve is flat, expectations are that the current short-term inflation rate will remain essentially unchanged over time. When the yield curve is downward sloping, investors expect inflation rates to be lower in the future. Recall from Figure 8.2 that the shape of the yield curve in March 1980 was downward sloping. Thus, investors believed that the double-digit inflation rates prevailing in 1980 were expected to decline in the future. In contrast, the relatively flat yield curve in November 1998 suggested that investors expected the low inflation rates in late 1998 to remain at low levels in the future and that the economy would continue to grow at a moderate rate.

The upward-sloping yield curve in November 2001 occurred at the end of the 2001 recession. The yield curve continued to be upward sloping in November 2003 as economic activity continued to increase. A flattening of the yield curve by October 2006 caused some concern about the possibility of a slowdown in economic activity and preceded the 2007–09 financial crisis. By October 2008, the yield curve, while at historically low interest rates for short maturities, was upward sloping, suggesting hope for future recovery.

To differentiate yield curve shapes in terms of Equations 8.1 and 8.2, first recall that the liquidity and the default risk premiums are zero for Treasury securities. Thus, Equation 8.2 for Treasury securities becomes Equation 8.1 plus a maturity risk premium (MRP). However, the expectations theory in its purest form also assumes the MRP to be zero. Given this assumption, we have reduced Equation 8.2 back to Equation 8.1 such that the yield curve reflects only the real rate (RR) of interest plus the expectation for an inflation premium (IP) over the life of the security.

Let's assume that the current rates of interest or yields are: one-year Treasury bills = 7 percent; two-year Treasury notes = 8 percent; and ten-year Treasury bonds = 9 percent. Using a 3 percent real rate of return, we have the following relationships:

Maturity	r	=	RR	+	IP
1-year	7%	=	3%	+	4%
2-year	8%	=	3%	+	5%
10-year	9%	=	3%	+	6%

Thus, the inflation rate is expected to be 4 percent over the next year. However, the inflation rate is expected to average 5 percent per year over the next two years; or if inflation is 4 percent the first year, then the rate for the second year must be more than 5 percent. Working with simple averages, 5 percent average inflation times two years means that the total inflation will be 10 percent. Thus, 10 percent less 4 percent means that inflation in the second year must be 6 percent.

For years three through ten, inflation must exceed 6 percent annually to average 6 percent over the ten-year period. We can find the simple average by starting with the fact that inflation will be 60 percent (6 percent times 10 years) over the full ten-year period, and 60 percent less the 10 percent for the first two years means that cumulative inflation for the last eight years will be 50 percent. Then, dividing 50 percent by eight means that inflation will have to average 6.25 percent over years three through ten. In summary, we have:

TIME PERIOD	AVERAGE INFLATION		NUMBER OF YEARS		CUMULATIVE INFLATION
Year 1	4%	×	1	=	4%
Year 2	6%	×	1	=	6%
Years 3–10	6.25%	×	8	=	50%
Total inflation					60%
Total years					10
Average inflation (60% ÷ 10 years)					6%

These are only simple arithmetic averages. Technically, we have ignored the impact of the compounding of inflation rates over time. The concept of compounding is presented in Chapter 9, which focuses on the time value of money.

The **liquidity preference theory** holds that investors or debt instrument holders prefer to invest short term so that they have greater liquidity and less maturity or interest rate risk. Lenders also prefer to lend short term because of the risk of higher inflation rates and greater uncertainty about default risk in the future. Borrowers prefer to borrow long term so that they have more time to repay loans. The net result is a willingness to accept lower interest rates on short-term loans as a trade-off for greater liquidity and lower interest rate risk.

The **market segmentation theory** holds that securities of different maturities are not perfect substitutes for one another. For example, because of their demand and other deposit liabilities, commercial banks concentrate their activities on short-term securities because of their demand and other deposit liabilities. On the other hand, the nature of insurance company and pension fund liabilities allows these firms to concentrate holdings in long-term securities. Thus, supply-and-demand factors in each market segment affect the shape of the yield curve. Thus, in some time periods interest rates on intermediate-term Treasury securities may be higher (or lower) than those for both short-term and long-term treasuries.

INFLATION PREMIUMS AND PRICE MOVEMENTS

Actions or factors that change the value of the money unit or the supply of money and credit affect the whole economy. The change affects first the supply of loanable funds and interest rates and, later, both the demand for and the supply of goods in general. **Inflation**, as previously defined, is an increase in the price of goods or services that is not offset by an increase in quality. Recall than when investors expect higher inflation rates, they will require higher nominal interest rates so that a real rate of return will remain after the inflation. A clearer understanding of investor expectations about inflation premiums can be had by first reviewing past price movements, then exploring possible types of inflation.

---

liquidity preference theory
states that investors are willing to accept lower interest rates on short-term debt securities that provide greater liquidity and less interest rate risk

market segmentation theory
states that interest rates may differ because securities of different maturities are not perfect substitutes for each other

CONCEPT CHECK

What is the expectations theory in terms of the term structure of interest rates?

What is the liquidity preference theory?

What is the market segmentation theory?

inflation
occurs when an increase in the price of goods or services is not offset by an increase in quality

GLOBAL DISCUSSION

HISTORICAL INTERNATIONAL PRICE MOVEMENTS

Changes in the money supply or in the amount of metal in the money unit have influenced prices since the earliest records of civilization. The money standard in ancient Babylon was in terms of silver and barley. The earliest available price records show that one shekel of silver was equal to 240 measures of grain. At the time of Hammurabi (about 1750 B.C.), a shekel in silver was worth between 150 and 180 measures of grain, while in the following century it declined to 90 measures. After Persia conquered Babylonia in 539 B.C., the value of the silver shekel was recorded as between 15 and 40 measures of grain.

Alexander the Great probably caused the greatest inflationary period in ancient history when he captured the large gold hoards of Persia and took them to Greece. Inflation was high for some years, but twenty years after Alexander's death, a period of deflation began and lasted over fifty years.

The first recorded cases of deliberate currency debasement (lowering the value) occurred in the Greek city-states. The government would debase currency by calling in all coins and issuing new ones containing less of the precious metals. This must have been a convenient form of inflation, for there are many such cases in the records of Greek city-states.

Ancient Rome

During the Punic Wars, devaluation led to inflation as the heavy bronze coin was reduced in stages from one pound to one ounce. Similar inflation occurred in Roman history. Augustus brought so much precious metal from Egypt that prices rose and interest rates fell. From the time of Nero, debasements were frequent. The weight of gold coins was gradually reduced, and silver coins had baser metals added to them so that they were finally only 2 percent silver. Few attempts were made to arrest or reverse this process of debasement of coins as the populace adjusted to the process. When Aurelian tried to improve the coinage by adding to its precious metal content, he was resisted so strongly that armed rebellion broke out.

The Middle Ages Through Modern Times

During the Middle Ages, princes and kings debased the coinage to get more revenue. The rulers of France used this ploy more than others, and records show that profit from debasement was sometimes greater than the total of all other revenues.

An important example of inflation followed the arrival of Europeans in America. Gold and silver poured into Spain from Mexico and Peru. Since the riches were used to buy goods from other countries, they were distributed over the continent and to England. Prices rose in Spain and in most of Europe but not in proportion to the increase in gold and silver stocks. This was because trade increased and because many people hoarded the precious metals.

Paper money was not used generally until the end of the seventeenth century. The first outstanding example of inflation due to the issuing of an excessive amount of paper money was in France. In 1719, the government gave Scottish banker John Law a charter for a bank that could issue paper money. The note circulation of his bank amounted to almost 2,700 million livres (the monetary unit in use at that time in France), against which he had coin of only 21 million livres and bullion of 27 million livres. Prices went up rapidly, but they fell just as fast when Law's bank failed. Afterward, the money supply was again restricted.

The next outstanding period of inflation was during the American (1775–83) and French (1789–99) Revolutions. For example, France's revolutionary government issued paper currency in huge quantities. This currency, called assignats, declined to 0.5 percent of its face value.

Spectacular inflation also took place in Germany in 1923, when prices soared to astronomical heights. During World War II, runaway inflation took place in China and Hungary, as well as in other countries.

INFLATION IN THE UNITED STATES

Monetary factors have often affected price levels in the United States, especially during major wars.

Revolutionary War

The war that brought the United States into being was financed mainly by inflation. The Second Continental Congress had no real authority to levy taxes and thus found it difficult to raise money. As a result, the congress decided to issue notes for $2 million. It issued more and more

CONCEPT CHECK

What do we mean by the term inflation?

What was the first example of rapid inflation after paper money began being used?

notes until the total rose to over $240 million. The individual states issued $200 million more. Since the notes were crudely engraved, counterfeiting was common, adding to the total of circulating currency. Continental currency depreciated in value so rapidly that the expression "not worth a continental" became a part of the American language.

War of 1812

During the War of 1812, the government tried to avoid repeating the inflationary measures of the Revolutionary War. However, since the war was not popular in New England, it was impossible to finance it by taxation and borrowing. Paper currency was issued in a somewhat disguised form: bonds of small denomination bearing no interest and having no maturity date. The wholesale price index, based on 100 as the 1910–1914 average prices, rose from 131 in 1812 to 182 in 1814. Prices declined to about the prewar level by 1816 and continued downward as depression hit the economy.

Civil War

The Mexican War (1846–1848) did not involve the total economy to any extent and led to no inflationary price movements. The Civil War (1861–1865), however, was financed partly by issuing paper money. In the war's early stages, the U.S. Congress could not raise enough money by taxes and borrowing to finance all expenditures; therefore, it resorted to inflation by issuing U.S. Notes with no backing, known as greenbacks. In all, $450 million was authorized. Even though this was but a fraction of the cost of the war, prices went up substantially. Wholesale prices on a base of 100 increased from 93 in 1860 to 185 in 1865. Attempts to retire the greenbacks at the end of the war led to deflation and depression in 1866. As a result, the law withdrawing greenbacks was repealed.

World War I

Although the U.S. government did not print money to finance World War I, it did practice other inflationary policies. About one-third of the cost of the war was raised by taxes and two-thirds of the cost by borrowing. The banking system provided much of this credit, which added to the money supply. People were even persuaded to use Liberty Bonds as collateral for bank loans to buy other bonds. The wholesale price index rose from 99 in 1914 to 226 in 1920. Then, as credit expansion was finally restricted in 1921, it dropped to 141 in 1922.

World War II and the Postwar Period

The government used fewer inflationary policies to finance World War II. Nevertheless, the banking system still took up large sums of bonds. By the end of the war, the debt of the federal government had increased by $207 billion. Bank holdings of government bonds had increased by almost $60 billion. Prices went up by only about one-third during the war because they were held in check after the first year by price and wage controls. They then rose rapidly when the controls were lifted after the war. In 1948, wholesale prices had risen to 236 from a level of 110 in 1939.

Wholesale prices increased during the Korean War and again during the 1955–1957 expansion in economic activity as the economy recovered from the 1954 recession. Consumer goods prices continued to move upward during practically the entire postwar period, increasing gradually even in those years in which wholesale prices hardly changed.

Recent Decades

Figure 8.3 shows the consumer price index (CPI) for all items, and a related consumer price measure when food and energy are excluded, since the early 1970s. Wholesale consumer goods prices again increased substantially when the Vietnam War escalated after mid-1965. Prices continued upward after American participation in the Vietnam War was reduced in the early 1970s. After American participation in the war ended in 1974, prices rose at the most rapid levels since World War I. Inflation was worldwide in the middle 1970s; its effects were much worse in many other industrial countries than in the United States.

As the 1970s ended, economists realized the full impact of a philosophy based on a high inflation rate. Many economists thought high inflation could keep unemployment down permanently, even though history shows that it does not. The government's efforts to control interest rates by increasing the money supply reinforced people's doubts that such policies would reduce inflation and high interest rates. By October 1979, the Federal Reserve System abandoned this

INTERNET ACTIVITY

Go to the Web site of the Council of Economic Advisors, http://www.whitehouse.gov/cea/pubs.html, and access the Economic Report of the President. Next access the statistical appendix tables, and find current inflation rates based on the consumer price index for all items and when food and energy prices are excluded.

FIGURE 8.3
Consumer Price Index

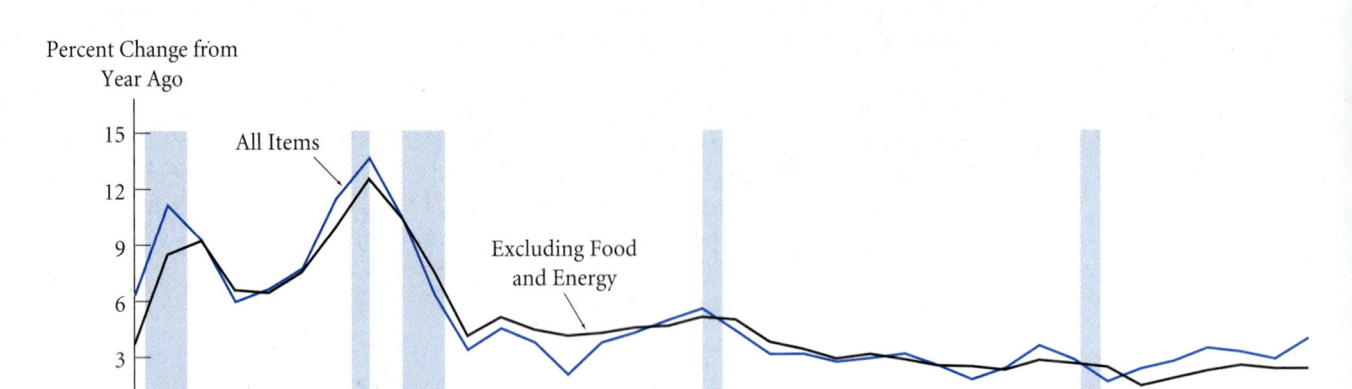

Source: *Economic Report of the President*, selected issues, and http://www.stlouisfed.org.

failed approach to interest rate control and adopted a policy of monetary growth control. The result was twofold. First, there was a far greater volatility in interest rates as the Federal Reserve concentrated on monetary factors. Second, during the first three quarters of 1980, some monetary restraint was exercised. This monetary restraint depressed production and employment. The Federal Reserve System quickly backed off from this position of restraint, and by the end of 1980 a far greater level of monetary stimulus had driven interest rates to new peaks.

By this time, the prime rate had risen to 21.5 percent and three-month Treasury bills had doubled in yield from their midyear lows. These high interest rates had a profound negative effect on such interest-sensitive industries as housing and automobiles. The Fed reversed the rapid growth of money supply throughout 1981 and until late in 1982. Unemployment climbed as the effects of monetary restraint were imposed on the economy, but the back of inflation was broken. By the end of 1982, economic recovery was in place, along with an easing of monetary restraint.

Figure 8.3 shows that inflation stayed at moderate levels beginning in 1983 and continuing through most of the remainder of the 1980s until near the end of the decade. After peaking in 1990 above a 6 percent annual rate, the CPI stayed at about 3 percent until 1997, when the inflation rate dropped even further. In early 1994, the Fed moved toward a tighter monetary policy in an effort to keep inflation from rising. As the country finished the 1990s and moved into the early twenty-first century, inflation rates remained at relatively low levels. For 2008, the CPI for all items was 3.9 percent, reflecting a record high price of oil. The alternative CPI measure, adjusted to exclude food and energy, was 2.3 percent for 2008. Since then, the CPI has declined, and inflation remained at historically low levels as the decade of the 2000s came to an end.

CONCEPT CHECK

What happened to inflation in the United States during the 1980s and the 1990s?

What happened to inflation in the United States during the first part of the twenty-first century?

TYPES OF INFLATION

Inflation may be associated with a change in costs, a change in the money supply, speculation, and so-called administrative pressures.

Price Changes Initiated by a Change in Costs

The price level can sometimes increase without the original impulse coming from either the money supply or its velocity. If costs rise faster than productivity increases, as when wages go up, businesses with some control over prices will try to raise them to cover the higher costs. Such increases are likely to be effective when the demand for goods is strong compared to the supply. The need for more funds to meet production and distribution at higher prices usually causes the money supply and velocity to increase. This type of inflation is called **cost-push inflation,** as this rise in prices comes from the cost side, not from increases in the money supply. Prices may not go up, however, if the monetary authorities restrict credit expansion. In that case, only the most efficient businesses will have enough demand to operate profitably. As a result, some resources will be unemployed.

cost-push inflation
occurs when prices are raised to cover rising production costs, such as wages

demand-pull inflation *occurs during economic expansions when demand for goods and services is greater than supply*

Cost-push inflation is different from inflation caused by an increase in the money supply, which is called **demand-pull inflation** and may be defined as an excessive demand for goods and services during periods of economic expansion as a result of large increases in the money supply. In practice, both aspects of inflation are likely to occur at the same time, since cost-push inflation can occur only in industries in which labor negotiations are carried out industry-wide and in which management has the ability to increase prices.

Demand-pull inflation may also be caused by changes in demand in particular industries. The demand for petroleum, for example, may be greater than demand in general, so that prices rise in this industry before they rise generally. The first raise is likely to be in the basic materials themselves, leading to increased profits in the industries that produce them. Labor will press for wage increases to get its share of the total value of output, and thus labor costs also rise. Price rises in basic industries lead to price increases in the industries that use their products. Wage increases in one major industry are also likely to lead to demands for similar increases in other industries and among the nonorganized workers in such industries. The process set into motion can lead to general changes in prices, provided the monetary authorities do not restrict credit so as to prevent it.

Price Changes Initiated by a Change in the Money Supply

The way in which factors that affect prices relate to one another is quite complex. The following discussion considers the adjustments that take place when the primary change is in the money supply or its velocity. Of course, more complex relationships arising out of changes in both the money supply and the goods side of the equation during business cycles could also take place.

An increase in the supply or velocity of money can cause several types of inflation. Inflation may result when the supply of purchasing power increases. Government deficits financed by creating deposits or private demands for funds may initiate this type of inflation. If this happens when people and resources are not fully employed, the volume of trade goes up; prices are only slightly affected at first. As unused resources are brought into use, however, prices will go up. When resources such as metals become scarce, their prices rise. As any resource begins to be used up, the expectation of future price rises will itself force prices up because attempts to buy before such price rises will increase demand above current needs. Since some costs will lag—such as interest costs and wages set by contract—profits will rise, increasing the demand for capital goods.

Once resources are fully employed, the full effect of the increased money supply will be felt on prices. Prices may rise out of proportion for a time as expectations of higher prices lead to faster spending and so raise the velocity of money. The expansion will continue until trade and prices are in balance at the new levels of the money supply. Velocity will probably drop somewhat from those levels during the period of rising prices, since the desire to buy goods before the price goes up has disappeared.

Even if the supply of money is increased when people and resources are fully employed, prices may not go up proportionately. Higher prices increase profits for a time and so lead to a demand for more capital and labor. Thus, previously unemployed spouses, retired workers, and similar groups begin to enter the labor force. Businesses may use capital more fully by having two or three shifts use the same machines.

Demand-pull inflation traditionally exists during periods of economic expansion when the demand for goods and services exceeds the available supply of such goods and services. A second version of inflation also associated with increases in the money supply occurs because of monetization of the U.S. government debt. Recall from Chapter 5 that the Treasury finances government deficits by selling U.S. government securities to the public, commercial banks, or the Federal Reserve. When the Federal Reserve purchases U.S. government securities, reserves must be created to pay for the purchases. This, in turn, may lead to higher inflation because of an increase in money supply and bank reserves.

Speculation and Administrative Inflation

speculative inflation *caused by the expectation that prices will continue to rise, resulting in increased buying to avoid even higher future prices*

When an increased money supply causes inflation, it can lead to the additional price pressure called **speculative inflation.** Since prices have risen for some time, people believe that they will keep on rising. Inflation becomes self-generating for a time because, instead of higher prices resulting in lower demand, people may buy more to get goods before their prices go still higher, as happened in the late 1970s. This effect may be confined to certain areas, as it was to land prices in the 1920s Florida land boom or to security prices in the 1928–1929 stock market boom. Such a price rise leads to an increase in velocity as speculators try to turn over their funds as rapidly as possible and many others try to buy ahead of needs before there are further price rises.

For three decades, until the early 1980s, price pressures and inflation were continual despite occasional policies of strict credit restraint. During this long period, in fact, prices continued upward in recession periods, though at a slower rate than in prosperity periods. The need to restrain price rises hampered the Fed's ability to promote growth and fight recessions. Prices and other economic developments during this period led many to feel that the economy had developed a long-run *inflationary bias*. However, the continued low inflation rates in the late 1980s and the 1990s may have curtailed these beliefs, at least for a while.

Those economists who believe that long-run inflationary bias will continue do so on the basis of the following factors. First, prices and wages tend to rise during periods of boom in a competitive economy. This tendency is reinforced by wage contracts that provide escalator clauses to keep wages in line with prices and by wage increases that are sometimes greater than increases in productivity. Second, during recessions, prices tend to remain stable rather than decrease. This is because major unions have long-run contracts calling for annual wage increases no matter what economic conditions are at the time. The tendency of large corporations to rely on nonprice competition (advertising, and style and color changes) and to reduce output rather than cut prices also keeps prices stable. Furthermore, if prices do decline drastically in a field, the government is likely to step in with programs to help take excess supplies off the market. There is little doubt that prices would decline in a severe and prolonged depression. Government takes action to counter resulting unemployment, however, before the economy reaches such a level. Thus we no longer experience the downward price pressure of a depression.

The inflation resulting from these factors is called **administrative inflation.** This is to distinguish it from the type of inflation that happens when demand exceeds the available supply of goods, either because demand is increasing faster than supply in the early stages of a recovery period or because demand from monetary expansion by the banking system or the government exceeds available supply.

Traditional monetary policy is not wholly effective against administrative inflation. If money supplies are restricted enough, prices can be kept in line; this will lead to long-term unemployment and slow growth. It is also difficult for new firms and small growing firms to get credit since lending policies are likely to be conservative. The government must develop new tools to deal with administrative inflation effectively.

administrative inflation
the tendency of prices, aided by union-corporation contracts, to rise during economic expansion and to resist declines during recessions

CONCEPT CHECK

What is the difference between cost-push inflation and demand-pull inflation?

What is meant by the terms speculative inflation and administrative inflation?

FINANCE PRINCIPLE

default risk
risk that a borrower will not pay interest and/or principal on a loan when due

DEFAULT RISK PREMIUMS

Investors are said to be "risk averse"; that is, they expect to be compensated with higher returns for taking on more risk in the form of greater uncertainty about return variability or outcome. This is the pillar of finance, known as the risk-return principle, or "higher returns are expected for taking on more risk" principle. **Default risk** is the risk that a borrower will not pay interest and/or repay the principal on a loan or other debt instrument according to the agreed contractual terms. The consequence may be a lower-than-expected interest rate or yield or even a complete loss of the amount originally lent. The premium for default risk will increase as the probability of default increases.

To examine default risk premiums for debt securities, it is necessary to hold some of the other risk premiums constant. By referring to Equation 8.2 we can develop a procedure for measuring that portion of a nominal interest rate (r) attributable to default risk. Recall that the nominal interest rate is a function of a real interest rate, an inflation premium, a default risk premium, a maturity risk premium, and a liquidity risk premium.

First, we constrain our analysis to the long-term capital markets by considering only long-term Treasury bonds and long-term corporate bonds. By focusing on long-term securities, the maturity risk will be the same for all the bonds and can be set at zero for analysis purposes. We have also said that the liquidity premium is zero for Treasury securities because they can be readily sold without requiring a substantial price discount. Corporate securities are less liquid than Treasury securities. However, we can minimize any possible liquidity premiums by considering the bonds of large corporations. This also allows us to set the liquidity premium at zero for analysis purposes.

For the following example, assume that the real rate is 3 percent, the nominal interest rate is 8 percent for long-term Treasury bonds, and high-quality corporate bonds have a 9 percent nominal interest rate. Using Equation 8.2, we have:

$$r = RR + IP + DRP + MRP + LP$$
$$9\% = 3\% + 5\% + DRP + 0\% + 0\%$$
$$DRP = 9\% - 3\% - 5\% - 0\% - 0\% = 1\%$$

Since the 8 percent Treasury bond represents the risk-free rate of interest, subtracting the 3 percent real rate results in a long-term average annual inflation premium of 5 percent. Another way of looking at the default risk premium (assuming zero maturity risk and liquidity premiums) is that it is the difference between the interest rates on the risky (corporate) and risk-free (Treasury) securities. In our example, we have:

$$DRP = 9\% - 8\% = 1\%$$

Thus investors require a 1 percent premium to hold or invest in the corporate bond instead of the Treasury bond.

Another corporate bond with a higher default risk may carry an interest rate of, say, 11 percent. If the other assumptions used above are retained, the DRP would be:

$$11\% = 3\% + 5\% + DRP + 0\% + 0\%$$
$$DRP = 11\% - 3\% - 5\% - 0\% - 0\% = 3\%$$

Alternatively, we could find DRP as follows:

$$DRP = 11\% - 8\% = 3\%$$

Thus, to get investors to invest in these riskier corporate bonds, a default risk premium of 3 percentage points must be offered above the interest rate or yield on Treasury bonds.

The examination of actual default risk premiums in Table 8.4 shows long-term interest rates for Treasury bonds and two corporate bonds with different degrees of default risk. The characteristics of corporate bonds are discussed in Chapter 10, but here it can be said that one way potential default risk is measured is through bond ratings. The highest rating, Aaa, indicates the lowest likelihood of default. Investors in these bonds require a small default risk premium over Treasury bonds. Baa-rated bonds have higher default risks but still are considered to be of reasonably high quality. **Investment grade bonds** have ratings of Baa or higher and meet financial institution (banks, pension funds, insurance companies, etc.) investment standards.

investment grade bonds ratings of Baa or higher that meet financial institution investment standards

In March 1980, the default risk premium on corporate Aaa bonds over twenty-year Treasuries was 0.5 percentage point (i.e., 13.0% – 12.5%). The default risk premium of the highest-quality corporate bonds over Treasury bonds generally falls in the range of 0.5 to 0.80 percentage point. In fact, the default risk premium was about 0.8 percentage point in March 1982 when the economy was in a deep recession. The default risk premium on Aaa-rated corporate bonds had increased to unusually high 1.7 percentage points in November 2001, reflecting an economic downturn and concerns about terrorism in the United States. However, by November 2003, the

TABLE 8.4

Default Risk Premiums on Corporate Bonds at Selected Dates (%)

	MARCH 1980	MARCH 1982	NOV. 2001	NOV. 2003	OCT. 2006	OCT. 2008
Aaa-rated corporate bonds	13.0	14.6	7.0	5.7	5.5	5.2
Less: 20-year Treasury bonds	12.5	13.8	5.3	5.2	4.9	4.2
Equals: default risk premium on Aaa bonds	.5	.8	1.7	.5	.6	1.0
Baa-rated corporate bonds	14.5	16.8	7.8	6.7	6.4	6.3
Less: 20-year Treasury bonds	12.5	13.8	5.3	5.2	4.9	4.2
Equals: default risk premium on Baa bonds	2.0	3.0	2.5	1.5	1.5	2.1

Source: *Statistical Supplement to the Federal Reserve Bulletin,* various issues, and http://www.stlouisfed.org.

CAREER PROFILES

JOEL RASSMAN

Senior Vice President, Chief Financial Officer, Toll Brothers, Inc.

BA, University of New York—City College
Certified Public Accountant

"Interest rate changes affect our business in several ways."

Q: *What type of company is Toll Brothers?*
A: Toll Brothers, Inc., the nation's leading builder of luxury homes, operates in twenty-one states. The publicly traded company builds customized single-family and attached homes and develops country club and/or golf course communities and active-adult communities. We operate our own architectural, engineering, mortgage, title, land development and land sale, home security, landscape, lumber distribution, house component assembly, and manufacturing units.

Q: *What are your general responsibilities as CFO at Toll Brothers?*
A: I oversee Wall Street relationships, investor relations, finance, borrowing and bank relationships, treasury functions, taxes, accounting, audit, and risk management. I also serve as an internal consultant for many other aspects of the business.

Q: *How do changing levels of interest rates affect the home-building industry?*
A: Interest rate changes affect our business several ways. Most homebuyers use mortgages to finance their acquisition. If long-term interest rates rise, so do a buyer's monthly payments, and fewer families can afford a home. Changing rates also affect the costs of owning a home versus renting an apartment. Because first-time homebuyers tend to have less disposable income, they are much more sensitive to changing interest rates. Luxury homebuyers buying their third or fourth homes are generally less sensitive. Also, the spread between long-term and short-term rates affects homebuyers' choice of fixed-rate or variable-rate mortgages. Because we borrow to finance our business, our interest costs on floating-rate debt change as rates fluctuate.

Q: *What external funding does Toll Brothers use to finance its activities, and how do interest rates change your financing strategy?*
A: We use many funding sources to finance our business. We have issued new stock in the public markets and used most types of debt instruments: convertible subordinated debentures, bonds, notes, bank term loans and revolving credit, and mortgages for our commercial operations and fixed asset financing. We determine which vehicle to use by analyzing the market and comparing costs of each alternative, choosing the vehicle that minimizes costs while best matching risk and related life of the asset. As a business, you should not finance long-term risk with short-term money.

Q: *What skills make you good at your job?*
A: I understand how business, taxes, finance, and accounting interrelate. Arranging financing that meet the needs of the borrower and lender/investor requires knowledge of capital markets, bank markets, and investors' needs. Patience and understanding other people's needs is a must, as is willingness to listen to others. Most better ideas come from new ideas with successful existing practices. It's also important to think out of the box and look for innovative ways of solving problems. Equally important is the fact that I enjoy what I do.

Q: *How should someone prepare for a career in real estate finance?*
A: Real estate finance is a broad field with such varied opportunities that multiple paths can lead to success. Find an environment that lets you experience different types of transactions and develop multiple skills and a mentor who will explain the reasons behind each transaction. In the right environment you learn something new every day—I still do after thirty-four years in real estate, often from questions people ask.

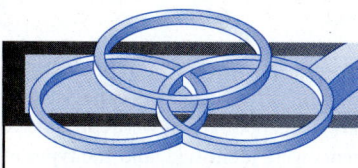

APPLYING FINANCE TO...

INSTITUTIONS AND MARKETS

Depository institutions make profits by achieving a spread between the interest rates they pay individuals on savings accounts and the interest rates they charge businesses and other individuals for loans. Interest rates are also important to financial institutions, such as insurance companies and pension funds, that accumulate premiums and contributions and invest these proceeds in government and corporate securities for the benefit of their policyholders and employees. The government depends on financial institutions holding or owning an important portion of the U.S. Treasury securities issued to finance the national debt

INVESTMENTS

Interest rates are set in the financial markets based on the supply and demand for loanable funds. The cost or price of home mortgage loans depends on the supply and demand for such loans in the mortgage markets. Interest rates offered on Treasury debt securities reflect a real rate of interest and an expected inflation premium. Corporate bond borrowers must pay a default risk premium above the interest rate being offered on government debt securities. Corporate issuers of high-quality investment-grade bonds pay lower default risk premiums relative to issuers of lower-quality bonds. Observed interest rates may also reflect a maturity risk premium and/or a liquidity premium.

FINANCIAL MANAGEMENT

The prevailing level of interest rates is particularly important to financial managers. When interest rates are high, businesses will find it less profitable to borrow from financial institutions or in the securities markets because investment in inventories, plant, and equipment will look less attractive. Likewise, when interest rates are relatively low, loans are generally readily available and stock prices are usually high. Thus, financial managers often find it attractive to grow their businesses during periods when funds to finance the expansion activities can be borrowed at relatively low interest rates or when they can issue new shares of their common stocks at relatively high prices.

INTERNET ACTIVITY

Go to the Web site of the Federal Reserve Bank of St. Louis, http://www.stlouisfed.org, and access the FRED database. Find current interest rates for long-term Treasury bonds, as well as Aaa and Baa corporate bonds, and indicate the size of default risk premiums.

ETHICAL ISSUES

high-yield or junk bonds
bonds that have a relatively high probability of default

CONCEPT CHECK
What is default risk?
What is a default risk premium and how is it calculated?

premium on Aaa-rated corporate bonds over the interest rate on twenty-year Treasury bonds was only 0.5 percentage point, which is considered to be low, historically speaking. The October 2006 risk premium for Aaa-rated bonds remained low at a 0.6 percentage point differential over twenty-year Treasury bonds. By October 2008, when the U.S. was in the midst of the 2007–09 financial crisis, the risk premium for Aaa-rated bonds had increased to 1.0 percentage point.

The default risk premiums on Baa corporate bonds are generally better indicators of investor pessimism or optimism about economic expectations than are those on Aaa bonds. More firms fail or suffer financial distress during periods of recession than during periods of economic expansion. Thus, investors tend to require higher premiums to compensate for default risk when the economy is in a recession or is expected to enter one. Notice in Table 8.4 that the risk premium on Baa-rated bonds was 2 percentage points in March 1980 (14.5% − 12.5%) and then increased to 3 percentage points in March 1982, when a deep recession existed. The default risk premium on Baa-rated bonds was 2.5 percentage points in November 2001 and reflected concerns about the slowing of economic activity in the United States and continued uncertainty after the terrorist attack on September 11, 2001. However, by November 2003 the risk premium on Baa-rated corporate debt had dropped to a relatively low 1.5 percentage points. As of October 2006, the risk premium on Baa-rated corporate debt remained at 1.5 percentage points over the interest rate on twenty-year Treasury bonds. The Baa-rated financial premium increased to 2.1 percentage points by October 2008, due to the financial crisis in the United States.

Sometimes corporations issue bonds with ratings lower than Baa. These are called **high-yield or junk bonds** because they have a substantial probability of default. While many institutional investors are restricted to investing in only investment-grade (Baa-rated or higher) corporate debt, others are permitted to invest in high-yield, high-risk corporate debt. Recall the discussion in Chapter 3 about the savings and loan associations crisis that was caused in part by corporate defaults on high-yield or junk bonds that were held by S&Ls. Michael Milken, who was at Drexel Burnham Lambert at the time, was instrumental in getting those S&Ls and other institutions allowed to purchase junk bonds to do so. Some individuals would argue that the purchasers of junk bonds were sophisticated enough to make rational risk-return decisions; *caveat emptor*—let the buyer beware. Other individuals charged that unethical and illegal behavior on the part of the marketers of junk bonds contributed to the failure of many of the issuers of the bonds as well as the purchasers (particularly S&Ls) of the bonds. In 1989, Milken was sent to prison and Drexel Burnham Lambert went bankrupt.

SUMMARY

This chapter began by illustrating how interest rates change given shifts in demand and/or supply curves. The loanable funds theory for explaining interest rates was presented. Then the following determinants of market interest rates were discussed: real rate of interest, inflation premium, default risk premium, maturity risk premium, and liquidity premium.

Three types of U.S. Treasury securities (bills, notes, and bonds) were identified and described. Then, the term structure of interest rates was defined and depicted with a yield curve graph. Next, the three theories used to explain the term structure–expectations, liquidity preference, and market segmentation–were presented. Major historical price movements were identified, and the types of inflation—cost-push, demand-pull, speculative, and administrative—were described. The final topic focused on how default risk premiums are estimated and what causes them to change over time.

KEY TERMS

administrative inflation
cost-push inflation
dealer system
default risk
default risk premium
demand-pull inflation
expectations theory
high-yield or junk bonds
inflation
inflation premium
interest rate
interest rate risk
investment grade bonds
liquidity preference theory
liquidity premium
loanable funds theory
market segmentation theory
marketable government securities
maturity risk premium
nominal interest rate
nonmarketable government securities
real rate of interest
risk-free rate of interest
speculative inflation
term structure
Treasury bills
Treasury bonds
Treasury notes
yield curve

DISCUSSION QUESTIONS

1. What is the "interest rate," and how is it determined?

2. Describe how interest rates may adjust to an unanticipated increase in inflation.

3. Identify major periods of rising interest rates in U.S. history, and describe some of the underlying reasons for these interest rate movements.

4. How does the loanable funds theory explain the level of interest rates?

5. What are the main sources of loanable funds? Indicate and briefly discuss the factors that affect the supply of loanable funds.

6. Indicate the sources of demand for loanable funds, and discuss the factors that affect the demand for loanable funds.

7. What are the factors, in addition to supply and demand relationships, that determine market interest rates?

8. What are the types of marketable obligations issued by the Treasury?

9. Explain the mechanics of issuing Treasury bills, indicating how the price of a new issue is determined.

10. Describe the dealer system for marketable U.S. government obligations.

11. What is the tax status of income from federal obligations?

12. Describe any significant changes in the ownership pattern of federal debt securities in recent years.

13. What have been the recent developments in the maturity distribution of marketable interest-bearing federal debt?

14. Describe the process of advance refunding of the federal debt.

15. What is the term structure of interest rates, and how is it expressed?

16. Identify and describe the three basic theories used to explain the term structure of interest rates.

17. Describe the process by which inflation took place historically before modern times.

18. Discuss the early periods of inflation based on the issue of paper money.

19. What was the basis for inflation during World Wars I and II?

20. Discuss the causes of the major periods of inflation in American history.

21. Explain the process by which price changes may be initiated by a general change in costs.

22. How can a change in the money supply lead to a change in the price level?

23. What is meant by the speculative type of inflation?

24. What is meant by a default risk premium?

25. How can a default risk premium change over time?

EXERCISES

1. Go to the Federal Reserve Bank of St. Louis website at http://www.stlouisfed.org, and find interest rates on U.S. Treasury securities and on corporate bonds with different bond ratings.

   a. Prepare a yield curve or term structure of interest rates.
   b. Identify existing default risk premiums between long-term Treasury bonds and corporate bonds.

2. As an economist for a major bank, you are asked to explain a substantial increase in the price level when neither the money supply nor the velocity of money has increased. How can this occur?

3. As an advisor to the U.S. Treasury, you have been asked to comment on a proposal for easing the burden of interest on the national debt. This proposal calls for the elimination of federal taxes

on interest received from Treasury debt obligations. Comment on the proposal.

4. As one of several advisors to the secretary of the U.S. Treasury, you have been asked to submit a memo in connection with the average maturity of the obligations of the federal government. The basic premise is that the average maturity is far too short. As a result, issues of debt are coming due with great frequency and need constant reissue. On the other hand, the economy shows signs of weakness. It is considered unwise to issue long-term obligations and absorb investment funds that might otherwise be invested in employment-producing construction and other private-sector support. Based on these conditions, what course of action do you recommend to the secretary of the U.S. Treasury?

5. Assume a condition in which the economy is strong, with relatively high employment. For one reason or another, the money supply is increasing at a high rate, with little evidence of money creation slowing down. Assuming the money supply continues to increase, describe the evolving effect on price levels.

6. Assume you are employed as an investment advisor. You are working with a retired individual who depends on her income from her investments to meet her day-to-day expenditures. She would like to find a way of increasing the current income from her investments. A new high-yield or junk bond issue has come to your attention. If you sell these high-yield bonds to a client, you will earn a higher-than-average fee. You wonder whether this would be a win-win investment for your retired client, who is seeking higher current income, and for you, who would benefit in terms of increased fees. What would you do?

PROBLEMS

1. Assume investors expect a 2.0 percent real rate of return over the next year. If inflation is expected to be 0.5 percent, what is the expected nominal interest rate for a one-year U.S. Treasury security?

2. A one-year U.S. Treasury security has a nominal interest rate of 2.25 percent. If the expected real rate of interest is 1.5 percent, what is the expected annual inflation rate?

3. A ten-year U.S. Treasury bond has a 3.50 percent interest rate, while a same maturity corporate bond has a 5.25 percent interest rate. Real interest rates and inflation rate expectations would be the same for the two bonds. If a default risk premium of 1.50 percentage points is estimated for the corporate bond, determine the liquidity premium for the corporate bond.

4. A thirty-year U.S. Treasury bond has a 4.0 percent interest rate. In contrast, a ten-year Treasury bond has an interest rate of 3.7 percent. If inflation is expected to average 1.5 percentage points over both the next ten years and thirty years, determine the maturity risk premium for the thirty-year bond over the ten-year bond.

5. A thirty-year U.S. Treasury bond has a 4.0 percent interest rate. In contrast, a ten-year Treasury bond has an interest rate of 2.5 percent. A maturity risk premium is estimated to be 0.2 percentage points for the longer maturity bond. Investors expect inflation to average 1.5 percentage points over the next ten years.
   a. Estimate the expected real rate of return on the ten-year U.S. Treasury bond.
   b. If the real rate of return is expected to be the same for the thirty-year bond as for the ten-year bond, estimate the average annual inflation rate expected by investors over the life of the thirty-year bond.

6. You are considering an investment in a one-year government debt security with a yield of 5 percent or a highly liquid corporate debt security with a yield of 6.5 percent. The expected inflation rate for the next year is expected to be 2.5 percent.
   a. What would be your real rate earned on either of the two investments?
   b. What would be the default risk premium on the corporate debt security?

7. Inflation is expected to be 3 percent over the next year. You desire an annual real rate of return of 2.5 percent on your investments.
   a. What nominal rate of interest would have to be offered on a one-year Treasury security for you to consider making an investment?
   b. A one-year corporate debt security is being offered at 2 percentage points over the one-year Treasury security rate that meets your requirement in (a). What would be the nominal interest rate on the corporate security?

8. Find the nominal interest rate for a debt security given the following information: real rate = 2 percent, liquidity premium = 2 percent, default risk premium = 4 percent, maturity risk premium = 3 percent, and inflation premium = 3 percent.

9. Find the default risk premium for a debt security given the following information: inflation premium = 3 percent, maturity risk premium = 2.5 percent, real rate = 3 percent, liquidity premium = 0 percent, and nominal interest rate = 10 percent.

10. Find the default risk premium for a debt security given the following information: inflation premium = 2.5 percent, maturity risk premium = 2.5 percent, real rate = 3 percent, liquidity premium = 1.5 percent, and nominal interest rate = 14 percent.

11. Assume that the interest rate on a one-year Treasury bill is 6 percent and the rate on a two-year Treasury note is 7 percent.
    a. If the expected real rate of interest is 3 percent, determine the inflation premium on the Treasury bill.
    b. If the maturity risk premium is expected to be zero, determine the inflation premium on the Treasury note.
    c. What is the expected inflation premium for the second year?

12. A Treasury note with a maturity of four years carries a nominal rate of interest of 10 percent. In contrast, an eight-year Treasury bond has a yield of 8 percent.
    a. If inflation is expected to average 7 percent over the first four years, what is the expected real rate of interest?
    b. If the inflation rate is expected to be 5 percent for the first year, calculate the average annual rate of inflation for years 2 through 4.
    c. If the maturity risk premium is expected to be zero between the two Treasury securities, what will be the average annual inflation rate expected over years 5 through 8?

13. The interest rate on a ten-year Treasury bond is 9.25 percent. A comparable-maturity Aaa-rated corporate bond is yielding 10 percent. Another comparable-maturity, but lower-quality, corporate bond has a yield of 14 percent, which includes a liquidity premium of 1.5 percent.

   a. Determine the default risk premium on the Aaa-rated bond.
   b. Determine the default risk premium on the lower-quality corporate bond.

14. A corporate bond has a nominal interest rate of 12 percent. This bond is not very liquid and consequently requires a 2 percent liquidity premium. The bond is of low quality and thus has a default risk premium of 2.5 percent. The bond has a remaining life of twenty-five years, resulting in a maturity risk premium of 1.5 percent.

   a. Estimate the nominal interest rate on a Treasury bond.
   b. What would be the inflation premium on the Treasury bond if investors required a real rate of interest of 2.5 percent?

15. Challenge Problem Following are some selected interest rates.

MATURITY OR TERM	RATE	TYPE OF SECURITY
1 year	4.0%	Corporate loan (high quality)
1 year	5.0%	Corporate loan (low quality)
1 year	3.5%	Treasury bill
5 years	5.0%	Treasury note
5 years	6.5%	Corporate bond (high quality)
5 years	8.0%	Corporate bond (low quality)
10 years	10.5%	Corporate bond (low quality)
10 years	8.5%	Corporate bond (high quality)
10 years	7.0%	Treasury bond
20 years	7.5%	Treasury bond
20 years	9.5%	Corporate bond (high quality)
20 years	12.0%	Corporate bond (low quality)

   a. Plot a yield curve using interest rates for government default risk-free securities.
   b. Plot a yield curve using corporate debt securities with low default risk (high quality) and a separate yield curve for low-quality corporate debt securities.
   c. Measure the amount of default risk premiums, assuming constant inflation rate expectations and no maturity or liquidity risk premiums on any of the debt securities for both high-quality and low-quality corporate securities based on information from (a) and (b). Describe and discuss why differences might exist between high-quality and low-quality corporate debt securities.
   d. Identify the average expected inflation rate at each maturity level in (a) if the real rate is expected to average 2 percent per year and if there are no maturity risk premiums expected on Treasury securities.
   e. Using information from (d), calculate the average annual expected inflation rate over years 2 through 5. Also calculate the average annual expected inflation rates for years 6 through 10 and for years 11 through 20.
   f. Based on the information from (e), reestimate the maturity risk premiums for high-quality and low-quality corporate debt securities. Describe what seems to be occurring over time and between differences in default risks.

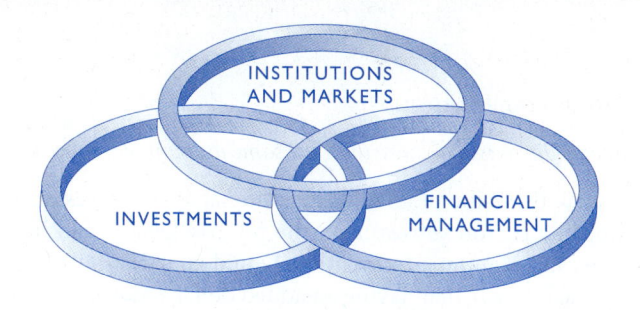

CHAPTER 9

Time Value of Money

Chapter Learning Objectives:

AFTER STUDYING THIS CHAPTER YOU SHOULD BE ABLE TO:

- Explain what is meant by "the time value of money."
- Describe the concept of simple interest and the process of compounding.
- Describe discounting to determine present values.
- Find interest rates and time requirements for problems involving compounding or discounting.
- Describe the meaning of an ordinary annuity.
- Find interest rates and time requirements for problems involving annuities.
- Calculate annual annuity payments.
- Make compounding and discounting calculations using time intervals that are less than one year.
- Describe the difference between the annual percentage rate and the effective annual rate.
- Describe the meaning of an annuity due (in the Learning Extension).

Where We Have Been...

In Chapter 8, you learned how interest rates are determined in the financial markets. The supply of and demand for loanable funds were discussed along with the determinants of market or "nominal" interest rates. You should recall that the determinants are the real rate of interest, an inflation premium, and a default risk premium for risky debt. A maturity risk premium adjusts for differences in lives or maturities, and there also may be a liquidity premium. You also learned about the characteristics of U.S. government debt securities and the term or maturity structure of interest rates. You now should know how inflation premiums and price movements affect interest rates, as well as why default risk premiums exist and how they are measured.

Where We Are Going...

Chapter 10 focuses on the characteristics and valuations of bonds and stocks. You will learn about the long-term external financing sources available to and used by businesses. You will then explore the characteristics and features of both debt and equity capital. Next, the general principles of valuation, which build on the time value of money (covered in this chapter), and how bonds and stocks are valued will be covered. Calculating rates of return is the last topic in Chapter 10. In Chapter 11 you will focus on the characteristics and operation of primary and secondary securities markets. Chapter 12, the last chapter in Part 2, will focus on financial return and risk concepts.

How This Chapter Applies to Me...

You probably have experienced the need to save money to buy an automobile or to pay for your tuition. Your savings grow more rapidly when you can earn interest on previously earned interest in addition to interest on the starting amount of your savings. This is known as compounding and means that the longer you save the faster your savings will grow and the larger will be your down payment on your automobile purchase or the more money you will have for your tuition. An understanding of compounding also will be useful to you when investing in stocks and bonds and planning for eventual retirement.

Most of us would agree that if other things are equal:

> More money is better than less money.

Most of us also would agree:

Money today is worth more than the same amount of money received in the future.

Of course, the value of an additional dollar is not necessarily the same for all individuals. For example, a person subsisting at the poverty level would likely find an added dollar to be worth more in "economic terms" than would an extra dollar to a millionaire or billionaire. It is probably safe to say that having an added dollar today has more "economic worth" to you or us than it would to Bill Gates, the founder and CEO of the Microsoft Corporation. At the same time, his personal desire or drive for accumulating more dollars is likely to be greater than your desires.

This chapter makes no attempt to consider the economic or psychic values of more money to a specific individual. Rather, it concentrates on the principle of finance, initially presented in Chapter 1, stating that "money has a time value." The focus here is on how money can grow or increase over time, as well as how money has a lower worth today if one has to wait to receive the money sometime in the future. This occurs because one loses the opportunity of earning interest on the money by not being able to save or invest the money today.

Financial calculators or spreadsheet software programs will perform the calculations and procedures discussed in this chapter. However, the calculation procedures are first described in detail to enhance the understanding of the logic involved in the concepts of the time value of money. By learning to work the problems the "long way," using step-by-step calculations, following the steps given for financial calculators, spreadsheet programs, and tables-based calculations should make more sense. Students are encouraged to explore using multiple problem-solving methods.

FINANCE PRINCIPLES

time value of money
math of finance whereby interest is earned over time by saving or investing money

present value
value today of a savings amount or investment

future value
value at a specified time or date in the future of a savings amount or investment

BASIC CONCEPTS

To understand the pricing and valuation of bonds, stocks, and real asset investments, we must first understand some basic finance math concepts. The **time value of money** is the math of finance whereby interest is earned over time by saving or investing money. Money can increase or grow over time if we can save (invest) it and earn a return on our savings (investment). Let's begin with a savings account illustration. Assume you have $1,000 to save or invest; this is your *principal*. The **present value** of a savings or an investment is its amount or value today. For our example, this is your $1,000.

A bank offers to accept your savings for one year and agrees to pay to you an 8 percent interest rate for use of your $1,000. This amounts to $80 in interest (0.08 × $1,000). The total payment by the bank at the end of one year is $1,080 ($1,000 principal plus $80 in interest). This $1,080 is referred to as the future value or value after one year. The **future value** of a savings amount or investment is its value at a specified time or date in the future. In general word terms, we have:

$$\text{Future value} = \text{Present value} + (\text{Present value} \times \text{Interest rate})$$

or

$$\text{Future value} = \text{Present value} \times (1 + \text{Interest rate})$$

In our example, we have:

$$\text{Future value} = \$1,000 + (\$1,000 \times 0.08)$$
$$= \$1,080$$

or

$$\text{Future value} = \$1,000 \times 1.08$$
$$= \$1,080$$

simple interest
interest earned only on the investment's principal

Let's now assume that your $1,000 investment remains on deposit for two years but that the bank pays only **simple interest,** which is interest earned only on the investment's principal. In word terms, we have:

$$\text{Future value} = \text{Present value} \times [1 + (\text{Interest rate}) \times (\text{number of periods})]$$

CONCEPT CHECK

What is the time value of money?

What do we mean by present value and future value?

What is simple interest?

For our example, this becomes:

$$\text{Future value} = \$1{,}000 \times [1 + (0.08 \times 2)]$$
$$= \$1{,}000 \times 1.16$$
$$= \$1{,}160$$

Another bank will pay you a 10 percent interest rate on your money. Thus, you would receive $100 in interest ($1,000 × 0.10) or a return at the end of one year of $1,100 ($1,000 × 1.10) from this second bank. While the $20 difference in return between the two banks ($1,100 versus $1,080) is not great, it has some importance to most people. For a two-year deposit for which simple interest is paid annually, the difference increases to $40. The second bank would return $1,200 ($1,000 × 1.20) to you versus $1,160 from the first bank. If the funds were invested for ten years, we would accumulate $1,000 × [1 + (0.08 × 10)] or $1,800 at the first bank. At the second bank we would have $1,000 × [1 + (0.10 × 10)] or $2,000, a $200 difference. This interest rate differential between the two banks will become even more important when we introduce the concept of compounding.

COMPOUNDING TO DETERMINE FUTURE VALUES

Compounding is an arithmetic process whereby an initial value increases or grows at a *compound interest* rate over time to reach a value in the future. **Compound interest** involves earning interest on interest in addition to interest on the principal or initial investment. To understand compounding, let's assume that you leave the investment with a bank for more than one year. For example, the first bank accepts your $1,000 deposit now, adds $80 at the end of one year, retains the $1,080 for the second year and pays you interest at an 8 percent rate. The bank returns your initial deposit plus accumulated interest at the end of the second year. How much will you receive as a future value? In word terms, we have:

compounding
arithmetic process whereby an initial value increases or grows at a compound interest rate over time to reach a value in the future

compound interest
earning interest on interest in addition to interest on the principal or initial investment

$$\text{Future value} = \text{Present value} \times [(1 + \text{Interest rate}) \times (1 + \text{Interest rate})]$$

For our two-year investment example, we have

$$\text{Future value} = \$1{,}000 \times (1.08) \times (1.08)$$
$$= \$1{,}000 \times 1.1664$$
$$= \$1{,}166.40$$
$$= \$1{,}166 \text{ (rounded)}$$

A timeline also can be used to illustrate this two-year example as follows:

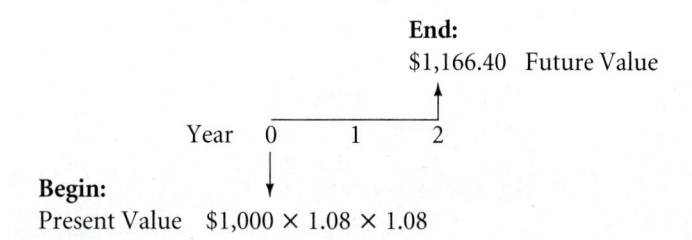

End:
$1,166.40 Future Value

Year 0   1   2

Begin:
Present Value $1,000 × 1.08 × 1.08

Thus, for a one-year investment, the return would be $1,080 ($1,000 × 1.08), which is the same as the return on a simple-interest investment, as was previously shown. However, a two-year investment at an 8 percent compound interest rate will return $1,166.40, compared to $1,160 using an 8 percent simple interest rate.

The compounding concept also can be expressed in equation form as

$$FV_n = PV(1 + r)^n \qquad (9.1)$$

where FV is the future value, PV is the present value, r is the interest rate, and n is the number of periods in years. For our $1,000 deposit, 8 percent, two-year example, we have

$$FV_2 = \$1{,}000(1 + 0.08)^2$$
$$= \$1{,}000(1.1164)$$
$$= \$1{,}166.40$$
$$= \$1{,}166 \text{ (rounded)}$$

If we extend the time period to ten years, the $1,000 deposit would grow to:

$$FV_{10} = \$1,000(1 + 0.08)^{10}$$
$$= \$1,000(2.1589)$$
$$= \$2,158.90$$
$$= \$2,159 \text{ (rounded)}$$

Texas Instruments (TI) and Hewlett Packard (HP) make two popular types of financial calculators. However, they are programmed differently.[1] Reference is made to the use of TI and HP calculators when discussing calculator solutions throughout the remainder of this chapter. Other available financial calculators are usually programmed like either the TI or HP calculators. What is important is that if you are going to use a financial calculator to solve time value of money problems, you must understand how your particular calculator works.

Most financial calculators are programmed to readily find future values. Typically, financial calculators will have a present value key (PV), a future value key (FV), a number of time periods key (N), an interest rate key (usually designated %i), and a compute key (usually designated as CPT). If you have a financial calculator, you can verify the future value result for the ten-year example.

First, clear any values stored in the calculator's memory. Next, enter 1000 and press the PV key (some financial calculators require that you enter the present value amount as a minus value because it is an investment or outflow). Then, enter 8 and press the %i key (most financial calculators are programmed so that you enter whole numbers rather than decimals for the interest rate). Next, enter 10 for the number of time periods (usually years) and press the N key. Finally, press the CPT key followed by the FV key to calculate the future value of 2,158.93, which rounds to $2,159. Actually, financial calculators are programmed to calculate answers to twelve significant digits.

Financial Calculator Solution:

Inputs: 10   8   1000
         N   %i   PV

Press: CPT   FV

Solution: 2158.93

Computer spreadsheet programs also are available for finding future values. Following is the same problem solved using *Microsoft's Excel* spreadsheet program. For presentation purposes, the solution only for the two-year version of the problem is shown. That is, how much would you accumulate after two years if you invested $1,000 at an 8 percent interest rate with annual compounding?

Spreadsheet Solution:

	A	B	C	D
1	Interest Rate	0.08		
2	Time Period	0	1	2
3	Cash Flow	1000		
4	Future Value (FV)		1080.00	1166.40
5				
6	Cash Flow fx Calc	-1000	0	0
7	Financial Function			
8	FV Solution			$1,166.40

---

1. For problems involving PVs and FVs, HP calculators require one of the values to be entered as a negative. In contrast, both PVs and FVs are entered as positive values in TI calculators, and the internal program makes one of the values negative for calculation purposes. Other TI and HP differences when entering data also are noted later in this chapter.

SMALL BUSINESS PRACTICE
Calculating Rates of Return for Venture Capitalists and Other Investors

Venture capitalists represent an important source of financing for small businesses. Venture capitalists, of course, are in the business of providing financial capital to small businesses with the expectation of earning a return on their investments commensurate with the risks associated with those investments. A typical "exit strategy" of venture capitalists is to maintain an investment in a firm for approximately five years and, if the investment is successful, then sell the firm to another company or take the firm public in an initial public offering (IPO).

A venture capitalist usually will invest in a small business by either taking a direct ownership position in the form of common stock or by accepting the firm's bond plus an "equity kicker" or the right to purchase a certain portion of the firm (e.g., 50 percent). For example, let's assume that a venture capitalist invests $5 million in a firm. In return, the venture capitalist receives shares of stock representing 50 percent ownership in the firm. Let's assume that the firm can be sold for $40 million at the end of five years. What will be the rate of return that the venture capitalist will earn on the $10 million investment? The present value is $5 million and the future value is $20 million (i.e., $40 million times .5, or 50 percent). Since, we know the time period is five years, we solve for the interest rate r. Using a financial calculator results in a compound interest rate (%i) of 32.0 percent.

What would have been the venture capitalist's rate of return if the firm had been sold for $40 million at the end of six years instead of at the end of five years? Again, the present value is $5 million, the future value is $20 million, and the time period is six years. Solving for the interest rate yields 26.0 percent. Thus, if the sale of the firm is delayed by one year, the compound rate of return on the venture capitalist's investment drops 6 percentage points from 32 percent down to 26 percent.

We set up our spreadsheet with descriptive labels in cells A1 through A4. We then solve the compound interest problem by placing the interest rate in decimal form (0.08) in Cell B1. The time periods are placed on Row 2, beginning with period 0 (the current period) in Cell B2 and so forth. The cash flow of 1,000 (an investment) is listed in cell B3. In this simple problem, we first replicate the basic "by hand" calculations in spreadsheet format and the future value calculations beginning in C4 and continuing to D4.

In Cell C4, we place the formula =B3*(1+B1), which reflects compounding the $1,000 investment at 8 percent interest for one year. Cell D4 shows compounding of the investment at 8 percent for a second year and can be calculated as C4*(1+B1), so compounding at an 8 percent interest rate results in a future value of $1,166.40 after two years. Of course, we could have made the FV calculation in one step as =B3*(1+B1)^2, which also produces 1,166.40.

Excel and other spreadsheet programs have built-in "financial functions" so that spreadsheet solutions do not have to be calculated the "long way." The bottom portion of the spreadsheet solution example illustrates the use of the financial function for future value. Here we enter the cash flow in time period zero as −1000 to reflect an outflow and a present value. Click on the Excel financial wizard (*fx*) icon, then Financial, then FV, then OK to bring up the dialogue box where the FV components for the problem at hand are requested. The equation is FV(Rate, Nper, Pmt, PV, Type). The Rate is 0.08; Nper is the number of time periods (2 in the preceding example); Pmt is 0, since there are no periodic payments; PV is −1000; and Type is 0, reflecting that payments occur at the end of the period. Thus we would have: FV(0.08,2,0,−1000,0). Clicking OK results in an FV of $1,166.40, or $1,166 rounded. Of course, rather than inserting numbers, one could insert specific cell references in the FV function.

If the investment had been compounded for ten years, the FV function inputs would have been FV(0.08,10,0,−1000,0). Clicking OK would result in an answer of $2,158.92, or $2.159 rounded.

In addition, tables have been prepared to simplify the calculation effort if financial calculators or spreadsheet programs are not available. Equation 9.1 can be rewritten as:

$$FV_n = PV(FVIF_{r,n}) \quad (9.2)$$

where the $(1 + r)^n$ part of Equation 9.1 is replaced by a future value interest factor (FVIF) corresponding to a specific interest rate and a specified time period.

Table 9.1 shows FVIF values carried to three decimal places for a partial range of interest rates and time periods. (Table 1 in the Appendix is a more comprehensive FVIF table.) Let's use Table 9.1 to find the future value of $1,000 invested at an 8 percent compound interest rate for a ten-year period; notice that at the intersection of the 8 percent column and ten years, we find an FVIF of 2.159. Putting this information into Equation 9.2 gives the following solution.

TABLE 9.1
Future Value Interest Factor (FVIF) of $1

YEAR	5%	6%	7%	8%	9%	10%
1	1.050	1.060	1.070	1.080	1.090	1.100
2	1.102	1.124	1.145	1.166	1.188	1.210
3	1.158	1.191	1.225	1.260	1.295	1.331
4	1.216	1.262	1.311	1.360	1.412	1.464
5	1.276	1.338	1.403	1.469	1.539	1.611
6	1.340	1.419	1.501	1.587	1.677	1.772
7	1.407	1.504	1.606	1.714	1.828	1.949
8	1.477	1.594	1.718	1.851	1.993	2.144
9	1.551	1.689	1.838	1.999	2.172	2.358
10	1.629	1.791	1.967	2.159	2.367	2.594

Table-based Solution:

$$FV_{10} = \$1{,}000(2.159)$$
$$= \$2{,}159$$

INTERNET ACTIVITY

Go to the Chase Bank Web site, http://www.chase.com. Under the "Personal Banking" heading, go to "CDs" and identify the interest rates being paid on certificates of deposit (CDs) of various maturities and amounts.

Further examination of Table 9.1 shows how a $1 investment grows or increases with various combinations of interest rates and time periods. For example, if another bank offers to pay you a 10 percent interest rate compounded annually, notice that the FVIF at the intersection of 10 percent and ten years would be 2.594, making your $1,000 investment worth $2,594 ($1,000 × 2.594). Now the difference between the 8 percent and 10 percent rates is much more significant at $435 ($2,594 − $2,159) than the $200 difference that occurred with simple compounding over ten years. Thus, we see the advantage of being able to compound at even slightly higher interest rates over a period of years.

The compounding or growth process also can be depicted in graphic form. Figure 9.1 shows graphic relationships among future values, interest rates, and time periods. For example, notice how $1 will grow differently over a ten-year period at 5 percent versus 10 percent interest rates. Of course, if no interest is being earned, then the initial $1 investment will remain at $1 no matter how long the investment is held. At a 10 percent interest rate, the initial $1 grows to $2.59 (rounded) after ten years. This compares with $1.63 (rounded) after ten years if the interest rate is only 5 percent. Notice that the future value increases at an increasing rate as the interest rate is increased and as the time period is lengthened.

FIGURE 9.1
Future Value, Interest Rate, and Time Period Relationships

INFLATION OR PURCHASING POWER IMPLICATIONS

The compounding process described in the preceding section does not say anything about the purchasing power of the initial $1 investment at some point in the future. As seen, $1 growing at a 10 percent interest rate would be worth $2.59 (rounded) at the end of ten years. With zero inflation, you could purchase $2.59 of the same quality of goods after ten years relative to what you could purchase now. However, if the stated or *nominal* interest rate is 10 percent and the inflation rate is 5 percent, then in terms of increased purchasing power, the "net" or differential compounding rate would be 5 percent (10 percent – 5 percent) and $1 would have an inflation-adjusted value of $1.63 after ten years. This translates into an increased purchasing power of $0.63 ($1.63 – $1.00).

Also note that if the compound inflation rate is equal to the compound interest rate, the purchasing power would not change. For example, if in Figure 9.1 both the inflation and interest rates were 5 percent, the purchasing power of $1 would remain the same over time. Thus, to make this concept operational, subtract the expected inflation rate from the stated interest rate and compound the remaining (differential) interest rate to determine the change in purchasing power over a stated time period. For example, if the interest rate is 10 percent and the inflation rate is 3 percent, the savings or investment should be compounded at a differential 7 percent rate. Turning to Table 9.1, we see that $1 invested at a 7 percent interest rate for ten years would grow to $1.967 ($1.97 rounded) in terms of purchasing power. Of course, the actual dollar value would be $2.594 ($2.59 rounded).

Financial contracts (e.g., savings deposits, bank loans) in countries that have experienced high and volatile inflation rates sometimes have been linked to a consumer price or similar inflation index. Such actions are designed to reduce the exposure to inflation risk for both savers and lenders. Since the interest rate they receive on their savings deposits will vary with the rate of inflation, savers receive purchasing power protection. As inflation rises, so will the rate of interest individuals receive on their savings deposits such that purchasing power will be maintained.

Bank lenders are similarly protected against changing inflation rates, since the rates they charge on their loans will also vary with changes in inflation rates. At least in theory, banks will be able to maintain a profit spread between the interest rates they pay to savers and the higher interest rates they lend at to borrowers because inflation affects both financial contracts. Of course, if the borrowers are business firms, they need to be able to pass on higher prices for their products and services to consumers to be able to maintain profit margins when interest rates are rising along with increases in inflation.

CONCEPT CHECK
What is compounding?
What is compound interest?

DISCOUNTING TO DETERMINE PRESENT VALUES

Most financial management decisions involve present values rather than future values. For example, a financial manager who is considering purchasing an asset wants to know what the asset is worth now rather than at the end of some future time period. The reason that an asset has value is because it will produce a stream of future cash benefits. To determine its value now in time period zero, we have to discount or reduce the future cash benefits to their present value. **Discounting** is an arithmetic process whereby a future value decreases at a compound interest rate over time to reach a present value.

Let's illustrate discounting with a simple example involving an investment. Assume that a bank or other borrower offers to pay you $1,000 at the end of one year in return for using $1,000 of your money now. If you are willing to accept a zero rate of return, you might make the investment. Most of us would not jump at an offer like this! Rather, we would require some return on our investment. To receive a return of, say, 8 percent, you would invest less than $1,000 now. The amount to be invested would be determined by dividing the $1,000 that is due at the end of one year by one plus the interest rate of 8 percent. This results in an investment amount of $925.93 ($1,000 ÷ 1.08), or $926 rounded. Alternatively, the $1,000 could have been multiplied by 1 ÷ 1.08, or 0.9259 (when carried to four decimal places) to get $925.90, or $926 rounded.

Let's now assume that you will not receive the $1,000 for two years and the compound interest rate is 8 percent. What dollar amount (present value) would you be willing to invest? In word terms, we have:

discounting
arithmetic process whereby a future value decreases at a compound interest rate over time to reach a present value

Present value = Future value × {[1 ÷ (1 + Interest rate)] × [1 ÷ (1 + Interest rate)]}

For our two-year investment example, we get

$$\begin{aligned}\text{Present value} &= \$1{,}000 \times (1 \div 1.08) \times (1 \div 1.08) \\ &= \$1{,}000 \times (0.9259) \times (0.9259) \\ &= \$1{,}000 \times 0.8573 \\ &= \$857.30\end{aligned}$$

A timeline also can be used to illustrate this two-year example as follows:

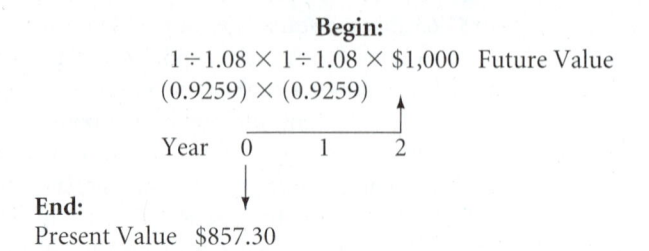

Begin:
$1 \div 1.08 \times 1 \div 1.08 \times \$1{,}000$ Future Value
$(0.9259) \times (0.9259)$

Year   0   1   2

End:
Present Value $857.30

Thus, for a one-year investment, the present value would be $925.90 ($1,000 × 1 ÷ 1.08), or 0.9259. A two-year investment would have a present value of only $857.30 ($1,000 × 0.9259 × 0.9259).

The discounting concept can be expressed in equation form as:

$$PV = FV_n \div (1 + r)^n$$

or

$$PV = FV_n[1 \div (1 + r)^n] \tag{9.3}$$

where the individual terms are the same as those defined for the future value equation. Notice that the future value equation has simply been rewritten to solve for the present value. For the $1,000, 8 percent, two-year example, we have:

$$\begin{aligned}PV &= \$1{,}000[1 \div (1 + 0.08)^2] \\ &= \$1{,}000(1 \div 1.1164) \\ &= \$1{,}000(0.8573) \\ &= \$857.30 \\ &= \$857 \text{ (rounded)}\end{aligned}$$

If we extend the time period to ten years, the $1,000 future value would decrease to:

$$\begin{aligned}PV &= \$1{,}000[1 \div (1 + 0.08)^{10}] \\ &= \$1{,}000(1 \div 2.1589) \\ &= \$1{,}000(0.4632) \\ &= \$463.20 \\ &= \$463 \text{ (rounded)}\end{aligned}$$

Most financial calculators are programmed to readily find present values. As noted, financial calculators typically have a present value (PV) key, a future value (FV) key, a number of time periods (N) key, an interest rate (%i) key, and a compute (CPT) key. If you have a financial calculator, you can verify the present value result for the ten-year example. First, clear the calculator. Then, enter 1000 (or –1000 for some calculators to find a positive PV) and press the FV key, enter 8 and press the %i key, and enter 10 and press the N key. Finally, press the CPT key followed by the PV key to calculate the present value of 463.19, which rounds to $463.

Financial Calculator Solution:

Inputs:	10		8		1000	
		N		%i		FV
Press:		CPT		PV		
Solution:		463.19				

Excel or another spreadsheet program also can be used to find present values. For a simple present value problem, we show the calculation by hand in spreadsheet format, as well as using the preprogrammed PV financial function. What would be the present value of receiving $1,000 two years from now if the annual discount rate is 8 percent?

Spreadsheet Solution:

	A	B	C	D
1	Interest Rate	0.08		
2	Time Period	0	1	2
3	Cash Flow	0	0	1000
4	Present Value	857.34	925.93	
5				
6	Cash Flow fx Calc	0	0	-1000
7	Financial Function			
8	PV Solution:	$857.34		

When making the calculation by hand, we enter 0.08 as the interest rate in Cell B1, then the time periods beginning with 0 in Cell B2 and so forth, and a cash flow of 1000 in Cell D3. In Cell C4 we insert the equation =D3/(1+B1)^1 and get 925.93. Then, in Cell B4 we enter the equation = C4/(1+B1)^1, with the result being 857.34. Of course, we could have solved for the present value in one step by entering in Cell B4 the equation =D3/(1+B1)^2 and found 857.34 directly.

The bottom portion of the spreadsheet solution example illustrates the use of the Excel's Financial Function called present value (PV). In order to get a positive PV value, we enter –1000 as the cash flow in time period 2. Click on the Excel financial wizard (*fx*) icon, then Financial, then PV, and then OK to bring up the dialogue box where the PV components for the problem at hand are requested. The equation is PV(Rate, Nper, Pmt, FV, Type). The Rate is 0.08; Nper is the number of time periods, or 2 in this example; Pmt is zero since there are no periodic payments; FV is –1000; and Type is 0, reflecting that payments occur at the end of the period. This equates to PV(0.08,2,0,–1000,0). Clicking OK results in a PV of $857.34, or $857 rounded. Because the PV function in Excel is programmed to give a negative number when there is a positive future value, much like the PV solutions on most calculators, we entered the FV as a negative number to get a positive PV. Of course, rather than inserting numbers, one could insert specific cell references in the PV function.

If the investment had been discounted for ten years, the PV function inputs would have been: PV(0.08,10,0,–1000,0). Clicking OK would result in an answer of $463.19, or $463 rounded.

In addition, tables have been prepared to simplify the calculation effort if financial calculators or computer programs are not available. Equation 9.3 can be rewritten as:

$$PV = FV_n \, (PVIF_{r,n}) \qquad (9.4)$$

where the $1 \div (1 + r)^n$ part of Equation 9.3 is replaced by a present value interest factor (PVIF) corresponding to a specific interest rate and a specified time period.

Table 9.2 shows PVIF values for a range of interest rates and time periods. (Table 2 in the Appendix is a more comprehensive PVIF table.) Let's use Table 9.2 to find the present value of $1,000 invested at an 8 percent compound interest rate for a ten-year period. Notice that at the intersection of the 8 percent column and ten years, we find a PVIF of 0.463. Putting this information in Equation 9.4 gives the following.

Table-based Solution:

$$PV = \$1,000(0.463)$$
$$= \$463$$

Further examination of Table 9.2 shows how a $1 investment decreases with various combinations of interest rates and time periods. For example, if another bank offers to pay interest at a 10 percent compound rate, the PVIF at the intersection of 10 percent and ten years would be 0.386, resulting in your $1,000 future value being worth an investment of $386 ($1,000 × 0.386). The difference in required investments needed to accumulate $1,000 at the end of ten years between 8 percent and 10 percent interest rates is $77 ($463 − $386). In essence, the present value of a future value decreases as the interest rate increases for a specified time period.

TABLE 9.2
Present Value Interest Factor (PVIF) of $1

YEAR	5%	6%	7%	8%	9%	10%
1	.952	.943	.935	.926	.917	.909
2	.907	.890	.873	.857	.842	.826
3	.864	.840	.816	.794	.772	.751
4	.823	.792	.763	.735	.708	.683
5	.784	.747	.713	.681	.650	.621
6	.746	.705	.666	.630	.596	.564
7	.711	.665	.623	.583	.547	.513
8	.677	.627	.582	.540	.502	.467
9	.645	.592	.544	.500	.460	.424
10	.614	.558	.508	.463	.422	.386

The discounting process also can be depicted in graphic form. Figure 9.2 shows graphic relationships among present values, interest rates, and time periods. For example, notice how a $1 future value will decrease differently over a ten-year period at 5 percent versus 10 percent interest rates. Of course, at a zero interest rate, the present value remains at $1 and is not affected by time. If no interest is being earned, the $1 future value will have a present value of $1 no matter how long the investment is held. At a 5 percent interest rate, the present value of $1 declines to $0.61 (rounded) if an investor has to wait ten years to receive the $1. This compares with a present value of $1 of only $0.39 (rounded) if the interest rate is 10 percent and the investor must wait ten years to receive $1. Notice that the present value decreases at an increasing rate as the interest rate is increased and as the time period is lengthened.

CONCEPT CHECK
What is discounting?

EQUATING PRESENT VALUES AND FUTURE VALUES

Notice that Equations 9.1 and 9.3 are two ways of looking at the same process involving compound interest rates. That is, if we know the future value of an investment, we can find its present value and vice versa. For example, an initial investment of $1,000 will grow to $1,116.40

FIGURE 9.2
Present Value, Interest Rate, and Time Period Relationships

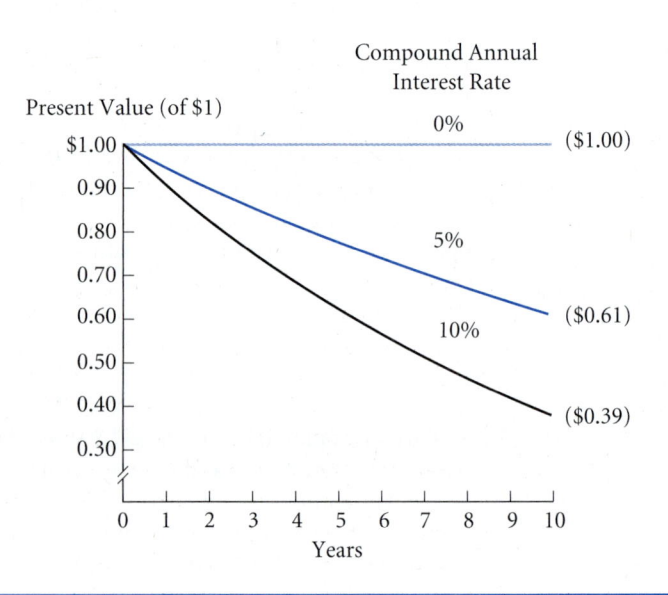

PERSONAL FINANCIAL PLANNING
So You Want to Be a Millionaire?

A million dollars can be acquired in a number of ways. Probably the easiest legal way is to inherit it. Those of us who won't benefit that way must save a portion of our disposable personal income and then live long enough to take advantage of compounding interest. For example, if you could invest $10,000 now (at the end of time period zero), the following combinations of annual compound interest rates and time periods would make you a millionaire.

INTEREST RATE (%)	TIME (YEARS)
5	94.4
10	48.3
15	33.0
20	25.3

Notice that at a 5 percent compound rate it would take more than ninety-four years to accumulate $1 million. This is probably not acceptable (or possible) for most of us. Even if we could compound our interest at a 20 percent annual rate, it would take a little more than twenty-five years to become a millionaire.

An alternative approach would be to create an investment annuity of $10,000 per year. Now let's show the time required to become a millionaire under the assumption of an ordinary annuity where the first investment will be made one year from now:

INTEREST RATE (%)	TIME (YEARS)
5	36.7
10	25.2
15	19.8
20	16.7

With this approach the time required, particularly at higher interest rates, is more feasible. Compounding at 5 percent would still require making annual investments for nearly thirty-seven years to accumulate $1 million. At 10 percent, it would take a little more than twenty-five years to attain that goal. Of course the most critical factor, which might be easier said than done, is the ability to come up with $10,000 per year out of disposable personal income. Good luck!

---

at the end of two years if the interest rate is 8 percent. Note that to reduce the impact of rounding errors, we are carrying our calculations here to four decimal places:

$$FV_2 = \$1,000(1 + 0.08)^2$$
$$= \$1,000(1.1664)$$
$$= \$1,166.40$$

Now, what is the present value of a $1,166.40 future value is if we must wait two years to receive the future value amount and if the interest rate is 8 percent? The solution would be:

$$PV = \$1,166.40[1 \div (1 + 0.08)^2]$$
$$= \$1,166.40(1 \div 1.1664)$$
$$= \$1,166.40(0.8573)$$
$$= \$1,000$$

Thus, an investor should be indifferent about receiving a $1,000 present value now or a $1,166 future value two years from now if the compound interest rate is 8 percent.

CONCEPT CHECK
How do present values and future values relate or equate to each other?

FINDING INTEREST RATES AND TIME REQUIREMENTS

Recall the four variables from the future value (9.1 and 9.2) and present value (9.3 and 9.4) equations: PV = present value, FV = future value, r = interest rate, and n = number of periods. As long as we know the values for any three of these variables, we can solve for the fourth or unknown variable. This is accomplished by using a financial calculator, a financial function in a spreadsheet program, or tables.

SOLVING FOR INTEREST RATES

INTERNET ACTIVITY
Go to the Citibank Web site, http://www.citibank.com, and identify the types of credit cards available to individuals and the prevailing interest rates on the credit cards.

Assume that the present value of an investment is $1,000, the future value is $1,403, and the time period is five years. What compound interest rate would be earned on this investment?

This problem can be solved using a financial calculator. If a financial calculator is used, enter PV = 1000, FV = 1403, N = 5, and press CPT followed by the %i key to find an r of 7.01, or 7 percent rounded (some calculators may require either the PV entry or FV entry to be negative).

216 PART TWO • Investments

Financial Calculator Solution:

Inputs: 5   1000   1403
           N   PV   FV

Press: CPT   %i

Solution: 7.01

A second way of solving for the interest rate is with a spreadsheet program using a financial function. Excel has a financial function called RATE that makes it possible to solve quickly for the interest rate. Click on the financial wizard (*fx*), then on Financial, then RATE. Entering the requested data and clicking OK gives the following solution.

Spreadsheet Solution:

$$= \text{RATE(Nper, Pmt, PV, FV, Type)}$$
$$= \text{RATE}(5, 0, -1000, 1403, 0)$$
$$= 7.01\%$$

The number of periods (Nper) is 5, there are zero periodic payments (Pmt), the present value (PV) is entered as -1000, the future value (FV) is 1403, and the Type is zero, since cash flows occur at the end of a time period.

Table-based Solution:

The interest rate answer also can be found by setting up the problem using Equation 9.2 and Table 9.1 as follows:

$$FV_5 = PV(FVIF_{r,5})$$
$$\$1{,}403 = \$1{,}000(FVIF_{r,5})$$
$$FVIF_{r,5} = 1.403$$

Since we know that the number of time periods is five, we can turn to Table 9.1 and read across the year-five row until we find FVIF of 1.403. Notice that this occurs under the 7 percent column, indicating that the interest rate r is 7 percent.

We also can work the problem using Equation 9.4 and Table 9.2 as follows:

$$PV = FV_5(PVIF_{r,5})$$
$$\$1{,}000 = \$1{,}403(PVIF_{r,5})$$
$$PVIF_{r,5} = 0.713$$

Turning to Table 9.2, we read across the year-five row until we find the PVIF of 0.713. This occurs under the 7 percent column, indicating that the interest rate r is 7 percent.

SOLVING FOR TIME PERIODS

Now let's assume an investment has a present value of $1,000, a future value of $1,403, and an interest rate of 7 percent. What length of time does this investment involve?

This problem can be solved using a financial calculator and entering PV = 1000 (or -1000), FV = 1403, and %i = 7 and then pressing the CPT key followed by the N key to find an n of 5.01, or 5 years rounded.

Financial Calculator Solution:

Inputs: 7   1000   1403
          %i   PV   FV

Press: CPT   N

Solution: 5.01

Spreadsheet Solution:

The number of time periods can also be determined by using the Excel financial function called NPER. Following the sequence described and clicking on the NPER financial function we have:

$$= \text{NPER}(\text{Rate},\text{Pmt},\text{PV},\text{FV},\text{Type})$$
$$= \text{NPER}(.07,0,-1000,1403,0)$$
$$= 5.00$$

The interest rate is 7 percent, there are no payments, the present value is −1000, the future value is 1403, and type is zero.

Table-based Solution:

The answer can also be found by using Equation 9.2 and Table 9.1 as follows:

$$FV_n = PV(FVIF_{7\%,n})$$
$$\$1,403 = \$1,000(FVIF_{7\%,n})$$
$$FVIF_{7\%,n} = 1.403$$

Since we know the interest rate is 7 percent, we can turn to Table 9.1 and read down the 7 percent column until we find the FVIF of 1.403. Notice that this occurs in the year-five row, indicating that the time period n is five years.

We also can work the problem using Equation 9.4 and Table 9.2 as follows:

$$PV = FV_n(PVIF_{7\%,n})$$
$$\$1,000 = \$1,403(PVIF_{7\%,n})$$
$$PVIF_{7\%,n} = .713$$

Turn to Table 9.2, we read down the 7 percent column until we find the PVIF of 0.713. This occurs at the year-five row, indicating that the time period n is five years.

RULE OF 72

Investors often ask, "How long will it take for my money to double in value at a particular interest rate?" Table 9.1 illustrates the process for answering this question. We pick a particular interest rate and read down the table until we find an FVIF of 2.000. For example, at an 8 percent interest rate, it will take almost exactly nine years (note the FVIF of 1.999) for an investment to double in value. At a 9 percent interest rate, the investment will double in about eight years (FVIF of 1.993). An investment will double in a little over seven years (FVIF of 1.949) if the interest rate is 10 percent.

A shortcut method referred to as the **Rule of 72** can be used to approximate the time required for an investment to double in value. This method is applied by dividing the interest rate into the number 72 to determine the number of years it will take for an investment to double in value. For example, if the interest rate is 8 percent, 72 divided by 8 indicates that the investment will double in value in nine years. Notice that this is the same conclusion drawn from Table 9.1. Likewise, at an interest rate of 10 percent it will take approximately 7.2 years (72 ÷ 10) for an investment to double in value. It is important to be aware that at very low or very high interest rates, the Rule of 72 does not approximate the compounding process as well and thus a larger estimation error occurs in the time required for an investment to double in value.

FUTURE VALUE OF AN ANNUITY

The previous discussion focuses on cash payments or receipts that occurred only as lump sum present and future values. However, many finance problems involve equal payments or receipts over time, referred to as *annuities*. More specifically, an **annuity** is a series of equal payments (receipts) that occur over a number of time periods.

An **ordinary annuity** exists when the equal payments (receipts) occur at the end of each time period.[2] For example, suppose you want to invest $1,000 per year for three years at an 8 percent interest rate. However, since you will not make your first payment until the end of the first year, this will be an ordinary annuity.

Rule of 72
used to approximate the time required for an investment to double in value

CONCEPT CHECK
How is the Rule of 72 used?

annuity
a series of equal payments (receipts) that occur over a number of time periods

ordinary annuity
equal payments (receipts) occur at the end of each time period

annuity due
exists when equal periodic payments occur at the beginning of each time period

---

2. An *annuity due* exists when equal periodic payments start at the end of time period zero, or in other words at the beginning of each time period. Annuity due problems are discussed in Learning Extension 9.

This problem also can be illustrated using a timeline as follows:

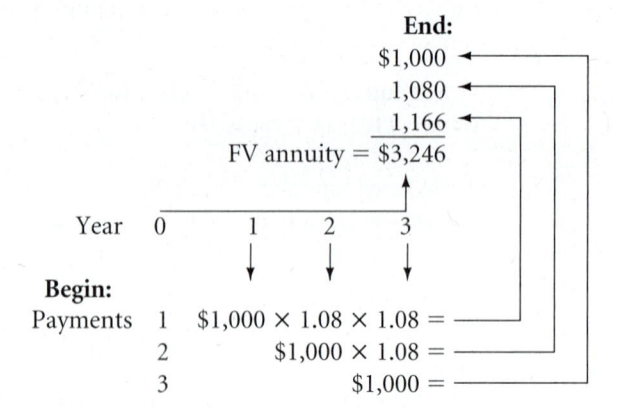

```
                                              End:
                                              $1,000
                                              1,080
                                              1,166
                                     FV annuity = $3,246

         Year    0        1        2        3
                          ↓        ↓        ↓
       Begin:
       Payments  1    $1,000 × 1.08 × 1.08 =
                 2           $1,000 × 1.08 =
                 3                  $1,000 =
```

Notice that to calculate the future value of this ordinary annuity we must add the future values of the first payment ($1,166), the second payment ($1,080), and the third payment ($1,000). This results in a future value of $3,246. To summarize, since the first payment is made at the end of the first year, it is compounded for two years. The second payment is compounded for one year and the third payment earns zero interest since the payment is made at the end of the third year.

The future value of this annuity can also be determined by making the following computations:

$$\begin{aligned} \text{FV ordinary annuity} &= \$1{,}000\,(1.08)^2 + \$1{,}000(1.08)^1 + \$1{,}000(1.08)^0 \\ &= \$1{,}000\,(1.166) + \$1{,}000(1.080) + \$1{,}000(1.000) \\ &= \$1{,}000\,(3.246) \\ &= \$3{,}246 \end{aligned}$$

While the computational process was relatively easy for the three-year ordinary annuity example, the required calculations become much more cumbersome as the time period is lengthened. As a result the following equation was derived for finding the future value of an ordinary annuity (FVA):

$$FVA_n = PMT\{[(1 + r)^n - 1] \div r\} \quad (9.5)$$

where PMT is the periodic equal payment, r is the compound interest rate, and n is the total number of periods. Inserting the data from the preceding three-year annuity example results in:

$$\begin{aligned} FVA_3 &= \$1{,}000\{[(1 + 0.08)^3 - 1] \div 0.08\} \\ &= \$1{,}000[(1.2597 - 1) \div 0.08] \\ &= \$1{,}000(3.246) \\ &= \$3{,}246 \end{aligned}$$

Most financial calculators are programmed to readily find future values of annuities. In addition to the previously identified keys, financial calculators also will have a payments (PMT) key for purposes of working problems involving ordinary annuities. The result for the three-year ordinary annuity can be verified using a financial calculator.

First, clear the calculator. Next, enter –1000 (for both TI and HP calculators) and press the PMT key. Then, enter 8 and press the %i key, and enter 3 and press the N key. Finally, press the CPT key and then the FV key to calculate the FVA of 3246.40, which rounds to $3,246. Note that because this problem involves a periodic outflow of $1,000, most financial calculators require that the payment be entered as a negative number to solve for a positive FVA.

Financial Calculator Solution:

Inputs:	3	8	−1000
	N	%i	PMT
Press:	CPT	FV	
Solution:	3246.40		

Spreadsheet programs also are available for finding future values of annuities. Following is a solution using an Excel spreadsheet and future value (FV). The difference here is that we have a constant periodic payment.

Spreadsheet Solution:

	A	B	C	D	E
1	Interest Rate	0.08			
2	Time Period	0	1	2	3
3	Cash Flow	0	-1000	-1000	-1000
4					
5	Financial Function				
6	FV Solution:				$3,246.40

We solve for the future value of the annuity as follows:

$$= FV(\text{Rate,Nper,Pmt,PV,Type})$$
$$= FV(.08, 3, -1000, 0, 0)$$
$$= \$3,246.40$$

In addition, tables have been prepared to simplify the calculation effort if financial calculators or computer programs are not available. Equation 9.5 can be rewritten as:

$$FVA_n = PMT(FVIFA_{r,n}) \quad (9.6)$$

where the $[(1 + r)^n - 1] \div r$ part of Equation 9.5 is replaced by a future value interest factor of an annuity (FVIFA) corresponding to a specific interest rate and a specified time period.

Table-based Solution:

Table 9.3 shows FVIFA values for a partial range of interest rates and time periods. (Table 3 in the Appendix is a more comprehensive FVIFA table.) Let's use Table 9.3 to find the future value of an ordinary annuity involving annual payments of $1,000, an 8 percent interest rate, and a three-year time period. Notice that at the intersection of the 8 percent column and three years, we find a FVIFA of 3.246. Putting this information into Equation 9.6 gives:

$$FVA_3 = \$1,000(3.246)$$
$$= \$3,246$$

Further examination of Table 9.3 shows how a $1 annuity grows or increases with various combinations of interest rates and time periods. For example, if $1,000 is invested at the end of each year (beginning with year one) for ten years at an 8 percent interest rate, the future value of the annuity would be $14,487 ($1,000 × 14.487). If the interest rate is 10 percent for ten years, the future value of the annuity would be $15,937 ($1,000 × 15.937). These results demonstrate the benefits of higher interest rates on the future values of annuities.

CONCEPT CHECK
What is an annuity?
What is an ordinary annuity?

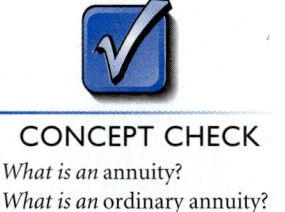

TABLE 9.3
Future Value Interest Factor (FVIFA) for a $1 Ordinary Annuity

YEAR	5%	6%	7%	8%	9%	10%
1	1.000	1.000	1.000	1.000	1.000	1.000
2	2.050	2.060	2.070	2.080	2.090	2.100
3	3.152	3.184	3.215	3.246	3.278	3.310
4	4.310	4.375	4.440	4.506	4.573	4.641
5	5.526	5.637	5.751	5.867	5.985	6.105
6	6.802	6.975	7.153	7.336	7.523	7.716
7	8.142	8.394	8.654	8.923	9.200	9.487
8	9.549	9.897	10.260	10.637	11.028	11.436
9	11.027	11.491	11.978	12.488	13.021	13.579
10	12.578	13.181	13.816	14.487	15.193	15.937

PRESENT VALUE OF AN ANNUITY

Many present value problems also involve cash flow annuities. Usually these are ordinary annuities. Let's assume that we will receive $1,000 per year beginning one year from now for a period of three years at an 8 percent compound interest rate. How much would you be willing to pay now for this stream of future cash flows? Since we are concerned with the value now, this becomes a present value problem.

We can illustrate this problem using a timeline as follows:

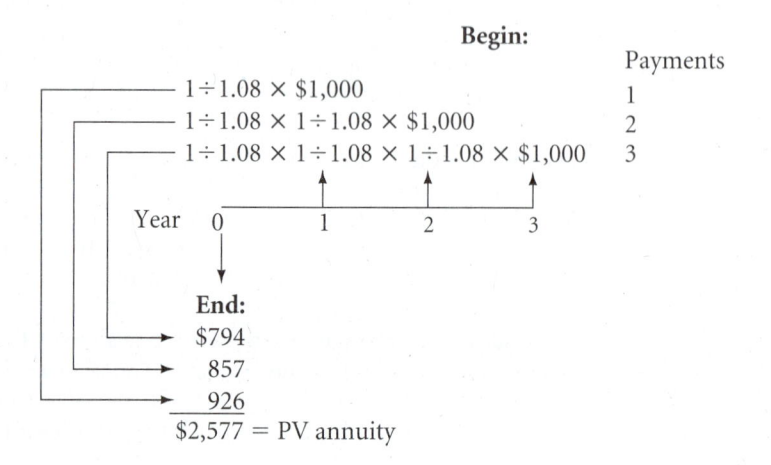

```
                                        Begin:
                                                        Payments
              1 ÷ 1.08 × $1,000                            1
              1 ÷ 1.08 × 1 ÷ 1.08 × $1,000                 2
              1 ÷ 1.08 × 1 ÷ 1.08 × 1 ÷ 1.08 × $1,000      3

   Year   0        1        2        3

          End:
          $794
           857
           926
         $2,577 = PV annuity
```

Notice that to calculate the present value of this ordinary annuity we must sum the present values of the first payment ($794), the second payment ($857), and the third payment ($926). This results in a present value of $2,577.

We also can find the present value of this annuity by making the following computations:

$$\begin{aligned}
\text{PV ordinary annuity} &= \{\$1,000[1 \div (1.08)^1]\} + \{\$1,000[1 \div (1.08)^2]\} \\
&\quad + \{\$1,000[1 \div (1.08)^3]\} \\
&= [\$1,000(0.926)] + [\$1,000(0.857)] \\
&\quad + [\$1,000(0.794)] \\
&= \$1,000(2.577) \\
&= \$2,577
\end{aligned}$$

While the computational process was relatively easy for the preceding three-year ordinary annuity example, the required calculations become much more cumbersome as the time period is lengthened. As a result the following equation was derived for finding the present value of an ordinary annuity (PVA):

$$PVA_n = PMT\{[1 - (1 \div (1 + r)^n)] \div r\} \qquad (9.7)$$

where the various inputs are the same as previously defined. Inserting the data from the preceding three-year annuity example results in:

$$\begin{aligned}
PVA_3 &= \$1,000\{[1 - (1 \div (1 + 0.08)^3)] \div 0.08\} \\
&= \$1,000[(1 - 0.7938) \div 0.08] \\
&= \$1,000(0.2062 \div 0.08) \\
&= \$1,000(2.577) \\
&= \$2,577
\end{aligned}$$

Most financial calculators are programmed to readily find present values of annuities. The result for the three-year present value of an ordinary annuity problem can be verified with a financial calculator. First, clear the calculator. Next, enter 1000 for a TI calculator (or −1000 for an HP calculator) and press the payments (PMT) key. Then, enter 8 and press the %i key, and enter 3 and press the N key. Finally, press the CPT key followed by the PV key to calculate the PVA of 2577.10, which rounds to $2,577.

Financial Calculator Solution:

Inputs:	3	8	1000
	N	%i	PMT
Press:	CPT	PV	

Solution: 2577.10

Spreadsheet programs also are available for finding present values of annuities. Following is an Excel spreadsheet solution.

Spreadsheet Solution:

	A	B	C	D	E
1	Interest Rate	0.08			
2	Time Period	0	1	2	3
3	Cash Flow	0	-1000	-1000	-1000
4					
5	Financial Function				
6	PV Solution:	$2,577.10			

Use the previously described present value (PV) financial function provided by Excel as follows:

$$= PV(Rate, Nper, Pmt, FV, Type)$$
$$= PV(.08, 3, -1000, 0, 0)$$
$$= \$2{,}577.10$$

In addition, tables have been prepared to simplify the calculation effort if financial calculators or computer programs are not available. Equation 9.7 can be rewritten as:

$$PVA_n = PMT(PVIFA_{r,n}) \qquad (9.8)$$

where the $\{1 - [1 \div (1 + r)^n]\} \div r$ part of Equation 9.7 is replaced by a present value interest factor of an annuity (PVIFA) corresponding to a specific interest rate and a specified time period.

Table-based Solution:
Table 9.4 shows PVIFA values for a partial range of interest rates and time periods. (Table 4 in the Appendix is a more comprehensive PVIFA table.) Let's use Table 9.4 to find the present value of an ordinary annuity involving annual payments of $1,000, an 8 percent interest rate, and a three-year time period. Notice that at the intersection of the 8 percent interest rate column and three years, we find a PVIFA of 2.577. Putting this information into Equation 9.8 gives:

$$PVA_3 = \$1{,}000(2.577)$$
$$= \$2{,}577$$

Further examination of Table 9.4 shows how the present value of a $1 annuity decreases with various combinations of interest rates and time periods. For example, if $1,000 is paid at the end of each year (beginning with year one) for ten years at an 8 percent interest rate, the present value of the annuity would be $6,710 ($1,000 × 6.710). If the interest rate is 10 percent for ten years, the present value of the annuity would be $6,145 ($1,000 × 6.145). These results demonstrate the costs of higher interest rates on the present values of annuities.

CONCEPT CHECK
How do we find the present value of an annuity?

INTEREST RATES AND TIME REQUIREMENTS FOR ANNUITIES

How to find or solve for interest rates or time periods for problems involving a lump sum present value or future value was discussed previously in this chapter. That originally involved working with four variables: PV = present value, FV = future value, r = interest rate, and n = number of periods. A fifth variable is now added to reflect payments (PMT) involving annuities.

TABLE 9.4
Present Value Interest Factor (PVIFA) for a $1 Ordinary Annuity

YEAR	5%	6%	7%	8%	9%	10%
1	0.952	0.943	0.935	0.926	0.917	0.909
2	1.859	1.833	1.808	1.783	1.759	1.736
3	2.273	2.673	2.624	2.577	2.531	2.487
4	3.546	3.465	3.387	3.312	3.240	3.170
5	4.329	4.212	4.100	3.993	3.890	3.791
6	5.076	4.917	4.767	4.623	4.486	4.355
7	5.786	5.582	5.389	5.206	5.033	4.868
8	6.463	6.210	5.971	5.747	5.535	5.335
9	7.108	6.802	6.515	6.247	5.995	5.759
10	7.722	7.360	7.024	6.710	6.418	6.145

SOLVING FOR INTEREST RATES

Assume that the future value of an ordinary annuity is $5,751, the annual payment is $1,000, and the time period is five years. What is the interest rate for this problem?

A financial calculator also could be used to solve this problem if either the FV or PV of the ordinary annuity is known. If you have a financial calculator and you know the future value, enter FV = 5751, PMT = –1000 (for both TI and HP calculators), and N = 5. Press the CPT key followed by the %i key to find an r of 7 percent. (Note: Some financial calculators will give an error message if the 1000 PMT is entered as a positive number. If the present value of the ordinary annuity is known instead of the future value, the preceding procedure would be followed except that PV = 4100 would be entered instead of the future value amount.)

Financial Calculator Solution:

Inputs: 5 [N]   –1000 [PMT]   5751 [FV]

Press: [CPT]   [%i]

Solution: 7.00

Spreadsheet Solution:

Excel's RATE financial function also can be used to solve this interest rate of an annuity problem, much as the function was used elsewhere in this chapter for problems without periodic payments. The financial function solution would be:

$$= \text{RATE(Nper,Pmt,PV,FV,Type)}$$
$$= \text{RATE}(5,-1000,0,5751,0)$$
$$= 7.00\%$$

Table-based Solution:

The answer can be found by setting up the problem using Equation 9.6 and Table 9.3 as follows:

$$FVA_5 = PMT(FVIFA_{r,5})$$
$$\$5{,}751 = \$1{,}000(FVIFA_{r,5})$$
$$FVIFA_{r,5} = 5.751$$

Since we know that the number of time periods is five, we can turn to Table 9.3 and read across the year-five row until we find the FVIFA of 5.751. Notice that this occurs under the 7 percent column, indicating that the interest rate r is 7 percent.

Let's now assume that we know that the present value of the preceding ordinary annuity is $4,100. We could then find the interest rate for the problem using present value annuity tables as follows:

$$PVA_5 = PMT(PVIFA_{r,5})$$
$$\$4{,}100 = \$1{,}000(PVIFA_{r,5})$$
$$PVIFA_{r,5} = 4.100$$

Turning to Table 9.4, we read across the year-five row until we find the PVIFA of 4.100. This occurs under the 7 percent column, indicating that the interest rate r is 7 percent.

SOLVING FOR TIME PERIODS

Let's assume that the future value of an ordinary annuity is $5,751, the annual payment is $1,000, and the interest rate is 7 percent. How long would it take for your $1,000 annual investments to grow to $5,751?

We can solve this problem using a financial calculator. We know that the future value of the ordinary annuity is $5,751, so enter FV = 5751, PMT = –1000, %i = 7, and press the CPT key followed by the N key to find an n of five years. If we knew the present value of the annuity instead of the future value, we could work the problem by substituting the PV for the FV.

Financial Calculator Solution:

Inputs:	7	–1000	5751
	%i	PMT	FV
Press:	CPT	N	
Solution:	5.00		

Spreadsheet Solution:

Excel's NPER financial function also can be used to solve for the number of periods in an annuity problem, much as we used the function earlier for problems without periodic payments. The financial function solution would be:

$$= \text{NPER}(\text{Rate,Pmt,PV,FV,Type})$$
$$= \text{NPER}(.07, -1000, 0, 5751, 0)$$
$$= 5.00$$

Table-based Solution:

The problem also can be set up by using Equation 9.6 and Table 9.3 as follows:

$$\text{FVA}_n = \text{PMT}(\text{FVIFA}_{7\%,n})$$
$$\$5,751 = \$1,000(\text{FVIFA}_{7\%,n})$$
$$\text{FVIFA}_{7\%,n} = 5.751$$

Since we know the interest rate is 7 percent, we can turn to Table 9.3 and read down the 7 percent column until we find FVIFA of 5.751. Notice that this occurs in the year-five row, indicating that the n time period is five years.

If we knew the present value of the above ordinary annuity was $4,100, we could also work the problem using Equation 9.8 and Table 9.4 as follows:

$$\text{PVA}_n = \text{PMT}(\text{PVIFA}_{7\%,n})$$
$$\$4,100 = \$1,000(\text{PVIFA}_{7\%,n})$$
$$\text{PVIFA}_{7\%,n} = 4.100$$

Turning to Table 9.4, we read down the 7 percent column until we find PVIFA of 4.100. This occurs at the year-five row, indicating that the n time period is five years.

CONCEPT CHECK
What is the process for solving for either interest rates or time period requirements for annuities?

DETERMINING PERIODIC ANNUITY PAYMENTS

EXAMPLES INVOLVING ANNUAL PAYMENTS

It is necessary in many instances to determine the periodic equal payment required for an annuity. For example, you may wish to accumulate $10,000 at the end of five years from now by making equal annual payments beginning one year from now. If you can invest at a compound 6 percent interest rate, what will be the amount of each of your annual payments?

This is a future value of an ordinary annuity problem. Using a financial calculator, the annual payment (PMT) would be found as follows:

Financial Calculator Solution:

Inputs: 6   5   10000
             %i   N   FV

Press: CPT   PMT

Solution: 1773.96

Spreadsheet Solution:
Excel's PMT financial function also can be used to solve for the annual payment amount. The financial function solution would be:

$$= \text{PMT}(\text{Rate},\text{Nper},\text{PV},\text{FV},\text{Type})$$
$$= \text{PMT}(.06,5,0,-10000,0)$$
$$= \$1{,}773.96$$

Table-based Solution:
Equation 9.6 and Table 9.3 also can be used, as follows:

$$\text{FVA}_n = \text{PMT}(\text{FVIFA}_{r,n})$$
$$\$10{,}000 = \text{PMT}(\text{FVIFA}_{6\%,5})$$
$$\$10{,}000 = \text{PMT}(5.637)$$
$$\text{PMT} = \$1{,}773.99$$
$$= \$1{,}774 \text{ (rounded)}$$

The FVIFA factor of 5.637 is taken from Table 5.3 at the intersection of the 6 percent column and the year-five row.

As another example, we might want to find the equal payment necessary to pay off, or amortize, a loan. An **amortized loan** is repaid in equal payments over a specified time period. Let's assume that a lender offers you a $20,000, 10 percent interest rate, three-year loan that is to be fully amortized with three annual payments. The first payment will be due one year from the loan date, making the loan an ordinary annuity. How much will you have to pay each year?

This is a present value problem because the $20,000 is the value or amount of the loan now. The annual payment can be found with a financial calculator, a financial function in a spreadsheet program, or via a table-based approach using Equation 9.8 and Table 9.4 as follows:

$$\text{PVA}_n = \text{PMT}(\text{PVIFA}_{10\%,3})$$
$$\$20{,}000 = \text{PMT}(2.487)$$
$$\text{PMT} = \$8{,}041.82$$
$$= \$8{,}042 \text{ (rounded)}$$

amortized loan
a loan repaid in equal payments over a specified time period

The PVIFA factor of 2.487 is taken from Table 9.4 at the intersection of the 10 percent column and the year-three row.

Table 9.5 illustrates the repayment process with a **loan amortization schedule,** which shows the breakdown of each payment between interest and principal, as well as the remaining balance after each payment. Since the interest rate is 10 percent, the first year interest will total $2,000 ($20,000 × 0.10). Subsequent interest payments are based on the remaining loan balances, which are smaller each year (also referred to as the *declining balance*). Since $6,042 ($8,042 − $2,000) of the first year's $8,042 payment is used to repay part of the principal, the second year's interest payment will only be $1,396 ($13,958 × 0.10). The third and last payment covers the final year's interest of $731 plus the remaining principal balance.

loan amortization schedule
a schedule of the breakdown of each payment between interest and principal, as well as the remaining balance after each payment

TABLE 9.5

Sample Loan Amortization Schedule

YEAR	ANNUAL PAYMENT	INTEREST PAYMENT	PRINCIPAL REPAYMENT	LOAN BALANCE
0	—	—	—	$20,000
1	$8,042	$2,000	$6,042	13,958
2	8,042	1,396	6,646	7,312
3	8,042	731	7,311*	0

*Because of rounding, the final principal repayment is off by $1.

REAL ESTATE MORTGAGE LOANS WITH MONTHLY PAYMENTS

As initially discussed in Chapter 1 and further covered in Chapter 7, the traditional residential real estate mortgage loan has been a 30-year fixed interest rate mortgage loan requiring equal monthly payments that would pay off or amortize the loan over its life. Let's assume that you want to borrow $100,000 for 30 years and the current interest rate is 6 percent. The mortgage requires you to make equal monthly payments so that the loan will be paid-in-full at maturity. What will be your monthly payment? We begin by first determining that you will have to make 360 (12 times 30 years) monthly payments. Since the annual interest rate is 6 percent, you will pay .50 percent (6 percent divided by 12) interest per month. With this information, we can calculate your monthly payment using a financial calculator as follows:

Financial Calculator Solution:

Inputs: .50   360   −100000
         %i   N   PV

Press: CPT   PMT

Solution: 599.55

You would need to make a $599.55 monthly payment.

Of course, Excel's PMT financial function also can be used to solve for the monthly payment amount.

Spreadsheet Solution:

The financial function solution would be:

$$= PMT(Rate, Nper, PV, FV, Type)$$
$$= PMT(.005, 360, -100000, 0, 0)$$
$$= 599.55$$

Unfortunately, due to rapidly rising housing prices during the decade prior to 2006, many home buyers needed increasingly larger loans to make their real property purchases. For example, a $200,000 fixed-rate mortgage loan would result in a much higher monthly payment compared to a $100,000 loan. Rework the above financial calculator and spread sheet solutions using a PV of −200000. The resulting doubling of the monthly payment to $1,199.10 means that fewer potential home buyers could qualify for these larger loans.

While the need for larger loans was increasing, many lenders—in part encouraged by government officials—also were willing to make subprime mortgage loans to individuals with poor credit scores or ratings in order to increase home ownership. These developments encouraged the increasing use of adjustable-rate mortgages (ARMs). Recall that an ARM typically has an interest rates tied to the bank prime rate or the Treasury bill rate, either of which normally is lower than long-term interest rates on fixed-rate mortgage loans, making it easier for borrowers with low credit scores and/or those wanting to borrow larger amounts to get mortgage loans.

Some lenders further offered initial below-market "teaser" rates such as 1 or 2 percent for the first year or so on their ARM mortgage loans. Of course, when the "teaser" rate period ends, the ARM interest rate adjusts to the then current market rate causing the possibility of a dramatic increase in monthly payments. Clearly lenders lent (and individuals borrowed) mortgage loans characterized by high default risks.

FINANCIAL CRISIS

CONCEPT CHECK

What is an amortized loan?

What is a loan amortization schedule?

MORE FREQUENT COMPOUNDING OR DISCOUNTING INTERVALS

In many situations, compounding or discounting may occur more often than annually. For example, recall from the beginning of this chapter the $1,000 that could be invested at one bank at an 8 percent annual interest rate for two years. Remember that the future value at the end of two years was:

$$FV_2 = \$1,000(1.08)^2$$
$$= \$1,000(1.166)$$
$$= \$1,166.40$$

Now let's assume that another bank offers the same 8 percent interest rate but with semiannual (twice a year) compounding. We can find the future value of this investment by modifying Equation 5.1 as follows:

$$FV_n = PV(1 + r \div m)^{n \times m} \tag{9.9}$$

where m is the number of compounding periods per year. For this problem:

$$FV_2 = \$1,000(1 + 0.08 \div 2)^{2 \times 2}$$
$$= \$1,000(1.04)^4$$
$$= \$1,000(1.1699)$$
$$= \$1,169.90$$

Thus, by compounding semiannually the future value would increase by $3.50.

The more-frequent-than-annual compounding process can be described operationally as follows. First, divide the annual interest rate of 8 percent by the number of times compounding is to take place during the year (0.08 ÷ 2 = 0.04). We also need to increase the total number of periods to reflect semiannual compounding. To do this, multiply the number of years for the loan times the frequency of compounding within a year (2 years × 2 = 4 periods).

Previously in this chapter, it was shown that a $1,000 investment at an 8 percent interest rate would grow to $2,158.92 or $2,159 (rounded) at the end of ten years. However, if semiannual compounding had been available the future value of the $1,000 investment would have been:

$$FV_{20} = \$1,000(1.04)^{20}$$
$$= \$1,000(2.1911)$$
$$= \$2,191.10$$

The following subsection shows how the financial calculator solution would be found.

Financial Calculator Solution:

Inputs: 20 4 1000
         N   %i PV

Press: CPT FV

Solution: 2191.12

Spreadsheet Solution:
The Excel FV function inputs would be:

$$= FV(0.04, 20, 0, -1000, 0)$$
$$= \$2,191.12$$

Table-based Solution:
The future value interest factor (FVIF) can also be found in Table 1 in the Appendix. When a three decimal place table is used, the factor is 2.191 with a future value of $2,191 (rounded). Notice that semiannual compounding will result in $32 more than the $2,159 earned with annual compounding. It follows that more frequent compounding, such as quarterly or monthly, produces even higher earnings.

CONCEPT CHECK

What is the process for compounding or discounting more frequently than annually?

ETHICAL ISSUES

usury
the act of lending money at an excessively high interest rate

annual percentage rate (APR)
determined by multiplying the interest rate charged per period by the number of periods in a year

effective annual rate (EAR)
measures the true interest rate when compounding occurs more frequently than once a year

INTERNET ACTIVITY

Go to the Board of Governors of the Federal Reserve Web site, http://www.federalreserve.gov, access "Consumer Information" and then "Consumer Credit," and describe some of the resources and tools that are available to consumers.

The process described also applies to discounting problems when discounting occurs more frequently than annually. The use of financial calculators and spreadsheet programs are more expedient as the frequency of compounding or discounting within a year increases.

COST OF CONSUMER CREDIT

UNETHICAL LENDERS

Throughout history there have been many examples of individuals being charged exorbitant interest rates on loans. There is a word, *usury*, for this type of action. **Usury** is the act of lending money at an excessively high interest rate. Lenders who exhibited such unethical behavior were sometimes referred to as "loan sharks." Lenders, of course, are in the business of making a rate of return on the money that they have to lend. Without question lenders deserve to earn a fair rate of return to compensate them for their time and the risk that the borrower will not repay the interest and/or principal on time or in full.

In Chapter 8, we defined this added compensation as a risk premium above the prevailing risk-free rate. Good ethical behavior is consistent with treating borrowers honestly and fairly. However, because of the existence of unethical lenders, various laws have made usury illegal. While it is illegal to charge usurious rates of interest, some unscrupulous lenders still try to behave unethically when making loans to consumers. Congress passed the *Consumer Credit Protection Act of 1968*, which prohibits excessively high-priced credit transactions. Regulation Z enacts the Truth in Lending section of the act, whereby the Federal Reserve has the responsibility of making consumers aware of the costs of alternative forms of credit. Lenders must disclose all loan costs (interest amounts, service charges, loan and finder fees, etc.), as well as the *annual percentage rate* of charge or interest. It is unfortunate, but a fact of life, that because of the unethical behavior of some lenders laws must be enacted to protect consumers.

APR VERSUS EAR

Banks, finance companies, and other lenders are required by the Truth in Lending law to disclose their lending interest rates on credit extended to consumers. Such a rate is called a contract or stated rate, or more frequently, an **annual percentage rate (APR)**. The method of calculating the APR on a loan is set by law. The APR is the interest rate r charged per period multiplied by the number of periods in a year m:

$$APR = r \times m \qquad (9.10)$$

Thus, a car loan that charges interest of 1 percent per month has an APR of 12 percent (i.e., 1 percent times 12 months). An unpaid credit card balance that incurs interest charges of 1.5 percent per month has an APR of 18 percent (1.5 times 12 months).

However, the APR misstates the true interest rate. The **effective annual rate (EAR),** sometimes called the *annual effective yield*, is the true opportunity cost measure of the interest rate, as it considers the effects of periodic compounding. For example, say an unpaid January balance of $100 on a credit card accumulates interest at the rate of 1.5 percent per month. The interest charge is added to the unpaid balance; if left unpaid, February's balance will be $101.50. If the bill remains unpaid through February, the 1.5 percent monthly charge is levied based on the total unpaid balance of $101.50. In other words, interest is assessed on previous months' unpaid interest charges. Thus, since interest compounds, the APR formula will *understate* the true or effective interest cost. This will always be true, except in the special case where the number of periods is one per year—that is, in annual compounding situations.

If the periodic interest charge r is known, the EAR is found by using Equation 9.11:

$$EAR = (1 + r)^m - 1 \qquad (9.11)$$

where m is the number of periods per year. If the APR is known instead, divide the APR by m and use the resulting number for r in Equation 9.11.[3]

---

[3]. Some financial calculators are preprogrammed with an "interest rate conversion" function, with which one can easily switch between an EAR (sometimes called EFF% for the "effective" rate) and the APR.

CAREER PROFILES

BRUCE ELIOT
Portfolio Manager
Helix Investment Partners

BA Economics
Claremont Men's College
MBA Finance
University of Chicago

"We take a resource, the money of our clients, and produce a product, which is the return on their investment."

Q: *Before you took your current position, you worked in the business valuation field. What is that?*
A: There are a number of circumstances when the owner of a business may need to determine the value of his or her firm. For instance, if I were going to sell part of the ownership of my company to someone else, I'd need to know how to price it; or if I were going to use it as collateral for a loan, I'd need to demonstrate the value to the lender.

Q: *How did you determine a company's value?*
A: There are several methods. Sometimes we would look for similar firms that had been sold recently and use those as comparisons, or we'd look for similar firms that are publicly traded and look at the value of their stock. In other cases we would look at their present value from a cash flow perspective.

Q: *Describe that process.*
A: It's not unlike the process you would use to determine the value of a stock or bond. We'd look at the discounted value of the projected cash flow for the next five years and then the terminal value, which is the amount you would expect to sell the business for in five years, again discounted to present value.

Q: *Now you're a portfolio manager.*
A: Right. I basically invest other people's money. In a way it's like a manufacturing business. We take a resource and the money of our clients, and we produce a product, which is the return on their investment. We manage about $180 million currently.

Q: *How do you decide what to invest in?*
A: Our investment strategy could be described as fairly complex. We look for firms with quite specific capital conditions. We look at their existing debt (bonds) and their existing equity (stock) values. When we see a certain relationship between those values, we see an opportunity to make a positive return. Applying our strategy, we will often end up buying a company's bonds and selling its stock short.

Q: *Why would this strategy work?*
A: In very simple terms, when we see certain stock and bond values, we conclude that there is a misvaluation, that the stock is overpriced relative to the bond, for instance. So if we're right, we're able to take advantage of that misvaluation by buying the underpriced security and shorting the overpriced one. As I said, it's a fairly complex strategy.

Q: *What do you do on a daily basis?*
A: I spend essentially the entire day on the telephone, discussing the value of securities, mostly with brokers. Since the bonds we buy are not traded on an exchange like stocks, I may need to call four or five sources for those bonds to determine the going price. The other piece of my job is to manage the existing portfolio, making day-to-day adjustments based on the changing values of securities. Using the metaphor of a manufacturing business, I adjust the settings on the production line so the products are manufactured correctly.

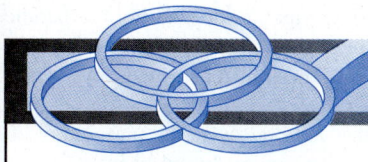

APPLYING FINANCE TO...

INSTITUTIONS AND MARKETS

Depository institutions offer savings accounts and certificates of deposit (CDs) to individual savers. To entice individuals to save with them, these financial institutions often state annual percentage rates but compound the interest more frequently than once a year. The result is that the effective annual rate (EAR) is higher than the stated annual percentage rate (APR). Of course, since most financial institutions depend on the spread between their cost of obtaining funds and their lending rates, they must balance the effective annual rates at which they borrow and lend. Credit card loans typically provide for monthly compounding so that the EAR is higher than the APR.

INVESTMENTS

Most financial decisions are based on the rate at which an investment is compounded or a future value is discounted. Savers are interested in growing or compounding their savings over time and know the longer an investment can compound the more rapidly it will grow in value at a specified interest rate. Investors make plans, based on the compound rates of return they expect to earn on their investments, about when they can buy a home, when they can send their children to college, and when they can retire. The ability to compound interest more frequently than once a year means that investors can reach their goals sooner or at lower interest rates.

FINANCIAL MANAGEMENT

Financial managers borrow from banks and issue debt to raise funds to maintain and grow their firms. While some business loans are simple interest loans, others take the form of fully amortized loans, whereby annuity payments are composed of a declining interest portion and a rising principal repayment portion over the life of the loan. Investors, of course, expect to earn compound rates of return on their debt and equity investments held for more than a year. Financial managers accordingly must invest funds in capital projects that will generate excess cash flows sufficient in amount to provide investors with their expected rates of return.

As an example of the effective annual rate concept, let's find the true annual interest cost of a credit card that advertises an 18 percent APR. Since credit card charges are typically assessed monthly, m (the number of periods per year) is 12. Thus, the monthly interest rate is:

$$r = APR \div m = 18\% \div 12 = 1.5\%$$

From Equation 9.11, the EAR is:

$$(1 + 0.015)^{12} - 1 = 1.1956 - 1 = 0.1956, \text{ or } 19.56\%$$

The true interest charge on a credit card with an 18 percent APR is really 19.56 percent!

When the annual stated rate stays the same, more frequent interest compounding helps savers earn more interest over the course of a year. For example, is it better to put your money in an account offering (option 1) 8 percent interest per year, compounded quarterly, or (option 2) 8 percent interest per year, compounded monthly?

Compounding interest quarterly means that the bank is paying interest four times a year to its depositors. Option 1 involved four periods per year and a periodic interest rate r of 8 percent divided by 4, or 2 percent. Every dollar invested under option 1 will grow to $1.0824 [$1(1 + 0.02)^4] after one year's time. Another way of expressing this is that the effective annual rate of 8 percent compounded quarterly is 8.24 percent.

Under option 2, the relevant time period is one month and the periodic interest rate is 8 percent ÷ 12, or 0.67 percent. Every dollar invested under option 2 will grow to $1.0830 [$1(1 + 0.0067)^{12}]. Thus, the effective annual rate of 8 percent compounded monthly is 8.30 percent.

As option 2 gives the depositor more interest over the course of a year, depositors should choose it over option 1. This example illustrates that, for the same APR or stated rate, more frequent compounding increases the future value of an investor's funds more quickly.

CONCEPT CHECK

What is the annual percentage rate (APR) on a loan?

What is the effective annual rate (EAR) on a loan?

SUMMARY

This chapter has introduced the reader to the concept of the time value of money, which is the basis of many financial applications. It began with an explanation and illustration of simple interest, whereby one starts with a present value amount as it grows to a future value in one time period. Then, compounding interest over several time periods to determine future values was discussed. This was followed with a discussion and illustrations of the concept of discounting to determine present values, then how to find interest rates and time requirements were covered in problems involving future and present values.

Future value problems involving ordinary annuities were described and the calculation process illustrated. This was followed with a section on how to calculate the present value of an ordinary annuity. Solving for either interest rates or time periods was then discussed in problems involving annuities. The next section focused on how to determine annual annuity payments. This is particularly useful for finding periodic payments for loans, such as traditional fixed-rate home mortgages, that are amortized (repaid in equal payments) over their lives.

The last two sections of the chapter addressed how to handle more frequent compounding or discounting intervals and a comparison of two interest rate concepts, the annual percentage rate versus the effective annual rate.

The Learning Extension that follows covers the meaning of an annuity due and will illustrate some annuity due problems.

KEY TERMS

amortized loan
annual percentage rate (APR)
annuity
annuity due
compounding
compound interest
discounting
effective annual rate (EAR)

future value
loan amortization schedule
ordinary annuity
present value
Rule of 72
simple interest
time value of money
usury

DISCUSSION QUESTIONS

1. Briefly describe the time value of money.
2. Explain simple interest.
3. Describe the process of compounding and the meaning of compound interest.
4. Briefly describe how inflation or purchasing power impacts stated or nominal interest rates.
5. What is discounting? Give an illustration.
6. Briefly explain how present values and future values are related.
7. Describe the process for solving for the interest rate in present and future value problems.
8. Describe the process for solving for the time period in present and future value problems.
9. How can the Rule of 72 be used to determine how long it will take for an investment to double in value?
10. What is an ordinary annuity?
11. Briefly describe how to solve for the interest rate or the time period in annuity problems.
12. Describe the process for determining the size of a constant periodic payment that is necessary to fully amortize a loan such as a home mortgage.
13. Describe compounding or discounting that is done more often than annually.
14. What is usury, and how does it relate to the cost of consumer credit?
15. Explain the difference between the annual percentage rate and the effective annual rate.

EXERCISES

1. Go to the Federal Reserve Web site, http://www.federalreserve.gov. Go to "Economic Research and Data," and access "Recent Statistical Releases" and the "Consumer Credit." Find average interest rates charged by commercial banks on new automobile loans, personal loans, and credit card plans.
    a. Compare the average level of interest rates among the three types of loans.
    b. Access "Historical Data" and then "Consumer Credit," and compare trends in the cost of consumer credit provided by commercial banks over the past three years.
2. Go to the Federal Reserve Web site, http://www.federalreserve.gov. Go to "Economic Research and Data," and access "Recent Statistical Releases" and the "Consumer Credit." Determine current interest rates charged by auto finance companies on new automobile loans. Also compare the trend in the cost of loans from auto finance companies over the past three years.
3. Assume that your partner and you are in the consumer lending business. A customer, talking with your partner, is discussing the possibility of obtaining a $10,000 loan for three months. The potential borrower seems distressed and says he needs the loan by tomorrow or several of his relatively new appliances will be repossessed by the manufacturers. You overhear your partner saying that that in order to process the loan within one day there will be a $1,000 processing fee so that $11,000 in principal will have to be repaid in order to have $10,000 to spend now. Furthermore, because the money is needed now and is for only three months the interest charge will be 6 percent per month. What would you do?

PROBLEMS

1. Find the future value one year from now of a $7,000 investment at a 3 percent annual compound interest rate. Also calculate the future value if the investment is made for two years.

2. Find the future value of $10,000 invested now after five years if the annual interest rate is 8 percent.
   a. What would be the future value if the interest rate is a simple interest rate?
   b. What would be the future value if the interest rate is a compound interest rate?

3. Determine the future values if $5,000 is invested in each of the following situations:
   a. 5 percent for ten years
   b. 7 percent for seven years
   c. 9 percent for four years

4. You are planning to invest $2,500 today for three years at a nominal interest rate of 9 percent with annual compounding.
   a. What would be the future value of your investment?
   b. Now assume that inflation is expected to be 3 percent per year over the same three-year period. What would be the investment's future value in terms of purchasing power?
   c. What would be the investment's future value in terms of purchasing power if inflation occurs at a 9 percent annual rate?

5. Find the present value of $7,000 to be received one year from now assuming a 3 percent annual discount interest rate. Also calculate the present value if the $7,000 is received after two years.

6. Determine the present values if $5,000 is received in the future (i.e., at the end of each indicated time period) in each of the following situations:
   a. 5 percent for ten years
   b. 7 percent for seven years
   c. 9 percent for four years

7. Determine the present value if $15,000 is to be received at the end of eight years and the discount rate is 9 percent. How would your answer change if you had to wait six years to receive the $15,000?

8. Determine the future value at the end of two years of an investment of $3,000 made now and an additional $3,000 made one year from now if the compound annual interest rate is 4 percent.

9. Assume you are planning to invest $5,000 each year for six years and will earn 10 percent per year. Determine the future value of this annuity if your first $5,000 is invested at the end of the first year.

10. Determine the present value now of an investment of $3,000 made one year from now and an additional $3,000 made two years from now if the annual discount rate is 4 percent.

11. What is the present value of a loan that calls for the payment of $500 per year for six years if the discount rate is 10 percent and the first payment will be made one year from now? How would your answer change if the $500 per year occurred for ten years?

12. Determine the annual payment on a $500,000, 12 percent business loan from a commercial bank that is to be amortized over a five-year period.

13. Determine the annual payment on a $15,000 loan that is to be amortized over a four-year period and carries a 10 percent interest rate. Also prepare a loan amortization schedule for this loan.

14. You are considering borrowing $150,000 to purchase a new home.
    a. Calculate the monthly payment needed to amortize an 8 percent fixed-rate 30-year mortgage loan.
    b. Calculate the monthly amortization payment if the loan in (a) was for 15 years.

15. Assume a bank loan requires an interest payment of $85 per year and a principal payment of $1,000 at the end of the loan's eight-year life.
    a. How much could this loan be sold for to another bank if loans of similar quality carried an 8.5 percent interest rate? That is, what would be the present value of this loan?
    b. Now, if interest rates on other similar quality loans are 10 percent, what would be the present value of this loan?
    c. What would be the present value of the loan if the interest rate is 8 percent on similar-quality loans?

16. Use a financial calculator or computer software program to answer the following questions:
    a. What would be the future value of $15,555 invested now if it earns interest at 14.5 percent for seven years?
    b. What would be the future value of $19,378 invested now if the money remains deposited for eight years and the annual interest rate is 18 percent?

17. Use a financial calculator or computer software program to answer the following questions:
    a. What is the present value of $359,000 that is to be received at the end of twenty-three years if the discount rate is 11 percent?
    b. How would your answer change in (a) if the $359,000 is to be received at the end of twenty years?

18. Use a financial calculator or computer software program to answer the following questions:
    a. What would be the future value of $7,455 invested annually for nine years beginning one year from now if the annual interest rate is 19 percent?
    b. What would be the present value of a $9,532 annuity for which the first payment will be made beginning one year from now, payments will last for twenty-seven years, and the annual interest rate is 13 percent?

19. Use a financial calculator or computer software program to answer the following questions.
    a. What would be the future value of $19,378 invested now if the money remains deposited for eight years, the annual interest rate is 18 percent, and interest on the investment is compounded semiannually?
    b. How would your answer for (a) change if quarterly compounding were used?

20. Use a financial calculator or computer software program to answer the following questions.
    a. What is the present value of $359,000 that is to be received at the end of twenty-three years, the discount rate is 11 percent, and semiannual discounting occurs?
    b. How would your answer for (a) change if monthly discounting were used?

21. What would be the present value of a $9,532 annuity for which the first payment will be made beginning one year from now,

payments will last for twenty-seven years, the annual interest rate is 13 percent, quarterly discounting occurs, and $2,383 is invested at the end of each quarter?

22. Answer the following questions.

   a. What is the annual percentage rate (APR) on a loan that charges interest of .75 percent per month?

   b. What is the effective annual rate (EAR) on the loan described in (a)?

23. You have recently seen a credit card advertisement stating that the annual percentage rate is 12 percent. If the credit card requires monthly payments, what is the effective annual rate of interest on the loan?

24. A credit card advertisement states that the annual percentage rate is 21 percent. If the credit card requires quarterly payments, what is the effective annual rate of interest on the loan?

25. **Challenge Problem** [Note: A computer spreadsheet software program or a financial calculator that can handle uneven cash flow streams will be needed to solve the following problems. The following cash flow streams are expected to result from three investment opportunities.

YEAR	INVESTMENT STABLE	INVESTMENT DECLINING	INVESTMENT GROWING
1	$20,000	$35,000	$10,000
2	20,000	30,000	15,000
3	20,000	20,000	20,000
4	20,000	5,000	30,000
5	20,000	0	50,000

   a. Find the present values at the end of time period zero for each of these three investments if the discount rate is 15 percent. Also find the present values for each investment using 10 percent and 20 percent discount rates.

   b. Find the future values of these three investments at the end of year five if the compound interest rate is 12.5 percent. Also find the future values for each investment using 2.5 percent and 22.5 percent compound rates.

   c. Find the present values of the three investments using a 15 percent annual discount rate but with quarterly discounting. Also find the present values for both semiannual and monthly discounting for a 15 percent stated annual rate.

   d. Find the future values of the three investments using a 12.5 percent annual compound rate but with quarterly compounding. Also find the future values for both semiannual and monthly compounding for a 12.5 percent stated annual rate.

   e. Assume that the present value for each of the three investments is $75,000. What is the annual interest rate (%i) for each investment?

   f. Show how your answers would change in (e) if quarterly discounting takes place.

   g. Assume that the future value for each of the three investments is $150,000. What is the annual interest rate (%i) for each investment? [Note: (e) and (g) are independent of each other.]

   h. Show how your answers would change in (g) if quarterly compounding takes place.

LEARNING EXTENSION 9

Annuity Due Problems

FUTURE VALUE OF AN ANNUITY DUE

In contrast with an ordinary annuity, an *annuity due* exists when the equal periodic payments occur at the beginning of each period. Let's return to the example used in the "Future Value of an Annuity" section in this chapter. Recall that the problem involved a three-year annuity, $1,000 annual payments, and an 8 percent interest rate. However, let's assume that the first payment now is made at the beginning of the first year, namely at time zero. This will allow the first $1,000 payment to earn interest for three years, the second payment to earn interest for two years, and the third payment to earn interest for one year.

The calculation process to find the future value of this annuity due problem can be demonstrated as follows:

$$\begin{aligned} \text{FV annuity due} &= \$1{,}000(1.08)^3 + \$1{,}000(1.08)^2 + \$1{,}000(1.08)^1 \\ &= \$1{,}000(1.260) + \$1{,}000(1.166) + \$1{,}000(1.080) \\ &= \$1{,}000(1.260 + 1.166 + 1.080) \\ &= \$1{,}000(3.506) \\ &= \$3{,}506 \end{aligned}$$

Notice that by making the first payment now the future value of this annuity at the end of three years will be $3,506. This contrasts with a future value of $3,246 if payments are delayed by one year, as would be the case with an ordinary annuity.

Table-based Solution:
Equation 9.6 can be easily modified to handle annuity due problems as follows:

$$\text{FVAD}_n = \text{PMT}(\text{FVIFA}_{r,n})(1 + r) \qquad \text{(LE9.1)}$$

where FVAD is the future value of an annuity due and the $(1 + r)$ factor effectively compounds each payment by one more year to reflect the fact that payments start at the beginning of each period. In this problem, the annual payment is $1,000, the time period is three years, and the interest rate is 8 percent. Using Equation LE9.1, the future value of this annuity due would be:

$$\begin{aligned} \text{FVAD}_3 &= \$1{,}000(\text{FVIFA}_{8\%,3})(1 + 0.08) \\ &= \$1{,}000(3.246)(1.08) \\ &= \$1{,}000(3.506) \\ &= \$3{,}506 \end{aligned}$$

The FVIFA of 3.246 comes from Table 9.3 at the intersection of the 8 percent interest rate column and the year-three row.

Annuity due problems also can be solved with financial calculators. In fact, most financial calculators have a DUE key (or a switch) for shifting payments from the end of time periods to the beginning of time periods. If you have a financial calculator, you can verify the future value of an annuity due result for the three-year annuity problem. First, clear the calculator. Next, enter −1000 (for both TI and HP calculators) and press the PMT key. Then enter 8 and press the %i key, and enter 3 and press the N key. Finally, instead of pressing the CPT key, press the DUE key followed by the FV key to find the future value of an annuity due of 3506.11, which rounds to $3,506.

Financial Calculator Solution:

Inputs: 3   8   −1000
           N   %i   PMT

Press: DUE   FV

Solution: 3506.11

Spreadsheet Solution:
The future value of an annuity due problem is solved by again using Excel's future value (FV) financial function, but adjusting for when the cash flows occur, as follows:

$$= FV(Rate, Nper, Pmt, PV, Type)$$
$$= FV(.08, 3, -1000, 0, 1)$$
$$= \$3,506.11$$

Note that the "Type" value was given a "1" to indicate the beginning of period cash flows. Recall that previously we used a "0" value in "Type" to reflect cash flows occurring at the end of each time period.

PRESENT VALUE OF AN ANNUITY DUE

Occasionally, you will have to do present-value annuity due problems. For example, leasing arrangements often require the person leasing equipment to make the first payment at the time the equipment is delivered. Let's illustrate by assuming that lease payments of $1,000 will be made at the beginning of each year for three years. If the appropriate interest rate is 8 percent, what is the present value of this annuity due leasing problem?

The calculation process to find the present value of this annuity due problem can be demonstrated as follows:

$$\text{PV annuity due} = \$1,000[1 \div (1.08)^0] + \$1,000[1 \div (1.08)^1] + \$1,000[1 \div (1.08)^2]$$
$$= \$1,000(1.000) + \$1,000(0.926) + \$1,000(0.857)$$
$$= \$1,000(2.783)$$
$$= \$2,783$$

Notice that by making the first payment now, the present value of this annuity is $2,783. This contrasts with a present value of $2,577 if payments are delayed by one year, as would be the case with an ordinary annuity.

Table-based Solution:
Equation 9.8 can be easily modified to handle annuity due problems as follows:

$$PVAD_n = PMT(PVIFA_{r,n})(1 + r) \qquad (LE9.2)$$

where PVAD is the present value of an annuity due and the $(1 + r)$ factor effectively compounds each payment by one more year to reflect the fact that payments start at the beginning of each period.

In the preceding problem, the annual payment is $1,000, the time period is three years, and the interest rate is 8 percent. Using Equation LE9.2, the present value of this annuity due would be:

$$PVAD_3 = \$1,000[(PVIFA_{8\%,3})(1 + 0.08)]$$
$$= \$1,000[(2.577)(1.08)]$$
$$= \$1,000(2.783)$$
$$= \$2,783$$

The PVIFA of 2.577 comes from Table 9.4 at the intersection of the 8 percent interest rate column and the year-three row. Present value annuity due problems also can be solved with computer software programs and financial calculators.

If you have a financial calculator, you can verify the present value of an annuity due result for the preceding three-year annuity problem. First, clear the calculator. Next, enter 1000 for TI calculators (or –1000 for HP calculators) and press the PMT key. Then enter 8 and press the %i key, and enter 3 and press the N key. Finally, instead of pressing the CPT key, press the DUE key followed by the PV key to find the present value of an annuity due of 2783.26, which rounds to $2,783.

Financial Calculator Solution:

Inputs: 3   8   1000
           [N]   [%i]   [PMT]

Press: [DUE]   [PV]

Solution: 2783.26

Spreadsheet Solution:

The present value of an annuity due problem is solved by again using Excel's present value (PV) financial function, but adjusting for when the cash flows occur, as follows:

$$= PV(Rate, Nper, Pmt, FV, Type)$$
$$= PV(.08, 3, -1000, 0, 1)$$
$$= \$2{,}783.26$$

Note that the "Type" value was given a "1" to indicate beginning of period cash flows. Recall that previously we used a "0" value in "Type" to reflect cash flows occurring at the end of each time period.

INTEREST RATES AND TIME REQUIREMENTS FOR ANNUITY DUE PROBLEMS

Tables containing FVIFA and PVIFA factors are not readily available for annuity due problems. Thus, it is better to use a spreadsheet program or a financial calculator when trying to find the interest rate for an annuity due problem. Let's assume that the future value of an annuity due problem is $6,153, each payment is $1,000, and the time period is five years. What is the interest rate on this problem? If you have a financial calculator, enter: FV = 6153, PMT = −1000, and N = 5. Press the DUE key and the %i key to find an r of 7 percent.

Financial Calculator Solution:

Inputs: 5   −1000   6153
           [N]   [PMT]   [FV]

Press: [DUE]   [%i]

Solution: 7.00

Spreadsheet Solution:

Excel's RATE financial function also can be used to solve for the interest rate involving an annuity due problem. The process is very similar to the one used for an ordinary annuity problem, except that a "1" value in "Type" is entered to indicate that cash flows occur at the beginning of each time period. The financial function solution would be:

$$= RATE(Nper, Pmt, PV, FV, Type)$$
$$= RATE(5, -1000, 0, 6153, 1)$$
$$= 7.00\%$$

The n time periods involved in an annuity due problem also can be determined using either a computer software program or a financial calculator. For example, in the preceding problem let's assume we know the interest rate is 7 percent, the future value is $6,153, and the payment is $1,000 (entered as −1000). What we don't know is the number of time periods required. We can solve for N as follows:

Financial Calculator Solution:

Inputs: 7   −1000   6153
            %i   PMT   FV

Press: DUE   N

Solution: 5.00

Spreadsheet Solution:
Excel's NPER financial function also can be used to solve for the number of periods in an annuity due problem. However, in contrast with an ordinary annuity, a value of "1" for "Type" must be entered to indicate that the cash flows occur at the beginning of the time periods. The financial function solution would be:

$$= \text{NPER}(\text{Rate},\text{Pmt},\text{PV},\text{FV},\text{Type})$$
$$= \text{NPER}(.07,-1000,0,6153,1)$$
$$= 5.00$$

Of course the same process could be used for finding either interest rates or the number of time periods if the present value of the annuity due instead of the future value were known. This would be done by substituting the PV value for the FV value in financial calculator or spreadsheet calculations.

QUESTIONS AND PROBLEMS

1. Assume you are planning to invest $100 each year for four years and will earn 10 percent per year. Determine the future value of this annuity due problem if your first $100 is invested now.

2. Assume you are planning to invest $5,000 each year for six years and will earn 10 percent per year. Determine the future value of this annuity due problem if your first $5,000 is invested now.

3. What is the present value of a five-year lease arrangement with an interest rate of 9 percent that requires annual payments of $10,000 per year with the first payment being due now?

4. Use a financial calculator to solve for the interest rate involved in the following future value of an annuity due problem. The future value is $57,000, the annual payment is $7,500, and the time period is six years.

5. **Challenge Problem** (Note: This problem requires access to a spreadsheet software package or a financial calculator that can handle uneven cash flows.) Following are the cash flows for three investments (originally presented in end-of-chapter problem 24) that actually occur at the beginning of each year rather than at the end of each year.

YEAR	INVESTMENT STABLE	INVESTMENT DECLINING	INVESTMENT GROWING
1	$20,000	$35,000	$10,000
2	20,000	30,000	15,000
3	20,000	20,000	20,000
4	20,000	5,000	30,000
5	20,000	0	50,000

a. Find the present values at the end of time period zero for each of these three investments if the discount rate is 15 percent.

b. Find the future values of these three investments at the end of year five if the compound interest rate is 12.5 percent.

c. Assume that the present value for each of the three investments is $75,000. What is the annual interest rate (%i) for each investment?

d. Assume that the future value for each of the three investments is $150,000. What is the annual interest rate (%i) for each investment? [Note: (c) and (d) are independent of each other.]

CHAPTER 10

Bonds and Stocks: Characteristics and Valuations

Chapter Learning Objectives:

AFTER STUDYING THIS CHAPTER, YOU SHOULD BE ABLE TO:
- Identify the major sources of external long-term financing for corporations.
- Describe major characteristics of corporate bonds.
- Identify the reasons why investors seek stocks for an investment vehicle.
- Describe major characteristics of preferred stock and common stock.
- Describe the process for issuing dividends by a firm.
- Explain how financial securities are valued in general and specifically for bonds and stocks.

Where We Have Been...

The financial system is composed of a number of participants—banks, insurance companies, credit unions, and individuals, among others. Some borrow or lend funds; others seek to sell or purchase ownership rights, or common stock, in firms. We've seen how investors are willing to give up their money today in the expectation of receiving a return in the future that will exceed the inflation rate and that will reward them for the risk of their investment. Time-value-of-money principles (present value, future value) help both borrowers and lenders determine items such as how much to borrow, repayment schedules, and the return on an investment.

Where We Are Going...

Bonds and stocks are traded in securities markets, which will be the topic of Chapter 11. We tie together the concepts of expected return, risk, and valuation in Chapter 12 when we discuss financial risk and return concepts. Additional sources of funds for business financing will be discussed in Chapter 16, Short-term Business Financing.

How Does This Chapter Apply to Me...

Time value of money is one of the most important concepts in finance. Here we will see applications of time value concepts to the investor and how an investor can evaluate a firm's prospects and estimate appropriate prices for its securities. Greater depth and detail will be presented in an investments course. Many investors lack the time or ability to analyze securities, so they will purchase a mutual fund, which is a professionally managed investment pool. As a financial manager, this chapter will introduce you to various types of capital market securities and their features, so you will know more about the financing choices facing firms.

There is a famous Mark Twain quote about financial markets:

> October. That month is especially dangerous for investing in stocks. Other dangerous months include August, January, June, March, November, July, February, April, December, May and September.

That pretty much covers them all! In this chapter we'll begin to learn about financial markets and the characteristics of stocks and bonds.

Borrowing money brings with it the obligation to repay the debt. Individuals and firms who do not repay their borrowing may find themselves unable to borrow again in the future and, worse yet, filing for bankruptcy. But prudent use of debt by issuers can help finance the purchase of capital, equipment, houses, and so forth. We'll learn more about the corporate decision to borrow in a future chapter. In this chapter, we'll begin to learn about the characteristics of bonds from an investor's perspective.

Investing in the stock market is, for many, the best means available for enjoying the benefits of corporate wealth creation. As firms grow in size, profitability, market share, and market value, the value of the shares of stock many times grow, too. This helps investors to meet their financial goals, such as preparing to meet the needs of paying for the college education of a small child or their own retirement. In this chapter, we'll discuss common stock, preferred stock, and principles behind how to value equity.

In Chapter 2, we described *financial assets* as claims against the income or assets of individuals, businesses, and governments. Businesses obtain long-term external financial capital either by borrowing or by obtaining equity funds. Long-term borrowing can be privately negotiated or be obtained by issuing debt obligations called bonds. Equity capital may be obtained by finding new partners with financial capital to invest or through the public markets by issuing shares. This chapter describes the characteristics of bonds and applies the time-value-of-money techniques from Chapter 9 to see how to value bonds. In the following chapter we'll discuss the characteristics of stocks and tools used to value them.

financial assets
claims against the income or assets of individuals, businesses, and governments

LONG-TERM EXTERNAL FINANCING SOURCES FOR BUSINESSES

Businesses obtain long-term financing from internal funds, which are generated from profits, and external funds, which are obtained from capital markets. Some firms will have little need for external funds. They may be able to generate sufficient internal funds to satisfy their need for capital, or they may require little investment in fixed assets (for example, firms operating in service industries). Other businesses, such as high-technology firms that experience rapid growth, cannot generate enough internal funds for their capital needs and may be forced to seek financing, often from the capital markets.

The proportion of internal to external financing varies over the business cycle. During periods of economic expansion, firms usually rely more on external funds because the funds needed for investment opportunities outstrip the firms' ability to finance them internally. During periods of economic contraction the reverse is true. As profitable investment opportunities become fewer, the rate of investment is reduced and reliance on external capital markets decreases.

Long-term funds are obtained by issuing corporate bonds and stocks. Table 10.1 shows that the total of new security issues amounted to more than $2,600 billion in 2006 but to about $1,100 billion in 2008 due to a steep recession and financial market anxiety. Most of the annual funds raised from security issues come from corporate bond sales. In fact, corporate bonds accounted for approximately 90 percent of total new security issues from 1995 to 2008. Firms issue more bonds than equities for two basic reasons. First, as we will see in Chapter 18, it is cheaper to borrow than to raise equity financing. Second, bonds and other loans have a maturity date, when they expire or come due; at times, new bonds are sold to repay maturing ones. Equity, on the other hand, never matures. Firms can repurchase their outstanding stock, or the shares of one firm may be merged or acquired by another firm. That is the reason the "net issues" line for common stocks shows negative numbers. Over the time period covered in the table, corporations have been net repurchasers, rather than net issuers, of new equity.

Table 10.1 further shows that corporations have been annually raising approximately 90 percent of their publicly held long-term debt funds by selling their bonds through public issues in the United States. The second important method of raising long-term debt funds is through private sales or placements in the United States. Public security issues are offered for sale to all investors, must be approved by the Securities and Exchange Commission (SEC), and are accompanied by public disclosure of the firm's financial statements and other information. Private placements are sold to specific qualified investors and do not go through SEC scrutiny, nor do they require public disclosure of company information. Since private sales are "private," we do not have good data on these sales over time.

INTERNET ACTIVITY

Examine recent financing activity and data at the Federal Reserve Board and Securities Exchange Commission Web sites,
http://www.federalreserve.gov and http://www.sec.gov.

TABLE 10.1
Public Offerings of Bonds and Stocks ($ billions)

	2003 AMOUNT	2003 PERCENT	2004 AMOUNT	2004 PERCENT	2005 AMOUNT	2005 PERCENT	2006 AMOUNT	2006 PERCENT	2007 AMOUNT	2007 PERCENT	2008 AMOUNT	2008 PERCENT	AVERAGE
New Security Issues													
Corporate Bonds	1692.3	93.2%	1923.1	92.9%	2323.7	95.3%	2500.8	95.5%	2220.5	92.9%	865.6	80.7%	91.7%
Public offerings, Corporate Stocks	123.3	6.8%	147.6	7.1%	115.3	4.7%	118.6	4.5%	168.6	7.1%	206.8	19.3%	8.3%
Total	**1815.6**	**100.0%**	**2070.7**	**100.0%**	**2439.0**	**100.0%**	**2619.4**	**100.0%**	**2389.1**	**100.0%**	**1072.4**	**100.0%**	**100.0%**
Bonds by Type of Offering													
Public, domestic	1579.3	93.3%	1737.3	90.3%	2141.5	92.2%	2296.5	91.8%	2002.7	90.2%	748.7	86.5%	90.7%
Sold Abroad	112.9	6.7%	185.8	9.7%	182.2	7.8%	204.2	8.2%	217.8	9.8%	116.9	13.5%	9.3%
Total	**1692.2**	**100.0%**	**1923.1**	**100.0%**	**2323.7**	**100.0%**	**2500.7**	**100.0%**	**2220.5**	**100.0%**	**865.6**	**100.0%**	**100.0%**
Stocks by Type of Offering													
Common shares issued	123.3		147.6		115.3		118.6		168.6		206.8		
Common shares repurchased	102.6		165.9		434.1		721.3		999.8		587.6		
Net issues	20.7		−18.3		−318.8		−602.7		−831.2		−380.8		
Retained earnings (internal financing) by corporations	376.5		397.3		440.0		497.5		403.4		440.0		
Net long term financing raised	2,089.5		2,302.1		2,444.9		2,395.6		1,792.7		924.8		
Net percent from bonds		81.0%		83.5%		95.0%		104.4%		123.9%		93.6%	96.9%
Net percent from common stock		1.0%		−0.8%		−13.0%		−25.2%		−46.4%		−41.2%	−20.9%
Net percent from internal financing		18.0%		17.3%		18.0%		20.8%		22.5%		47.6%	24.0%
		100.0%		**100.0%**		**100.0%**		**100.0%**		**100.0%**		**100.0%**	**100.0%**

Source: *Federal Reserve Bulletin* (tables 1.46, 1.57), *Economic Report of the President* (Table B-90), various issues.

FIGURE 10.1
Net Percent of Financing from Bonds, New Stock Issues, and Retained Earnings, 1995–2008

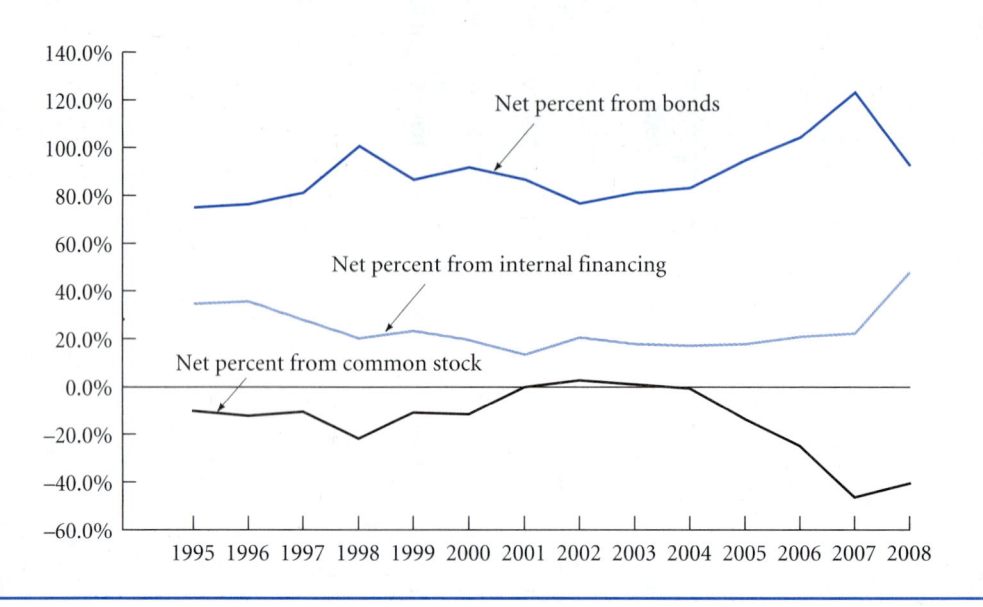

GLOBAL DISCUSSION

CONCEPT CHECK
Which security is more frequently issued, stocks or bonds?

Why would a U.S. firm issue bonds overseas?

How important are internal equity and external equity as a financing source for U.S. corporations?

par value (face value)
principal amount that the issuer is obligated to repay at maturity

coupon payments
interest payments paid to the bondholders

U.S. firms may also borrow funds overseas. This percentage varies over this time frame, from 4.5 percent in 2001 to over 15 percent in 2000. There are four reasons why U.S. firms raise funds outside of the United States. First, if they have overseas plants or factories, it may make financial sense to raise funds in the country in which the plant is built. Second, financing costs, such as interest rates, are sometimes lower overseas, although the recent downtrend in overseas financing may be due to lower interest rates in the United States. Third, if securities are issued outside of the United States, the issuer avoids the costly and time-consuming SEC approval process. Fourth, the growing number of large bond offerings (issues of $1 billion or more at one time) causes issuers to seek access to the global capital markets to find buyers.[1]

The bottom of Table 10.1 and Figure 10.1 show the mix between external (bonds and stocks) and internal (retained profits) financing for U.S. corporations. Because of merger, acquisition, and stock buyback activity, external public equity has fallen in recent years (this trend began in the 1980s). To make up for the shortfall, publicly issued bonds have increased relative to retained earnings as a funding source. Since the late 1990s, about 90 percent of net financing have come from bonds.

DEBT CAPITAL

A debt agreement is really a contract between lenders and the firm. As such, holders of debt capital have certain rights and privileges not enjoyed by the firm's owners (those holding shares of common stock) in a corporation. A debt holder may force the firm to abide by the terms of the debt contract even if the result is reorganization or bankruptcy of the firm. The periodic interest payments due to the holders of debt securities must be paid or else the creditors can force the firm into bankruptcy. Table 10.2 summarizes important characteristics of bonds, which we'll be reviewing in this section.

Except for rarely issued perpetuities[2], all debt issues have maturity dates when issuers are obligated to pay the bond's principal (*par value* or *face value*) to bondholders. In the United States, par value is usually $1,000 for corporate bonds. All but zero-coupon issues pay interest, called **coupon payments**. If a bond has an 8 percent coupon and a par value of $1,000, it pays

---

1. Gregory Zuckerman, "Cautious Bond Investors Have Issuers Thinking Big," *Wall Street Journal* (July 27, 1998), pp. C1, C23.
2. A perpetuity is a bond without a maturity date. Its owners and heirs receive interest payments in perpetuity as long as the firm exists.

TABLE 10.2
Common Elements of Bonds

Represent borrowed funds
Contractual agreement between a borrower and lender (indenture)
Senior claim on assets and cash flow
No voting rights
Par value
Having a bond rating improves the issue's marketability to investors
Covenants
Interest:	Tax deductible to the issuing firm
	Usually fixed over the issue's life but can be variable as the indenture allows coupon rate on new issues affected by market interest rates and bond rating
Maturity:	Usually fixed; can be affected by convertibility, call and put provisions, sinking fund, extendibility features in the indenture
Security:	Can have senior claim on specific assets pledged in case of default or can be unsecured(debenture or subordinated [junior claim] debenture)

annual interest of 8 percent of $1,000 or 0.08 × $1,000 = $80. A bond with a 10 percent coupon would pay interest of $100 per year. Eurobonds, bonds issued in Europe, pay a single annual coupon interest payment. In the United States, bonds pay interest semiannually; an 8 percent coupon will pay interest of $40 every six months during the life of the bond.

Bondholders have the legal status as creditors, not owners, of the firm. As such, they have priority claims on the firm's cash flows and assets. This means that bondholders must receive their interest payments before the firm's owners receive their dividends. In case of bankruptcy, the debt holders must receive the funds owed to them before funds are distributed to the firm's owners. Because of this first claim on a firm's cash flow and assets, debt is a less risky investment than equity.

Offsetting the advantages of owning debt is its lower return. The interest payments creditors receive usually are considerably less over a period of years than the returns received by equity holders. Also, as long as the corporation meets its contractual obligations, the creditors have little choice in its management and control, except for those formal agreements and restrictions that are stated in the loan contract.

Long-term corporate debt securities fall into two categories: secured obligations and unsecured obligations. A single firm can have many types of debt contracts outstanding. Although ownership of many shares of stock may be evidenced by a single stock certificate, the bondholder has a separate security for each bond owned. Bonds can be either registered or bearer bonds. Bonds currently issued in the United States are **registered bonds,** in that the issuer knows the bondholders' names and interest payments are sent directly to the bondholder. **Bearer bonds** have coupons that are literally 'clipped' from the side of the bond certificate and presented, like a check, to a bank for payment. Thus, the bond issuer does not know who is receiving the interest payments. Bearer bonds are more prevalent outside of the United States. Regulations prevent their issuance in the United States, primarily because unscrupulous investors may evade income taxes on the clipped coupons.

Bonds can be sold in the public market, following registration with the SEC, and traded by investors. There is a 'private' market too; bonds can be sold in a private placement to qualified investors, typically institutional investors such as insurance companies and wealthy individuals. We should note that other forms of debt capital exist in addition to bonds. Businesses can borrow from banks; a popular source of debt financing is commercial finance companies, which will be further discussed in Chapter 16.

WHO BUYS BONDS?

The U.S. Treasury has a Treasury Direct program to sell Treasury securities directly to individual investors, but the main buyers of Treasury bonds are large institutions, such as pension funds or insurance companies, which hold them for investment purposes; others, such as investment banks, may purchase them and then resell them to smaller investors.

---

registered bonds
the issuer knows the names of the bondholders and the interest payments are sent directly to the bondholder

bearer bonds
have coupons that are literally clipped and presented, like a check, to the bank for payment; the bond issuer does not know who is receiving the interest payments

SMALL BUSINESS PRACTICE
Financing Sources for the Start-Up Firm

So you want to start your own business? All businesses require some initial financial capital to carry out the firm's operations. A service business requires less financial capital than would a manufacturing business. Both need working capital in the form of inventories and possibly accounts receivable if sales are made on credit terms. In addition, a manufacturing business requires fixed assets to manufacture the products that are to be sold.

Now that you have decided to start a new business, where are you going to get the necessary financial capital? First, you use your own assets. You may have some accumulated savings to use and/or have some financial assets in the form of stocks and bonds that can be sold. Second, you can turn to family and friends for financial support. You can either borrow from family members and friends or offer them a partial ownership (equity) position in the firm.

A small business can sometimes get outside financing from business angels or venture capitalists. Angels are wealthy individuals who provide financial capital to small businesses, usually during their early development. Venture capitalists organize partnerships that specialize in providing debt and equity capital to small businesses in their development and early expansion stages. The partners in a venture capital pool typically include insurance companies, endowment funds, and other institutional investors.

After a firm begins operations, some financing may be obtained from customers and/or suppliers. Large customers may be willing to 'lend' to you in the form of advance 'partial payments' on products that have not yet been completed. Suppliers often will give small businesses 'credit,' in some cases for several months, on purchases of materials and supplies. Bank financing is another source of possible outside financing for the small business once operations have begun. The federal government through the Small Business Administration provides an additional source of financing for small businesses. Many states and local communities also provide financing assistance to small businesses.

INTERNET ACTIVITY
Learn more about these financing options by visiting http://www.treasurydirect.gov, http://www.smartnotes.com, and http://www.internotes.com.

trust indenture
contract that lists the various provisions and covenants of the loan arrangement

ETHICAL ISSUES

trustee
individual or organization that represents the bondholders to ensure the indenture's provisions are respected by the bond issuer

covenants
impose additional restrictions or duties on the firm

Similarly, corporate debt markets are oriented toward the large institutional investor who can purchase millions of dollars of bonds at a time. But several innovative firms, such as IBM, UPS, Caterpillar, and GE Capital, initiated programs in recent years to sell $1,000 par value bonds directly to the retail, or individual, investor. Called SmartNotes, medium-term notes, or direct access notes (depending on the issuer and the investment banker selling them), the programs target small investors who have only a few thousand rather than millions to invest in bonds.

BOND COVENANTS

The **trust indenture** is an extensive document and includes in great detail the various provisions and covenants of the loan arrangement. A **trustee** represents the bondholders to ensure the bond issuer respects the indenture's provisions. In essence, the indenture is a contract between the bondholders and the issuing firm. The indenture details the par value of the issue, its maturity date, and coupon rate. A bond indenture may also include **covenants,** which can impose restrictions or extra duties on the firm.

Examples of covenants include stipulations that the firm must maintain a minimum level of net working capital[3], keep pledged assets in good working order, and send audited financial statements to bondholders. Others include restrictions on the amount of the firm's debt, its dividend payments, the amount and type of additional covenants it may undertake, and asset sales.

These examples illustrate the purpose of covenants: to protect the bondholders' stake in the firm. Bonds have value, first, because of the firm's ability to pay coupon interest and, second, because of the value of the assets or collateral backing the bonds in case of default. Without proper covenant protection, the value of a bond can decline sharply if a firm's liquidity and assets depreciate or if its debt grows disproportionately to its equity. These provisions affect the bond rating (discussed below) of the issue and the firm's financing costs, since bonds giving greater protection to the investor can be sold with lower coupon rates. The firm must decide if the restrictions and duties in the covenants are worth the access to lower-cost funds.

Covenants are important to bondholders. Holders of RJR-Nabisco bonds owned high-quality, A-rated bonds prior to the firm's takeover in 1988 by a leveraged buyout. After the buyout, large quantities of new debt were issued; RJR-Nabisco's original bonds were given a lower rating and fell by 17 percent in value. Lawsuits by disgruntled bondholders against the takeover were unfruitful. The courts decided that the bondholders should have sought protection against such increases

---

3. This is a measure of a firm's ability to repay short-term bills as they come due. Net working capital will be discussed further in Chapter 15 (Managing Working Capital) and Chapter 16 (Short-term Business Financing).

CONCEPT CHECK

Why are bond returns expected to be lower than stock returns?

Are covenants important to bond investors? Why or why not?

bond ratings
assess both the collateral underlying the bonds as well as the ability of the issuer to make timely payments of interest and principal

ETHICAL ISSUES

in the firm's debt load by seeking appropriate covenant language before investing, rather than running to the courts after the fact to correct their mistake. Covenants are the best way for bondholders to protect themselves against dubious management actions or decisions. For example, some bonds allow the investor to force the firm to redeem them if the credit rating falls below a certain level; others, such as Deutsche Telekom's $14.5 billion issue in 2000, increase the coupon rate (in this case by fifty basis points or 0.50 percentage points) if the bond rating falls below an "A" rating. We'll discuss bond ratings in the next section.

BOND RATINGS

Most bond issuers purchase **bond ratings** from one or more agencies such as Standard & Poor's (S&P), Moody's, or Fitch. For a one-time fee of about $25,000, the rater examines the credit quality of the firm (e.g., its ability to pay the promised coupon interest), the indenture provisions, covenants, and the expected trends of firm and industry operations. From its analysis and discussions with management, the agency assigns a bond rating (as shown in Table 10.3) that indicates the likelihood of default (nonpayment of coupon or par value or violation of the bond indenture) on the bond issue.[4] In addition, the rating agency commits to continually reexamine the issue's risk. For example, should the financial position of the firm weaken or improve, S&P may place the issue on its *Credit Watch* list with negative or positive implications. Shortly thereafter, S&P will either downgrade, upgrade, or reaffirm the original rating.

Despite the initial cost and the issuer's concern of a lower-than-expected rating, a bond rating makes it much easier to sell the bonds to the public. The rating acts as a signal to the market that an independent agency has examined the qualities of the issuer and the bond issue and has determined that the credit risk of the bond issue justifies the published rating. An unrated bond issue will likely obtain a cool reception from investors. Investors may have good reason to wonder, "What is the firm trying to hide? If this really was an attractive bond issue, the firm would have had it rated." In addition, certain types of investors, such as pension funds and insurance companies, may face restrictions against purchasing unrated public debt.

TABLE 10.3
Examples of Bond Rating Categories

MOODY'S	STANDARD & POORS	FITCH	
Aaa	AAA	AAA	Best quality, least credit risk
Aa1	AA+	AA+	High quality, slightly more risk than a top-rated bond
Aa2	AA	AA	
Aa3	AA–	AA–	
A1	A+	A+	Upper-medium grade, possible future credit quality difficulties
A2	A	A	
A3	A–	A–	
Baa1	BBB+	BBB+	Medium-quality bonds
Baa2	BBB	BBB	
Baa3	BBB–		
Ba1	BB+	BB+	Speculative issues, greater credit risk
Ba2	BB	BB	
Ba3	BB–	BB–	
B1	B+	B+	Very speculative, likelihood of future default
B2	B	B	
B3	B–	B–	
Caa	CCC	CCC	Highly speculative, either in default or high likelihood of going into default
Ca	CC	CC	
C	C	C	
	D	DDD	
		DD	
		D	

---

4. For a review of S&P's rating process, see G. Hessol, "Financial Management and Credit Ratings," *Midland Corporate Finance Journal* (Fall 1985), pp. 49–52.

junk bonds or high-yield bonds
bonds with ratings that are below investment grade, that is, that are Ba1, BB+, or lower

INTERNET ACTIVITY

Learn about the rating agencies and their processes at the following Web sites:
http://www.standardandpoors.com,
http://www.moodys.com, and
http://www.fitchratings.com.

A bond's security or collateral provisions (discussed below) affect its credit rating. Bonds with junior or unsecured claims receive lower bond ratings, leading investors to demand higher yields to compensate for the higher risk. Thus, bond issues of a single firm can have different bond ratings if their security provisions differ.

Viewing Table 10.3, investment grade bonds are those with ratings of Baa3, BBB-, or better. They are called "investment grade" as historically investors (both individuals and managed funds, such as bank trust department portfolios and pension funds) were allowed to invest in such bonds. Bonds below "investment grade" were deemed too risky for such conservative portfolios and were not allowed to be held.

Times and regulations change, however, and bonds that are below investment grade, that is, that have ratings of Ba1, BB+, or lower, have gained a spot in many investment portfolios. Known as **junk bonds** or (euphemistically) **high-yield bonds**, they are higher risk, but offer higher expected returns, and do have benefits in lowering unsystematic risk in diversified portfolios. Formerly, issuing companies would seek the highest bond rating possible for new issues for two reasons. First, having high-rated debt added prestige to the company; an AAA-rated firm was viewed as being well managed, financially stable, and strong. In addition, such bonds gave the appearance of a safe investment and as they were investment-grade would find demand by investors such as trust departments and pension funds. The second main reason for seeking a high bond rating is that the higher rating saves the firm interest expense as coupon rates on highly-rated bonds are lower (because of the risk-expected return tradeoff) than lower-rated bonds.

The growth of the high-yield sector of the bond market has attracted both investors and issuers. Some firms prefer to issue debt rather than dividend-paying common stock as interest payments are tax-deductible to the issuer. Others, as part of the firm's financial strategy, have issued bonds and used the funds to repurchase shares of common stock. Investors have noted that having junk bonds in a portfolio offers potential return enhancements and may help to diversify risk.

Over time, the stigma attached to "junk" bonds has diminished. Both issuers and investors are more amenable to these securities. For example, in 1980 less than a third of S&P-rated bonds were not investment-quality—and many of those were "fallen angels," that is, bonds that were originally issued as investment grade but whose rates fell into the junk category because the issuing firm ran into financial difficulty.

By the late 1980s, more than half of rated debt was in the high-yield category, and by 2007, over 70 percent of S&P-rated firms had junk bonds outstanding. The number of AAA and AA-rated companies fell from 17 percent of issuers in 1980 to only 2 percent in 2007; B-rated bonds, on the other hands, have grown from 7 percent of issues in 1980 to over 40 percent of issues in 2007. Only four nonfinancial firms had an AAA rating in mid-2010: Automatic Data Processing, ExxonMobil, Johnson & Johnson, and Microsoft.[5]

BONDHOLDER SECURITY

An important attribute of a bond issue that affects its rating is the security, collateral, or assets that are pledged to back the bond issue. In case the bond issuer defaults and misses a payment of coupon interest or principal, the collateral can be sold and distributed to the bond investors. It helps make their investment in the issue more secure. There are a number of different types of bonds, each offering different levels of security to their investors.

Mortgage bonds, despite their name, are not secured by home mortgages! Rather, they are backed or secured by specifically pledged property of a firm. As a rule, the mortgage applies only to real estate, buildings, and other assets classified as real property. For a corporation that issues bonds to expand its plant facilities, the mortgage usually includes only a lien, or legal claim, on the facilities to be constructed.

---

[5]. Reuters, "S&P strips Pfizer's AAA rating on Wyeth acquisition", October 16, 2009, accessed at http://www.reuters.com/article/companyNews/idUKN1636373320091016 on October 17, 2009; Sereno Ng, "Junk Turns Golden, but May Be Laced With Tinsel, *The Wall Street Journal*, January 4, 2007, pp. C1, C2; Nicholas Riccio, "The Rise Of 'B' Rated Companies And Their Staying Power As An Asset Class," S&P's *CreditWeek*, January 3, 2007.

When a parcel of real estate has more than one mortgage lien against it, the first mortgage filed for recording at the appropriate government office, generally the county recorder's office, has priority. The bonds outstanding against the mortgage are known as *first mortgage bonds.* The bonds outstanding against all mortgages subsequently recorded are known by the order in which they are filed, such as second or third mortgage bonds. Because first mortgage bonds have priority with respect to asset distribution if the business fails, they generally provide a lower yield to investors than the later liens. An *equipment trust certificate* is a type of mortgage bond that gives the bondholder a claim to specific "rolling stock" (movable assets), such as railroad cars or airplanes. The serial numbers of the specific items of rolling stock are listed in the bond indenture and the collateral is periodically examined by the trustee to ensure its proper maintenance and repair.

There are two basic types of mortgage bonds. A *closed-end mortgage bond* does not permit future bond issues to be secured by any of the assets pledged as security under the closed-end issue. Alternatively, an *open-end mortgage bond* is one that allows the same assets to be used as security in future issues. As a rule, open-end mortgages usually stipulate that any additional real property acquired by the company automatically becomes a part of the property secured under the mortgage. This provides added protection to the lender.

Debenture bonds are unsecured obligations and depend on the general credit strength of the corporation for their security. They represent no specific pledge of property; their holders are classed as general creditors of the corporation equal with the holders of promissory notes and trade creditors. Debenture bonds are used by governmental bodies and by many industrial and utility corporations. The riskiest type of bond is a *subordinated debenture.* As the name implies, the claims of these bondholders are subordinate, or junior, to the claims of debenture holders. Most junk bonds or high-yield bonds, which we discussed earlier, are subordinated debentures.

Another bond market innovation is "asset securitization." Securitization involves issuing bonds whose coupon and principal payments arise from another existing cash flow stream. Suppose a mortgage lender by virtue of previously issued mortgages has a steady cash flow stream coming into the firm. By selling bonds that use that cash flow stream as collateral, the mortgage banker can receive funds today rather than waiting for the mortgages to be paid off over time.[6] Principal and interest on the newly issued bonds will be paid by homeowners' mortgage payments; in essence, the mortgage payments will "pass through" the original mortgage lender to the investor who purchased the mortgage-backed securities. Not all the interest payments are passed on, however; the mortgage lender will be paid a servicing fee from these cash flows to compensate them for collecting the mortgage payments and distributing them to the bond holders.

Securitization allows the original lender to reduce its risk exposure, as any homeowner defaults are now a risk borne by the investor. In addition, the lender receives new funds, which can, in turn, form the basis for new loans and new issues of mortgage-backed securities. In 2007–2008, the agency issues of this arrangement become clearly known. It led to efforts to encourage loans of questionable quality ("subprime" mortgage loans) as the loans would be packaged, sold to others, and the originator would reap a commission while selling poor-quality loans to others.

Many other cash flow streams are amenable to securitization. Payment streams based on credit card receivables and auto loans have been packaged as bonds and sold to investors. Music artists who collect royalties from past recordings have taken advantage of securitization. In 1997, British rock star David Bowie initiated this trend by his involvement in a $55 million bond deal in which royalty rights from his past recordings were pooled and sold to investors. Interest on the bonds will be paid by the royalty cash flow generated by compact disk, radio playtime and music and ringtone downloads.[7] Other innovations include offering bonds backed by pools of insurance contracts. Interest on such bonds is paid from the policy premiums of the contract

---

first mortgage bonds backed or secured by specifically pledged property of a firm (real estate, buildings, and other assets classified as real property)

equipment trust certificate gives the bondholder a claim to specific 'rolling stock' (movable assets), such as railroad cars or airplanes

closed-end mortgage bond does not permit future bond issues to be secured by any of the assets pledged as security to it

open-end mortgage bond allows the same assets to be used as security in future issues

debenture bonds unsecured obligations that depend on the general credit strength of the corporation for their security

ETHICAL ISSUES

subordinate debenture claims of these bonds are subordinate or junior to the claims of the debenture holders

---

6. Collateralized bonds pledge securities to protect bondholders against loss in case of default. An example of collateralized bonds is collateralized mortgage obligations (CMOs) sold by firms and agencies involved in the housing market. The CMO is backed by a pool of mortgages. Frank J. Fabozzi, *Fixed Income Analysis* (New Hope, PA; Frank J. Fabozzi Associates, 2000) and Frank J. Fabozzi with Steven V. Mann, ed., *The Handbook of Fixed-Income Securities*, 7th edition, (Chicago, IL: McGraw-Hill, 2005).

7. Karen Richardson, "Bankers Hope For a Reprise of 'Bowie Bonds'" *The Wall Street Journal*, August 23, 2005, pp. C1, C3; anonymous, "Iron Maiden Bank Finishes $30 Million Sale of Bonds," *Wall Street Journal* (February 9, 1999), p. C23.I.S., "Bowie Ch-Ch-Changes the Market," *CFO* (April 1997); see also Patrick McGeehan, "Rock 'n' Roll Bonds Tap Investors' Faith in Future Royalties," *Wall Street Journal* (February 10, 1998), p. C21.

holders. Many times, however, these bonds have provisions for future payoffs that are affected by the existence of catastrophes such as hurricanes or earthquakes.[8]

TIME TO MATURITY

A straight bond will have a set time to maturity. That is, it will pay coupon interest every six months until the bond matures, at which time the final interest payment is made and the bond's par value is paid to investors. But a variety of features can affect the bond's final maturity.

Geography can play a role. U.S. firms routinely issue bonds with ten- to thirty-year maturities (and even longer in some instances). Bonds in the European market rarely extend their maturity past the seven-to-ten-year range, but this may change over time as European firms are starting to access the capital markets more and rely on bank debt less for their longer-term financing needs.[9]

A *convertible bond* can be changed or converted, at the investor's option, into a specified number of shares of the issuer's common stock (defined as the bond's *conversion ratio*). The conversion ratio is set initially to make conversion unattractive. If the firm meets with success, however, its stock price will rise and the bond's price will be affected by its *conversion value* (the stock price times the conversion ratio) rather than just its value as a straight bond. For example, suppose a firm has just issued a $1,000 par value convertible bond. Its conversion ratio is 30 and the stock currently sells for $25 a share. The conversion value of the bond is 30 × $25/share or $750. It makes sense to hold onto the bond rather than convert a bond with a purchase price of about $1,000 into stock that is worth only $750. Should the stock's price rise to $40, the bond's conversion value will be 30 × $40/share or $1,200. Now it may be appropriate for an investor to convert his bond into the more valuable shares. Why would a firm issue convertible bonds? Some may do so as way to raise equity at a time when either the firm's stock or the overall stock market is out of favor. By selling convertible bonds, they can raise capital now and erase the debt from their books when the bonds are converted after the stock price rises.

Callable bonds can be redeemed prior to maturity by the firm. Such bonds will be called and redeemed if, for example, a decline in interest rates makes it attractive for the firm to issue lower coupon debt to replace high-coupon debt. A firm with cash from successful marketing efforts or a recent stock issue also may decide to retire its callable debt.

Most indentures state that, if called, callable bonds must be redeemed at their **call prices**, typically par value plus a call premium of one year's interest. Thus, to call a 12 percent coupon, $1,000 par value bond, an issuer must pay the bondholder $1,120.

Investors in callable bonds are said to be subject to **call risk**. Despite receiving the call price, investors are usually not pleased when their bonds are called away. As bonds are typically called after a substantial decline in interest rates, the call eliminates their high coupon payments; investors will have to reinvest the proceeds in bonds that offer lower yields.

In order to attract investors, callable bonds must offer higher coupons or yields than noncallable bonds of similar credit quality and maturity. Many indentures specify a **call deferment period** immediately after the bond issue during which the bonds cannot be called.

Putable bonds (sometimes called *retractable bonds*) allow investors to force the issuer to redeem them prior to maturity. Indenture terms differ as to the circumstances when an investor can "put" the bond to the issuer prior to the maturity date and receive its par value. Some bond issues can be put only on certain dates. Some can be put to the issuer in case of a bond rating downgrade.[10] The put option allows the investor to receive the full face value of the bond, plus accrued interest. Since this protection is valuable, investors "pay" for it in the form of a lower coupon rate.

Extendable notes have their coupons reset every two or three years to reflect the current interest rate environment and any changes in the firm's credit quality. At each reset, the investor may accept the new coupon rate (and thus effectively extend the maturity of the investment) or put the bonds back to the firm.

An indenture may require the firm to retire the bond issue over time through payments to a sinking fund. A **sinking fund** requires the issuer to retire specified portions of the bond issue over time. This provides for an orderly and steady retirement of debt over time. Sinking funds are more common in bonds issued by firms with lower credit ratings. A higher-quality issuer

---

GLOBAL DISCUSSION

convertible bond
can be changed or converted, at the investor's option, into a specific number of shares of the issuer's common stock

conversion ratio
number of shares into which a convertible bond can be converted

conversion value
stock price times the conversion ratio

callable bonds
can be redeemed prior to maturity by the issuing firm

call price
price paid to the investor for redemption prior to maturity, typically par value plus a call premium of one year's interest

call risk
risk of having a bond called away and reinvesting the proceeds at a lower interest rate

call deferment period
specified period of time after the issue during which the bonds cannot be called

putable bonds (retractable bonds)
allow the investor to force the issuer to redeem the bonds prior to maturity

extendable notes
have their coupons reset every two or three years to reflect the current interest rate environment and any changes in the firm's creditworthiness; the investor can accept the new coupon rate or put the bonds back to the firm

---

8. Patrick McGeehan, "Investment Banks Are Moving Fast to Offer Securities Backed by Pools of Insurance Policies," *Wall Street Journal* (June 15, 1998), p. C4.
9. Aline van Duyn, "Euro Corporate Bonds Give the Dollar a Run for its Money," *Financial Times* (June 29, 2001), p. 16.
10. Another way to offer protection in the face of a ratings downgrade is for the issues' coupon rate to rise to compensate for the higher credit risk.

sinking fund
requirement that the firm retire specific portions of the bond issue over time

may have only a small annual sinking fund obligation due to a perceived ability to repay investor's principal at maturity.

INCOME FROM BONDS

A typical bond will pay a fixed amount of interest each year over the bond's life. As we noted above, U.S. bonds pay interest semi-annually while Eurobonds pay interest annually.

Although most bonds pay a fixed coupon rate, some bonds have coupon payments that vary over time. The bond's indenture may tie coupon payments to an underlying market interest rate so that the interest payment will always be a certain level above or will be a specified percentage of a market interest rate, such as the ten-year Treasury note rate. Others, such as the Deutsche Telekom bond issue mentioned above, will have a coupon rate that will increase if the bond's rating falls.

Zero coupon bonds pay no interest over the life of the bond. The investor buys the bond at a steep discount from its par value; the return to the investor over time is the difference between the purchase price and the bond's par value when it matures. A drawback to taxable investors is that the IRS assumes interest is paid over the life of the bond so the investor must pay tax on interest he or she doesn't receive. Because of these tax implications, zero coupon bonds are best suited for tax-exempt investment accounts, such as IRAs, or tax-exempt investment organizations, such as pension funds.

Why would an investor purchase a zero-coupon bond? Many bond investors have long-term time horizons before the invested funds are needed (to pay for a child's college education, personal retirement, or other financial goals). Such investors will not spend the bond's coupon interest when it is received; they will re-invest it in other securities. When these investors purchase regular bonds, they face the risk of not knowing what the return will be on the re-invested coupons over the life of the bond. Interest rates may rise, fall, or cycle up and down over the life of the investment. Zero coupon bonds eliminate this uncertainty by, in essence, locking in the return (the difference between the price paid and the par value) when the bond is purchased.

A large risk faced by bond investors is an unexpected change in inflation. An unexpected increase in inflation can cause lower real returns to an investor as the bond's fixed interest rate does not adjust to varying inflation. In 1997, the U.S. Treasury offered an innovation to investors in U.S. debt: inflation-protected Treasury notes.[11] Issued in $1,000 minimum denominations, the principal value of the notes change in accordance with changes in the consumer price index (CPI).[12]

Here's how Treasury Inflation Protected Securities (TIPS) work: Interest payments are computed based upon the inflation-adjusted principal value. In times of rising consumer prices, both the principal value and interest payments rise in line with inflation. Should the CPI fall, the principal amount is reduced accordingly. As an example, suppose an inflation-indexed note with a $1,000 par value is sold at a 3 percent interest rate. If inflation over the next year is 4 percent, the principal value rises to $1,000 plus 4 percent or $1,040. The annual interest payment will be 3 percent of $1,040, $0.03 \times \$1,040$, or $31.20. With 4 percent inflation, the principal rises by 4 percent ($1,000 to $1,040) as well as the interest ($30 to $31.20).

Although the principal is not paid until the note matures, the IRS considers the year-by-year change in principal as taxable income in the year in which the change in value is made. In the above example, the investor will pay taxes on $71.20—the $31.20 in interest received and the $40 increase in principal value. Because of this, these bonds will be most attractive to tax-exempt or tax-deferred investors, such as pension funds and individual IRA accounts.[13] To make the inflation protection more affordable to smaller investors, in 1998 the U.S. Treasury announced plans to offer inflation-protected U.S. savings bonds.[14]

---

11. Inflation-adjusted bonds have been offered by other countries for some time. For example, Israel first offered these securities in 1955; the UK in 1981; Australia in 1985; Canada in 1991; and Sweden in 1994.

12. Because of the initial popularity of the inflation-adjusted T-notes, some federal agencies (Federal Home Loan Bank Board, TVA) have issued inflation-indexed notes as well.

13. Gregory Zuckerman, "Inflation-Indexed Bonds Attract Fans," *Wall Street Journal* (May 20, 1999) p. C1; Pu Shen, "Features and Risks of Treasury Inflation Protection Securities," Federal Reserve Bank of Kansas City *Economic Review* (first quarter, 1998), pp. 23–38.

14. In addition, several corporations, such as Merrill Lynch, Morgan Stanley, Household International, Fannie Mae, and Sallie May, have issued inflation-protected bonds. Several banks, for example LaSalle Bank and Standard Federal Bank, have inflation-protected certificates of deposit. See Aaron Lucchetti, "Inflation Rears its Head . . . If Only on New Bond Issues," *Wall Street Journal* (January 28, 2004) pp. C1, C4; Christine Richard, "Corporations, Banks Issue Debt With an Inflation-Wary Hook," *Wall Street Journal* (September 24, 2003), p. C5.

CONCEPT CHECK

What information does a bond rating give to investors?

How does a collateralized bond differ from a mortgage bond?

Which offer investors greater protection: a mortgage bond, a debenture, or a subordinated debenture? Why?

Explain what a conversion feature does on a bond. What does it mean when a bond is callable?

GLOBAL DISCUSSION

Eurodollar bonds
dollar denominated bonds sold outside the United States

Yankee bonds
dollar denominated bonds issued in the United States by a foreign issuer

global bonds
generally denominated in U.S. dollars and marketed globally

Why are there so many variations in bondholder security, maturity, and income payouts among bond issues? For the same reason why there are different computers, carbonated beverages, and pizza: namely, to meet different needs in the market, or in the case of bonds, to meet the needs of different types of borrowers and lenders. Some borrowers reduce borrowing costs by offering lenders better collateral; other want to maintain flexibility (or they have no collateral to offer) so they issue debentures and pay higher interest rates. From the lenders' perspective, zero-coupon bonds may be attractive as they eliminate reinvestment risk (the risk of reinvesting coupon income at lower interest rates). Similarly, sinking funds, call, put, or convertibility provisions are attractive to different investors in ever-changing market environments.

GLOBAL BOND MARKET

Many U.S. corporations have issued Eurodollar bonds. **Eurodollar bonds** are dollar-denominated bonds that are sold outside the United States. Because of this, they escape review by the SEC, somewhat reducing the expense of issuing the bonds. Eurodollar bonds usually have fixed coupons with annual coupon payments. Most mature in five to ten years, so they are not attractive for firms that want to issue long-term debt. Most Eurodollar bonds are debentures. This is not a major concern to investors, as only the largest, financially strongest firms have access to the Eurobond market. Investors *do* care that the bonds are sold in bearer form, because investors can remain anonymous and evade taxes on coupon income. Some researchers believe that this is the main reason that Eurodollar bond interest rates are low relative to U.S. rates.[15]

U.S. firms aren't the only issuers of securities outside their national borders. For example, foreign firms can issue securities in the United States if they follow U.S. security registration procedures. **Yankee bonds** are U.S. dollar-denominated bonds that are issued in the United States by a foreign issuer. Some issuers find the longer maturities of Yankees attractive to meet long-term financing needs. While Eurodollar bonds typically mature in five to ten years, Yankees may have maturities as long as thirty years. Nonetheless, the euro (€) is becoming a strong competitor to the U.S. dollar for firms that want to raise funds in a currency that has broad appeal to many investors.[16]

Increasingly, the international bond market is ignoring national boundaries. A growing number of debt issues are being sold globally. In 1989, the World Bank was the first issuer of **global bonds.** Global bonds usually are denominated in U.S. dollars. As they are marketed globally, their offering sizes typically exceed $1 billion. In addition to the World Bank, issuers include the governments of Finland and Italy and corporations such as Deutsche Telekom ($14.5 billion raised), Ford Motor Credit ($8.6 billion), Tecnost International Finance (Neteherlands) ($8.3 billion), AT&T ($8 billion), Glitnir Bank (Iceland) ($1.25 billion), and Wal-Mart ($5.8 billion).

READING BOND QUOTES

Figure 10.2 shows some of the bond quotation information that is available in the financial press or websites such as http://finance.yahoo.com and http://wsjmarkets.com. The exhibit highlights a bond quote for a hypothetical bond issued by Ford Motor Credit, the subsidiary of Ford Motor that raises funds to finance car loans and leases.

The ticker symbol (F) refers to Ford's common stock; in stock trading ticker symbols are used as a shorthand notation rather than full company names. The Ford Credit bond has a coupon rate of 7.000 percent. If its par value is $1,000, as are most corporate bonds, then Ford Credit pays interest of 7 percent of $1,000, or 0.0700 × 1,000 = $70.00 per year or $35.00 every six months.

FIGURE 10.2
Sample Bond Quotation

COMPANY (TICKER)	COUPON	MATURITY	LAST PRICE	LAST YIELD	SPREAD	UST	EST. $ VOL (000S)
Ford Motor Credit (F)	7.000	2013	105.296	6.252	236	5	230,068

---

15. W. Marr and J. Trimble, "The Persistent Borrowing Advantage of Eurodollar Bonds: A Plausible Explanation," *Journal of Applied Corporate Finance* (Summer 1988), pp. 65–70.

16. Aline van Duyn, "Euro Corporate Bonds Give the Dollar a Run for its Money," *Financial Times* (June 29, 2001), p. 16.

CHAPTER TEN • Bonds and Stocks: Characteristics and Valuations

PERSONAL FINANCIAL PLANNING
Investing in Ladders and Barbells

As a first introduction to stocks and bonds, this chapter is filled with applications to personal finance. From knowledge about the different types of stocks and bonds to how to read the stock and bond listings in the paper to basic valuation principles, all these tools and concepts can be used by individual investors as well as professionals.

Let's look at one application for a bond investor. Because of the "seesaw effect," lower interest rates cause bond prices to rise and higher interest rates causes lower bond prices. But the yield curve doesn't just shift up and down over time. Sometimes it twists: this means that short-term rates rise while long-term rates are stable or falling or long-term rates rise while short-term rates are stable or falling. To avoid having their holdings hit by sudden moves in short-term or long-term rates, some investors employ a 'ladder' strategy.

This strategy invests an equal amount of money in bonds over a range of maturities, so interest rate cycles will average out over the business cycle to reduce the bond investor's risk. Other chose a 'barbell' approach, with approximately equal amounts of short-term bonds and long-term bonds purchased. By clumping holdings at either end of the maturity spectrum, the investor hopes to smooth out the effect of interest rate fluctuations on his bond portfolio.

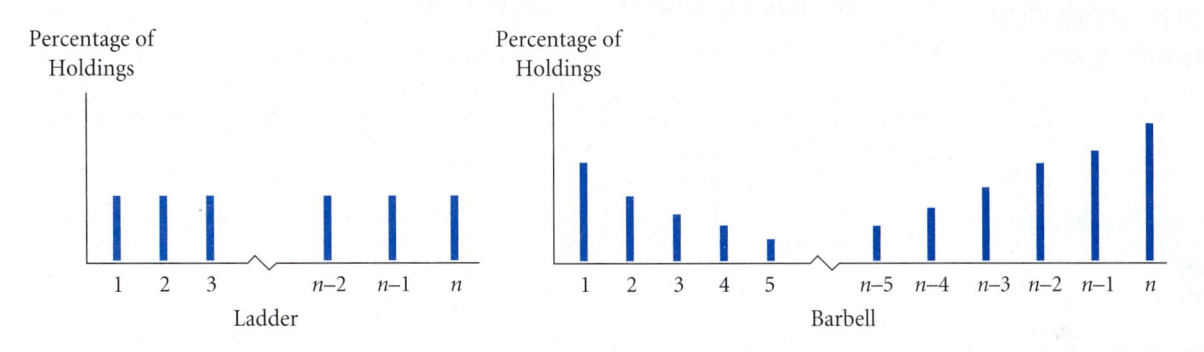

The bond matures (that is, the principal repayment comes due) on October 1, 2013. The "Last Price" reports the closing price of the bond, expressed as a percentage of par value. Since its par value is $1,000, a closing price 105.296 percent of par gives a value for the bond of $1,052.96.

A commonly used term that is simple to compute is the current yield of a bond. We calculate current yield by dividing the annual coupon interest by the current price. The Ford Credit bond's current yield is $70.00/$1,052.96 = 6.65 percent. The current yield does not adequately represent the return on a bond investment is it considers income return only and ignores price changes.

The yield to maturity is a better measure of investor return on a bond and is shown by the "Last Yield" in Figure 10.2. Yield to maturity represents an estimate of the investor's return on the bond if it was purchased today and held to maturity. We calculate the yield to maturity using the bond's coupon, par value, last price, and time to maturity. Later we will learn to compute a bond's yield to maturity. Here the yield is presented to us as 6.252 percent.

The "Estimated Spread" is the difference between the yield to maturity on the Ford Credit bond and a similar maturity U.S. Treasury bond. Here, the spread is 236 basis points or 2.36 percent (one basis point represents 0.01 percentage points). The spread is computed from the yield to maturity on a Treasury security that matures in five years, as seen by the number under the "UST" column. Since any corporate bond is riskier than Treasury securities because of default or credit risk, the spread will always be positive. Since the Ford Credit bond has a yield to maturity of 6.252 percent, the five-year Treasury security must have a yield to maturity of about 6.252 percent − 2.36 percent = 3.89 percent.

The "Vol" column represents actual bond trading volume in thousands of dollars for this Ford Credit bond. The market value (quantity traded times last price) of the trading volume is $230,068,000. With a last price of $1,052.96, the approximate number of this type of Ford Credit bond that traded is $230,068,000/$1,052.96 = 218496.

A typical price quote in the financial pages for Treasury bonds is:

RATE	MATURITY MO/YR	BID	ASKED	CHG.	ASKED YLD
4.000	Feb 14	100:27	100:28	−1	3.89

INTERNET ACTIVITY

Learn more about the bond market and prices at www.bonds-online.com and www.investinginbonds.com.

CONCEPT CHECK

What is a current yield?

What does the "Est. Spread" mean in the Ford Credit bond quote in Figure 10.2?

corporate equity capital
financial capital supplied by the owners of a corporation

stock certificate
certificate showing an ownership claim of a specific company

The coupon rate for the bond is 4.000 percent of par value, meaning that a $1,000 par value bond will pay $40 of interest annually, in two semi-annual payments of $20. The bond matures in February of 2014. Treasury bond prices are expressed as percentages of par value and in 32nds of a point. The bid price, which is the price received by investors selling bonds, is 100 27/32 percent of par, or $1,008.4375. The ask price, which is paid by investors purchasing the bonds, is 100 28/32 of par or $1,008.75. The bid-ask spread represents dealer profit, or $0.3125 per $1,000 par value bond. Spreads are often an indicator of how liquid a security is; the narrower the bid-ask spread, the greater the liquidity (and, usually, the greater the trading volume). The change in price from the previous day was −1/32 of a percentage point. The yield to maturity, based on the asked price, is 3.89 percent. Note that this is the same bond used as the "UST" bond in the Ford Credit quote in Table 10.1. The five-year Treasury security yield to maturity we estimated above agrees with the data in the Treasury security quote.[17]

CORPORATE EQUITY CAPITAL

Corporate equity capital is the financial capital supplied by the owners of a corporation. This ownership claim is represented by the ***stock certificate,*** as shown in Figure 10.3, although today most record-keeping is done electronically. Shares are usually traded 100 shares at a time (called a "round lot") or multiples thereof.

When a stockholder sells his or her shares, the broker forwards the assigned stock certificate to the company and the secretary of the corporation destroys it. A new certificate is issued to the new owner, whose name will then be carried on the stock record. For larger corporations an official transfer agent, generally a trust company or a bank, is appointed for this task. The larger corporations may also have an independent stock registrar to supervise the transfer of securities. When an investor sells stock, the stock certificate must be delivered to the stockbroker within

FIGURE 10.3
Common Stock Certificates

---

17. A fine point: the asked yield in the Treasury security quote will slightly understate the true yield to maturity. It is determined by computing the semiannual yield given the coupon payments, ask price, and par value and then doubling it. To be exact, we would compound the semiannual yield over two half-year periods. That is, if the reported Asked Yield is 3.89 percent, the computed semiannual yield is 3.89/2, or 1.945 per cent. Compounding this over two semiannual periods gives a truer estimate of the yield to maturity, $(1 + 0.01945)^2 - 1$, which equals 3.93 percent.

three business days (called T + 3). When stock is purchased, adequate funds must be brought to the broker within three business days. As technology advances, so do regulations; in past years the requirement was T + 5; it is now T + 3; in the planning stages is the requirement for T + 1 for settling trades. Instantaneous settlement, called STP or straight through processing, will occur when all systems are electronically tied together.

Stock certificates can be kept in the owner's name and in his or her possession. Many investors find it convenient, however, to keep their stock holdings in *street name.* Stock held in street name is kept in the name of the brokerage house, but the broker's accounting system keeps track of dividends, proxy voting, and so on. Some investors find it convenient to keep shares in street name; there is no need for the investor to safeguard the certificates, and delivery of the certificates within the T + 3 time frame is automatic.

Equity securities of the corporation may be grouped broadly into two classes: common stock and preferred stock. We discuss each below.

> *street name*
> allows stock to be held in the name of the brokerage house

COMMON STOCK

Common stock (see Table 10.4) represents ownership shares in a corporation. Ownership gives common stockholders certain rights and privileges that bondholders do not have. Common shareholders can vote to select the corporation's board of directors. The board of directors, in turn, exercises general control over the firm. In addition to voting for the board, common shareholders may also vote on major issues facing the firm, such as corporate charter changes and mergers.

> *common stock*
> represents ownership shares in a corporation

The common shareholders have a claim on all business profits that remain after the holders of all other classes of debt and equity securities have received their coupon payments or returns. But the firm may wish to retain some of those profits to reinvest in the firm to finance modernization, expansion, and growth. When so declared by the board of directors, owners of a firm's common stock receive dividend payments. The dividend is typically a cash payment that allows shareholders to receive some income from their investment. To many investors, an attractive characteristic of common stock dividends is their potential to increase over time. As a firm achieves success, its profits should grow and the shareholders can expect to see the dollar amount of their dividends rise. Of course, success and growth are not guaranteed! A firm may experience poor earnings or losses, in which case shareholders bear the risk of smaller dividends or even the elimination of dividend payments until the firm's financial situation improves.

The common stockholders have the lowest standing when a business venture is liquidated or fails. All creditors, bond holders, and preferred stockholders must, as a rule, be paid in full before common stockholders receive proceeds from liquidation. As with dividends, all bankruptcy or liquidation proceeds remaining after prior obligations are settled accrue to the common stockholders, but it is rare when the proceeds of an asset sale from a bankrupt corporation fulfill the claims of creditors and preferred stockholders. Common stockholders generally receive little, if anything, from liquidation proceedings. The common stockholders, therefore, are affected hardest by business failure, just as they enjoy the primary benefits of business success.

TABLE 10.4
Elements of Common Stock

- Represents an ownership claim
- Board of Directors oversees the firm on behalf of the shareholders and enforces the corporate charter
- Voting rights for Board members and other important issues allowed by the corporate charter
- Lowest claim on assets and cash flow
- Par value is meaningless, many firms have very low or no-par stock
- Dividends: Received only if declared by the firm's Board
  Are paid out from after-tax earnings and cash flow; they are not tax deductible
  Dividends are taxable when received by the shareholder
  Can vary over time
- Maturity: Never; stock remains in existence until firm goes bankrupt, merges with another firm, or is acquired by another firm

par value
stated value of a stock; accounting and legal concept bearing no relationship to a firm's stock price or book value

The common stock of a corporation may be assigned a **par value**, or stated value, in the certificate of incorporation. It usually bears little relationship to the current price or book value of the stock. It is used mainly for accounting purposes and some legal needs.[18]

Common stock may be divided into special groups, generally Class A and Class B, in order to permit the acquisition of additional capital without diluting the control of the business. When a corporation issues two classes of common stock, it will often give voting rights to only one class, generally Class B. Except for voting, owners of Class A stock will usually have most, if not all, of the other rights and privileges of common stockholders. Issuing nonvoting equity securities is opposed by some government agencies, including the Securities and Exchange Commission, because it permits the concentration of ownership control. The New York Stock Exchange refuses to list the common stock of corporations that issue nonvoting classes of common stock.

At times, different stock classes are created following an acquisition of one corporation by another. For example, General Motors' Class E shares and Class H shares were issued in the past to help finance GM's acquisition of EDS and Hughes Aircraft, respectively. The dividends on GM's Class E and H shares were related to the earnings of their respective subsidiary.

ADRs, or American Depository Receipts, represent shares of common stock that trade on a foreign stock exchange. The receipts can be traded on U.S. exchanges. We'll learn more about ADRs in Chapter 11, Securities Markets.

CONCEPT CHECK

What rights and privileges do common shareholders have that bondholders do not?

What extra risks do shareholders face that bondholders do not?

PREFERRED STOCK

preferred stock
equity security that has preference, or a senior claim, to the firm's earnings and assets over common stock

Preferred stock (see Table 10.5) is an equity security that has a preference, or senior claim, to the firm's earnings and assets over common stock. Preferred shareholders must receive their fixed dividend before common shareholders can receive a dividend. In liquidation, the claims of the preferred shareholders are to be satisfied before common shareholders receive any proceeds. In contrast with common stock, preferred stock generally carries a stated fixed dividend. The dividend is specified as either a percentage of par value or as a fixed number of dollars per year. For example, a preferred stock may be a 9 percent preferred, meaning that its annual dividend is 9 percent of its par or stated value. In such cases, unlike common stock, a preferred stock's par value does have important meaning, much like par value for a bond! The dividend for no-par preferred stock is stated in terms of a dollar amount, for example, preferred as to dividends in the amount of $9 annually. The holder of preferred stock accepts the limitation on the amount of dividends as a fair exchange for the priority held in the earnings and assets of the company.

Thus, unlike with common stock, the par value of a preferred stock is important: dividends often are expressed as a percentage of par and the par value represents the holder's claim on corporate assets in case of liquidation. Additionally, when shares of preferred stock are first issued, the initial selling price is frequently close to the share's par value.[19]

TABLE 10.5
Elements of Preferred Stock

- Does not represent an ownership claim
- No voting rights unless dividends are missed
- Claim on assets and cash flow lies between those of bondholders (specifically, subordinated debenture holders) and common shareholders
- Par value is meaningful as it can determine the fixed annual dividend
- Dividends: Annual dividends are stated either as a dollar amount or as a percentage of par value
    Received only if declared by the firm's board
    Are paid out from after-tax earnings and cash flow; they are not tax deductible
    Dividends are taxable when received by the shareholder
    May be cumulative
- Maturity: Unless it has a callable or convertible feature, the stock never matures; it remains in existence until firm goes bankrupt, merges with another firm, or is acquired by another firm

---

18. To show further that par value has little significance, consider that most states permit corporations to issue no-par stock.

19. A recent innovation is *hybrid capital*, a security that is concerned equity for accounting purposes but whose payments to security holders are tax-deductible to the firm—thus it appears to be a perfect combination of advantages of both equity and debt. The details of issuing such capital can be difficult and involve aspects of accounting treatment, securities law, and bank regulation and so are beyond the scope of our discussion.

CHAPTER TEN ○ Bonds and Stocks: Characteristics and Valuations

---

cumulative preferred stock
requires that before dividends on common stock are paid, preferred dividends must be paid not only for the current period, but also for all previous periods in which preferred dividends were missed

noncumulative preferred stock
makes no provision for the accumulation of past missed dividends

callable preferred stock
gives the corporation the right to retire the preferred stock at its option

convertible preferred stock
has a special provision that makes it possible to convert it to common stock of the corporation, generally at the stockholder's option

participating preferred stock
allows preferred shareholders to receive a larger dividend under certain conditions when common shareholder dividends increase

---

CONCEPT CHECK

How is preferred stock similar to a bond? To common stock?

What is meant by the term "cumulative" preferred stock?

Because preferred stocks are frequently nonvoting, many corporations issue them as a means of obtaining equity capital without diluting the control of the current stockholders. Unlike coupon interest on bonds, the fixed preferred stock dividend is not a tax-deductible expense. A major source of preferred stock issues are regulated public utilities, such as gas and electric companies. For regulated firms, the nondeductibility of dividends is not as much of a concern as for other firms, because the utilities' tax payments affect the rates they are allowed to charge.

For foreign firms to issue preferred stock, they must do so in the United States. The U.S. security markets are the only public financial markets in which preferred stock is sold.

Preferred stock may have special features. For example, it may be cumulative or noncumulative. **Cumulative preferred stock** requires that before dividends on common stock are paid, preferred dividends must be paid not only for the current period but also for all previous periods in which preferred dividends were missed. It is important to remember that, unlike debt holders, the preferred stockholders cannot force the payment of their dividends. They may have to wait until earnings are adequate to pay dividends. Cumulative preferred stock offers some protection for periods during which dividends are not declared.

Noncumulative preferred stock, on the other hand, makes no provision for the accumulation of unpaid dividends. The result may be that management may be tempted to declare preferred dividends only when it appears that sufficient earnings are available to pay common stock dividends as well. Practically all modern preferred stock is cumulative.

Callable preferred stock gives the corporation the right to retire the preferred stock at its option. **Convertible preferred stock** has a special provision that makes it possible to convert it to common stock of the corporation, generally at the stockholder's option. This, like many of the special features that preferred stock may have, exists primarily to attract investors to buy securities at times when distribution would otherwise be difficult. Preferred stock that is both cumulative and convertible is a popular financing choice for investors purchasing shares of stock in small firms with high growth potential.

Participating preferred stock allows preferred shareholders to participate with common shareholders when larger dividend payouts are available. Holders get a larger dividend, if sufficient earnings exist and if common shareholders will be getting a dividend larger than the preferred shareholders. It is a rarely used feature except in some private equity and venture capital investments.

The one tax advantage of preferred stock goes to corporate investors who purchase another firm's preferred. When one corporation buys stock of another firm, 70 percent of the dividend income received by the corporation is exempt from taxes. Thus, for every $100 of dividend income, only $30 is taxable to an investing corporation.

READING STOCK QUOTES

Information on stock prices is available for a number of print resources (such as *The Wall Street Journal* and other newspapers with financial sections) and the Internet. Figure 10.4 shows stock quotation information that is available on these print and online resources.

The information from print sources reflects trading that occurred on the previous business day; online information many times reflects current trading information but with a 15–20 minute delay in reporting. Information, such as that presented in Figure 10.4, is available on stock prices, recent trends or volatility in prices, the dividend paid by the company, and its earnings per share.

For example, Figure 10.4 shows Microsoft's ticker symbol, MSFT. Tickers are shorthand notation for a stock. Rather than keying in a firm's full name many times only the ticker need be entered to obtain information. Microsoft's stock is traded on the NASDAQ, an over-the-counter exchange we'll discuss in Chapter 11. At the time this information was accessed, the most recent trade for Microsoft stock was for $30.00 a share. If a round lot (100 shares) was purchased at this price the cost of purchasing the shares would be $30.00 × 100 shares = $3,000 plus any commissions. The price of Microsoft stock rose 37 cents from the end of the previous trading day; that means the closing or final price of the previous trading day was 37 cents lower, namely $30.00 − 0.37 = $29.63. If only the price of the final trade of the day is reported (as may be the case for newspaper listings) it appears under the label of "close" to represent the day's closing price for the stock.

FIGURE 10.4
Stock Quotation Information

FIRM NAME: MICROSOFT	TICKER: MSFT
Market: Nasdaq	YTD range: $15.15–$30.14
Last Trade: $30.00	52 week range: $14.87–$30.14
Change: 0.37	Volume (1000s): 56501
	P/E: 19.5
	Dividend: $0.52
	Dividend Yield: 1.70%

Source: http://finance.yahoo.com, http://www.marketwatch.com, http://moneycentral.msn.com accessed November 23, 2009

Looking at the information in the second column, we see that Microsoft's stock price has varied from a low of $15.15 to a high of $30.14 over the course of the year (YTD means year to date). Over the past 52 weeks, however, Microsoft's stock has varied from a low price of $14.87 to a high of $30.14. This wide range (the high price is double the low price) is not uncommon. Review for yourself the 52-week ranges of different stocks from a current issue of *The Wall Street Journal*.

The previous trading day, approximately 56,501,000 shares of Microsoft stock were traded. Many times, the volume is printed in terms of 1,000s (56501) or 100s (565010) in order to save space.

The column labeled PE gives the price/earnings ratio of the stock. This value is computed by dividing the firm's latest annual earnings per share into its current stock price. Newspaper stock listings report only integer values of P/E ratios, so they would list Microsoft's P/E ratio as 24. Using the stock's price and the P/E ratio, we can estimate Microsoft's earnings per share:

$$\text{Price/EPS} = 19.5 = (\$30.00)/\text{EPS}; \text{ so our approximation for EPS is } \$1.54$$

Next, the table lists the twelve-month dividend paid by the firm; Microsoft paid $0.52 per share in dividends to its owners over the past twelve months. The final piece of information in the table is the dividend yield of the stock. The dividend yield is calculated as the stock's annual dividend divided by its current price. Since the current price is $30.00, the dividend yield is $0.52/$30.00, or 1.73 percent. In most listings this may be rounded to 1.7 percent.

Dots (. . .) or "NA" will appear as the dividend or dividend yield for some stocks. This indicates that the firm did not pay dividends in the previous twelve months. Similarly, lack of a number for the firm's P/E indicates a firm with a negative net income.

As we saw in earlier in this chapter, bonds have many different characteristics with respect to time to maturity, coupon income payouts, callable, put options, and so forth. With only a few exceptions, equity has fewer variations. Except for some variations across preferred equity issues (callable, participating, convertible) or different voting rights and dividend rights for common stock, there are not many variations of publicly traded equity issues.

INTERNET ACTIVITY
Get stock price quotes online and learn more about stock investing at http://www.fool.com and http://finance.yahoo.com.

CONCEPT CHECK
What does the "volume" notation mean in Figure 10.4?

What dividend does Microsoft pay its common shareholders?

What does the P/E ratio indicate?

What do tracking stocks track?

dividend reinvestment plans (DRIPS) *allow shareholders to easily purchase additional shares with their dividends*

DIVIDENDS AND STOCK REPURCHASES

The process of paying coupon interest on bonds is rather straightforward; it is a payment that is legally required under the terms of the bond's indenture. Only when a firm contacts the trustee that it will not be able to pay the required interest because of financial difficulty does the process become complex and legalistic.

Dividends, as we've learned, are not a legal obligation of the firm and as such may be skipped, decreased, increased, stopped, and started according to the collective wisdom of the corporation's board of directors. When they are paid, they are typically paid on a quarterly basis, four times in the course of a year.

Many firms offer shareholders the choice to receive a check for the amount of their dividends or to re-invest the dividends in the firm's stock. **Dividend reinvestment plans (DRIPS)** allow shareholders to purchase additional shares automatically with all or part of the investor's dividends. Fractional shares can be purchased and DRIP purchases have no or very low commissions.

Suppose an investor owns sufficient shares to receive $10 in dividends on a stock from its quarterly declared dividend. If the stock price is $25, the DRIP program allows the investor to purchase $10/$25 or 0.40 share of the firm's stock. If the stock price is $8, the investor's reinvested dividends will purchase $10/$8 or 1.25 shares of the stock.

If the investor favors the stock and wants to continue holding it, participating in a DRIP is an easy way of purchasing additional shares over time without any direct cash outlay. It also allows income returns to be reinvested to facilitate compounding returns over time. However, as with all dividends, the declared dividend is taxable as income. Whether the dividends are received as cash or reinvested, the investor must pay taxes on them.

HOW DO FIRMS DECIDE ON THE DOLLAR AMOUNT OF DIVIDENDS?

dividend payout ratio
dividends per share divided by earnings per share

Most firms that issue dividends try to maintain a consistent **dividend payout ratio,** which is dividends per share divided by earnings per share. Microsoft's dividend payout ratio, using the information from Figure 10.4 and our calculations, is its dividend of $0.52 per share divided by our calculation of earnings per share, $1.54:

Dividend payout ratio = $0.52 / $1.54 = 0.34 or 34 percent.

How about the case of a firm that wants to start paying dividends? Microsoft's decision to start paying dividends in 2003 was prompted by its cash balance of $48 billion; its decision to pay a special dividend totaling $30 billion to shareholders in 2004 arose as its cash balance had risen to $60 billion. Suffice it to say, most firms that initiate dividends do not generate as much cash as does Microsoft.

A key component of the "how much?" decision is: what level of dividends is sustainable over time? A firm does not want to announce it will begin paying dividends only at a later time to have to reduce or eliminate the dividend due to the need to conserve cash. Dividends are thought to send a signal to investors about managements' view of the future cash-generating ability of the firm. Managers—and the board of directors—have private information about the strategies, competitive responses, and opportunities facing the firm that the investing public does not know. Thus if the firm decides to increase dividends, that is a positive signal or indicator to the financial markets that management believes the future looks stable, or improving, for the firm. A reduction in dividends is taken to be a pessimistic indicator of the firm's future, so firms try to set dividends so future reductions are unlikely given their current perspective on the firm's future.

Thus, most firms that start paying dividends will do so at a rather low level—perhaps just a penny a share. The fact that management and the board are sufficiently confident to issue a dividend is a positive signal to the financial markets. Over time, as the firm generates more cash, the firm will increase its dollar amount of dividends per share as well as its dividend payout ratio. After a while, the firm will determine a "target" dividend payout ratio that it seeks to maintain over time. However, dividends will not automatically rise along with earnings. If future earnings rise, dividends will not increase until the board feels the higher level of earnings are sustainable over time (remember, firms do not want to ever cut the dollar amount of the dividends per share if they can avoid it). If the higher earnings appear to be sustainable over time the firm will adjust the dividends per share accordingly toward the "target" dividend payout ratio.[20] Some call this the **target dividend payout policy.**

target dividend payout policy
the dividend payout ratio adjusts over time to a target level set by management

special dividend
an extra dividend declared by the firm over and above its regular dividend payout

Some firms follow a different dividend strategy of consistently paying a low regular dividend but declaring a **special dividend** when times are particularly good. For a firm in a cyclical industry, with sales and earnings that are highly variable, this may be a strategy to conserve cash during industry recessions while maintaining the low but stable regular dividend. Shareholders are rewarded when rising earnings allow the company to declare an extra or special dividend.

---

20. Discussions of dividend policy theories and practice are available in Julio Brandon and David L. Ikenberry, "Reappearing Dividends," *Journal of Applied Corporate Finance,* Fall 2004, 16 (4), 89–100 and Alon Brav, John R. Graham, Campbell R. Harvey, and Roni Michaely, "Payout Policy in the 21st Century" (April 2003). NBER Working Paper No. W9657. Available at SSRN: http://ssrn.com/abstract=398560.

residual dividend policy
dividends vary over time based on the firm's excess funds

constant payout ratio
the declared dividends are a constant percentage of the firm's earnings

While such a dividend policy may help management control their cash balance, investors, who generally prefer certainty to uncertainty, do not favor such a strategy.

Other dividend payment strategies suffer from the same drawback of creating investor uncertainty due to variable dividend levels. The **residual dividend policy** states that dividends will vary based upon how much excess funds the firm has from year to year. Under a **constant payout ratio** strategy the firm pays a constant percentage of earnings as dividends, so as earnings rise and fall so does the dollar amount of dividends. Please note that this is not the same as the target payout policy. The firm adjusts dividends around the target over time, depending on earnings sustainability; some years the actual payout ratio will exceed the target and others will be under it in order to have stable, predictable changes in dividends. The constant payout ratio maintains the payout ratio at the expense of varying dollar amount of dividends per share.

The board of directors and management will consider several factors as they examine the level of dividend payout. Some of these factors are:

- Ability of the firm to generate cash to sustain the level of dividends. Recall that investors do not react well to reductions in dividends. If a dividend level is thought to be unsustainable, the firm's stock price will fall as investors sell the stock.

- Legal and contractual considerations: Dividends, when they are paid, reduce a firm's equity. A firm cannot pay dividends if doing so will reduce the firm's equity below the par value of the common stock. In addition, a bond's indenture (or loan agreement with a bank) may restrict the dollar amount of dividends to ensure adequate cash is available to pay loan interest and principal.

- Growth opportunities. Growing firms require capital—they will likely want to reinvest all profits into the company to help finance expansion, movement into new products or markets. Growing firms may seek additional funds from loans, bond issues, and new issues of stock. It is unlikely firms facing growth opportunities will want to initiate or significantly increase their dividends.

- Cost of other financing sources. Dividends are paid, for the most part, from internally generated funds—that is, cash that remains after the firm's bills, interest, and taxes are paid. If a firm has the ability to easily raise low-cost external financing sources it will be better able to maintain a higher level of dividends. Firms that can raise outside financing only by paying high interest rates or by issuing new shares of stock will likely have lower levels of dividends.

- Tax rates. Prior to 2003, dividend income was viewed as unattractive by some investors. Why? Because dividend income was taxed as income, at the investors' marginal income tax rate, which exceeded 30% (combined federal and state tax rates) for many. But the Jobs and Growth Tax Relief Reconciliation Act of 2003 reduced the top federal tax rate on dividends from 38% to 15%, the same as the top rate on long-term capital gains. Although surveys of financial officers indicate that tax rates are not a "first-order concern" when setting dividends, on the aggregate firms markedly increased dividends after the law was passed.

CONCEPT CHECK

Why is the decision to reduce dividends not well received by investors?

What policies might a board follow in setting a firm's dividend?

What five influences affect a board's dividend decision?

In addition to giving cash dividends to shareholders, the firm's board of directors can announce other decisions, such as a stock dividend or stock split, that, at first glance, appear to give extra shares and wealth to shareholders. In reality, as we shall see in the next section, their effect on the value of a firm's stock and the wealth of shareholders is zero. But there is one other decision the board can make with respect to the firm's shares that will positively affect shareholders: a stock buy-back, or share repurchase program. We'll examine stock dividends, splits, and repurchases below.

STOCK DIVIDENDS AND STOCK SPLITS

stock dividend
a dividend in which investors receive shares of stock rather than cash

A **stock dividend** is what it sounds like: a dividend paid with shares of stock rather than cash. Rather than mention a dollar figure, the announcement will state that the firm is distributing a 5 percent (or "X" percent) stock dividend. But a stock dividend has no net effect on the wealth of the shareholders. To see why, consider the following:

CUL8R Incorporated stock is currently priced at $10 a share, and there are 100,000 shares outstanding; the total market value of the firm is $10 × 100,000 or $1 million. Suppose you own 1,000 shares, so you own 1 percent of the shares outstanding and the value of your holdings is $10 × 1,000 shares or $10,000. CUL8R's board has declared a 10 percent stock dividend, so now you own 1,100 shares.

Are you any richer? The answer is no: you still own 1 percent of the shares outstanding, and the value of your CUL8R holdings is still $10,000. You own 1,100 shares, but the number of shares outstanding is now 10 percent larger, too. There are now 110,000 total shares and you still own 1 percent of this total. Nothing has happened to the value or the earnings ability of the firm with this paper transaction so the firm's stock price will fall and will equal $1 million / 110,000 shares or approximately $9.09. There are some account entries that will affect the firm's equity account, but the total amount of equity in the accounting statements will remain the same.[21] The bottom line is a stock dividend distributes nothing to shareholders and removes nothing from the firm. No value is transferred.

A **stock split** has a similar effect. The firm distributes extra shares for every share owned in a stock split. For example, a firm may announce a two-for-one stock split; this has the effect of doubling the number of shares outstanding and doubling the holdings of each investor, but as in the case of a stock dividend, the net effect on investor wealth is zero. You may own twice as many shares, but the stock price will be cut in half leaving your ownership stake (both in terms of value and percentage owned) the same as it was before the stock split. Occasionally, a firm will announce a "reverse split" in which multiple shares are combined to form one new share. For example, a one-for-four reverse split means four old shares are now equal to one new share. When this happens, the stock price will change so once again there is no change in the investor's wealth.

You may have noted that there is not much of a difference between a stock split and a stock dividend. They both involve paper transactions in which the number of shares is increased but prices adjust downward to maintain investor wealth at a constant level. By way of accounting convention, a distribution of 5 shares for 4 (a 25 percent stock dividend) is considered to be a stock split; a distribution of less than five for four (less than a 25 percent stock dividend) is considered to be a stock dividend.[22]

SHARE REPURCHASES

Rather than distribute funds to shareholders in the form of earnings, a firm can repurchase its shares. Why would a firm repurchase its shares of stock? Small purchases (relative to the total amount of shares outstanding) acquire shares used in management stock option incentive programs, in which managers can purchase shares of stock at prespecified prices (more will be said about this Chapter 13, Business Organization and Financial Data). Other firms purchase shares of their own stock to use in stock-based acquisitions of other firms. That is, they repurchase shares from current shareholders and then distribute them to owners of a newly acquired firm.

A major reason is to reward longer-term shareholders by enhancing the value of the firm's shares. Increases in stock prices are not taxed until the shares are sold, and if the shares have been held longer than one year, the maximum tax on the increase in value (called a capital gain) is 15 percent. This tax savings is thought to be a major reason by some researchers for the increase in stock repurchases in recent years.

Another reason for stock repurchases: the firm has the cash and sees its own stock as one of its most attractive investment alternatives. Rather than investing in expanding the business to new markets, the firm's Board of Directors and top managers believe the firm's stock is undervalued and offers potential returns. The stock can be purchased now at what is perceived to be a low price and re-issued later, after the stock price rises. This is literally a firm "putting its money where its mouth is." This was a popular reason given for stock repurchases during the 2000–2002 stock market decline. On the other hand, it is an indicator that management is doing a poor job in identifying new corporate strategies for increasing the stock's value.

This section discussed the process of declaring and issuing dividends on equity securities. The following section applies the Chapter 9 time value of money principles to expected cash flows from bond and equity investments. The process of valuation is important to business managers considering ways to issue securities as well as to investors who must make security buy and sell decisions.

---

stock split
the firms distributes additional shares for every share owned

CONCEPT CHECK

What is the difference between a stock dividend and a stock split?

Why might a firm decide to repurchase shares of its common stock?

What is the tax advantage to investors if funds are used to repurchase shares rather than to pay dividends?

---

21. The firm's combined value of its par value and additional paid-in capital accounts will rise by the market value of the stock dividend but the firm's retained earnings account will decline by this account, so the firm's equity account remains constant.

22. There is a distinction in what happens to the equity account in the case of a stock split. For a stock split, the only change is to the number of shares outstanding and to the stock's par value (if any). None of the dollar amounts in the equity accounts change. So if a firm has 100,000 shares outstanding of $1 par value stock and it announces a two-for-one stock split, the number of share outstanding becomes 200,000 and the par value becomes $0.50.

VALUATION PRINCIPLES

In Chapter 9, we learned how to find the present value of a series of future cash flows. The present value represents the current worth of the future cash flows. In other words, it represents the price someone would be willing to pay today in order to receive the expected future cash flows. For example, we saw an investor would be willing to pay $2,577 in order to receive a three-year annuity of $1,000 at an 8 percent discount rate.

All securities are valued on the basis of the cash inflows that they are expected to provide to their owners or investors. Thus mathematically, we have:

$$\text{price} = [CF_1/(1+r)^1] + [CF_2/(1+r)^2] + \cdots + [CF_n/(1+r)^n] \tag{10.1}$$

or

$$\text{price} = \sum_{t=1}^{n} [CF_t/(1+r)^t] \tag{10.1a}$$

that is, value or current price should equal the present value of expected future cash flows. Recall from Chapters 8 and 9 that the r represents the appropriate discount rate or the rate of return required by investors. For securities with no default risk (such as Treasury bonds), the r reflects the combination of the real risk free rate and expected inflation as measured by the nominal risk-free interest rate. For securities with default risk such as the bonds and stocks issued by corporations, the r represents a nominal risk-free rate plus a premium to reflect default risk.

For illustration purposes, let's assume that a security is expected to pay its owner $100 per year for five years. Let's also assume that investors expect a 10 percent annual compound rate of return on this investment. The 10 percent rate is based on a risk-free rate of 6 percent plus a 4 percent default risk premium. Now let's ask: what should be the security's current or present value?

The answer can be determined by using present value tables, a financial calculator, or a computer software program. For example, using Table 2 (Present Value of $1) in the book's appendix, we can identify the appropriate present value interest factors (PVIF) at 10 percent as follows:

YEAR	CASH FLOW	×	PVIF @ 10%	=	PRESENT VALUE
1	$100		0.909		$ 90.90
2	100		0.826		82.60
3	100		0.751		75.10
4	100		0.683		68.30
5	100		0.621		62.10
					price = $379.00

Thus, the current or present value of the security at a 10 percent discount rate should be $379.

Notice how the table above resembles a spreadsheet. Indeed, spreadsheets are powerful tools for developing models to evaluate bonds and stocks. Using Excel we can create a table to do this calculation:

	A	B	C	D
1				
2	Interest rate:	10%		
3	Number of years:	5		
4				
5	Year	Cash Flow	PVIF	Present Value
6	1	$100	0.909	$90.91
7	2	$100	0.826	$82.64
8	3	$100	0.751	$75.13
9	4	$100	0.683	$68.30
10	5	$100	0.621	$62.09
11				$379.08

where the present value interest factor formula in cell C6 is: $= 1/(1+B2)\wedge A6$. In cell C6, the present value interest factor is computed is $1/(1 + 0.10)^1$ or 0.909 (to three decimal places). In cell C7, the interest rate remains the same, but the exponent changes to reflect the fact that the cash flow is discounted back two years: $= 1/(1+B2)\wedge A7$. The spreadsheet calculates this as $1/(1 + 0.10)^2$ or 0.826. We use the SUM function to add the numbers in cell D11: $=$ SUM(D6:D10).

Of course, since the security's cash flow reflects a $100 five-year annuity, we could have used Table 4 (Present Value of a $1 Ordinary Annuity) in the book's appendix to determine the security's present value as follows:

$$\text{price} = \text{cash flow annuity} \times \text{PVIFA @ 10\%}$$
$$= \$100 \times 3.791$$
$$= \$379.10$$

where PVIFA refers to the present value interest factor of an annuity. Notice that there is a slight rounding error due to the use of three-digit tables.

The security's present value also can be determined by using a financial calculator as follows. First, clear the calculator's memory. Next, enter 100 (or -100 depending on the calculator) using the annuity or payments (PMT) key. Then, enter 10 and press the %i key and enter 5 and press the N key. Finally, press the compute (CPT) key followed by the present value (PV) key to calculate the security's current value of $379.08.

Financial Calculator Solution:

Inputs:	5	10	-100
	N	%i	PMT
Press:	CPT	PV	
Solution:	379.08		

Excel's PV function can compute the present value of an annuity, too. Recall the PV function has the form: PV (periodic interest rate, number of periods, payment, future value, type). To solve for this five-year annuity, we can use the Excel spreadsheet:

	A	B
1	Interest rate:	10%
2	Number of years:	5
3	Cash flow	$100
4		
5	Present value of the annuity:	-$379.08

where the Excel function in cell B5 will be: $=$PV(B1,B2,B3,0,0). Cell B1 contains the interest rate; the number of years in the annuity, 5, is found in cell B2; and the periodic annuity payment, $100, is in cell B3. The desired future savings (future value) is zero for the current problem. Since we are computing a regular annuity, we can either omit the final item or enter "0" in the final position. The Excel PV function returns a negative number. Recalling the cash flow diagrams from Chapter 9, if the $100 annuity represents cash inflows to an investor, the present value must represent an outflow, namely, the price an investor is willing to pay in order to receive a five-year annuity of $100. By convention, cash outflows are negative numbers and inflows are positive. Should you prefer not to have a negative present value number, simply insert a negative sign before the PV command: =−PV(B1,B2,B3,0,0) so the spreadsheet returns a positive present value:

	A	B
1	Interest rate:	10%
2	Number of years:	5
3	Cash flow	$100
4		
5	Present value of the annuity:	$379.08

CONCEPT CHECK

What is the relationship between the present value of future cash flows and the price an investor should be willing to pay for a security?

What does r represent in equation 10.1?

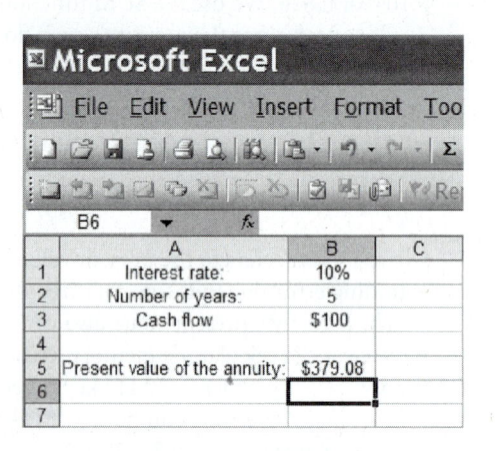

Now we are ready to determine the values of bonds. Conceptually, bond valuation is very similar to many of the present value examples covered in Chapter 9.

VALUATION OF BONDS

Corporate and government bonds usually provide for periodic payments of interest plus the return of the amount borrowed or par value when the bond matures. Equation 10.1 can be modified to incorporate these bond cash flows.

DETERMINING A BOND'S PRESENT VALUE

The value of a bond with annual coupon payments can be expressed as follows:

$$\text{Price} = \text{PV (expected future cash flows)}$$
$$= [C_1/(1 + r_b)^1] + [C_2/(1 + r_b)^2] + \cdots$$
$$+ [C_n/(1 + r_b)^n] + [Par_n/(1 + r_b)^n] \quad (10.2)$$
$$= \sum_{t=1}^{n}[C_t/(1 + r_b)^t] + [Par_n/(1 + r_b)^n] \quad (10.2a)$$
$$= \text{PV (coupon annuity)} + \text{PV (principal)}$$

where
- Price = the bond's value now or in period zero,
- C = the coupon payment,
- Par = the bond's principal amount,
- r_b = the rate of return required by investors on this quality or risk-class of bonds, given its bond rating; if coupons are paid semi-annually, this is the semiannual required rate of return.

In words, we use both Equation 9.7 (present value of an annuity) and equation 9.3 (present value of a single amount) to compute a bond's price. We first find the present value of the bond's expected coupon payments. Second, we compute the present value of the bond's principal payment. Third, we add these two present values together to find the bond's price. A point to watch for is the type of bond we are dealing with; Eurobonds pay coupon interest once a year, whereas American bonds pay interest twice a year, delivering one-half of the annual coupon to bondholders every six months. Thus, for American bonds, we need to adjust the calculation of Equation 10.2a for semiannual cashflows. In this circumstance, n, the number of periods, equals

$$n = 2 \times \text{the number of years until maturity}$$

and the required rate of return, r_b, is the rate that compounds to equal the market interest rate:

$$(1 + \text{market rate}) = (1 + r_b)^2$$

That is, the market rate is the effective interest rate (EAR) in equation 9–11; the bond's required periodic rate is found by:

$$r_b = (1 + \text{market rate})^{1/2} - 1$$

Most corporate bonds are issued in $1,000 denominations. To illustrate how a corporate bond's value is calculated, let's assume that a bond with $1,000 face value has a coupon rate of 8 percent and a ten-year life before maturity. Thus an investor will receive $80 ($1,000 × 0.08) annually; for U.S. corporate bonds, half of this annual amount, $40, will be paid every six months with the $1,000 paid at the end of ten years. We determine the bond's present value based on the interest rate required by investors on similar quality bonds. Let's assume investors require an 8.16 percent rate of return on bonds of similar quality.

With semi-annual coupons, the number of periods is 20 (2 × 10 years) and the periodic interest is:

$$r_b = (1 + \text{market rate})^{1/2} - 1 = (1 + 0.0816)^{1/2} - 1 = 0.04 \text{ or } 4.0 \text{ percent}$$

We need to discount the $40 coupon annuity portion of the bond at the PVIFA at 4 percent for twenty periods, which is 13.590 (see Table 4 in the book's appendix). Since the $1,000 principal will be received only at the end of twenty periods, we use 0.456, the PVIF at 4 percent for twenty years from Table 2 in the Appendix.[23]

Taking these together, we have:

$$\begin{aligned} \$40 \times 13.590 &= \$543.60 \\ \$1,000 \times 0.456 &= \underline{456.00} \\ \text{Bond value} &= \$999.60 \end{aligned}$$

which rounds to $1,000. Thus the bond is worth $1,000 and will remain so as long as investors require the 8.16 market rate of return on bonds of this maturity and risk.

Rather than use tables, we can compute bond prices using a financial calculator's functions or with spreadsheets. The spreadsheet format below shows the price of the above bond is $1,000.00:

	A	B
2	Computing Bond Price using EAR (effective annual rate)	
3	Coupon Rate	8.00%
4	Number of years until maturity	10.00
5	Number of coupon payments per year	2.00
6	Par Value	$1,000.00
7	Market rate	8.16% (EAR)
8		
9	Compute periodic interest rate:	4.00% equals [(1 + B7)^(1/B5)] minus 1
10	Compute number of periods:	20.00 equals B4 * B5
11	Compute coupon cash flow:	$40.00 equals (B3 *B6)/B5
12		
13	Bond price	$1,000.00 equals -PV(B9, B10, B11, B6, 0)

---

23. For bonds paying semi-annual coupons, we must not think in terms of the number of years but rather the number of periods. Because the 4 percent periodic rate of return is a semi-annual rate, we use twenty semi-annual periods of time in both the coupon and par value present value calculations.

As an alternative, we can use ten years as the time frame for the par value calculation, but only if we use the annualized market interest rate of 8.16 percent as the discount rate. Doing so, the present value of the $1,000 par value is $1,000 × (1/1.0816)^{10} = $1,000 × 0.456 = $456.00, the same value as we received using the semi-annual rate of 4 percent over twenty semi-annual periods.

However, what if investors required a 10.25 percent return, or yield, on bonds of similar quality? The bond must then fall in price to compensate for the fact that only $80 in annual interest is received by the investor. A market return of 10.25 percent corresponds to a semi-annual return of $(1 + 0.1025)^{1/2} - 1 = 0.05$ or 5.0 percent. The appropriate discount factors at 5 percent for twenty years from Tables 2 and 4 in the Appendix would be:

$$40 \times 12.462 = \$498.48$$
$$\$1,000 \times 0.377 = \underline{377.00}$$
$$\text{Bond value} = \$875.48$$

Using the above spreadsheet and changing the value of cell B7 from 8.16 percent to 10.25 percent, we easily find the new price of the bond, $875.38. The spreadsheet's price is more accurate as interest factors from the financial tables are rounded to only three decimal places. The benefit of this calculation with spreadsheets is clear; once we appropriately design the spreadsheet, we can change our inputs or assumptions and see the effect on the bond's price.

	A	B	C	D
2	Computing Bond Price using EAR (effective annual rate)			
3	Coupon Rate	8.00%		
4	Number of years until maturity	10.00		
5	Number of coupon payments per year	2.00		
6	Par Value	$1,000.00		
7	Market rate	10.25%	(EAR)	
8				
9	Compute periodic interest rate:		5.00% equals [(1 + B7)^(1/B5)] minus 1	
10	Compute number of periods:		20.00 equals B4 * B5	
11	Compute coupon cash flow:		$40.00 equals (B3 *B6)/B5	
12				
13	Bond price		$875.38 equals -PV(B9, B10, B11, B6, 0)	

Thus, an investor would be willing to pay about $875 (rounded) for the bond. Although annual coupon payment remains at $80, a new investor would earn a 10.25 percent return because she or he would pay only $875 now and get back $1,000 at the end of ten years. A bond that sells below par value, such as this one, is said to be selling at a *discount* and is called a *discount bond.* Someone who purchases this discount bond today and holds it to maturity will receive, in addition to the stream of coupon interest payments, a gain of $125, the difference between the bond's price ($875) and its principal repayment ($1,000).

discount bond
bond that is selling below par value

A bond's price will reflect changes in market conditions while it remains outstanding. With its fixed 8 percent coupon rate, this bond will no longer be attractive to investors when alternative investments are yielding 10.25 percent. The bond's market price will have to fall in order to offer buyers a combined return of 10.25 percent from the coupon payments and the par value. Thus, bond prices fall as interest rates rise.

If investors required less than an 8 percent (e.g., 6.09 percent) return for bonds of this quality, then the above-described bond would have a value greater than $1,000; investors would find the bond's 8 percent coupon attractive when other bonds are offering closer to 6 percent. If it was selling to yield a return of 6.09 percent to investors, the bond's price will rise to $1,149.08 (check this on your own). When a bond's price exceeds its par value, it is selling at a *premium*, and it is called a *premium bond.* The investor who holds the bond until maturity will receive the above-market coupon payments of 8 percent per year, offset by a loss of $149 (the difference between its purchase price and par value). In most cases where the bond sells at a premium, interest rates have fallen

premium bond
bond that is selling in excess of its par value

CHAPTER TEN ● Bonds and Stocks: Characteristics and Valuations 263

after the bond's issue. This bond's 8 percent coupon rate makes it very attractive to investors; buying pressure increases its price until its overall yield matches the market rate of 6.09 percent.

CALCULATING THE YIELD TO MATURITY[24]

yield to maturity (YTM)
return on a bond if it is held to maturity

Many times, rather than compute price, investors want to estimate the return on a bond investment if they hold it until it matures (this is called the *yield to maturity* or *YTM*). Financial calculators and computer spreadsheet packages, such as Excel, can be used to find the exact return. An approximate answer for the yield to maturity can be obtained by using the following formula:

$$\text{Approximate yield to maturity} = \frac{\text{Annual interest} + \dfrac{\text{par} - \text{price}}{\text{No. of years until maturity}}}{\dfrac{\text{par} + \text{price}}{2}} \quad (10.3)$$

The numerator of Equation 10.3 equals the annual coupon interest plus a straight-line amortization of the difference between the current price and par value. It represents an approximation of the annual dollar return the bondholder expects to receive, as over time the bond's value will rise or fall so it equals its par value at maturity. This estimated annual return is divided by the average of the bond's par value and its current price to give us an approximate yield or percentage return if the bond is held until maturity.

From the example above, we know that if the bond can be purchased for $875, it offers investors a 10.25 percent return. Let's use Equation 10.3 to estimate the approximate yield to maturity if we know the price is $875, annual coupons are $80, and the bond matures in ten years with a par value of $1,000:

$$\text{Approximate yield to maturity} = \frac{\$80 + \dfrac{\$1000 - \$875}{10}}{\dfrac{\$1000 + \$875}{2}}$$

$$= 0.0987 \text{ or } 9.87 \text{ percent}$$

The approximate answer of 9.87 percent is somewhat close to the exact yield to maturity of 10.25 percent but certainly shows the approximate nature of the formula.

Of course, the use of a financial calculator will give us a precise answer for the yield to maturity. We illustrate the calculation process for a ten-year (or, rather, twenty-period) bond paying interest of $40 per period and a $1,000 principal repayment at maturity. First, we assume the bond is currently trading at $1,000. Second, we assume the price to be $875.48.

Financial Calculator Solution: $1,000 Current Price

Inputs:	20	1,000	40	1,000
	N	PV	PMT	FV

Press: CPT %i

Solution: 4.00

A periodic return of 4 percent is the same as an annual yield to maturity of 8.16 percent.[25] Now let's see the yield to maturity when the bond is trading at $875.48:

---

24. The yield to maturity calculation assumes that all coupon cash flows are reinvested at the YTM throughout the bond's life. The realized compound yield (RCY) calculation allows the investor to compute the expected return on a bond using another, perhaps more realistic return, for how the bond's coupons are reinvested. The RCY calculation is done in two steps. First, the future value of all the bond's cash flows is computed using the assumed reinvestment rate. Second, the rate that equates the bond's current price and the future value of cash flows is calculated; this rate is the RCY.

For example, a bond investor may expect interest rates to fall so the reinvestment rate is expected to fall to 6.09 percent on ten-year bonds. That means the $40 semi-annual coupons are likely to be reinvested at a semi-annual rate of only 3 percent. After ten years (or twenty periods), the future value of the $40 coupons will be $40 × 26.870 (FVIFA factor for 3 percent and twenty years from Table 3 in the Appendix) or $1,074.80. Adding the par value we'll receive at that time, the future value of all the bond's cash inflows is $2,074.80. If the current price of the bond is $1,000, the annual RCY is found by solving the future value equation for r: $FV = PV(1 + r)^n = \$2,074.80 = 1,000(1 + r)^{10}$. Solving for r, the realized compound yield is 7.57 percent.

25. Annualized yield to maturity = $(1 + 0.04)^2 - 1 = 0.0816$ or 8.16 percent.

Financial Calculator Solution: $875.48 Current Price

Inputs:	20	875.48	40	1,000
	N	PV	PMT	FV

Press: CPT %i

Solution: 5.00

This corresponds to an annual yield to maturity of 10.25 percent.[26]

Given what we know about bonds and our time value of money techniques, the following will be true, if all other influences are kept constant:

- The larger the coupon interest, the higher the bond's price. We've already seen that with a yield to maturity of 8.16 percent, a ten-year bond that pays annual interest of $80 will have a present value or price of $1,000. A bond that is identical except it has a 10 percent coupon rate will have a price of $50 × 13.590 + $1,000 × 0.456 = $1,135.50.

- The more frequent the coupon payments (e.g., semi-annually instead of annually), the higher the bond's price, as some cash flows occur sooner in time than they would otherwise. For example, with semi-annual coupon payments the 8 percent coupon bond is worth $1,000 when the market interest rate is 8.16 percent. If this bond were a Eurobond, with annual coupon payments, its price would be slightly lower, at $989.34 (check this answer using Equations 9.3 and 9.7).

- The higher the yield to maturity, the lower the price of the bond; the lower the yield to maturity, the higher the bond's price. We have already seen this; when a ten-year bond with an 8 percent coupon sells at an 8.16 percent yield to maturity, its price is $1,000; when it sells at a 10.25 percent yield to maturity, its price is $875; its price is $1,149 when the yield to maturity falls to 6.09 percent. More risky bonds (those with lower bond ratings) will have higher required yields and will sell at lower prices or with higher coupon rates.

CONCEPT CHECK

How do you go about computing a bond's price?

What is a discount bond? A premium bond?

Given two bonds identical in all respects except one pays coupons annually and the other pays coupons semi-annually, which one will have the higher price? Why?

RISK IN BOND VALUATION

Investors in domestic bonds face three types of risk: credit risk, interest rate risk, and reinvestment rate risk. Investors in foreign bonds are subject to two additional risks: political risk and exchange rate risk.

Credit Risk

The cash flows to be received by bond market investors are not certain; like individuals, corporate debtors may pay interest payments late or not at all. They may fail to repay principal at maturity. To compensate investors for this **credit risk** or **default risk,** rates of return on corporate bonds are higher than those on government securities with the same terms to maturity.

Government securities are presumed to be free of credit risk. In general, as investors perceive a higher likelihood of default, they demand higher default-risk premiums. Since perceptions of a bond's default risk may change over its term, the bond's yield to maturity may also change, even if all else remains constant. Firms such as Moody's, Standard & Poor's, and Fitch provide information on the riskiness of individual bond issues through their bond ratings. The bond rating is a measure of a bond's default risk.

credit risk (default risk)
the chance of nonpayment or delayed payment of interest or principal

The default risk premium is measured by the difference in the yield to maturity, or spread, of two bonds of equal time to maturity. If a ten-year Treasury note has a yield of 5.4 percent and a ten-year Baa-rated corporate bond has a yield of 7.4 percent, the Baa-Treasury spread of 2.0 percentage points represents the default risk premium earned by investors who are willing to carry the extra risk of a Baa-rated bond.

Credit risk spreads are not constant; they fluctuate based upon credit conditions and investors' willingness to take on risk. In good economic times when investors are optimistic,

---

26. We can design a spreadsheet to incorporate the inputs and calculation of equation 10.3. We can also use several Excel functions (IRR, YIELD, YIELDMAT) to compute the exact yield to maturity, but their application is too advanced for the current discussion.

FIGURE 10.5
Credit Risk Spreads

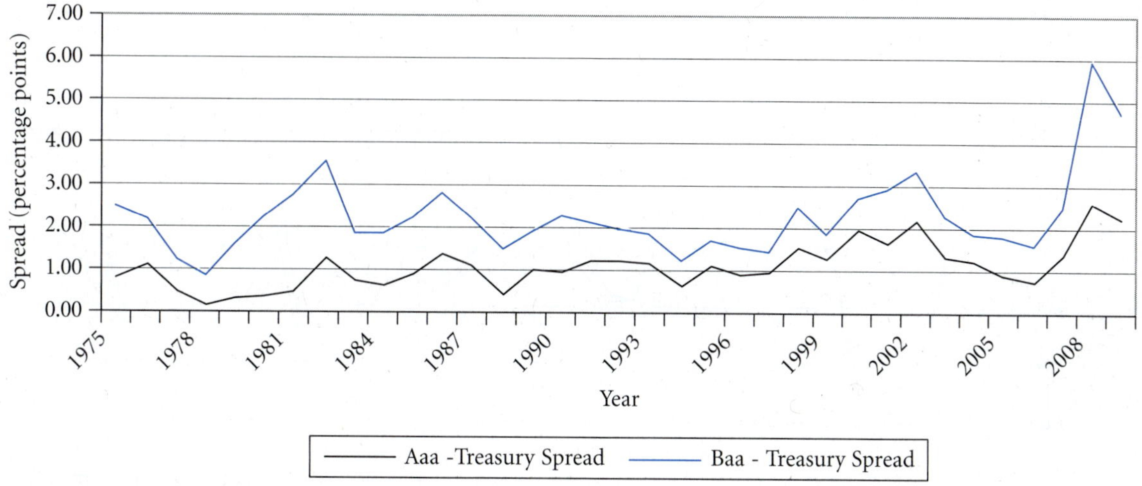
7.00
6.00
5.00
4.00
3.00
2.00
1.00
0.00
Spread (percentage points)
1975
1978
1981
1984
1987
1990
1993
1996
1999
2002
2005
2008
Year
Aaa -Treasury Spread
Baa - Treasury Spread

FINANCIAL CRISIS

spreads generally narrow; in uncertain times or in a recession, there is a "flight to quality" as investors prefer safer securities and credit spreads widen. Figure 10.5 shows the behavior of spreads between Baa-rated bonds and Treasuries and Aaa-rated bonds and Treasuries over time. During the 2007–2009 financial crisis credit spreads widened to near-record levels. During this time, particular in fall 2008, investors fled from risky securities and sought safety in Treasury securities.

ETHICAL ISSUES

Ethics plays a role in determining a bond's rating. If management, through fraud or accounting gimmickry, makes a firm appear more profitable or financially stable, the firm's bonds may have higher bond ratings than they should. After accounting irregularities were discovered at Enron, which at the time was one of the largest energy firms in the United States, its bond rating dropped to "junk" levels and its bank loans came due as a result of failing to meet its loan covenants.

Interest Rate Risk

As we introduced in the discussion of premium and discount bonds, bond prices change in response to changes in interest rates. We know the general level of interest rates in an economy does not remain fixed, it fluctuates. For example, interest rates will change in response to changes in investors' expectations about future inflation rates. In Figure 10.6 we can see that the "seesaw effect" means that a rise in interest rates renders the fixed coupon interest payments on a bond less attractive, lowering its price. Therefore, bondholders are subject to the risk of capital loss from such interest rate changes should the bonds have to be sold prior to maturity.

A longer term to maturity, all else equal, increases the sensitivity of a bond's price to a given change in interest rates, as the discount rate change compounds over a longer time period. Similarly, a lower coupon rate also increases the sensitivity of the bond's price to market interest rate changes. This occurs because lower coupon bonds have most of their cash flow occurring further into the future, when the par value is paid.

FIGURE 10.6
Relationship Between Current Interest Rates and Bond Prices: The Seesaw Effect

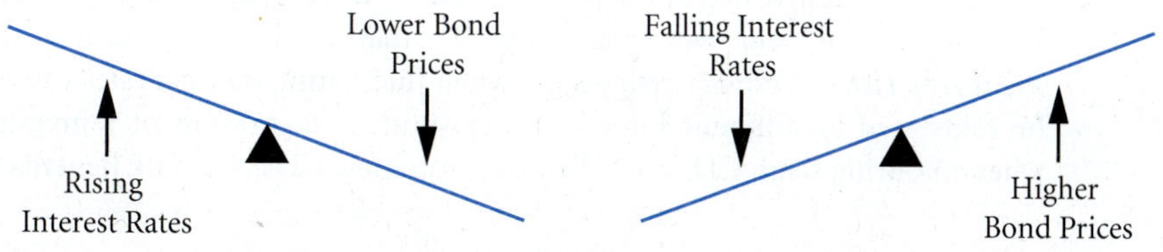
Lower Bond Prices
Rising Interest Rates
Falling Interest Rates
Higher Bond Prices

FIGURE 10.7

Horizon (Time) Spreads on Treasury Securities

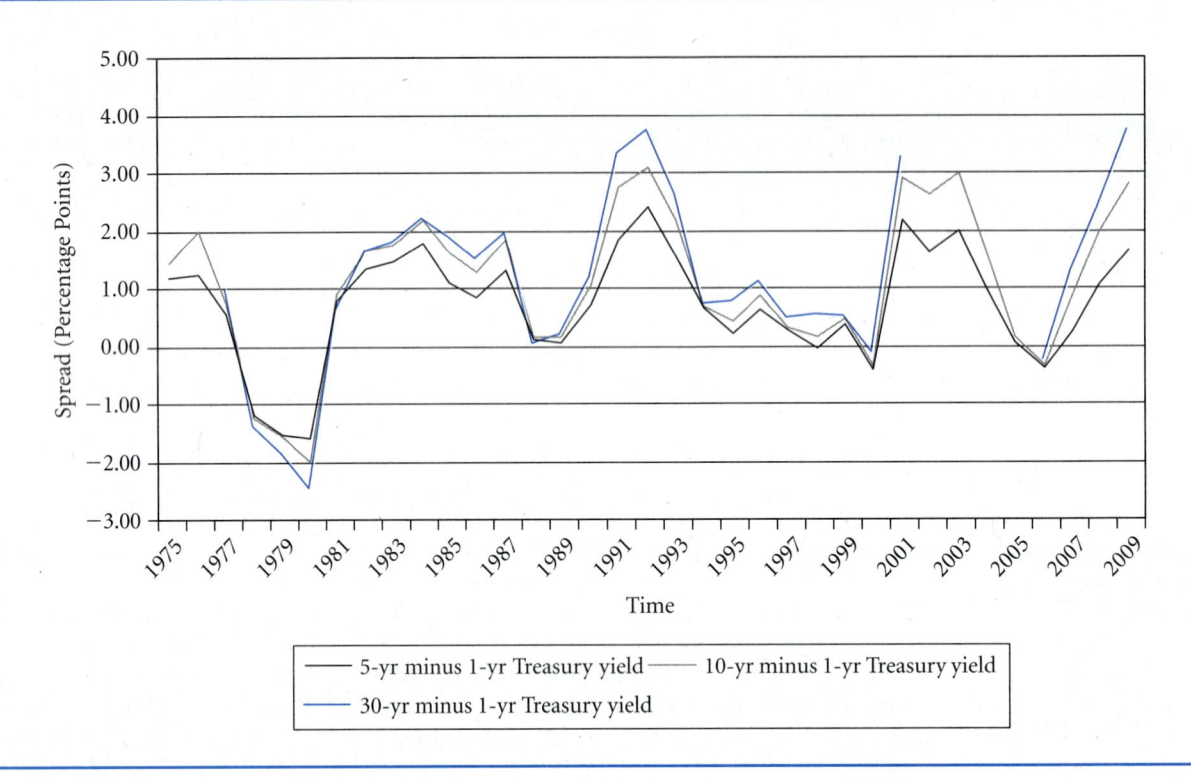

— 5-yr minus 1-yr Treasury yield   — 10-yr minus 1-yr Treasury yield
— 30-yr minus 1-yr Treasury yield

interest rate risk
fluctuating interest rates lead to varying asset prices. In the context of bonds, rising (falling) interest rates result in falling (rising) bond prices

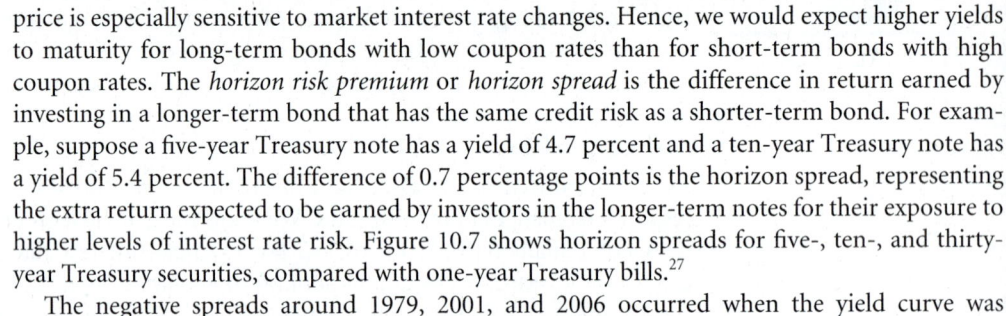

Because of **interest rate risk,** investors will demand a larger risk premium for bonds whose price is especially sensitive to market interest rate changes. Hence, we would expect higher yields to maturity for long-term bonds with low coupon rates than for short-term bonds with high coupon rates. The *horizon risk premium* or *horizon spread* is the difference in return earned by investing in a longer-term bond that has the same credit risk as a shorter-term bond. For example, suppose a five-year Treasury note has a yield of 4.7 percent and a ten-year Treasury note has a yield of 5.4 percent. The difference of 0.7 percentage points is the horizon spread, representing the extra return expected to be earned by investors in the longer-term notes for their exposure to higher levels of interest rate risk. Figure 10.7 shows horizon spreads for five-, ten-, and thirty-year Treasury securities, compared with one-year Treasury bills.[27]

The negative spreads around 1979, 2001, and 2006 occurred when the yield curve was inverted, when short-term rates exceeded long-term rates. This typically happens before a recession begins, when short-term rates are rising because of inflationary pressures at the time. In 1983–1985, 1992, and 2009, the yield curve steepened—meaning rates on longer-term Treasury securities rose far above those of short-term Treasury securities. In the cases such as 2008–2009, the financial crisis created a flight-to-quality even within Treasuries as institutional and corporate funds poured into T-bills, the safest U.S. investment.

FINANCIAL CRISIS

Reinvestment Rate Risk

The return an investor receives from a bond investment equals the bond's yield to maturity only if the coupon payments can be reinvested at a rate equal to the bond's yield to maturity. Recall the form of the interest factor in bond price (Equation 10.2): $(1 + r_b)^n$. This assumes that all the cash flows are reinvested at the periodic rate r_b. If the coupons are reinvested at a lower rate, the investor's actual yield over time will be less than the bond's yield to maturity. Thus, **reinvestment rate risk** or **rollover risk** occurs when fluctuating interest rates cause coupon payments to be reinvested at different interest rates. Another illustration of reinvestment rate risk occurs when maturing bank CDs are rolled over into new CDs. The risk benefits the investor when the

reinvestment rate risk (rollover risk)
fluctuating interest rates cause coupon or interest payments to be reinvested at different interest rates over time

---

27. The U.S. Treasury did not issue thirty-year securities in 2002–2005

new CD rate is higher than the maturing CD rate; it works against the investor when the new CD rate is lower. It is this risk that zero coupon securities eliminate, as they have no intermediate cash flows requiring reinvestment.

Risks of Nondomestic Bonds

Investors in nondomestic securities face a number of risks beyond those of domestic securities. Among these are political risk and exchange rate risk. **Political risk** can affect a bond investor in a number of ways. A foreign government may block currency exchanges, preventing the investor from repatriating coupon income. Social unrest may lead a foreign corporation to default on its bonds. Of course, exchange rate changes will cause fluctuations in the values of cash flows in terms of U.S. dollars; this is called *exchange rate risk.*

GLOBAL DISCUSSION

political risk
actions by a sovereign nation to interrupt or change the value of cash flows accruing to foreign investments

exchange rate risk
fluctuating exchange rates lead to varying levels of U.S. dollar-denominated cash flows

VALUATION OF STOCKS

All securities are valued on the basis of the cash inflows that they are expected to provide to their owners or investors. As we saw in the previous chapter and in the above bond discussion:

$$\text{price} = [CF_1/(1+r)^1] + [CF_2/(1+r)^2] + \cdots + [CF_n/(1+r)^n] \quad (10.1)$$

or

$$\text{price} = \sum_{t=1}^{n}[CF_t/(1+r)^t] \quad (10.1a)$$

CONCEPT CHECK

What risks do domestic bond investors face?

What is the seesaw effect?

What special risks do investors in foreign bonds face?

that is, value or current price should equal the present value of expected future cash flows. Earlier we applied this general formula to the case of bond pricing. The cash flows from a typical bond are straightforward: the bond has a known and definite life, has fixed coupon payments paid on a regular basis, pays a known par value or principal when the bond matures, and should have a discount rate (yield to maturity) close to that of bonds with similar credit ratings.

Although the principle for determining an appropriate stock price is the same as that for determining a bond price, equity does not offer the certainty of bond cash flows. Common and preferred stocks are generally assumed to have infinite lives. For common stock, relevant cash flows (dividend payments) will likely be variable over time. Finally, determining an appropriate rate at which to discount future dividends is difficult. Despite these difficulties, in this section we will see that the present value of all future dividends should equal a stock's current price, and that some simplifying assumptions can make the task of determining stock value much easier. Our discussion in this section focuses on common stock. As we will see, the method for valuing preferred stock is a special case of common stock valuation.

It may seem rather strange to treat the stock price as nothing more than the present value of all future dividends. Who buys stock with no intention of ever selling it, even after retirement? Investors generally buy stock with the intention of selling it at some future time ranging from a few hours to thirty years or longer. Despite the length of any one investor's time horizon, the current price of any dividend-paying common stock should equal the present value of all future dividends:[28]

$$\text{price} = \sum_{t=1}^{n}[D_t/(1+r_s)^t] \quad (10.4)$$

What if a corporation currently pays no dividends and has no plans to pay dividends in the foreseeable future? The value of this company's stock will not be zero. First, just because the

---

28. Here is the intuition behind this statement. A stock is purchased today, in year T, with the plan of selling it in year T + 1. What should its current price be? The current price should equal the present value of dividends over year T and the selling price in year T + 1.

What will be the price of the stock in year T + 1? Suppose another investor plans on buying the stock at the beginning of year T + 1 and selling it a year later in year T + 2. As before, the price of the stock at the beginning of year T + 1 should be the present value of the dividends paid in year T + 1 plus the selling price in year T + 2.

Through substitution, today's price will be the present value of the dividends in year T and T + 1 plus the expected selling price in year T + 2. We can continue extending this exercise through many years: year T + 3, T + 4, and so on. The result is that today's stock price will be the sum of the present value of future dividends.

firm has no plans to pay dividends does not mean that it never will. To finance rapid growth, young firms often retain all their earnings; when they mature, they often begin paying out a portion of earnings as dividends. Second, although the firm may not pay dividends to shareholders it may be generating cash (or have the potential to do so). The firm's new owner can claim the cash or profits if the firm is acquired or merged, so its current price should reflect this value. Third, at the very least, the firm's stock should be worth the per-share liquidation value of its assets; for a going concern, the firm is worth the discounted cash flow value that can be captured by an acquirer.

Estimating all future dividend payments is impractical. Matters can be simplified considerably if we assume that the firm's dividends will remain constant or will grow at a constant rate over time.

VALUING STOCKS WITH CONSTANT DIVIDENDS

If the firm's dividends are expected to remain constant, so that $D_0 = D_1 = D_2 \ldots$, we can treat its stock as a perpetuity. We know that preferred stock dividends are constant over time, so this situation is most applicable for valuing shares of preferred stock. The present value of a perpetuity is the cash flow divided by the discount rate. For stocks with constant dividends, this means Equation 10.4 becomes

$$P_0 = D_0/r_s \tag{10.5}$$

Many preferred stocks are valued using Equation 10.5 since preferred stocks typically pay a constant dollar dividend and do not usually have finite lives or maturities. For example, if the FY Corporation's preferred stock currently pays a $2.00 dividend and investors require a 10 percent rate of return on preferred stocks of similar risk, the preferred stock's present value is:

$$P_0 = \$2.00/0.10 = \$20.00$$

For a preferred stock with no stated maturity and a constant dividend, changes in price will occur only if the rate of return expected by investors changes.

VALUING STOCKS WITH CONSTANT DIVIDEND GROWTH RATES

Many firms have sales and earnings that increase over time; their dividends may rise, as well. If we assume that a firm's dividends grow at an annual rate of g percent, next year's dividend, D_1, will be $D_0(1 + g)$; the dividend in two years' time will be $D_0(1 + g)^2$. Generalizing, we have

$$D_t = D_0(1 + g)^t$$

Equation 10.4 now can be shown in expanded form as:

$$P_0 = [D_0(1 + g)]/(1 + r_s) + [D_0(1 + g)^2]/(1 + r_s)^2 + [D_0(1 + g)^3]/(1 + r_s)^3 + \cdots$$

As long as the dividend growth rate g is less than the discount rate r_s, each future term will be smaller than the preceding term. Although technically there are an infinite number of terms, the present value of dividends received farther and farther into the future become closer and closer to zero. By accepting the fact that the sum of all these terms is finite, Equation 10.4 becomes

$$P_0 = D_1 / (r_s - g) \tag{10.6}$$

Gordon model (constant dividend growth model) a means of estimating common stock prices by assuming constant dividend growth over time

This result is known as the **Gordon model** or the **constant dividend growth model.** The model assumes that a dividend is currently being paid and that this dividend will grow or increase at a constant rate over time. Of course, the assumption of constant growth in dividends may not be realistic for a firm that is experiencing a period of high growth (or negative growth, that is, declining revenues). Neither will constant dividend growth be a workable assumption for a firm whose dividends rise and fall over the business cycle.

Let's assume that the cash dividend per share for XYZ Company for last year was $1.89 and is expected to be $2.05 at the end of this year. This represents a percentage increase of 8.5 percent [($2.05 − $1.89)/$1.89]. If investors expect a 12 percent rate of return, then the estimated current stock value (P_0) would be:

$$P_0 = \$1.89(1.085) / (0.12 - 0.085) = (\$2.05/0.035) = \$58.59$$

Thus, if investors believed that the cash dividends would grow at a 8.5 percent rate indefinitely into the future and expected a 12 percent rate of return, they would pay $58.59 for the stock.

A simple spreadsheet can compute stock price using the constant growth assumption:

	A	B
2	Constant dividend growth model	
4	Current dividend	$1.89
5	Expected dividend growth rate	8.50%
6	Required rate of return	12.00%
8	Estimated stock price	$58.59 =B4*(1+B5)/(B6-B5)

From this discussion, we can see that there are four major influences on a stock's price. First is the firm's earnings per share, and second is the firm's dividend payout ratio; together, they determine a firm's dollar amount of dividends. The third influence is the firm's expected growth rate in dividends, which will itself be affected by a number of firm, industry, and economic influences. Fourth is the shareholders' required return; from Chapter 8, we know this return is itself affected by the real interest rate in the economy, the expected inflation rate, and a risk premium to compensate investors for purchasing risky equities.

We can use the constant dividend growth model to solve for any of the four unknown variables (price, dividends, required return, and growth) as long as the other three are known. For example, rearranging Equation 10.4, we can use the market price of the stock to calculate the market's required return for the stock:

$$r_s = D_1/P_0 + g$$

that is, the dividend yield plus the expected growth rate. Similarly, using an estimate for the required return, we can estimate the market's consensus estimate for future dividend growth:

$$g = (P_0 \cdot r - D_0)/(P_0 + D_0)$$

This is especially valuable as a check against over-optimism on the part of investors when valuing a growth stock, that is, one whose earnings are expected to continue growing at a fast rate over time. At the height of the Internet stock bubble in 1999–2000, stocks of technology firms were priced assuming that 20–30 percent growth or higher was expected indefinitely. Such growth is not possible for long periods of time, so it was only a matter of time that their stock prices tumbled after slower sales resulted in slower earnings and cash flow growth for these firms.

INTERNET ACTIVITY

Examine estimates on the future earnings of firms at http://www.zacks.com and http://www.whispernumber.com. Another great resource of stock analysis is http://www.fool.com.

RISK IN STOCK VALUATION

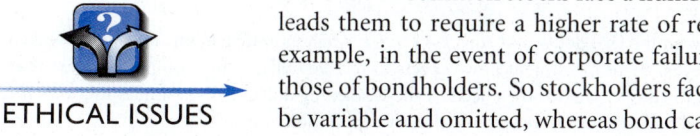

Investors in common stocks face a number of risks that bondholders do not. This additional risk leads them to require a higher rate of return on a firm's stock than on its debt securities. For example, in the event of corporate failure, the claims of stockholders have lower priority than those of bondholders. So stockholders face a greater risk of loss than bondholders. Dividends can be variable and omitted, whereas bond cash flows have a legal obligation to be met.

ETHICAL ISSUES

CONCEPT CHECK

What challenges must be faced when determining a value for a firm's common shares?

What risks do shareholders face that can lead to fluctuations in share values?

Poor ethical decisions and poor management are another source of risk for stock investors in that such decisions can lower future cash flows and raise the required rate of return demanded by future investors. Accounting gimmickry and decisions by self-serving managers (more will be said about this in Chapter 11) can hurt stock prices, as happened with Enron, WorldCom, and Tyco. Poor customer/supplier relations, allegations of poor-quality products, and poor communications, as occurred between Ford Motor Company and one of its tire suppliers, Firestone, hurt both companies and their shareholders.

If the general level of interest rates rises, investors will demand a higher required rate of return on stocks to maintain their risk premium differential over debt securities. This will force stock prices downward. Therefore, stockholders risk losses from any general upward movement of market interest rates.

Also, future dividends, or dividend growth rates, are not known with certainty at the time stock is purchased. If poor corporate performance or adverse general economic conditions lead investors to lower their expectations about future dividend payments, this will lower the present value of shares of the stock, leaving the stockholder with the risk of capital loss. Stock analysts systematically review economic, industry, and firm conditions in great detail to gain insight into corporate growth prospects and the appropriate level of return that an investor should require of a stock.

VALUATION AND THE FINANCIAL ENVIRONMENT

The price of an asset is the present value of future cash flows; the discount rate used in the present value calculation is the required rate of return on the investment. Future cash flows of firms and the required returns of investors are affected by the global and domestic economic environments and the competition faced by firms. Slower sales or higher expenses can harm a firm's ability to pay its bond interest or dividends or to reinvest in its future growth. Besides affecting cash flows, these can affect investors' required rates of return by increasing risk premiums or credit spreads. Inflation pressures and capital market changes influence the level of interest rates and required returns.

INTERNET ACTIVITY

Read analysis and expectations of overseas economic activity from sites such as http://www.morganstanley.com (search for "Global Economic Forum") and download exchange rate data from sites such as https://www.federalreserve.gov/Releases/.

GLOBAL ECONOMIC INFLUENCES

Two main overseas influences will affect firms.[29] First is the condition of overseas economies. Growth in foreign economies will increase the demand for U.S. exports. Similarly, sluggish foreign demand will harm overseas sales and hurt the financial position of firms doing business overseas. The rate of economic growth overseas can affect the conditions faced by domestic firms, too, as growing demand globally may make it easier to raise prices and sluggish demand overseas may lead to intense competition in the U.S. market.

The second influence is the behavior of exchange rates, the price of a currency in terms of another currency. A change in exchange rates over time has two effects on the firm. Changing exchange rates lead to higher or lower U.S. dollar cash flows from overseas sales, more competitively priced import goods, or changing input costs. Thus, changing exchange rates affect profitability by influencing sales, price competition, and expenses. Second, changing exchange rates affect the level of domestic interest rates. Expectations of a weaker U.S. dollar can lead to higher U.S. interest rates; to attract capital, U.S. rates will have to rise to compensate foreign investors for expected currency losses because of the weaker dollar.[30] Conversely, a stronger dollar can result in lower U.S. interest rates.

---

29. By "overseas," we refer to events outside of the domestic economy, whether water separates the countries or not. Thus, although we share a land border, to a U.S. firm the economies of Canada and Mexico are overseas economies.

30. To understand this effect, suppose initially the exchange rate between the U.S. dollar and euro is $1 = €1. Analysts anticipate the dollar will weaken over the year to $1 = €0.95. The European investor who invests €1 for every $1 of investment now expects to receive dollars worth only €0.95 next year. The investor will require a higher expected return on his U.S. investment to compensate for the effects of the weakening dollar. This is similar to a U.S. investor seeking protection from anticipated inflation by increasing the required rate of return to reflect inflationary expectations.

INTERNET ACTIVITY

The Economic Report of the President is available on the Internet, as are its data tables; see also the Economics Briefing Room of the White House http://www.whitehouse.gov/issues/economy. Other good sources of domestic economic analysis and data include the Federal Reserve's Web site, http://www.federalreserve.gov; see especially the Beige Book analysis of economic conditions across the regions of the country. The St. Louis Federal Reserve's Web site, http://www.stlouisfed.org, has links to the FRED database and to education and analysis sites.

INTERNET ACTIVITY

Some industry analyses and information is available on Web sites such as http://finance.yahoo.com and www.hoovers.com. Other helpful information on industries is available from trade groups. Use of a Web search engine can help you find these sources.

CONCEPT CHECK

How can the growth of overseas economies affect the value of a U.S. firm's stock?

Why do stock and bond investors need to be aware of expectations in the exchange rate market?

How do fiscal policy, monetary policy, and consumer spending affect the outlook for securities markets?

How does competition affect a firm's profits over time?

DOMESTIC ECONOMIC INFLUENCES

Individuals can spend only what they have (income and savings) or what their future earning capacity will allow them to borrow. Consumption spending (spending by individuals for items such as food, cars, clothes, computers, and so forth) comprises about two-thirds of gross domestic product, GDP, in the United States. Generally, higher disposable incomes (that is, income after taxes) lead to higher levels of consumption spending. Higher levels of spending mean inventories are reduced and companies need to produce more and hire additional workers to meet sales demand. Corporations will spend to obtain supplies and workers based upon expectations of future demand. Similarly, they will invest in additional plant and equipment based upon expected future sales and income. Economic growth results in higher levels of consumer spending and corporate investment, which in turn stimulates job growth and additional demand. Slow or negative growth can lead to layoffs, pessimistic expectations, and reduced consumer and corporate spending. These effects will directly influence company profits and cash flows.

Economic conditions affect required returns, too. Investors will be more optimistic in good economic times and more willing to accept lower risk premiums on bond and stock investments. In poor economic times, credit spreads will rise as investors want to place their funds in safer investments.

Governments shape the domestic economy by fiscal policy (government spending and taxation decisions) and monetary policy. These decisions may affect consumer disposable income (fiscal policy) and the level of interest rates and inflation expectations (monetary policy) and therefore affect the valuation of the bond and stock markets.

Some industry sectors are sensitive to changes in consumer spending. Sales by auto manufacturers, computer firms, and other manufacturers of high-priced items will rise and fall by greater amounts over the business cycle than food or pharmaceutical firms. Changes in interest rates affect some industries more than others, too: banks and the housing industry (and sellers of large household appliances) are sensitive to changes in interest rates more than, say, book and music publishers or restaurants.

INDUSTRY AND COMPETITION

A firm's profits are determined by its sales revenues, expenses, and taxes. We've already mentioned taxes and some influences on sales and expenses in our discussion of global and domestic economies, but industry competition and the firm's position within the industry will have a large impact on its ability to generate profits over time. Tight competition means it will be difficult to raise prices to increase sales revenue or profitability. Nonprice forms of competition, such as customer service, product innovation, and using technology to the fullest extent in the manufacturing and sales process, may hurt profits by increasing expenses if the features do not generate sufficient sales. Competition may not come only from similar firms; for example, a variety of "entertainment" firms, from music to theater to movies to sports teams, vie for consumers' dollars. Both trucking firms and railroads compete for freight transportation; cable and satellite firms compete in the home television markets (and for Internet service, along with telephone service providers). Changes in the cost and availability of raw materials, labor, and energy can adversely affect a firm's competitive place in the market.

The influences of competition and supply ultimately affect a firm's profitability and investors' perceptions of the firm's risk. This, in turn, will affect its bond and stock prices. The most attractive firms for investing will be firms with a competitive advantage over their rivals. They may offer a high-quality product, be the low-cost producer, be innovators in the use of technology, or offer the best customer support. Whatever the source of the advantage, if they can build and maintain their advantage over time, they will reap above-normal profits and be attractive investments.

TINA LONGFIELD
Associate, Investment Banking Division
Credit Suisse First Boston

BA, Accountancy, University of Illinois
MBA, University of Chicago Graduate School of Business

CAREER PROFILES

"Being a team player is a must."

Q: *How does an investment bank like Credit Suisse First Boston help clients set and implement financial strategy?*
A: Credit Suisse First Boston (CSFB) is a leading global investment bank serving institutional, corporate, government, and individual clients. Its businesses include securities underwriting, sales and trading, investment banking, private equity, financial advisory services, investment research, venture capital, correspondent brokerage services, and asset management. We operate in over eighty-nine locations across more than thirty-seven countries on six continents.

Q: *What are your responsibilities as an associate at CSFB?*
A: I work in the firm's investment banking division, and specialize in technology companies. The technology group serves a wide range of clients, from large established companies to startups. As an associate in the corporate finance area, I work with our clients to help in such areas as determining alternative capital structures, choosing a financing strategy in ever-changing market environments, and introducing ideas for mergers and acquisitions. Of course, once a client chooses to implement a financing strategy, I work with a team to execute the transaction, such as an Initial Public Offering (IPO) or a Convertible Financing transaction. Business development—marketing ideas to potential clients—is also an important part of my job.

Q: *Is there a typical career path at investment banking firms?*
A: Yes, BAs enter an analyst program. After an intensive training program covering accounting, corporate finance, and financial modeling, you're often assigned to an industry, product, or geographical group where you learn to apply these basics and become an integral member of the group. At the end of two to three years, many analysts go to business school to earn their MBA. An investment bank also hires MBAs, who often have three or more years of work experience as associates. After several years of investment banking experience with a variety of clients and transactions, associates are considered for promotion to the next level, vice president.

Q: *Sounds like a challenging job. What skills do you need to be successful?*
A: Good analytical skills are, of course, helpful to provide both analysis and the interpretation of numbers. Being a team player is a must; we often work in small groups, which can change from transaction to transaction. Creativity and overall communication skills are very important, as is the ability to work in a fast-paced environment. As an analyst, it's an advantage to have introductory classes in finance, accounting, and economics, but it's not a necessity, because of the intensive training program everybody is put through. As you become more experienced, product and industry-specific knowledge, as well as the ability to see the big picture, are important, so you can provide the best advice on the range of financing and strategic alternatives available to the client.

Q: *What do you like best about your work?*
A: This job is always changing—no two days are the same. One day I could be working with a young private company looking to raise equity, and the next, I could be focused on helping a client sell a distressed unit of their company. One of the most rewarding experiences I probably have is the strategic dialogue I have with a lot of influential decision makers, who are looking to raise significant amounts of money and deciding how to put it to work. I also enjoy working with the people at CSFB. This job requires long hours, so liking your colleagues is a key factor in job satisfaction.

APPLYING FINANCE TO...

INSTITUTIONS AND MARKETS

Bond and stock trading occurs in capital markets. Some institutions, such as investment banks, facilitate trading of these securities and develop different variations (callable, putable) to meet the needs of different kinds of issuers and investors. For other institutions, bonds and stocks are another means of supplying capital in addition to bank loans, private placements, mortgages, and so forth to those needing access to funds.

INVESTMENTS

Bonds and stocks are tools used by investors; they are purchased in an attempt to meet an investor's goals and risk preferences over the investor's time horizon.

FINANCIAL MANAGEMENT

These securities are a source of long-term financing for asset acquisition, implementing long-term strategies, and for acquiring other firms.

SUMMARY

One purpose of this chapter has been to examine the characteristics of bonds and stocks. A second major purpose has been to determine security values by applying time value of money techniques to the cash flows that investors receive from bond and stock investments. The current price of the securities should equal the present value of future expected cash flows. If security prices are already known, these techniques can also be used to estimate investment returns.

Stock and debt offerings are major sources of long-term funds for businesses. Bonds offer investors a fixed income flow and priority in terms of liquidation. Bond covenants, which are found in the indenture, list some of the obligations of the issuer toward the bondholders. Bonds can be secured by corporate assets or be unsecured; unsecured bonds are called debentures. Bond ratings assess both the collateral underlying the bonds as well as the ability of the issuers to make timely payments of interest and principal. Bonds can be sold overseas by U.S. issuers; non-U.S. firms can issue bonds in the United States, as long as SEC requirements are fulfilled.

Most equity offerings are sales of common stock. Preferred stock gives holders preference over common shareholders with respect to dividends and liquidation, but unlike the common shareholders, the (usually) fixed dividend received by preferred shareholders does not allow them to enjoy the benefits of future profit growth. Many investors buy common shares expecting dividends to rise over time.

The financial system and the economic environment are inseparable inputs to analyzing stocks and bonds. Firms' cash flows—and the outlook for their stock and bond issues—are affected by the global economy and domestic economy as growth overseas and at home will affect demand for the firm's products and will affect its costs, too. Industry competition and technological change can make last year's "sure thing" become this year's bankruptcy filing. Changing demand and supply for funds, fluctuating exchange rates, and monetary policy will influence inflationary expectations and required returns on securities. Much of what was learned in economics and in Part 1 of this book has implications for the behavior of the bond and stock market over time.

KEY TERMS

bearer bonds
bond rating
call deferment periods
call price
call risk
callable bond
callable preferred stock
closed-end mortgage bond
common stock
constant payout ratio
conversion ratio
conversion value

convertible bond
convertible preferred stock
corporate equity capital
coupon payments
covenants
cumulative preferred stock
credit risk (default risk)
debenture bonds
discount bond
dividend payout ratio
dividend reinvestment plan (DRIP)
equipment trust certificate

Eurodollar bonds
exchange rate risk
extendable notes
face value
financial assets
first mortgage bonds
global bonds
Gordon model (constant dividend growth model)
interest rate risk
junk bonds or high-yield bonds
noncumulative preferred stock

open-end mortgage bond	reinvestment rate risk	stock split
par value	residual dividend policy	street name
participating preferred stock	retractable bonds	subordinated debenture
political risk	rollover risk	target dividend payout policy
preferred stock	sinking fund	trustee
premium bond	special dividend	trust indenture
putable bonds	stock certificate	Yankee bonds
registered bonds	stock dividend	yield to maturity (YTM)

DISCUSSION QUESTIONS

1. Describe the relationship between internal and external financing in meeting the long-term financial needs of a firm.

2. What are the major sources of long-term funds available to business corporations? Indicate their relative importance.

3. Why would firms raise capital in markets other than their domestic or home market?

4. Can only large institutional investors purchase bonds? Explain.

5. How does a TIPS bond differ from the typical U.S. Treasury security?

6. Describe what is meant by bond covenants.

7. What are bond ratings?

8. Briefly describe the types of bonds that can be issued to provide bondholder security.

9. What is meant by the following terms: convertible bonds, callable bonds, putable bonds, and Eurodollar bonds?

10. Why are investment-grade bonds given that name? Why are "junk bonds" also known as "high-yield bonds"?

11. Why might a firm want to maintain a high bond rating? What has been happening to bond ratings in recent years?

12. Why might an investor find a zero-coupon bond an attractive investment?

13. Briefly describe how securities are valued.

14. Describe the process for valuing a bond.

15. What is meant by the "yield to maturity" on a bond?

16. Briefly describe the types of risk faced by investors in domestic bonds. Also indicate the additional risks associated with nondomestic bonds.

17. What risk does a zero-coupon bond address?

18. According to the behavior of interest rates in Figure 10.5, were investors more concerned or less concerned about risk over the 2002–2006 time period? Explain.

19. What does it mean with the horizon spreads in Figure 10.7 dip below the X-axis? Why do some feel that this was not to be the case in 2006?

20. How do you think credit spreads behave over the course of the economic cycle?

21. What is a "flight to quality?" Under what economic conditions might we see this?

22. Why study stocks if the net amount of stock issues is negative?

23. Why should investors consider common stock as an investment vehicle if they have a long-term time horizon?

24. Why does dividend income growth exceed that of bond income growth over a period of time?

25. What is a capital gain? Is it taxed the same way as dividends?

26. "Taxes on capital gains can be deferred." Explain what this statement means.

27. Explain how a capital loss on the sale of a firm's stock can affect an investor's taxes.

28. What is a round lot of common stock?

29. Describe some of the characteristics of common stock.

30. List and briefly explain the special features usually associated with preferred stock.

31. How do firms decide how much of their earnings to distribute as dividends?

32. Explain how an investor may view a stock dividend, a stock split, and a stock repurchase plan with regards to the value of his stock holdings.

33. Briefly describe how securities are valued.

34. Describe the process for valuing a preferred stock.

35. Describe the process for valuing a common stock when the cash dividend is expected to grow at a constant rate.

36. Discuss the risks faced by common shareholders that are not related to the general level of interest rates.

37. Under what economic forecast would you believe an auto manufacturer would be a good investment? A computer manufacturer?

38. Discuss how changes in exchange rates can affect the outlook for both global and domestic firms.

39. What can looking at data on inventories tell us about the condition of the economy? Data on business expansion or investment plans?

40. Is industry competition good or bad if you are looking for attractive stock investments?

41. Give examples of firms you believe have been successful over time because they are industry leaders in quality; they are the low-cost producer; they are innovative; they offer superior customer service.

42. Energy prices are forecast to go higher. How would this affect your decision to purchase the stocks of
    a. ExxonMobil?
    b. American Airlines?
    c. Ford?
    d. Archer Daniels Midland, a food processor?

PROBLEMS

1. Compute the annual interest payments and principal amount for a Treasury Inflation-Protected Security with a par value of $1,000 and a 3 percent interest rate if inflation is 4 percent in year one, 5 percent in year two, and 6 percent in year three.

2. Judy Johnson is choosing between investing in two Treasury securities that mature in five years and have par values of $1,000. One is a Treasury note paying an annual coupon of 5.06 percent. The other is a TIPS which pays 3 percent interest annually.

   a. If inflation remains constant at 2 percent annually over the next five years, what will be Judy's annual interest income from the TIPS bond? From the Treasury note?

   b. How much interest will Judy receive over the five years from the Treasury note? From the TIPS?

   c. When each bond matures, what par value will Judy receive from the Treasury note? The TIPS?

   d. After five years, what is Judy's total income (interest + par) from each bond? Should she use this total as a way of deciding which bond to purchase?

3. Using the regular Treasury note of problem 2:

   a. What is its price if investors' required rate of return is 6.09 percent on similar bonds? Treasury notes pay interest semi-annually.

   b. Erron Corporation wants to issue five-year notes but investors require a credit risk spread of 3 percentage points. What is the anticipated coupon rate on the Erron notes?

4. Assume a $1,000 face value bond has a coupon rate of 8.5 percent, pays interest semi-annually, and has an eight-year life. If investors are willing to accept a 10.25 percent rate of return on bonds of similar quality, what is the present value or worth of this bond?

5. a. By how much would the value of the bond in Problem 4 change if investors wanted an 8 percent rate of return?

   b. A bond with the same par value and coupon rate as the bond in Problem 4 has fourteen years until maturity. If investors will use a 10.25 percent discount rate to value this bond, by how much should its price differ from the bond in Problem 4?

6. The Garcia Company's bonds have a face value of $1,000, will mature in ten years, and carry a coupon rate of 16 percent. Assume interest payments are made semi-annually.

   a. Determine the present value of the bond's cash flows if the required rate of return is 16.64 percent.

   b. How would your answer change if the required rate of return is 12.36 percent?

7. Judith, Inc. bonds mature in eight years and pay a semi-annual coupon of $55. The bond's par value is $1,000.

   a. What is their current price if the market interest rate for bonds of similar quality is 9.2 percent?

   b. A change in Fed policy increases market interest rates 0.50 percentage points from their level in part (a). What is the percentage change in the value of Judith, Inc. bonds from their value in part (a)?

   c. Better profits for Judith, Inc. reduces the market interest rate for its bonds to 9.0 percent. What is the percentage change in the value of Judith, Inc. bonds from the answer in part (b)?

8. Kamins Corporation has two bond issues outstanding, each with a par value of $1,000. Information about each is listed below. Suppose market interest rates rise 1 percentage point across the yield curve. What will be the change in price for each of the bonds? Does this tell us anything about the relationship between time to maturity and interest rate risk?

   Bond A: 5 years to maturity, 8 percent coupon, market interest rate is 9 percent

   Bond B: 12 years to maturity, 8 percent coupon, market interest rate is 9 percent

9. Billon Corporation has two bond issues outstanding, each with a par value of $1,000. Information about each is listed below. Suppose market interest rates rise 1 percentage point across the yield curve. What will be the change in price for each of the bonds? Does this tell us anything about the relationship between coupon rate and interest rate risk?

   Bond A: 10 years to maturity, 0 percent coupon, market interest rate is 9.62 percent.

   Bond B: 10 years to maturity, 10 percent coupon, market interest rate is 9.62 percent.

10. Koppen Corporation has two bond issues outstanding, each with a par value of $1,000. Information about each is listed below. Suppose market interest rates rise 1 percentage point across the yield curve. What will be the change in price for each of the bonds? Does this tell us anything about the relationship between frequency of cash flows and interest rate risk?

    Bond A: This bond is a Eurobond. It has 10 years to maturity, pays a 7 percent coupon, and the market interest rate is 11.3 percent.

    Bond B: This is a issued in the U.S. It has 10 years to maturity, pays a 7 percent coupon, and the market interest rate is 11.3 percent.

11. BVA Inc. has two bond issues outstanding, each with a par value of $1,000. Information about each is listed below. Suppose market interest rates rise 1 percentage point across the yield curve. What will be the change in price for each of the bonds? Does this tell us anything about the relationship between initial yield to maturity and interest rate risk?

    Bond A: 12 years to maturity, pays a 7 percent coupon, and the market interest rate on this BB-rated bond is 12.36 percent.

    Bond B: 12 years to maturity, pays a 7 percent coupon, and the market interest rate on this A-rated bond is 10.25 percent.

12. What is the approximate yield to maturity (use formula 10.3) and the exact yield to maturity (use a calculator) for the following bonds? Assume these are bonds issued in the U.S.

    a. 10 years to maturity, 6 percent coupon rate, current price is $950.

    b. 16 years to maturity, 0 percent coupon rate, current price is $339.

    c. 25 years to maturity, 8.5 percent coupon rate, current price is $1030.

13. On Thursday the following bond quotation appears in the newspaper. Interpret each item that appears in the quote and compute its current yield:

COMPANY (TICKER)	COUPON	MAT.	LAST PRICE	LAST YIELD	EST SPREAD	EST UST	$VOL (000s)
Wal-Mart Stores WMT	4.550	May 1, 2013	99.270	4.649	47	10	66,830

14. Perusing the corporate bond quotations, you write down some summary information:

COMPANY (TICKER)	COUPON	MAT	LAST PRICE	LAST YIELD	EST SPREAD	EST UST	$VOL (000S)
Wal-Mart Stores WMT	4.550	10 years	99.270	4.649	47	10	66,830
Wal-Mart Stores WMT	4.125	8 years	99.554	4.200	2	10	50,320
Liberty Media L	5.700	10 years	102.750	5.314	112	10	26,045
Ford Motor Credit F	7.250	8 years	107.407	6.012	183	10	22,863

a. Which company is the riskiest? Why?
b. Which bond has the highest default risk? Why?
c. Why would Wal-Mart have two bonds trading at different yields?
d. Compute the current yield for each of the four bonds.
e. Compute yield to maturity for each of the four bonds.

15. You run across the following bond quotation on a Friday.

RATE	MATURITY MO/YR	BID	ASKED	CHG.	ASKED YLD
7.500	Nov 24	131:06	131:07	−9	5.04

a. What kind of security is it?
b. Interpret the information contained in the quote.
c. Suppose a corporate bond with the same time to maturity has a credit risk spread of 250 basis points. What should be the yield to maturity for the corporate bond?

16. **Challenge Problem** A $1,000 face value bond issued by the Dysane Company currently pays total annual interest of $79 per year and has a thirteen-year life.

a. What is the present value, or worth, of this bond if investors are currently willing to accept a 10 percent annual rate of return on bonds of similar quality if the bond is a Eurobond?
b. How would your answer in (a) change if the bond is a U.S. bond?
c. How would your answer in (b) change if, one year from now, investors only required a 6.5 percent annual rate of return on bond investments similar in quality to the Dysane bond?
d. Suppose the original bond can be purchased for $925. What is the bond's yield to maturity?

17. **Challenge Problem**

a. You own a two-bond portfolio. Each has a par value of $1,000. Bond A matures in five years, has a coupon rate of 8 percent, and has an annual yield to maturity of 9.20 percent. Bond B matures in fifteen years, has a coupon rate of 8 percent and has an annual yield to maturity of 9.20 percent. Both bonds pay interest semi-annually. What is the value of your portfolio? What happens to the value of your portfolio if each yield to maturity rises by one percentage point?
b. Rather than own a five-year bond and a fifteen-year bond, suppose you sell both of them and invest in two ten-year bonds. Each has a coupon rate of 8 percent (semi-annual coupons) and has a yield to maturity of 9.20 percent. What is the value of your portfolio? What happens to the value of your portfolio if the yield to maturity on the bonds rises by one percentage point?

c. Based upon your answers to (a) and (b), evaluate the price changes between the two portfolios. Were the price changes the same? Why or why not?

18. **EXCEL** A bond with a par value of $1,000 has a coupon rate of 7 percent and matures in fifteen years. Using a spreadsheet program, graph its price versus different yields to maturity, ranging from 1 percent to 20 percent. Is the relationship between price and yield linear? Why or why not?

19. Global Cycles (GC) offers investors a DRIP program. An investor purchases 100 shares of GC at a price of $20 per share on January 2. How many shares will the investor own on December 31 if the following dividends are paid and the investor participates in the DRIP program (assume the firm allows fractional shares and accounts for them up to three decimal places)? If the stock's price is $27.50 on December 31, what is the value of her investment in GC?

March 1: dividend paid of $0.50 per share; stock price is $21
June 1: dividend paid of $0.50 per share; stock price is $22.5
September 1: dividend paid of $0.55 per share; stock price is $19
December 1: dividend paid of $0.55 per share; stock price is $25

20. If a stock's earnings per share are $2.00, what will be the dividend per share if the payout ratio is 40 percent? If the following year's earnings per share are $2.10, what will the payout ratio be if the firm wants to maintain dividend growth of 8 percent?

21. You purchased 200 shares of H2O Corporation stock at a price of $20. Consider each of the following announcements separately. What will the price of the stock be after each change? How many shares will you own? What will be the total value of your holdings (value of stock plus any income)?

a. The firm announces a 10 percent stock dividend.
b. The firm announces a two-for-one stock split.
c. The firm announces a $0.50 per share dividend (in your answer use the price of the stock on the exdividend date).
d. The firm announces it will repurchase 10 percent of its shares; you do not offer to sell any of your shares.

22. The Fridge-Air Company's preferred stock pays a dividend of $4.50 per share annually. If the required rate of return on comparable quality preferred stocks is 14 percent, calculate the value of Fridge-Air's preferred stock.

23. The Joseph Company has a stock issue that pays a fixed dividend of $3.00 per share annually. Investors believe the nominal risk-free rate is 4 percent and that this stock should have a risk premium of 6 percent. What should be the value of this stock?

24. The Lo Company earned $2.60 per share and paid a dividend of $1.30 per share in the year just ended. Earnings and dividends per share are expected to grow at a rate of 5 percent per year in the future. Determine the value of the stock:

a. if the required rate of return is 12 percent.
b. if the required rate of return is 15 percent.
c. Given your answers to (a) and (b), how are stock prices affected by changes in investor's required rates of return?

25. The French Thaler and Company's stock has paid dividends of $1.60 over the past 12 months. Its historical growth rate of dividends has been 8 percent, but analysts expect the growth to slow to 5 percent annually for the foreseeable future.

a. Determine the value of the stock if the required rate of return on stocks of similar risk is 15 percent.

b. If analysts believe the risk premium on the stock should be reduced by 2 percentage points, what is the new required rate of return on French Thaler and Company stock? How much should its price change from the answer you computed in part (a)?

26. Mercier Corporation's stock is selling for $95. It has just paid a dividend of $5 a share. The expected growth rate in dividends is 8 percent.

   a. What is the required rate of return on this stock?
   b. Using your answer to (a), suppose Mercier announces developments that should lead to dividend increases of 10 percent annually. What will be the new value of Mercier's stock?
   c. Again using your answer to (a), suppose developments occur that leave investors expecting that dividends will not change from their current levels in the foreseeable future. Now what will be the value of Mercier stock?
   d. From your answers to (b) and (c), how important are investors' expectations of future dividend growth to the current stock price?

27. The common stock of RMW Inc. is selling at $88 a share. It just paid a dividend of $4. Investors expect a return of 15 percent on their investment in RMW Inc. From this information, what is the expected growth rate of future dividends?

28. Lerman Company has preferred stock outstanding. It pays an annual dividend of $10. If its current price is $70, what discount rate are investors using to value the stock?

29. Interpret the following stock price quote. In addition, what are Sizzler's approximate earnings per share? What was the stock's closing price the previous day?

YTD % CHG	52 WEEKS HI	52 WEEKS LO	STOCK	SYM	DIV	YLD %	PE	VOL 100s	LAST	NET CHG
+17.3	7.13	5.00	Sizzlr	SZ	0.16	2.7	25	844	6	−0.25

30. **Challenge Problem** Ritter Incorporated just paid a dividend of $2 per share. Its management team has just announced a technological breakthrough that is expected to result in a temporary increase in sales, profits, and common stock dividends. Analysts expect the firm's per-share dividends to be $2.50 next year, $3 in two years, and $3.50 in three years. After that, normal dividend growth of 5 percent is expected to resume. If shareholders expect a 15 percent return on their investment in Ritter, what should the firm's stock price be?

31. **Challenge Problem** Tough times have hit the retail store chain of Brador, Inc. Analysts expect its dividend of $1.00 a share to fall by 50 percent next year and another 50 percent the following year before it returns to its normal growth pattern of 3 percent a year. If investors expect a return of 18 percent on their investment in Brador stock, what should its current stock price be?

32. **EXCEL** JW Corp has a dividend of $0.50. The dividend is growing at a 6 percent rate over time. Based on the stock's risk, investors require an 11 percent rate of return.

   a. Using the constant dividend growth model, what should the stock's price be?
   b. Estimate the firm's dividends for the next ten years and find their present value. What proportion of the stock's price is based upon dividends that are expected to occur more than ten years into the future?
   c. What proportion of the firm's price is based upon dividends that are expected to occur more than five years into the future?

33. **EXCEL** A firm's dividends are expected to grow 20 percent a year for the next five years and then trend downward by 3 percentage points per year until they stabilize at a constant growth rate of 5 percent. The current dividend is $0.80 a share and the stock's required rate of return is 13 percent. What should its current price be? If these growth expectations come to pass, what will its price be four years from now? Eight years from now?

LEARNING EXTENSION 10

Annualizing Rates of Return

An investment provides two sources of returns: income and price changes. Bonds pay coupon interest (income), and as we saw in Chapter 10, fluctuating market interest rates can lead to changing bond prices and capital gains or losses. Stocks may pay dividends (a source of investor income) and rise or fall in value over time, leading to capital gains or losses. Such is the case with other investment vehicles such as real estate or mutual funds.

HOLDING PERIOD RETURNS

The dollar return on a single financial asset held for a specific time, or holding period, is given by:

$$\text{Dollar return} = \text{Income received} + \text{Price change} \quad \text{(LE 10.1)}$$

Suppose during the time Amy held a share of stock, she received dividends of $2 while the stock price rose from a purchase price of $25 to its current level of $30. Should Amy sell the stock today, her dollar return would be:

$$\text{Dollar return} = \text{Income received} + \text{price change}$$
$$= \$2 + (\$30 - \$25)$$
$$\$7 = \$2 + \$5$$

She received $2 in dividends and the value of her investment rose by $5 for a total dollar return of $7. To compare this investment return with others, it is best to measure the dollar return relative to the initial price paid for the stock. This percentage return is simply the dollar return divided by the initial price of the stock:

$$\text{Percentage return} = (\text{Dollar return}/\text{Initial price}) \quad \text{(LE 10.2)}$$

Amy's percentage return was:

$$\text{Percentage return} = (\text{Dollar return}/\text{Initial price}) = (\$7/\$25) = 0.28 \text{ or } 28 \text{ percent}$$

ANNUALIZED RATES OF RETURN

To compare accurately the returns on one investment with another, they should be measured over equal time periods, such as a year, a month, or a day. By convention, most investors use annual returns as a means by which to compare investments. To *annualize a return* means to state it as the annual return that would result in the observed percentage return. Equation LE 10.3 gives us a formula for determining annualized returns:

$$\text{Annualized return} = (1 + \text{percentage return})^{1/n} - 1 \quad \text{(LE 10.3)}$$

where n is the number of years an investment was held. For a one-year example, Amy's annualized return is the same as her percentage return. This can be shown as follows:

$$\text{Annualized return} = (1 + 0.28)^{1/1} - 1$$
$$= (1.28)^1 - 1 = 1.28 - 1 = 0.28 \text{ or } 28 \text{ percent}$$

Notice that the superscript fraction 1/1 indicates that Amy's investment was for one year.

When investments are held for longer than one year, the fraction becomes less than one, indicating that the percentage return must be spread over a longer time period. For example, if Amy's investment was purchased two years ago, her annualized return would be:

$$\text{Annualized return} = (1 + 0.28)^{1/2} - 1$$
$$= (1.28)^{0.5} - 1 = 1.131 - 1 = 0.131 \text{ or } 13.1 \text{ percent}$$

Also notice that the annualized return is not just the 28 percent total return divided by two years or 14 percent, which would be a simple average annual return. Rather, the annualized return measured by Equation LE 10.3 also captures the compounding or discounting effects of holding investments longer than one year.

It should now be apparent that as the investment-holding period lengthens, the annualized return gets progressively smaller. For example, let's now assume that Amy earned her 28 percent total return over a period of four years. Her annualized return would be calculated as:

$$\text{Annualized return} = (1 + 0.28)^{1/4} - 1$$
$$= (1.28)^{0.25} - 1 = 1.064 - 1 = 0.064 \text{ or } 6.4 \text{ percent}$$

A financial calculator can be used to simplify the calculation effort, as follows:

Financial Calculator Solution: 1-Year Investment

Exponent	$1/n = 1/1 = 1$						
Input	1.28	Y^x	then	1	$=$	-1	$=$
Solution	0.28						

Financial Calculator Solution: 2-Year Investment

Exponent	$1/n = 1/2 = 0.5$						
Input	1.28	Y^x	then	0.5	$=$	-1	$=$
Solution	0.131						

Financial Calculator Solution: 4-Year Investment

Exponent	$1/n = 1/4 = 0.25$						
Input	1.28	Y^x	then	0.25	$=$	-1	$=$
Solution	0.064						

Annualized returns also can be calculated for investments that are held for less than one year. Let's assume that Amy held her investment for only nine months while earning a percentage return of 28 percent. What would be Amy's annualized return under this scenario?

$$\text{Annualized return} = (1 + 0.28)^{1/(9/12)} - 1$$
$$= (1.28)^{1/0.75} - 1 = (1.28)^{1.33} - 1 = 1.389 - 1 = 0.389 \text{ or } 38.9 \text{ percent}$$

Because most individual and institutional investors are interested in comparing annualized returns, it is important that you know how to compute percentage returns and how to annualize them.

PROBLEMS

1. Given the information below, compute annualized returns:

ASSET	INCOME	PRICE CHANGE	INITIAL PRICE	TIME PERIOD
A	$2	$6	$29	15 months
B	0	10	40	11 months
C	50	70	30	7 years
D	3	−8	20	24 months

2. Given the information below, compute annualized returns:

ASSET	PURCHASE PRICE	CURRENT PRICE	INCOME RECEIVED	TIME PERIOD
A	$20	$26	$2	75 weeks
B	15	18	0.40	3 months
C	150	130	0	2 years
D	3.50	3.00	0.20	8 months

CHAPTER 11

Securities Markets

Chapter Learning Objectives:

AFTER STUDYING THIS CHAPTER, YOU SHOULD BE ABLE TO:
- Describe the processes and institutions used by businesses to distribute new securities to the investing public.
- Outline the recent difficulties and changes in structure of the investment banking industry.
- Describe how securities are traded among investors.
- Identify the regulatory mechanisms by which the securities exchanges and the over-the-counter markets are controlled.
- Explain influences that affect broker commissions.

Where We Have Been... For the savings process to work, funds must be routed from savings to the users of funds. Banks and other financial institutions assist with this process; so do securities markets. Chapter 10 introduced us to the characteristics of stocks and bonds, how they can be priced using time value concepts, and the risks that investors face when holding them. Supply and demand forces in financial markets set market prices for securities. Interest rates and asset prices rise and fall based upon investors' and issuers' desires to buy and sell securities.

Where We Are Going... The process of raising funds in securities markets is important for business firms. A firm's ability to raise funds will be the topic of future chapters: long-term fund raising is the focus of Chapter 18's capital structure discussion and short-term financing is discussed in Chapter 16.

How Does This Chapter Apply to Me... Securities markets—typically the secondary markets such as the New York Stock Exchange—are in the news every day. Stock and bond indexes reflect the changing values of securities over time. Investors' decisions and reactions to news events lead to changes in interest rates, bond prices, and stock prices. Movements in market prices affect personal wealth. Many people make decisions, either through direct investment or through their decisions regarding where to place their 401(k) or Individual Retirement Account (IRA) investments that involve the securities markets. As a financial manager, the trend in your firm's stock price over time, relative to competitors and the overall market, is a reflection of how investors view your firm's prospects.

The goal of every investor is to:

Buy low and sell high.

Will Rogers, the famous American humorist, gave his own thoughts on how to succeed in investing:

Buy a stock that will go up in value. If it doesn't go up, don't buy it!

Of course, the ability to buy securities at a low price and to sell them at a higher price is the goal of every investor, but it isn't easy to do. In this chapter we'll learn how securities are issued, about the different markets in which they are traded, and how investors can buy and sell securities.

ISSUING SECURITIES: PRIMARY SECURITIES MARKETS

primary market
original issue market in which securities are initially sold

FINANCIAL CRISIS

secondary market
market in which securities are traded among investors

flotation
initial sale of newly issued debt or equity securities

initial public offering (IPO)
initial sale of equity to the public

investment bankers (underwriters)
assist corporations by raising money through the marketing of corporate securities to the securities markets

public offering
sale of securities to the investing public

private placement
sale of securities to a small group of private investors

due diligence
detailed study of a corporation

prospectus
highly regulated document that details the issuer's operations and finances and must be provided to each buyer of a newly issued security

Recall from Chapter 1 that newly created securities are sold in the **primary market** while existing securities are traded in the **secondary market.** The initial sale of newly issued debt or equity securities is called a **flotation;** the initial sale of equity to the public is called an **initial public offering (IPO).** To raise money, corporations usually use the services of firms called **investment bankers,** or **underwriters,** whose main activity is marketing securities and dealing with the securities markets. Investment bankers act as intermediaries between corporations and the general public when corporations want to raise capital. Investment banks, for the most part, were separate, stand-alone firms. After the 2007–09 Financial Crisis, most investment banks either failed (Bear Stearns, Lehman Brothers) or were purchased by stronger financial institutions (such as Bank of America's acquisition of Merrill Lynch). Current investment banking firms include Bank of America (Bank of America Merrill Lynch), Barclays (Barclays Capital), Citigroup, Goldman Sachs, JPMorgan Chase (J.P. Morgan), and Morgan Stanley, among others.

PRIMARY MARKET FUNCTIONS OF INVESTMENT BANKERS

Although the specific activities of investment bankers differ depending upon their size and financial resources, the functions of investment bankers include originating, underwriting, and selling newly issued securities.

Originating

Most of the larger investment banking firms engage in originating securities. As an originator, the investment bank seeks to identify firms that may benefit from a **public offering,** which is a sale of securities to the investing public, or a **private placement,** which is a sale of securities to a small group of private investors. The Securities and Exchange Commission (SEC) regulates the public offering process. The private placement process has fewer regulations, but the securities can only be sold to investors who meet certain SEC-regulated guidelines for wealth and investment knowledge. Most of this section will focus on the role of an investment bank in a public offering.

Once the investment bank identifies a firm that may want to sell securities, the investment bank attempts to sell itself to the issuer as the best investment bank to handle the offering.[1] Once an agreement is reached, the investment bank makes a detailed study (called **due diligence**) of the corporation. The investment bank uses this information in order to determine the best means of raising the needed funds. The investment banker will recommend the types, terms, and offering price of securities that should be sold.[2] He or she also aids the corporation in preparing the registration and informational materials required by the Securities and Exchange Commission.

One important and carefully regulated piece of information is the **prospectus,** which details the issuer's finances and must be provided to each buyer of the security. Some of the questions one chief financial officer used to quiz prospective investment banking partners for his firm's IPOs are listed in Table 11.1. These questions cover several of the underwriting, selling, and aftermarket aspects of the going-public process, which we will discuss below.

Another piece of advice the investment bank gives firms who want to have an initial public offering is when to go public. At times, the investing public is particularly interested in firms operating in certain industries or that develop certain technologies. Firms that go public in "hot" IPO markets—when investors are anxious to buy new issues and prices are bid up, sometimes, to twice or three times their initial offering price—are likely to receive better prices for their shares than if they go public in a "cold" market, when investors are less receptive to new stock issues.

---

1. For one firm's process of selecting an investment banker, see Alix Nyberg, "The Tough Go Shopping," *CFO* (January 2001), pp. 89–93; Orin C. Smith, "Wanted: The Right Investment Banker," *Financial Executive* (November/December 1994), pp. 14–18. Mr. Smith describes his firm's experience of "going public" when he was chief financial officer of Starbucks Coffee Company.

2. Chapter 18, Capital Structure and the Cost of Capital, will detail some of the items a firm and its investment bank will consider before deciding the type of securities to be sold.

TABLE 11.1
Selections from One Firm's Quiz for Potential Investment Banking Firms Interested in Doing Its IPO

1. How would you position our company in relation to the market and its competition?
2. What companies would you choose as comparable companies from a valuation standpoint? How do you value our company and why?
3. Explain your pricing strategy for our firm's public offering, and contrast it with at least four other recent IPOs that you have managed or comanaged.
4. How frequently will research reports be published during the two years following the offering? Present examples of your research frequency for other IPOs in the last two years.
5. Under what circumstances would you stop research coverage of the company? Have you dropped coverage of any companies you have taken public in the last three years?
6. Please prepare a table that demonstrates your trading performance post-IPO for five or six high-profile IPOs that you have managed in the last 12 to 18 months.

Source: Based upon Alix Nyberg, "The Tough Go Shopping," *CFO* (January 2001), p. 90.

Underwriting

Investment bankers not only help to sell securities to the investing public, they also sometimes assume the risk arising from the possibility that such securities may not be purchased by investors. This occurs when the investment banker enters into an **underwriting agreement** with the issuing corporation. As shown in Figure 11.1, with an underwriting agreement, securities are purchased at a predetermined or "firm commitment" price by the underwriters, who then sell them to investors at the **offer price.** The difference between the offer price and the price paid by the investment bank is called a **spread.** The spread is revenue to the investment bank, which is used to cover its expenses and to provide a profit from its underwriting activities.

The issuer has virtually no price risk in a firm commitment offering once the offer price is set. The issuer receives the proceeds from the sale immediately, which it can then spend on the purposes outlined in the prospectus. The investment bank carries, or underwrites, the risk of fluctuating stock prices. The investment bank carries the risk of loss, or at least the possibility of a smaller spread than expected, should the market's perception of the issuer change or an economic event (such as an unexpected attempt by the Fed to increase interest rates) result in a stock market decline before the investment bank can sell all the securities; but as we shall see in a later section, the phenomenon of "underpricing" or first-day price increases for IPOs is prevalent and reduces the possibility of an investment banker losing money on a firm commitment underwriting.

Another means of offering securities is called best-effort selling. Under a **best-effort agreement,** investment bankers try to sell the securities of the issuing corporation, but they assume no risk for a possible failure of the flotation. The investment bankers are paid a fee or commission for those securities they sell. The best-effort agreement is typically used when the investment bankers anticipate that there may be some difficulty in selling the securities and they are unwilling to assume the underwriting risk. From the perspective of investors, an investment bank putting its money at risk with a firm commitment underwriting agreement would be preferable. Investors should view a best-effort offering with some concern. If the investment banker is not willing to support the firm's security sale, why should other investors?

Firms that are already public and wish to raise additional funds have several choices. They can sell additional securities by using the underwriting process, as discussed above. They can also

underwriting agreement
contract in which the investment banker agrees to buy securities at a predetermined price and then resell them to investors

offer price
price at which the security is sold to the investors

spread
difference between the offer price and the price paid by the investment bank

best-effort agreement
agreement by the investment banker to sell securities of the issuing corporation; assumes no risk for the possible failure of the flotation

FIGURE 11.1
Diagram of a Firm Commitment Underwriting

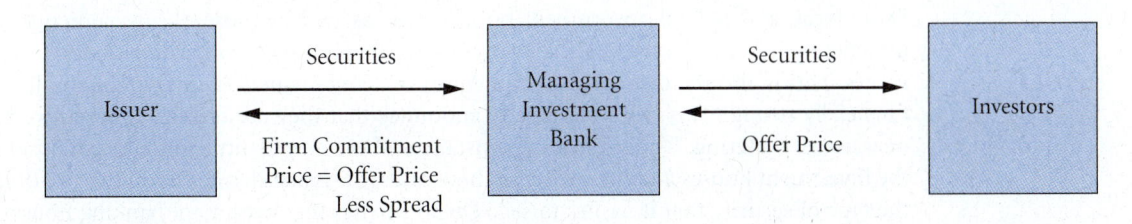

Issuer →Securities→ Managing Investment Bank →Securities→ Investors
Issuer ←Firm Commitment Price = Offer Price Less Spread← Managing Investment Bank ←Offer Price← Investors

choose to use shelf registration, sell securities to a private party, have a rights offering, or seek competitive bids. We discuss each of these below.

Shelf Registration

The Securities and Exchange Commission's (SEC) Rule 415 allows firms to register security issues (both debt and equity) and then "put them on the shelf" for sale any time over the succeeding two years. Once registered, the securities can be offered for sale by submitting a short statement to the SEC whenever the firm needs the funds or market conditions are attractive. The **shelf registration** process saves issuers both time and money. There is no cost or penalty for registering shelf securities and then not issuing them. Filing fees are relatively low, and the firm can take some securities from the shelf, sell them immediately through one underwriter, and later sell more with another underwriter. Not every firm can use shelf registration. Firms must meet several size, credit quality, and ethics requirements:

1. The market value of the firm's common stock must be at least $150 million.
2. It must have made no defaults on its debt in the previous three years.
3. The firm's debt must be investment grade (rated BBB or better).
4. The firm must not have been found guilty of violating the Securities Exchange Act of 1934 in the previous three years.

> **shelf registration**
> allows firms to register security issues (both debt and equity) with the SEC and have them available to sell for two years

ETHICAL ISSUES

Sell Securities to a Private Party

A publicly held firm can choose to sell securities in a private placement. To keep current shareholders from suspecting any "sweetheart deals," privately placed equity is typically sold at a slight premium to the stock's current market price.

Private equity sales may occur if the firm is the rumored or actual target of a hostile takeover. Management may try to stall the takeover or stop it by selling a large block of voting stock to an investor or syndicate that seems friendlier. Occasionally news stories contain articles of rumored deals involving firms in financial difficulty that are seeking equity infusions to keep them afloat.

Private placements of equity may also fulfill a need for an emergency infusion of equity. Since the shares are not being sold in a public offering, the private placement avoids SEC registration and subsequent publicity. The private sale must follow other SEC regulations, however. The firm must disclose the sale after it occurs, and the private investors must meet SEC requirements as "accredited investors." Basically, accredited investors are those who are considered knowledgeable enough or sufficiently strong enough financially to invest without the protection provided by the SEC's registration process. Accredited investors can include wealthy individuals with investment experience as well as financial institutions, such as insurance companies and pension funds.

Rights Offerings

Under the charters of some corporations, if additional shares of common stock—or any security that may be converted to common stock—are to be issued, the securities must be offered for sale first to the existing common stockholders. That is, the existing shareholders have **pre-emptive rights** to purchase newly issued securities. The purpose of this regulation is to permit existing stockholders to maintain their proportional share of ownership. Once popular in the United States, rights offerings among public corporations became infrequent during the 1980s and 1990s, although they are still used among privately held firms. On the other hand, rights offerings remain popular among public firms in Europe.

> **pre-emptive rights**
> rights of existing shareholders to purchase any newly issued shared

Competitive Bidding

State, local, and federal government bond issues, as well as those of governmental agencies, usually require competitive bidding by investment bankers before awarding underwriting agreements. This is also the case for debt and equity securities issued by some public utilities. Large, financially strong firms will occasionally announce that they are seeking competitive bids on a new security offering. Under these circumstances, there may be little initial negotiation between the investment houses and the issuer. In these cases, the issuer decides upon the size of issue and the type of security that it wishes to sell. Then it invites the investment banking houses to offer bids for handling the securities. The investment-banking group offering the highest price for the securities, while also providing information showing it will be able to carry through a successful flotation, will usually be awarded the contract.

A great deal of disagreement has existed about the relative advantages and disadvantages of competitive bidding by investment banking houses. Investment bankers strongly contend that the continuing advice they give is essential to an economical and efficient distribution of an issuer's primary market securities. Others contend that competitive bidding enables corporations to sell their securities at higher prices than would otherwise be the case.

A variation of competitive bidding—which usually occurs when issuers seek bids solely from investment banking firms—is the **Dutch auction** bidding process, which allows smaller firms and individual investors to purchase securities. The U.S. Treasury uses a Dutch auction; some IPOs use the Dutch auction mechanism too. Most notable was the Google stock public offering in 2004. The process begins when the issuer and its investment banks determine a price range for the stock. After setting up an account with one of the underwriters, investors place bid prices for the number of shares they want to purchase via Internet, fax, or telephone. Bidders can place bids outside the price range if they believe demand will be high (higher bid price) or weak (lower bid price) than expected by underwriters. At the close of the bidding period, the underwriters determine the highest bid, or clearing price, at which all the offered shares are sold.

For example, suppose a firm, Yoogle, wants to issue 100 million shares in a Dutch auction IPO. For a simple example, assume only five bids are made.

> **Dutch auction**
> an offering process in which investors bid on prices and number of securities they wish to purchase; the securities are sold at the highest price that allows all the offered securities to be sold

> **INTERNET ACTIVITY**
> Go to http://www.openipo.com to visit a site of an investment bank (W.R. Hambrecht & Co.) that uses Dutch auctions in initial public offerings it underwrites.

BIDDER	PRICE	NUMBER OF SHARES
A	$20.50	25 million
B	$20.47	25 million
C	$20.45	25 million
D	$20.43	25 million
E	$20.40	25 million

The clearing price is $20.43; the number of shares to be purchased at that price or higher allows all the offered shares to be sold. Investors A, B, C, and D will be able to purchase their desired number of shares, and investor E will receive no shares in the IPO.

If two or more investors place bids at the clearing price, the offering firm can make one of three choices. First, they can increase the offering size to absorb the extra demand; second, they can sell shares on a pro rata basis to the lowest bidders; and third, they can sell shares on a pro rata basis to all successful bidders. To illustrate, here is what would happen if investors D and E had each placed a bid of $20.43 for 25 million shares. At the clearing price of $20.43, there are orders for 125 million shares, but only 100 million shares are offered. Under the first option, Yoogle can decide (if the prospectus gives Yoogle permission to do so) to increase the offering size to 125 million shares and sell the desired amounts to each investor. With the second option, Yoogle allocates 75 million shares to bidders A, B, and C, and splits the remaining 25 million shares between bidders D and E in proportion to the size of their bids. Since they both wanted the same number of shares, the remaining shares are divided evenly with bidders D and E each receiving 12.5 million shares. Under the third option, with 100 million shares to sell and clearing price demand for 125 million, each investor receives 100/125 or 80 percent of their desired number of shares. That is, bidders A, B, C, D, and E will receive 25 million × 0.80 shares, or 20 million shares, each.

Selling

The amount of securities sold in public offerings is quite large. In 2003, over $5.3 trillion of equity and debt was raised; in 2006, over $7.6 trillion worth of debt and equity securities were sold in the primary market. This fell to about $4.4 trillion in the recessionary market of 2008.[3] To assist the underwriting and best-effort process, the majority of large investment-banking houses maintain "retail" outlets throughout the nation. Retail selling is selling to individual investors. There are also many independent retail brokerage outlets not large or financially strong enough to engage in major originating and underwriting functions. These independents may be able to assist the major investment banks in selling new issues. Like the underwriters, they depend upon the resale of securities at a price above their cost to cover expenses and provide profit from operations. A few of the

---

3. The first issue of *The Wall Street Journal* each year contains a summary of the prior years' largest IPOs and leading underwriting firms.

FIGURE 11.2
A Security Offering Announcement, or Tombstone

This announcement is under no circumstances to be construed as an offer to sell or as a solicitation of an offer to buy any of these securities. The offering is made only by the Prospectus.

New Issue   December 5, 1995

10,350,000 Shares

BOSTON MARKET — Home Style Meals

Boston Chicken, Inc.

Common Stock

Price $34.50 Per Share

Copies of the Prospectus may be obtained from any State or jurisdiction in which this announcement is circulated from only such of the undersigned or other dealers or brokers as may lawfully offer these securities in such State or jurisdiction.

Merrill Lynch & Co.   **Alex. Brown & Sons**
                                                            Incorporated

Dean Witter Reynolds Inc.	A.G. Edwards & Sons, Inc.	Goldman, Sachs & Co.
Montgomery Securities	Morgan Stanley & Co. Incorporated	Oppenheimer & Co., Inc.
Piper Jaffray Inc.	Prudential Securities Incorporated	Schroder Wertheim & Co.
Smith Barney Inc.		Nesbitt Burns Securities Inc.
Arnhold and S. Bleichroeder, Inc.	J. C. Bradford & Co.	Equitable Securities Corporation
EVEREN Securities, Inc.	Hanifen, Imhoff Inc.	Interstate/Johnson Lane Corporation
Janney Montgomery Scott Inc.	Edward D. Jones & Co.	Ladenburg, Thalmann & Co. Inc.
Legg Mason Wood Walker Incorporated	Principal Financial Securities, Inc.	Pryor, McClendon, Counts & Co., Inc.
Rauscher Pierce Refsnes, Inc.	Wessels, Arnold & Henderson, L.L.C.	Wheat First Butcher Singer

---

large investment banking houses do not sell to individuals. Rather, they confine their activities entirely to originating, underwriting, and selling securities to institutional investors. Institutional investors are large investors such as insurance companies, pension funds, investment companies, and other large financial institutions.

Regulatory authorities permit announcements of security offerings to be placed in newspapers and other publications. These announcements, called **tombstones,** are very restricted in wording and must not seem to be soliciting sales. An announcement is shown in Figure 11.2. Note that this tombstone is careful to point out that "This is neither an offer to sell nor a solicitation of an offer to buy any of these securities." The word "tombstone" apparently derives from the small amount of information it provides and the large amount of white space it features. Boston Chicken was seeking to sell 10.35 million shares of common stock at an offer price of $34.50 a share. The underwriters are shown on the bottom of the announcement.

tombstones
announcements of securities offerings

syndicate
group of several investment banking firms that participate in underwriting and distributing a security issue

aftermarket
period of time during which members of the syndicate may not sell the securities for less than the initial offering price

market stabilization
intervention of the syndicate to repurchase securities in order to maintain their price at the offer price

INTERNET ACTIVITY
Review recent offerings and position openings at investment banking firms such as Merrill Lynch (http://www.ml.com) and Morgan Stanley (http://www.morganstanley.com).

CONCEPT CHECK
What are the three primary market functions of investment banks?

How does an underwriting agreement differ from a best effort offering?

What is a tombstone ad?

underpricing
represents the difference between the aftermarket stock price and the offering price

---

The investment bank or banks chosen to originate and handle a flotation are called the lead bankers. In the issue shown in Figure 11.2, the two firms listed at the top, Merrill Lynch and Alex. Brown, are the lead bankers. These lead bankers formed a **syndicate** of several investment banking firms to participate in the underwriting and distribution of the issue. Syndicate members are listed under the lead bankers, in alphabetical order, in the tombstone ad. For very large issues, many firms may be part of the syndicate. For an $8 billion Kraft Foods IPO in 2001, about 75 firms—including the lead bankers—were part of the syndicate. Visa's IPO, the largest ever at the time ($17 billion offering) had 15 firms in its syndicate.

The period after a new issue is initially sold to the public is called the **aftermarket**. This period may vary from a few hours to several weeks. During this period, the members of the syndicate may not sell the securities for less than the offering price. Investors who decide to sell their newly purchased securities may depress the market price temporarily, so the syndicate steps in to buy back the securities in order to prevent a larger price drop. This is called **market stabilization**. Although the Securities Exchange Act of 1934 prohibits manipulation of this sort by all others, underwriters are permitted to buy shares if the market price falls below the offering price. If market stabilization is allowed for a particular issue, it must be stipulated in the prospectus. If part of an issue remains unsold after a period of time, for example thirty days, members may leave the syndicate and sell their securities at whatever price the market will allow. The lead underwriter decides when the syndicate is to break up, freeing members to sell at the prevailing market price.

As an example of underwriting risk, at times the lead banker is left holding many more shares of an offering than it would like.[4] Merrill Lynch and its investment funds once owned over one-half of outstanding shares of First USA Inc., a credit card company, more than three months after its initial public offering. Bond offerings can turn sour because of unexpected interest rate increases in the economy or credit deterioration by the firm. Convertible bonds—bonds that can be converted to shares of common stock at predetermined prices—are sometimes shunned by investors if the conversion and other features are not to their liking. Rumors were that J.P. Morgan was left owning 80 percent of a convertible bond offering in 2000 for LSI Logic, a semiconductor firm; this was at the peak of the technology bull market. As the bear market continued into 2001, other firms (including CFSB, Salomon Smith Barney, and Merrill Lynch) were still holding large stakes of convertible bond issues.[5] But underwriting is a lucrative business, earning firms multiple billions of dollars in fees.

COST OF GOING PUBLIC

One of the drawbacks of going public is its cost. The issuing firm faces direct out-of-pocket costs for accountants' and lawyers' fees, printing expenses, and filing fees.

In addition, the firm faces two additional costs, which together represent the difference between the market value of the firm's shares in the aftermarket and the actual proceeds the firm receives from the underwriters. The first of these costs is the spread, as discussed earlier. The second cost, **underpricing**, represents the difference between the aftermarket stock price and the offering price. Underpricing represents money left on the table or money the firm could have received had the offer price better approximated the aftermarket value of the stock. For example, suppose a firm raises $15 million by selling one million shares at an offer price of $15. By the close of trading on the first day, the firm's stock price is $20. The firm's market value rose (20 − 15) × 1 million shares or $5 million. Had the securities originally been offered at $20, the firm might have received an additional $5 million for the stock. Some would argue that the firm left $5 million "on the table," financing it could have received had the stock been priced better; or to view it another way, if the offer price had been $20, the firm could have raised $15 million by selling only 750,000 shares.

Studies of IPOs in the United States find that firms' IPOs are, on average, underpriced more if it is a smaller issue, if it is issued by a technology firm, if the firm has benefited from venture capital financing, and if the issue's underwriters are more prestigious.[6] Underpricing is not only

---

4. Alexandra Peers and Craig Torres, "Underwriters Hold Huge Stakes in IPOs," *The Wall Street Journal* (August 12, 1992), p. C1.

5. Suzanne McGee, "First Boston's 'Son of Tyco' Deal Goes Sour," *The Wall Street Journal* (February 15, 2001), pp. C1, C16; Gregory Zuckerman, "Stalled Convertible: J. P. Morgan Is Left Holding $400 Million of LSI Bond Issue," *The Wall Street Journal* (March 2, 2000), pp. C1, C19.

6. For reviews of these studies, see Jay R. Ritter, "Investment Bank and Securities Issuance," in George Constantinides, Milton Harris, and Rene Stulz, editors, *Handbook of the Economics of Finance*, North-Holland (2002).

TABLE 11.2
Average initial returns for 45 countries

COUNTRY	SAMPLE SIZE	TIME PERIOD	AVG. INITIAL RETURN
Argentina	20	1991–1994	4.4%
Australia	1,103	1976–2006	19.8%
Austria	96	1971–2006	6.5%
Belgium	114	1984–2006	13.5%
Brazil	180	1979–2006	48.7%
Bulgaria	9	2004–2007	36.5%
Canada	635	1971–2006	7.1%
Chile	65	1982–2006	8.4%
China	1,394	1990–2005	164.5%
Cyprus	51	1999–2002	23.7%
Denmark	145	1984–2006	8.1%
Finland	162	1971–2006	17.2%
France	686	1983–2006	10.7%
Germany	652	1978–2006	26.9%
Greece	363	1976–2005	25.1%
Hong Kong	1,008	1980–2006	15.9%
India	2,811	1990–2007	92.7%
Indonesia	321	1989–2007	21.1%
Iran	279	1991–2004	22.4%
Ireland	31	1999–2006	23.7%
Israel	348	1990–2006	13.8%
Italy	233	1985–2006	18.2%
Japan	2,579	1970–2007	40.5%
Korea	1,417	1980–2007	57.4%
Malaysia	350	1980–2006	69.6%
Mexico	88	1987–1994	15.9%
Netherlands	181	1982–2006	10.2%
New Zealand	214	1979–2006	20.3%
Nigeria	114	1989–2006	12.7%
Norway	153	1984–2006	9.6%
Philippines	123	1987–2006	21.2%
Poland	224	1991–2006	22.9%
Portugal	28	1992–2006	11.6%
Russia	40	1999–2006	4.2%
Singapore	441	1973–2006	28.3%
South Africa	118	1980–1991	32.7%
Spain	128	1986–2006	10.9%
Sri Lanka	115	1987–2007	48.9%
Sweden	406	1980–2006	27.3%
Switzerland	147	1983–2006	29.3%
Taiwan	1,312	1980–2006	37.2%
Thailand	459	1987–2007	36.6%
Turkey	282	1990–2004	10.8%
United Kingdom	3,986	1959–2006	16.8%
United States	12,007	1960–2007	16.9%

Source: from Tim Loughran, Jay R. Ritter, and Kristian Rydquist, Initial Public Offerings: International Insights, *Pacific-Basin Finance Journal* (June 1994), vol. 2, pp. 165–199, updated November 18, 2008, available on http://bear.cba.ufl.edu/ritter/ipodata.htm.

a U.S. occurrence; Table 11.2 shows that studies in many countries find large first-day returns to IPOs, indicating underpricing. Why underpricing occurs is a matter of debate among researchers; it evidently isn't dependent upon a country's security markets, regulations, or trading mechanisms since it occurs in so many different countries. Some theories that have been proposed include cases where some investors have better information (presumably via their own research) than others regarding the attractiveness of an IPO; in order to give incentive for the uninformed investors to continue to purchase primary market equity offerings, they on average

flotation costs
composed of direct costs, the spread, and underpricing

INTERNET ACTIVITY

Jay Ritter of the University of Florida's Warrington College of Business is a leading academic researcher on IPOs. His Web site, http://bear.cba.ufl.edu/ritter/index.html, offers data and recent research findings on IPOs.

INTERNET ACTIVITY

Web sites of firms involved in the Internet IPO market include W. R. Hambrecht & Co. (http://www.wrhambrecht.com). An information source on public offerings is http://www.ipo.com.

INTERNET ACTIVITY

Visit the site of a firm that facilitates Internet bond offerings:
http://www.internotes.com.

must earn profits via underpricing. Other theories deal with irrational investor behavior: investors who want to purchase shares but are unable to in the public offering frantically bid up the prices of shares to purchase them from those who did purchase IPO shares.

Together, these three costs—direct costs, the spread, and underpricing—are the **flotation costs** of an IPO. The flotation costs of an issue depend upon a number of factors, including the size of the offering, the issuing firm's earnings, its industry, and the condition of the stock market. The flotation costs, relative to the amount raised, are usually lower for a firm commitment offering than a best-efforts offering. Best-efforts offerings have higher costs for two reasons. First, it is typically higher-risk firms that utilize best-efforts offerings, so the banker charges higher fees to compensate for his extra efforts. Second, on average, best-efforts offerings raise smaller amounts of money (so the fixed costs of preparing the offering are spread over fewer shares sold). One study found for U.S. corporations the average costs for initial public offerings (IPOs) of equity, not including underpricing, averaged 11.0 percent of the proceeds. For seasoned equity offerings (SEOs), that is, follow-on equity offerings of firms that already have public equity outstanding, these costs averaged 7.1 percent. For convertible bonds, the costs averaged 3.8 percent. For straight debt issues, issuing costs average 2.2 percent, although they were sensitive to the credit rating of the issue.[7]

Studies have shown that underpricing varies over time and with IPO volume. In addition, IPO volume is cyclical: periods of frantic IPO activity alternate with periods when few firms go public. There is a close relationship between IPO volume and underpricing. Periods of "hot IPO markets" have heavy IPO volume with large underpricing; periods of low IPO volume or "cold IPO markets" show less underpricing. The data in Table 11.3 show these patterns since 1980. Note the hot IPO markets in the late 1990s and the cooler markets in the early 1980s, late 1980s, and after the turn of the millennium.

Innovations Among Investment Banking Firms

As we saw in Chapter 10, investment banking firms have tried to meet the needs of both issuers and investors by developing many variations of "debt" and "equity." As far as the process of underwriting is concerned, the Internet has had an impact, albeit relatively minor, on public offerings. Some firms have tried using the Internet as a means to sell securities to small investors and to reduce the amount of under pricing of securities. Most investment banks are large, well capitalized firms. Investors who receive IPO shares in an offering are typically large institutional clients of the investment banks and their favored retail customers (those with large brokerage accounts who do a lot of trading). The Internet has the potential to make investors more equal by allowing them to bid for shares in Dutch auctions. By selling shares to the highest bidders, all investors are treated equally; if a small investor bids a higher price than an investment bank, she will receive her requested number of shares first. Second, by seeking bids, the hope is the average price received by the issuing firm will exceed the price they would receive in a firm commitment underwriting. Bond offerings have been made available on the Internet, too. Internotes is a firm and a name given to bonds sold via the Internet. Corporations, government agencies, and municipalities have issued bonds using the internet.[8]

Another means of going public for a private firm to merge with or acquire a public firm. This is how the New York Stock Exchange "went public"; they purchased the publicly-held electronic communications network (ECN) firm, Archipelago Holdings.

OTHER FUNCTIONS OF INVESTMENT BANKING FIRMS

Investment banking firms engage in many activities beyond their primary function of distributing long-term security instruments. For example, they have traditionally dominated the commercial paper market. Commercial paper is an important source of short-term financing for business that we will discuss in Chapter 16. Through buying and selling commercial paper,

---

[7]. Inmoo Lee, Scott Lochhead, Jay Ritter, and Quanshui Zhao, "The Costs of Raising Capital," *Journal of Financial Research*, vol. 19, no. 1 (Spring 1996).

[8]. Rachel Koning, "Chicago Bonds Go Straight to Buyers," *The Wall Street Journal*, September 15, 2005, page D2; Emily S. Plishner, "E-bonds: Will They Fly?," *CFO* (March 2001), pp. 87–92; Terzah Ewing, "Too Hot an IPO? Andover.net's 252% Pop Raises Questions About Underwriter's 'Dutch Auction,'" *The Wall Street Journal* (December 9, 1999), pp. C1, C23; John Thackray, "A Kinder, Gentler IPO?," *CFO* (October 1999), pp. 41–42; Silvia Ascarelli, "Investment Bank Niche Thrives for Online IPOs," *The Wall Street Journal* (October 18, 1999), p. A431.

TABLE 11.3
Number of Offerings and Average First-Day Returns (Underpricing) of Initial Public Offerings in 1975–2008

YEAR	NUMBER OF OFFERINGS	AVERAGE FIRST-DAY RETURN
1975	12	−1.5
1976	26	1.9
1977	15	3.6
1978	20	11.2
1979	39	8.5
1980	75	13.9
1981	197	6.2
1982	81	10.7
1983	521	9.0
1984	222	2.5
1985	216	6.2
1986	480	5.9
1987	341	5.6
1988	128	5.4
1989	119	7.9
1990	112	10.5
1991	287	11.7
1992	395	10.1
1993	505	12.7
1994	412	9.8
1995	461	21.1
1996	687	17.0
1997	483	13.9
1998	317	20.1
1999	487	69.6
2000	385	55.4
2001	81	13.7
2002	70	8.6
2003	68	12.4
2004	186	12.2
2005	169	9.8
2006	164	11.3
2007	160	13.5
2008	21	6.4

First-day returns are computed as the percentage return from the offering price to the first closing market price.
Source: Jay R. Ritter, "Some Factoids About the 2008 IPO Market," unpublished (May 11, 2009), http://bear.cba.ufl.edu/ritter/IPOs2008Factoids.pdf.

INTERNET ACTIVITY

An overview of various regulations and the EDGAR (Electronic Data Gathering and Retrieval) system for required SEC filings can be found at http://www.sec.gov.

investment bankers assist with the short-term cash flow needs of many businesses. Three investment banking firms dominate commercial paper activities. They are Goldman, Sachs & Co., Merrill Lynch & Co., and Credit Suisse.

In recent years, merger and acquisition (M & A) activities have increased in importance for many investment-banking firms. Firms with strong M & A departments compete intensely for the highly profitable activity of corporate mergers or acquisitions. Investment banking firms act on behalf of corporate clients in identifying firms that may be suitable for merger. Very large fees are charged for this service.

Other activities of investment bankers include the management of pension and endowment funds for businesses, colleges, churches, hospitals, and other institutions. In many cases, officers of investment banking firms are on the boards of directors of major corporations. In this capacity, they are able to offer financial advice and participate in the financial planning of the firm. Investment bankers also provide financial counseling on a fee basis.

Not all investment bankers engage in every one of these activities. The size of the firm largely dictates the various services it provides. Some firms, known as *boutiques*, specialize in only a few activities, such as mergers or underwriting IPOs for high-technology firms.

ETHICAL ISSUES

broker
one who assists in the trading process by buying or selling securities in the market for an investor

dealer
satisfies the investor's trades by buying and selling securities from its own inventory

blue-sky laws
protect the investor from fraudulent security offerings

CONCEPT CHECK

Describe the costs of "going public" by issuing shares of common stock.

What is the difference between a broker and a dealer?

What are some of the regulations that investment banks must follow?

INVESTMENT BANKING REGULATION

Federal regulation of investment banking is administered primarily under the provisions of the Securities Act of 1933. The chief purposes of the act are (1) to provide full, fair, and accurate disclosure of the character of newly issued securities offered for sale and (2) to prevent fraud in the sale of such securities. The first purpose is achieved by requiring that the issuer file a registration statement with the Securities and Exchange Commission and deliver a prospectus to potential investors. The SEC, however, does not pass judgment on the investment merit of any securities. It is illegal for a seller of securities to represent the SEC's approval of a registration statement as a recommendation of investment quality. The philosophy behind the Securities Act of 1933 is that the most effective regulatory device is the requirement that complete and accurate information be disclosed for securities on which investment decisions may be made. Although the SEC does not guarantee the accuracy of any statement made by an issuer of securities in a registration statement or prospectus, legal action may be taken against officers and other representatives of the issuing company for any false or incorrect statements. Full disclosure is, therefore, instrumental in accomplishing the second purpose, that of fraud prevention.

The Securities Exchange Act of 1934 established the Securities and Exchange Commission (SEC) and gave it authority over the securities markets. All brokers and dealers doing business in the organized markets must register with the SEC. A **broker** assists the trading process by buying or selling securities in the market for an investor. A **dealer** satisfies investors' trades by buying and selling securities from his own inventory. In addition, attempts to manipulate securities prices were declared illegal.

In addition to federal regulation of investment banking, most states have **blue-sky laws** to protect investors from fraudulent security offerings. Blue-sky laws apparently get their name from the efforts of some unscrupulous operators who, if not restricted, would promise to sell investors pieces of the blue sky. Because state laws differ in their specific regulations, the federal government is the primary regulator of investment banking. The most common violation of state blue-sky laws is that of misrepresenting the financial condition and asset position of companies.

The Glass-Steagall Act of 1933 ended the ability of commercial banks to act as underwriters of newly issued securities. There were many commercial bank failures during the Great Depression, and there was thought to be evidence at the time that some of the failures resulted from the underwriting activities and poor equity investments of banks. With the passage of the Gramm-Leach-Bliley Act, the walls between commercial banking and investment banking are falling and the traditional boundaries among insurance, commercial banks, investment banks, and other financial institutions are becoming blurrier.

SMALL BUSINESS PRACTICE
Business Angels: Who Are They?

Business angels are private investors who provide start-up capital for small businesses. Although they are wealthy individuals, angels seldom invest more that $100,000 in a firm. The annual investment in the angel market is estimated to be $20 billion. In addition to providing financing, angels provide valuable advice and sometimes help with the preparation of business plans. Robert Gaston completed a survey of over 400 angel investors for the Small Business Administration and found the following. Angels typically are entrepreneurs and over 80 percent are business owners or managers. Angels will consider small investments, are usually older than the individuals they are trying to help, and are the largest source of small business financial capital. Iris Lorenz-Fife in *Financing Your Business* (Prentice-Hall, 1997) provides valuable advice on how to attract angels, how to react when angels respond, and a checklist for the small business person to examine in terms of deciding whether angels are right for you.

Angels usually identify small business investment opportunities through word of mouth referrals from bankers, accountants, lawyers, and business consultants. Angels are attracted to individuals who have the drive to succeed. When an angel responds to a business plan, make sure that you spell out the amount, timing, and length of the investment. Also, the degree of involvement of the angel in the firm's operations should be spelled out in advance.

TRADING SECURITIES—SECONDARY SECURITIES MARKETS

The primary market, we have learned, is where securities are first issued; the issuer sells the securities in an offering to investors. Any trading of the securities thereafter occurs in the secondary market. The secondary markets provide liquidity to investors who wish to sell securities. It is safe to say that, were it not for secondary securities markets for trading between investors, there would be no primary market for the initial sale of securities. Selling securities to investors would be difficult if investors had no easy way to profit from their holdings or no way to sell them for cash. They allow investors to shift their assets into different securities and different markets. Secondary markets provide pricing information, thus providing a means to evaluate a firm's management and for management to determine how investors are interpreting its actions. The secondary market for securities has two components: organized security exchanges, which have physical trading floors, and the over-the-counter market, a network of independent dealers and agents who communicate and trade electronically rather than on a trading floor. The New York Stock Exchange is the prime example of an organized exchange while NASDAQ is an over-the-counter market.

A firm that fares poorly is penalized by pressure placed on the firm's management by its stockholders as market prices of its securities fall in the secondary market. In addition, when such a firm seeks new capital, it will have to provide a higher expected return to investors. The position of a firm's management becomes increasingly vulnerable as business deteriorates. Ultimately the firm's directors may replace management, or the firm may be a target of a takeover attempt.

ORGANIZED SECURITY EXCHANGES

An organized securities exchange is a location with a trading floor where all trading takes place under rules created by the exchange. Organized exchanges in the United States include the New York Stock Exchange (NYSE; this is part of the NYSE-Euronext group following a 2007 merger of a U.S. and European stock exchange) as well as several regional exchanges, such as the Boston, Chicago, Cincinnati, Philadelphia, and Pacific Stock Exchanges. The regionals trade both local and national issues, including *dual-listed* stocks—those traded on more than one exchange. Another national exchange, the American Stock Exchange, was merged into NYSE Euronext in 2008; it is now part of the larger stock exchange and in 2009 was renamed NYSE Amex Equities. The "branding" function of marketing works in finance as well as the NYSE Euronext firm seeks to take advantage of the stature and goodwill of the "NYSE" brand in such renaming.

The organized stock exchanges use the latest in electronic communications. This helps to ensure an internally efficient trading mechanism where orders are tracked and processed quickly. It ensures that prices on the different exchanges are identical, so a trader cannot *arbitrage*, or purchase a security on one exchange at one price while selling it on another, at a different price, to lock in a riskless profit. The present methods of transmitting information within cities and between cities are in sharp contrast to the devices used before the introduction of the telegraph in 1844. Quotations were conveyed between New York and Philadelphia through signal flags in the daytime and light signals at night from high point to high point across New Jersey in as little as ten minutes.

Because of its relative importance and because in most respects its operations are typical of those of the other exchanges, the New York Stock Exchange, sometimes called the "Big Board," will provide the basis for the following description of exchange organization and activities.

STRUCTURE OF THE NEW YORK STOCK EXCHANGE

Like all the stock exchanges in the nation, the objective of the New York Stock Exchange is to provide a convenient meeting place where buyers and sellers of securities or their representatives may conduct business. In addition, the New York Stock Exchange provides facilities for the settlement of transactions, establishes rules for the trading processes and the activities of its members, provides publicity for the transactions, and establishes standards for the corporations whose securities are traded on the exchange.

There are three basic types of members: designated market makers, **floor brokers,** and registered traders. In turn, there are two variations of floor brokers: house brokers and independent brokers.

floor brokers
independent brokers who handle the commission brokers' overflow

house (commission) brokers
act as agents to execute customers' orders for securities purchases and sales

independent brokers
independent brokers who handle the commission brokers' overflow

registered traders
buy and sell stocks for their own account

designated market makers (DMM)
assigned dealers who have the responsibility of making a market in an assigned security

INTERNET ACTIVITY

LaBranche and Company is a NYSE designated market maker; their Web site is http://www.labranche.com. Names of other DMMs, are available on the NYSE Web site, http://www.nyse.com/pdfs/03 allocation_policy_instructions_.pdf.

ETHICAL ISSUES

Supplemental Liquidity Provider (SLP)
assigned dealers who have a responsibility of trading in an assigned security to increase liquidity on NYSE-listed stocks

---

The largest group of members on the New York Stock Exchange is the house (sometimes called commission) brokers. The key function of **house brokers** is to act as agents to execute customers' orders for securities purchases and sales. In return the broker receives a commission for the service. Merrill Lynch owns several seats used by their house brokers. **Independent brokers** handle the house brokers' overflow. When trading volume is particularly heavy, house brokers will ask an independent broker to help them in handling their orders. **Registered traders** are individuals who purchase a seat on the exchange to buy and sell stocks for their own account. Since they do their own trading, they do not pay any commissions. They may also be on retainer from a brokerage house, often a regional firm that does not want its own seat on the exchange.

Designated market markers (DMMs), or assigned dealers, have the responsibility of making a market in an assigned security. Each stock is assigned to a DMM[9], who has a trading post on the exchange floor. The DMM selects the opening price at the start of trading each day, based upon the previous day's closing price and the backlog of buy and sell orders that exist. As a market maker, the DMM maintains an inventory of the security in question and stands ready to buy or sell to maintain a fair and orderly market. That means they must be ready to purchase shares of their assigned stock when there are many sellers and they must be willing to sell shares when traders want to buy. Exchange regulations require the DMM to maintain an orderly market, meaning that trading prices should not change by more than a few cents (stocks are traded in decimals, so the smallest difference in price can be one cent). The designated market marker maintains bid-and-asked prices for the security, and the margin between the two prices represents the DMM's potential gross profit. The bid price is that price the buyer is willing to pay for the securities (thus, it represents the investors' selling price). The ask price is the price at which the owner is willing to sell securities (thus, it represents the investors' purchase price). If the current bid price from brokers is 50.00 and the current ask price is 50.05, the DMM may enter a bid of 50.02 or 50.03 or a lower ask price in order to lower the spread and maintain market order.

A recent innovation to the NYSE is a new set of traders called **Supplemental Liquidity Providers** (SLPs). Their purpose is to help add liquidity to the NYSE trading floor—that is, supplement the work of the DMM by buying and selling shares throughout the day. To be an SLP, the firm must present the best bid or offer prices in their assigned securities at least 5 percent of the trading day. The NYSE pays the liquidity providers a rebate when they execute a trade. The goal is for the SLPs to generate more bid and ask prices and to lead to tighter bid-ask spreads and greater liquidity in the stock market.

A penny may not seem like much, but an extra penny per share profit on the billion shares traded each day on the NYSE can add to a sizable sum. In the past, trading in listed stocks was supervised by "specialists" rather than DMMs or SLPs. Specialists, which did several of the functions of the current DMMs, had access to order flow information—that is, expected orders, called limit orders that would be forthcoming should prices change (we discuss limit orders in a few pages). Specialist firms were accused of placing their own interests above that of their customers by "front running." Front running occurred when a specialist traded to take advantage of information they have (but others do not) about large buy or sell orders that will soon be placed. An example would be buying a stock for $23.27 knowing in a few minutes a customer will place a large buy order which will likely push the price higher to $23.30 or $23.32.

Another example of profiting from trades is "negative obligation," that is, when a specialist intervened in a trade when their assistance is unnecessary. It occurs when a specialist purchased shares from a seller and then immediately sold them to a buyer at a higher price. The specialist should have allowed the two traders to trade between themselves without the specialist making a profit. In 2004, the NYSE and SEC fined five specialist firms $240 million for such tactics. The NYSE received sanctions, too, from the Securities and Exchange Commission and was forced to add staff and funds to increase its oversight of regulations and trading. The new DMM structure lessens the chance of such unfair trading activity.

Other exchanges face ethics issues, too. In the late 1990s, two dozen firms involved in NASDAQ trading were accused of setting unfairly high trading commissions and were fined a total of $900 million.

---

9. More correctly, the listed firm chooses which specialist firm to use. The five designated market markers are: Banc of America Specialists, Barclays Capital, Kellogg Specialist Group, LaBranche & Co., and Spear, Leeds and Kellogg Specialists.

INTERNET ACTIVITY

Learn about the different exchanges and their listing requirements at http://www.nyse.com, http://www.amex.com, and http://www.nasdaq.com. Many international exchanges are available on the Web, too. See, for example, the Toronto Stock Exchange, http://www. tsx.com; exchanges in the United Kingdom, http://www.londonstockexchange.com and www.ftse.com; the Tokyo Stock Exchange, http://www.tse.or.jp/english/index.htm; and the Frankfort Stock Exchange, http://www. deutsche-boerse. com. Links to many more are available at www.world-exchanges.org (World Federation of Exchanges).

bid
price offered by a potential buyer

ask
price requested by the seller

spread
difference between the bid and ask prices

CONCEPT CHECK

How do secondary securities markets assist the function of primary markets?

Describe the four types of members of the New York Stock Exchange.

market order
open order of an immediate purchase or sale at the best possible price

Listing Securities

All securities must be listed before they may be traded on the New York Stock Exchange. To qualify for listing its security, a corporation must meet certain requirements regarding profitability, total value of outstanding stock, or stockholder's equity. Over time the NYSE revamped its listing standards in an attempt to attract more high-growth firms (which had been favoring the NASDAQ over-the-counter market for listings) and more foreign companies.[10] The corporation also pays a fee for the privilege of being listed. The original listing fee ranges from $150,000–250,000. Continuing annual fees range from $35,000–$500,000, depending on the number of outstanding shares. The acceptance of the security by the exchange for listing on the Big Board does not constitute endorsement of its quality.

SECURITY TRANSACTIONS

Buying and selling securities is similar to buying and selling other items in a negotiated market. Whether you want to sell a house or a car, you have a price you are asking potential buyers to pay. Buyers of your house or car will likely not want to pay your price but will offer their own price, a bid, to see if you will agree to sell your item for a lower price. In security transactions, potential buyers place **bid** prices, as in an auction, and sellers have their **ask** prices. The difference between the lower bid and higher ask is the **spread**. The narrower the spread, the more liquid the market and the quicker a transaction can be made.

Internet sites inform us (with a time delay, unless you purchase access to real-time data) what the bid and ask prices are for a security throughout the day. For example, a quote from such a site for Microsoft stock may show:

$$\text{Bid: } 30.42 \times 50900$$
$$\text{Ask: } 30.43 \times 50800$$

This means there is demand for 50,900 shares by potential buyers at that point during the day and the highest bid price for Microsoft shares is $30.42. There are 50,800 shares offered for sell at that time and the lowest asking price is $30.43. With trading in pennies, this is the tightest spread possible since only one cent separates the bid and ask prices. This shows Microsoft stock, at least in this snapshot of time, is quite liquid.

Investors can place a number of different types of orders to buy or sell securities. In order to trade, they need to contact a stock brokerage firm where they can set up an account. The investor can then specify the type of order to be placed as well as the number of shares to be traded in specific firms. Securities orders to buy and sell can be market, limit, or stop-loss orders.

Market Order

An order for immediate purchase or sale at the best possible price is a **market order**. The brokerage firm that receives an order to trade shares of stock listed on the New York Stock Exchange at the best price possible transmits the order to its New York office, where the order is transmitted to its commission broker on the floor of the exchange.

Limit Order

In a **limit order**, the maximum buying price (limit buy) or the minimum selling price (limit sell) is specified by the investor. For example, if a commission broker has a limit buy order at 50 from an investor and other brokers have ask prices higher than 50, the order could not be filled at that moment. The broker will wait until a price of 50 or less becomes available. Of course, if the price of the stock progresses upward rather than downward, the order will not be completed. Limit orders may be placed to expire at the end of one day, one week, one month, or on a good-until-canceled basis.

Stop-Loss Order

A **stop-loss order** is an order to sell stock at the market price when the price of the stock falls to a specified level. The stockholder may protect gains or limit losses due to a fall in the price of the stock by placing a stop-loss order at a price a few points below the current market price. For

---
10. The listing standards for both U.S. firms and non-U.S. firms can be found on the NYSE website: http://www.nyse.com/regulation/nyse/1147474807344.html

example, an investor paying $50 for shares of stock may place a stop-loss order at a price of $45. If the price does fall to $45, the commission broker sells the shares for as high a price as possible. This order does not guarantee a price of $45 to the seller, since by the time the stock is actually sold a rapidly declining stock price may have fallen to well below $45. On the other hand, if the stock price does not reach the specified price, the order will not be executed.

These orders can be used to protect profits. If the stock increases in price after its purchase, the investor can cancel the old stop-loss order and issue a new one at a higher price.

Short Sale

A **short sale** is sale of securities that the seller does not own. An investor will want to short a stock if she feels the price will decline in the future. Shares of the stock are borrowed by the broker and sold in the stock market. In the event that a price decline does occur, the short seller covers the resulting short position by buying enough stock to repay the lender. If any dividends are paid during the time the stock is shorted, the short seller must pay the dividends owed on the borrowed shares.

As an example, suppose Amy thinks AT&T's stock price will fall in the future because of intense competition in the telecommunications industry. She contacts her broker, for example Merrill Lynch, and gives instructions to sell 100 shares of AT&T short. The broker in turn arranges to borrow the necessary stock, probably from another Merrill Lynch investor who has their stock in **street name,** meaning they keep their stock certificates at the brokerage firm rather than taking personal possession of them. Having sold the borrowed stock, the brokerage house keeps the proceeds of the sale as collateral. In our example, if the securities were sold at $40, Merrill Lynch will keep the proceeds from the 100 shares, $4,000, in Amy's account. Let's say the stock drops to a price of $36 and Amy wants to cover her short position. She tells her broker to buy 100 shares, which costs her $3,600. Merrill Lynch returns the newly purchased shares to the account from which they were borrowed. Amy sold $4,000 worth of stock and purchased $3,600 worth of stock after it fell in price; the difference, $400, is Amy's profit, ignoring brokerage commissions. The person from whose account the shares were borrowed will never know that they were borrowed; Merrill Lynch's internal record keeping will keep track of all such transactions.

If the price of AT&T stock rises, the short seller must still cover her short position at some future time. If the price rises to $45 a share and the position is closed, Amy will pay $4,500 to purchase 100 shares to cover her position. Amy will suffer a loss of $4,000–$4,500 or $500 from her short sale.

Because short sales have an important effect on the market for securities, the SEC regulates them closely. Heavy short sale trades can place undue pressure on a firm's stock price. Among the restrictions on short sales is one relating to selling only on an uptick. This means that a short sale can take place only when the last change in the market price of the stock from transaction-to-transaction was an increase. For example, if the most recent transaction prices were 39.95, 39.95, 40.00, 40.00, 40.00, the short sale would be allowed as the last price change was an increase. A short sale would not be allowed if the most recent transactions prices were, for example, 40.07, 40.01, 40.00 or 40.10, 40.00, 40.00, since the most recent price change was a decrease.

In addition, both Federal Reserve System and New York Stock Exchange regulations require the short seller to maintain a margin or deposit of at least 50 percent of the price of the stock with the broker. Loans of stock are callable on 24 hours' notice.

Buying on Margin

Buying on margin means the investor borrows money and invests it along with his own funds in securities. The securities so purchased become collateral for the loan. The **margin** is the minimum percentage of the purchase price that the investor must pay in cash. In other words, margin is the ratio of the investor's equity (own money) to the market value of the security. In order to buy on margin, the investor must have a margin account with the brokerage firm, which in turn arranges the necessary financing with banks.

Margin trading is risky; it magnifies the profits as well as the losses from investment positions. For example, suppose an investor borrows $20,000 and combines it with $30,000 of his own money to purchase $50,000 worth of stocks. His initial margin is 60 percent ($30,000 of his own money divided by the $50,000 value of the securities). Should the market value of his stock rise 10 percent to $55,000, the value of his equity rises to $35,000:

---

limit order
maximum buying price (limit buy) or the minimum selling price (limit sell) specified by the investor

stop-loss order
order to sell stock at the market price when the price of the stock falls to a specified level

short sale
sale of securities that the seller does not own

street name
an investor's securities are kept in the name of the brokerage house to facilitate record keeping, settlement, safety against loss or theft, and so on

buying on margin
investor borrows money and invests it along with his own funds in securities

margin
minimum percentage of the purchase price that must represent the investor's equity or unborrowed funds

Market value of securities:	$55,000
Less: borrowed funds	$20,000
Value of investor's position:	$35,000

This increase in value to $35,000 represents a gain of 16.7 percent ($5,000/$30,000). A 10 percent rise in the stock's value increased the value of the investor's position by 16.7 percent because of the use of margin.

Margin also magnifies losses. If the value of the securities falls by 10 percent to $45,000, the value of the investor's equity would fall to $25,000:

Market value of securities:	$45,000
Less: borrowed funds	$20,000
Value of investor's position:	$25,000

This loss in value to $25,000 represents a loss of 16.7 percent. A 10 percent fall in the stock's value decreased the value of the investor's position by 16.7 percent because of the use of margin.

Should the value of the securities used as collateral in a margin trade begin to decline, the investor may receive a **margin call** from the brokerage firm. The investor will face a choice of either closing out the position or investing additional cash to increase the position's equity or margin. If the market price of the pledged securities continues to decline and the investor fails to provide the new margin amount, the brokerage house will sell the securities. Under current Federal Reserve regulations, investors must have an **initial margin** of at least 50 percent when entering into a margined trade. The minimum **maintenance margin** to which the position can fall is 25 percent before the broker will have to close out the position. Depending upon the individual investor's creditworthiness, a brokerage firm can impose more stringent margin requirements.

The combination of falling prices, margin calls, and sales of securities can develop into a downward spiral for securities prices. This kind of spiral played an important role in the stock market crash of 1929. At that time there was no regulatory restraint on margin sales and, in fact, margins of only 10 percent were common. An outcome of this was the Securities Act of 1933 and the Securities Exchange Act of 1934 to regulate short sales, margin trading, and the process of issuing and trading securities.

margin call
investor faces the option of either closing the position or investing additional cash to increase the position's equity or margin

initial margin
initial equity percentage

maintenance margin
minimum margin to which an investment may fall before a margin call will be placed

Record Keeping

When a trade takes place, the information is sent to a central computer system, which, in turn, sends the information to display screens across the nation. This consolidated report includes all transactions on the New York Stock Exchange as well as those on the regional exchanges and other markets trading NYSE-listed stocks. Trades can be for a **round lot** of 100 shares or an **odd lot**, a trade of less than 100 shares.[11] The details of the purchase transaction are also sent to the central office of the exchange and then to the brokerage office where the order was originally placed. Trade information is also sent to the registrar of the company whose shares were traded. The company needs this information so new certificates can be issued in either the name of the investor or the brokerage firm (if the shares are to be kept in street name). Likewise, records will be updated so dividends, annual reports, and shareholder voting material can be sent to the proper person.

A security is bought in *street name* when the brokerage house buys the security in its own name on behalf of the investor. The advantage of this is that the investor may sell the securities by simply phoning the broker without the necessity of signing and delivering the certificates. New regulations imposed in 1995 require stock trades to be settled in three days. Before this regulation, settlement did not have to take place until five days after the trade. This "T + 3" requirement means funds to purchase shares or stock certificates of shares that were sold must be presented to the stock broker within three days of the stock trade. This shorter settlement time should make street name accounts more appealing to investors. Plans are underway for a "T + 1" one-day settlement requirement and hopes exist for an all-electronic process that would make settlement immediate.

round lot
sale or purchase of 100 shares

odd lot
sale or purchase of less than 100 shares

INTERNET ACTIVITY
Examples of how trades are placed can be found on the Web sites of several exchanges, including
http://www.nyse.com and http://www.nasdaq.com.

---

11. For a few high-priced stocks listed on the New York Stock Exchange, a round lot is ten shares.

program trading
technique for trading stocks as a group rather than individually, defined as a minimum of at least 15 different stocks with a minimum value of $1 million

CONCEPT CHECK

How does a limit order differ from a stop order?

How does a short sale work? What does "buying on margin" mean?

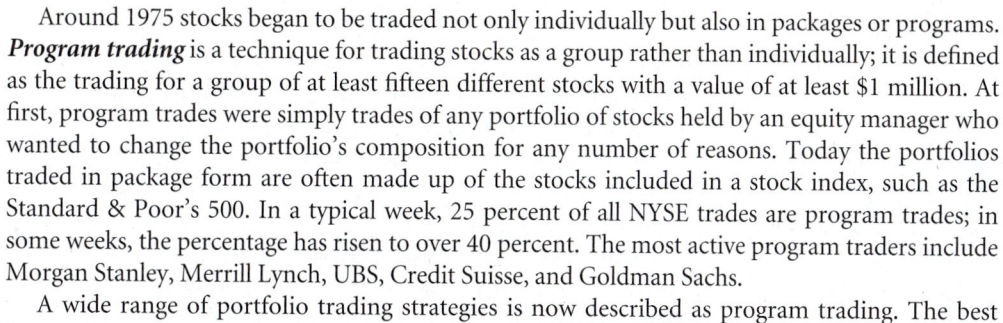

Around 1975 stocks began to be traded not only individually but also in packages or programs. **Program trading** is a technique for trading stocks as a group rather than individually; it is defined as the trading for a group of at least fifteen different stocks with a value of at least $1 million. At first, program trades were simply trades of any portfolio of stocks held by an equity manager who wanted to change the portfolio's composition for any number of reasons. Today the portfolios traded in package form are often made up of the stocks included in a stock index, such as the Standard & Poor's 500. In a typical week, 25 percent of all NYSE trades are program trades; in some weeks, the percentage has risen to over 40 percent. The most active program traders include Morgan Stanley, Merrill Lynch, UBS, Credit Suisse, and Goldman Sachs.

A wide range of portfolio trading strategies is now described as program trading. The best known form of program trading is known as *index arbitrage*, when traders buy and sell stocks with offsetting trades in futures and options in order to lock in profits from price differences between these different markets.[12] Program traders use computers to keep track of prices in the different markets and to give an execution signal when appropriate. At the moment the signal is given, the orders for the stocks are sent directly to the NYSE trading floor for execution by the proper designated market maker. The use of computers allows trades to be accomplished more quickly. This can cause problems if price movements trigger simultaneous sales orders by a number of large program traders. A serious plunge in market prices may occur. As a result, efforts have been made to control some aspects of program trading by limiting its use on days when the Dow Jones Industrial Average rises or falls more than 10 percent.

Over-the-Counter Market

In addition to the organized exchanges, the other major secondary market for securities trading is the over-the-counter market or OTC. The largest OTC market is the NASDAQ system; "NASDAQ" stands for National Association of Securities Dealers Automated Quotation system. Although it trades more than twice as many issues as the NYSE, the OTC is composed mainly of stocks of smaller firms, although companies such as Intel, Microsoft, Novell, and Apple Computer are listed on it.

There are several differences between the organized exchanges and the OTC market. Organized exchanges have a central trading location or floor, such as the NYSE trading floor on Wall Street in New York City. The OTC is a telecommunications network linking brokers and dealers that trade OTC stocks. The organized exchanges have designated market makers that make markets and control trading in listed stocks; the OTC has no DMMs. Instead, OTC dealers buy from and sell for their own account to the public, other dealers, and commission brokers. In a sense, they operate in the manner of any merchant. They have an inventory, composed of the securities in which they specialize, that they hope to sell at a price enough above their purchase price to make a profit. The OTC markets argue that theirs is a competitive system, with multiple dealers making a market in a company's stock.

INTERNET ACTIVITY
The NASDAQ Web site is http://www.nasdaq.com.

To trade in an OTC stock, an investor contacts his broker, who then checks a computer listing of dealers for that particular stock. After determining which dealer has the highest bid price or lowest ask price, the broker contacts the dealer to confirm the price and to execute the transaction.

The OTC market is regulated by the Maloney Act of 1938. This act amended the Securities Exchange Act of 1934 to extend SEC control to the OTC market. The law created the legal basis for OTC brokers and dealers to form national self-regulating trade associations. This was one instance where business itself requested government regulation. It stemmed from the fact that honest dealers in the investment field had little protection against bad publicity resulting from the unscrupulous practices of a few OTC dealers. Under this provision one association, the Financial Industry Regulatory Authority (FINRA) has been formed.[13] All rules adopted by FINRA must be reported to the SEC. The SEC has the authority to take away any powers of the FINRA.

ETHICAL ISSUES

The FINRA has established a lengthy set of rules and regulations intended to ensure fair practices and responsibility on the part of the association's members. Any broker or dealer engaged in OTC activities is eligible to become a member of the FINRA as long as it can prove a record of responsible operation and the broker or dealer is willing to accept the FINRA code of ethics.

---

12. Futures and options are discussed in this chapter's Learning Extension.
13. Prior to 2007, this organization was known as National Association of Security Dealers (NASD).

Third and Fourth Security Markets

It should not be surprising that an activity as broad as the security market would give rise to special arrangements. Despite their names, the third and fourth markets are two additional types of secondary markets that have evolved over time.

The **third market** is a market for large blocks of listed shares that operates outside the confines of the organized exchanges. In the third market, blocks of stock (units of 10,000 shares) are traded OTC. The participants in the third market are large institutions (such as mutual funds, insurance companies, and pension funds) that often need to trade large blocks of shares. Brokers assist the institutions in the third market by bringing buyers and sellers together and, in return, receive a fee.

The **fourth market** is even further removed from the world of organized securities trading. Electronic communications networks, or ECNs, are computerized trading systems that automatically match buy and sell orders at specified prices. Certain large institutional investors arrange purchases and sales of securities among themselves without the benefit of a broker or dealer. They subscribe to an electronic network in which offers to buy or sell are made known to other subscribers. The offers are made in code, and institutions wishing to accept a buy or sell offer know the identity of the other party only upon acceptance of the offer. A fee is paid to the network provider when the trade is completed. Those who support fourth-market trading argue that transfers are often quicker and more economical, but the confidentiality is also an important feature to many firms.

third market
market for large blocks of listed stocks that operates outside the confines of the organized exchanges

fourth market
large institutional investors arrange the purchase and sale of securities among themselves without the benefit of broker or dealer

INTERNET ACTIVITY
Examples of ECNs are Instinet, http://www.instinet.com, and Arcavision (now part of the NYSE), http://www.arcavision.com.

CONCEPT CHECK
How does trading OTC differ from trading at the New York Stock Exchange?

How do the third and fourth markets differ from the New York Stock Exchange?

WHAT MAKES A GOOD MARKET?

NYSE, NASDAQ, third market, fourth market—what are the requirements for a good market? What makes one market better for trading than another for a certain type of transaction?

Competition exists in our product markets. For example, the local Wal-Mart store is a market place for buying and selling goods—except that Wal-Mart is the lone seller and we, the consumers, are the buyers. Other large stores nearby compete for the consumer dollar, wanting you to enter their store and to "trade" with them.

Competition exists among exchanges, too. NYSE, NASDAQ, and others are encouraging firms to list their shares with them so the exchange benefits from the trading volume. For example, NYSE has been perceived as listing only quality firms that have many shareholders and a history of financial success. NASDAQ has allowed smaller firms and firms without a financial track record to list with them. NASDAQ's emphasis over time on technology (as trading occurs via market makers and computers rather than in a physical location) has attracted many "high tech" firms to list their shares on NASDAQ, such as Microsoft, Intel, Cisco Systems, and Dell Computer.

One exchange will boast of quicker execution of trades to encourage investors to trade securities on their exchange rather than a competitor. For example, NASDAQ has argued its technology will allow faster trade execution than NYSE's DMM system. Over time, NYSE has responded by automating some trades that did not require interaction with a DMM.

A good market will have four characteristics: liquidity, quick and accurate execution of trades, reasonable listing requirements, and low costs. Let's discuss each of these in turn:

A market is liquid if trades are executed quickly at a price close to fair market value. Generally, a market needs to have breadth and depth in order to be liquid.

A market has depth if it can absorb large buy and sell orders with disrupting prices. This may mean there are investors with deep pockets willing to take the opposite side of a large trade or there are many traders each of whom is willing to help execute the trade. A broad market, or one with breadth, attracts many traders. In general, having many traders makes a market more competitive; a few large traders may be able to set prices in their own favor rather than allowing competitive forces determine price levels. Generally, trading is more liquid if the difference between the bidder's buy and the seller's ask price is small. Otherwise, large price jumps can occur, depending on how anxious a trader is to execute his buy or sell order.

The second characteristic, quick and accurate execution of trades, is reasonably self-explanatory. The quicker the sale or purchase is executed, the quicker the investor can receive confirmation and know the transaction price. Studies have indicated that small stock transactions done electronically

PERSONAL FINANCIAL PLANNING
Stock Market Indexes

"What did the market do today?" is an often-heard question in financial circles. Although the question sounds ambiguous (which market?), the speakers and their intended listener know which market: the stock market, specifically the performance of the Dow Jones Industrial Average (DJIA). As we mention in the chapter, the DJIA is comprised of only thirty firms, but they are thirty very large firms whose market capitalization (that is, the number of shares multiplied by the stock price) is quite large compared to those of other firms. There are literally dozens of stock market indexes, and even more examples of indexes abound for the bond markets.

Why are indexes so popular? There are several reasons. First, they are a means of representing the movement and returns to the overall market or a segment of the market. The DJIA 30, S&P 500, and Wilshire 5000 are measures of stock market performance. The NYSE, AMEX, and NASDAQ indexes measure performance of the New York, American, and OTC stock markets.

Second, indexes are a useful comparison when you want to benchmark the performance of a portfolio. If your investment advisor recommends a portfolio of stocks that rose 10 percent in value while the S&P 500 rose 20 percent, you may feel that his recommendations were not very good. On the other hand, if his selections were all OTC stocks and the NASDAQ index rose only 5 percent, you may judge his performance more favorably.

Third, indexes are gaining popularity as investments themselves. Rather than try to invest to "beat the market," which is difficult to do (as we'll see in Chapter 12 with the discussion of efficient capital markets), more and more investors are coming to believe the saying, "if you can't beat them, join them." They are choosing to invest in the stocks and bonds that comprise an index in the hope of matching the index's performance over time. Many mutual funds exist so the small investor can do this quickly and easily just by purchasing shares of the mutual fund.

---

average one-tenth of a second to execute whereas larger transactions can take up to 10 seconds.[14] Size of the trade, the liquidity of the stock, and the venue affect the transaction time. Computer trading is quickest, NYSE DMM trading is the slowest, and NASDAQ dealers lie in between. But good recordkeeping is needed, too, to verify the price of the transactions. Portfolio managers (to measure the performance of their stock selections) and individual traders (for tax records) need accurate transactions records.

Thirdly, reasonable listing requirements allow investors to know the quality of the firms that are listed. The NYSE has the highest standards, in terms of stock ownership, earnings, and cash flow. But many firms that could meet the NYSE standards decide to list their shares elsewhere, believing costs may be cheaper and investor trade execution faster on another exchange. Nonetheless, the average size and profitability is lower for NASDAQ firms than NYSE firms. The "pink sheet" (an OTC market, now computerized, that started trading speculative issues listed on pink sheets of paper)[15] has no listing fees and its quotes are provided only by dealers making a market in the stock. Its securities will be fairly speculative.

Finally, a good market will offer reasonable listing fees to issuers (lest they price themselves out of the market for listings) and low costs to investors. Costs to investors include the commissions paid for stock or bond purchases but also "hidden" costs. One hidden cost is lack of breadth (i.e., few traders), so that the buyer must pay the higher ask price of the security (or the seller must accept the lower bid price). Another hidden cost is price pressure, which is another indicator of a market that lacks good liquidity. Price pressure occurs when a large trade moves the market (i.e., causes the market price to change) before it can be fully executed. Professional traders learn to parcel out large trades into smaller trades and to work with several dealers or market makers in order to minimize price changes that occur because of the large transaction. But a market that can absorb such trades is a benefit to investors.

A WORD ON COMMISSIONS

It costs money to trade securities. About the only market participants that don't pay commissions are the exchange designated market makers, supplemental liquidity providers, and registered traders on the NYSE and dealers in OTC stocks.

Stock commissions vary from brokerage firm to brokerage firm. Some brokerage firms, called "full-service" brokerages, not only assist your trades but also have research staffs that analyze

CONCEPT CHECK
What are four characteristics of a good market?

How do market breadth and market depth differ?

---

14. Gregory Crawford, "Inconsistency Haunts Investor Equity Trades, Report Says," *Pensions and Investments*, January 9, 2006, p. 28.
15. "Yellow sheets" refer to over-the-counter bond market quotations for smaller and lower quality bond issues.

INTERNET ACTIVITY

*Merrill Lynch (http://www.ml.com) is a full service broker; Charles Schwab (http://www.schwab.com) is a premier discount broker that offers stock trading, some research, mutual funds, annuities, and life insurance. An example of an online broker is E*TRADE (http://www.etrade.com).*

CONCEPT CHECK

What factors affect the size of a commission on a trade?

Why has stock trading on the Internet increased so rapidly in recent years?

firms and make recommendations on which stocks to buy or sell. Their analysts write research reports that are available to the firm's brokerage customers. Examples of full-service brokerages include Merrill Lynch, A.G. Edwards, and Morgan Stanley.

"Discount" brokerages are for investors who just want someone to do their stock transactions. Investors who do not desire or need the extra services of a full-service broker use discounters. The stereotypical discount investor makes his or her own investment decisions and wishes to trade at the lowest possible costs. Examples of discount brokerages include Brown and Company, Charles Schwab, Muriel Siebert, and Olde Discount. With low overhead costs and offers of basic services, stock trading on some Internet-based brokerages are quite inexpensive, even compared to discount brokers. Falling commissions and ease of access make online trading attractive to those who make their own investment decisions. Trading commissions for some online brokerages are under $7 a trade.

Commissions on security trades depend upon several additional factors. Commissions generally are lower on more liquid securities (more actively traded securities or securities with a popular secondary market). Commissions generally are higher, as a proportion of the market value of the securities purchased, for smaller trades that involve fewer shares or lower-priced shares. Many brokerages charge a minimum commission that may make small trades relatively costly. They also charge a transaction fee to cover their costs of processing the trade. Others assess fees if your account is inactive for a year; in other words, even if you don't trade, you still pay the broker some fees. As with so many other things in life, a wise investor will shop around for the brokerage firm and broker that best meets his or her particular needs.

It is possible to buy shares of some companies without going through a stock broker. Some firms sell their shares directly to the public; this is called *direct investing*. Other firms allow shareholders to add to their stock holdings through dividend reinvestment plans; as the name implies, the shareholder's dividends are used to purchase shares (including partial or fractional shares) of the firm.

SECURITY MARKET INDEXES

If one listens to the radio, watches television, or reads the newspaper, the words "Dow Jones Industrial Average" or "Standard & Poor's 500 Stock Index" will be encountered daily. The thirty stocks that are part of the Dow Jones Industrial Average are listed in Table 11.4. You are probably familiar with most of their names.

Market indexes are useful for keeping track of trends in an overall market (such as the NYSE index, which tracks all stocks listed in the NYSE), a sector (the S&P 400 industrials summarizes the movements in 400 stocks of industrial firms), or specific industries (Dow Jones' various industry indexes, such as those for banks, autos, chemicals, retail, and many others). Market indexes exist for many different countries' securities markets, including a variety of both stock and bond market indexes.

There are many ways in which an index can be constructed; the previous paragraph shows that indexes can cover different security market segments. Indexes also can be computed in different ways. For example, the Dow Jones Industrial Average of thirty large "blue-chip" stocks is based upon a sum of their prices; it is an example of a price-weighted index. The S&P 500 stock index is computed in part by summing the market values—the stock price times the

TABLE 11.4
Stocks in the Dow Jones Industrial Average (as of July 2010)

Alcoa	American Express	AT&T
Bank of America	Boeing	Caterpillar
Chevron	Cisco Systems	Coca-Cola
DuPont	ExxonMobil	General Electric
Hewlett Packard	Home Depot	IBM
Intel	Johnson & Johnson	JPMorgan Chase
Kraft Foods	McDonalds	Merck
Microsoft	3M	Pfizer
Procter and Gamble	Travelers	United Technologies
Verizon	WalMart	Walt Disney

number of shares outstanding—of the 500 component stocks; it is an example of a value-weighted index. Still other indexes are based upon other computational schemes.

The 500 stocks comprising the S&P 500 are not the largest 500 firms or the 500 stocks with the largest market values. A nineteen-member committee of Standard & Poor's Corporation selects the stocks in the index. The committee tries to have each industry represented in the S&P 500 index in proportion to its presence among all publicly traded stocks. Most of the changes that occur in the S&P 500 index occur because of firms' mergers, acquisitions, or bankruptcies. Because it is an index based upon market values, large market value firms, or "large capitalization" stocks as they are called, are the main influences on the index's movements over time.

Bond indexes exist, too; Barclays (Treasury bonds) and Merrill Lynch (corporates) publish bond indexes that show trends in their respective markets. As the U.S. Treasury stopped selling the thirty-year bond from 2002–2005, indexes will favor intermediate-term treasury securities, longer-term agencies, and corporate bonds.

FOREIGN SECURITIES

The growth in the market value of foreign securities has occurred because of general economic expansion, deregulation of exchange rates, and liberalization of regulations of equity markets. The integration of the world's markets is emphasized by the fact that many securities are listed on several markets. The London Stock Exchange, for example, has over 500 foreign listings, of which about 200 are U.S. firms. The major U.S. stock markets, the NYSE and NASDAQ, trade about 600 foreign stocks. Foreign stocks can be traded in the United States if they are registered with the Securities and Exchange Commission.

Why would foreign companies raise funds in the United States? The reason is similar to the reason U.S. firms will tap overseas markets: to gain access to new funding sources and to finance overseas assets with overseas financing. But there is one other reason that foreign companies want a presence in the U.S. capital markets: their breadth and depth. Companies can find an audience for their shares and raise huge amounts of capital. Some leading world economies have stock markets that are all but ignored by their citizens. Germans prefer the safety of savings accounts and bonds; only 13 percent own stocks. Only 7 percent of Japanese own shares.[16] One reason for this is government pension systems, which diminish the need to invest long-term for one's retirement. Another is a culture that favors conservative investment strategies.

Investors and professional money managers have found it increasingly important to diversify their investments among the world's markets. Such diversification makes possible a broader search for investment values and can reduce the risk in investment portfolios.[17]

Investment in foreign shares by U.S. investors may be facilitated through the use of **American depository receipts** or **ADRs** for short. These ADRs are traded on our exchanges and are as negotiable as other securities. They are created when a broker purchases shares of a foreign company's stock in its local stock market. The shares are then delivered to a U.S. bank's local custodian bank in the foreign country. The bank then issues depository receipts. There is not necessarily a one-to-one relationship between shares and depository receipts; one depository receipt may represent five, ten, or more shares of the foreign company's stock. ADRs allow U.S. investors to invest in foreign firms without the problems of settling overseas trades or having to personally exchange currencies. ADRs are traded in dollars, and dividends are paid in dollars as well. A **global depository receipt (GDR)** is similar to an ADR, but it is listed on the London Stock Exchange. U.S. investors can buy GDRs through a broker in the United States.

As securities markets become more global, more and more foreign firms will seek to have their shares or ADRs listed on a U.S. exchange. There are nearly 2,200 ADRs from ninety countries, although significant trading occurs in only a small portion of them.[18] Leading ADRs include telecom firms Nokia (Finland), Ericsson (Sweden), Vodafone (U.K.) and oil firms BP (U.K.) and Royal Dutch Petroleum (Netherlands). Listing an ADR allows U.S. investors more

GLOBAL DISCUSSION

INTERNET ACTIVITY
The Bank of New York developed the ADR index (see it on the Internet at http://www.adrbnymellon.com).

American depository receipt (ADR)
receipt that represents foreign shares to U.S. investors

global depository receipt (GDR)
listed on the London Stock Exchange; facilitates trading in foreign shares

CONCEPT CHECK
What does an index measure?
What are ADRs?

---

16. Sara Calian and Silvia Ascorelli, "Europeans Lose Love for Stocks," *The Wall Street Journal* (May 12, 2004), p.C1; and Craig Karmin, "The Global Shareholder," *The Wall Street Journal* (May 8, 2000), p. R4.

17. The topic of diversification and its effect on the risk of an investment portfolio will be discussed in Chapter 12.

18. Craig Karmin, "ADR Issuance Surges as Firms Abroad Tap Market for Capital," *The Wall Street Journal* (December 8, 2000), p. C12.

CAREER OPPORTUNITIES IN FINANCE
Field: Securities Markets

Opportunities
Individuals and institutions invest in stocks and bonds to finance assets and to create wealth. Many times, as with large corporations, these investments for any given day may be in the millions of dollars. Most investors, however, have neither the time nor the resources to properly plan these investments. Instead, investors turn to securities specialists to plan and execute investment decisions.

Jobs like these require that individuals have the ability to make sound decisions quickly under heavy pressure. For those who excel, though, the opportunities are limitless. Brokerage firms, bank trust departments, and insurance companies typically hire professionals in this field.

Jobs
Account Executive, Securities Analyst

Responsibilities
An *account executive*, or securities broker, sells stocks and bonds to individual and institutional customers, as well as manages client funds consistent with client risk-taking objectives. In addition, an account executive must actively pursue new clients and learn about new investment possibilities. Securities firms typically hire account executives to fill entry-level positions. A *securities analyst* includes being a securities analyst or a securities trader for brokerage firms. A securities analyst must evaluate the value of stocks and bonds and present this information to, or act on this information for, investors.

Education
A strong background in finance, economics, and marketing is necessary for these jobs. In addition, these jobs require the ability to communicate and negotiate effectively.

---

easily to trade a foreign firm's shares. It also gives the foreign firm easier access to a large pool of U.S. investment capital. There is an ADR Index to track price trends.

ETHICAL ISSUES

INSIDE INFORMATION AND OTHER ETHICAL ISSUES

The capital markets are successful in allocating capital because of their integrity. Should investors lose confidence in the fairness of the capital markets, all will lose; investors lose an attractive means for investing funds and issuers will lose access to low-cost public capital.

Some persons who deal in securities and have access to nonpublic or private information about mergers, new security offerings, or earnings announcements may be tempted to trade to take advantage of this information. Taking advantage of one's privileged access to information can lead to large profits from timely purchases or sales (or short sales) of securities. In the United States, taking advantage of private "inside" information is thought to be unfair to other investors. These factors, combined with the ease with which inside information can be used, explain why insider trading is not allowed under provisions of the Securities Exchange Act of 1934.

The most obvious opportunity for insider trading is that for personnel of a corporation who, by virtue of their duties, have knowledge of developments that are destined to have an impact on the price of the corporation's stock. But "insiders" are not limited to corporate personnel. Investment bankers, by virtue of their relationship with such corporations, may be aware of corporate difficulties, major officer changes, or merger possibilities. They, too, must take great care to avoid using such information illegally. Even blue-collar workers at printing firms that print prospectuses or merger offers have been found guilty of trading on private information based upon what they have read from their presses.

Because the insider-trading law is not very clear, it is often difficult to tell when it is illegal to turn a tip into a profit. For example, a stock analyst may discover, through routine interviews with corporate officers, information destined to have an impact on the price of the company's stock. Such information conveyed to the analyst's clients may be, and has been considered to be, insider trading. The almost frantic efforts of large firms to control insider trading is understandable in light of the damage that can occur to their reputations. It is understandable, too, that the SEC has resorted to very strong efforts to resolve the question that continues to exist with respect to a meaningful and fair definition of insider information. After all, it is the investing public without access to this information that pays the price for insider information abuses. Regulation FD mandates full disclosure of material nonpublic information, which was sometimes disclosed to a select few, such as security analysts or large institutional investors. Insight into higher or lower earnings, for example, could result in those receiving the information—and their clients—trading securities to make a profit (or avoid a loss) at the expense of others not privileged to have access to the information. Regulation FD mandates that if a company official discloses material nonpublic information to certain individuals, it must announce the information to all via public disclosure.

Another breach of investor confidence can occur via "churning." Churning is when a broker constantly buys and sells securities from a client's portfolio in an effort to generate commissions. Rather than making decisions that are in the client's best interest, frequent commission-generating trades may be made by brokers with selfish motives. There are some times when frequent trading may be appropriate, but it should occur only within the clients' investing guidelines and with the client's interests at heart.

Unfortunately, the millions of dollars paid in fees for investment banking fees result in occasional scandal by some who make poor choices. In 2003, several investment-banking firms were fined $1.4 billion for ethical lapses. Evidence showed stock analysts, whose stock recommendations should be unbiased, were sometimes rewarded for writing favorable reports to attract investment banking clients. Recall the first-day returns from IPOs in Table 11.3; in another ethical lapse, some banks allocated IPO shares to top officers of their client firms—or to firms they wanted to attract as clients. Allocating shares that may enjoy a quick "pop" in price is a means of bribing clients. In addition to paying large fines, firms must separate stock research from investment banking practices and offer clients independent investment research written by analysts from other firms. Because ethics and integrity are at the center of fair and well-functioning securities markets, major professional certifications, such as the Chartered Financial Analyst (CFA®) and Certified Financial Planner(CFP™), have ethics as a central part of their certification programs.

CHANGES IN THE STRUCTURE OF THE STOCK MARKET

In an effort to increase the technological and informational efficiency of the stock market, the SEC has actively promoted major changes in the structure of stock market activities and institutions. Many of the changes proposed have long met with resistance from existing interests, especially the NYSE. However, many of the SEC's recommendations have been adopted and many more will be instituted in due time. The NYSE, which many times resisted change that would de-emphasize its former specialist trading structure, gained new leadership in 2003 and since then has been embracing technology and globalization. As NASDAQ founder Gordon Macklin said in 1987, "How long do you think people are going to stand in a marble hall and trade?"[19]

Indeed, an important change relates to electronic technology. Technology exists to link organized exchanges and OTC markets electronically. The SEC would like to see the stock market take the form of one giant trading floor, all at the command of the broker. The broker would be able to tell which market has the best quote on each stock by punching buttons on the quotation machine. Bid and asked prices on covered stocks would be available in all markets. In a step toward this, NASDAQ offers "dual-listing" to NYSE firms, meaning that NYSE-listed stocks can choose to have their shares listed on NASDAQ. Instituted in 2004, the first firms to take advantage of dual listing were Apache Corp (stock symbol: APA), Cadence Design Systems (CDN), Charles Schwab Corp. (SCH), Countrywide Financial (CFC), Hewlett-Packard (HPQ), and Walgreens (WAG).

Technology can link national markets to one another, worldwide. Long the purview of national market regulators, stock exchanges are now reaching across national boundaries to link up and in some cases merge with other exchanges. The New York Stock Exchange and Euronext, a major European exchange, agreed in 2006 to a merger. In 2007, the NASDAQ owned over 25% of the London Stock Exchange and was seeking its own merger with it. In addition to Euronext, alliances or cross-ownership agreements exist between the NYSE and the National Stock Exchange of India and between the NYSE and the Tokyo Stock exchange; also, the Tokyo Stock Exchange has made alliance agreements with the Singapore Exchange and the Korea Exchange.[20] Look for this trend to continue!

The goal of global alliances and mergers is to make international investing and the raising of capital easier. One goal of the NYSE–Euronext merger is to cross-list shares on the two exchanges; this will make it easier for U.S. investors to trade securities listed on Euronext and for European investors to trade U.S. stocks. Higher commissions, currency translation, and difficulties in

---

19. Stephen Miller, "Gordon Macklin, 1928–2007: Ushering in Age of the Electronic Stock Market," *The Wall Street Journal*, February 3, 2007, p. A8.
20. Gaston F. Ceron, "NYSE and Tokyo Tie a Knot," *The Wall Street Journal*, February 1, 2007, p. C2.

CAREER PROFILES

JOHN MURPHY
Independent Floor Broker,
New York Stock Exchange

BA History/Business
St. Bonaventure University

"I pay $130,000 a year for the privilege of making trades."

Q: *What does an Independent Floor Broker do?*
A: I buy and sell stocks on the floor of the New York Stock Exchange. The "independent" means I'm not an employee of any of the big brokerage houses. I'm self-employed.

Q: *For whom are you making trades?*
A: I have a few of my own clients, and I make trades for them, but the vast majority of my business is overflow for larger brokers. When Merrill Lynch, for instance, has so many customer orders that its own floor traders can't get them all executed in a timely fashion, I am given a portion of the orders to execute for them. Then Merrill pays me a commission for the work I've done.

Q: *Describe what happens on a trade.*
A: Let's say Merrill has a customer that wants to buy 2,000 shares of company X stock at $20 per share or less. Merrill would give me a piece of paper with those instructions. I would then go to the specific area of the floor where company X is traded. I would ask the DMM in company X stock what price people are willing to sell that stock for. If the has a seller at $20 per share or less, he executes the trade.

Q: *What actually happens when it is executed?*
A: The DMM records Merrill as the buyer and whoever the seller is, the number of shares, and the price, and that's pretty much it. I would then go on to the next order. Now if my order is for a larger volume of shares, say 200,000 shares, I may need to stay there for a while executing a bunch of smaller trades. It might take 50 separate trades to come up with 200,000 shares, and I want to make these buys at the lowest possible cost. If I can save an eighth of a point on each share, that's a savings of $25,000.

Q: *Do you only trade certain stocks?*
A: No, I move all over the floor during the course of the day. I might trade 25 to 30 different issues on a given day, and that may involve several hundred individual orders.

Q: *Sometimes we see the Chicago Board of Trade on television, with traders yelling out bids and making hand signals to each other. Is the NYSE like that?*
A: Not really. In fact, many trades, especially smaller ones, are completed via computer instead of by a trader on the floor. The DMM matches up buy and sell orders from brokerages on his computer screen. It's not as wild as the Board of Trade, but it still can get pretty hectic. Recently the trading volume on the exchange has been quite high, which means everyone on the floor has lots of trades to execute as quickly as possible. If prices are moving up or down quickly, the urgency is even greater.

Q: *Do you own a seat on the exchange?*
A: No. There is a finite number of seats, or memberships, on the exchange. To make trades there you need to either buy a seat, which costs more than a million dollars now, or lease one, which is what I do. I pay $130,000 a year for the privilege of making trades.

APPLYING FINANCE TO...

INSTITUTIONS AND MARKETS

One can easily argue that securities markets exist because of the development of financial institutions and intermediaries over time to collect and allocate capital. In particular, investment banks and brokerage houses help firms and governments raise funds in the public and private markets. They assist investors who want to trade securities and help to provide liquidity to the financial system.

INVESTMENTS

Investors and analysts need to know the different ways to trade (long, short, margin) in securities markets and the risks of each. It is their desire to trade that creates a need for the securities markets and the institutions which facilitate their trading. New information is quickly evaluated by investors as a whole and reflected in changing market prices.

FINANCIAL MANAGEMENT

Firms raise capital in the primary markets. Initial public offerings and secondary offerings are an important undertaking for financial managers who take their firms public; others in private firms will arrange private placements or loans from banks, insurance companies, and other institutions. Securities markets set the interest rates and security prices for the firm; these are a reflection of the quality of the firm, risk, and investors' expectations of future cash flows.

---

settling trades are large hindrances to investing overseas; efficiencies in having global alliances will make investing in overseas firms easier, quicker, and less expensive.

The European Community is moving toward greater integration of its financial services, too. Markets in Financial Instruments Directive (MiFID) has the goal of a creating a single market for investment services across the European Union as well as creating a single set of regulations for financial services firms. MiFID has three main objectives: (a) to create a single EU market for investment services, (b) to coordinate responses to innovations in the securities markets, and (c) to increase protection for investors in a cross-country market.

Electronic trading has been occurring for some time; NASDAQ has an electronic European exchange that it hopes will be the forerunner of an all-European exchange. Another European electronic exchange, Virt-X, is a joint effort of the Swiss exchange and London's Trade-point trading platform.

Which model—NYSE's or the electronic trading—is better? For the most part, both systems work to give investors swift trade execution and the best price available. For quicker trades, some will give the advantage to an electronic market. For the best price (lowest price for buyers, highest price for sellers) some argue that NYSE's DMMs or SLPs can intervene to offer better prices to traders. For clearing large trades, the advantage goes to the NYSE; it has more trading volume and offers greater liquidity for handling large transactions.

Highly automated securities exchanges now exist in the major money-center cities of the world, permitting trading on a global basis. Because of varying time zones, trading is now possible twenty-four hours a day. Trading and settlement (issuing securities and collecting funds) go hand-in-hand; currently the United States has a T + 3 settlement standard, meaning all stock trades have to be settled in cash within three business days. With advancing technology, a standard of T + 1, next-day settlement, may become regulatory reality by the middle of the decade.

SUMMARY

The accumulation of funds by business establishments to finance plant, equipment, and working capital is a necessary process of an industrial society. In this chapter, we described the role of the investment banking industry in facilitating this process. The accumulation of funds is supported by the existence of a secondary market for securities. The constant buying and selling of securities not only provides the investor with the confidence that his or her investment is liquid and can be converted easily to cash but also provides information to the firm's managers. Businesses that prosper are rewarded by securities that enjoy price increases. The secondary market is made up principally of the organized securities exchanges and the over-the-counter markets. Investing in foreign securities can take place by using ADRs.

Trading on the basis of inside or private information is illegal in U.S. markets, although such trading is accepted as the norm in some overseas securities markets. In the United States, ethical norms are such that society frowns upon those who, by virtue of their position or access to information, take advantage of their shareholders for personal gain.

KEY TERMS

- aftermarket
- American depository receipt (ADR)
- ask price
- best-effort agreement
- bid price
- blue-sky laws
- broker
- buying on margin
- commission brokers
- dealer
- designated market markets (DMMs)
- due diligence
- Dutch auction
- floor brokers
- flotation
- flotation costs
- fourth market
- global depository receipt (GDR)
- house brokders
- independent brokers
- initial margin
- initial public offering (IPO)
- investment bankers
- limit order
- maintenance margin
- margin
- margin call
- market maker
- market order
- market stabilization
- odd lot
- offer price
- pre-emptive rights
- primary market
- private placement
- program trading
- prospectus
- public offering
- registered traders
- round lot
- secondary market
- shelf registration
- short sale
- spread
- stop-loss order
- street name
- Supplemental Liquidity Providers (SLPs)
- syndicate
- third market
- tombstones
- underpricing
- underwriters
- underwriting agreement

DISCUSSION QUESTIONS

1. Why do corporations employ investment bankers?
2. Identify the primary market functions of investment bankers.
3. Discuss how investment bankers assume risk in the process of marketing securities of corporations. How do investment bankers try to minimize these risks?
4. Briefly describe the process of competitive bidding and discuss its relative advantages and disadvantages.
5. Explain market stabilization.
6. Identify the costs associated with going public.
7. Briefly describe how investment banking is regulated.
8. Describe the inroads into investment banking being made by commercial banks.
9. In 2003, several investment banking firms were fined $1.4 billion for ethics abuses related to the underwriting process. Will this be a deterrent for ethical lapses?
10. What are some of the characteristics of an organized securities exchange?
11. Describe the types of members of the New York Stock Exchange.
12. Why is there a difference between bid and ask prices at some point in time for a specific security?
13. Describe the differences among the following three types of orders: market, limit, and stop loss.
14. What is a short sale?
15. Describe buying on margin.
16. What is program trading?
17. Describe several differences between the organized exchanges and the over-the-counter (OTC) market.
18. What factors differentiate a "good market" from a "poor market"?
19. A security's liquidity is affected by what influences?
20. Why may a stock trade that takes 1 second to execute be preferable to a trade that takes 9 seconds to execute?
21. How do the third and fourth markets differ from other secondary markets?
22. What are some factors that influence the commission on a stock trade with a broker?
23. Give some examples of market indexes. Why are there so many different indexes?
24. What are American Depository Receipts (ADRs)?
25. Why is it illegal to trade on insider information?
26. What is Regulation FD, and how does it affect security trading?
27. Visit the Web site of the CFA Institute, http://www.cfainstitute.org. Type the word "ethics" into the site's search function. Discuss, in your own words, the ethics issues that the CFA Institute is analyzing or discussing.
28. Visit the Web site of the CFP Board, http://www.cfp.net. Type the word "ethics" into the site's search function. Describe a few of the pages that appear from the search.
29. What are the advantages of having a specialist-based or DMM (open outcry) trading system? An electronic trading system?
30. Discuss this statement: "Technology and globalization are two current forces impacting stock exchanges."

PROBLEMS

1. You are the president and chief executive officer of a family owned manufacturing firm with assets of $45 million. The company articles of incorporation and state laws place no restrictions on the sale of stock to outsiders. An unexpected opportunity to expand arises that will require an additional investment of $14 million. A commitment must be made quickly if this opportunity is to be taken. Existing stockholders are not in a position to provide the additional investment. You wish to maintain family control of the firm regardless of which form of financing you might undertake. As a first step, you decide to contact an investment banking firm.

   a. What considerations might be important in the selection of an investment banking firm?
   b. A member of your board has asked if you have considered competitive bids for the distribution of your securities compared with a negotiated contract with a particular firm. What factors are involved in this decision?
   c. Assuming that you have decided upon a negotiated contract, what are the first questions that you would ask of the firm chosen to represent you?
   d. As the investment banker, what would be your first actions before offering advice?
   e. Assuming the investment banking firm is willing to distribute your securities, describe the alternative plans that might be included in a contract with the banking firm.
   f. How does the investment banking firm establish a selling strategy?
   g. How might the investment banking firm protect itself against a drop in the price of the security during the selling process?
   h. What follow-up services will be provided by the banking firm following a successful distribution of the securities?
   i. Three years later, as an individual investor, you decide to add to your own holding of the security but only at a price that you consider appropriate. What form of order might you place with your broker?

2. In late 2010, you purchased the common stock of a company that has reported significant earnings increases in nearly every quarter since your purchase. The price of the stock increased from $12 a share at the time of the purchase to a current level of $45. Notwithstanding the success of the company, competitors are gaining much strength. Further, your analysis indicates that the stock may be overpriced based on your projection of future earnings growth. Your analysis, however, was the same one year ago and the earnings have continued to increase. Actions that you might take range from an outright sale of the stock (and the payment of capital gains tax) to doing nothing and continuing to hold the shares. You reflect on these choices as well as other actions that could be taken. Describe the various actions that you might take and their implications.

3. Which of the following securities is likely to be the most liquid according to this data? Explain.

STOCK	BID	ASK
R	$39.43	$39.55
S	13.67	13.77
T	116.02	116.25

4. You purchased shares of Broussard Company using 50 percent margin; you invested a total of $20,000 (buying 1,000 shares at a price of $20 per share) by using $10,000 of your own funds and borrowing $10,000. Determine your percentage profit or loss under the following situations (ignore borrowing costs, dividends, and taxes). In addition, what would the percentage profit and loss be in these scenarios if margin were not used?

   a. the stock price rises to $23 a share
   b. the stock price rises to $30 a share
   c. the stock price falls to $16 a share
   d. the stock price falls to $10 a share

5. Currently the price of Mattco stock is $30 a share. You have $30,000 of your own funds to invest. Using the maximum margin allowed, what is your percentage profit or loss under the following situations (ignore dividends and taxes)? What would the percentage profit or loss be in each situation if margin were not used?

   a. you purchase the stock and it rises to $33 a share
   b. you purchase the stock and it rises to $35 a share
   c. you purchase the stock and it falls to $25 a share
   d. you purchase the stock and it falls to $20 a share

6. The Trio Index is comprised of three stocks, Eins, Zwei, and Tri. Their current prices are listed below.

STOCK	PRICE AT TIME (t)
Eins	$10
Zwei	$20
Tri	$40

   a. Between now and the next time period, the stock prices of Eins and Zwei increase 10 percent while Tri increases 20 percent. What is the percentage change in the price-weighted Trio Index?
   b. Suppose instead that the price of Eins increases 20 percent while Zwei and Tri rise 10 percent. What is the percentage change in the price-weighted Trio Index? Why does it differ from the answer to part a?

7. The four stocks below are part of an index. Using the information below:

   a. Compute a price-weighted index by adding their prices at time t and time $t + 1$. What is the percentage change in the index?
   b. Compute a value-weighted index by adding their market values at time t and time $t + 1$. What is the percentage change in the index?
   c. Why is there a difference between your answers to (a) and (b)?

STOCK	# OF SHARES OUTSTANDING	PRICE AT TIME (t)	PRICE AT TIME ($t + 1$)
Eeny	100	10	15
Meeny	50	20	22
Miney	50	30	28
Moe	20	40	42

8. The Quad Index is comprised of four stocks, Uno, Dos, Tres, and Fore.

a. Given the data below on the number of shares outstanding and their share prices at time (t) and time ($t + 1$), what is the percentage change in the Quad Index if it is calculated as a price-weighted index? As a value-weighted index?

STOCK	# OF SHARES OUTSTANDING	PRICE AT TIME (t)	PRICE AT TIME ($t + 1$)
Uno	1000	$10	$11
Dos	500	20	21
Tres	250	40	42
Fore	100	50	60

b. Instead of the prices shown above, suppose we switch the prices for Uno and Fore. That is, Uno's stock price is $50 at time ($t$) and it rises to $60 by time ($t + 1$) and Fore's stock price rises from $10 to $11 over the same time frame. What is the percentage change in the Quad Index if it is computed as a price-weighted index? As a value-weighted index?

c. Explain similarities or differences in your answers to parts (a) and (b).

9. A U.S. firm wants to raise $10 million of capital so it can invest in new technology. How much will it need to raise in order to net $10 million, using the average costs of raising funds in the chapter?

10. A U.S. firm wants to raise $15 million by selling 1 million shares at a net price of $15. We know that some say that firms "leave money on the table" because of the phenomenon of underpricing.

a. Using the average amount of underpricing in U.S. IPOs, how many fewer shares could it sell to raise these funds if the firm received a net price per share equal to the value of the shares at the end of the first day's trading?

b. How many less shares could it sell if the IPO was occurring in Germany?

c. How many less shares could it sell if the IPO was occurring in Korea?

d. How many less shares could it sell if the IPO was occurring in Canada?

11. Below are the results of a Dutch auction for an IPO of Bagel's Bagels, a trendy bagel and coffee shop chain. Bagel's is offering 50 million shares.

BIDDER	BID PRICE	NUMBER OF SHARES
Matthew	$50.25	15 million
Kevin	49.75	20 million
Amy	49.45	20 million
Megan	49.00	10 million

a. What will be the clearing price?

b. How many shares will each bidder receive if Bagel's allocates shares on a pro rata basis to all the successful bidders?

12. Boneyard Biscuits' Dutch auction for an IPO was a great success. The firm offered 100 million shares. Bids appear below.

BIDDER	BID PRICE	NUMBER OF SHARES
Manahan	$25.25	25 million
Campbell	24.95	30 million
Maloney	24.75	25 million
Touma	24.40	10 million
Clark	24.40	30 million
Fry	24.25	15 million

a. What is the clearing price?

b. What options do Boneyard and its underwriters have for allocating shares? How many shares will each bidder receive under each option?

13. **EXCEL** Develop a spreadsheet to do the dollar amount and percentage profit and loss calculations in questions 4 and 5. Use as inputs to the spreadsheet the amount of your funds you are investing, the initial margin percentage, the maintenance margin percentage, and the stock's price. In addition, have the spreadsheet calculate the stock price at which you'll receive a margin call.

14. **EXCEL** Expand the spreadsheet of problem 13 to consider one extra source of return and one extra cost to using margin. Specifically, modify the spreadsheet to include expected dividends per share and the cost of the margin loan (stated in APR format).

Assume that Broussard Corporation pays a dividend of $0.50 per share, Mattco pays an annual dividend of $0.80 per share, and the margin loan rate is 6 percent.

15. **EXCEL** Adjust the spreadsheet and its calculations in problem 13 for one more complication: have the length of the holding period (in quarters) be one of the spreadsheet's inputs. Compute the annualized return if the holding period for Mattco stock were (a) three months and (b) six months.

16. **Challenge Problem** Get stock price data from http://finance.yahoo.com/ for ten stocks in the Dow Jones Industrial Average for the prior ten days and use these prices to compute a price-weighted index for each of these ten days. Chart the performance of your index versus the DJIA over this time period. How closely do they track one another? What is the total percentage change in each index? Comment on the differences in performance over this time frame.

Size and Age of the Firm

The size and age of a company and stage in its financial life cycle may also influence management's short-term/long-term financing mix decisions. A new company's only source of funds may be the owner and possibly his or her friends. Some long-term funds may be raised by mortgaging real estate and buying equipment on installment, and some current borrowing may be possible to meet seasonal needs. As a business grows, it has more access to short-term capital from finance companies and banks. Further along, its growth and good record of profitability may enable a business to arrange longer-term financing with banks or other financial agencies such as insurance companies. At this stage in its financial development, it may also expand its group of owners by issuing stock to people other than the owner and a few friends.

Growth and Profitability

The growth prospects of a company also have an effect on financing decisions. If a company is growing faster than it can generate funds from internal sources, it must give careful consideration to a plan for long-term financing. Even if it can finance its needs in the current situation from short-term sources, it may not be wise to do so. Sound financial planning calls for raising long-term funds at appropriate times. A firm that is generating cash profits will need less outside financing than one that is less profitable. The internally generated cash flows can help pay bills in a timely manner, thus requiring less short-term financing.

Some examples of ratios of current liabilities to total assets are presented in Figure 16.6. Google has a low amount of short-term financing as it is flush with cash from recent stock offerings and its profits. Con Ed, a regulated utilty, has an asset base that is mainly fixed so it uses relatively little short-term financing. McDonald's, which relies on long-term facility leases or franchisee funds for financing its stores, also has a relatively low amount of current liabilities. Dell has a relatively high amount of short-term financing in Figure 16.6; it is well-known for its focus on liquidity with its just-in-time inventory and production environment. It has very little long-term debt financing as it relies mainly on short-term financing for its large amount of current assets.

FIGURE 16.6

Current Liabilities Divided by Total Assets for Selected Firms

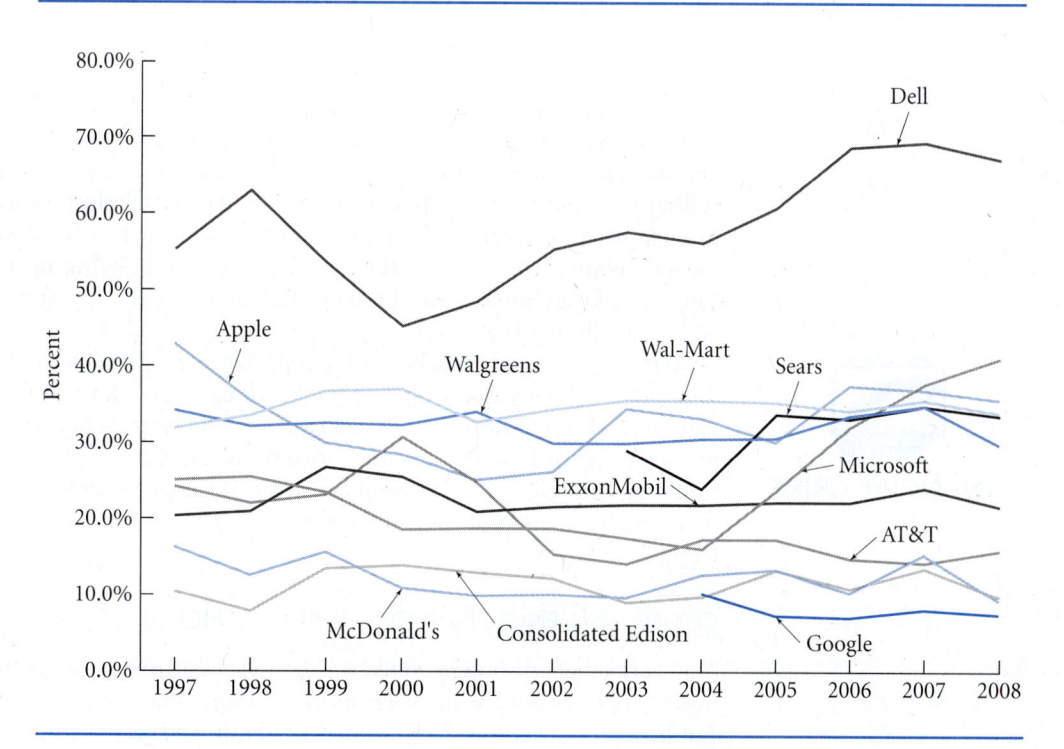

Seasonal Variation

Our earlier discussion of Figure 16.3 pointed out that seasonal variations in sales affect the demand for current assets. Inventories are built up to meet seasonal needs, and receivables rise as sales increase. The peak of receivables will come after the peak in sales, the intervening time depending on the credit terms and payment practices of customers. Accounts payable will also increase as inventories are purchased. The difference between the increase in current assets and accounts payable should be financed by short-term borrowing because the need for funds will disappear as inventories are sold and accounts receivable are collected. When a need for additional funds is financed by a short-term loan, such a loan is said to be self-liquidating since funds are made available to repay it as inventories and receivables are reduced.

Sales Trend

A firm's sales trend affects the financing mix. As sales grow, fixed assets and current assets also must grow to support the sales growth, as depicted in Figure 16.3. This need for funds is ongoing unless the upward trend of sales is reversed.

If asset growth is initially financed by short-term borrowing, the outstanding borrowings will continue to rise as sales rise. The amount of debt may rise year by year as the growth trend continues upward. After a while the current ratio will drop to such a level that no financing institution will provide additional funds. The only alternative then is long-term financing. Long-term financing often rises to reduce excess levels of short-term financing.

As we learn later in this chapter, short-term financing can be increased over time in relatively small increments, if needed, by applying for loans and negotiating with borrowers, as seen in Panel A of Figure 16.7. Long-term external financing, however, is "lumpy." Because of the time and cost of floating a bond or stock issue or negotiating a long-term loan or private placement, long-term securities are usually issued only in large quantities, as seen in Panel B of Figure 16.7.

Cyclical Variations

The need for current funds increases when there is an upswing in the business cycle or the sales cycle of an industry. Since the cycle is not regular in timing or degree, it is hard to predict exactly how much, or for how long, added funds will be needed. The need should be estimated for a year ahead in the budget and checked quarterly. When the sales volume of business decreases, the need for funds to finance accounts receivable and inventory will decrease as well. It is possible, however, that for a time during the downturn the need for financing will increase temporarily. This will occur if the cash conversion cycle lengthens as receivables are collected more slowly and inventories move more slowly and drop in value.

If cyclical needs for funds are met by current borrowing, the loan may not be self-liquidating in a year. There are hazards in financing these needs on a short-term basis. The lending institution may demand payment of all or part of the loan as business turns down. Funds may be needed more than ever at this stage of the cycle, and the need may last until receivables can be collected and inventory can be reduced. Firms in cyclical industries should use a more conservative approach that makes use of long-term financing. Major U.S automobile firms, in a highly cyclical business, prepare for the next recession by building up cash reserves. Ford Motor Company, for example, went through $10 billion in cash during the 1990–1991 recession and $8.5 billion during 1999–2001.

At the beginning of 2006, before the 2007–2009 recession and credit crisis hit, Ford and its car financing subsidiary had over $39 billion in cash and short-term marketable securities as a cushion. General Motors had over $50 billion and DaimlerChrysler had $7.1 billion in cash and marketable securities. For these latter two firms, the cash was insufficient as GM filed for bankruptcy and received a U.S. government rescue financing package. DaimlerChrysler was sold by its German parent firm, received government bailout funds, and is now known as Chrysler Group LLC.

OTHER INFLUENCES IN SHORT-TERM FINANCING

There are other advantages to using short-term borrowing rather than other forms of financing. Short-term borrowing offers more flexibility than long-term financing, since a business can borrow only those sums needed currently and pay them off if the need for financing

FIGURE 16.7

Patterns of Short-term and Long-term Financing Needs Over Time for a Growing Firm

Panel A: Pattern of Short-Term Financing

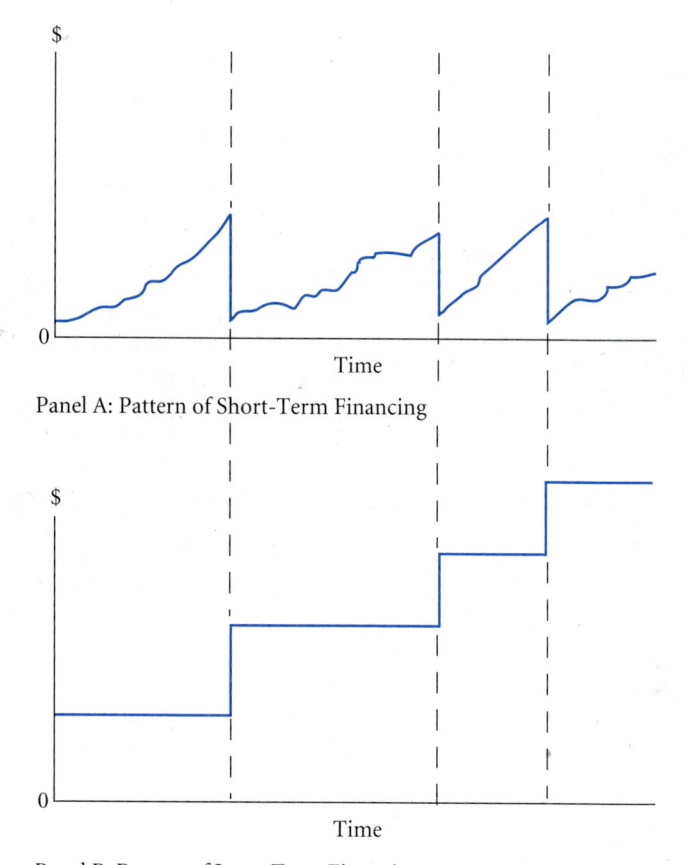

Panel B: Pattern of Long-Term Financing

diminishes. Long-term financing cannot be retired so easily and it may include a prepayment penalty, as is the case with the call premium for callable bonds. If an enterprise finances its growing current asset requirements entirely through long-term financing during a period of general business expansion, it may be burdened with excess funds and financing costs during a subsequent period of general business contraction. Using short-term financing along with long-term financing creates a financial flexibility that is not possible with long-term financing alone.

Short-term financing has advantages that result from continuing relationships with a bank or other financial institution. The firm that depends almost entirely on long-term financing for its needs will not enjoy the close relationship with its bank that it might otherwise. A record of frequent borrowing and prompt repayment to a bank is an extremely important factor in sound financial management. A bank will make every effort to accommodate regular business customers who do this. The enterprise that has not established this type of working relationship with its bank will scarcely be in a position to seek special loans when it has emergency needs. The credit experience of a business with short-term financing may be the only basis on which its potential long-term lenders will be able to judge it. Hence, the business that intends to seek long-term loans may wish to establish a good credit reputation based on its short-term financing.

Offsetting these advantages of short-term financing is the need for frequent renewals. Even though short-term credit is usually easy to obtain, time and effort must be spent at frequent intervals because of the short duration of these loans—and when sales revenues decline, a great deal of negotiation may be required to receive needed credit.

Frequent maturities also create an added element of risk. The bank or finance company can call the loan whenever it is due. The bank may not want to roll over a loan. Borrowing costs also may rise if short-term interest rates increase. A company in a temporary slump due to the business cycle or some internal problem could possibly work out its problems in time with adequate financing. If the company had acquired funds on a long-term basis, it might have a better chance of resolving its problems. On the other hand, if it relies heavily on short-term financing, its loans may be reduced or not renewed, which may make it nearly impossible to recover and might even lead to liquidation.

Now that we have an understanding of short-term/long-term financing strategies and factors that affect the relative use of short-term financing, we turn our attention toward various sources of short-term financing. Short-term financing sources include bank loans, trade credit or accounts payable, and commercial paper, among others. Financial managers should recall the five C's discussed in Chapter 15's section on accounts receivable management: the ability to obtain short-term financing is made easier for firms with acknowledged character (ethics), the capacity to pay bills, a strong capital base, collateral to act as security for loans, and favorable conditions in the economy and the firm's industry.

CONCEPT CHECK

List the major influences on a firm's short-term financing mix decision.

What other influences can affect a firm's level of short-term financing?

PROVIDERS OF SHORT-TERM FINANCING

Businesses can attempt to obtain short-term financing from a number of different providers and methods. Some are financial institutions, such as banks, which lend to firms for both working capital and long-term purposes (such as equipment loans). But other providers of financing include the firm's suppliers (trade credit), other corporations (commercial finance companies), and the financial markets (commercial paper), and when a small business is deemed "too risky" for a bank loan, they may be able to obtain financing by way of a government loan guarantee through the U.S. Small Business Administration. We discuss each of these in turn.

COMMERCIAL BANK LENDING

Although many banks require a pledge of specific assets, the unsecured loan still remains the primary type of loan arrangement. The stated rate on such loans is based on the bank's **prime rate** or the interest rate a bank charges its most creditworthy customers. Interest rates on loans typically are stated in terms of the prime rate plus a risk differential, such as prime +2 percent. Loan papers will call this prime plus 2 or simply P + 2. Higher-risk borrowers will have higher differentials to compensate the bank for lending to riskier customers

prime rate
interest rate the bank charges its most creditworthy customers

Bank Lines of Credit

A business and a bank often have an agreement regarding the amount of credit that the business will have at its disposal. The loan limit that the bank establishes for each of its business customers is called a **line of credit.** The cost for a line of credit is the interest rate for the period during which money is actually borrowed.

Under a line of credit, the business does not wait until money is needed to negotiate the loan. Rather, it files the necessary financial statements and other evidences of financial condition with the bank prior to the need for credit. The banker is interested in how well the business has fared in the past and its probable future because the line of credit generally is extended for a year at a time. The banker may require that other debts of the business be subordinated to, or come after, the claim of the bank. Banks also usually require their business customers to "clean up" their lines of credit for a specified period of time each year—that is, to have no outstanding borrowing against the credit line, usually for a minimum of two weeks. This ensures that the credit line is being used for short-term financing purposes rather than for long-term needs.

Continued access to a line of credit may be subject to the approval of the bank if there are major changes in the operation of a business. A major shift or change in management personnel or in the manufacture or sale of particular products can greatly influence the future success of a company. Hence, the bank, having contributed substantially to the financial resources of the business, is necessarily interested in these activities. The bank may also seek information on the business through organized credit bureaus, through contact with other businesses having dealings with the firm, and through other banks.

line of credit
loan limit the bank establishes for each of its business customers

TABLE 16.1
Merging Banks

BANKS IN EXISTENCE SOMETIME DURING 1990–2010	SURVIVING BANKS IN 2010 AFTER MERGERS
J.P. Morgan Manufacturers Hanover Trust Chemical Bank Chase Manhattan Bank Banc One First Chicago NBD Bancorp	JPMorgan Chase
Bank of America Continental Bank Security Pacific Nations Bank Barnett Bank Boston Bay Bank Fleet Shawmut Fleet Boston LaSalle Bank	Bank of America
Wells Fargo First Union Signet CoreStates Norwest Corporation Wachovia	Wells Fargo

In the event that the business needs more money than was anticipated at the time the line of credit was set up, it may request the bank to increase the limit on its line of credit. It must be prepared, however, to offer very sound evidence of the need for additional funds and the ability of the business to repay the increased loan from business operations. A request for an increased line of credit frequently occurs when a business is growing and needs more capital to make its growth possible. Banks, following the principle of maturity-matching discussed previously, generally insist that expansion be financed with long-term funds, but they may assist growth by temporarily providing a part of the increased needs. The business that is unable to obtain additional unsecured credit from its bank may seek a loan secured with collateral from the bank or other lenders. These other forms of borrowing are discussed later in this chapter.

Bank mergers have affected the ability of firms to obtain credit lines. Table 16.1 lists over twenty large banks that were in existence, in one form or another, from 1990 to 2010; by 2010 they had merged into only three banks. That doesn't mean, however, that the larger banks are eager participants in meeting the line of credit needs of larger firms; fewer banks has meant tighter credit and higher fees.[4] A survey of corporate financial officers found that 78 percent believed the mergers reduced the number of loans and 72 percent had fears of "monopolistic pricing" by merged banks. Fortunately, as the field of banking changes to one of financial services, other entities, such as commercial finance companies, insurance companies, and even some mutual funds are starting to lend to firms and to take the place of the traditional banking relationship.

Although the practice is diminishing, some banks require that a **compensating balance** of 10 to 20 percent of unsecured loans outstanding be kept on deposit by the business. The most frequently cited justification for this requirement is that, because banks cannot lend without deposits, bank borrowers should be required to be depositors. But compensating balances are also a means of increasing the effective cost of borrowing by increasing the amount on which interest is computed.

compensating balance requirement that 10 to 20 percent of a loan be kept on deposit at the bank

---

[4]. Jathon Sapsford and Paul Sherer, "Fewer Banks Means Costlier Credit Lines," *The Wall Street Journal*, March 14, 2001, pp. C1, C16.

Computing Interest Rates

Chapter 9, "The Time Value of Money," illustrated how to use time value of money concepts to calculate interest rates. The same concepts can be used to calculate the true cost of borrowing funds from a bank. If, for example, Global Manufacturing can borrow $10,000 for six months at 8 percent APR, the six-month interest cost will be 8 percent/2 × $10,000, or $400. Global will repay the $10,000 principal and $400 in interest after six months. As we learned in Chapter 9, the true or effective interest rate on this loan is

$$\text{EAR} = (1 + \text{APR}/m)^m - 1 \qquad (16.1)$$

or

$$(1 + 0.08/2)^2 - 1 = 0.0816, \text{ or } 8.16 \text{ percent.}$$

discounted loan
borrower receives the principal less the interest at the time the loan is made; the principal is repaid at maturity

At times banks will discount a loan. A **discounted loan** is one in which the borrower receives the principal less the interest at the time the loan is made. At maturity, the principal is repaid. Discounting has the effect of reducing the available funds received by the borrower while raising the effective interest rate. If Global's loan is discounted, Global will receive $9,600 ($10,000 less $400) and will repay $10,000, in essence paying $400 interest on the $9,600 funds received. This is a periodic rate of $400/$9,600, or 4.17 percent.[5] The effective annual rate is $(1 + 0.0417)^2 - 1$, or 8.51 percent, an increase of 0.35 percentage points over the undiscounted loan.

When a loan is discounted, a firm has to borrow more money than the amount it really needs. To counteract the effect of discounting, to acquire $10,000 in usable funds they will have to borrow $10,000/(1 − 0.04) or $10,416.67. When a loan of $10,416.67 is discounted at a six-month rate of 4 percent, the net proceeds to Global will be $10,000 (that is, $10,416.67 − [0.04][10,416.67] = $10,000). In general, to receive the desired usable funds, the loan request must equal:

$$\text{Loan request} = \text{Desired usable funds}/(1 - \text{discount}). \qquad (16.2)$$

INTERNET ACTIVITY
Examine bank Web sites and learn about their offerings to small and medium businesses and large corporations. Include in your search the Web sites of local banks in your area as well as large banks such as http://www.jpmorganchase.com and http://www.bankofamerica.com.

A loan with a compensating balance is similar to a discounted loan as far as its effect on the effective interest rate and usable funds is concerned. Compensating balances are equivalent to discounting when the firm currently has no money on deposit at the bank. The firm's loan request should be large enough so that after funds are placed in the compensating balance it will have the usable funds it desires. For compensating balance loans, Equation 16.2 becomes:

$$\text{Loan request} = \frac{\text{Desired usable funds}}{(1 - \text{compensating balance requirement})} \qquad (16.3)$$

which is identical to Equation 16.2, except the discount percent is replaced by the compensating balance percentage.

Revolving Credit Agreements

The officers of a business may feel rather certain that an agreed-upon line of credit will provide the necessary capital requirements for the coming year, but the bank is not obligated to continue to offer the credit line if the firm's financial condition worsens. Line of credit agreements usually allow the bank to reduce or withdraw its extension of credit to the firm.

revolving credit agreement
legal obligation of the bank to provide up to the agreed upon borrowing limit

The well-established business with an excellent credit rating may be able to obtain a **revolving credit agreement.** A revolving credit agreement is a commitment in the form of a standby agreement for a guaranteed line of credit. Unlike a line of credit, a revolving credit agreement is a legal obligation of the bank to provide funds up to the agreed-upon borrowing limit during the time the agreement is in effect. In addition to paying interest on borrowed funds for the period of the loan, the business must pay a commission or fee to the bank based on the unused portion of the credit line, or the money it has "on call" during the agreement period. This fee is usually between 0.25 and 0.50 percent of the unused amount of the line.[6]

---

5. This periodic rate can also be computed using our Chapter 9 concepts. We know that: $FV = PV (1 + r)^n$. Since FV equals $10,000 (the amount to be repaid), PV equals $9,600 (the usable funds received after discounting), and n is 1 for our six-month time frame, we have: $10,000 = $9,600 $(1 + r)^1$. Solving for r, we see the periodic interest rate is 4.17 percent.

6. Banks are a major participant in the commercial paper market (discussed later in this chapter) as they frequently support this market by offering paper issuers a line of credit or an arrangement similar to the revolving credit agreement described above to act as a secondary source of funds for repaying its commercial paper loans.

CONCEPT CHECK

How does a bank line of credit differ from a revolving credit agreement?

What does it mean to "clean up" a line of credit?

What is a discounted loan?

What happens to the borrower's effective interest rate when the loan is discounted?

To compute the effective cost of a revolving agreement, the joint effect of interest on borrowed funds and the commitment fee on the unborrowed portion of the agreement must be considered. Suppose Global has a one-year $1 million revolving credit agreement with a local bank. The annual interest rate on the agreement is 9 percent with a commitment fee of 0.40 percent on the unborrowed portion. Global expects to have average outstanding borrowings against the revolver of $300,000. Over the year, the interest cost on the average amount borrowed is 0.09 × $300,000 or $27,000. The commitment fee on the average unborrowed portion is 0.0040 × $700,000, or $2,800. With total interest and fees of $29,800 ($27,000 + $2,800) on average borrowings of $300,000, the expected annual cost of the revolver is $29,800/$300,000, or 9.93 percent.

Small Business Administration

The Small Business Administration (SBA) was established by the federal government to provide financial assistance to small firms that are unable to obtain loans through private channels on reasonable terms. Created in 1953, the SBA provides a wide variety of services in addition to loan guarantees through its more than 100 field offices.

The reason businesses use SBA loan guarantees is explained by the stated objectives of the SBA: to enable deserving small businesses to obtain financial assistance otherwise not available through private channels on reasonable terms. When the SBA was established, it was recognized that the economic development of the nation depended in large part on the freedom of new business ventures to enter into active operation. Yet the increased concentration of investable funds with large institutional investors, such as life insurance companies, investment companies, and others, made it increasingly difficult for new and small business ventures to attract investment capital. The lack of a track record made loans hard to obtain from traditional bank sources.

It is important to note that the Small Business Administration does not make loans, rather it guarantees them. Under their 7(a) loan program the SBA will guarantee up to 85 percent of the loan amount for loans of $150,000 or less. Loans larger than $150,000 up to $2 million can obtain a guarantee of up to 75 percent. The loan guarantee means a bank can lend a sum to a small business owner but only have a small portion of the funds at risk. In case of default, the SBA will repay the loan. For example, a bank lending $100,000 under the SBA loan guarantee program has 85 percent of the loan guaranteed by the SBA. This means that only 15 percent, or $15,000, of their funds is at risk. In case the borrower cannot repay the loan, the SBA will reimburse the bank for up to $85,000 in case of default.

If a firm is able to obtain financing elsewhere, its loan application to the SBA is rejected. An applicant for a loan must prove that funds needed are not available from any bank, that no other private lending sources are available, that issuing securities is not practicable, that financing cannot be arranged by disposing of business assets, and that the personal credit of the owners cannot be used. These loans may not be used for paying existing creditors or for speculative purposes.

In addition to its business-lending activities, the SBA is responsible for several related financial activities. These include loans to development companies, disaster loans, lease guarantees, surety bond support, minority enterprise programs, procurement assistance, and support for investment companies that service small businesses.

SBA working capital loans are limited to seven years, while regular business loans have a maximum maturity of twenty-five years. It also sets a maximum allowable rate that banks can charge on guaranteed loans. These rates are adjusted periodically by the SBA to reflect changes in market conditions.

INTERNET ACTIVITY

Learn about financing opportunities for small businesses through the Small Business Administration at www.sba.gov.

CONCEPT CHECK

How can the Small Business Administration help a firm obtain short-term financing?

TRADE CREDIT FROM SUPPLIERS

The most important single form of short-term business financing is the credit extended by one business organization to another. Accounts receivable together with longer-term notes receivable taken by manufacturers, wholesalers, jobbers, and other businesses that sell products or services to businesses—are known as trade credit.

The establishment of trade credit is the least formal of all forms of financing. It involves only an order for goods or services by one business and the delivery of goods or performance of service by the selling business. The purchasing business receives an invoice stating the terms of

SMALL BUSINESS PRACTICE
Bank Financing for Small Businesses

Getting a small business bank loan today is much harder than it was in the 1980s. Bankers are making greater demands on entrepreneurial or venture firms. More comprehensive financial statements must be provided and more collateral (such as equipment or working capital in the form of inventories or receivables) pledged. Banks lend at the "prime rate," which is their best rate to larger businesses. In contrast, small businesses are asked to pay two or more points above prime. For example, if the prime rate is 8 percent, small businesses will have to pay interest rates of 10 percent or more to obtain bank loans.

Iris Lorenz-Fife in her book *Financing Your Business* (Prentice Hall, 1997) lists the five most common reasons given by bankers when they decide not to make loans to small businesses. The first reason is the "owner's equity is too low relative to the size of the loan that is requested." The second reason relates to the "value of the collateral being offered is too low or unreliable." A third reason is that the "firm is a one-person business with no adequate managerial backup." A fourth reason centers on the belief that the business "will need more time to repay the loan than the bank's usual terms." The fifth reason for rejecting a loan application from a small business is that the banker believes that the small business owner/manager "has inadequate managerial experience or ability."

If you have a small business loan application rejected by a bank, you should ask the banker why it was rejected. You also should ask what changes in the application would be necessary to be successful in obtaining a bank loan.

---

the transaction and the time period within which payment is to be made. The purchaser adds the liability to accounts payable. The seller adds the claim to accounts receivable. In some situations, the seller may insist on written evidence of liability on the part of the purchaser. Such written evidence is usually in the form of a note that is payable by the purchaser and is considered as a note receivable by the seller. Before a business organization delivers goods or performs a service for another business, it must determine the ability and willingness of the purchaser to pay for the order.[7] The responsibility of such credit analysis in most businesses belongs to the credit manager.

Terms for Trade Credit

Sales may be made on terms such as cash, E.O.M. (end of month), M.O.M. (middle of month), or R.O.G. (receipt of goods). Or such terms as 2/10, net 30 may be offered, which means the purchaser may deduct 2 percent from the purchase price if payment is made within ten days of shipment; if not paid within ten days, the net amount is due within thirty days. Such **trade discounts** to purchasers for early payment are common and are designed to provide incentive for prompt payment of bills. Occasionally, sellers offer only net terms such as net 30 or net 60.

*trade discounts
provided to purchasers as an incentive for early or prompt payment of accounts*

A cash sale, contrary to its implication, usually involves credit. This is because the purchaser is often permitted a certain number of days within which to make payment. For example, a sale of merchandise in which the purchaser is permitted up to ten days to pay may be considered a cash transaction, but credit is outstanding to the purchaser for that time. Even for the firm that purchases products entirely on a cash basis, the volume of accounts payable outstanding on its books at any one time may be large.

Cost of Trade Credit

When trade credit terms do not provide a discount for early payment of obligations, there is no cost to the buyer for such financing. Even when discounts are available, it may seem that there is no cost for trade credit since failing to take the early payment discount simply requires the purchaser to pay the net price. There is a cost involved, however, when a discount is not taken. For example, with terms of 2/10, net 30, the cost is the loss of the 2 percent discount that could have been taken if payment were made within the ten-day period.

To compare the cost of trade credit and bank credit, the cost of the trade credit must be placed on an annual interest rate basis. For example, if the terms of sale are 2/10, net 30, the cost of trade credit is the loss of the 2 percent discount that the purchaser fails to take if she or he extends the payment period from ten days up to thirty days. The lost 2 percent is the cost of trade credit for those twenty days. If we also consider that it is the discounted price (invoice price minus the percentage discount) that is being financed, the approximate effective cost (EC) is:

---

7. We discussed the process of credit evaluation in Chapter 15.

$$EC = \frac{\% \text{ discount}}{100\% - \% \text{ discount}} \times \frac{365 \text{ days}}{\text{Credit period} - \text{discount days}} \quad (16.4)$$

For our 2/10, net 30 example,

$$EC = \frac{2\%}{100\% - 2\%} \times \frac{365}{30 - 10} = 2.04\% \times 18.25 = 37.2\%$$

This shows that the cost of trade credit typically is far in excess of bank rates. Thus it is usually worthwhile to borrow funds to take advantage of cash discounts on trade credit. Failure to take advantage of the trade discount is the same as borrowing from the vendor at the effective cost.[8]

The cost of trade credit in most lines of business activity is high when discounts are missed. However, it should not be assumed that high cost necessarily makes trade credit an undesirable source of short-term financing. It can be, in fact, the most important form of financing for small and growing businesses that are unable to qualify for short-term credit through customary financial channels.

The firm in a weak financial condition will find trade credit more readily available than bank credit. The bank stands to gain only the interest on the loan if repayment is made, but it will lose the entire sum loaned if the borrower's obligation is not met. The manufacturer or merchant, on the other hand, has a profit margin on the goods sold. If the purchaser fails to meet the obligation, the seller loses at most the cost of the goods delivered to the purchaser.

COMMERCIAL FINANCE COMPANIES

The first commercial finance company in the United States was chartered about 100 years ago. Since that time, the number of these institutions has increased to more than five hundred. Some of these organizations are small, offering limited financial services to their customers, while others have vast resources and engage in broadly diversified programs of business lending.

A **commercial finance company** is an organization without a bank charter that advances funds to businesses by (1) discounting accounts receivable, (2) making loans secured by chattel mortgages on machinery or liens on inventory, or (3) financing deferred-payment sales of commercial and industrial equipment. These companies also are known as commercial credit companies, commercial receivables companies, and discount companies.

Commercial finance companies, such as CIT Group, Celtic Capital, and GE Capital, offer many of the same services as commercial banks for financing accounts receivable and inventory. Lending funds based upon the amount of a firm's accounts receivable balances was, in fact, originated by commercial finance companies and only later was adopted by commercial banks. Both consumer and business financing can be obtained from firms such as General Electric Capital Corporation and Ford Motor Credit Company.

Commercial finance companies grew to their present number because they were completely free to experiment with new and highly specialized types of credit arrangements. Also, state laws concerning lending on the basis of accounts receivable were generally more favorable to these nonbanking organizations. A third influence is that they were able to charge high enough rates to make a profitable return on high-risk loans. Frequently these rates were far above rates bankers were permitted to charge.

In addition to financing accounts receivable and inventories, commercial finance companies provide a vast amount of credit for businesses by financing commercial vehicles, industrial and

---

CONCEPT CHECK
What is trade credit?
What is the cost of trade credit?
Is it usually more or less expensive than bank financing?

commercial finance company
organization without a bank charter that advances funds to businesses

INTERNET ACTIVITY
The Commercial Finance Association is a trade association for commercial finance companies. Learn more about the industry at http://www.cfa.com.

---

[8]. Astute readers will note that these popular formulas do not take period-by-period compounding into account. The true effective cost can be determined as follows:

$$\text{Effective cost} = \left(1 + \frac{\% \text{ discount}}{100\% - \% \text{ discount}}\right)^{365/(\text{Credit period} - \text{discount days})} - 1$$

In the text example, we have:

$$\text{True effective cost} = \left(1 + \frac{2\%}{100\% - 2\%}\right)^{365/(30-10)} - 1$$

$$= (1.0204)^{365/20} - 1$$
$$= 1.446 - 1 = 0.446 \text{ or } 44.6 \text{ percent}$$

farm equipment, and other types of business credit. The Commercial Finance Association estimates the total volume of business credit outstanding by the commercial finance companies to be almost $600 billion.[9]

The equity position of commercial finance companies is considerably greater than that of banks. However, these organizations do not operate on equity capital alone. Additional long-term capital is acquired by selling debenture, or unsecured, bonds. In addition, commercial banks lend a large volume of money at wholesale rates to commercial finance companies, which in turn lend it to business borrowers at retail rates. Nonbank financial intermediaries, as well as commercial and industrial firms, often find it advantageous to invest their temporary surplus funds in the commercial paper of commercial finance companies. These sources of short-term funds permit the commercial finance companies to meet their peak loan demands without having too much long-term debt, only part of which would be used during slack lending periods.

When viewing the high interest rates (sometimes as high as 15 to 20 percent) for commercial finance company loans, the question may arise: Why would a borrower, under any circumstances, use these companies? As a matter of fact, a business that has ample current assets and is in a highly liquid position may be well advised to rely on other sources of short-term financing. When business is most brisk and growth possibilities most favorable, the need for additional short-term funds becomes unusually pressing, just as it is when customers are slow in paying their bills and the company needs cash.

A business will typically first request an increase in its bank line of credit. Failing this, an additional loan from a bank may be secured by pledging either inventory or receivables as collateral. However, not all banks actively engage in this type of financial arrangement. Thus it may be necessary to deal with a commercial finance company. Commercial finance companies are able to operate through a system of branches on a regional or national basis, unhampered by restrictions on bank branch operations. Therefore, they can acquire the volume of business necessary to cover overhead and provide the needed diversification of risks for high-risk financing. Several bank holding companies have purchased or established commercial finance companies to take advantage of their special operating characteristics.

COMMERCIAL PAPER

A final source of short-term financing is not a specific type of lender but is the financial markets itself. Large U.S. corporations of high credit quality can issue or sell **commercial paper,** which is a short-term promissory note. This means the notes are backed solely by the credit quality of the issuer; there is no security or collateral behind them. Commercial paper may be sold directly by the issuer to financial institutions or other investors. Alternatively, it can be sold to commercial paper houses or dealers who purchase the promissory notes to resell them to individuals or businesses. A fee based on the amount of notes purchased, charged to the issuer of the notes, provides the basic income of commercial paper dealers. With about $1.1 trillion outstanding in early 2010 trading in this short maturity form of debt is about one-half of what it was before the financial crisis began in late 2007 annually. Fears of financial uncertainly can send shockwaves through the commercial paper market, as we saw in 2007–2008. The commercial paper market all but dried up as investors fled to the safety of Treasury securities in the fear of possible financial system meltdown. Many firms were able to access commercial paper financing only after the Fed stepped in to provide liquidity and backing to the market.[10]

A firm that wishes to obtain funds from a commercial paper house must have an unquestioned reputation for sound operation. First the commercial paper house makes a thorough investigation of the firm's financial position. If it appears that the notes of the firm can be sold with little difficulty, an agreement is made for the outright sale of a block of the firm's promissory notes to the commercial paper house. They, in turn, will resell these notes as quickly as possible to banks, managers of pension funds, business corporations that have surplus funds, or other investors. The notes are usually prepared in denominations of $100,000 or more with

CONCEPT CHECK

What is a commercial finance company?

How does a commercial finance company raise funds to lend to borrowers?

commercial paper
short-term promissory note sold by high-credit-quality corporations; notes are backed solely by the credit quality of the issuer

FINANCIAL CRISIS

---

9. R.S. Carmichael & Co., Inc. and Commercial Finance Association, *Annual Asset-Based Lending and Factoring Surveys, 2008,* issued May 6, 2009; accessed at https://www.cfa.com/eweb/Docs/2008_ABL_Factoring_Non-Member_Report.pdf on January 14, 2010.

10. The Commercial Paper Funding Facility is described at http://www.federalreserve.gov/monetarypolicy/cpff.htm.

INTERNET ACTIVITY

Visit Sungard's trading system Web site at https://mm2.sungard.net. For a variety of financial market information, see the Bloomberg Web site at http://www.bloomberg.com.

maturities ranging from a few days to 270 days.[11] The size of the notes and the maturities, however, can be adjusted to suit individual investor requirements.

Commercial paper is sold on a discount basis. Dealers will pay the borrower the face amount of the notes minus the interest charge and a fee that is usually between 0.02 and 0.05 percent. The interest charge is determined by the general level of prevailing rates in the money market and the strength of the borrowing company. When these notes are resold to banks and other lenders, only the prevailing interest charge is deducted from the face value of the notes. Hence, the commercial paper dealer receives the fee as compensation for the negotiation and intermediation.

Commercial paper is no longer sold only through dealers or brokers. Investors can now buy commercial paper online through an electronic trading system. The first firm to offer its paper online was Ford Motor Company on a commercial paper trading system designed by CS First Boston. Since then, others have developed online commercial paper systems to facilitate the direct issue of paper to investors. In recent years, the most successful of them has been SunGard's Transaction Network. Online issuance of paper allows issuers to cut in half the fees usually collected by dealers.

Commercial paper is issued by large, well-known, and financially stable firms; only they have the ability to raise large sums of short-term financing quickly and with a bank's backing.[12] Many of the borrowers of commercial paper are financial firms such as commercial finance companies; they seek to finance their own lending and leasing operations by raising short-term funds through commercial paper. They will borrow at the commercial paper rate and then lend the funds to others at higher interest rates.

Suppose Global Manufacturing wants to issue $100,000 of commercial paper that will mature in nine months (270 days). The placement fee is 0.10 percent and the interest charge will be 7.5 percent over the nine-month period. To compute Global's effective financing cost we must determine the net proceeds or usable funds that Global will obtain from the sale as well as the total interest charges they will pay. The net proceeds will be the $100,000 raised minus the interest less the placement fee:

$$\text{Net proceeds} = \$100{,}000 - [(0.075)(\$100{,}000)] - [(0.0010)(\$100{,}000)]$$
$$= \$100{,}000 - \$7{,}500 - \$100$$
$$= \$92{,}400$$

The interest charge is 0.075 × $100,000, or $7,500, and the placement fee is $100 for total expenses of $7,600. The nine-month financing cost for the commercial paper issue is:

$$\text{9-month cost} = \$7{,}600/\$92{,}400 = 0.0823, \text{ or } 8.23 \text{ percent}$$

The annualized cost of the commercial paper issue will be

$$(1 + 0.0823)^{12/9} - 1 = 0.1111 \text{ or } 11.11 \text{ percent}$$

The most important reason to a firm for issuing commercial paper is that the cost of borrowing is generally less than regular bank rates. The reason for the lower rates is that only the largest, most financially stable firms can issue commercial paper. And unlike banks, which typically service a geographic region, commercial paper is sold by dealers to investors worldwide, so international short-term rates help determine commercial paper rates rather than bank loan committees. Also, the need for compensating bank balances that increase interest costs on short-term bank loans is avoided. Loan restrictions on the amount that can be borrowed from a single bank also may favor the issuance of commercial paper by large corporations.

Like bonds, commercial paper is rated. The rating is important to the issuer, because the higher the rating, the lower is the interest expense. Industrial firms and other nonbank lenders often purchase commercial paper as a more profitable alternative to Treasury bills for investing excess cash.

---

11. Commercial paper has a maximum maturity of 270 days, as SEC regulations require that securities with maturities exceeding 270 days must go though the costly and time-consuming SEC registration process.

12. Banks are a major player in the commercial paper market, as they frequently offer issuers a line of credit equal to their amount of paper outstanding. Up until 1999, this was a requirement for S&P to award its top A-1 rating to a firm issuing paper. S&P now considers all sources of liquidity that can be used to redeem the paper.

CONCEPT CHECK

What is commercial paper?

How is commercial paper sold?

What advantages are there to a firm in issuing commercial paper instead of getting a bank loan?

Commercial paper provides a yield slightly above that of short-term government securities as we saw in Figure 15.6 in the previous chapter. Although commercial banks were historically the main purchasers of commercial paper, it is now actively held by industrial corporations, money market mutual funds, and other lenders.

Many top-rated U.S. commercial paper issuers can also issue paper overseas. The European commercial paper (Euro CP) market offers advantages to commercial paper issuers just as the Eurodollar bond market offers advantages over the U.S. bond market. There is no SEC regulation of the Euro CP market, so commercial paper maturities are generally a little longer and interest costs lower. In addition, Euro CP is available only to the "cream" of the commercial paper issuers, so no ratings are needed. Investors already know who the safest issuers are. So not having to pay for a rating also makes the Euro CP market attractive to those firms that are able to use it.

ADDITIONAL VARIETIES OF SHORT-TERM FINANCING

We've reviewed several types of short-term financing in our discussion of financing providers. For example, in our prior discussion of banks we discussed lines of credit, revolving credit agreements, and SBA loan guarantees. Suppliers offer trade credit. The financial markets offer the ability to sell commercial paper. In this section, we discuss other important varieties of short-term financing. For the most part, these financing arrangements are available both from banks and commercial finance companies and are forms of secured financing. **Secured lending** (also called *asset-based lending*) means that there is some collateral or security backing the loan that can be claimed or sold by the lender if the borrower defaults. We have seen this type of lending before in Chapter 10's discussion of mortgage bonds. In this section, we examine the use of asset-based lending for short-term financing purposes.

ACCOUNTS RECEIVABLE FINANCING

The business that does not qualify for an unsecured bank loan or that has emergency needs for funds in excess of its line of credit may decide to use its accounts receivable as a way to raise needed funds. Two methods exist for using accounts receivable as a form of asset-based lending. First, the firm can borrow against its accounts receivable balances. This is called **pledging** accounts receivable. Second, it can sell its accounts receivable to a firm called a **factor;** thus, selling accounts receivable balances is called *factoring*.

There are many similarities between these two methods of using accounts receivable to raise funds but there are a number of differences. We'll discuss the general process of each before reviewing the differences between them.

pledging or pledge
obtain a short-term loan by using accounts receivable as collateral

factor
engages in accounts receivable financing by purchasing accounts and assuming all credit risks

Pledging Accounts Receivable

Rather than wait until its customers pay on each of their accounts, a firm can pledge its accounts and get a loan. By so doing, the firm obtains funds sooner, albeit at a cost. The word "accounts" in accounts receivable is plural. When a firm pledges its accounts receivable, each customer's account is reviewed to see if it is sufficiently creditworthy to be security or collateral for a loan. The lender—usually a bank or finance company—gives close attention to the borrower's collection experience on its receivables and to certain characteristics of its accounts receivable.

The bank may spot-check the receivables of the firm and may in some cases analyze each account to determine how quickly the firm's customers make payments. It is also important for the bank to know something about these customers; it will probably check on their credit ratings from a source such as Dun and Bradstreet. Their ability to pay their debts will strongly influence how well the business applying for the loan will be able to collect payment.

In addition, the bank studies the type and quality of goods that are sold. If the merchandise is inferior, there may be objections from the customers and hence slower payment of bills or sales returns. Accounts receivable are of little value as security for a loan if large quantities of merchandise are returned and the amount of accounts receivable is reduced accordingly.

Generally, a loan based on accounts receivable will be no more than 80 percent of the gross receivables. This amount should be reduced by any discounts allowed to customers for quick payment and by the normal percentage of merchandise returns. If there is reason to believe that many of the loan applicant's customers are not suitable risks, or if adequate credit ratings are not available, the bank will lend a lower percentage of the face value of the receivables. Additionally, if a customer is a large proportion of the firm's credit sales, the percentage lent against that account may be less than usual; this protects the bank in case a large customer of the firm experiences financial difficulties, which may, in turn, create subsequent cash flow problems for the supplying firm.

Pledging accounts receivable is not a simple process. The firm's accounts receivable are reviewed by the bank to determine their level and if they are acceptable to form the basis for a loan. At the time the loan is made, individual accounts on the ledger of the business are designated clearly as having been pledged for the bank loan. Only those accounts suitable for collateral purposes for the bank are designated. When these accounts are paid in full or become unsatisfactory, they are replaced by other accounts.

Pledging accounts receivable involves sending invoices and funds (either electronically or paper) back and forth between the firm, its customers, and the bank offering the loan. For example, the bank receives copies of all shipping invoices to show that the goods have been shipped and an account receivable is valid. Thus not only is invoice material transferred from firm to customer but also from firm to bank. Similarly, there are several transfers of funds. First the bank lends funds to the firm. Second, the firm's customers make payments on the pledged receivables. Third, the firm sends such payments to the bank to repay the loan.

It is usually more expensive to pledge receivables than to borrow funds from a bank. Under a pledged receivables arrangement the firm pays interest on the loan (namely the funds advanced to it) and a separate fee to cover the extra work needed for such a loan. The bank must periodically check or audit the books of the business to see that it is, in fact, living up to the terms of the agreement and sending customer payments to it in a timely basis. As customers pay their bill on the pledged account that has been assigned for the loan, the proceeds must be turned over to the bank. The bank also reserves the right to make a direct audit of the business' books from time to time and to have an outside accounting firm examine the books periodically.

Factoring Accounts Receivable

Pledging involves borrowing against receivables balances; factoring involves selling the accounts. A financing firm called a factor purchases the accounts receivable outright and assumes all credit risks. Under **maturity factoring,** the firm selling its accounts receivable is paid on the normal collection date or net due date of the account. Under **advance factoring,** the factor pays the firm for its receivables before the account due date.

maturity factoring
firm selling its receivables is paid on the normal collection date or net due date of the account

advance factoring
factor pays the firm for its receivables before the account due date

Under a factoring arrangement, customers whose accounts are sold are notified that their bills are payable to the factor. The task of collecting on the accounts is thus shifted from the seller of the accounts to the factor. Some factors include GE Capital, Platinum Funding, and units of several large banks.

Factoring can be done *with recourse* or *without recourse*. With recourse, the factor can return an unpaid account to the firm and any funds advanced for that account must be returned to the factor. Without recourse, the accounts are sold to the factor and any bad or slow-paying accounts are the factor's responsibility.

Rather than just occasionally selling accounts to the factor, many times the factor becomes a partner with the firm. A typical arrangement has the factor become the firm's credit department. That is, all requests to sell goods on credit to new and existing customers are routed to the factor for approval, thus saving the firm time and expense in hiring, training, staffing, and running its own credit department. Members of the factor's credit department not only must be extremely prompt and accurate in their credit analyses but also, because they work closely with the firm's clients, must retain the goodwill of the companies that use its services.

Should the factor reject a credit request from a new customer of the firm—or reject a request to increase an existing credit limit on an existing customer of the firm—the firm can always choose to extend the credit itself. In such cases, the firm will keep those accounts on its books and have to service the accounts—send bills, collect payments, and deal with any slow or nonpayers.

To use a factor, a contract is drawn establishing the duties and obligations of the seller and the factor. The contract provides that the accepted accounts be assigned to the factor for payment and that sales invoices to these customers, together with the original shipping documents, be delivered daily to the factor along with information on all credits, allowances, and returns of merchandise.

INTERNET ACTIVITY

Learn about factors and other asset-based lenders by visiting Web sites such as http://www.gecapital.com, http://www.gecfo.com, http://www.textronfinancial.com, and http://www.celticcapital.com.

The contract includes the conditions under which accounts may be sold to the factor, such as type of firm, geographic area of the customer, and acceptable credit ratings. Another important part of the contract is the collection procedures to be followed in case a customer is slow in paying their bill. As we saw in Chapter 15, collecting accounts receivable can be a costly process, especially when a customer is alienated by aggressive collection efforts. A firm will want to know what collection process the factor follows as future sales may be lost if the factor is too aggressive.

The charge for factoring has two components. First, interest is charged on the money advanced. Second, a factoring commission or service charge is figured as a percentage of the face amount of the receivables. This charge typically ranges from 1.5 percent to 3 percent of the face amount of the accounts financed. Factors will typically lend 80 percent of the remainder although they may reduce the amount of the loan anywhere from 5 to 15 percent of the total amount of receivables factored to make adjustments, such as for merchandise that is returned to the seller. This portion of the receivables is returned to the seller if it is not needed for adjustment purposes.

For example, suppose a firm is owed $70,000 by a customer that rarely pays its bills any sooner than 60 days after the invoice. Assuming the customer meets the factor's credit standards, the firm will receive 80 percent of the $70,000, or $56,000, within a day or two of accepting the account. If the interest rate for a 60-day account is 2 percent and the factoring fee is 3 percent, the cost of the factoring arrangement will be $3,500 (5 percent of $70,000). Assuming the customer pays its bill in full on day 60, the firm receives an additional $10,500 which is the amount of the invoice ($70,000) less the advance ($56,000) less the combined factoring and interest costs ($3,500). Thus, the firm collects $66,500 of the original $70,000 invoice; $56,000 was received after a one or two day delay and the remainder was received around day 60.

Although a factor's services may be used by a firm that is unable to secure financing through customary channels, financially strong companies also may at times use these services to good advantage. In fact, factors are of greatest benefit to companies that enjoy very strong sales and growth. We have noted that during such periods companies experience extreme shortages of working capital. The sale of receivables without recourse (that is, sellers do not have to repay any funds received from the factor in the case of a bad debt) has the effect of substituting cash for accounts receivable. This may make even greater growth and profitability possible in the long run.

Some firms factor their receivables for other reasons. First, the cost of doing business through credit sales is definite and can be determined in advance because the factor assumes all risks of collection. This is, in effect, a form of credit insurance. Second, factoring eliminates expenses, including bookkeeping costs, the maintenance of a credit department, and the expenses of collecting delinquent accounts. A further advantage, but of a less tangible nature, is that factoring frees the management of a business from concern with financial matters and permits it to concentrate on production and distribution. Factoring has become increasingly important in supporting export sales. The firm that is unfamiliar with the problems of financing international shipments of goods is relieved of such details by factoring foreign receivables.

GLOBAL DISCUSSION

Although factoring services are regarded highly by some businesses, others object to their use. The two reasons cited most frequently are the cost and the implication of financial weakness. The cost of factoring is unquestionably higher than the cost of borrowing from a bank on the basis of an unsecured loan. However, it is difficult to conclude that the net cost is higher. The elimination of overhead costs that would otherwise be necessary plus the reality that management need not concern itself with financial matters may completely offset the additional cost involved in factoring.

Few industries are affected by factors as much as retailing. Factors guarantee payment to suppliers of many large retail firms. With such guarantees, suppliers ship goods to the retailers, confident that they will get paid. Should factors refuse to guarantee payments to suppliers because the factors believe a retailer to be on shaky financial ground, a retailing firm can find itself with no merchandise to sell. Thus, predictions about poor finances can become a self-fulfilling prophecy. Once one factor hesitates to stand behind a retailer's credit, they all turn their backs on the retailer since no one factor wants to be left alone supporting a financially troubled firm. Factors act as an early warning signal of a retailer's real or imagined financial deterioration. In 1995, Bradlees, a discount retailer, filed for Chapter 11 bankruptcy protection

TABLE 16.2
Comparison of Pledging and Factoring Accounts Receivable

PLEDGING ACCOUNTS RECEIVABLE	FACTORING ACCOUNTS RECEIVABLE
It is a loan against Accounts Receivable	It is a sale of Accounts Receivable
Accounts Receivable balances remain on the balance sheet	Sold Accounts Receivable balances are removed from the balance sheet
Customer payment is made to firm, which then submits the payment to the bank	Customer pays the factor
Firm makes each credit decision	Factor makes the credit decision; firm can always choose to extend credit on its own
Charges: • interest rate on loan • audit fees for periodic review of accounts, payments Additional cost: paper and funds flow between firm and bank	Charges: • interest rate on funds advanced • service charge

CONCEPT CHECK

What are two types of accounts receivable financing?

What is meant by pledging receivables and how does it differ from factoring?

What are the advantages of using a factor? What are the disadvantages?

after factors refused to guarantee Bradlees' receivables to its suppliers. A few months later Caldor, another discount retailer, filed for bankruptcy protection for the same reason: the factors would not support it. When factors refuse to accept a retailer's credit, the retailer's suppliers face a decision: whether to continue shipping and taking the risk of nonpayment by the financially troubled retailer or to stop shipping and possibly lose a client. With the bankruptcy filings in recent years of retail stores such as Federated Department Stores, Allied Stores, Macy's, Jamesway, Bradlees, and Caldor, it appears that the suppliers are choosing to listen to the factors.[13]

There are many similarities between pledging and factoring. To help differentiate them, Table 16.2 summarizes some of their differences.

INVENTORY LOANS

A business may use its inventory as collateral for a loan in much the same manner that it may borrow on its receivables. The bank evaluates the physical condition of the firm's inventory and the inventory's general composition. Staple items that are in constant demand serve well as collateral for a loan. Style and fashion items such as designer clothes are not as acceptable as collateral except for brief periods. Firms that use inventory as collateral usually do so because they are not in a position to obtain further funds on an unsecured basis.

The bank may protect itself when lending to a business by having a **blanket inventory lien,** or a claim against inventory when individual items are indistinguishable, as may be the case with grain or clothing items. For such loans, a borrower may receive only 60 to 80 percent of the inventory's value in a loan. A manufacturer's work-in-process inventory may receive only 20 to 30 percent of its value.

blanket inventory lien
claim against a customer's inventory when the individual items are indistinguishable

trust receipt
lien against specific identifiable items in inventory

warehouse receipt
inventory is placed in a bonded warehouse for safekeeping; items are removed as they are paid for

In other cases, when goods can be clearly identified, a **trust receipt** may be used. Money is borrowed against specific items in inventory. This method of financing, sometimes called "floor plan financing," is used by car dealerships and appliance stores, where inventory items financed by trust receipts can be identified by serial number. Under a trust receipt arrangement, the bank retains ownership of the goods until they are actually sold in the regular course of business. Audits are simply a matter of checking serial numbers of inventory items to determine if items held against a trust receipt have been sold.

In some cases when inventory is used as collateral, the bank may insist that the inventory be placed in a bonded and licensed warehouse. The **warehouse receipt** issued by the warehouse is then turned over to the bank, which holds it until the loan is repaid.

---

13. Joseph Pereira, "Bradlees Seeks Bankruptcy Protection, But Denies it is Facing Liquidity Crisis," *The Wall Street Journal*, June 26, 1995, p. A10; Susan Pulliam and Laura Bird, "Concern Rises about Retailer Caldor's Ability to Deal with Cutthroat Rivalry; Stock Sinks," *The Wall Street Journal*, August 24, 1995, p. C2; Laura Bird, "Caldor Files for Bankruptcy Protection in Face of Weak Sales, Jittery Suppliers," *The Wall Street Journal*, September 19, 1995, p. A3; Roger Lowenstein, "Lenders' Stampede Tramples Caldor," *The Wall Street Journal*, October 26, 1995, p. C1.

field warehouse
an enterprise establishes a warehouse on the grounds of the borrowing business establishment

It is frequently inconvenient for a business to deliver large, bulky items of inventory to a warehouse for storage. Using **field warehouses** solves this problem. A field warehousing enterprise has the power to establish a field warehouse on the grounds of the borrowing business establishment. Field warehouses differ from the typical public warehouse in that (1) they serve a single customer: that customer on whose property the field warehouse is established and (2) they exist only until the loan is repaid.

In setting up a field warehouse, the warehouse operator usually must first obtain a lease on that portion of the property to be used for warehousing purposes. Then he or she must establish fences, barriers, walks, and other postings to indicate clear possession of the property. This is done to avoid accidental or deliberate removal of stored items during the general course of business operations. A guard may be posted to check on the safety of the warehoused goods or a room may be sealed and the seal inspected periodically to make sure the company is honoring its agreement.

There also must be a complete statement of the commodities or items that are to be warehoused, and agreements must be made about the maintenance of the property, proper fire precautions, insurance, and other necessary physical requirements. Under certain circumstances, the warehouse operator is authorized to release a certain quantity of goods by the day, week, or month to make possible a rotation of merchandise. Under this arrangement, physical inventories must be taken from time to time.

Field warehouses are in operation throughout the United States but are concentrated in the Central and Pacific Coast regions. Canned goods, miscellaneous groceries, lumber, timber, and building supplies fill about two-fifths of all field warehouses in this country. Those banks that make loans involving commodities will generally accept field warehouse receipts as collateral.

Inventory loans are somewhat more expensive than unsecured loans to business borrowers. The higher cost is due in part to the cost of warehousing operations and also because the borrower's credit rating may be low. Bank interest rates for warehouse loans ordinarily are somewhat higher than for unsecured loans.[14] In addition, a warehouse fee of 1 to 2 percent of the loan, depending on size and other factors, must be paid.

Technology can assist the valuing of inventory, especially if the inventory is equipment.[15] Digital writing and recording devices, such as digital cameras, allow items to be photographed and the information saved electronically for later recall. Business-to-business auction sites and even eBay auction prices have been used to estimate an item's value.[16]

INTERNET ACTIVITY
Have you visited http://www.ebay.com to look for items of interest? Do a search for items that may comprise excess inventory. Another business-oriented site is http://www.salvagesale.com.

LOANS SECURED BY STOCKS AND BONDS

Stocks and bonds often are used as collateral for short-term loans. These securities are welcomed as collateral primarily because of their marketability and their value. If the securities are highly marketable and if their value is high enough to cover the amount of the loan requested even if the stock's price goes down somewhat, a banker will not hesitate to extend a loan. Securities listed on one of the national exchanges are preferred because frequent price quotations are available. Banks usually will loan from 60 to 70 percent of the market value of listed stocks and from 70 to 80 percent of the market value of high-grade bonds.

Only assignable stocks and bonds are eligible for this type of collateral financing, with the exception of nonassignable U.S. savings bonds. When assignable securities are placed with a bank, a stock or bond power is executed that authorizes the bank to sell or otherwise dispose of the securities should it become necessary to do so to protect the loan.

OTHER FORMS OF SECURITY FOR BANK LOANS

Security for short-term bank loans also may include such things as the cash surrender value of life insurance policies, guarantee of a loan by a party other than the borrower, notes, and acceptances.

---

14. Inventory loans, like receivable loans, are also made by commercial finance companies. Their interest rates usually are higher than those charged by banks.
15. Firms can also obtain loans against the firm's equipment used in its operations as well as what might be manufactured or sold from inventory.
16. Hilary Rosenberg, "Mining the Balance Sheet," *CFO*, May 2001, pp. 103–108; Robert S. MacDonald, "Technology Tools Used in the Equipment Appraisal Process," *The Secured Lender*, August 2001, p. 8.

Life Insurance Loans

Small businesses frequently find it possible to obtain needed short-term bank loans by pledging the cash surrender value, or the amount they will receive on cancellation, of the owner's life insurance policies. The policies must be assignable, and many insurance companies insist that their own assignment forms be used for such purposes. Because of the safety afforded the bank by the cash surrender values, these loans usually carry a lower interest rate than loans on other types of business collateral. Another reason for the favorable rates is that the borrower could borrow directly from the insurance company. Even so, bank interest rates are many times higher than those of insurance companies to their policyholders. As a result, there has been an increase in the number of these loans made by insurance companies.

Co-maker Loans

Many small businesses find it necessary to provide the bank with a guarantor in the form of a cosigner to their notes. It is expected that the cosigner has a credit rating at least as satisfactory as, and usually far better than, the firm requesting the loan.

Acceptances

Another type of receivable instrument that arises out of the sale of merchandise and that may be sold to a bank is the acceptance. An *acceptance* is a receivable from the sale of merchandise on the basis of a draft or bill of exchange drawn against the buyer or the buyer's bank. The accepted draft or bill of exchange is returned to the seller of the merchandise where it may be held until the date payment is due. During this period, the business may discount such acceptances with its bank. Again, the seller is contingently liable for these discounted acceptances. The use of the banker's acceptance is discussed in detail in Chapter 6 in connection with an international shipment of goods.

> *acceptance*
> receivable from the sale of merchandise on the basis of a draft or bill of exchange drawn against the buyer or the buyer's bank

THE COST OF SHORT-TERM FINANCING

For most asset-based and unsecured loans, a simple method can be used to combine the interest expenses and fees to determine the true interest cost of a short-term loan. Fortunately, it is a process we discussed earlier in this chapter when we examined commercial paper. Here we break it down into steps and then present an example.

First, determine the amount to be borrowed. Discounted loans or bank loans with compensating balances will need to use Equations 16.2 and 16.3 to determine the amount.

Second, determine the interest expenses on the borrowed funds. This is the interest rate multiplied by the amount borrowed.

Third, determine the fees and other expenses associated with using the financing source. We know, for example, that factors charge a service fee, inventory loans may carry warehouse charges, and pledged loans usually carry extra fees because of the extra analysis done by the lender.

Fourth, estimate the net proceeds. This may be the same as the amount borrowed, but in the case of discounted loans (such as commercial paper) the net proceeds will be less than the amount borrowed.

Fifth, to estimate the financing cost, divide the sum of the interest expenses and fees (steps 2 and 3) by the net proceeds (step 4). Annualize this rate, if necessary.

Here's an example. Fluoridated Manufacturing is considering short-term financing choices. A factor is willing to advance FM 80 percent of its receivables and charge it a 2 percent fee to compensate it for analyzing the receivables and determining which it will purchase. FM estimates they will pay 12 percent APR in order to receive cash an average of 45 days earlier. The current receivables balance is $10,000.

Let's do the analysis step-by-step:

1. Determine the amount to be received. With receivables of $10,000 and an advance rate of 80 percent, FM will receive $10,000 × 0.80 = $8,000.

2. Determine the interest expense. With a 12 percent APR the daily interest charge is 0.12/365. Factoring allows FM to receive its funds an average of 45 days sooner, so the interest expense is $8,000 × (0.12/365) × 45 = $118.36.

CAREER PROFILES

DAVE LOCKARD
Corporate Manager
Fath Management

BS Accounting
University of Notre Dame
Certified Public Accountant

"I wear lots of hats."

Q: *Describe the firm you work for.*
A: Fath Management is a privately owned real estate management company. We own and operate about forty properties, almost all apartment buildings or complexes, in four states. In all, we have about 7,000 residential units.

Q: *What is your role there?*
A: I wear lots of hats. I set the operating budgets for our properties, approve significant expenditures, oversee hiring and firing, negotiate contracts for services like waste removal, manage our insurance needs, set company policies and salary guidelines, manage our banking relationships, and evaluate properties that we may want to purchase, among other things.

Q: *You "manage banking relationships." What does that involve?*
A: Most of our properties are purchased via bank loans. Because interest rates are relatively low right now, we are continually looking for opportunities to refinance our loans at lower rates. That's basically a cost-justification issue—can we save enough in interest expense to compensate for the refinancing fees we would face? Every time there's a fall in interest rates it opens up the possibility of refinancing more of our loans. And then there are new loans when we buy new properties, of course.

Q: *Describe the acquisition process.*
A: We are not acquiring as many new properties now as we did several years ago, but we are always open to that possibility. I've developed a computer spreadsheet model that we use to assess the financial potential of a property. We use this model to identify the properties that fit best with our strategy and have the potential to generate the rate of return we need. Then we take a closer look at those properties, their condition, and the neighborhoods. If we decide to purchase a property, we go to a local or regional bank and negotiate a loan.

Q: *What information do you provide the bank to secure the financing?*
A: We would provide information about the specific property—the projected cash flow, our plans for renovation or improvement, and so on—as well as information about Fath's overall financial position, our operating results, and credit history. There's another side to our interaction with banks, too. Banks compete for customers just like any other business. In many cases, banks will come to us offering special deals on certain types of loans, which may encourage us to take a closer look at an acquisition we might not have pursued otherwise.

Q: *What skills do you use most in your job?*
A: The ability to understand and resolve problems is essential in this job. A lot of issues come up that you could never foresee and you need to be able to determine the right course of action and implement it right away. You have to be able to consider the impact of your actions so that you don't create new problems when you solve an existing one. These problems make the job difficult, but interesting, too. I like the variety of issues that I get involved in.

3. Determine the fees and other expenses. The factor's fee is 2 percent for basing a loan on a receivables balance of $10,000. The fees are 0.02 × $10,000 = $200.
4. Estimate the net proceeds. There is no discounting, so in this case the net proceeds will be $8,000. We assume FM will pay the fees out of pocket. The net proceeds will be smaller if the $200 in fees is deducted by the factor from the loan amount.
5. The financing cost is $118.36 + $200 = $318.36 with net proceeds of $8,000. The percentage cost is: $318.36/$8,000 = 0.0398 or 3.98% for 45 days of financing. The annualized rate is $(1 + 0.0398)^{365/45} - 1 = 0.3724$ or 37.24 percent.

The above process should help determine the financing cost of virtually any lending arrangement, whether by a bank, commercial finance company, factor, or other source of short-term finance.

APPLYING FINANCE TO...

INSTITUTIONS AND MARKETS

We've seen in earlier chapters how the financial markets determine financing rates. Interest rates facing borrowers depend on the risk-free rate and a risk premium. Financial institutions have developed many ways to meet the short-term financing needs of firms, including instruments offering different maturities, security (collateral) requirements, and control—that is, who actually "supervises" the collateral—arrangements.

INVESTMENTS

Just as a capital market investor reviews the creditworthiness of a bond issuer and the share price appreciation potential of a company, similar care must be taken when analyzing a firm seeking a short-term loan or other financing arrangement. The primary concern will be the firm's ability to generate cash to repay the short-term loan. Cash generation, not sales or accounting profits, will be paramount.

FINANCIAL MANAGEMENT

Managers must balance the opportunity cost of excess cash with the costs of paying short-term financing rates and the dangers of a credit crunch when short-term financing dries up. A firm's treasurer wants to maintain liquidity, which includes the firm's access to short-term financing sources, at all times.

SUMMARY

Working capital, it has been said, is the grease that keeps the wheels turning in a company. Inventories are needed to meet customer demands for the firm's products. When they are sold, accounts receivable are created that will one day be converted into cash. This cash is used to pay suppliers, workers, creditors, taxes, and shareholder dividends. A firm without working capital is a firm unlikely to remain in business.

There are two classes of working capital: permanent, or the minimum necessary for smooth company operations, and temporary, which occurs because of seasonal or cyclical fluctuations in sales demand. A company financing strategy that uses long-term sources to finance its working capital is a conservative strategy that reduces profits but increases liquidity. An aggressive strategy that uses more short-term financing has less liquidity but may increase company profits. Several influences affect managers' decisions on how the firm should be financed, including the characteristics of the firm's industry, its asset base, seasonality, sales cycles, and sales trends.

Firms have many possible sources of short-term financing, from bank loans (including lines of credit and revolving credit), commercial paper, to trade credit. Care should be taken by the treasurer to evaluate the cost of each financing source by calculating its effective annual cost, by incorporating all interest charges and fees into the analysis, and by comparing the principal of the loan with the actual usable funds received. Asset-backed financing—such as pledging, factoring receivables, or using inventory as collateral—are usually higher-cost financing sources, primarily because smaller, less creditworthy firms rely on them for financing.

KEY TERMS

acceptance
advance factoring
asset-based lending
blanket inventory lien
commercial finance company
commercial paper
compensating balance
discounted loan

factor
field warehouse
line of credit
maturity factoring
maturity-matching approach
net working capital
pledge
prime rate

revolving credit agreement
secured lending
trade discounts
trust receipt
warehouse receipt
working capital

DISCUSSION QUESTIONS

1. What is net working capital? Briefly describe the financing implications when net working capital is positive.

2. What are "permanent" current assets? How do "temporary" current assets differ from permanent current assets?

3. Explain the strategies businesses can use to finance their assets with short-term and long-term funds.

4. What influences affect the nature of the demand for short-term versus long-term funds?

5. Explain how a conservative approach to financing a firm's assets is a low-risk/low-expected-return strategy whereas an aggressive approach to financing is a high-risk/high-expected-return strategy.

6. Prepare a list of advantages and disadvantages of short-term bank borrowing over other short-term financing sources.

7. What is meant by an unsecured loan? Are these loans an important form of bank lending?

8. Explain what a bank line of credit is.

9. Explain how discounting and compensating balances affect the effective cost of bank financing.

10. Describe the revolving credit agreement and compare it with the bank line of credit.

11. When might a business seek accounts receivable financing?

12. What safeguards may a bank establish to protect itself when it lends on the basis of a customer's receivables pledged as collateral for a loan?

13. When a business firm uses its inventory as collateral for a bank loan, how is the problem of storing and guarding the inventory accomplished for the bank?

14. What is trade credit? Briefly describe some of the possible terms for trade credit.

15. What are the primary reasons for using trade credit for short term financing?

16. Under what circumstances would a business secure its financing through a commercial finance company?

17. Describe how a factor differs from a commercial finance company in terms of accounts-receivable financing.

18. Why would a business use the services of a factor?

19. How does the Small Business Administration provide financing to businesses?

20. What is commercial paper, and how important is it as a source of financing?

21. Is commercial paper a reliable source of financing? Why or why not?

22. How is changing technology changing the methods of raising short-term funds?

PROBLEMS

1. A supplier is offering your firm a cash discount of 2 percent if purchases are paid for within ten days; otherwise the bill is due at the end of sixty days. Would you recommend borrowing from a bank at an 18 percent annual interest rate to take advantage of the cash discount offer? Explain your answer.

2. Assume that you have been offered cash discounts on merchandise that can be purchased from either of two suppliers. Supplier A offers trade credit terms of 3/20, net 70, while supplier B offers 4/15, net 80. What is the approximate effective cost of missing the cash discounts from each supplier? If you could not take advantage of either cash discount offer, which supplier would you select?

3. Obtain a current issue of the Federal Reserve Bulletin, or review a copy from the Fed's Web site (http://www.federalreserve.gov) or the St. Louis Fed's Web site (http://www.stlouisfed.org), and determine the changes in the prime rate that have occurred since the end of 2000. Comment on any trends in the data.

4. Compute the effective cost of not taking the cash discount under the following trade credit terms:

    a. 2/10 net 40
    b. 2/10 net 50
    c. 3/10 net 50
    d. 2/20 net 40

5. What conclusions can you make about credit terms from reviewing your answers to Problem 4?

6. Your firm needs to raise funds for inventory expansion.

    a. What is the effective annual rate on a loan of $150,000 if it is discounted at a 12 percent stated annual rate and it matures in five months?
    b. How much must you borrow to obtain usable funds of $150,000?
    c. What is the effective annual rate if you borrow the funds computed in (b)?

7. Bank A offers loans with a 10 percent stated annual rate and a 10 percent compensating balance. You wish to obtain $250,000 in a six month loan.

    a. How much must you borrow to obtain $250,000 in usable funds? Assume you currently do not have any funds on deposit at the bank. What is the effective annual rate on a six month loan?
    b. How much must you borrow to obtain $250,000 in usable funds if you currently have $10,000 on deposit at the bank? What is the effective annual rate on a six-month loan?
    c. How much must you borrow to obtain $250,000 in usable funds if you currently have $30,000 on deposit at the bank?
    d. What is the effective annual rate on a six-month loan?

8. Compute the effective annual rates of the following:

    a. $1 million maturing in 90 days with a stated annual rate of 6 percent. Fees are 0.02 percent of the principal.
    b. $15 million maturing in 60 days with a stated annual rate of 7.6 percent. Fees are 0.05 percent of the principal.
    c. $500,000 maturing in 180 days with a stated annual rate of 8.25 percent. Fees are 0.03 percent of the principal.
    d. $50 million maturing in 210 days with a stated annual rate of 6.5 percent. Fees are 0.10 percent of the principal.

9. Construct a spreadsheet that computes the effective annual rates on the commercial paper offerings. Inputs to the spreadsheet should

include the dollar amount of paper to be issued, the number of days the paper is outstanding, the stated annual rate, and fees. All paper is sold on a discount basis. Use it to find the effective annual rates in problem 8.

10. Wonder Dog Leash Company is examining their accounts receivable patterns. Wonder's customers are offered terms of 1/10 net 30. Of their receivables, $150,000 is current, $75,000 is 1 month overdue, $30,000 is two months overdue, and $20,000 is over two months overdue.

    a. What proportion of Wonder's customers pay their bills on time?
    b. What is the effective cost of Wonder's terms of trade credit?
    c. What might happen to their receivables balance if they changed their terms to 1/15 net 30? To 2/10 net 30?

11. Wonder Dog Leash Company is seeking to raise cash and is in negotiation with Big Bucks finance company to pledge their receivables.

    BB is willing to loan funds against 75 percent of current (that is, not overdue) receivables at a 15 percent annual percentage rate (see the aging of receivables in problem 10). To pay for its evaluation of Wonder's receivables, BB charges a 2.5 percent fee on the total balance of current receivables.

    a. If the average term of a loan is 30 days, what is the effective interest rate if Wonder pledges its receivables?
    b. What is the effective rate if Wonder negotiates a loan of 45 days with no other changes in the loan's terms?

12. Michael's Computers is evaluating proposals from two different factors that will provide receivables financing. Big Fee Factoring will finance the receivables at an APR of 8 percent, discounted, and charges a fee of 4 percent. High Rate Factoring offers an APR of 14 percent (nondiscounted) with fees of 2 percent. The average term of either loan is expected to be 35 days. With an average receivables balance of $250,000, which proposal should Michael's accept?

13. Michael's Computers' local bank offers the firm a 12-month revolving credit agreement of $500,000. The APR of the revolver is 12 percent with a commitment fee of 0.5 percent on the unused portion.

    Over the course of a year Michael's chief financial officer believes they will have an average balance of $280,000 on the revolving credit agreement, with a low of $50,000 and a high of $450,000. What is the annual effective cost of this proposed agreement?

14. Banc Two wants to attract Michael's Computers, Inc. to become a customer. Their sales force contacts Michael's and offers them line of credit financing. The credit line will be for $500,000 with a one month "clean-up" period. The APR on borrowed funds is 11 percent. Banc Two will offer the line of credit if Michael's opens an account and maintains an average balance of $100,000 over the next twelve months. As in problem 13, ignoring compensating balances, Michael's CFO believes its financing needs will average $280,000 monthly over the next year with a low monthly need of $50,000 and a high need forecast of $450,000.

    a. Will the line of credit satisfy Michael's needs for short-term funds?
    b. How much money will Michael's draw-down from the credit line during a low use month?
    c. How much will Michael's need to borrow in a month before it maximizes its use of the line of credit?
    d. What is the average cost to Michael's of using the credit line for a year?

15. Montcalm Enterprises is seeking bids on short-term loans with area banks. It expects its average outstanding borrowings to equal $320,000. Which of the following terms offers Montcalm the lowest effective rate?

    a. Town Bank: revolving credit agreement for $500,000 with a 15 percent APR, 0.5 percent commitment fee on the unused portion.
    b. Village Bank: revolving credit agreement for $400,000 with a 12 percent APR, 1.0 percent commitment fee on the unused portion and a 10 percent compensating balance requirement based on the size of the bank's commitment.

16. Beckheart is seeking financing for its inventory. Safe-proof Warehouses offers space in their facility for Beckheart's inventory. They offer loans with a 15 percent APR equal to 60 percent of the inventory. Monthly fees for the usage of the warehouse are $500 plus 0.5 percent of the inventory's value. If Beckheart has saleable inventory of $2 million,

    a. how much money can the firm borrow?
    b. what is the interest cost of the loan in dollars over a year?
    c. what is the total amount of fees to be paid in a year?
    d. what is the effective annual rate of using Safe-proof to finance Beckheart's inventory?

17. CDRW is evaluating an inventory financing arrangement with DVD Banks. CDRW estimates an average monthly inventory balance of $800,000. DVD Bank is offering a 12 percent APR loan on 75 percent of the value of the inventory. DVD's inventory storage and evaluation fees will be 1 percent a month on the total value of the inventory. What is the annual effective rate of the inventory loan?

18. Which of the following offer the lowest effective rate for Wolf Howl jackets? Assume Wolf Howl will need to borrow $800,000 for 180 days.

    a. A 14 percent APR bank loan
    b. A 13 percent APR, discounted bank loan.
    c. 12.5 percent APR with fees of 1 percent for receivables financing.
    d. A $2 million revolving credit agreement with an APR of 12 percent, a commitment fee of 0.5 percent on the unused balance, and a 10 percent compensating balance requirement.

19. **Challenge Problem** Visit a firm's Web site and obtain historical quarterly balance sheet information from it or from its SEC EDGAR filings (http://www.walmart.com and http://www.walgreens.com may be two good sites to use). Record quarterly balance sheet data for several years in a spreadsheet. Over time, compute and graph the firm's financing mix (for example, by computing the ratio of current liabilities to total assets) and asset mix (by computing the ratio of current assets to total assets). What happens to the firm's financing mix and asset mix over time? Do the financing and asset mix ratios move together over time? Are any seasonal effects in the firm's working capital position and financing evident? What conclusions can you draw about the firm's use of short-term financing?

20. **Challenge Problem** Use the information below for this problem. Comfin Company has estimates on its level of current and total assets for the next two years:

    a. Estimate the levels of permanent and temporary current assets for Comfin over these months. Find the average amount for fixed assets, permanent current assets, and temporary current assets in year 201X and year 201X + 1.

b. What average amounts of short-term and long-term financing should Comfin have during each year if it wants to follow a maturity-matching financing strategy over time?

c. What average amounts of short-term and long-term financing should Comfin have during each year if it wants to follow an aggressive financing strategy over time?

d. Suppose Comfin's cost of short-term funds is 8 percent and its cost of long-term funds is 15 percent. Use your answers in (b) and (c) to compute the cost of each strategy.

e. What are the pro and con arguments toward each strategy in terms of profitability, risk, and company liquidity?

Comfin Company data for problem 20.

YEAR 201X	JAN	FEB	MAR	APR	MAY	JUNE	JULY	AUG	SEPT	OCT	NOV	DEC
Total Assets	$500,000	$475,000	$460,000	$470,000	$475,000	$485,000	$495,000	$555,000	$600,000	$650,000	$700,000	$750,000
Current Assets	$250,000	$220,000	$199,900	$204,698	$204,392	$208,980	$213,459	$262,829	$307,085	$351,227	$395,251	$439,156
YEAR 201X + 1												
Total Assets	$600,000	$570,000	$552,000	$564,000	$570,000	$582,000	$594,000	$660,000	$720,000	$780,000	$840,000	$900,000
Current Assets	$350,000	$350,000	$352,100	$359,302	$365,608	$373,020	$380,541	$397,171	$412,915	$428,773	$444,749	$460,844

• CHAPTER 17 •

Capital Budgeting Analysis

Chapter Learning Objectives:

AFTER STUDYING THIS CHAPTER, YOU SHOULD BE ABLE TO:
- Explain how the capital budgeting process should be related to a firm's mission and strategies.
- Identify and describe the five steps in the capital budgeting process.
- Identify and describe the methods or techniques used to make proper capital budgeting decisions.
- Explain how relevant cash flows are determined for capital budgeting decision purposes.
- Discuss how a project's risk can be incorporated into capital budgeting analysis.

Where We Have Been...

In Chapter 13, at the beginning of the financial management section of this book, we considered how firms will have a mission or vision statement—a reason for being. This current chapter will examine how firms can "put feet to their words" and make decisions to purchase fixed assets and pursue strategies to help them fulfill their mission. The previous two chapters examined how a firm should manage and finance its current assets. Now our focus will shift to fixed assets.

Where We Are Going...

Once a firm decides which fixed assets and corporate strategies to pursue, it must finance them. This will be the focus of Chapter 18, "Capital Structure and the Cost of Capital."

How Does This Chapter Apply to Me...

Capital budgeting analysis is a framework for evaluating all business decisions; it is not only a tool for the "financial" types. Proper analysis will identify relevant cash flows and an appropriate discount rate to reflect the risk of the strategy and will compare the benefits and costs of the project by considering the time value of money. It causes managers to consider more than a "feel good" or "sounds right" criterion for investing in projects. Whether the investment is one in a business strategy, building a new warehouse, seeking fuel-efficient methods of doing business, upgrading information technology systems, or investing in human resources, we should try to quantify the benefits and cost of these choices in order to evaluate them properly.

To achieve success over time, a firm's managers must identify and invest in

projects that provide positive net present values

to maximize shareholder wealth. Good ideas become good strategies when the numbers—cash flow forecasts—show the likelihood of shareholder wealth increasing because of the project. The value of the firm will rise when a capital investment provides the firm with positive cash flows after the amount of the investment has been recovered, the cost of obtaining the necessary financing has been paid, and the timing of the project's cash flows has been taken into consideration.

As first discussed in Chapter 13, every firm should have a vision or mission—a reason for being. To successfully implement its mission, a firm needs to have a competitive advantage. A competitive advantage is the reason why a firm's customers are willing to purchase its products or services rather than another firm's. Large corporations spend millions on researching their customers and competitors to gather information they can use to maintain or expand their competitive advantage. Integral to the process of trying to maintain or expand a firm's competitive advantage are its decisions of what products to offer and what markets or market segments to serve.

capital budgeting
process of identifying, evaluating, and implementing a firm's investment opportunities

Capital budgeting is the process of identifying, evaluating, and implementing a firm's investment opportunities. Capital budgeting seeks to identify projects that will enhance a firm's competitive advantage and by so doing increase shareholders' wealth. By its nature, capital budgeting involves long-term projects, although capital budgeting techniques also can be applied to working capital decisions.[1] Capital budgeting projects usually require large initial investments and may involve acquiring or constructing plant and equipment. A project's expected time frame may be as short as a year or as long as twenty or thirty years. Projects may include implementing new production technologies, new products, new markets, or mergers. Given their size and duration, the projects undertaken by the firm should reflect its overall strategy for meeting future goals. Given the length of most projects, time value of money concepts should be used to evaluate them.

The typical capital budgeting project involves a large upfront cash outlay, followed by a series of smaller cash inflows and outflows, but the project's cash flows, including the total upfront cost of the project, are not known with certainty before the project starts. The firm must evaluate the size, timing, and risk of the project's cash flows to determine if it enhances shareholder wealth.

The profitability of a firm is affected to the greatest extent by the success of its management in making capital budget investment decisions. A fixed-asset decision will be sound only if it produces a stream of future cash inflows that earns the firm an acceptable rate of return on its invested capital.

CONCEPT CHECK
What is capital budgeting?
Why is it important to a firm?

MANAGEMENT OF FIXED ASSETS

Fixed-asset management requires financial managers to compare capital expenditures for plant and equipment against the cash flow benefits that will be received from these investments over several years. When properly adjusted benefits exceed expenditures, these projects will help increase the firm's value.

Investment in assets provides the basis for a firm's earning power or profitability. Plant, equipment, training, and infrastructure are employed to manufacture inventories or provide services that will be sold for profit, produce cash inflows, and enhance the firm's value. Proper capital budgeting decisions must be made by the financial manager for this to occur. The types of decisions include whether to replace existing equipment with new equipment, whether to expand existing product lines by adding more plant and equipment similar to that in use, and whether to expand into new product areas requiring new types of assets.

mutually exclusive projects
selecting one project precludes others from being undertaken

independent projects
projects not in direct competition with one another

Capital budgeting decisions can involve mutually exclusive or independent projects. As an example of *mutually exclusive projects,* two or more machines that perform the same function may be available from competing suppliers, possibly at different costs and with different expected cash benefits. The financial manager is responsible for choosing the best of these alternatives since only one can be chosen. Selecting one project precludes the other from being undertaken. **Independent projects** are not in direct competition with one another. They are to be evaluated based on their expected effect on shareholder wealth. All such projects that enhance shareholder wealth should be included in the firm's capital budget.

In this chapter, we focus on only a small part of what is a very complex topic. We present an overview of the capital budgeting process and some techniques that are used to evaluate potential investments. Then we briefly discuss the process of estimating the cash flows that are expected to occur from a capital budgeting project. We then cover how a project's risk can affect the evaluation process.

CONCEPT CHECK
What kinds of asset decisions can be made with capital budgeting analysis?

A firm is considering two capital budgeting projects. How will the decision to do or not do each project be affected by whether the projects are independent or mutually exclusive?

IDENTIFYING POTENTIAL CAPITAL BUDGET PROJECTS

From Chapter 10, we know that the market value of an investment is the present value of future cash flows to be received from the investment. The net benefit, or the **net present value**, of an investment is the present value of a project's cash flows minus its cost:

net present value
present value of a project's cash flows minus its cost

$$\text{Net present value} = \text{Present value of cash flows} - \text{Cost of the project} \qquad (17.1)$$

---

[1]. See Terry S. Maness and John T. Zietlow, *Short-Term Financial Management,* Mason, OH: Thomson South-Western, 2005; Ned C. Hill and William Sartoris, *Short-Term Financial Management,* 3rd ed., Englewood Cliffs, N.J.: Prentice-Hall, 1995.

Should the net present value be positive (the investor pays less than the market value of the investment), the owner's wealth increases by the amount of the net present value. If, for example, the present value of an asset's cash flows is $100 and we can purchase it now for only $80, our wealth rises by $20. If instead we were foolish enough to pay $130 for the investment, our wealth will fall by $30. To maximize shareholder wealth, we need to find assets or capital budgeting projects that have positive net present values.

Where do businesses find attractive capital budgeting projects? Business managers need to search for projects that are related to the firm's present lines of business or future plans. It would be foolish, for example, for a computer manufacturer to consider investing in land and mining equipment to prospect for gold. Despite management beliefs about future trends in gold prices and despite their confidence in their ability to find gold, such a project is far afield from the firm's current markets, products, and expertise.

Businesses should seek guidance to focus their search for capital budgeting projects. One popular corporate planning tool, **MOGS** (for *M*ission, *O*bjectives, *G*oals, and *S*trategies), develops project plans that fit well with firm plans. A firm should have a MOGS plan, or something similar to it, in place to give direction to company planning and to help the firm's officers identify potential capital budgeting projects.

MOGS
Mission, Objectives, Goals, and Strategies

Over time managers define and redefine the firm's mission, objectives, goals, and strategies. This long-term plan provides a foundation for the next five to ten years of operating plans for the firm. The long-term plan is operationalized, or implemented, in the annual capital budget. To develop the capital budget, managers must find investment opportunities that fit within the overall strategic objectives of the firm; its position within the various markets it serves; government fiscal, monetary, and tax policies; and the leadership of the firm's management. Attractive capital budgeting projects take the firm from its present position to a desired future market position and, as a consequence, maintain or increase its shareholders' wealth.[2]

SWOT analysis examines a firm's *s*trengths, *w*eaknesses, *o*pportunities, and *t*hreats. It can help managers identify capital budgeting projects that allow the firm to exploit its competitive advantages or prevent others from exploiting its weaknesses.

SWOT analysis
A review of a firm's internal strengths and weaknesses and its external opportunities and threats

Strengths and weaknesses come from the firm's internal abilities, or lack thereof. Strengths give the firm a comparative advantage in the marketplace. Perceived strengths can include good customer service, high-quality products, strong brand image and customer loyalty, innovative R&D efforts, market leadership, or strong financial resources. Once identified, strengths can also be used to correct or mitigate a firm's weaknesses. Weaknesses give competitors opportunities to gain advantages over the firm. Once weaknesses are identified, the firm can select capital investments to mitigate or correct them. For example, a single-country producer who finds it difficult to compete in a global market can try to achieve global economies of scale (that is, achieve "global scale") by making investments that will allow it to export or produce its product overseas.

FINANCIAL CRISIS

Opportunities and threats represent external conditions that affect the firm such as competitive forces, new technologies, government regulations, and domestic and international economic trends. The 2007–2009 recession affected economies and firms around the globe. Those firms with strong brands and adequate liquidity survived; others—such as U.S. firms General Motors, Chrysler, and AIG—needed government bailouts or went bankrupt, such as Bear Stearns. As another example, consumers tend to favor "green" technology and are willing to pay a premium price for it. Changing environmental regulation and "cap and trade" programs are opportunities to some (wind energy firms) and threats to others (coal-fired utility plants).

Where do positive NPV projects come from? From economics we learn that economic profits in a competitive market are zero (recall that zero economic profits implies that the firm is earning a fair accounting return on its invested capital). In a competitive marketplace, we should be suspicious of any capital budgeting project that appears to have a positive net present value. Any positive economic profit or positive net present value must arise from one or two sources.

---

2. For a seminal piece on the role of value maximization in a firm versus stakeholder theory or the "balanced scorecard," see Michael C. Jensen, "Value Maximization, Stakeholder Theory, and the Corporate Objective Function," *Journal of Applied Corporate Finance*, Fall 2001, vol. 14, no. 5, pp. 8–21.

One source is a market imperfection or inefficiency (such as an entry barrier or monopoly situation) that prevents competition from driving the net present value to zero. The second source involves cost-saving projects that allow the firm to reduce costs below their current level. Some possibilities of such projects include:

Economies of scale and high capital requirements typically go together. High sales volumes are sometimes needed to cover large fixed costs of plant and equipment. Scale economies occur as average production cost declines with rising output per period. Any new entrant must (1) have available financing to construct a large-scale factory and (2) be able to sell in sufficient quantity to be cost competitive. These requirements can prevent entry and promote positive net present values.

Product differentiation can also generate positive net present values. Differentiation comes from consumers' belief in a difference between firms' products, whether there is a real difference or not. Differentiation leads to an imperfect market where a firm can set higher prices. Potential sources of differentiation include advertising and promotion expenditures to create "branding," R&D, and quality differences.

Absolute cost advantages can place competitors at a cost disadvantage. A firm that enters a market early can learn about the production and distribution process first making its use of assets, technology, raw inputs, and personnel more efficient than that of competitors. The firm can frequently cut costs and prices, and maintain market leadership. Similar advantages can result from possessing proprietary technology that is protected by patents. Early entry into foreign markets can allow the firm to gain experience over its competitors as it can more effectively make inroads into new markets and start to build customer loyalty.

Differences in access to distribution channels can also produce unique advantages by reducing competitors' access to consumers. Shelf space is limited at retail outlets, and store owners are understandably hesitant to take space from a current supplier and give it to a new entrant. A motivated and well-trained sales force may keep competitors from chipping away at a firm's market share. Next time you are at the grocery store, take a look at the varieties of breakfast cereal produced by the large firms in the industry!

Government policy can hinder new and potential entrants and give existing competitors unique advantages. An increasing regulatory burden on an industry can discourage entry by increasing both the complexity and the costs of entry. Domestic industries can seek import quotas to limit the extent of foreign entry and competition. Of course, similar quotas by other countries, perhaps raised in retaliation to the domestic quotas, can hurt the firm that initially sought protection. The policy of a foreign government toward nondomestic producers, as well as the stability of the government, can contribute to the political risk of investing or doing business overseas.

CONCEPT CHECK

What does "net present value" mean?

Should a firm invest in any line of business that looks attractive? Why or why not?

How can SWOT analysis be used to identify capital budgeting projects?

List five sources of positive net present value projects.

CAPITAL BUDGETING PROCESS

The capital budgeting process involves the preparation and analysis of a business case request for funding and usually consists of the following five stages:

1. Identification
2. Development
3. Selection
4. Implementation
5. Follow-up

The **identification stage** involves finding potential capital investment opportunities and identifying whether a project involves a replacement decision and/or revenue expansion. The **development stage** requires estimating relevant cash inflows and outflows. It also involves discussing the pros and cons of each project. Development sometimes requires asking what the strategic impact will be of not doing the project.

The third **selection stage** involves applying the appropriate capital budgeting techniques to help make a final accept or reject decision. In the **implementation stage,** projects that are accepted must be executed in a timely fashion. Finally, decisions need to be reviewed periodically

identification stage
finding potential capital investment opportunities and identifying whether a project involves a replacement decision and/or revenue expansion

development stage
requires estimating relevant cash inflows and outflows

selection stage
applying appropriate capital budgeting techniques to help make a final accept or reject decision

implementation stage
executing accepted projects

follow-up stage
a stage in the capital budgeting process during which managers track, review, or audit a project's results

GLOBAL DISCUSSION

INTERNET ACTIVITY

Details of investments can be seen in annual reports and news releases, both of which can be accessed via the firms' Web sites,
http://www.wellsfargo.com,
http://www.merck.com,
http://www.dell.com, and
http://www.chick-fil-a.com.

with a *follow-up* analysis to determine whether they are meeting expectations. If disappointing results occur, it is sometimes necessary to terminate or abandon previous decisions.

The multinational corporation (MNC) must go through the same capital budgeting process just described. In addition, however, MNCs need to consider possible added political and economic risks when making their decisions. Risk adjustments may be necessary because of the possibility of seizure of assets, unstable currencies, and weak foreign economies. MNCs also must consider the impact of foreign exchange controls and foreign tax regulations on a project's cash flows in relation to the final amounts that may be paid to the parent firm.

In Chapter 13, we stated how a company's mission should guide management in making investment decisions as they strive to meet goals and maximize shareholder wealth. We looked at several firms' mission statements in Chapter 13; now, let's briefly review some of the capital projects in which the firms are investing.

Wells Fargo: This financial institution is implementing a number of strategies to cross-sell products with a special emphasis on home equity loans. It has acquired a number of financial institutions in recent years, including Wachovia and banks located in various states. Technology investments improve its online financial services capabilities and improve customer service. Wells Fargo's strategy is to increase customer loyalty and to increase customer satisfaction with bank visits.

Merck: As a pharmaceutical company, its future relies on investing in research and developing a portfolio of products to meet the health needs of consumers. It initiates, curtails, expands, and shepherds a variety of formulations through the FDA drug approval process in order to maintain and grow its future cash flows. In late 2009, it recently completed its acquisition of Schering-Plough.

Dell: Growth in sales, both in the U.S. and abroad, show that Dell is making progress on its mission, which deals with customer experience and product development. Dell invests funds with customer service and satisfaction in mind. It has been successful, as witnessed by the many awards Dell has won for the quality and reliability of its products and services. It has diversified and its offerings now include printers, digital music players, and monitors—as well as a new entry into the smart phone line of business.

Chick-fil-A: Growth in sales and earnings in the restaurant industry comes mainly via new innovative products, opening new outlets, and acquisitions. Its award-winning ad campaigns—featuring cows encouraging us to "Eat Mor Chikin" have also helped sales.

Capital budget decisions require a great deal of analysis. Information generation develops three types of data: internal financial data, external economic and political data, and nonfinancial data. These data are used to forecast financial data that are used to estimate a project's cash flows.

Table 17.1 lists data items that may need to be gathered in the information generation stage, depending on the size and scope of the project. Many economic influences can directly impact

TABLE 17.1
Examples of Data Needed in Project Analysis

EXTERNAL ECONOMIC AND POLITICAL DATA
External economic and political data
Business cycle stages
Inflation trends
Interest rates trends
Exchange rate trends
Freedom of cross-border currency flows
Political stability and environment
Regulations
Taxes

INTERNAL FINANCIAL DATA	NONFINANCIAL DATA
Investment costs (fixed assets and working capital)	Distribution channels
Market studies and estimates of revenues, costs, cash flows	Quantity, quality of labor force in different global locations
Financing costs (cost of capital)	Labor-management relations
Transportation costs	Status of technological change in the industry
Publicly available information on competitor's plans, operating results	Competitive analysis of the industry, potential reaction of competitors

the success of a project by affecting sales revenues, costs, exchange rates, and overall project cash flows. Regulatory trends and political environment factors, in both the domestic and foreign economies, may help or hinder the success of proposed projects.

Financial data relevant to the project are developed from sources such as marketing research, production analysis, and economic analysis. Using the firm's research and internal data, analysts estimate the cost of the investment, working capital needs, projected cash flows, and financing costs. If public information is available on competitors' lines of business, this also should be incorporated into the analysis, to help estimate potential cash flows and to determine the effects of the project on the competition.

Nonfinancial information relevant to the cash flow estimation process includes data on the means used to distribute products to consumers, quality and quantity of the labor force, dynamics of technological change in the targeted market, and information from a strategic analysis of competitors. Analysts should assess the strengths and weaknesses of competitors and how they will react if the firm undertakes its own project.

To illustrate, in mid-1998 a strike against General Motors caused GM management to reexamine its capital budgeting plan. General Motors had been planning to invest $21 billion in its U.S. plants between 1998 and 2002. The prospect of poor labor relations and inefficient union work rules was giving GM leaders second thoughts about its planned U.S. capital investment.[3] Political risks affect overseas projects; delays have occurred in developing oil fields in Kazakhstan and Turkmenistan because the projects involve building an oil pipeline across politically unstable or unfriendly countries to get the oil to waterways and to oil tankers.[4] A surprise by competitors who introduced a seven-seat model in the European compact minivan market caused Ford to abandon its plans to introduce a five-seat model, after several years and many millions had been spent on design efforts.[5]

Table 17.1 lists some of the information that firms may use to evaluate capital spending projects. For a specific industry example, oil and gas companies ranked the following items from most important to least important on their effect on capital spending decisions:

1. Forecasts of natural gas prices
2. Forecasts of crude oil prices
3. Forecasted demand for natural gas
4. Forecasted demand for crude oil
5. Availability and cost of outside funds to finance projects
6. Regulatory requirements or constraints on projects
7. Tax considerations

Natural gas prices and demand and crude oil prices and demand determine company revenues. Higher prices (demand) will result in higher sales revenues and, all else being constant, higher profits. Moreover, since oil and gas are substitute products, oil producers will be interested in natural gas price and demand trends and vice versa. With large oil companies spending billions of dollars a year on capital spending, the ability to raise external funds is a consideration should additions to retained earnings be insufficient to finance all of the attractive projects. Because of environmental concerns, oil and gas production is heavily regulated. The intricacies of the tax code also affect oil and gas investment decisions. Not only do U.S. income taxes affect these companies, but so do depreciation and oil and gas depletion allowances, tax codes of the different countries in which they drill, tax credits for taxes paid to different jurisdictions, and so on. Firms sometimes plan for growing capital budgets when oil and gas prices are low, in order to take advantage of future price upswings

---

3. Micheline Maynard, "GM May Rethink Plant Investments," *USA Today*, June 18, 1998, p. 1B.
4. Hugh Pope, "Scramble for Oil in Central Asia Hits Roadblocks," *The Wall Street Journal*, March 13, 1998, p. A12.
5. Scott Miller, "Ford Scraps Plans for Compact Minivan, Years in Planning, in Cost-Cutting Effort," *The Wall Street Journal*, February 14, 2000, p. A18.

INTERNET ACTIVITY
Visit the Environmental Protection Agency's SmartWay program to see what programs exist to help businesses lower transportation costs: http://www.epa.gov/smartway/.

and to trim spending when prices are high, since they don't want to overextend themselves before oversupply occurs and prices fall.[6]

In recent years, energy prices in general—and oil in particular—have become higher and more volatile. This trend has led many companies in energy-intensive sectors to consider new ways of designing how they operate and to initiate capital budgeting projects that will help lower energy costs. Indeed, many sectors of the economy are trying to become more "green" and to incorporate sustainability as a major focus of their business strategies.[7] In this context, "sustainability" refers not so much as to keeping the business operating into the distant future but for the business to use materials for indefinite periods without causing environmental damage or depleting resources. The focus of such projects is to reduce waste and to conserve natural resources. Sustainable strategies will seek to use renewable resources. Whereas some fear we may someday deplete oil reserves in the future, there is less concern over naturally renewable (and potentially carbon-reducing) energy sources such as wind, wave, solar, and nuclear energy and biofuels from corn, soybeans, algae, and so forth.

Such concerns are large for transportation-related industries—not just for trucking, railroad, and airline carriers but for the users of such services, such as much of the retail sector and capital goods sector. When fuel costs are low, just-in-time inventory systems with daily shipments make sense to keep inventory costs down. But higher energy prices will be passed on by shippers and suppliers—so inventory storage and warehouse decisions take prominence over JIT efficiency. Some estimate that corporate supply-chain transportation costs consumes about 7 percent of energy in developed economies. As a result, firms are looking at ways to lower costs and dependence on oil by upgrading truck fleets with auxiliary power systems, tire-inflation sensors, and better aerodynamics. They are considering projects to replace large trucks with smaller more fuel-efficient vehicles for deliveries into congested areas. Smaller warehouses closer together rather than megawarehouses miles from the products' final destination may help lower transportation costs, too. Even loading a truck becomes a science to try to use the available space as efficiently as possible to reduce trips and energy costs.

CONCEPT CHECK
What are the five stages of the capital budgeting process?

Depending upon energy price trends, it may also affect exports and imports. High fuel bills will lead to lower corporate profits and some pass-through to consumers. Industries that heavily import goods from overseas may want to consider the energy benefits for producing those goods at home rather than paying higher shipping costs.

CAPITAL BUDGETING TECHNIQUES

FINANCE PRINCIPLE

Appropriate methods or techniques are required to evaluate capital budgeting projects so proper wealth-maximizing decisions can be made. The techniques used should reflect the time value of money since cash outlays for plant and equipment occur now, while the benefits occur in the future. Five methods—net present value, internal rate of return, modified internal rate of return, profitability index, and the payback period—are utilized widely. Of these four methods, the payback period is the *least* preferable, because it does not take the time value of money into account.

NET PRESENT VALUE

The net present value (NPV) method is arguably the best method to use to evaluate capital budgeting projects. A project's net present value is calculated as the present value of all cash flows for the life of the project less the initial investment or outlay, as we saw in Equation 17.1. It considers the time value of money and includes all of the project's cash flows in the analysis. In addition, its value measures the project's dollar impact on shareholder wealth. The NPV measures the expected dollar change in shareholder wealth from doing the project. That is, a

---

6. Thaddeus Herrick, "Big Oil Firms Trim Exploration Spending," *The Wall Street Journal,* September 26, 2000, p. A2; Anne Reifenberg, "Big Oil Opens Capital-Spending Spigot for Overseas Projects Amid Price Slump," *The Wall Street Journal,* January 3, 1996, p. A2.
7. Vincent Ryan, "Sucking It Up," *CFO,* April 2008, pp. 66–73; S. L. Mintz, "What Goes Down Will Come Up," *CFO,* December 2008, pp. 51–55.

TABLE 17.2
Cash Flow Data for Projects A and B

YEAR	PROJECT A	PROJECT B
1	$5,800	$4,000
2	5,800	4,000
3	5,800	8,000
4	5,800	10,000
5	5,800	10,000

project with an NPV of $1 million is expected to increase shareholder wealth by $1 million. Thus, projects with positive NPVs are expected to add to shareholder wealth while projects with negative NPVs should be shunned.

To apply the net present value method, we need to know the project's estimated cash flows and the required rate of return to discount the cash flow. We discuss methods of estimating cash flows in a future section. The required rate of return should reflect the cost of long-term debt and equity capital funds for projects with the same risk as the one under consideration. In the following example, we'll assume that the required rate of return, or ***cost of capital,*** is 10 percent. In Chapter 18, we review the process of determining the cost of capital in detail.

cost of capital
project's required rate of return

We apply the net present value technique to projects A and B. Their cash flows are shown in Table 17.2. Assuming a 10 percent cost of capital, the cash flows are multiplied by the 10 percent PVIF from Table 2 in the Appendix to get the present values shown in Table 17.3. Notice that there is no discount factor for the initial outlays because they occur before any time has passed (i.e., in year zero). Positive net present values are shown for both projects. This means that an investment in either project will add to shareholder wealth. However, project A, with the higher net present value of $1,982, is preferable to project B, which has a net present value of $988.

A positive NPV means the project's cash inflows are sufficient to repay the initial upfront (time zero) costs as well as the financing cost of 10 percent over the project's life. Since their NPVs are greater than zero, each project's return is greater than the 10 percent cost of capital.

Financial calculators can compute NPV. For example, for project A we can enter the following:

For HP 10 B II Financial Calculator:
$-20,000$ CF$_j$
5800 CF$_j$
5800 CF$_j$
5800 CF$_j$
5800 CF$_j$
5800 CF$_j$
10 i (interest rate key)

Pushing the NPV key next, we have a more exact answer for the NPV: $1,986.56.

TABLE 17.3
Net Present Value Calculations for Projects A and B

	PROJECT A				PROJECT B		
YEAR	CASH FLOW	× 10% PVIF	= PRESENT VALUE	CASH FLOW	× 10% PVIF	= PRESENT VALUE
0	−$20,000	1.000	−$20,000	−$25,000	1.000	−$25,000
1	5,800	0.909	5,272	4,000	0.909	3,636
2	5,800	0.826	4,791	4,000	0.826	3,304
3	5,800	0.751	4,356	8,000	0.751	6,008
4	5,800	0.683	3,961	10,000	0.683	6,830
5	5,800	0.621	3,602	10,000	0.621	6,210
			Net present value = $1,982			Net present value = $988

For the TI BA II Plus Financial Calculator:

TO	PRESS	DISPLAY
Select Cash Flow worksheet	CF	CFo = 0.00
Enter initial cash flow	20000 +/− ENTER	CFo = −20,000
Enter cash flow for first year	↓5800 ENTER	C01 = 5,800
	↓	F01 = 1.00
Enter cash flows for the second year	↓5800 ENTER	C01 = 5,800
	↓	F01 = 1.00
Enter cash flows for the third year	↓5800 ENTER	C01 = 5,800
	↓	F01 = 1.00
Enter cash flows for the fourth year	↓5800 ENTER	C01 = 5,800
	↓	F01 = 1.00
Enter cash flows for the fifth year	↓5800 ENTER	C01 = 5,800
	↓	F01 = 1.00

Computing NPV:

TO	PRESS	DISPLAY
Prepare to compute NPV	NPV	I = 0.00
Enter interest rate per period	10 ENTER	I = 10.00
Compute NPV	↓ CPT	NPV = 1,986.56

Doing this calculation for project B, we find its NPV is $992.01.

A shortcut method can be used to calculate the net present value for project A. Since the cash inflows form an annuity, we could have used the PVIFA at 10 percent for five years from Table 4 in the Appendix, which is 3.791. The net present value then can be calculated:

$$\$5,800 \times 3.791 = \$21,988 \text{ PV cash inflows}$$
$$-20,000 \text{ Initial outlay}$$
$$\$1,988 \text{ Net present value}$$

The $1,988 net present value figure using PVIFA differs slightly from the $1,982 using PVIF because of rounding the present value interest factors in the Appendix tables. When cash inflows are not in the form of an annuity, as in the case of project B, the longer calculation process shown in Table 17.3 must be used to find the net present value.

Projects with negative net present values are not acceptable to a firm. They provide returns lower than the cost of capital and would cause the value of the firm to fall. In our example, both projects A and B have positive NPVs that are acceptable. If they are mutually exclusive projects, managers should chose project A as its NPV, $1,986.56, is higher than Project B's NPV of $992.01. Clearly, it is important for the financial manager to make capital budgeting decisions on the basis of their expected impact on the firm's value.

Using Spreadsheet Functions

In addition to multiplying with factors found in a present value table or using a financial calculator, electronic spreadsheet packages such as Excel make the task of computing a net present value rather simple, too. Suppose we have the cash flows for project A in column B, rows 2 through 7 of an Excel spreadsheet:

	A	B	C
1	Time	Cash Flow	
2	0	-$20,000	
3	1	$5,800	
4	2	$5,800	
5	3	$5,800	
6	4	$5,800	
7	5	$5,800	
8	NPV =	$1,986.56	=NPV(10%,B3:B7) + B2

To compute the net present value, we can use Excel's NPV function, with modification. We need to modify its use because Excel's NPV does not calculate net present value as we do in this chapter. Excel's NPV function computes the sum of present values assuming the value in the first cell listed is to be discounted back one period, the value in the second cell is to be discounted back two periods, and so on. But most capital budgeting problems have a "time zero" or "current" investment that is not discounted; in our example, the investment of $20,000 at time zero is already expressed in present value terms.

To get around this problem, we use Excel's NPV function to find the sum of the present values in periods one through the end of the project (cells B3 through B7 in our case) and then add the initial negative investment cash outflow of $20,000 in cell B2. In the above example, in cell B8, we typed =NPV (10%, B3:B7) + B2 and the spreadsheet computes an exact value of the net present value, $1,986.56.

The NPV function has the form:

$$=NPV \text{ (discount rate, cell of time one cash flow : cell of last cash flow)}$$

The discount rate can be typed as a percentage (10%) or as a decimal equivalent (0.1). If you type in the "%" symbol, Excel assumes the number is a percentage, otherwise the decimal equivalent is assumed. Be careful: if you key in "10" rather than "10%" the spreadsheet will use a discount rate of 1000%!

INTERNAL RATE OF RETURN

We know from our discussion of bonds in Chapter 10 that there is an inverse relationship, or "seesaw effect," between bond prices and interest rates. As investors' required rates of return rise, bond prices fall; as investors' required rates of return fall, bond prices rise. A similar relationship exists between NPV and a firm's required rate of return or cost of capital on a project. For a given set of cash flows, a higher cost of capital will lead to a lower NPV; a lower cost of capital, however, will increase a project's NPV. Figure 17.1 shows this relationship, called the **NPV profile,** between NPV and the cost of capital. As the cost of capital on a project rises, the NPV changes from positive, to zero, to negative. The cost of capital at which the NPV is zero deserves special attention.

While the net present value method tells us that both projects A and B provide expected returns that are greater than 10 percent, we do not know the actual rates of return. The **internal rate of return (IRR) method** finds the return that causes the net present value to be zero, namely the point where the NPV profile crosses the x axis in Figure 17.1. Net present value will

CONCEPT CHECK
How is NPV computed?
What does the cost of capital represent?

NPV profile
the graphical relationship between a project's NPV and cost of capital

internal rate of return (IRR) method
return that causes the net present value to be zero

FIGURE 17.1
Relationship Between NPV and Discount Rates

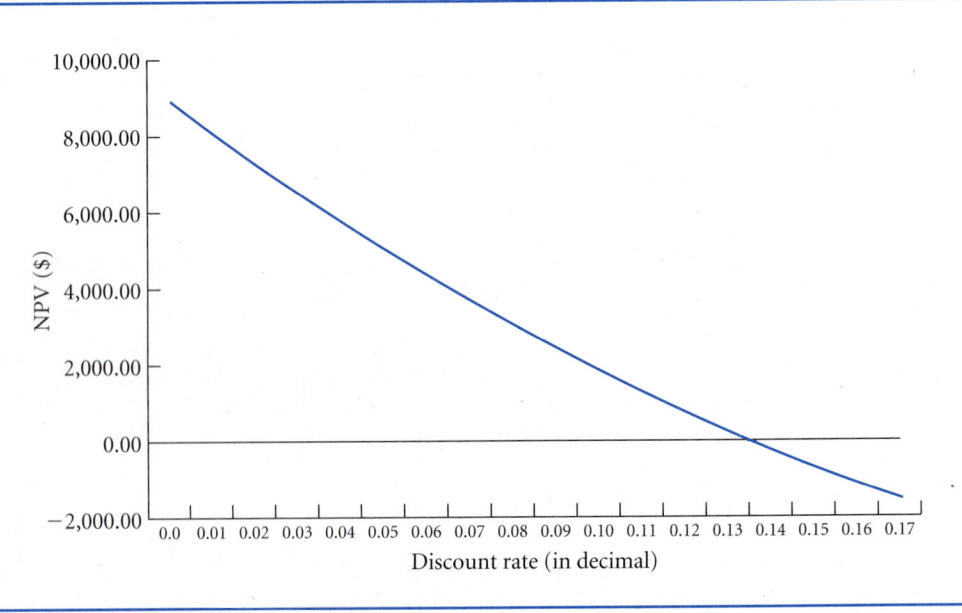

equal zero when the present value of the cash flows equals the project's initial investment, as seen in Equation 17.2:[8]

$$NPV = \sum_{t=1}^{n} CF_t/(1 + IRR)^t - \text{Initial Investment} = 0 \quad (17.2)$$

A trial-and-error process can be used to find the internal rate of return (IRR), but financial calculators and computer spreadsheets (such as Excel's IRR function) provide much quicker means of estimating internal rates of return.

Let's illustrate the IRR process first for project A. Because the cash inflows form an annuity, the IRR is easy to find. From Chapter 9, we know that

Present value of an annuity = PVIFA × annuity cash flow

Rearranging, we divide the initial capital budgeting outlay (PV annuity) by the cash inflow annuity amount to find the present value interest factor for an ordinary annuity:

PVIFA = PV annuity / Annual receipt

For Project A, the PVIFA is 3.448 ($20,000/5,800). We know this PVIFA of 3.448 is for five years. By turning to Table 4 in the Appendix, Present Value of a $1 Ordinary Annuity, we can read across the five-year row until we find a PVIFA close to 3.448. It falls between 3.605 (12 percent) and 3.433 (14 percent) but is much closer to the PVIFA at 14 percent. Thus, the internal rate of return for project A is a little less than 14 percent.

Of course, with financial calculators and computer spreadsheets there are other, more precise, ways to find internal rate of return. Using a financial calculator and project A's cash flows:

For HP 10 B II Financial Calculator:

$-20,000$ CF$_j$
5800 CF$_j$
5800 CF$_j$
5800 CF$_j$
5800 CF$_j$
5800 CF$_j$

Pushing the IRR key (for some calculators, you may need to push a shift or "2nd" key before pushing the IRR key). Doing so, we find the IRR is 13.82 percent.

For the TI BA II Plus Financial Calculator:

TO	PRESS	DISPLAY
Select Cash Flow worksheet	CF	CFo = 0.00
Enter initial cash flow	20000 +/− ENTER	CFo = −20,000
Enter cash flow for first year	↓ 5800 ENTER	C01 = 5,800
	↓	F01 = 1.00
Enter cash flows for the second year	↓ 5800 ENTER	C01 = 5,800
	↓	F01 = 1.00
Enter cash flows for the third year	↓ 5800 ENTER	C01 = 5,800
	↓	F01 = 1.00
Enter cash flows for the fourth year	↓ 5800 ENTER	C01 = 5,800
	↓	F01 = 1.00
Enter cash flows for the fifth year	↓ 5800 ENTER	C01 = 5,800
	↓	F01 = 1.00

Computing NPV:

TO	PRESS	DISPLAY
Prepare to compute IRR	IRR	IRR = 0.00
Compute internal rate of return	↓ CPT	IRR = 13.82

---

8. This method also is used to find the yield to maturity on bonds in Chapter 10.

We can illustrate how to determine the IRR two ways using spreadsheets. We will use project A, with its annuity cash flows, in these examples. First, we can successively compute values of NPV using different discount rates:

DISCOUNT RATE (%)	PROJECT A'S NPV
0	$9,000.00
1	$8,149.90
2	$7,338.07
3	$6,562.30
4	$5,820.57
5	$5,110.96
6	$4,431.71
7	$3,781.15
8	$3,157.72
9	$2,559.98
10	$1,986.56
11	$1,436.20
12	$907.70
13	$399.94
14	−$88.13
15	−$557.50
16	−$1,009.10
17	−$1,443.79

The NPV goes from positive to negative here, so the IRR must lie between 13 and 14 percent.

This shows the IRR is between 13 and 14 percent. This information can then be used as input into Excel's graphing capabilities and the NPV profile can be graphed. In fact, that is how we constructed Figure 17.1. The NPV profile gives us a visual perspective of how sensitive the net present value is to a change in the project's cost of capital or discount rate.

The second way to use the spreadsheet is to compute the internal rate of return directly by using Excel's IRR function. Let's assume the time 0 through time 5 cash flows for project A are in cells B2 through B7, as below. By keying =IRR(B2:B7) into a cell (B9, in this case), the spreadsheet will compute an exact value of the internal rate of return for project A:

In our example, the initial (time zero) cash flow is found in cell B2. Cell B7 contains the final cash inflow for time period five. Using the IRR function, we obtain an exact value for Project A's internal rate of return, 13.82 percent, the same as we found using a financial calculator.

The IRR function has the form: =IRR(cell of time zero cash flow : cell of last cash flow, initial estimate for the IRR). The last item, the initial estimate for the IRR, is optional and we did not use it in the above example for Project A. To input an initial guess we can use percentages (10%) or decimal equivalents (0.10). Many times, we can omit this initial guess and the IRR function will compute the internal rate of return without difficulty.

For project B, with its unequal cash flows, a financial calculator or spreadsheet program is the best to use. But a trial-and-error process can also be used to find the IRR for project B.

TABLE 17.4

Net Present Value Calculation for Project B Using a 12 Percent Discount Rate

YEAR	CASH FLOW	×	12% PVIF	=	PRESENT VALUE
0	−$25,000		1.000		−$25,000
1	4,000		0.893		3,572
2	4,000		0.797		3,188
3	8,000		0.712		5,696
4	10,000		0.636		6,360
5	10,000		0.567		5,670
				Net present value =	−$514

Discounting the cash flows at a 10 percent rate results in a positive net present value of $988, as calculated in Table 17.3. A positive net present value indicates that we need to try a higher discount rate, such as 12 percent, to find the discount rate that results in a zero NPV.[9] The 12 percent present value interest factors are taken from Table 2 in the Appendix, Present Value of $1. In Table 17.4, we calculate that when the cash flows are discounted at a 12 percent rate, the net present value becomes minus $514.

This indicates that the IRR actually falls between 10 and 12 percent. Since minus $514 is closer to zero than $988 is, you might guess that the IRR is a little above 11 percent. But to obtain an exact answer, we need to use a financial calculator or electronic spreadsheet. Doing so, we learn that project B's IRR is 11.3 percent.

Both projects A and B are acceptable because they provide returns higher than the 10 percent cost of capital. However, if the projects are mutually exclusive, we would select project A over project B because A's net present value is higher.[10]

NPV and IRR

The NPV and IRR methods will always agree on whether a project enhances or harms shareholder wealth. If a project returns more than its cost of capital, the NPV is positive. If a project returns less than its cost of capital, the NPV is negative. An issue with the use of IRR is that at times it will rank projects differently than the NPV. If that occurs, what decision should be made?

If the projects are independent, there is no real issue; the firm should do all projects with positive NPVs—or to state this similarly, the firm should do all projects with internal rates of return greater than their required returns.

If the projects are mutually exclusive, however, the decision should be made to follow the rankings created by the NPV method. The NPV measures the change in shareholder wealth that is expected to be generated by the project. As managers should try to maximize shareholder wealth, the project with the higher NPV—*not* the higher IRR—should be preferred.

A second issue with IRR is when the cash flows of a project alternate in sign—some positive, some negative. In such a case it is mathematically possible to have two—or more—IRRs! For example, consider the case of a project with an initial outlay of $100, a positive cash flow of $300 in year one, and a cash outflow of –$200 in year two because of shut-down costs. Such a project has two IRRs: 0 percent and 100 percent:

NPV at 0%: $-100 + 300/(1 + 0)^1 + -200/(1 + 0)^2 = -100 + 300 - 200 = 0$

NPV at 100%: $-100 + 300/(1 + 1.00)^1 + -200/(1 + 100.0)^2 = -100 + 150 - 50 = 0$

It is easy to think of a real-world project that may require substantial renovations or maintenance over time or that may have large end-of-life decommissioning or shut-down costs. Thus, for this reason NPV is the preferred approach rather than IRR.

---

9. Similar to the "seesaw effect" we learned in bond pricing, a higher discount rate results in a lower NPV, as seen in Figure 17.1.

10. For several reasons, a project with an NPV below that of another project may have a higher IRR than the competing project. That is why it is best to calculate each project's NPV in addition to the IRR. The project with the highest NPV is the one that is expected to add the most to shareholder wealth.

A common misconception is that the internal rate of return represents the compounded return on the funds originally invested in the project. What IRR really measures is the return earned on the funds that remain internally invested in the project (hence the name, *internal* rate of return). Some cash flows from a project are a return of the principal (original investment), while some pay a return on the remaining balance of funds invested in the project.

To show that the IRR measures the return earned on the funds that remain internally invested in a project, we present the following example. Martin and Barbara have decided to upgrade their business computer system to improve the quality and efficiency of their work. The initial investment is $5,000 and the project will save them $2,010.57 per year. The internal rate of return on the project has been determined to be 10 percent. We show how the IRR represents the return on the year-by-year unrecovered costs of the project.

Below is the cash flow schedule constructed for Martin and Barbara's computer upgrade project.

(1) YEAR	(2) BEGINNING INVESTMENT VALUE	(3) CASH INFLOW (SAVINGS)	(4) 10% RETURN ON THE INVESTED FUNDS (2) × 0.10	(5) REDUCTION IN THE INVESTED FUNDS (3) − (4)	(6) ENDING VALUE OF INVESTED FUNDS (2) − (5)
1	$5,000.00	$2,010.57	$500.00	$1,510.57	$3,489.43
2	3,489.43	2,010.57	348.94	1,661.63	1,827.80
3	1,827.80	2,010.57	182.78	1,827.79	0.01*

*Value is not 0.00 due to rounding.

This table shows that the yearly cash saving of $2,010.57 from the computer upgrade project represents both a return on the funds that remain invested (Column 4) and a reduction in the funds that remain invested in the project (Column 5). The project does not earn a 10 percent return, or $500 annually, on the initial $5,000 investment for all three years. The 10 percent IRR represents the return on the funds that remain invested in the project over its lifetime rather than each year's return on the original investment.

MODIFIED INTERNAL RATE OF RETURN

Modified internal rate of return (MIRR) solves some of the problems presented by IRR. MIRR rankings of mutually exclusive projects with comparably-sized initial investments will agree with the NPV rankings of those projects. Additionally, the MIRR calculation always gives a single answer—it will not give us multiple answers as the IRR approach sometimes does.

MIRR is calculated in a three-step process:

1. Using the required rate of return as the discount rate, find the present value of all cash outflows (for a conventional project, this will be just the initial cost of the project). This step converts all the cash outflows into a lump-sum present value at Time 0.
2. Using the required return as the reinvestment or compounding rate, compute the *future* value of each cash inflow as of the end of the project's life, time N, and add them together. This sum is sometimes called the **terminal value.** This step converts all inflows into a lump-sum future value at time N.
3. Find the discount rate that equates the present value of the outflows and the future value of the terminal value; this discount rate is the modified internal rate of return.

Figure 17.2 illustrates this process using the cash flow data from project A using a required return of 10 percent.

In the first step, the present value of the project's outflows is simply its initial investment, $20,000.

Second, we find the future value of each of the project's inflows as of the end of the fifth and final year of the project. The year one cash inflow of $5,800 is compounded over four years to the end of year five; its future value at the end of year five is $8,491.78. The year-two

CONCEPT CHECK

What is the relationship between the cost of capital and net present value?

What is the relationship between IRR and NPV?

What does the IRR measure?

modified internal rate of return (MIRR) method a technique that finds the return that equates the present value of a project's outflows to the future value of its inflows

FIGURE 17.2
MIRR for Project A

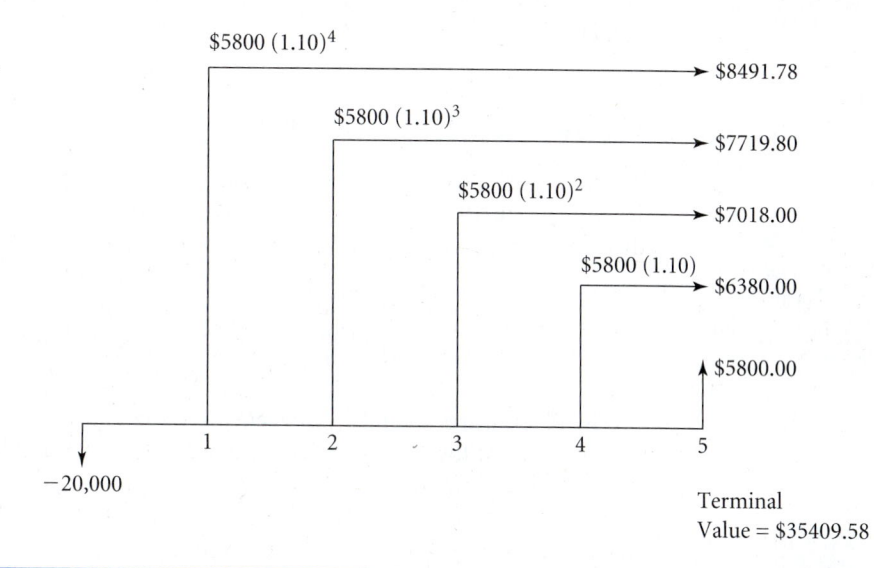

```
                $5800 (1.10)⁴
     ┌─────────────────────────────────────────→ $8491.78
     │          $5800 (1.10)³
     │     ┌───────────────────────────────────→ $7719.80
     │     │          $5800 (1.10)²
     │     │     ┌─────────────────────────────→ $7018.00
     │     │     │          $5800 (1.10)
     │     │     │     ┌───────────────────────→ $6380.00
     │     │     │     │
     │     │     │     │              ↑ $5800.00
     │     │     │     │              │
     │     1     2     3     4        5
     ↓
  −20,000                                    Terminal
                                             Value = $35409.58
```

cash flow is compounded for three years to the end of year five; its future value at the end of year five is $7,719.80. Similarly, we compute the future values for the year-three, four, and five cash inflows. The year five cash inflow needs no compounding as it occurs at the end of year five. Adding the future values together yields the sum $35,409.58; this is the project's terminal value.

Third, we find the discount rate that sets the present value of the outflows equal to the terminal value:

$$FV = PV(1 + r)^n = \$35{,}409.58 = \$20{,}000(1 + r)^5$$

Solving, we find the MIRR is 12.10 percent

Using a spreadsheet, Excel has a function, MIRR, to do this calculation:

	A	B	C
1	Time	Cash Flow	
2	0	-$20,000	
3	1	$5,800	
4	2	$5,800	
5	3	$5,800	
6	4	$5,800	
7	5	$5,800	
8	NPV =	$1,986.56	=NPV(10%,B3:B7) + B2
9	IRR =	13.82%	=IRR(B2:B7)
10	MIRR =	12.10%	=MIRR(B2:B7,10%,10%)

The MIRR function has the form: =MIRR(cell of time zero cash flow : cell of last cash flow, finance rate, reinvestment rate). The finance rate is the interest rate paid on borrowing to finance the cash outflows. The reinvestment rate is the rate used to compound, or to find the future value, of the cash inflows. We used the firm's required rate of return of 10 percent for both of these in this example.

Similar calculations show the MIRR for Project B is 10.86 percent. MIRR ranks project A (12.10 percent) higher than project B (10.86 percent); this is the same ranking as NPV gave the projects.

CONCEPT QUIZ

What is MIRR?

How does the MIRR method improve upon the IRR method?

profitability index (PI) or benefit/cost ratio
ratio between the present values of the cash flows and the project's cost

CONCEPT CHECK

What is the profitability index?

What is the relationship between the profitability index and the net present value?

The decision rule for MIRR is similar to that for IRR; a project is acceptable if its MIRR exceeds the project's minimum required return. A drawback to the MIRR is that it is a relative measure of attractiveness; it does not indicate the dollar amount by which projects change shareholder wealth.[11]

PROFITABILITY INDEX

Another discounted cash flow technique for evaluating capital budgeting projects is the **profitability index (PI)**, also called the **benefit/cost ratio**. The PI method computes the ratio between the present values of the inflows and outflows:

$$PI = \frac{\text{Present value of the cash flows}}{\text{Initial cost}} = \frac{\sum_{t=1}^{N} \frac{CF_t}{(1+r)^t}}{CF_0} \quad (17.3)$$

The PI measures the relative benefits of undertaking a project, namely the present value of benefits received for each dollar invested. A PI of 2, for example, means that the project returns a present value of $2 for every $1 invested. Since it would be foolish to invest in a project that returns less than a dollar for every dollar invested, the profitability index has a natural decision rule: accept a project that has a profitability index greater than 1.0; reject a project that has a PI less than 1.0.

Using the data in Table 17.3, we calculate the present value of project A's inflows to be $21,982. Since its initial cost is $20,000, project A has a profitability index of $21,982/$20,000, or 1.099. Project B's cash inflows have a present value of $25,988, so its profitability index is $25,988/$25,000, or 1.040.

The relationship between PI and NPV should be clear. Whenever NPV is positive, PI exceeds 1.0. Likewise, whenever NPV is negative, PI is less than 1.0. Thus, the NPV, IRR, and PI always agree on which projects would enhance shareholder wealth and which would diminish it.

CONFLICTS BETWEEN DISCOUNTED CASH FLOW TECHNIQUES

NPV, IRR, MIRR, and PI will *always* agree on whether a project should be accepted or rejected. So if the firm is considering only independent projects it makes little practical difference which method is used. All of them always give consistent decisions as to whether a given project would increase or decrease shareholder wealth.

When mutually exclusive projects are ranked from most attractive to least attractive, NPV may rate them differently than the other techniques. The main reason for this is that NPV measures one aspect of the project whereas IRR and PI measure another.

NPV measures the dollar change in shareholder wealth that arises from undertaking the project. As relative measures of project attractiveness, IRR and PI indicate the rate of profitability a project adds to shareholder wealth but not the actual dollar amount. A project with a lower IRR or PI may still add more to shareholder value than another mutually exclusive project if the projects have different cash flow patterns, time horizons, or sizes.

DIFFERENT CASH FLOW PATTERNS

Projects that provide larger cash flows in their early stages can seem to provide more funds than a project with more even cash flows. If the IRR exceeds the firm's required rate of return, the effects of compounding larger cash flows at a rate exceeding the required return may result in the IRR method ranking the project higher than the NPV method. Thus, projects with larger earlier cash flows may have higher IRR rankings than those with larger later cash flows.

---

11. The reason the MIRR ranks projects in the same order as the NPV method is because the MIRR is a transformation of the NPV calculation. The terminal value calculation in the MIRR method is equal to the future value of the present value of the inflows. For example, for project A, the present value of the inflows is $21,986.56. At the 10 percent required return, the future value of this amount in year 5 is $21,986.56(1.10)^5 = $35,409.57, which, with some rounding error, is the terminal value we computed above.

DIFFERENT TIME HORIZONS

A shorter project may free up invested funds sooner and consequently offer a higher IRR. A long-term project's cash flows will remain internally invested in the project for a longer period. Unless those future cash flows are quite large, the discounting process may reduce their perceived present value, eroding the IRR of the longer-term project. The IRR of a desirable project must exceed the project's required return; the NPV formula uses a lower discount rate so it values later cash flows more favorably than does the IRR calculation.

A quick example will show this point. Suppose project Short and project Long both require an initial investment of $100. In two years, project Short returns a lump sum of $200. Project Long lasts ten times longer and returns ten times more than Short; that is, Long will return a lump sum of $2,000 in 20 years. A quick calculation will confirm that Short has an IRR of 41.42 percent; Long has an IRR of 16.16 percent, but at a 10 percent cost of capital, Long's NPV ($197.29) exceeds that of Short ($65.29).

DIFFERENT SIZES

Projects with smaller initial investments may have higher PIs and IRRs, but their small size may appear to make them less attractive from an NPV perspective. For example, consider Projects Small and Large:

PROJECT	INITIAL OUTLAY	PV OF CASH FLOWS	NPV	PI
Small	$100.00	$150.00	$50	1.5
Large	1,000.00	1,100.00	$100	1.1

The NPV method ranks Project Large first because of its larger NPV, but PI ranks Project Small first.

Thus, rankings among capital budgeting projects may differ for the three reasons above. The discounted cash flow methods each provide a different perspective on project attractiveness, but since the goal of the decision process is to maximize shareholder wealth, the NPV approach remains preferred among the others.

PAYBACK PERIOD

The payback period method does not consider the time value of money. So why discuss it? Because it is simple to compute and it is still used by some firms. You need to know about this technique and to be able to explain why it should not be used to make investment decisions.

The ***payback period method*** determines the time in years it will take to recover, or "pay back," the initial investment in fixed assets. Management will choose the projects whose paybacks are less than a management-specified period.

In cases where the cash benefits form an annuity, the payback period is easily calculated:

$$\text{Payback period} = \text{Initial outlay}/\text{Annual cash inflow}$$

For project A we have:

$$\text{payback period} = \$20,000/\$5,800 = 3.4 \text{ years.}$$

The initial investment outflow for project B is $25,000. Cash inflows for project B will total $16,000 ($4,000 + $4,000 + $8,000) for the first three years. This leaves $9,000 ($25,000 − $16,000) still unrecovered. With a $10,000 cash flow expected in year four, it will take an additional 0.9 of a year ($9,000/$10,000) before the investment is fully recovered. Thus the payback period for project B is 3.9 years. Based solely on the payback period technique, project A would be chosen over project B because it recoups its investment more quickly.

However, the payback period evaluation method suffers from two basic drawbacks. First, the technique does not consider the time value of money. The second limitation is that all cash flows beyond the payback period are ignored. Notice that project B will return $10,000 in cash inflow in year five, which is substantially more than project A's fifth-year cash inflow. The possible significance of this difference is overlooked by the payback period method.

CONCEPT QUIZ

Why will projects with larger earlier cash flows tend to have higher IRRs?

Why will shorter projects tend to have higher IRRs?

Why might projects with smaller initial investments have higher IRRs and PIs than projects with larger initial investments?

---

payback period method determines the time in years it will take to recover, or pay back, the initial investment in fixed assets

SMALL BUSINESS PRACTICE
A Small Business Resource Center

Business Week has established The Small Business Resource Center. Access to this center is available to current Business Week subscribers on its Web site: http://www.businessweek.com/small-business/. The Center provides a variety of different types of information and also is interactive. A variety of resource information is available on such topics as market research, managing a workforce, finance, and technology.

In addition to information about resources available to small businesses, the Center provides services in the form of access to *Business Week* travel and career centers. Daily reports and breaking business stories are provided along with an Ask Enterprise feature that helps provide answers to questions posed by managers of small businesses.

Information relating to operating and financing a business at various life cycle stages is provided. For example, if you wish to start a new business, you can examine the forms that are necessary to begin operation. Information on financing and growing a business also is provided. Finally, information is provided for owner/managers who are either seeking to sell their firms or trying to find other ways to exit their businesses.

CONCEPT CHECK
What is the payback period?

Why is the payback period inferior to NPV as a method for selecting capital budgeting projects?

A large accounting firm conducted a study of store remodelings and renovations. Their findings are disturbing for some retailers: these investments may never pay for themselves. The study found that large discounters, such as Kmart and Target, have payback periods that average twenty years for renovation projects. The IRR on such projects range from 1 percent to 6 percent. For family-apparel specialty stores (such as Eddie Bauer), it was a different story. Their remodeling IRRs were as high as 67 percent with payback periods that averaged nineteen months. (The participants in the study were not revealed; the store names used above are only examples of stores in the different retail categories.)

The study concludes that having a good market position is more important than a renovation project. Poor returns on some stores' renovations apparently occurred because stores were trying to modernize in the face of new competition rather than realigning company strategy to respond to a successful competitor.[12]

DIFFERENCE BETWEEN THEORY AND PRACTICE

Thus far, this chapter has presented the basic concepts and techniques of capital budgeting. The capital budgeting process tries to identify projects that will maximize shareholder value. Using the firm's mission and objectives as a guide, managers seek to identify market or product segments where the firm can build, maintain, or expand a competitive advantage.

We have reviewed five capital budgeting techniques: net present value, internal rate of return, modified internal rate of return, profitability index, and the payback method. The first four use discounted cash flows to incorporate the time value of money into the analysis. The final method ignores time value considerations. Financial managers favor the use of discounted cash flow techniques.

Theory strongly suggests that analysts should evaluate capital budgeting projects using DCF techniques that incorporate all relevant cash flows, base decisions on clear and objective criteria, and indicate projects' impacts on shareholder wealth. The net present value method clearly satisfies these conditions better than other methods. Surveys of practitioners find, however, that NPV is not all that widely used; even more surprising is the continued popularity of non-DCF techniques as either primary or secondary evaluation methods.

Over time, studies have found that use of DCF techniques have become more prevalent among practitioners. Surveys indicate that IRR is the most favored capital budgeting analysis technique. The payback is especially popular as a secondary or supplementary method of analysis. One survey found that about 75 percent of CFOs use NPV, IRR, or both to evaluate capital budgeting projects. Surprisingly, over half of the firms computed the payback period, too, to help evaluate projects.[13] A survey of techniques used by multinational firms confirms these results.[14]

---

12. Christina Duff, "Discount Retailers Get No Quick Fix from Remodeling Stores, Study Says," *The Wall Street Journal*, March 27, 1995, p. A15C.
13. John R. Graham and Campbell R. Harvey, "The Theory and Practice of Corporate Finance: Evidence from the Field," *Journal of Financial Economics*, 2001, vol. 60, no. 1, 187–243.
14. M. Stanley and S. Block, "A Survey of Multinational Capital Budgeting," *Financial Review*, March 1984, pp. 36–54.

Why might real-world decision makers favor IRR and payback over net present value? One reason could be ignorance. Over time, surveys have shown that the use of discounted cash flow techniques has become more prevalent, perhaps because business schools have taught students the virtues of time value of money and NPV. The apparent sustaining power of IRR and payback techniques, however, suggests the possibility of other reasons. Let's examine several of them.

SAFETY MARGIN

Suppose an analyst tells you that the NPV of project Big is $100,000 while a competing project, project Small, has an NPV of $60,000. From our earlier discussion, you should select Big because of its larger NPV. But what if Big requires a $5 million investment while Small requires only a $600,000 investment? If the present value estimates of project Big cash flows are off by only 2 percent, the forecasted positive NPV becomes negative. The present value of Small's cash flows can deviate from plan by 10 percent before the project turns into a loser.

Suppose instead that the analyst tells you that Big's IRR is 10.5 percent, Small's IRR is 15 percent, and the required return is 10.0 percent. Would you feel confident that BIG is the more attractive project, despite its higher NPV? Perhaps not, as a small change in cash flows could push Big's actual IRR below 10 percent.

This rather contrived example illustrates why managers in the real world may prefer to use relative DCF measures such as the IRR or the profitability index. IRR and PI give the decision maker an intuitive feel for a project's "safety margin." The decision maker will sleep better at night after deciding to undertake a smaller project with a larger safety margin and reject a large project with a small safety margin. Most managers have seen reality defy forecasts and they know that an inadequate safety margin can make taking big investment risks unwise. Post-project audits can give the firm a better perspective on the accuracy or inaccuracy of its cash flow forecasting techniques. This information can help improve management's perspective on the safety cushion needed for a typical project.

MANAGERIAL FLEXIBILITY AND OPTIONS

The popularity of NPV and DCF techniques also suffers because they are difficult to apply in practice to projects that entail future investment opportunities or options. These techniques do not suit some situations in which managerial flexibility can be valuable. For example, if a project involves a joint venture, an R&D effort, or a move into new markets, management may face several choices once the project is underway. After seeing the initial results, management may decide to continue the project as planned, to expand its scope in the face of success, to decrease the scope of the project, to defer further investment, or to abandon the project completely. These kinds of decisions can help improve a project's potential for upside return while limiting its loss potential. Such flexibility is hard to model in terms of cash flows and discount rates. Payback periods, for example, may be useful as a means to give managers a general feel for how much time a project needs to at least break even and recover its costs.

Conflicts may arise when a firm tries to coordinate strategy analysis and shareholder value analysis. The numbers on the analyst's spreadsheet may fail to justify the actions that the corporate planner strongly feels will lead to competitive advantage and future investment opportunities. But strategic analysis and financial analysis, if properly applied, are compatible. More often than not, conflicts between these two sets of tools result from inadequate estimates of the cash flows from implementing a strategy. Unless the cash flows that result from a strategic plan are estimated correctly, good projects can be rejected on the basis of inaccurate NPVs or IRRs. The process of correctly estimating a project's cash flows is the subject of the next section.

CONCEPT QUIZ

What capital budgeting analysis techniques are the most popular primary and secondary evaluation methods among practitioners?

Why might managers prefer methods such as the IRR, PI, or payback method instead of NPV?

ESTIMATING PROJECT CASH FLOWS

This section reviews methods of developing such cash flow forecasts based on input from engineering, economic, and market analyses as well as from examination of the firm's competitive advantages.

ISOLATING PROJECT CASH FLOWS

stand-alone principle
analysis focuses on the project's own cash flows, uncontaminated by cash flows from the firm's other activities

To estimate properly the cash flows of a proposed capital budgeting project, the project must be viewed separately from the rest of the firm. This **stand-alone principle** ensures that analysts focus on the project's own cash flows, uncontaminated by cash flows from the firm's other activities. We should treat the project as its own minifirm and create financial statements that are specific to the project.

Relevant Project Cash Flows

The relevant cash flows of a project include its incremental after-tax cash flows, any cannibalization or enhancement effects, and opportunity costs.

incremental cash flows
represent the difference between the firm's after-tax cash flows with the project and the firm's after-tax cash flows without the project

Incremental After-Tax Cash Flows. The stand-alone principle requires the analyst to examine the future after-tax cash flows that occur only as a result of the project. These are the project's *incremental cash flows.* The cash flows are incremental as they represent the difference between the firm's after-tax cash flows with the project and its **base case**, or the after-tax cash flows without the project. To identify this difference, analysts must try to identify all cash flows that will rise or fall as a consequence of pursuing the future project. This includes any expected changes in revenues, expenses, and depreciation as well as investments in fixed assets and net working capital.

base case
firm's after-tax cash flows without the project

Managerial estimates need to be checked and verified as part of the capital budget review process; ethical lapses, such as inflating revenues and decreasing expenses to make a project look more attractive, may result in harm to the firm and reductions in shareholder wealth.

ETHICAL ISSUES

Estimating incremental after-tax cash flows for a project requires a more thorough analysis than determining the expected change in cash flows from the firm's current condition. If future strategic moves by competitors are expected to damage or eliminate a firm's competitive advantage, the firm's base case cash flow forecast should reflect this situation. A project's incremental cash flows would then reflect expected changes from this declining trend.

For example, a firm such as Intel must consider competitors' responses when it invests in R&D to develop new computer chips. Intel's base case must include the impact on its sales if it does not develop the next generation of computer chips first. In the fast-moving technology market, being second to market could mean billions of lost sales.

Intel has poured billions in factory improvement and expansion projects to increase its production capacity. The purpose is to maintain and increase Intel's competitive advantage over other chip manufacturers and to sustain cash flow growth. Greater capacity means greater economies of scale, lower costs, and better competitive position in the computer chip market. With forecasted chip demand experiencing double-digit growth rates each year, Intel needs additional capacity just to maintain its current market share of the chip market.

cannibalization
a project robs cash flow from the firm's existing lines of business

Cannibalization or Enhancement. *Cannibalization* occurs when a project robs cash flow from the firm's existing lines of business. When a soft-drink firm is thinking about introducing a new flavor or a new diet product, the project's incremental cash flows should consider how much the new offering will erode the sales and cash flows of the firm's other products. Corporate strategists reportedly considered how the introduction of Pepsi One, a new low-calorie cola soft drink product, would affect sales of Diet Pepsi and Pepsi-Cola.[15] Similarly, Intel engineers and strategists agonized for months before deciding it needed to design a new computer chip to try to advance the technology of its highly successful $\times$ 86 chip (the one that powers Pentium-class computers).[16]

enhancement
increase in the cash flows of the firm's other products that occur because of a new project

Enhancement is less common than cannibalization; it reflects an increase in the cash flows of the firm's other products that occur because of a new project. For example, adding a delicatessen to a grocery store may increase cash flows more than the deli sales alone if new deli customers also purchase grocery items.

opportunity cost
cost of passing up the next best alternative

Opportunity Costs. From economics, we know that an *opportunity cost* is the cost of passing up the next best alternative. For example, the opportunity cost of a building is its market value. By deciding to continue to own it, the firm is foregoing the cash it could receive from selling it. Economics teaches the TINSTAAFL principle: "there is no such thing as a free lunch." Capital budgeting analysis frequently applies this principle to existing assets.

---

15. Nikhil Deogun, "Pepsi Takes Aim at Coke With New One-Calorie Drink," *The Wall Street Journal*, October 5, 1998, p. B4.
16. David P. Hamilton, "Circuit Break:Gambling It Can Move Beyond PC, Intel Offers a New Microprocessor," *The Wall Street Journal*, May 29, 2001, pp. A1, A8.

sunk cost
project-related expense not dependent upon whether or not the project is undertaken

CONCEPT CHECK

What is the stand-alone principle?

What three categories of cash flows are relevant to measure for capital budgeting purposes?

What categories of cash flows are irrelevant for capital budgeting analysis?

If a firm is thinking about placing a new manufacturing plant in a building it already owns, the firm cannot assume that the building is free and assign it to the project at zero cost. The project's cash flow estimates should include the market value of the building as a cost of investing since this represents cash flows the firm cannot receive from selling the building.

Irrelevant Cash Flows

Now that we've examined some factors that influence cash flow estimates, let's look at some factors that should be excluded.

Sunk Costs. A *sunk cost* is a project-related expense that does not depend on whether or not the project is undertaken. For example, assume a firm commissioned and paid for a feasibility study for a project last year. The funds for the study are already committed and spent. The study's cost is not an incremental cash flow as it is not affected by the firm's future decision to either pursue or abandon the project. Therefore, the cost must be excluded from the project's cash flow estimates.

Financing Costs. It may seem important to account for financing cash flows such as interest and loan repayments, but there is a very good reason for excluding them from cash flow estimates. Capital budgeting analysis techniques explicitly consider the costs of financing a project when the analysis discounts project cash flows. As we shall discuss more fully in Chapter 18, a project's minimum required rate of return, or cost of capital, incorporates a project's financing costs.

APPROACHES TO ESTIMATING PROJECT CASH FLOWS

As an initial step of the financial analysis of a capital budgeting proposal, we should first construct year-by-year projected balance sheets and income statements for the project. Analysis of these forecasted statements tell us what the expected cash flows from the project will be. Changes over time in the project's working capital requirements or investment needs will represent cash inflows or outflows from the project. Similarly, the net income and noncash expenses from the project are part of the project's periodic cash flows too.

As discussed in Chapter 13, one of the financial statements that must be issued by public firms is the statement of cash flows. In this section, we use the format of the statement of cash flows to identify the periodic cash flows of a capital budgeting project.

Recall that a firm's statement of cash flows has three sections. The first, cash flows from operations, reports on cash generated by the firm's day-to-day manufacturing and marketing activities. The second section, cash flows from investments, usually involves data for investments in subsidiaries or the firm's plant and equipment. The third section lists the firm's financing cash flows, including sales and purchases of debt as well as dividend payments.

Using this format for a capital budgeting project, cash flows from operations summarize the sources of a project's operating cash flows. Cash flows from investing activities report a firm's fixed asset investments in the capital budgeting project. As explained earlier, cash flows from financing activities are excluded from a project's cash flow analysis since their impact is measured in the discount rate or cost of capital used to discount a project's cash flow.

Table 17.5 summarizes the similarities between company and project cash flow statements. The following sections explore these relationships in more detail.

CASH FLOW FROM OPERATIONS

Cash flow from operations is, quite simply, a measure of the cash entering and leaving the firm as a result of the firm's business. Cash flow from operations equals net income plus depreciation plus funds from sources arising from changes in current asset and liability accounts minus uses from changes in current asset and liability accounts for a given period of time. A period-by-period project income statement can estimate the net income from a project as in Table 17.6.

All sales revenues may not be cash inflows. For example, if customers buy the firm's products with credit, some of the increase in sales revenue may increase accounts receivable rather than cash. Similarly, not all costs reflect cash outflows. Such is the case if the firm buys supplies or raw materials on credit. Some expenses may be paid in cash and others may create changes in accounts payable. For reasons such as these, to compute cash flow we need to include an adjustment—the change in net working capital—to reflect such situations.

TABLE 17.5
Firm versus Project Statement of Cash Flows

THE FIRM'S CASH FLOW STATEMENT	A PROJECT'S CASH FLOW STATEMENT
Cash Flow from Operations	**Cash Flow from Operations**
Net Income	Net Income
+Depreciation	+ Depreciation
+current sources	+ current sources
−current uses	− current uses
Cash Flow from Investment Activities	**Cash Flow from Investment Activities**
−change in gross fixed assets	− Funds invested in the project's fixed assets
−change in investments	
Cash Flow from Financing Activities	**Cash Flow from Financing Activities**
−Dividends paid	Not applicable
+net new bond issues	
+net new stock issues	

TABLE 17.6
A Project Income Statement

Project sales	(generally a cash inflow)
− Project costs	(generally a cash outflow)
− Depreciation	(a non-cash expense)
EBIT = EBT	(earnings before interest and taxes, which also equals earnings before taxes as financing costs are ignored in cash flow analysis)
− Taxes	(a cash outflow)
Net income	

Depreciation is a noncash expense. Accounting rules allow us to compute taxable income by deducting depreciation expense from revenues although no cash leaves the firm. Since it is a noncash expense we add it back—after we compute net income—when we compute operating cash flows.

Thus, a project's operating cash flows are computed as:

Cash flow from operations = net income + depreciation − change in net working capital   (17.4)

where net income, as seen in Table 17.6, equals [sales − costs − depreciation − taxes]; if T represents the firm's tax rate, this relationship for net income becomes [(sales − costs − depreciation)(1 − T)].

In most cases of capital budgeting analysis, operating cash flow is calculated in part by using the traditional net working capital measure of current assets minus current liabilities. *This occurs since typically a project's cash flows are immediately returned to the firm. The project's balance sheet cash account always will be zero.* Thus, current sources and current uses can be summarized in the period-by-period change in a project's net working capital.[17]

A confusing point to some is "Why do we subtract the change in net working capital when computing operating cash flow?" To illustrate the reasoning for this, suppose current assets are $700 and current liabilities are $400; this means net working capital is $300. Cash comes into the firm if customers pay $200 of their accounts receivable. This reduces accounts receivable and current assets to $500 ($700 − $200 payment) and net working capital to $100 ($500 current assets − $400 current liabilities).[18] Thus, net working capital decreases when there is a source or

---

17. An exception to this rule is overseas projects. For internal financing purposes or because of currency restraints, some cash may remain with the overseas subsidiary. In this case, an overseas project's cash flows should include only the cash that is returned to the parent firm.

18. As noted in the prior paragraph, a capital budgeting project's balance sheet will typically always have a zero cash balance as all cash inflows are claimed by the firm and all cash outflows are paid by the firm.

inflow of operating cash to the firm. When we *subtract* this *negative* change in net working capital it becomes a *positive* addition to operating cash flow:

$$-(-\$200 \text{ change in net working capital}) = +\$200 \text{ change in operating cash flow.}$$

Conversely, suppose with $700 in current assets and $400 in current liabilities (and a net working capital of $700 − $400 = $300) we pay $150 in bills we owe to suppliers. Cash flows out of the firm and accounts payable falls by $150 as does current liabilities. The new value of current liabilities is $250 ($400 − $150), and the new value for net working capital is $700 − $250 = $450. Net working capital has risen +$150 from $300 to $450. Thus, net working capital increases when there is a use or outflow of operating cash from the firm. When we subtract this increase in net working capital it becomes a *reduction* to operating cash flow:

$$-(+\$150 \text{ change in net working capital}) = -\$150 \text{ change in operating cash flow.}$$

CONCEPT CHECK

How is the format of a firm's statement of cash flows correspond to that of a project's cash flow estimates?

Does an increase in net working capital increase or decrease operating cash flow? Explain.

When developing a project income statement, why does EBIT equal EBT?

CASH FLOW FROM INVESTMENT ACTIVITIES

Cash flow from investment activities will record the firm's period-by-period fixed asset investments in the capital project, namely the plant and equipment necessary to pursue the project. Cash flow from investments is usually negative at the beginning of a project as the firm spends cash to acquire, build, modify, or replace assets. The cash flow from investments may be positive at the end of a project if it sells assets for salvage value.

CASH FLOW FROM FINANCING ACTIVITIES

Capital budgeting analysis excludes cash flows from financing activities. As discussed earlier, relevant after-tax financing costs are incorporated into the discount rate used to discount estimated cash flows to the present.

AN EXAMPLE

Now let's look at an example. Suppose you are considering opening a campus ice cream shop. Your initial investment in depreciating assets will be $10,000, and your initial investment in net working capital (which will include such inventory items as cones, ice cream and toppings) will be $3,500. You forecast no future changes in net working capital. You will depreciate fixed assets on a straight-line basis over four years.[19]

The shop's forecasted net income is $0, $1,500, $2,500, and $4,000 over each of the next four years. At the end of four years, you expect to graduate with a bachelor's degree and some entrepreneurial work experience, and you will sell your enterprise to another student. You hope to be able to sell your business for $12,000. For simplicity, ignore any tax implications from the sale. What are the cash flows from this project?

It is sometimes easier to estimate cash flows if you construct a table, or use a spreadsheet, such as the one shown below. It summarizes, by year and by cash flow category, the project's incremental after-tax cash flows. For example, at the current time (year zero), the only expected cash flows are a $10,000 investment in fixed assets and a $3,500 outflow for net working capital. Depreciating the $10,000 in fixed assets on a straight-line basis over four years gives a yearly depreciation expense of $10,000/4 or $2,500.

Year one net income is expected to be $0; along with the $2,500 depreciation expense and no change in net working capital, year one's operating cash flow is estimated at $2,500. Since you anticipate no investing cash flows, year one's total cash flow is estimated to be $2,500.

The cash flows for years two, three, and four are computed similarly. In year four, the operating cash flows are supplemented by an investing cash flow of $12,000 from the sale of the business. Thus, year four's total cash flows sum to $18,500 : $4,000 from net income, $2,500 from depreciation, and $12,000 from the sale of the business.

---

19. Current income tax laws specify allowable methods for depreciating business assets. Accelerated depreciation methods are popular but they add an unnecessary layer of complexity to the discussion. Straight-line depreciation is a permitted method so we assume it in most of our discussions.

	OPERATING CASH FLOWS			INVESTING CASH FLOWS	
YEAR	NET INCOME +	DEPRECIATION −	CHANGE IN NWC	CHANGE IN FIXED ASSETS =	TOTAL CASH FLOW
0	$0	$0	$−3,500	$−10,000	$−13,500
1	0	2,500	0	0	2,500
2	1,500	2,500	0	0	4,000
3	2,500	2,500	0	0	5,000
4	4,000	2,500	0	12,000	18,500

If 12 percent is your required rate of return, the net present value of this endeavor is $7,236.90, so your personal wealth should rise from opening the ice cream shop.

DEPRECIATION AS A TAX SHIELD

Depreciation plays an important role in determining operating cash flow. As discussed above, it is a noncash expense. By deducting depreciation expense a firm lowers its pretax income (earnings before taxes or EBT), its tax bill, and its net income—and it increases its operating cash flow! A short example will show how this deduction *lowers* net income but *raises* operating cash flow.

Suppose JohnnyJim Products has $1,000 in sales and expenses for wages and supplies of $300. Let's see how a depreciation expense of $100 affects its profitability and its net income. Table 17.7 shows two income statements: one without depreciation expense and one with depreciation expense. To simplify the example we'll assume the change in net working capital is zero and that JohnnyJim's tax rate is 40 percent.

Using Equation 17.4, JohnnyJim's operating cash flow with depreciation is:

Cash flow from operations = net income + depreciation − change in net working capital

= $360 + $100 − $0 = $460

and its operating cash flow without depreciation is:

Cash flow from operations = net income + depreciation − change in net working capital

= $420 + $0 − $0 = $420

Although depreciation lowers its net income, JohnnyJim's operating cash flow is $40 higher with depreciation expense than without depreciation expense. The reason the operating cash flow with depreciation is $40 higher is because JohnnyJim's tax bill is $40 lower. By lowering earnings before taxes, noncash depreciation expense lowers a cash expense—taxes—by $40. This $40 reduction leads to an operating cash flow that is $40 higher than the case of no depreciation.

The $40 savings in taxes arises from a combination of the tax rate t and the depreciation expense. With a 40 percent tax rate, a depreciation expense of $100 increases expenses—and lowers taxes—by (0.40)($100) or $40.

This term, $(t)(\text{Depreciation})$, the tax rate multiplied by the depreciation expense, is called the **depreciation tax shield**. It represents the tax savings the firm receives from its noncash depreciation expense. With a 40 percent tax rate, a depreciation expense of $100 reduces a firm's tax bill by $40.

depreciation tax shield
tax reduction due to depreciation of fixed assets; equals the amount of the depreciation expense multiplied by the firm's tax rate

TABLE 17.7
JohnnyJim Projects Income Statements, With and Without Depreciation Expense

	WITH DEPRECIATION EXPENSE	WITHOUT DEPRECIATION EXPENSE
Sales	$1000	$1000
−Costs	−300	−300
−Depreciation	−100	0
EBT	$600	$700
−Taxes (40%)	240	280
Net Income	$360	$420

CONCEPT CHECK

How does depreciation affect a project's cash flows?

What is meant by the term depreciation tax shield?

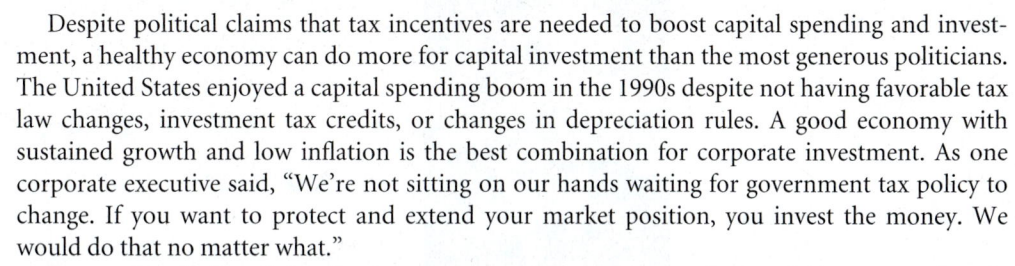

Despite political claims that tax incentives are needed to boost capital spending and investment, a healthy economy can do more for capital investment than the most generous politicians. The United States enjoyed a capital spending boom in the 1990s despite not having favorable tax law changes, investment tax credits, or changes in depreciation rules. A good economy with sustained growth and low inflation is the best combination for corporate investment. As one corporate executive said, "We're not sitting on our hands waiting for government tax policy to change. If you want to protect and extend your market position, you invest the money. We would do that no matter what."

Economists do favor incentives, such as a capital gains tax cut, that would increase savings in the economy. Greater savings, all else being constant, would mean lower interest rates, higher stock prices, and lower financing costs for firms buying plant and equipment.[20]

ETHICAL ISSUES

KEEPING MANAGERS HONEST

The fifth stage of the capital budgeting process we reviewed at the beginning of the chapter—the follow-up—is sometimes called the audit or control phase. In this stage, a firm's financial analysts track the spending and results of the firm's current capital budgeting projects.

Many firms review spending during the implementation stage of approved projects. Quarterly reports are often required in which the manager overseeing the project summarizes spending to date, compares it to budgeted amounts, and explains differences between the two. Such oversight during the implementation stage allows top managers to foresee cost overruns. Some firms require projects that are expected to exceed their budgets by a certain dollar amount or percentage to file new appropriation requests to secure the additional funds. Implementation audits allow managers to learn about potential trouble areas so future proposals can account for them in their initial analysis; implementation audits also give top management information on which managers generally provide the best estimates of project costs.

Besides implementation control, firms should also compare forecasted cash flows to actual performance after the project has been completed. This provides data regarding the accuracy over time of cash flow forecasts; this will permit the firm to discover what went right with the project, what went wrong, and why. Audits force management to discover and justify any major deviations of actual performance from forecasted performance. Specific reasons for deviations from budget are needed for the experience to be helpful to all involved.

An effective control system will record the names of the persons who make the estimates so top management can evaluate business units and managers on the accuracy of their estimates. Such a system pinpoints personal responsibility. If, for example, a department head estimates that a proposed expenditure would allow the department to reduce personnel by 10 percent, the department head can be questioned if the proposed cuts do not come to pass. Such a system will control intra-firm agency problems by helping to help reduce 'padding,' i.e., overestimating the benefits of favorite or convenient project proposals. This increases the incentives for department heads to manage in ways that help the firm achieve its goals.

The control or post-audit phase sometimes requires the firm to consider terminating or abandoning an approved project. The possibility of abandoning an investment prior to the end of its estimated useful or economic life expands the options available to management and reduces the risk associated with a decision that turns out to be a poor one. This form of contingency planning gives decision makers a second chance when dealing with the economic and political uncertainties of the future.

In a survey, researchers found that three-fourths of responding *Fortune* 500 firms audited their cash flow estimates.[21] Nearly all of the firms that performed audits compared initial investment outlay estimates with actual costs; all evaluated operating cash flow estimates; two-thirds audited salvage value estimates.

---

20. Joseph Spiers, "The Most Important Economic Event of the Decade," *Fortune*, April 3, 1995, pp. 33–40.
21. R. Pohlman, E. Santiago, and F. Markel, "Cash Flow Estimation Practices at Large Firms," *Financial Management*, Summer 1988, pp. 71–78.

CAREER PROFILES

TIM KISH
Vice President and Chief Financial Officer
Illumina Corp.

BBA, Accounting, Michigan State University
MBA, University of Minnesota.

"My role as Illumina's CFO is to maximize the shareholder value of the firm."

Q: *Please describe Illumina and its products.*

A: Illumina is a biotechnology company that develops next-generation tools for the large-scale analysis of genetic variation and function. The information provided by these tools will enable the development of personalized medicine by correlating genetic variation and function with particular disease states, allowing diseases to be detected earlier and more specifically and permitting better choices of drugs for individual patients.

Q: *What are your responsibilities as chief financial officer?*

A: My role as Illumina's CFO is similar to most other publicly held companies—to maximize the shareholder value of the firm. I have three broad job responsibilities: raising capital at reasonable rates to fund growth, spending the right amount of money on corporate activities that contribute to growth, and communicating the company's business strategies and results to the financial markets so that the company's intrinsic value is reflected in its stock price.

Q: *What skills do you need to accomplish these responsibilities?*

A: Successful financial managers must have strong analytical skills. They must understand trends at strategic, commercial and operational levels, as well as identify and help resolve financial and operating issues. Excellent interpersonal, communication, and persuasion skills are extremely important, too. CFOs do not control operating departments but must convey their business and financial expertise to motivate the behavior of the managers of those departments. They also need managerial and leadership skills so that they are seen as "influencers" in the organization and can develop a highly capable staff.

Q: *How do you make capital investment decisions at Illumina?*

A: Illumina first establishes an annual target amount for its anticipated capital expenditures based on the company's cash flow and the types of assets required to accomplish our corporate objectives. We then carefully review each new investment proposal to ensure that it is consistent with our strategic or operating plans at that time and that the value provided by the asset will exceed its cost by an acceptable margin. We use discounted cash flow analysis to determine if a project's future benefits exceed its total costs, making adjustments to incorporate risk. We also monitor the project once it is underway to make sure that actual costs and benefits are consistent with the original expectations.

Q: *What are the challenges of capital budgeting?*

A: Understanding how to deal with risk and uncertainty. To properly analyze the future value of a project, we have to make assumptions about alternative uses and project cash flows. In many cases, we can estimate the economic assumptions and alternatives within reasonable ranges. In those situations, we use special techniques to measure the risk that the project will have unfavorable economics.

CONCEPT CHECK

Why are audits important to project implementation?

What useful information can be discovered by comparing forecasted and actual cash flows?

Which type of cash flow—initial investments, operating flows, or salvage values—are the hardest to estimate?

About two-thirds of firms that performed audits claimed that actual initial investment outlay estimates usually were within 10 percent of forecasts. Only 43 percent of firms that performed audits could make the same claim with respect to operating cash flows. Over 30 percent of the firms confessed that operating cash flow estimates differed from actual performance by 16 percent or more.[22]

To be successful, the cash flow estimation process requires a commitment by the corporation and its top policy-setting managers; this commitment includes the type of management information system the firm uses to support the estimation process. Past experience in estimating cash flows, requiring cash flow estimates for all projects, and maintaining systematic approaches to cash flow estimation appear to help firms achieve success in accurately forecasting cash flows.

In volatile economic environments, such as the first decade of the 21st century, business professionals know that historical averages and point estimates are likely to be incorrect. The business environment is complex and is affected, as we saw in 2007–2009, by factors that are beyond a manager's control.

We introduced the concept of scenario analysis in Chapter 12 as a means to gauge outcomes in an uncertain future. More and more professionals at all levels of business have realized the value of playing "what if" scenarios and creating plans for what should be done if certain economic and business events occur.[23]

RISK-RELATED CONSIDERATIONS

The degree of risk associated with expected cash inflows may vary substantially among different investments. For example, a decision about whether to replace an existing machine with a new, more efficient machine would not involve substantial cash inflow uncertainty because the firm already has some operating experience with the existing machine. Likewise, expansion in existing product lines allows the firm to base cash flow expectations on past operating results and marketing data. These capital budgeting decisions can be made by discounting cash flows at the firm's cost of capital, or required rate of return, because they are comparable in risk to the firm's other assets.

Expansion projects involving new areas, new product lines, and overseas expansion are usually associated with greater cash inflow uncertainty. To compensate for this greater risk, financial managers use concepts based upon the tradeoff between risk and expected return. A higher-risk project needs to be evaluated using a higher required rate of return. To use a financial markets analogy, given the current return offered on safe short-term Treasury bills, investors will not want to invest in risky common stocks unless the expected returns are commensurate with the higher risk of stocks. Similarly, managers should not choose higher-risk capital budgeting projects unless the project's expected returns are in line with their risks.

The **risk-adjusted discount rate (RADR)** approach does this; it adjusts the required rate of return at which the analyst discounts a project's cash flows. Projects with higher (or lower) risk levels demand higher (or lower) discount rates. A project is expected to enhance shareholder wealth only if its NPV based on a risk-adjusted discount rate is positive.

risk-adjusted discount rate (RADR)
adjusts the required rate of return at which the analyst discounts a project's cash flows based on the project's risk

One way to determine project risk-adjusted discount rates is for the firm's managers to use past experience to create risk classes or categories for different types of capital budgeting projects. Each risk category can be given a generic description to indicate the types of projects it should include and a required rate of return or "hurdle rate" to assign those projects.[24]

An example is shown in Table 17.8, which assigns projects of average risk (or those whose risk is about the same as the firm's overall risk) a discount rate equal to the firm's cost of capital. That is, projects of average risk must earn an average return, as defined by the firm's cost of financing. Projects with below-average risk levels are discounted at a rate below the cost of capital. Projects of above-average risk must earn premiums over the firm's cost of capital to be acceptable.

---

22. In the last chapter, we argued that safety margin concerns may lead managers to prefer selection methods such as IRR and PI over NPV. With error rates such as these, it is easy to see why safety margins would concern analysts and decision makers.

23. Vincent Ryan, "Future Tense," *CFO*, December 2008, p. 37–42.

24. Another, more complicated technique, is to use the Capital Asset Pricing Model. A "beta" is calculated for each project based on analysis of firms in lines of business similar to that of the proposed project. The Security Market Line is used with the beta estimate to approximate the project's required return.

TABLE 17.8
Risk Categories, RMEN Corporation

Below-average risk:
　Replacement decisions that require no change, or only a minor change, in technology; no change in plant layout required
　Discount rate = Cost of capital − 2%

Average risk:
　Replacement decisions involving significant changes in technology or plant layout; all cost-saving decisions; expansions and improvements in the firm's main product lines
　Discount rate = Cost of capital

Above-average risk:
　Applied research and development; introduction of new products not related to major product lines; expansion of production or marketing efforts into developed economies in Europe and Asia
　Discount rate = Cost of capital + 2%

High risk:
　Expansion of production or marketing efforts into less-developed and emerging economies; introduction of products not related to any of the firm's current product lines
　Discount rate = Cost of capital + 5%

Subjectivity enters this process as management must decide the number of categories, the description of each risk category, and the required rate of return to assign to each category. Differences of opinion or internal firm politics may lead to controversy in classifying a project. Clearly defined category descriptions can minimize such problems.

For example, let's use the previously presented data for projects A and B to illustrate the use of risk-adjusted discount rates. Let's assume that project A and B are independent projects. Project A involves expansion in an existing product line, whereas project B is for a new product. The firm's cost of capital, 10 percent, would be the appropriate discount rate for project A. Recall that this would result in a net present value of $1,982.

In contrast, a higher discount rate for project B's cash flows of possibly 12 percent—the 10 percent cost of capital plus a 2 percentage point risk premium—might be judged appropriate by the financial manager. This would result in a net present value of −$514. Thus, on a risk-adjusted basis, project A would still be acceptable to the firm, but project B would be rejected. Making adjustments for risk differences is a difficult but necessary task if the financial manager is to make capital budgeting decisions that will increase the value of the firm.

SUMMARY

A firm's long-term success depends on its strategy and its competitors' actions. The capital budget allocates funds to different projects, usually long-term, that are primarily used to purchase fixed assets to help a firm build or maintain a competitive advantage.

The capital budgeting process is composed of five stages: identification, development, selection, implementation, and follow-up. Since the capital budgeting process involves the analysis of cash flows over time, it is best to examine projects using a selection technique that considers the time value of money. The net present value, internal rate of return, modified internal rate of return and profitability index are four such methods. A fifth method, the payback period, measures how quickly a project will pay for itself but ignores time value concerns. Of these selection methods, the net present value is the best, as it measures the dollar amount by which a project will change shareholder wealth.

Estimating cash flows is a difficult part of evaluating capital budgeting projects. Projected earnings must be converted into cash flows by using the methods discussed in this chapter. Depreciation expense acts as a tax shield, because it reduces a project's tax bill and works to increase a project's after-tax cash flows.

By focusing solely on numbers, financial analysts of capital budgeting projects can lose sight of the strategic importance behind the analysis. On the other hand, strategists need to be made aware of the need for shareholder value-enhancing projects. Analysts must be sure the financial analysis includes the correct base case, includes cannibalization and competitor retaliation effects, and includes proper risk adjustments. As with financial market investments, corporate investments should include risk/expected return considerations. Higher-risk projects should be evaluated using higher discount rates.

The next chapter examines how firms can estimate their cost of capital. This is important, as the cost of financing the firm will be used as the discount rate for evaluating average-risk capital budgeting projects.

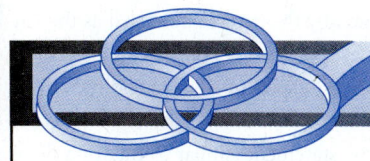

APPLYING FINANCE TO...

INSTITUTIONS AND MARKETS

Financial institutions and markets play an indirect role in the capital budgeting process. The participants comprising the markets use the flow of information from the firm and its competitors, as well as economic and industry conditions, to evaluate firms. Their analysis and reactions are seen in the firm's stock price changes and bond rating changes. In turn, market return expectations are used to determine the discount rate in the net present value calculation. This process will be covered in detail in Chapter 18.

INVESTMENTS

Investors, security analysts, and portfolio managers are continually evaluating a firm's performance. Investment in projects likely to return a positive net present value is a sign of forward-thinking managers who have shareholder interests at heart. Stock price and bond ratings respond favorably to a firm's wealth-maximizing capital budgeting and resource allocation decisions.

FINANCIAL MANAGEMENT

A way to operationalize shareholder wealth maximization is to identify and select projects that are expected to have positive net present values. Managers must properly use capital budgeting evaluation techniques, adjust project evaluation for risk, and seek to invest in projects that enhance shareholder value.

KEY TERMS

base case
cannibalization
capital budgeting
cost of capital
depreciation tax shield
development stage
enhancement
follow-up stage
identification stage
implementation stage
incremental cash flow
independent projects
internal rate of return (IRR) method
modified internal rate of return (MIRR) method
MOGS
mutually exclusive projects
net present value (NPV)
NPV profile
opportunity cost
payback period method
profitability index (PI)
risk-adjusted discount rate (RADR)
selection stage
stand-alone principle
sunk cost
SWOT analysis

DISCUSSION QUESTIONS

1. What is capital budgeting? Briefly describe some characteristics of capital budgeting.

2. Why is proper management of fixed assets crucial to the success of a firm?

3. How do "mutually exclusive" and "independent" projects differ?

4. Where do businesses find attractive capital budgeting projects?

5. Briefly describe the five stages in the capital budgeting process.

6. Identify some capital budgeting considerations that are unique to multinational corporations.

7. What kinds of financial data are needed to conduct project analysis?

8. What kinds of nonfinancial information are needed to conduct project analysis?

9. What is meant by a project's net present value? How is it used for choosing among projects?

10. Identify the internal rate of return method and describe how it is used in making capital budgeting decisions.

11. How does the modified internal rate of return measure improve upon the IRR measure?

12. Describe the term "profitability index," and explain how it is used to compare projects.

13. Why do the NPV, IRR, and profitability index technique sometimes rank projects differently?

14. Describe the payback period method for making capital budgeting decisions.

15. Why might managers want to use other techniques besides NPV to make capital budgeting decisions?

16. How is the "stand-alone principle" applied when evaluating whether to invest in projects?

17. What are the three types of relevant cash flows to be considered in analyzing a project?

18. Label each of the following as a cannibalization effect, enhancement effect, or neither. Explain your answers.

   a. A computer manufacturer seeks to produce a high quality engineering work station, thinking that consumers will believe the firm's standard PC products will also be of higher quality.

   b. An airline offers taxicab service to and from the airport.

   c. A gas station adds service bays and a small convenience store.

   d. A mainframe computer manufacturer begins to sell personal computers.

e. A snack food manufacturer starts marketing a new line of fat-free snacks.

f. A firm seeks to export its products to foreign countries.

19. What types of cash flows are considered irrelevant when analyzing a project?

20. "Our firm owns property around Chicago that would be an ideal location for the new warehouse, and since we already own the land, there isn't any cash flow needed to purchase it." Do you agree or disagree with this statement? Explain

21. "Our bank will finance the product expansion project with at a loan interest rate of 10 percent. Make sure the project's cash flow estimates include this interest expense." Do you agree or disagree? Explain.

22. Classify each of the following as a sunk cost, an opportunity cost, or neither.

   a. The firm has spent $1 million thus far to develop the next-generation robotic arm; it is now examining whether the project should continue.

   b. A piece of ground owned by the firm can be used as the site for a new facility.

   c. It is anticipated another $200,000 of R&D spending will be needed to work out the bugs of a new software package.

23. How is a project's cash flow statement similar to that of a firm? How is it different?

24. Why is the change in net working capital included in operating cash flow estimates?

25. Why is depreciation considered to be a "tax shield"?

26. What is a way to keep managers accountable for their capital budgeting forecasts and estimates?

27. What is a risk-adjusted discount rate? How are risk-adjusted discount rates determined for individual projects?

PROBLEMS

1. Find the NPV and PI of a project that costs $1,500 and returns $800 in year one and $850 in year two. Assume the project's cost of capital is 8 percent.

2. Find the NPV and PI of an annuity that pays $500 per year for eight years and costs $2,500. Assume a discount rate of 6 percent.

3. Find the IRR of a project that returns $17,000 three years from now if it costs $12,000.

4. Find the IRR and MIRR of a project if it has estimated cash flows of $5,500 annually for seven years if its year-zero investment is $25,000 and the firm's minimum required rate of return on the project is 10 percent.

5. For the following projects, compute NPV, IRR, MIRR, profitability index, and payback. If these projects are mutually exclusive, which one(s) should be done? If they are independent, which one(s) should be undertaken?

	i. A	B	C	D
Year 0	−1,000	−1,500	−500	−2,000
Year 1	400	500	100	600
Year 2	400	500	300	800
Year 3	400	700	250	200
Year 4	400	200	200	300
Discount rate	10%	12%	15%	8%

6. The Sanders Electric Company is evaluating two projects for possible inclusion in the firm's capital budget. Project M will require a $37,000 investment while project O's investment will be $46,000. After-tax cash inflows are estimated as follows for the two projects:

YEAR	PROJECT M	PROJECT O
1	$12,000	$10,000
2	12,000	10,000
3	12,000	15,000
4	12,000	15,000
5	15,000	

a. Determine the payback period for each project.

b. Calculate the net present value and profitability index for each project based on a 10 percent cost of capital. Which, if either, of the projects is acceptable?

c. Determine the internal rate of return and modified internal rate of return for Projects M and O.

7. AA Auto Parts Company has a corporate tax rate of 34 percent and depreciation of $19,180. Compute its depreciation tax shield.

8. A project is estimated to generate sales revenue of $10 million with expenses of $9 million. No change in net working capital is expected. Marginal profits will be taxed at a 35 percent rate. If the project's operating cash flow is $1 million, what is the project's depreciation expense? Its net income?

9. Compute operating cash flows for the following:

   a. A project that is expected to have sales of $10,000, expenses of $5,000, depreciation of $200, an investment of $50 in net working capital, and a 20 percent tax rate.

   b. A project has the simplified project income statement below. In addition, assume that the project requires a $75 investment in net working capital.

Sales	$925.00
−Costs	−315.00
−Depreciation	−100.00
EBIT=EBT	510.00
−Taxes (at 34%)	−173.40
Net Income	336.60

   c. For a capital budgeting proposal, assume this year's cash sales are forecast to be $220, cash expenses $130, and depreciation $80. Assume the firm is in the 30 percent tax bracket.

10. A machine can be purchased for $10,500, including transportation charges, but installation costs will require $1,500 more. The machine is expected to last four years and produce annual cash revenues of $6,000. Annual cash operating expenses are expected

to be $2,000, with depreciation of $3,000 per year. The firm has a 30 percent tax rate. Determine the relevant after-tax cash flows and prepare a cash flow schedule.

11. Use the information in Problem 10 to do the following:
   a. Calculate the payback period for the machine.
   b. If the project's cost of capital is 10 percent, would you recommend buying the machine?
   c. Estimate the internal rate of return for the machine.

12. The Brassy Fin Pet Shop is considering an expansion. Construction will cost $90,000 and will be depreciated to zero, using straight-line depreciation, over five years. Earnings before depreciation are expected to be $20,000 in each of the next five years. The firm's tax rate is 34 percent.
   a. What are the project's cash flows?
   b. Should the project be undertaken if the firm's cost of capital is 11 percent?

13. The following is a simplified project annual income statement for Ma & Pa Incorporated for each year of an eight-year project. Its upfront cost is $2,000. Its cost of capital is 12 percent.

Sales	$925.00
less cash expenses	310.00
less depreciation	250.00
Earnings before taxes	$365.00
Less taxes (at 35%)	127.75
Net income	$237.25

   a. Compute the project's after-tax cash flow.
   b. Compute and interpret the project's NPV, IRR, profitability index, and payback period.

14. **Challenge Problem** Annual savings from Project X include a reduction of ten clerical employees with annual salaries of $15,000 each, $8,000 from reduced production delays, $12,000 from lost sales due to inventory stock-outs, and $3,000 in reduced utility costs. Project X costs $250,000 and will be depreciated over a five-year period using straight-line depreciation. Incremental expenses of the system include two new operators with annual salaries of $40,000 each and operating expenses of $12,000 per year. The firms' tax rate is 34 percent.
   a. Find Project X's initial cash outlay.
   b. Find the project's operating cash flows over the five-year period.
   c. If the project's required return is 12 percent, should it be implemented?

15. **Challenge Problem** You are considering becoming a franchisee with the Kopy-Kopy Copy and Pizza Delivery Service. For $50,000 they give you training and exclusive territorial rights.
    Equipment can be purchased through the home office for an additional $50,000, all of which will be straight-line depreciated. The home office estimates your territory can generate $100,000 in sales volume in the first year and that sales will grow 10 percent in each of the following four years, at which time you plan on selling the business for $50,000, after tax. From reading their brochures and talking to several other franchisees, you believe that costs, excluding depreciation, are about 60 percent of sales. You also know that the home office requires you to pay a 15 percent royalty on your gross sales revenue.
    Using a 30 percent tax rate and a 10 percent return requirement, how will this opportunity affect your personal wealth?

16. **Challenge Problem** The ice cream shop described in the text has been a smash success. Customers from the next college town are pleading with you to open one closer to them. Based on your operating experience and knowledge of local real estate, you believe that opening a new ice cream shop will require an investment of $20,000 in fixed assets and $3,000 in working capital. Fixed assets will be straight-line depreciated over five years. Preliminary market research indicates that sales revenue in the first year should be about $50,000 and that variable costs, excluding depreciation, will be about 80 percent of sales. To be on the safe side, you assume sales revenue will not change over the next five years. At the end of five years, you estimate you can sell your business, after-tax, for $25,000. Using a 28 percent tax rate and a 12 percent required return, should you expand?

17. **Challenge Problem** Sensitivity analysis involves changing one variable at a time in a capital budgeting situation and seeing how NPV changes. Perform sensitivity analysis on the each of the following variables in Problem 16 to determine its effect on NPV.
    a. Sales can be 10 percent higher or lower than expected each year.
    b. Expenses may be 10 percent higher or lower than expected each year.
    c. Your initial investment in fixed assets and working capital may be 50 percent higher than originally estimated.

18. Project R requires an investment of $45,000 and is expected to produce after-tax cash inflows of $15,000 per year for five years. The cost of capital is 10 percent.
    a. Determine the payback period, the net present value, and the profitability index for Project R. Is the project acceptable?
    b. Now, assume that the appropriate risk-adjusted discount rate is 14 percent. Calculate the risk-adjusted net present value. Is the project acceptable after adjusting for its greater risk?
    c. Calculate the internal rate of return.

19. Assume the financial manager of the Sanders Electric Company in Problem 6 believes that Project M is comparable in risk to the firm's other assets. In contrast, there is greater uncertainty concerning Project O's after-tax cash inflows. Sanders Electric uses a 4 percentage point risk premium for riskier projects. The firm's cost of capital is 10 percent.
    a. Determine the risk-adjusted net present values for Project M and Project O, using risk-adjusted discount rates where appropriate.
    b. Are both projects acceptable investments? Which one would you choose?

20. The BioTek Corporation has a basic cost of capital of 15 percent and is considering investing in either or both of the following projects. Project HiTek will require an investment of $453,000, while Project LoTek's investment will be $276,000. The following after-tax cash flows (including the investment outflows in year zero) are estimated for each project.

YEAR	PROJECT HITEK	PROJECT LOTEK
0	$-453,000	$-276,000
1	132,000	74,000
2	169,500	83,400
3	193,000	121,000
4	150,700	54,900
5	102,000	101,000
6	0	29,500
7	0	18,000

a. Determine the present value of the cash inflows for each project and then calculate their net present values by subtracting the appropriate dollar amount of capital investment. Which, if either, of the projects is acceptable?
b. Calculate the internal rates of return for Project HiTek and Project LoTek. Which project would be preferred?
c. Now assume that BioTek uses risk-adjusted discount rates to adjust for differences in risk among different investment opportunities. BioTek projects are discounted at the firm's cost of capital of 15 percent. A risk premium of 3 percentage points is assigned to LoTek-type projects, while a 6 percentage point risk premium is used for projects similar to HiTek. Determine the risk-adjusted present value of the cash inflows for LoTek and HiTek and calculate their risk-adjusted net present values. Should BioTek invest in either, both, or neither project?

LEARNING EXTENSION 17

Estimating Project Cash Flows

How are cash flow estimates developed? In this section we present a practical overview of how an analyst develops the data to estimate cash flows.

PROJECT STAGES AND CASH FLOW ESTIMATION

A typical project encompasses three stages. First there is the initial outlay or investment. Second is the operating life of the project, be it market expansion, a building, or technology. The final stage is at the end of the project's useful life. For projects involving fixed assets or business lines, this can involve selling assets and reclaiming working capital. But for projects that have an indefinite life—such as business expansion—a few years of careful cash flow estimations may give way in the third stage to an estimate of terminal value—that is, what the present value of project cash flows might be far into the future. We'll examine each of the three stages below.

INITIAL OUTLAY

The first cash flow estimate is the initial investment in the project. Engineering estimates may be available for projects that require designing or modifying equipment and buildings. Engineers will examine preliminary designs or architectural sketches and estimate the quantities of various materials needed. Estimates of purchases, transportation costs, and construction expenses can be developed based on current market prices.

Another means of estimating the acquisition or construction cost of a project is to solicit bids from various construction or equipment manufacturers based upon a preliminary set of design specifications. An approximate cost can be determined through discussions with bidding firms. If the firm is large enough that it has an in-house engineering or real estate acquisition staff, this expertise can also be tapped to estimate relevant costs.

The expense of developing cost estimates is a sunk cost. That money is spent and gone whether or not the proposed project is accepted; it should not be included in the project's cash flow estimates. However, the initial outlay estimate must consider opportunity costs if the project will use property or equipment presently owned by the firm.

The investment cost estimate may have to be adjusted if the project involves replacing an asset with another, presumably newer and more cost efficient model. If the old asset is going to be sold, the investment outlay must be reduced by the after-tax proceeds from the sale of the old asset. We will shortly discuss some of the specifics of adjusting for salvage value.

Finally, even though a project's initial outlay may directly involve property and equipment (investing cash flows), it may also have implications for net working capital (operating cash flows). For example, if a project affects the firm's production process, inventory levels

CONCEPT CHECK

How can a firm estimate the initial investing cash flows for a project?

When might a project's initial outlays include changes in net working capital?

may change. New raw materials needs may affect accounts payable. These kinds of expected changes in net working capital must be included as part of the initial outlay.

CASH FLOWS DURING THE PROJECT'S OPERATING LIFE

Operating cash flows can be estimated using Equation 17.4. The practical difficulty, of course, is determining the amounts for sales, costs, depreciation, taxes, and net working capital changes to enter into the calculations.

A project with the main purpose of reducing costs should have a presumed impact on sales of zero. Expected cost savings can be derived from engineering estimates or production management techniques. Suppliers can often estimate the potential cost savings from new machines or processes, but these sales claims may not be wholly trustworthy; the careful manager runs independent tests and trial runs, preferably at the plant that will house the new project, to verify any claims.

One asset often replaces another in cost-saving projects. This can involve a difference in depreciation schedules between the old and new asset (not to mention salvage value differences), which the analyst must incorporate into the analysis. More will be said about this point later in the chapter when we review an example.

CONCEPT CHECK

How can operating cash flow estimates be developed for cost-saving projects?

How can operating cash flow estimates be developed for revenue-expanding projects?

Revenue-enhancing or revenue-sustaining projects build or protect a firm's competitive advantage or extend its market penetration. Market researchers can provide detailed data about new products or features and the costs to develop them to help the financial analyst construct cash flow estimates. Such research may include sales forecasts or information on price, quantity, and quality trends in the market segment. If the project concerns one of the firm's current products, the production staff can often provide data to estimate the cost implications of greater sales. If the project involves a new product offering, engineers or the production staff should be able to provide production cost estimates. Depreciation expense can be estimated from the estimated initial investment outlay for the property or equipment needed for the project.

Net working capital may be expected to change over the course of the project's life. Operating cash flow estimates must reflect these changes in net working capital.

SALVAGE VALUE AND NWC RECOVERY AT PROJECT TERMINATION

If the project is expected to have a definite life span, the analysis must consider the salvage value of the project's assets. Any increases in net working capital in the course of a project are generally assumed to be recovered by the firm and converted to cash at the project's end.

Any property or equipment that is expected to be sold, either for use by someone else or for scrap, will generate inflows. The cash flow for the sale will have to be adjusted to account for tax implications if the asset's selling price differs from its book value.

INTERNET ACTIVITY

Some firms sell old equipment on auction sites, such as http://www.ebay.com, in order to recover final or "salvage" cash flows at the end of a project's term. Another more business-oriented site is http://www.salvagesale.com.

Book value (BV) represents an asset's original cost less accumulated depreciation. At the end of a project, if the selling price of an asset equals its book value there is no need for tax adjustments; the after-tax cash flow equals the selling price.

If the asset's selling price exceeds its book value, then in effect the asset was depreciated too quickly on the firm's books. The amount of the recovered depreciation (Price − BV) is taxed at the firm's marginal tax rate for ordinary income. Thus, the tax owed the government is t(Price − BV). The total after-tax proceeds will be Price − t(Price − BV), that is, the selling price less the tax obligation.

If the selling price is less than the asset's book value, the firm suffers a loss. This loss reflects failure to depreciate the asset's book value quickly enough. The firm's taxable income is reduced by the amount of the loss, and taxes will be reduced by t(Price − BV).

Note that if t(Price − BV) is positive, the firm owes taxes, reducing the after-tax proceeds of the asset sale; if t(Price − BV) is negative, the firm reduces its tax bill, in essence increasing the after-tax proceeds of the sale. When t(Price − BV) is zero, the transaction causes is no tax adjustment to be made. Thus, a general relationship for the after-tax salvage value is:

$$\text{After-tax salvage value} = \text{Price} - t(\text{Price} - \text{BV}) \qquad (\text{LE17.1})$$

Let's look at an example. Assume that an asset originally cost $100, had an expected life of 10 years, and was depreciated on a straight-line basis. Seven years later, the firm must determine the after-tax cash flow from selling the asset if the selling price is (a) $50, (b) $30, or (c) $15. Assume the marginal tax rate for ordinary income is 34 percent.

The first thing we need to do is determine the asset's book value; then Equation LE17.1 can be used to compute cash flows for three situations. With an original cost of $100 and straight-line depreciation over ten years, its yearly depreciation expense is $100/10 = $10. As seven years have passed, accumulated depreciation is now $70 (7 × $10/year), so the asset's book value is $100 minus $70, or $30.

If the asset's sale price is $50, the firm has recovered some past depreciation and it must reduce the salvage value cash flow by the resulting tax liability. The after-tax salvage value is Price − t(Price − BV) = $50 − 0.34($50 − $30) = $43.20.

If the asset's sale price is $30, this price equals the book value. According to Equation LE17.1, the after-tax salvage value is $30: Price − t(Price − BV) = $30 − 0.34($30 − $30) = $30.

If the asset's sale price is $15, the firm suffers a loss as the price is below book value. This means the salvage value cash flow will rise above $15 by the amount of the subsequent tax savings. The after-tax cash flow equals Price − t(Price − BV) = $15 − 0.34($15 − $30) = $20.10.

By their nature, after-tax salvage values are difficult to estimate as both the salvage value and expected future tax rate are uncertain. As a practical matter, if the project termination is many years in the future, the present value of the salvage proceeds will be small and inconsequential to the analysis. If necessary, however, the analyst can try to develop a salvage value forecast in two ways. First, one could try to tap the expertise of those involved in secondary market uses of the asset. Second, one could try to forecast future scrap material prices for the asset. Typically, the after-tax salvage cash flow is calculated using the firm's current tax rate as an estimate for the future tax rate.

The problems of estimating values in the distant future become worse when the project involves a major strategic investment that the firm expects to maintain over a long period of time. In such a situation, the firm may estimate annual cash flows for a number of years (say, ten years) and then attempt to estimate the project's value as a going concern at the end of this time horizon. One method the firm can use to estimate the project's going-concern value is the constant dividend growth model discussed in Chapter 10:

$$\text{Price}_{\text{horizon}} = \frac{\text{Dividend}_{\text{horizon}+1}}{r - g} \qquad \text{(LE17.2)}$$

The "salvage value" of the project is its going-concern value at the end of the time horizon; the dividend is its expected operating cash flow one year past the horizon. The required rate of return, r, is the project's required return. The expected growth rate, g, is the analyst's estimate of the constant growth rate for operating cash flows after the horizon.

CONCEPT CHECK

How is a project's salvage value affected by taxes?

How can salvage value be estimated?

How may net working capital affect a project's terminal cash flow?

APPLICATIONS

In this section, we review practical applications of cash flow estimation for a revenue expanding project, for a cost saving project, and in setting a bid price.

CASH FLOW ESTIMATION FOR A REVENUE EXPANDING PROJECT

Let's examine a firm's decision to build an addition to a present plant in response to a forecast showing rising sales. For simplicity, we'll assume construction for the addition occurs in year zero. The plant has an expected useful life of five years and can be sold for $1 million at the end of the project. We need to determine the initial outlay, the incremental after-tax operating cash flow, and the salvage value for the project. We will assume the project's minimum required return is 10 percent and its tax rate is 40 percent.

Initial Outlay The upfront expenses include those that are depreciable for tax purposes and those that are not depreciable. Depreciable outlays include construction labor, materials, preparation and transportation of materials, and equipment in the plant addition. For this example, we'll assume depreciable outlays are $4.5 million in year zero. Other expenses include costs for additional workers to operate the new plant and expenses associated with hiring, relocating, and training the workers. As with other expenses, this cost is deducted from the project's year zero taxable income. The plant managers estimate that these costs will total $0.4 million after-tax.

As seen in Table LE17.1, the initial after-tax outlays are $4.9 million in year zero. Of this cost, $4.5 million is depreciable while the remaining $0.4 million is expensed in year zero.

Incremental After-tax Operating Cash Flows For simplicity, assume that the incremental sales and costs arising from the plant addition project will be constant over the five-year life of the addition. Sales are expected to rise by $3.0 million and costs will increase by $0.635 million.

TABLE LE17.1
Initial Outlays For Plant Addition Project ($ Millions)

	$t = 0$
Depreciable Outlays	−$4.5
Expensed Cash Outlays, after tax	−0.4
	−$4.9

Using straight-line depreciation, the depreciable outlays of $4.5 million will increase the firm's depreciation expense by $4.5 million/5 years, or $0.90 million per year.

The expected increase in sales volume and production will require more working capital. Net working capital is expected to rise by $0.1 million in year one as the plant goes online. In year five, the plant addition will cease operations and the firm will recover the $.1 million.[25]

Table LE17.2 presents this data in income statement format and calculates the operating cash flows using Equation 17.4.

Salvage Value In year five, the project will generate a cash inflow as the firm receives the after-tax salvage value of the plant addition and the resale value of equipment from the addition. These items will be fully depreciated by the end of year five, that is, their book values will be zero. Their collective market value was given as $1.0 million, so the after-tax salvage value cash flow is

$$\text{Price} - t(\text{Price} - \text{BV}) = \$1.0 \text{ million} - 0.4(\$1.0 \text{ million} - 0) = \$0.600 \text{ million}$$

Is the Project Beneficial to Shareholders? Table LE17.3 summarizes the expansion project's incremental cash flows: the net initial outlay, after-tax operating cash flows, and salvage value determine if the project will increase shareholder wealth. Table LE17.3 uses this information to compute the present values of the cash flows, using a 10 percent required return, for the NPV calculation. Since the project's NPV is positive, the plant expansion project should be undertaken; shareholders will benefit from it.

Calculating the project's operating cash flow through direct application of Equation 17.4:

(Sales − Costs − Depreciation) (1 − t) + Depreciation − change in net working capital =
($3.000 − 0.635 − $0.900) (1 − 0.40) + $0.900 − $0.100 = $1.679 for year one

With no further changes in net working capital, the operating cash flow for years two through four is

$$\text{OCF} = (\$3.000 - 0.635 - \$0.900)(1 - 0.40) + \$0.900 - \$0 = \$1.779$$

TABLE LE17.2
Project Income Statement, for Years 1 through 5 ($ millions)

Sales	$3.000
−Costs	−0.635
−Depreciation	−0.900
EBT	$1.465
−Taxes (40%)	−0.586
Net income	$0.879

Operating Cash Flow Estimates Using Equation 17.4, spreadsheet format:

	YEAR 1	YEARS 2–4	YEAR 5
Tax rate:	40%		
Sales	$3.000	$3.000	$3.000
−Cost	−$0.635	−$0.635	−$0.635
−Depreciation	−$0.900	−$0.900	−$0.900
SUM	$1.465	$1.465	$1.465
× (1−t)	$0.879	$0.879	$0.879
+Depreciation	$0.900	$0.900	$0.900
−change NWC	−$0.100	$0.000	$0.100
Operating CF	$1.679	$1.779	$1.879

---

25. The funds, will be recovered as inventory is sold, accounts receivable are collected, and raw material accounts payable are paid in full.

TABLE LE17.3
Cash Flow Summary and NPV Calculation (millions of dollars)

YEAR	INITIAL OUTLAY	OPERATING CASH FLOWS	SALVAGE VALUE	TOTAL INCREMENTAL CASH FLOWS	PVIF (10%)	PV OF CASH FLOWS
0	$-4.9	$ 0.000	$ 0.0	$-4.90	1.0000	$-4.90
1	0.0	1.679	0.0	1.679	0.9091	1.53
2	0.0	1.779	0.0	1.779	0.8264	1.47
3	0.0	1.779	0.0	1.779	0.7513	1.34
4	0.0	1.779	0.0	1.779	0.6830	1.22
5	0.0	1.879	0.6	2.479	0.6209	1.54

NPV = $ 2.20

And with the net working capital recovery, operating cash flow in year five is:

$$\text{OCF} = (\$3.000 - 0.635 - \$0.900)(1 - 0.40) + \$0.900 - (-\$0.1) = \$1.879$$

CASH FLOW ESTIMATION FOR A COST-SAVING PROJECT

For a cost-saving project, the incremental cash flows are usually the difference between the cash flows of two mutually exclusive investments: (1) keeping the existing capital equipment and (2) purchasing new equipment. Suppose that a firm is considering a project to replace an older computer system with a more cost-efficient model. The decision depends on the difference between the cash flows that arise from the initial investment in the new equipment, the operating cash flows, and the salvage values.

Initial Investment Outlay The total cost of the investment consists of the total outlay required to purchase and prepare the new computer for operation less the after-tax salvage value of the older model. For simplicity, let's assume that the expected useful life of the new computer, three years, equals the expected remaining useful life of the old system.

Table LE17.4 lists the depreciable cash outlays. Added to the purchase price of $7,700 are transportation, hookup, and modification costs, which result in a total depreciable cost of $12,000. Table LE17.4 also shows the after-tax salvage cash flow of the old system of $3,600. This brings the initial total cash outlay for this project to $12,000 minus $3,600, or $8,400.

Incremental After-Tax Operating Cash Flows For a cost-saving project, it is safe to assume the incremental sale revenues are zero, so if the firm's revenues are $500,000, they will not change after the project is done. Suppose the estimated costs of operating the old system and the new system are as follows:

	t = 1	t = 2	t = 3
Old computer system	$3,000	$3,500	$4,000
New computer system	$500	$2,000	$3,000

TABLE LE17.4
Total Outlays

CASH OUTFLOWS ON THE NEW COMPUTER	
Purchase price	$7,700
Transportation	1,800
Hookup cost	200
Office modification	2,300
Total depreciable outlays	$12,000

CASH INFLOWS FROM DISPOSAL OF OLD COMPUTER	
After-tax salvage value	$3,600

INITIAL INVESTMENT OUTLAY	
Cash outflows for new computer	$12,000
Cash inflow from disposal of old computer	-$ 3,600
Initial investment outlay	$ 8,400

TABLE LE 17.5
Incremental After Tax Operating Cash Flows

YEAR 1 TAX RATE: 40%	OLD SYSTEM	NEW SYSTEM	INCREMENTAL CASH FLOWS (NEW − OLD)
Sales	$500,000	$500,000	$0
− Cost	−$3,000	−$500	$2,500
− Depreciation	−$2,000	−$4,000	−$2,000
SUM	$495,000	$495,500	$500
× (1−t)	$297,000	$297,300	$300
+ Depreciation	$2,000	$4,000	$2,000
− change NWC	$0	$0	$0
Operating CF	$299,000	$301,300	$2,300

YEAR 2 TAX RATE: 40%	OLD SYSTEM	NEW SYSTEM	INCREMENTAL CASH FLOWS (NEW − OLD)
Sales	$500,000	$500,000	$0
Cost	−$3,500	−$2,000	$1,500
Depreciation	−$2,000	−$4,000	−$2,000
SUM	$494,500	$494,000	−$500
× (1−t)	$296,700	$296,400	−$300
+ Depreciation	$2,000	$4,000	$2,000
− change NWC	$0	$0	$0
Operating CF	$298,700	$300,400	$1,700

YEAR 3 TAX RATE: 40%	OLD SYSTEM	NEW SYSTEM	INCREMENTAL CASH FLOWS (NEW − OLD)
Sales	$500,000	$500,000	$0
Cost	−$4,000	−$3,000	$1,000
Depreciation	−$2,000	−$4,000	−$2,000
SUM	$494,000	$493,000	−$1,000
× (1−t)	$296,400	$295,800	−$600
+ Depreciation	$2,000	$4,000	$2,000
− change NWC	$0	$0	$0
Operating CF	$298,400	$299,800	$1,400
Summary:	t = 1	t = 2	t = 3
Incremental after-tax OCF	$2,300	$1,700	$1,400

The incremental depreciation charge is the difference between depreciation charges on the new computer and those on the old one. Using straight-line depreciation, the new computer's depreciation will be its cost of $12,000 divided by 3 years, or $4,000 per year. The future depreciation of the old computer depends on the depreciation method the firm selected at the time of purchase. Assuming that the firm acquired the old computer two years earlier at a cost of $10,000 expecting a life of five years, its straight-line annual depreciation charges are $2,000 per year.

We will assume that replacing one computer system with another will have no impact on the firm's current assets and current liabilities. Thus, changes in net working capital will be zero.

Using a 40 percent tax rate and the above information on sales, costs, depreciation, and net working capital, Table LE17.5 applies Equation 17.4 to estimate operating cash flows.

In Table LE17.5, we apply Equation 17.1 to each year. For example, for the first year we list the operating cash flow components for the old system: costs of $3,000, depreciation of $2,000, and no change in net working capital. We do the same for the new system: costs of $500, depreciation of $4,000, and no change in net working capital. The incremental operating cash flow of replacing computer systems in the first year is $2,300. Similarly, we find the incremental operating cash flows for year two is $1,700 and year three is $1,400.

Terminal Cash Flows At the end of the third year, we will assume that the new computer will have a market value of $1,000 whereas the old computer, if kept, will be worthless. Since the old computer system will have a book value and a market value of $0, its after-tax salvage value is $0.

TABLE LE17.6

Cash Flow Summary and NPV Calculation

YEAR	INITIAL OUTLAY	OPERATING CASH FLOWS	SALVAGE VALUE	TOTAL INCREMENTAL CASH FLOWS	PVIF (10%)	PV OF CASH FLOWS
0	−$8,400	$0	$0	$8,400	1.0000	−$8,400
1	0	2,300	0	2,300	0.9091	2,091
2	0	1,700	0	1,700	0.8264	1,405
3	0	1,400	600	2,000	0.7513	1,503
					NPV =	− $3,401

The new computer's book value will be zero after three years. Its after-tax salvage value will be the selling price of $1,000 less the tax obligation of $400 [0.4($1,000 − $0)], or $600. The incremental salvage value cash flow will be $600 (new computer) − $0 (old computer), or $600.

Is the Project Beneficial to Shareholders? Table LE17.6 summarizes the incremental cash flows: the net initial outlay, the after-tax operating cash flows, and the salvage value. Assuming a 10 percent minimum required rate of return, the net present value is –$3,401. The computer replacement project is unacceptable because the negative NPV indicates that the project would decrease shareholder wealth by $3,401.

SETTING A BID PRICE

Often a corporation or government that needs a fixed asset or service will solicit bids for its manufacture. The firm's request for proposals (RFP) will list the desired attributes and specifications of the item. Firms will respond to the RFP with the hope of winning the solicitor's approval by verifying that it can produce the item at the lowest cost. The firm that makes the lowest bid will most likely win the contract.

Before placing a bid in response to an RFP, a firm's financial analysts must first determine the price that will allow the firm to cover its costs and earn a sufficient return so its shareholders aren't harmed. Putting it another way, the bidding firm must determine the minimum price at which the project will have a zero NPV. Any bid below this price would result in a negative NPV and hurt the firm's shareholders. In order to determine the minimum bid price, the analyst must work backward to develop cash flow estimates consistent with a zero NPV and then convert the cash flow estimates into a unit price.

Suppose you are the chief financial officer for You-go, Inc., a manufacturer of high-quality, motorized bicycles. An RFP from a large city is seeking bids for motorized bicycles for use by police officers on patrol. Your firm's motorized bicycles will require special modifications to make them suitable for police work. Among other requirements, the RFP notes that 100 bicycles will have to be delivered each year for the next three years. Assume You-go's required return on such projects is 20 percent and the firm's tax rate is 40 percent.

Initial Investment Outlay To increase production to meet the city's request and to properly modify the cycles for police use, the firm's plant and equipment will need to be expanded at a cost of $120,000 this year. It will cost about $10,000, after tax, to hire and train new workers. Net working capital needs are expected to increase $40,000 this year, as well. The firm will recover this increase in net working capital in the third year as it fills the production requirement.

This brings the total investment to $170,000, including $120,000 in depreciable assets. These assets will be straight-line depreciated over the three years of the project's life; thus, depreciation expense is expected to be $120,000/3, or $40,000 per year.

If the firm wins the bid, labor costs are expected to rise by $50,000 per year. Raw materials expenses will rise by $20,000 per year. Thus, expenses will increase by $70,000 annually as a result of this project.

Salvage Value The salvage value of the specialized equipment needed for this project is expected to be only $20,000 after three years. Since the assets will be fully depreciated to a book value of $0 at the end of three years, the after-tax proceeds from their sale will be $20,000 − 0.4($20,000 − $0) = $12,000.

TABLE LE1 7.7

Cash Flow Summary

YEAR	INITIAL OUTLAY	OPERATING CASH FLOWS	SALVAGE VALUE	TOTAL INCREMENTAL CASH FLOWS
0	−$170,000	$0	$0	−$170,000
1	0	X	0	X
2	0	X	0	X
3	0	X + $40,000	$12,000	X + $52,000

Estimating Yearly Operating Cash Flows Table LE17.7 summarizes the information that is known so far. The initial outlay totals $170,000 in year zero, and salvage value is $12,000 in year three. The operating cash flows are unknown now, but they will increase by $40,000 in year three due to the recovery of net working capital.

To make this information easier to work with, let's simplify the information presented in the table. Let's add the *present value* of the year three cash inflow of $52,000 to the initial cash outflow of $170,000. This gives a present value of the known cash flows of:

$$-\$170,000 + \$52,000(1/1.20)^3 = -\$139,907.41$$

This removes the effects of the salvage value and the recovery of net working capital from the project's annual cash flows. The cash flows in years one through three are now a three-year annuity, with a net year zero investment of $139,907.41 in present value terms:

Year	Cash flow
0	−$139,907.41
1	X
2	X
3	X

The net present value of this series of cash flows is the present value of the three year $X annuity less $139,907.41. To determine the minimum operating cash flow that will leave shareholder wealth unharmed, we set NPV to zero and solve for X

$$\text{NPV} = 0 = (\$X)(\text{PVIFA for 3 years, 20\%}) - \$139,907.41.$$

Using interest factor table or a financial calculator, the PVIFA for three years and 20 percent is 2.1065; solving for $X, we find the operating cash flow annuity is $66,417.58.

Using this minimum operating cash flow, we can work backward to determine the minimum sales revenue consistent with a zero-NPV bid. Recall the project's annual costs are $70,000, its annual depreciation expense is $40,000, and the firm's tax rate is 40 percent. We can ignore the change in net working capital as we've already incorporated that in the analysis in Table LE17.7 and the cash flow estimate of $66,417.58. Using equation 17.4 and simplifying we have:

$$\text{Operating cash flow} = (\text{Sales} - \text{Costs} - \text{Depreciation})(1 - t) + \text{Depreciation} - \text{change in net working capital}$$

$$\$66,417.58 = (\text{Sales} - \$70,000 - \$40,000)(1 - 0.40) + \$40,000 - 0$$
$$\$66,417.58 = (\text{Sales} - \$110,000)(0.60) + \$40,000$$
$$\$66,417.58 = (\text{Sales})(0.60) - \$66,000 + \$40,000$$
$$\$66,417.58 = (\text{Sales})(0.60) - \$26,000$$
$$\$92,417.58 = (\text{Sales})(0.60)$$

Solving for Sales to find the minimum total sales revenue, we see that Sales equals $92,417.58/0.60 = $154,029.30 per year. Dividing total annual sales by 100 cycles gives us the minimum bid per cycle, $1,540.29. This unit price represents the lowest price the firm can bid without adversely affecting shareholder wealth.

We see from these applications that to approach a cash flow estimation problem, we should first estimate initial cash outlay, including property and equipment expenditures, necessary

SUMMARY

Estimating cash flows is a difficult part of evaluating capital budgeting projects. Projected earnings, expenses, and fixed asset investments must be converted into cash flows by using the methods discussed in this chapter.

DISCUSSION QUESTIONS

1. What information sources are used to develop estimates for a project's
   a. initial outlays?
   b. operating life?
   c. salvage value?
2. Why might there be tax implications when an asset is sold at the termination of a capital budgeting project?
3. Explain the process to estimating cash flows for a revenue-enhancing project.
4. Explain the process to estimating cash flows for a cost-saving project.
5. Explain the process to estimating a bid price by estimating zero-NPV cash flow needs.

PROBLEMS

1. Suppose the Quick Towing Company purchases a new tow truck. The old truck had a book value of $1,000 and was sold for $1,420. If Quick Towing is in the 34 percent marginal tax bracket, what is the tax liability on the sale of the truck? What is the after-tax cash flow on the sale?

2. Hammond's Fish Market just purchased a $30,000 fork lift truck. It has a five-year useful life. The firm's tax rate is 25 percent.
   a. If the fork lift is straight-line depreciated, what is the firm's tax savings from depreciation?
   b. What will be its book value at the end of year three?
   c. Suppose the fork-lift can be sold for $10,000 at the end of three years. What is its after-tax salvage value?

3. Lisowski Laptops is examining the possibility of manufacturing and selling a notebook computer that is compatible with both PCs and Macintosh systems and that can receive television signals. Its estimated selling price is $2,500. Variable costs (supplies and labor) will equal $1,500 per unit, and fixed costs per year would approximate $200,000. Up-front investments in plant and equipment will total $270,000, which will be straight-line depreciated over three years. The initial working capital investment will be $100,000 and will rise proportionately with sales. Bill, the CEO, forecasts sales of the laptop will be 50,000 units the first year, 60,000 units the second, and 45,000 units the third year, at which time product life cycles would require closing down production of the model. At that time, the market value of the project's assets will be about $70,000. LL's tax rate is 40 percent and its required return on projects such as this one is 17 percent. Should Lisowski Laptops offer the new computer?

4. Preston Industries' current sales volume is $100 million a year. Preston is examining the advantages of EDI (electronic data interchange). The technology will allow Preston to electronically communicate with suppliers and customers, send and receive purchase orders, invoices, and cash. It will save Preston money by lowering costs in the purchasing, customer service, accounts payable, and accounting departments. Initial estimates are that savings will equal $100,000 a year. Investment in EDI technology will include $500,000 in depreciable expenses and $100,000 in nondepreciable expenses. Assets will be depreciated on a straight-line basis for four years. Implementation of EDI is expected to reduce Preston's net working capital by $200,000. Because of changing technology, Preston's president, Carol, wants to estimate the effect of switching to EDI on shareholder wealth over a four-year time horizon assuming that advances in technology will make the equipment worthless at the end of four years. At a 30 percent tax rate and 13 percent required rate of return, should Preston Industries switch to EDI?

5. Bart and Morticia, owners of the prestigious Gomez-Addams Office Towers, are concerned about high heating and cooling costs and client complaints of temperature variation within the building. They commissioned an engineering study by Frasco-Prew Associates to identify the cause of the problems and suggest corrective action. Frasco-Prew's basic recommendation is that a new HVAC (heating, ventilation, and air conditioning) system, featuring electronic climate control, be installed in the Towers. Over the next four years, the engineers estimate a new system will reduce heating and cooling costs by $125,000 a year. Cost of the new system will be $500,000 and can be depreciated over four years. Using a 25 percent tax rate

and a 14 percent required return, should Bart and Morticia change the HVAC system? Use a four-year time horizon.

6. Casey's Baseball Bats is planning to begin exporting their product to the Asian market. They estimate up-front expenses of $1 million this year (year 0) and $3 million next year (year 1). Operating cash flows in years two, three, and four will be (in dollars) $100,000, $200,000, and $400,000, respectively. After year four, they expect operating cash flows to grow at 10 percent a year indefinitely. If 15 percent is the required return on the project, what is its NPV?

7. The No-Shoplift Security Company is interested in bidding on a contract to provide a new security system for a large department store chain. The new security system would be phased into 10 stores per year for five years. No-Shoplift can purchase the hardware for $50,000 per installation. The labor and material cost per installation is approximately $15,000. In addition, No-Shoplift will need to purchase $100,000 in new equipment for the installation, which will be depreciated to zero using the straight-line method over five years. This equipment will be sold in five years for $25,000. Finally, an investment of $50,000 in net working capital will be needed. Assume that the relevant tax rate is 34 percent. If the No-Shoplift Security Company requires a 10 percent return on its investments, what price should it bid?

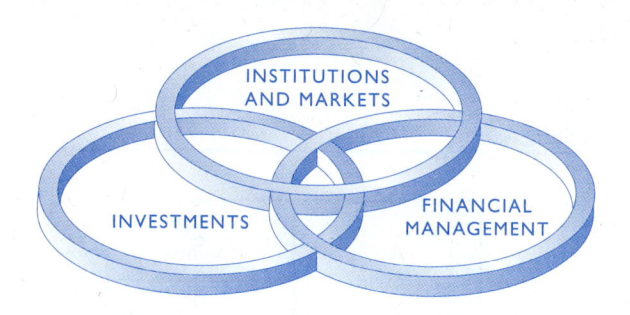

CHAPTER 18

Capital Structure and the Cost of Capital

Chapter Learning Objectives:

AFTER STUDYING THIS CHAPTER, YOU SHOULD BE ABLE TO:

- Explain how capital structure affects a firm's capital budgeting discount rate.
- Explain how a firm can determine its cost of debt financing and cost of equity financing.
- Explain how a firm can estimate its cost of capital.
- Explain how a firm's growth potential, dividend policy, and capital structure are related.
- Explain how EBIT/eps analysis can assist management in choosing a capital structure.
- Describe how a firm's business risk and operating leverage may affect its capital structure.
- Describe how a firm's degree of financial leverage and degree of combined leverage can be computed and explain how to interpret their values.
- Describe the factors that affect a firm's capital structure.

Where We Have Been...

We have seen how a firm can choose a short-term or long-term financing strategy (Chapter 16) and familiarize itself with the workings of the financial markets, security pricing, and IPOs (Chapters 10 and 11). Part of the financing decision depends on the firm's asset needs. New asset purchases, restructurings, or corporate strategies may lead to the need for new financing or a new financing strategy for the firm. Likewise, changes in financial market conditions (due to fluctuations in interest rates, stock price, or exchange rates) may make new financial strategies look appealing.

Where We Are Going...

We've gone full circle now. Part 1 of this text, "Institutions and Markets," discussed the purpose, evolution, and working of financial institutions. Part 2, "Investments," showed how these institutions and the financial markets work to bring together suppliers and users of capital, how interest rates are determined on a variety of financial instruments, how securities markets work, how securities are priced, and how risk and return influence investor decisions and security prices. Part 3, "Financial Management," has reviewed financial statements and financial decisions in the context of businesses. And what inputs do firms use to help guide their long-term financing decisions and corporate strategies? As we see in this chapter, none other than information from the financial system and financial markets.

How Does This Chapter Apply to Me...

High levels of consumer debt are used as a harbinger of tough economic times ahead. Similar to a firm, individuals have a capital structure, too. Add up your assets; subtract any debts; the balance is your net worth or "equity." Your own personal capital structure is your mixture of debt and equity that is used to finance what you own and your lifestyle. Like a firm, use of debt without the ability to make interest payments and to reduce the principal can lead to financial distress. The best use of debt for individuals is similar to that of firms: use in moderation and only to help purchase assets with the potential to grow in value, such as a house. Right now, you may be using student loans to finance an investment in yourself—your education. Because of your education, your future earnings potential is expected to be greater than it otherwise would be and gives you the ability to repay the loan.

FIGURE 18.1
The Balance Sheet

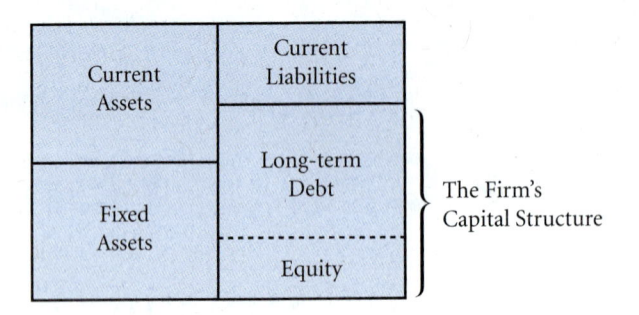

In Shakespeare's play *Hamlet*, the elder Polonius counsels his son Laertes:

Neither a borrower nor a lender be.

We can tell that Polonius did not study modern-day finance! Lending money, in the form of buying bonds or putting money in a bank account, can be an attractive investment strategy for some, and businesses often find themselves needing to borrow or raise funds for short periods (which was the topic of Chapter 16) or longer periods. This chapter looks at the analysis a firm should do when funds are needed for longer periods.

The previous chapters described the capital budgeting process. We learned how to estimate a project's cash flows and how to use techniques, such as NPV and IRR, for evaluating projects. In Chapter 17 we assumed that the project's discount rate, or its cost of capital, was given. In this chapter, we'll explain how managers can estimate their firm's cost of capital for an "average risk" project. This discount rate is adjusted up or down, as we learned in Chapter 17, depending on the project's risk.

Before managers can estimate the cost of capital, two inputs are needed. First, the cost of each financing source needs to be determined. Second, they must determine the appropriate financing mix to use to fund the firm. Once these are known, managers can estimate the firm's weighted average cost of capital.

A firm's mix of debt and equity used to finance its assets defines the firm's **capital structure**, as seen in Figure 18.1. In this chapter, we first review the importance of a firm's capital structure and how the capital structure and the costs of each financing source can be combined to provide an estimate of the weighted average cost of capital (WACC). We'll examine the interrelationship among a firm's growth rate, its dividend policy, and its capital structure decisions. Then we'll review the influences that affect a firm's choice of a capital structure over time.

capital structure
firm's mix of debt and equity

WHY CHOOSE A CAPITAL STRUCTURE?

Obviously, a target capital structure is important as it determines the proportion of debt and equity used to estimate a firm's cost of capital. There is, however, a second, even more important reason. The firm's **optimum debt/equity mix** minimizes the firm's **cost of capital,** which in turn helps the firm to maximize shareholder wealth.

For example, suppose a firm expects cash flows of $20 million annually in perpetuity. Each of the three capital structures shown in Table 18.1 has a different weighted average cost of capital. Following the perpetuity valuation rule from Chapter 9, firm value is computed by dividing the expected cash flow by the firm's cost of capital under each capital structure. Capital Structure 2 in the following table minimizes the cost of capital at 8 percent, which in turn maximizes the value of the firm at $250 million.

cost of capital
minimum acceptable rate of return to a firm on a project

optimum debt/equity mix
proportionate use of debt and equity that minimizes the firm's cost of capital

A nonoptimal capital structure with either too much or too little debt leads to higher financing costs, and the firm will likely reject some capital budgeting projects that could have increased shareholder wealth with an optimal financing mix. For example, suppose a firm has a minimum cost of capital of 8 percent, but poor analysis leads management to choose a capital structure that

TABLE 18.1
Capital Structure Options

	CAPITAL STRUCTURE 1	CAPITAL STRUCTURE 2	CAPITAL STRUCTURE 3
Debt	25.0%	40.0%	70.0%
Equity	75.0%	60.0%	30.0%
Weighted Average Cost of Capital	10.0%	8.0%	12.5%

Firm value under
 Capital Structure 1: $20 million/0.10 = $200 million
 Capital Structure 2: $20 million/0.08 = $250 million
 Capital Structure 3: $20 million/0.125 = $160 million

results in a 10 percent cost of capital. It would then reject an average risk project that costs $100,000 and returns cash flows of $26,000 in years one through five at a 10 percent cost of capital (NPV = −$1,434). This project would be acceptable at the minimum possible cost of capital of 8 percent (NPV = $3,818).

There is another, more intuitive way to see the importance of finding the optimal capital structure. A project's NPV represents the increase in shareholders' wealth from undertaking a project. From Chapter 10, we know there is an inverse relationship between value and discount rates (the "seesaw effect"). Thus, a lower weighted average cost of capital gives higher project net present values and results in higher levels of shareholder wealth.

TRENDS IN CORPORATE USE OF DEBT

The ratio of long-term debt to GDP for U.S corporations grew during the 1960s until, as seen in Figure 18.2, the mid-1970s, exceeding 35 percent only for limited occasions. But the relative use of debt then rose until 1989, peaking at a nearly 45 percent of GDP. Many firms restructured themselves financially during the 1980s. Some did so in attempts to lower their cost of capital by

FIGURE 18.2
Corporate Debt as a Percentage of GDP

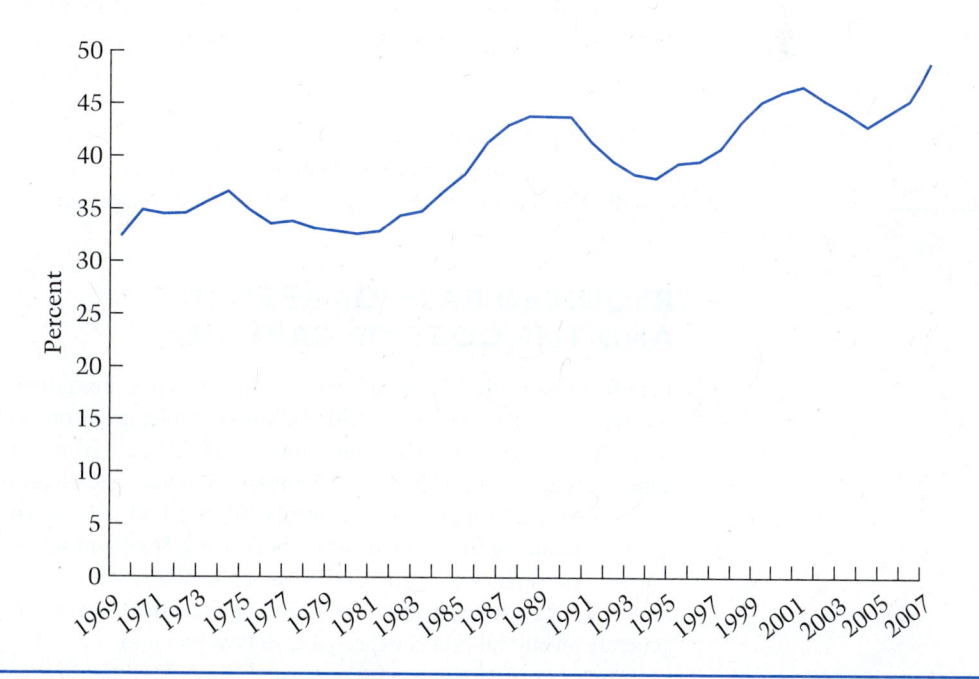

Source: GDP: *Economic Report of the President, 2009*, Table B-1, http://www.gpoaccess.gov/eop/tables09.html
Debt: *Flow of Funds Accounts*, Federal Reserve Board, Table of debt growth, borrowings, and debt outstanding. http://www.federalreserve.gov/releases/z1/Current/. (accessed January 15, 2010)

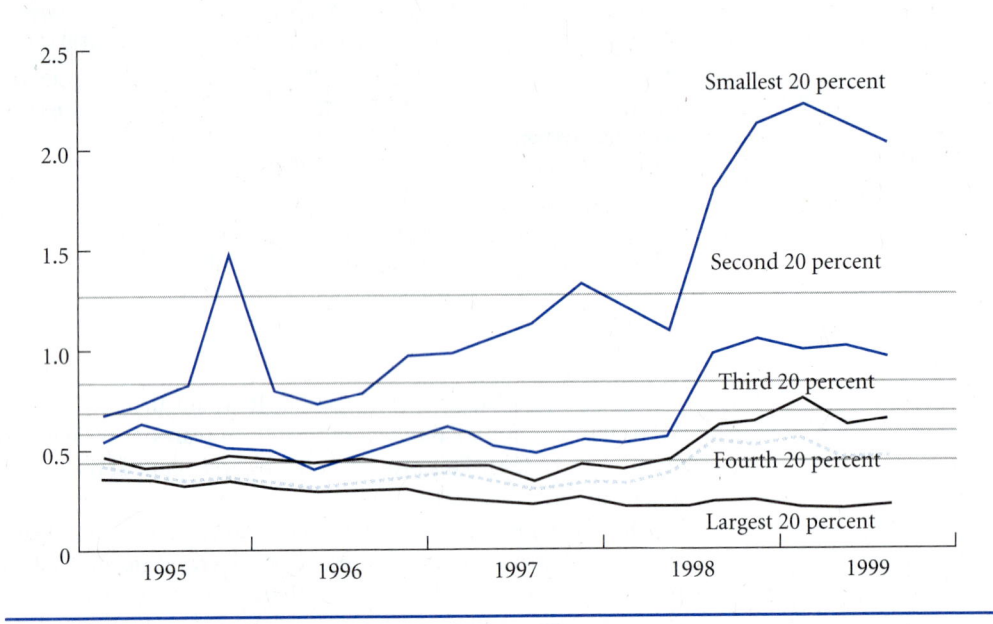

FIGURE 18.3
Ratios of Debt to Stock Market Equity for Different-Sized Firms

Source: Carol Osler and Gijoon Hong, "Rapidly Rising Corporate Debt: Are Firms Now Vulnerable to an Economic Slowdown?" *Current Issues in Economics and Finance*, vol. 6, no. 7, June 2000, Federal Reserve Bank of New York.

CONCEPT CHECK

What are the components of a firm's capital structure?

What is the relationship between a firm's cost of capital and firm value?

Have corporations been using a steady ratio of debt to equity over time?

taking advantage of the tax deductibility of interest by issuing debt to repurchase common stock, thereby increasing their debt to equity ratios. Other firms went private in the 1980s, fought off takeovers, or acquired other firms, financing the transactions with large amounts of debt. The surge in bankruptcies at the beginning of the 1990s shows the folly of such excessive use of debt.

Into the early 1990s, the ratio of debt to economic activity fell as firms issued equity to strengthen their balance sheets and to reduce the probability of financial distress due to overborrowing. But as the economy grew in the 1990s, so did the relative use of debt, until the economic slowdown in the early part of the new millennium started to reduce debt levels. From 2001 through the present, we see the same cycle: a recessionary economy causing firms to shed debt, only for the corporate economy to borrow again as the economy grew through 2007.

Figure 18.3 shows the relative use of debt to equity for different-sized firms in the latter part of the 1990s. The figure shows a fairly consistent pattern that smaller firms use relatively more debt than larger firms. This occurs because of the higher relative costs of equity for smaller firms as well as the better access to capital markets of the larger ones.

REQUIRED RATE OF RETURN AND THE COST OF CAPITAL

Investors in a project expect to earn a return on their investment. This expected return depends on current capital market conditions (for example, levels of stock prices and interest rates) and the risk of the project. The minimum acceptable rate of return of a project is the return that generates sufficient cash flow to pay investors their expected return.

To illustrate, suppose a firm wants to spend $1,000 on an average risk capital budgeting project, financing the investment by borrowing $600 and selling $400 worth of common stock. The firm must pay interest on the debt at a rate of 9 percent, while shareholders expect a 15 percent return on their investment. To compensate the firm's investors adequately, the project should generate an annual pretax expected cash flow equal to

$$\text{Lender's interest} + \text{Shareholders' return} = \text{Annual expected cash flow}$$
$$= (0.09)(\$600) + (0.15)(\$400)$$
$$= \$54 + \$60 = \$114$$

SMALL BUSINESS PRACTICE
Venture Capital as a Source of Financing for the Small Business

Venture capitalists usually are members of partnerships that consist of a few general partners. The typical venture capital partnership manages between $50 million and $100 million in assets. The general approach for raising investment funds for a venture capital firm is to set up a "venture capital fund" and seek financial commitments from investors to fund the "fund." It is common to organize a venture capital fund as a limited partnership in which the venture capitalist is the general partner and the other investors are limited investors. The general partner might invest 1 percent of the funds and the limited partners the remainder. Investors make an initial contribution and also commit to provide additional funds up to some stated maximum during the life of the fund, which is usually ten years. Often there is an option to extend the fund for two or three more years. At the end of a fund's life, cash and securities are distributed to the investors.

What are the sources of venture capital? According to *Venture Capital Journal*, pension funds provide well over one-third of annual venture capital funds. Second in importance as suppliers of venture capital are foundations and endowments, with 22 percent of the funds raised. Endowment contributions come largely from university endowments. Investments by insurance firms and bank portfolios play a major role, as do investments by high net worth individuals and families.

The project's minimum rate of return must then equal

$$\text{Minimum cash flow/Investment} = \text{Minimum rate of return}$$
$$= \$114/\$1{,}000 = 11.4 \text{ percent}$$

As another means to determine this, the expected return of each financing source could be weighted by its relative use. The firm is raising 60 percent of the project's funds from debt and 40 percent from equity. This results in a minimum pretax required return of

$$(0.60)(9\%) + (0.40)(15\%) = 11.4 \text{ percent}$$

Thus, the required rate of return on a project represents a weighted average of lenders' and owners' return expectations. Since a cash flow or return to an investor represents a cash outflow or a cost to the firm, *the minimum required rate of return is a weighted average of the firm's costs of various sources of capital.* Thus, the required rate of return on a project is equivalent to the project's cost of capital. It is this number that should be used as a discount rate when evaluating a project's NPV. *Required rate of return, cost of capital,* and *discount rate* are different terms for the same concept.

It is fair to ask: why is the minimum required return equal to a *weighted* average of financing costs? If a firm can finance a project using all debt at an interest cost of 8 percent, shouldn't the project be accepted if it has a positive NPV using an 8 percent discount rate or if its IRR exceeds 8 percent? The answer is no, not necessarily. Suppose this week a project of average risk is financed by borrowing at 8 percent and has an IRR of 9 percent, so the Board votes to accept the project. Next quarter, because the firm's debt ratios are high, the firm's Board decides to finance all new projects with equity. If the cost of equity is 15 percent and a potential project with average risk has an IRR of 12 percent, it will be turned down. It is hard to envision a Board that is maximizing the value of the firm accepting projects with 9 percent expected returns while rejecting projects with the same risk that have expected returns of 12 percent! That is why the weighted average cost of capital is used, so project acceptance is not subject to specifically how it is to be financed.

CONCEPT CHECK

What is the relationship between a project's cost of capital and its minimum required rate of return?

Why is a weighted average cost used instead of a project's specific cost of financing to determine whether it should be accepted or rejected?

COST OF CAPITAL

Relevant cash flows are incremental after-tax cash flows. To be consistent, these cash flows must be discounted using an incremental after-tax cost of capital. The firm's relevant cost of capital is computed from after-tax financing costs. Firms pay preferred and common stock dividends out of net income, so these expenses already represent after-tax costs to the firm. Because debt interest is paid from pretax income, however, the cost of debt requires adjustment to an after-tax basis before computing the cost of capital.

A project's incremental cash flows must also be discounted at a cost of capital that represents the incremental or marginal cost to the firm of financing the project, that is, the cost of raising one additional dollar of capital. Thus, the cost of debt and equity that determines the cost of capital must come not from historical averages or past costs, but rather from forward-looking projections of future costs. The firm's analysts need to evaluate investors' expected returns under likely market conditions and then use these expected returns to compute the firm's marginal future cost of raising funds by each method.

Conceptually, investors' required returns equal the firm's financing costs. The following sections use the valuation concepts for bonds and stocks from Chapter 10 to find investors' required returns on bonds, preferred stock, and common stock. We then adjust these required returns to reflect the firm's after-tax cost of financing.

COST OF DEBT

The firm's unadjusted cost of debt financing equals the yield to maturity on new debt issues, either a long-term bank loan or a bond issue. The yield to maturity represents the cost to the firm of borrowing funds in the current market environment. The firm's current financing costs determine its current cost of capital.

A firm can determine its cost of debt by several methods. If the firm targets an "A" rating (or any other bond rating), a review of the yields to maturity on A-rated bonds in Standard & Poor's Bond Guide can provide an estimate of the firm's current borrowing costs. Several additional factors will affect the firm's specific borrowing costs, including covenants and features of the proposed bond issue as well as the number of years until the bond or loan matures or comes due. It is important to examine bonds whose ratings and characteristics resemble those the firm wants to match.

In addition, the firm can solicit the advice of investment bankers on the cost of issuing new debt. Or if the firm has debt currently trading, it can use public market prices and yields to estimate its current cost of debt. The publicly traded bond's yield to maturity can be found using the techniques for determining the internal rate of return on an investment discussed in Chapters 9 and 10. Finally, a firm can seek long-term debt financing from a bank or a consortium of banks. Preliminary discussions with the bankers will indicate a ballpark interest rate the firm can expect to pay on its borrowing.

The yield estimate, however derived, is an estimate of the coupon rate on newly issued bonds (as bonds are usually issued with prices close to their par value) or the interest rate on a loan. Interest is a pretax expense, so the interest estimate should be adjusted to reflect the tax shield provided by debt financing. If YTM is the pretax interest cost estimate, the after-tax estimate is YTM times $(1 - T)$, where T is the firm's marginal tax rate.[1] Thus the after-tax cost of debt, k_d, is

$$k_d = YTM\,(1 - T) \qquad (18.1)$$

Suppose Global Manufacturing has a 40 percent marginal tax rate and it can issue debt with a 10 percent yield to maturity. Its after-tax cost of debt is 10 percent $(1 - 0.40) = 6$ percent.

COST OF PREFERRED STOCK

Chapter 10 explained how to model preferred stock as a perpetuity. The investor pays a price, P, for a share of preferred stock and in return expects to receive D_p of dividends every year, forever. Valuing the stock as perpetuity, the maximum price an investor will pay for a share is D_p/r_p, where r_p represents the rate of return required by investors in the firm's preferred stock. Rearranging the valuation equation to solve for r_p yields:

$$r_p = D_p/P$$

When issuing preferred stock, the firm will not receive the full price P per share; there will be a flotation cost of F_p per share.[2] Thus, the cost to the firm of preferred stock financing, k_p, is

$$k_p = D_p/(P - F_p) \qquad (18.2)$$

A firm wants to issue preferred stock that pays an annual dividend of $5 a share. The price of the stock is $55, and the cost of floating a new issue will be $3 a share. The cost of preferred stock to this firm is: $k_p = D_p/(P - F_p) = \$5/(\$55 - \$3) = 0.0962$, or 9.62 percent.

CONCEPT CHECK

How is a firm's after-tax cost of debt determined?

How is a firm's cost of preferred stock calculated?

---

1. In reality, this is an approximation. We know from Chapter 10 that the yield to maturity reflects both interest paid and the difference between market price and par value. Only the interest is tax-deductible to the firm. For coupon-paying bond issues, the coupon rate many times is set so that the market or offering price of the bonds is close to par. In these cases, Equation 18.1 is a close approximation to the cost of debt.

2. Flotation costs were discussed in Chapter 9.

COST OF COMMON EQUITY

Unlike debt and preferred stock, cash flows from common equity are not fixed or known beforehand and their risk is harder to evaluate. In addition, firms have two sources of common equity, retained earnings and new stock issues, and thus two costs of common equity. It may be clear that there is an explicit cost (dividends) associated with issuing new common equity, but even though the firm pays no extra dividends to use retained earnings, they are not a free source of financing. We must consider the opportunity cost of using funds that could have been given to shareholders as dividends.

Retained earnings are the portion of net income that the firm does not distribute as dividends. As owners of the firm, common shareholders have a claim on all of its net income, but they receive only the amount that the firm's board of directors declares as dividends.

From the shareholders' perspective, the opportunity cost of retained earnings is the return the shareholders could earn by investing the funds in assets whose risk is similar to that of the firm. Suppose, for example, that shareholders expect a 15 percent return on their investment in a firm's common stock. If the firm could not invest its retained earnings to achieve a risk-adjusted 15 percent expected return, shareholders would be better off receiving 100 percent of its net income as dividends. That way they can reinvest the funds themselves in similar-risk assets that can provide a 15 percent expected return.

To maximize shareholder wealth, management must recognize that retained earnings have a cost. That cost, k_{re}, is the return that shareholders expect from their investment in the firm. We will review two methods of estimating the cost of retained earnings. One method uses the security market line; the other uses the assumption of constant dividend growth.

Cost of Retained Earnings: Security Market Line Approach

Chapter 12's Learning Extension developed the security market line, or SML, which can provide an estimate of shareholder required return based on a stock's systematic risk. The security market line equation,

$$E(R_i) = RFR + \beta_i(R_{MKT} - RFR)$$

gives the required return as a combination of the risk-free return, RFR, and a risk premium that is the product of a stock's systematic risk, measured by β_i, and the market risk premium (R_{MKT} – RFR). The required shareholder return is the opportunity cost the firm must earn on its retained earnings. Thus, an estimate for the cost of retained earnings is:

$$k_{re} = E(R_i) = RFR + \beta_i(R_{MKT} - RFR) \tag{18.3}$$

For example, assume that the current T-bill rate is 4.5 percent and that analysts estimate that the current market risk premium is slightly above its historical average at 9.0 percent. Suppose also that analysts estimate Global Manufacturing's β to be 1.30. What is Global Manufacturing's cost of retained earnings using the SML approach?

All the information we need to apply Equation 18.3 was presented above:

$$k_{re} = E(R_i) = RFR + \beta_i(R_{MKT} - RFR) = 4.5\% + [(1.3)(9\%)] = 16.2 \text{ percent}$$

Using the security market line, Global Manufacturing's cost of retained earnings is 16.2 percent.

Cost of Retained Earnings: Constant Dividend Growth Model

Chapter 10 presented the constant dividend growth model to estimate a firm's stock price:

$$P = \frac{D_1}{r_{cs} - g} \tag{18.4}$$

where

P = the stock's price
g = the expected (constant) dividend growth rate
D_1 = next year's expected dividend (equal to the current dividend increased by g percent)
r_{cs} = the shareholders' required return on the stock

Rather than use the model to determine a price, however, we can substitute today's actual stock price for P and solve for the shareholders' required rate of return, r_{cs}:

$$k_{re} = r_{cs} = \frac{D_1}{P} + g \tag{18.5}$$

The shareholders' required return represents the firm's cost of retained earnings, k_{re}. The ratio D_1/P represents the current income yield to shareholders from their investment of P. From the firm's perspective, this ratio represents the ratio of dividends it pays to its current market value. The growth rate, g, represents shareholders' expected capital gain arising from dividend growth. From the firm's perspective, g can be viewed as an opportunity cost of raising equity today. It is expected to be able to sell equity at a g percent higher price next year.

COST OF NEW COMMON STOCK

To estimate the cost of new equity, we must modify Equation 18.5 to reflect extra cost to the firm of issuing securities in the primary market. The costs of issuing stock, or **flotation costs,** include the accounting, legal, and printing costs of offering shares to the public as well as the commission or fees earned by the investment bankers who market the new securities to investors. If the flotation cost is F per share, the cost of issuing new common stock, or k_n, is given by Equation 18.6:

$$k_n = \frac{D_1}{P - F} + g \tag{18.6}$$

> **flotation costs**
> *costs of issuing stock; includes accounting, legal, and printing costs of offering shares to the public as well as the commission earned by the investment bankers who market the new securities to investors*

Suppose a firm has just paid a dividend of $2.50 a share; its stock price is $50 a share; and the expected growth rate of dividends is 6 percent. The current dividend of $2.50 must be multiplied by a factor to reflect the expected 6 percent growth for D_1, next year's dividend. Using Equation 18.5, the cost of using retained earnings as a financing source is:

$$k_{cs} = \frac{2.50(1 + 0.06)}{\$50} + 0.06 = \frac{\$2.65}{\$50} + 0.06$$

$$= 0.053 + 0.06 = 0.113, \text{ or } 11.3 \text{ percent}$$

If new common stock is to be issued to finance the project and flotation costs are expected to be $4 per share, we need to use Equation 18.6 to estimate the cost of new common equity:

$$k_{cs} = \frac{2.50(1 + 0.06)}{\$50 - \$4} + 0.06 = \frac{\$2.65}{\$46} + 0.06$$

$$= 0.058 + 0.06 = 0.118, \text{ or } 11.8 \text{ percent}$$

The cost of using new common stock is 11.8 percent.

We learned about the concept of efficient markets in Chapter 12, namely that current market prices and interest rates reflect all known information as well as the market's expectations about the future. Financial managers can do little to "fight the market." If managers feel their financing costs are too high, it is usually the case that the market perceives risk that the managers are ignoring. The efficient market ensures that financing costs are in line with the market's perception of firms' risks and expected returns.

> **CONCEPT CHECK**
> *Should retained earnings be considered a source of free financing to the firm?*
>
> *How can the cost of retained earnings be determined for a firm? The cost of new common equity?*

WEIGHTED AVERAGE COST OF CAPITAL

We have seen how to compute the costs of the firm's basic capital structure components. Now we will combine the components to find the weighted average of the firm's financing costs.

The firm's **weighted average cost of capital (WACC)** represents the minimum required rate of return on its capital budgeting projects. It is found by multiplying the marginal cost of each capital structure component by its appropriate weight and summing the terms:

$$\text{WACC} = w_d k_d + w_p k_p + w_e k_e \tag{18.7}$$

> **weighted average cost of capital (WACC)**
> *represents the minimum required rate of return on a capital-budgeting project; it is found by multiplying the marginal cost of each capital structure component by its appropriate weight and summing the terms*

The weights of debt, preferred equity, and common equity in the firm's capital structure are given by w_d, w_p, and w_e, respectively. As the weighted average cost of capital covers all of the firm's capital financing sources, the weights must sum to 1.0.

The firm's cost of common equity, k_e, can reflect the cost of retained earnings, k_{re}, or the cost of new common stock, k_n, whichever is appropriate. Most firms rely on retained earnings to raise the common equity portion of their financial needs. If retained earnings are insufficient, they can issue common stock to meet the shortfall. In this case, k_n is substituted for the cost of common equity.

INTERNET ACTIVITY

Go to http://www.ibbotson.com and look for Ibbotson's Cost of Capital Center (it is now part of Morningstar). Review its various methodologies for determining capital costs and sample data.

CAPITAL STRUCTURE WEIGHTS

The weights in Equation 18.7 represent a specific intended financing mix. These target weights represent a mix of debt and equity that the firm will try to achieve or maintain over the planning horizon. As much as possible, the target weights should reflect the combination of debt and equity that management believes will minimize the firm's weighted average cost of capital. The firm should make an effort over time to move toward and maintain its target capital structure mix of debt and equity.

MEASURING THE TARGET WEIGHTS

As the firm moves toward a target capital structure, how will it know when it arrives? There are two ways to measure the mix of debt and equity in the firm's capital structure.

One method uses target weights based on the firm's book values, or balance sheet amounts, of debt and equity. The actual weight of debt in the firm's capital structure equals the book value of its debt divided by the book value of its assets. Similarly, the actual equity weight is the book value of its stockholders' equity divided by total assets. Once the target weights are determined, the firm can issue or repurchase appropriate quantities of debt and equity over time to move the balance sheet numbers toward the target weights.

A second method uses the market values of the firm's debt and equity to compare target and actual weights. The actual weight of debt in the firm's capital structure equals the market value of its debt divided by the market value of its assets. Similarly, the actual equity weight is the market value of the firm's stockholders' equity divided by the market value of its assets. Calculated in this way, bond and stock market price fluctuations, as well as new issues and security repurchases, can move the firm toward—or away from—its target.

Financial theory favors the second method as most appropriate. Current *market* values are used to compute the various costs of financing, so it is intuitive that *market*-based costs should be weighted by *market*-based weights.

The basic capital structure of a firm may include debt, preferred equity, and common equity. In practice, calculating the cost of these components is sometimes complicated by the existence of hybrid financing structures (e.g., convertible debt) and other variations on straight debt, preferred equity, or common equity.[3] A discussion of this advanced topic is beyond the scope of this book.

As an example, let's compute the weighted average cost of capital for Global Manufacturing. Assume that Global Manufacturing has determined that its target capital structure should include one-third debt and two-thirds common equity. Global Manufacturing's current after-tax cost of debt is 6.0 percent, and its current cost of retained earnings is 15.0 percent. What is Global Manufacturing's weighted average cost of capital, assuming that last year's operations generated sufficient retained earnings to finance this year's capital budget?

Since sufficient new retained earnings exist, Global Manufacturing will not need to issue shares to implement its capital budget. Thus, the cost of retained earnings will be used to estimate its weighted average cost of capital. The target capital structure is one-third debt and two-thirds common equity. Using Equation 18.7, Global Manufacturing's weighted average cost of capital is:

$$\text{WACC} = (1/3)(6.0 \text{ percent}) + (2/3)(15.0 \text{ percent})$$
$$= 12.0 \text{ percent}$$

Given current market conditions and Global Manufacturing's target capital structure weights, the firm should use a discount rate of 12.0 percent when computing the NPV for average risk projects.[4]

---

[3]. For insights into how to handle these more complex financing structures, see McKinsey & Company Inc., Tim Koller, Marc Goedhart, and David Wessels, *Valuation: Measuring and Managing the Value of Companies*, 4th ed. (Hoboken, NJ: Wiley, 2005), and Michael C. Ehrhardt, *The Search for Value* (New York: Oxford University Press, 2001), or most intermediate-level corporate finance textbooks.

[4]. For a good case study of estimating the cost of capital for firms in the food processing industry, see Samuel C. Weaver, "Using Value Line to Estimate the Cost of Capital and Industry Capital Structure," *Journal of Financial Education*, Fall 2003, vol. 29, pp. 55–71.

INTERNET ACTIVITY

A firm may have only one class of common stock but many bonds outstanding. Data on bonds outstanding for a specific firm can be found in the financial reports on firms' Web sites and Mergent's Bond Record, in your library, or on the Internet at http://www.mergent.com.

To compare Global Manufacturing's current capital structure with its target capital structure, let's assume that Global Manufacturing has two bond issues outstanding. One is rated AA and has a yield to maturity of 8.8 percent; the other is rated A and yields 9.5 percent. The firm also has preferred stock and common stock outstanding. The table below shows the current market prices and the number of shares or bonds outstanding. How does Global Manufacturing's current capital structure compare to its target?

SECURITY	CURRENT PRICE	NUMBER OUTSTANDING
AA bonds	$1,050	10,000 bonds
A bonds	1,025	20,000 bonds
Preferred stock	40	250,000 shares
Common stock	50	700,000 shares

To begin, Global Manufacturing's target capital structure of one-third debt and two-thirds common equity does not leave any room for preferred stock. Evidently Global Manufacturing's management has decided not to raise funds in the future with new preferred stock issues. Using the given information, let's compute the market values of Global Manufacturing's securities and their current market value weights and then compare these figures to Global Manufacturing's target capital structure. A security's market value is found by multiplying its market price by the number of bonds or shares currently outstanding. The figures in the previous table give these market values and weights:

SECURITY	MARKET VALUE ($ MILLIONS)	MARKET WEIGHT
AA bonds	$10.50	0.138
A bonds	20.50	0.270
Preferred stock	10.00	0.132
Common stock	35.00	0.460
Total	$76.00	1.000

CONCEPT CHECK

How is WACC computed?

Should market value or book value weights be used to compare a firm's current capital structure with its target capital structure?

Presently, Global Manufacturing's capital structure is comprised of 41 percent debt, about 46 percent common equity, and about 13 percent preferred equity. To move toward its target capital structure, Global Manufacturing may want to issue common stock and use the proceeds to purchase outstanding preferred stock and bonds. There is no need for Global Manufacturing to restructure its finances immediately. The flotation costs and administrative fees of such a program would be prohibitive. Some movement toward the target capital structure would occur if Global Manufacturing could identify several positive-NPV projects. Barring a market downtrend, these projects would increase its market value of equity. Also, it could use future additions to retained earnings to repurchase some outstanding debt or preferred equity.

INTERNET ACTIVITY

Cost of capital is included in the calculation of economic value added, a measure of firm performance developed by Stern Stewart & Co. Stern Stewart's Web site, http://www.sternstewart.com, contains information on the importance of the cost of capital as well as practitioner-oriented research reports.

WHAT DO BUSINESSES USE AS THEIR COST OF CAPITAL?

Surveys of U.S. firms find that most firms use after-tax weighted average costs of capital as their required rates of return for projects. Other methods include management-determined target returns or the cost of some specific source of funds. A survey of U.S.-based multinationals found, surprisingly, that half of them use a single firm-wide discount rate to evaluate projects, regardless of risk differences. The most popular method for estimating the cost of equity is the security market line approach; nearly 75 percent of firms use this method. Because of its assumption regarding growth, the constant dividend growth model is not used by many firms; only about 15 percent of firms in a 1999 survey used that method, about half the level found in a 1982 survey.[5]

---

5. John R. Graham and Campbell R. Harvey, "The Theory and Practice of Corporate Finance: Evidence from the Field," *Journal of Financial Economics*, Vol. 60, No. 1, 2001, pp. 187–243; Lawrence J. Gitman and Vincent Mercurio, "Cost of Capital Techniques Used by Major U.S. Firms: Survey and Analysis of Fortune's 1000," *Financial Management*, vol. 14, 1982, pp. 21–29.

FIGURE 18.4
Corporate Bond Yields, 1919–2009

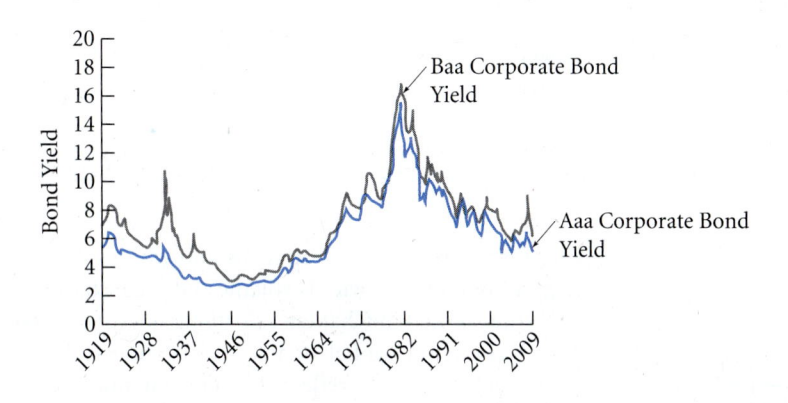

The student who has been watching the financial markets throughout the course—or possibility the past several years—may notice a potential problem with the formulas in this section. The cost of debt relies on current interest rates for a firm's debt. Similarly, the cost of equity relies on current estimates of beta (SML approach) or stock price. These values are always changing. Figure 18.4 shows a ninety-year history of investment-grade bond yields, and Figure 18.5 presents a three-year history of stock prices for one of the world's largest firms, ExxonMobil.

Although there are periods when corporate bond yields are relatively stable, the effects of the business cycle, Fed policy, and financial market risk premiums have resulted in more variability than stability with respect to interest rates in general and corporate bond yields in particular. Table 18.2 shows basic statistics about Aaa and Baa corporate bond yields over this time frame. Recalling our interpretation of the normal distribution from Chapter 12, we expect 65 percent of the time the yields on an Aaa corporate bond to fall within 3.17 and 8.66 percent (the average yield plus and minus one standard deviation); for Baa bonds, the yields is expected to fall 65 percent of the time within 4.22 and 10.01 percent. That's a fairly wide range!

Similarly, stock prices and annual returns show little stability. This is expected, since we learned in Chapter 12 that risk levels determined expected returns; if stock prices were stable, that would not reward investors over time with higher expected returns. Table 12.4 shows historical variability in stocks and other financial assets. In Chapter 12, we reviewed the histori-

FIGURE 18.5
ExxonMobil Stock Price January 2007-May 2010

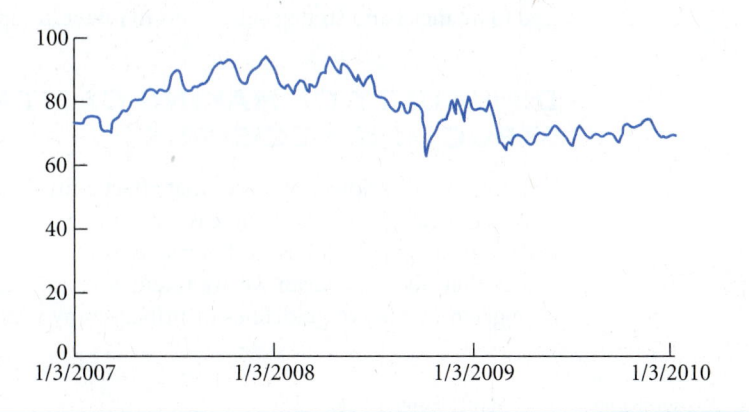

TABLE 18.2

Statistical Data on Aaa and Baa Corporate Bond Yields, 1919–2009

	AAA BOND	BAA BOND
Minimum	2.46	2.94
Maximum	15.49	17.18
Average	5.91	7.11
Median	5.24	6.75
Standard Deviation	2.74	2.90

cal returns and risk of Walgreens and Microsoft stock. In Figure 18.5, we see a similar story: ExxonMobil's stock price is volatile and is constantly changing.

As we learned in Chapter 12's discussion of efficient markets, some variability is expected as news—about the global or national economy, about a firm's industry, and about a specific firm—will be quickly reflected in current stock prices. Over the period shown in Figure 18.5 ExxonMobil's stock price ranged from $62.36 to $95. What may be surprising is these price extremes are separated by only ten months. During these three years, ExxonMobil's high price was in December 2007 and its low was in October 2008. Of course, the recession that occurred during that time frame had much to do with the decline of ExxonMobil's stock price.

What's a financial manager to do? Answer: focus on the longer-term, not on day-to-day market fluctuations.[6] Business cycles and financial market cycles come and go, and cost of capital calculations should take these variations into account over time—but not with daily revisions!

Rather than focus on the current day's interest rate or stock price, a longer-term perspective is needed. This is appropriate, as the capital investment under consideration is likely long-term as well. Today's costs matter most only if the firm needs to raise capital today by getting bank loans, issuing bonds, or issuing shares of stock. If internal funds (accumulated cash and retained earnings) can be used, the firm can use a longer-term average cost of capital that should better reflect the firm's history and prospects rather than current conditions. Some subjective adjustments may be appropriate because of risk perceptions in the financial markets (much like the cost of capital adjustments of project risk in Chapter 17). The firm will have historic information on the difference, or spread, between its cost of debt and cost of equity. Perhaps that spread is 4 percent. One way to check the reasonableness of a recent cost of capital calculation is to compare the cost of debt and cost of equity—does the new spread exceed 4 percent? Or is it under 4 percent? Financial managers can adjust the cost of capital used to evaluate projects based on both current financing costs and known—and reasonable—historical relationships between financial sources in light of current financial market concerns or "jitters."

Without such adjustments, the cost of capital may appear extremely large during market panics when interest rates spike and/or stock prices fall—such as during the 2007–2009 financial crisis. Financial market history has shown that the best time to invest—in financial assets if you are an individual or in your business and product if you are a manager—is during recessions. When others are pessimistic and slashing capital budgets, this is a great time to prepare for the coming business cycle upturn. Cost of capital calculations using current data may appear to rule out any such investing as the cost of capital will skyrocket as stock prices plunge. But keeping a longer-term view and using both current and historical stock/bond premium relationships may lead to financial and strategic decisions to invest in capital budgeting projects.

DIFFICULTY OF MAKING CAPITAL STRUCTURE DECISIONS

Examining the various influences that affect a firm's capital structure is not an easy task. Unlike NPV or operating cash flow, there is no formula we can use to determine the proportions of debt and equity a firm should use to finance its assets.

But that does not mean we are totally lost. Financial theory and research on firm behavior have given us a set of guidelines or principles by which to evaluate a firm's proper mix of debt

---

6. Randy Myers, "A Losing Formula," *CFO*, May 2009, pp. 17–18.

FIGURE 18.6
Long-term Debt Divided by Total Assets

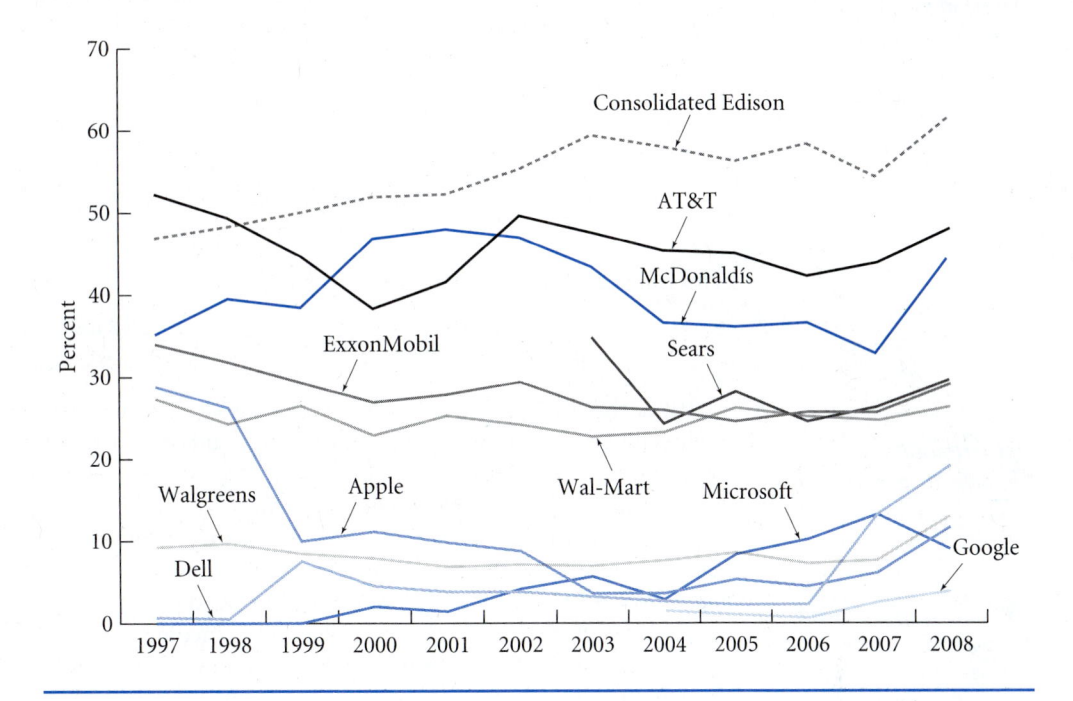

and equity. We also simplify the discussion by referring only to debt and equity, with little distinction between the various types of debt and equity. We discuss some of the variations in debt and equity later in the chapter.

In the following sections, we'll examine a number of interrelationships affecting a firm's capital structure decisions. First is the firm's growth rate. All else equal, a firm with higher growth levels will need to tap the capital markets more frequently than a slow- or no-growth firm. Second, given a firm's growth rate, the need for outside capital depends upon its return on assets and dividend policy. Again, all else equal, a firm with a larger return on assets can rely more on retained earnings as a source of financing and will favor equity over debt financing. A firm with a large dividend payout will need more outside capital to finance growth. Next we will examine some analytical tools and theories that have been advanced and tested to explain firms' capital structures.

Figure 18.3 showed how debt ratios—one indication of capital structure—can differ among different-sized firms. Figure 18.6 shows the ratio of long-term debt to total assets for several firms. The graph shows a wide variation in capital structures. Google, which went public in 2004 and then had a secondary equity offering in 2005, has little debt. Other technology firms (Apple, Dell, and Microsoft, whose true assets are software, ideas, and knowledge rather than brick and mortar) have low debt ratios. Walgreens also has a low ratio of long-term debt to assets but that is because they lease, rather than own, many of their stores to conserve capital. The firm with the highest level of debt relative to assets is Consolidated Edison. This is no surprise, since as a utility most of its asset base are fixed assets, which are more amenable to borrowing then ideas or software. In addition, since it is regulated, it will likely be able to charge electric rates sufficient to service the debt interest.

PLANNING GROWTH RATES

A firm's growth is in part determined by management's strategy to acquire or maintain market share in a growing or stable market. But management's plans for future sales, asset, and financing growth may not happen because of the competitive struggle in the marketplace. Growth that is faster or slower than expected may occur. A simple financial planning tool, the internal growth rate model, is available to determine just how quickly a firm can grow without running short of cash.

INTERNAL GROWTH RATE

internal growth rate
a measure of how quickly a firm can grow without needing additional outside financing

The **internal growth rate** measures how quickly a firm can increase its asset base over the next year without raising outside funds. It does not measure divisional growth, or break down total growth into domestic or international components. The internal growth rate gives a general, company-wide value.

It is equal to the ratio of the expected increase in retained earnings over the next year to the current asset base:

$$\frac{\text{Expected change in retained earnings}}{\text{Total assets}}$$

This can also be calculated as:

$$\text{Internal growth rate (g)} = \frac{(RR)(ROA)}{1 - (RR)(ROA)} \qquad (18.8)$$

RR is the firm's retention rate and ROA is its return on assets. The internal growth rate divides the product of these values by one minus this product.[7] The **retention rate** represents the proportion of every $1 of earnings per share that is retained by the firm; in other words, it is equal to one minus the **dividend payout ratio.**

retention rate
the proportion of each dollar of earnings that is kept by the firm

dividend payout ratio
the proportion of each dollar of earnings that is paid to shareholders as a dividend; equals one minus the retention rate

Suppose a firm pays out 40 percent of its earnings as dividends and has averaged a 15 percent return on assets over the past several years; how quickly can the firm grow without needing to tap outside financing sources? A 40 percent dividend payout ratio means that the firm's retention rate is 1.00 – 0.40 = 0.60. Of every dollar of net income, the firm distributes $0.40 as dividends and retains $0.60. With a 15 percent return on assets, Equation 18.8 tells us that the internal growth rate for the firm is:

$$\text{Internal growth rate} = \frac{(0.60)(0.15)}{1 - (0.60)(0.15)} = 0.099 \text{ or } 9.9 \text{ percent}$$

If it relies only on new additions to retained earnings to finance asset acquisition and maintains its past profitability and dividend pay out, the firm can increase its asset base by a little under 10 percent next year.[8]

The internal growth rate makes the restrictive assumption that the firm will pursue no outside sources of financing. Should the firm grow at its internal growth rate, its retained earnings account will continually rise (assuming profitable sales) while its dollar amount of debt outstanding will remain constant. *Thus, the relative amount of debt in its capital structure declines over time and the debt level will likely fall below its proportion in management's ideal financing mix.*

SUSTAINABLE GROWTH RATE

Perhaps a more realistic assumption would be to allow management to borrow funds over time to maintain steady capital structure ratios. As the stockholder's equity account rises from new additions to retained earnings, the firm issues new debt to keep its debt to equity ratio constant over time.

---

[7]. An end-of-chapter problem (number 13) invites you to derive this relationship.

[8]. Most managers plan and think in terms of sales dollars rather than size, so it may help to relate the internal growth rate to sales growth. If the firm's total asset turnover ratio is expected to remain constant into the foreseeable future, the growth in sales will equal the internal growth rate computed above. For example, suppose the total asset turnover ratio of 2.0 is expected to remain constant over the next few years:

$$\frac{\text{Sales}}{\text{TA}} = 2.0$$

Both sales and assets will rise at their respective growth rates:

$$\frac{\text{Sales}(1 + g_s)}{\text{TA}(1 + g_a)} = 2.0$$

Then

$$2.0 = \frac{(\text{Sales})(1 + g_s)}{(\text{TA})(1 + g_a)} = (2.0)\frac{(1 + g_s)}{(1 + g_a)}$$

This implies that $1 + g_s = 1 + g_a$, or that sales growth will equal asset growth.

sustainable growth rate
the estimate of how quickly a firm may grow by maintaining a constant mix of debt and equity

This rate of growth is the **sustainable growth rate.** It measures how quickly the firm can grow when it uses both internal equity and debt financing to keep its capital structure constant over time. It is computed as follows:

$$\text{Sustainable growth rate} = \frac{(RR)(ROE)}{1 - (RR)(ROE)}$$

As before, RR is the firm's retention rate, which is multiplied by ROE, its return on equity, divided by one minus this product.[9]

Suppose that the firm in the prior example maintains a debt to equity ratio of 1.0 (which is equivalent to an equity multiplier of 2.0) to minimize its financing costs. What would be the firm's sustainable growth rate? From the discussion in Chapter 14 of DuPont analysis, we know that ROE = ROA × equity multiplier.

Since the firm has a return on assets of 15 percent, its ROE equals 15 percent × 2 = 30 percent; with a retention rate of 0.60, the sustainable growth rate equals:

$$\text{Sustainable growth rate} = \frac{(0.60)(0.30)}{1 - (0.60)(0.30)} = 0.2195 \text{ or } 21.95 \text{ percent}$$

Thus, without outside financing, the firm can increase sales and assets by slightly under 10 percent; by maintaining a constant capital structure, the firm can grow by nearly 22 percent if it can maintain its levels of profitability and earnings retention.

EFFECTS OF UNEXPECTEDLY HIGHER (OR LOWER) GROWTH

The internal and sustainable growth rates are planning tools. These formulas cannot make a firm grow by a certain prescribed amount. Changing global competition, political, and credit market conditions can cause actual growth to deviate from planned growth.

The internal and sustainable growth rate relationships suggest that there are three measurable influences on growth: dividend policy (as reflected in the retention rate), profitability (as measured by ROA), and the firm's capital structure (as measured by the equity multiplier). A fourth influence that is much harder to measure is management's preferences and beliefs about the use of external financing rather than relying solely on changes in retained earnings. Should actual growth differ from planned growth, one or more of these factors will have to be adjusted either to prevent financial difficulty or to absorb excess funds.

Dividend Policy A reduction in the dividend payout ratio implies a higher retention rate and the ability for the firm to grow more quickly, if all else remains constant. Thus, a fast-growing firm may decide to maintain a low dividend payout (thereby increasing its addition to retained earnings) in an effort to finance its rapid growth. More mature, slower growing firms usually increase their dividend payout (and have smaller relative additions to retained earnings) as growth opportunities diminish.

Profitability Higher returns on assets generate more net income, larger additions to retained earnings, and faster growth, when all else is held constant. As we learned in the DuPont analysis discussion in Chapter 14,

$$ROA = \text{profit margin} \times \text{total asset turnover}$$

Management can attempt to change return on assets by influencing these factors should growth outpace or fall short of the planned rate.

Capital Structure The equity multiplier is determined by the firm's financing policy. A firm that uses a larger amount of debt can support a higher sustainable growth rate, when all else remains constant. If actual growth exceeds the sustainable growth rate, a firm can finance the difference by taking on additional debt.

One or more of these variables must deviate from planned levels to accommodate a difference between planned and actual growth. If a firm's actual growth exceeds the planned rate, management will have to reduce its dividend payout, increase profitability, use more debt, or use a combination of these options. If growth slows, the firm will need to increase its dividend payout,

---

CONCEPT CHECK

What does the internal growth rate measure?

What does the sustainable growth rate measure?

What causes the difference between them?

---

[9]. You have a chance to derive this relationship in one of the end-of-chapter problems (number 14).

reduce profitability, reduce its use of debt, or choose some combination of these alternatives. If outside financing is needed, the external financing needs calculation from Chapter 14 can help estimate the amount of funds needed.

The ability of the firm to grow is affected not only by management's strategy and by competitive conditions but by the firm's access to capital and levels of additions to retained earnings. Jointly, these influences of growth, dividend payout, and the amount of retained earnings determine the firm's need for outside capital. We first learned this in Chapter 14, when estimating a firm's external financing requirements.

As we saw then, a firm's external financing needs can come from short-term financing sources such as notes payable and drawing down lines of credit as well as spontaneous financing sources such as accounts payable. We reviewed influences on a firm's short-term/long-term financing mix in Chapter 16. Starting in the next section, we'll examine influences on a firm's long-term financing strategy.

EBIT/EPS ANALYSIS

As a first step in capital structure analysis, let's examine how different capital structures affect the earnings and risk of a firm in a simple world with no corporate income taxes. We use a tool of financial analysis called EBIT/eps analysis. **EBIT/eps analysis** allows managers to see how different capital structures affect the earnings and risk levels of their firms. Specifically, it shows the graphical relationship between a firm's operating earnings, or earnings before interest and taxes (EBIT), and earnings per share (eps). If we ignore taxes, these two quantities differ only by the firm's interest expense and by the fact that eps is, of course, net income stated on a per-share basis. Examining scenarios with different EBIT levels can help managers to see the effects of different capital structures on the firm's earnings per share.

EBIT/eps analysis allows managers to see how different capital structures affect the earnings and risk levels of their firms

Let's assume the Bennett Corporation is considering whether it should restructure its financing. As seen in Table 18.3, Bennett currently finances its $100 million in assets entirely with equity. Under the proposed change, Bennett will issue $50 million in bonds and use this money to repurchase $50 million of its stock (if the stock's price is $25 a share, Bennett will repurchase 2 million shares of stock). Bennett expects to pay 10 percent interest on the new bonds, for an annual interest expense of $5 million.

Assuming that Bennett's expected EBIT for next year is $12 million, let's see how the proposed restructuring may affect earnings per share. For simplicity, we ignore taxes in this example, so earnings per share (eps) will be computed as (EBIT − interest expense) divided by the number of shares. As shown in Table 18.4, the scenario analysis assumes that Bennett's EBIT will be either $12 million, 50 percent lower ($6 million), or 50 percent higher ($18 million). Figure 18.7 graphs the EBIT/eps combinations that result from the scenario analysis of the current and proposed capital structures. For lower EBIT levels, the current all-equity capital structure leads to higher earnings per share. At higher levels of EBIT, the proposed 50 percent equity, 50 percent debt capital structure results in higher levels of eps.

INDIFFERENCE LEVEL

Figure 18.7 clearly shows that the EBIT/eps lines cross. This means that, at some EBIT level, Bennett will be indifferent between the two capital structures, inasmuch as they result in the same earnings per share.

TABLE 18.3

Current and Proposed Capital Structures for the Bennett Corporation

	CURRENT	PROPOSED
Total assets	$100 million	$100 million
Debt	0 million	50 million
Equity	100 million	50 million
Common stock price	$25	$25
Number of shares	4,000,000	2,000,000
Interest rate	10%	10%

TABLE 18.4

Scenario Analysis with Current and Proposed Capital Structures

CURRENT—NO DEBT, 4 MILLION SHARES
(MILLIONS OMITTED)

	EBIT 50% BELOW EXPECTATIONS	EXPECTED	EBIT 50% ABOVE EXPECTATIONS
EBIT	$6.00	$12.00	$18.00
−I	0.00	0.00	0.00
NI	$6.00	$12.00	$18.00
eps	$1.50	$3.00	$4.50

PROPOSED—50% DEBT (10% COUPON), 2 MILLION SHARES
(MILLIONS OMITTED)

	EBIT 50% BELOW EXPECTATIONS	EXPECTED	EBIT 50% ABOVE EXPECTATIONS
EBIT	$6.00	$12.00	$18.00
−I	5.00	5.00	5.00
NI	$1.00	$7.00	$13.00
eps	$0.50	$3.50	$6.50

Under Bennett's current capital structure, earnings per share is computed as (EBIT − $0 interest)/4 million shares. Under the proposed structure, earnings per share is calculated as (EBIT − $5 million interest)/2 million shares. To find the level of EBIT where the lines cross, that is, where the combination of earnings per share and EBIT are the same under each capital structure, we set these two earnings per share values equal to each other and solve for EBIT:

$$\frac{EBIT - 0}{4} = \frac{EBIT - 5}{2}$$

Doing so, we learn that the earnings per share under the two plans are the same when EBIT equals $10 million.[10] When EBIT exceeds $10 million; the proposed, more highly leveraged capital structure will have the higher earnings per share. When EBIT is less than $10 million, the current, less leveraged capital structure will have the higher earnings per share.

The indifference level of $10 million in EBIT did not occur by chance. It equals the firm's interest cost of 10 percent multiplied by its total assets ($100 million). In other words, if the

FIGURE 18.7

EBIT/eps Analysis, Bennett Corporation

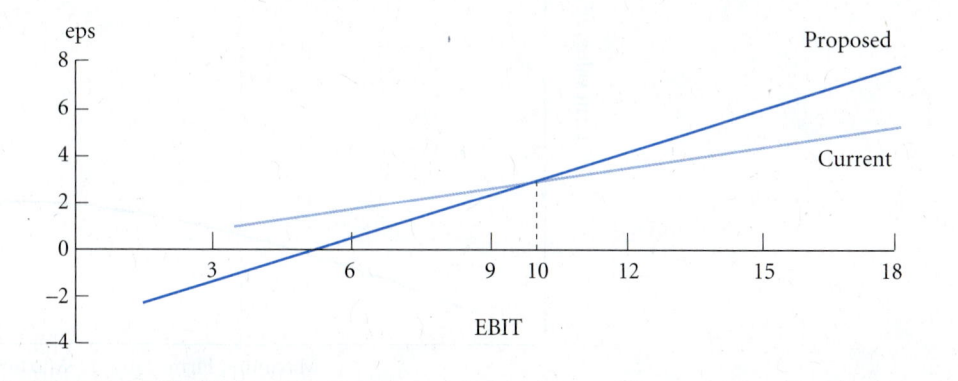

---

10. By cross-multiplying, 2 EBIT = 4 EBIT − 20. Solving for EBIT, we obtain EBIT = 10.

firm can earn an operating return on assets (EBIT/TA) greater than its interest cost, leverage is beneficial in that it results in higher earnings per share. If the firm's operating return on assets is less than its 10 percent interest cost, leverage is expensive relative to the firm's earning ability and results in lower earnings per share. If Bennett strongly believes that EBIT will meet expectations at $12 million, the proposed capital structure change is attractive.

EBIT/eps analysis has several practical implications. First, as seen, it shows the ranges of EBIT where a firm may prefer one capital structure over another. The firm may decide to increase or decrease its financial leverage depending on whether its expected EBIT is above or below the indifference EBIT level.

Second, EBIT is not constant over time; it will change, depending on sales growth, industry competitive conditions, and the firm's operating leverage. Variations in EBIT will produce variations in earnings per share. Should the expected EBIT of the firm lie above the indifference EBIT level, the firm's managers need to consider potential variation of earnings in their EBIT forecast. Depending on its uncertainty, management may decide to use a more conservative financing strategy with less debt.

This shows the drawback of using EBIT/eps analysis. It does not adequately capture the risk facing investors and how it affects shareholder wealth. We seek a capital structure that maximizes the value of the firm, not earnings per share. Although earnings per share may rise with financial leverage under certain values of EBIT, the value of earnings per share that maximizes firm value will likely be less than the maximum earnings per value. The firm's investors, both lenders and shareholders, consider the risk of cash flows when valuing investments. A relationship among debt, earnings per share, and firm value appears in Figure 18.8. Because of the risk of excessive debt, the maximum firm value occurs at a lower debt ratio than that of maximum earnings per share.

A firm's **business risk** is measured by its variability in EBIT over time. Business risk is affected by several factors, including the business cycle, competitive pressures, and the firm's operating leverage or its level of fixed operating costs. The following section reviews business risk and the combined effects of business and financial risk on management's choice of a capital structure.

business risk
measured by variability in EBIT over time

FIGURE 18.8
Firm Value, Earnings per Share, and Debt Ratios

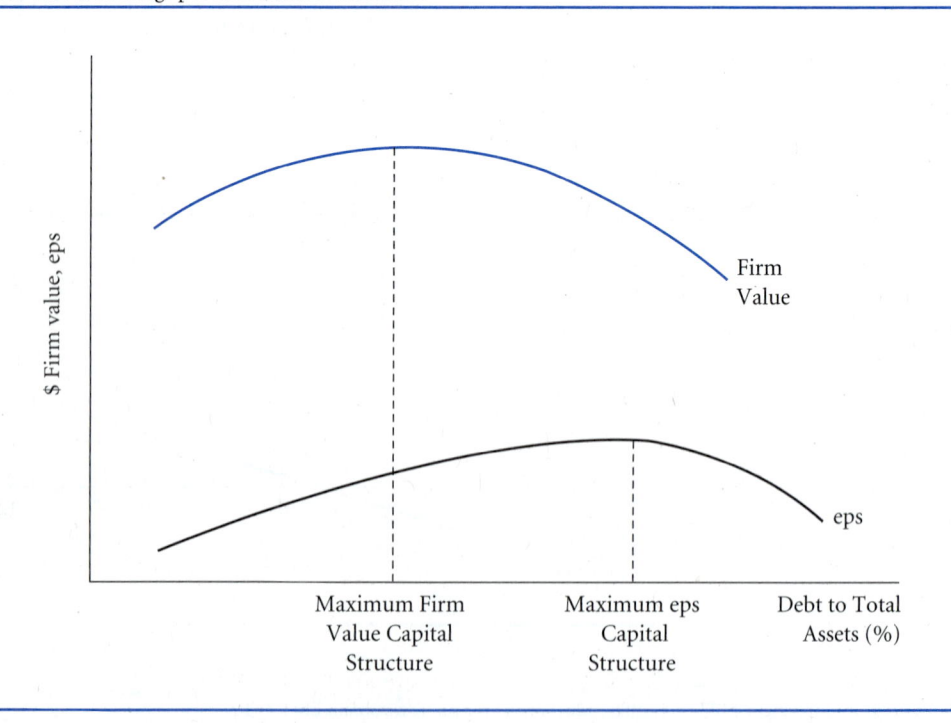

CONCEPT CHECK

How is EBIT/eps analysis useful to managers?

How might the expected level of EBIT and its potential variability affect a firm's capital structure?

COMBINED OPERATING AND FINANCIAL LEVERAGE EFFECTS

Business risk is determined by the products the firm sells and the production processes it uses. The effects of business risk are seen ultimately in the variability of operating income or EBIT over time. In fact, one popular measure of a firm's business risk is the standard deviation of EBIT.[11]

Table 18.5 shows a simplified income statement. Because business risk is measured by variability in EBIT, line items that affect business risk appear on the top half of the income statement, between sales revenue and EBIT. This suggests that a firm's business risk is affected by three major influences: unit volume or quantity sold, the relationship between selling price and variable costs, and the firm's fixed costs.

UNIT VOLUME VARIABILITY

Variability in the quantity sold of the firm's products or services will cause variation in sales revenue, variable costs, and EBIT. Fluctuating sales volumes can arise from a variety of factors, including pricing strategy from competitive products, new technologies or new products, customer impressions of product or service quality, and other factors affecting customer brand loyalty.

PRICE-VARIABLE COST MARGIN

A second factor affecting business risk is the firm's ability to maintain a constant, positive difference between price and per-unit variable costs. If the margin between price and cost fluctuates, the firm's operating income will fluctuate, too. Competitive pricing pressures, input supply shocks, labor union contracts, and other cost influences can cause the price-variable cost margin to vary over time, thus contributing to business risk.

FIXED COSTS

The variability of sales or revenues over time is a basic operating risk. Furthermore, when fixed operating costs, such as rental payments, lease payments, contractual employee salaries, and general and administrative overhead expenses exist, they create operating leverage and increase business risk. Since fixed costs do not rise and fall along with sales revenues, fluctuating revenues lead to variability in operating income or EBIT. As we learned in Chapter 14, the effect of operating leverage is that a given percentage change in net sales will result in a greater percentage change in operating income or earnings before interest and taxes (EBIT).

Operating leverage affects the top portion of a firm's income statement, as shown in Table 18.5. It relates changes in sales to changes in EBIT or operating income. We saw in Chapter 14

TABLE 18.5
Effects of Business Risk and Financial Risk on a Simplified Income Statement

IMPACT OF BUSINESS RISK (TOP HALF OF INCOME STATEMENT)	Sales revenue (equals price × quantity sold) Less variable costs (such as labor and materials; equals variable cost per unit × quantity) Less fixed costs (such as rent and depreciation expenses) Earnings before interest and taxes (operating income)
IMPACT OF FINANCIAL RISK (BOTTOM HALF OF INCOME STATEMENT)	Less interest expense (bank loans, bonds, other debt; a fixed expense as it is not dependent on sales) EBT (earnings before taxes) Less taxes (a variable expense, dependent on EBT) Net Income
	eps = Net Income/Number of Shares

---

[11]. To control for the effects of firm size when comparing different firms, some use the standard deviation of operating return on assets, that is, the standard deviation of EBIT/Total Assets.

that the effect of fixed operating costs on a firm's business risk can be measured by the degree of operating leverage (DOL). Equation 18.9 repeats these relationships from Chapter 14:

$$\text{DOL} = \frac{\text{Percentage change in EBIT}}{\text{Percentage change in Sales}} = \frac{\text{Sales} - \text{variable cost}}{\text{Sales} - \text{variable cost} - \text{fixed cost}} \quad (18.9)$$

In a similar fashion, when money is borrowed, financial leverage will be created as the firm will have a fixed financial obligation or interest to pay. Financial leverage affects the bottom half of a firm's income statement. A given percentage change in the firm's EBIT will produce a larger percentage change in the firm's net income or earnings per share. A small percentage change in EBIT may be levered or magnified into a larger percentage change in net income.

DEGREE OF FINANCIAL LEVERAGE

A firm's financial risk reflects its interest expense, or in financial jargon, its financial leverage. A quick way to determine a firm's exposure to financial risk is to compute its degree of financial leverage. The ***degree of financial leverage (DFL)*** measures the sensitivity of earnings per share to changes in EBIT:

degree of financial leverage (DFL)
measures the sensitivity of eps to changes in EBIT

$$\text{DFL} = \frac{\text{Percentage change in eps}}{\text{Percentage change in EBIT}} \quad (18.10)$$

This definition clearly suggests that DFL represents the percentage change in earnings per share arising from a 1 percent change in earnings before interest and taxes. For example, a DFL of 1.25 means that the firm's eps will rise (or fall) by 1.25 percent for every 1 percent increase (or decrease) in EBIT; a 1 percent change in EBIT becomes magnified to a 1.25 percent change in earnings per share.

There is a more straightforward way to compute a firm's degree of financial leverage that avoids handling percentage changes in variables. This formula is given in Equation 18.11:

$$\text{DFL} = \frac{\text{EBIT}}{\text{EBIT} - \text{I}} = \frac{\text{EBIT}}{\text{EBT}} \quad (18.11)$$

DFL equals the firm's earnings before interest and taxes (EBIT) divided by EBIT minus interest expense, or earnings before taxes (EBT).

Let's use Equation 18.11 to find the degree of financial leverage when EBIT equals $50 and interest expense equals $10, $20, and $0. When EBIT equals $50 and interest expense equals $10, DFL equals $50/($50 − $10) = 1.25.

When interest expense is $20, DFL equals $50/($50 − $20) = 1.67. Higher interest expense leads to greater financial risk and greater eps sensitivity to changes in EBIT.

When the interest expense is zero, the DFL is $50/($50 − $0) = 1.00. That is, the percentage change in eps will be the same as the percentage change in EBIT. Without any fixed financial cost, there is no financial leverage and there is no magnification effect.

TOTAL RISK

combined leverage
effect on earnings produced by the operating and financial leverage

Total earnings risk, or total variability in earnings per share, is the result of combining the effects of business risk and financial risk. As shown in Table 18.5, operating leverage and financial leverage combine to magnify a given percentage change in sales to a potentially much greater percentage change in earnings.

degree of combined leverage (DCL)
percentage change in earnings per share that results from a 1 percent change in sales volume

Together, operating and financial leverage produce an effect called **combined leverage**. A firm's ***degree of combined leverage (DCL)*** is the percentage change in earnings per share that results from a 1 percent change in sales volume:

$$\text{DCL} = \frac{\text{Percentage change in eps}}{\text{Percentage change in Sales}} \quad (18.12)$$

There is a straightforward relationship between the degrees of operating and financial leverage and the degree of combined leverage. A firm's degree of combined leverage is simply the product of its degree of operating leverage and its degree of financial leverage:[12]

$$DCL = DOL \times DFL \qquad (18.13)$$

The DCL represents the impact on earnings per share of the effects of operating leverage and financial leverage on a given change in sales revenue.

Let's illustrate this concept with a full income statement for this year and both a 10 percent decrease and a 10 percent increase in net sales for next year, as seen in Table 18.6.

We can estimate directly the individual effects of operating and financial leverage and their combined effects. First, from Chapter 14, the degree of operating leverage (DOL) is estimated as

$$DOL = \frac{\text{Sales} - \text{variable cost}}{\text{Sales} - \text{variable cost} - \text{fixed cost}}$$

$$= \frac{\$700,000 - \$420,000}{\$700,000 - \$420,000 - \$200,000} = \frac{\$280,000}{80,000} = 3.50$$

It should be noted that this is the same as the percentage change in EBIT (35 percent) divided by the percentage change in sales (10 percent) in Table 18.6:

$$DOL = \frac{35\%}{10\%} = 3.50$$

The degree of financial leverage (DFL) measures the impact of fixed financial expenses and is estimated as:

$$DFL = \frac{EBIT}{EBIT - 1}$$

Thus, DFL is equal to:

$$DFL = \frac{\$80,000}{\$80,000 - \$20,000} = \frac{\$80,000}{\$60,000} = 1.33$$

It should be noted that this is the same as the percentage change in eps (46.7 percent) divided by the percentage change in EBIT (35 percent) in Table 18.6:

$$DFL = \frac{46.7\%}{35.0\%} = 1.33$$

TABLE 18.6
Effects of Leverage on the Income Statement

	THIS YEAR	NEXT YEAR 10% SALES DECREASE	NEXT YEAR 10% SALES INCREASE
Net sales	$700,000	$630,000	$770,000
Less: variable costs (60% of sales)	420,000	378,000	462,000
Less: fixed costs	200,000	200,000	200,000
Earnings before interest and taxes	80,000	52,000	108,000
Less: interest expenses	20,000	20,000	20,000
Income before taxes	60,000	32,000	88,000
Less: income taxes (30%)	18,000	9,600	26,400
Net income	$42,000	$22,400	$61,600
Percent change in operating income (EBIT)		−35.0%	+35.0%
Percent change in net income		−46.7%	+46.7%

---

12. Recall that the degree of operating leverage is the percentage change in EBIT divided by the percentage change in sales; the degree of financial leverage is the percentage change in earnings per share divided by the percentage change in EBIT. Multiplying these two formulas gives the definition of DCL in Equation 18.12:

$$\frac{\text{Percentage change in EBIT}}{\text{Percentage change in sales}} \times \frac{\text{Percentage change in eps}}{\text{Percentage change in EBIT}} = DOL \times DFL = \frac{\text{Percentage change in eps}}{\text{Percentage change in sales}} = DCL$$

Finally, the degree of combined leverage (DCL) can be estimated by finding the product of the DOL and the DFL as follows:

$$\begin{aligned} DCL &= DOL \times DFL \\ &= 3.5 \times 1.33 \\ &= 4.66 \end{aligned}$$

Except for rounding, this is the same as the percentage change in eps (46.7 percent) divided by the percentage change in sales (10 percent): 46.7 percent/10 percent = 4.67.

By knowing the DCL factor, we can now estimate next year's change in net income, assuming no major change occurs in the income tax rate. This is done by multiplying the expected percentage change in net sales by the DCL of 4.67. For example, a 10 percent increase in net sales will increase net income by 46.7 percent (10 percent times the combined leverage factor of 4.67). Of course, combined leverage works in both directions, and a decline in net sales might place the firm in a difficult financial position. A 10 percent decline in sales will be expected to reduce net income and eps by 46.7 percent.

The use of both operating and financial leverage produces a compound impact when a change in net sales occurs. Thus, from an overall risk perspective, it is important for the financial manager to use operating and financial leverage to form an acceptable combined leverage effect.

For example, if a firm's stockholders do not like large amounts of risk, a firm with a high degree of operating leverage may attempt to keep financial leverage low. In other words, it will use relatively less debt and more equity to finance its assets. Likewise, a firm with low business risk (that is, steady sales and low fixed operating expenses), such as an electric utility, can support a higher degree of financial leverage and use relatively more debt financing. There is no evidence that firms adjust their DOLs and DFLs to match some standard degree of combined leverage, but their relationship does imply a potential trade-off between a firm's business and financial risk.

CONCEPT CHECK

What are the effects of financial leverage on earnings per share?

What is the degree of combined leverage? How is it related to DOL and DFL?

INSIGHTS FROM THEORY AND PRACTICE

An insight from our discussion of combined leverage is that a firm with greater business risk may be inclined to use less debt in its capital structure, while a firm with less business risk may use more debt in its capital structure. Theories of financial researchers have shed light on additional influences on the capital structure decision.

TAXES AND NONDEBT TAX SHIELDS

Interest on debt is a tax-deductible expense whereas stock dividends are not; dividends are paid from after-tax dollars. This gives firms a tax incentive to use debt financing.

But in reality there are limits to the benefits of tax-deductible debt. Business risk leads to variations in EBIT over time, which can lead to uncertainty about the firm's ability to fully use future interest deductions. For example, if a firm has a negative or zero operating income, an interest deduction provides little help; it just makes the pretax losses larger. Firms in lower tax brackets have less tax incentive to borrow than those in higher tax brackets.

In addition, firms have other tax-deductible expenses besides interest. Various cash and noncash expenses such as depreciation, R&D, and advertising expenses can reduce operating income. Thus, the tax deductibility of debt becomes less important to firms with large nondebt tax shields. Foreign tax credits, granted by the U.S. government to firms that pay taxes to foreign governments, also diminish the impact of the interest deduction.

BANKRUPTCY COSTS

The major drawback to debt in the capital structure is its legal requirement for timely payment of interest and principal. As the debt/total asset ratio rises, or as earnings become more volatile, the firm will face higher borrowing costs, driven upward by bond investors requiring higher yields to compensate for additional risk.

bankruptcy costs
explicit and implicit costs associated with financial distress

static tradeoff hypothesis
a theory that states firms attempt to balance the benefits of debt versus its disadvantages to determine an optimal capital structure

INTERNET ACTIVITY

Professor Edward Altman's Web site contains links to research on bond default rates and financial distress: http://www.stern.nyu.edu/~ealtman.

A rational marketplace will evaluate the probability and associated costs of bankruptcy for a levered firm. **Bankruptcy costs** include explicit expenses such as legal and accounting fees and court costs, along with implicit costs such as the use of management time and skills in trying to prevent and escape bankruptcy. It is also difficult to market the firm's products and keep good people on staff when the firm is teetering on the brink of bankruptcy.[13] An efficient market will evaluate the present value of the expected bankruptcy costs and reduce its estimate of the value of the firm accordingly.

The **static tradeoff hypothesis** states that firms will balance the advantages of debt (its lower cost and tax-deductibility of interest) with its disadvantages (greater possibility of bankruptcy and the value of explicit and implicit bankruptcy costs). This is illustrated in Figure 18.9. At low levels of debt, increasing the use of debt is beneficial because debt's lower cost helps to lower the weighted average cost of capital and to increase the firm's value. But further increases in debt beyond the optimal capital structure level actually reduce firm value, as investors' perceptions of the increased cost of bankruptcy outweigh the tax benefits of additional debt.

Bond ratings, discussed in Chapter 10, help guide both investors and managers in evaluating the risk of increasing debt to the capital structure. Studies have shown the probability of financial distress and bankruptcy rises as a firm's bond ratings decline. Some firms use their bond rating as a guide for their capital structure decision, for example, maintaining debt at a level consistent with an "A" bond rating. To preserve some financing flexibility, firms may try to keep their debt ratios lower than that necessary to maintain their target debt rating. This way, should they need to raise additional debt, they can do so and still be able to maintain their desired rating.

Table 18.7 shows that the decline in senior debt ratings over time among U.S. firms. In 1980, 50 percent of firms with rated senior debt had a rating of "A" or higher. In 1999, in good economic times, only 18 percent of firms had an "A" rating or better; by 2006 the proportion had sunk lower to 11 percent. Of course, this has the opposite effect on low-rated issues; the percentage of junk bonds (rated BB or lower) has swelled from 32 percent in 1980 to 71 percent in 2006. Several factors may account for this decline in credit quality, including more risk-tolerant investors, more

FIGURE 18.9
The Static Tradeoff Hypothesis: Weighted Average Cost of Capital versus Debt Ratio

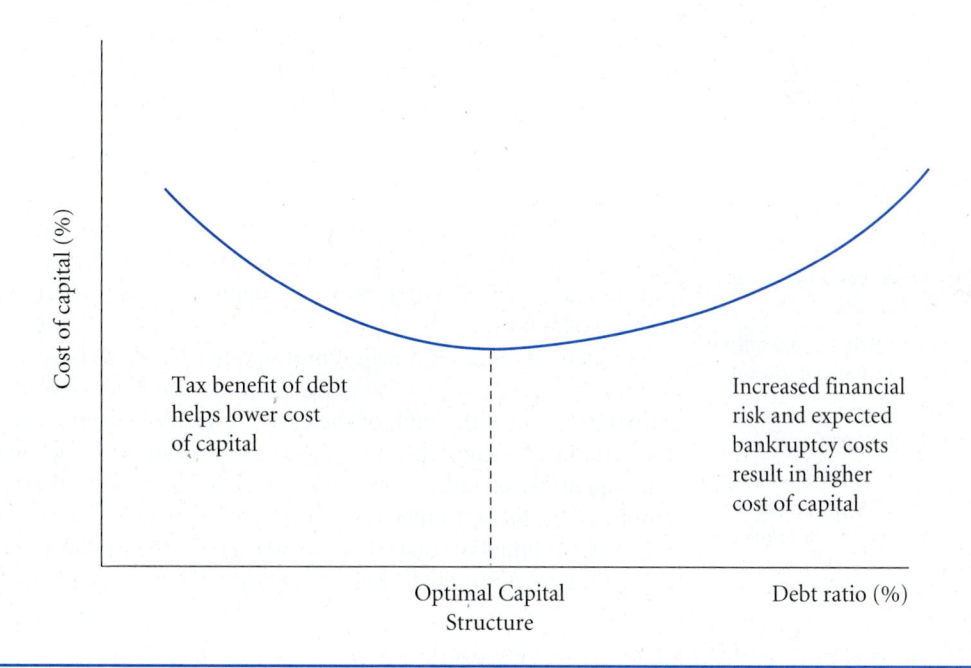

---

13. Potential customers shy away from a financially troubled firm in fear that it may not survive to provide warranty service or spare parts for their products. Customers may also fear that financial distress may lead management to reduce customer service or product maintenance (witness the decline in ridership for an airline when it declares bankruptcy). Good employees with marketable skills may decide to change jobs rather than risk unemployment due to business failure.

TABLE 18.7

Distribution of U.S. Industrial Senior Debt Ratings, various years

RATING	PERCENTAGE OF FIRMS WITH RATING IN 1980	PERCENTAGE OF FIRMS WITH RATING IN 1999	PERCENTAGE OF FIRMS WITH RATING IN 2006
AAA/AA	17	5	2
A	33	13	9
BBB	18	20	18
BB	22	24	25
B	7	32	42
CCC/D	3	6	4

Sources: Serena Ng, "Junk Turns Golden, but May Be Laced With Tinsel," *The Wall Street Journal*, January 4, 2007 pp. C1, C2; David Lindorff, "Who Needs a Triple A?" *Treasury and Risk* Management, May/June 2000, pp. 47–48.

risk-taking corporate managers, and perceptions of lower bankruptcy costs. In 2010, only four corporations were AAA-rated: ADP, ExxonMobil, Johnson & Johnson, and Microsoft.[14]

AGENCY COSTS

From Chapter 13 we know agency costs are restrictions placed on corporate managers in order to limit their discretion. They basically measure the cost of distrust between investors and management. To protect bondholders, covenants may require the firm to maintain a minimum level of liquidity or they may restrict future debt issues, future dividend payments, or certain forms of financial restructuring. Agency costs may also take the form of explicit expenses, such as a requirement that the firm's finances be periodically audited.

The cost to the firm's shareholders of excessive covenants and interference with management discretion will likely cause firms to shy away from excessive debt in the United States. In other words, the relationship between the level of agency costs and firm debt will look similar to that of bankruptcy costs and firm debt in Figure 18.9. The joint effect of bankruptcy and agency costs will reduce the optimal level of debt financing for a firm below the level that would be appropriate if agency costs were zero.

The situation may be different for non-U.S. companies. Agency costs may differ across national borders as a result of different accounting principles, banking structures, and securities laws and regulations. Firms in the United States and United Kingdom use relatively more equity financing than firms in France, Germany, and Japan—which use relatively more debt financing. Some argue that these apparent differences can be explained by differences in equity and debt agency costs across the countries.[15] For example, agency costs of equity seem to be lower in the United States and the United Kingdom. These countries have more accurate systems of accounting than the other countries, with higher auditing standards. Dividends and financial statements are distributed to shareholders more frequently, as well, which allows shareholders to monitor management more easily.

Germany, France, and Japan, on the other hand, all have systems of debt finance that may reduce the agency costs of lending. In these countries, a bank can hold an equity stake in a corporation, meet the bulk of the corporation's borrowing needs, and have representation on the corporate board of directors. Corporations can own stock in other companies and also have representatives on other companies' boards. Companies frequently get financial advice from groups of banks and other large corporations with which they have interlocking directorates. These institutional arrangements greatly reduce the monitoring and agency costs of debt; thus, debt ratios are substantially higher in France, Germany, and Japan.[16]

GLOBAL DISCUSSION

CONCEPT CHECK

As a firm's use of nondebt tax shields rises, how might its use of debt change?

How do bankruptcy costs affect a firm's optimal capital structure?

How do agency costs affect a firm's capital structure?

Why might a firm with many fixed assets use more debt financing relative to a dot-com firm?

---

14. A fifth firm, Pfizer, was AAA-rated but was downgraded in AA due to the debt and cash flow aspects of its 2009 acquisition of Wyeth Labs. See Ben Steverman, "Pfizer Loses Its Triple-A Credit Rating," http://www.businessweek.com/investing/insights/blog/archives/2009/10/pfizer_loses_it.html, accessed January 16, 2010.

15. See J. Ruttherford, "An International Perspective on the Capital Structure Puzzle," *Midland Corporate Finance Journal*, Fall 1985, pp. 60–72. For a perspective on several countries in the Asia Pacific region, see Rataporn Deesomsak, Krishna Paudyal, and Gioia Pescetto, "The Determinants of Capital Structure: Evidence from the Asia Pacific Region," *Journal of Multinational Financial Management*, vol. 14, issue 4–5, 2004, pp. 387–405.

16. Substantially higher debt ratios still exist in these countries after allowing for differences in accounting principles.

A FIRM'S ASSETS AND ITS FINANCING POLICY

Firms' asset structures and capital structures are related because of agency costs and bankruptcy costs. Evidence shows that firms with fungible, tangible assets (i.e., assets in place that can be easily sold and used by another firm, such as railroad cars or automobiles) use more debt financing than firms with many intangible assets. Examples of intangible assets include growth opportunities, the value of the firm's R&D efforts, and customer loyalty that is built and maintained through large advertising expenditures.

Agency costs and bankruptcy costs impose lighter burdens on financing for investments in tangible assets. It is much easier for a lender to monitor the use of tangible assets, such as physical plant and equipment. Well-developed accounting rules govern methods for tracking the values of such assets. Also, tangible assets can be sold and reused and they will not lose all of their value following a period of financial distress. Such is not necessarily the case for intangible assets whose value mainly resides within the firm.

THE PECKING ORDER HYPOTHESIS

One perspective on firms' capital structure decisions is based on repeated observations of how corporations seem to raise funds over time. The theory behind this perspective is based on the belief that management knows more about the firm and its opportunities than does the financial marketplace and that management does not want to be forced to issue equity when stock prices are depressed.

Evidence shows that corporations rely mainly on additions to retained earnings to finance growth and capital budgeting projects. If they need outside financing, firms typically issue debt first, as it imposes lower risk on the investor than equity, and it has a lower cost to the corporation. Should a firm approach its debt capacity, it may well favor hybrid securities, such as convertible bonds, over common stock. As a last resort, the firm will issue common equity. Thus, the firm has a financing "pecking order," rather than a goal to maintain a specific target debt/equity ratio over time.

Under this **pecking order hypothesis,** financial theory implies that firms have no optimal debt/equity ratios.[17] Instead, they follow the pecking order, exhausting internal equity (retained earnings) first and resorting to external equity (new issues of common stock) as a last resort. Observed debt ratios represent nothing more than the cumulative result of a firm's need to use external financing over time and reflect the joint effects of growth, attractive investment opportunities, and dividend policy.

Under the pecking order hypothesis, firms with higher profitability should have lower debt ratios, as these firms' additions to retained earnings reduce their need to borrow. Under the static tradeoff hypothesis, a firm with higher profitability should have a lower probability of bankruptcy and a higher tax rate, thus leading to *higher* debt ratios. Most empirical evidence resolves this conflict in favor of the pecking order hypothesis; studies find that more profitable firms tend to have lower debt ratios.

pecking order hypothesis
a theory that states managers prefer to use additions to retained earnings to finance the firm, then debt, and (as a final resort) new equity

MARKET TIMING

Like the pecking order hypothesis, this perspective is based upon observations of how firms raise funds in practice. The **market timing hypothesis** states that firms try to time the equity market by issuing stock when their stock prices are high and repurchasing shares when stock values are low.[18] Research studies have found that firms prefer to issue stock when earnings expectations by the market are over-optimistic. Managers have admitted that over- and undervaluation of their stock is an important consideration in issuing equity.[19] Researchers argue that firms, after issuing or repurchasing equity in apparent attempts to time the equity market, do not move the firm back to its former capital structure over time. Rather, low-leverage firms are those that were, on balance, successful in raising funds when their equity market values were high; high-leverage firms, on average, are those that raised funds when their equity market values were low.

market timing hypothesis
firms try to time the market by selling common stock when their stock price is high and repurchasing shares when their stock price is low

---

17. Stewart C. Myers and Nicholas S. Majluf, "Corporate Financing and Investment Decisions When Firms Have Information That Investors Do Not Have," *Journal of Financial Economics*, vol. 13, 1984, pp. 187–221; Stewart C. Myers, "The Capital Structure Puzzle," *Journal of Finance*, vol. 39, 1984, pp. 575–592.

18. Malcolm Baker and Jeffrey Wurgler, "Market Timing and Capital Structure," *Journal of Finance*, vol. 57, no. 1, February 2002, pp. 1–32.

19. John R. Graham and Campbell R. Harvey, "The Theory and Practice of Corporate Finance: Evidence from the Field," *Journal of Financial Economics*, vol. 60, 2001, pp. 187–243.

INTERNET ACTIVITY

Cutting-edge research on capital structure issues and many other finance topics can be found from the links on www.cob.ohio-state.edu/fin, the home page of the Finance Department at Ohio State University. Another site, http://www.cfo.com, contains items of interest on financing and other corporate finance topics.

An apparent implication of both the pecking order and market timing hypotheses is that the firm has no optimal capital structure. What implication does this have for computing a cost of capital and using it to evaluate capital budgeting projects? The answer: hardly any. Recall that the weighted average cost of capital represents the minimum required return on a firm's average-risk capital budgeting projects. The target capital structure weights reflect *management's* impression of a capital structure that is *sustainable* in the long run and that allows financing flexibility over time. Using the target structure and current financing costs, management can compute the weighted average cost of capital. The cost of capital calculation is paramount; should a firm fail to earn an appropriate return on its capital budgeting projects, shareholder wealth and firm value will decline.

Part of the uncertainty over which theoretical perspective may be correct arises from capital structure choices that depart from "plain vanilla" debt and equity. Firms have devised a myriad of financing flavors, as we discuss next.

BEYOND DEBT AND EQUITY

Bright Wall Street investment bankers have introduced many variations on these two themes in attempts to market new and different instruments to meet the needs of many kinds of issuers and investors.[20] Today firms can choose among various types of security issues, as we saw in Chapter 10. Consequently many firms have several layers of debt and several layers of equity on their balance sheets.

Debt can be made convertible to equity. Its maturity can be extended, or shortened, at the firm's option. Debt issues can be made senior or subordinate to other debt issues. Coupon interest rates can be fixed, float up or down along with other interest rates, or be indexed to a commodity price.[21] Some bond issues do not even pay interest. Corporations can issue bonds in the United States or overseas. Bonds can be sold alone, or with warrants attached that allow the bond investor to purchase shares of common stock at predetermined prices over time.

Likewise, equity variations exist. Preferred stock has a claim on the firm that is junior to the bondholder claim but senior to the common shareholder claim. Preferred stock can pay dividends at a fixed or a variable rate.

Even types of common stock can differ. Firms can have different classes of common equity. Some classes can provide holders with higher levels of dividend income. Some classes may have superior voting rights. Examples of such firms include Google, Facebook, Ford, and Visa. Firms have issued separate classes of equity to finance acquisitions, distributing part of the acquired firm's earnings as dividends to holders of that particular class of stock. Such was the case with General Motors. It issued its Class E stock to finance its acquisition of EDS in the 1980s; dividends on the Class E shares were determined by the earnings of the EDS subsidiary.

All these variations of debt and equity give the firm valuable flexibility. Corporate financial managers' decisions about the structure of a security issue may be more difficult now, but these choices also can allow them to lower the cost of capital and increase firm value.[22]

CONCEPT CHECK

What is the pecking order hypothesis?

What is the marketing timing hypothesis?

Describe some differences that can exist among security issues.

GUIDELINES FOR FINANCING STRATEGY

We have covered a lot of ground and a lot of controversy in this chapter. Let's now summarize the practical implications of these discussions and list the influences of both theory and real-world evidence on a firm's capital structure decisions.

---

20. Finance is not just finance; it sometimes involves marketing research and analysis. Wall Street firms serve two basic sets of customers: issuers and investors. By designing innovative securities to better meet their customers' needs, investment bankers can exploit market niches by being the first mover in a new product area. Such innovation will attract business, enhance income, and increase the firm's reputation among market players.

21. For example, a silver-mining firm whose profits and cash flow are quite sensitive to the market price of silver can reduce its financial leverage by issuing bonds that pay interest at a rate that is related to silver price fluctuations.

22. An accessible review of issues related to capital structure and cost of capital is available in Zander's 8-part series "WACC: Practical Guide for Strategic Decision-Making" found on http://www.gtnews.com/feature/122.cfm. Zanders, Treasury and Finance Solutions, is a European-based consulting firm. Their series on WACC was featured on the gtnews website March 2006–March 2007.

Business Risk

Firms in the same industry will generally face the same business risks. Many financial managers confess that they examine their competitors' capital structures to help determine if their own financial strategies are appropriate. A firm's degree of operating leverage affects the amount of debt it can issue. Firms with highly variable EBIT can ill afford to issue large amounts of debt, as the combined effects of high business and financial risk may imperil the future of the firm. In general, greater EBIT variability reduces the firm's reliance on debt.[23]

Taxes and Nondebt Tax Shields

Under current tax regulations, the debt interest deduction is a strong influence in favor of debt. The tax incentive for debt financing can diminish as a firm accumulates nondebt tax shields, such as depreciation expense, R&D, and large advertising outlays.

Mix of Tangible and Intangible Assets

Agency costs and bankruptcy costs can make debt less attractive as a financing alternative for firms with relatively large amounts of intangible assets such as goodwill, customer loyalty, R&D, and growth opportunities.

Financial Flexibility

Frequently the greatest concern among financial managers is maintaining access to capital. Without the ability to raise financing, a firm may have to pass up attractive investment opportunities, or a temporary cash crunch may push it to the edge of default. Loss of financial flexibility can disrupt the firm more than the strictest bond covenants. Some firms seek financial flexibility by maintaining financial slack or unused debt capacity. One way to do this is to try to maintain an investment-grade bond rating over time or to maintain large lines of credit.

It may be good to have financing that can be eliminated if it is no longer needed. The firm can arrange for debt financing with a maturity matching the expected period of need. For maturity matching, debt holds an important advantage over preferred stock or common stock financing because equity securities do not have a stated maturity that makes it possible to retire them conveniently. We should also note that a lease arrangement for fixed assets is advantageous because the lease term may be set to coincide with the duration of the need for the assets.

Control of the Firm

Common shareholders receive dividends and have voting control of the firm. Additional equity issues will likely reduce per-share dividends and dilute control. If shareholders worry about control, they may force a firm to use more debt financing and less external equity financing.

Profitability

Firms with above-average profitability can reduce flotation costs and restrictive debt covenants by relying on internal equity to finance capital budgeting projects. More profitable firms tend to use less debt financing.

Financial Market Conditions

A firm can minimize its financing costs by issuing debt when interest rates are near cyclical lows, especially if economists forecast rising rates in the future. Likewise, it is advantageous to issue stock when stock prices are high rather than depressed.

Management's Attitude Toward Debt and Risk

When push comes to shove, it is people—the management team—who ultimately make decisions about financing policy. Some management teams may be more conservative and hesitant to issue debt, while others may be more aggressive and willing to increase the firm's financial leverage. Their judgment and expectations for the firm's financial future will affect the firm's capital structure.

> **CONCEPT CHECK**
> *What influences affect a firm's choice of a capital structure?*

---

23. Securities can reduce the adverse effects of price swings that might otherwise contribute to business risk. Bonds with coupons that rise and fall with changes in commodity prices, market interest rates, or foreign currencies can help mitigate the effects of EBIT variations on net income. Firms can reduce political risk exposure from their foreign operations by financing foreign assets with host country bank loans or debt issues.

CAREER PROFILES

JEFF YINGLING
Managing Director, Corporate Finance
Morgan Stanley Dean Witter

BBA, Finance
University of Notre Dame
MBA, Finance
University of Chicago

"We definitely have ups and downs with the markets."

Q: *What is your primary responsibility?*
A: My job is to initiate and maintain investment banking relationships with clients in the utility and telecommunications industries.

Q: *What do you do for these clients?*
A: Our primary role is to help them raise capital through the issuance of equity or debt. We also advise on mergers, acquisitions, and divestitures.

Q: *Explain what happens when the client decides to publicly offer common stock.*
A: We work with the client to assemble the necessary information to register the offering with the Securities and Exchange Commission, analyze the value of the company to determine the price at which to offer the security, and coordinate a series of "road shows" where we and the client present information to potential investors. These road shows help generate awareness and demand for the upcoming stock issue. We also underwrite the issue, which means that we buy the stock for an agreed-upon price upfront. The client gets that money minus our commission. Then it's up to our sales force to sell the stock at the higher public offering price.

Q: *What are the major differences between issuing equity as you've just described and selling debt?*
A: There are lots of similarities, but one major difference is the timeline. A stock issue generally takes a number of weeks. A bond issue can be concluded in a very short time if necessary. That's because it's much less complicated to determine the value of a bond. Its cash flows, which are a function of the prevailing market interest rates and the credit rating of the company, are known at the time of sale. The value of a common stock issue, on the other hand, is much more subjective because it relates to the value of the Company's future earnings and cash flow, which obviously cannot be known in advance. There are many more variables to consider, so it takes longer to analyze.

Q: *What is the normal entry-level point in investment banking?*
A: Someone with an undergraduate degree would normally start as an analyst. An MBA would normally start as an associate. These positions involve the detail-level responsibilities in a transaction such as document preparation, number crunching, and the specifics of the road shows. Each deal is handled by a team of several people, depending on its size and complexity. The work of the analysts and associates is overseen by a more senior person.

Q: *Do the fluctuations of the markets affect your success?*
A: Very much so. When interest rates are low and equity values are high it is much easier for a company to raise money or complete a merger or acquisition, which means there is more business for us. When the markets are weak, our job is more difficult and the competition is more spirited. We definitely have ups and downs with the markets.

APPLYING FINANCE TO...

INSTITUTIONS AND MARKETS

A firm's capital structure is affected by the costs it faces from raising capital. Depository institutions and investment banks funnel savings to those wanting to raise funds. They do so in a way that helps to lower flotation and other transactions costs associated with raising funds, thereby making it easier for firms to raise capital. Security analysts and bond rating agencies convey opinions to investors regarding the attractiveness of a firm's securities.

INVESTMENTS

Dividends and the price appreciation potential in equity are attractive to many investors. Investors examine a firm's prospects and then "vote with their dollars" by deciding which investments look most attractive from a risk/expected return trade-off. The market prices of a firm's securities and the ratings given the firm's bonds are used as inputs into the firm's decision making process because they determine the cost of financing the firm's assets and therefore are a cost the firm must consider in its capital budgeting decisions.

FINANCIAL MANAGEMENT

Financial managers need to listen to the market. Trends in interest rates will affect the choice of short-term and long-term borrowing by the firm. Changes in stock price that differ from those of the overall market or the firm's industry group send positive or negative messages to managers about how investors evaluate the firm's future prospects. Financial capital is not cheap; the cost of financing assets, whether in the form of higher inventory or equipment, must be part of the firm's investment decisions.

SUMMARY

The capital structure decision is a very difficult, but a very important, one for managers to make. An inappropriate mix of debt and equity can lead to higher financing costs for a firm, which in turn will hurt shareholders' wealth. Once a target capital structure is selected, the cost of each financing source must be estimated before the weighted average cost of capital can be computed. We review how to estimate the cost of debt, cost of preferred stock, the cost of retained earnings, and the cost of new common equity.

This chapter reviewed several tools that can be used to examine a firm's capital structure, including EBIT/eps analysis, business risk, financial risk, and combined leverage. We reviewed findings of several studies, both theoretical and empirical, relating to influences on the capital structure decision, including management's desire to balance the benefits and drawbacks of debt, financing pecking orders, market timing, and agency cost issues, among others.

KEY TERMS

bankruptcy costs
business risk
capital structure
combined leverage
cost of capital
degree of combined leverage (DCL)

degree of financial leverage (DFL)
dividend payout ratio
EBIT/eps analysis
flotation costs
internal growth rate
market timing hypothesis

optimum debt/equity mix
pecking order hypothesis
retention rate
static tradeoff hypothesis
sustainable growth rate
weighted average cost of capital (WACC)

DISCUSSION QUESTIONS

1. What is a firm's capital structure?

2. Explain why determining a firm's optimum debt to equity mix is important.

3. Briefly describe the trends that have occurred in the corporate use of debt.

4. What is EBIT/eps analysis? What information does it provide managers?

5. Describe the term "indifference level" in conjunction with EBIT/eps analysis.

6. Describe how a firm's business risk can be measured and indicate how operating leverage impacts business risk.

7. How is financial leverage created? Describe how the degree of financial leverage is calculated.

8. Briefly explain the concepts of business risk, operating leverage, and financial leverage in terms of an income statement.

9. How might the following influences affect a firm's business risk (consider each separately)?

   a. Imports increase the level of competition
   b. Labor costs decline
   c. Healthcare costs (provided for all employees) increase
   d. The firm's proportion of Social Security and unemployment insurance taxes rises
   e. Adoption of new technology allows the firm to produce the same output with fewer employees

10. How might the following influences affect a firm's financial risk (consider each separately)?

a. Interest rates on the firm's short-term bank loans are reduced
b. The firm refinances a mortgage on one of its buildings at a lower interest rate
c. Tax rates decline
d. The firm's stock price rises
e. The firm suffers a sales and operating income decline

11. What is meant by the degree of combined leverage?

12. Describe how the degree of combined leverage can be determined by the degrees of operating and financial leverage.

13. Briefly explain how the factors of flexibility and timing affect the mix between debt and equity capital.

14. How do corporate control concerns affect a firm's capital structure?

15. The management of Albar Incorporated has decided to increase the firm's use of debt from 30 percent to 45 percent of assets. How will this affect its internal growth rate in the future? Its sustainable growth rate?

16. A booming economy creates an unexpectedly high sales growth rate for a firm with a low internal growth rate. How can the firm respond to this unplanned sales increase?

17. What is the relationship between a firm's cost of capital and investor required rates of return?

18. How can a firm estimate its cost of debt financing?

19. Describe how the cost of preferred stock is determined.

20. Describe two methods for estimating the cost of retained earnings.

21. How does the cost of new common stock differ from the cost of retained earnings?

22. What is the weighted average cost of capital? Describe how it is calculated.

23. Should book value weights or market value weights be used to evaluate a firm's current capital structure weights? Why?

24. How does management's strategy toward corporate growth and dividends affect its capital structure policy?

25. If a firm is eligible to receive tax credits, how might that affect its use of debt?

26. Describe the reasoning behind the static tradeoff hypothesis.

27. How do agency costs affect a firm's optimal capital structure? How can differences in agency costs explain capital structure differences across countries?

28. How do you expect the capital structures of two firms to differ if one is involved in steel production and the other designs software to solve business problems?

29. What implications might the pecking order and market timing hypotheses have for an optimal capital structure? Is the weighted average cost of capital still an important concept under these hypotheses?

PROBLEMS

1. AQ&Q has EBIT of $2 million, total assets of $10 million, stockholders' equity of $4 million, and pretax interest expense of 10 percent.
    a. What is AQ&Q's indifference level of EBIT?
    b. Given its current situation, might it benefit from increasing or decreasing its use of debt? Explain.
    c. Suppose we are told AQ&Q's average tax rate is 40 percent. How does this affect your answers to (a) and (b)?

2. URA, Incorporated, has operating income of $5 million, total assets of $45 million, outstanding debt of $20 million, and annual interest expense of $3 million.
    a. What is URA's indifference level of EBIT?
    b. Given its current situation, might URA benefit from increasing or decreasing its use of debt? Explain.
    c. Suppose forecasted net income is $4 million next year. If it has a 40 percent average tax rate, what will be its expected level of EBIT? Will this forecast change your answer to (b)? Why or why not?

3. Stern's Stews, Inc., is considering a new capital structure. Its current and proposed capital structures are:

	CURRENT	PROPOSED
Total assets	$150 million	$150 million
Debt	25 million	100 million
Equity	125 million	50 million
Common stock price	$50	$50
Number of shares	2,500,000	1,000,000
Interest rate	12%	12%

Stern's Stews' president expects next year's EBIT to be $20 million, but it may be 25 percent higher or lower. Ignoring taxes, perform an EBIT/eps analysis. What is the indifference level of EBIT? Should Stern's Stews change its capital structure? Why or why not?

4. Faulkner's Fine Fries, Inc. (FFF), is thinking about reducing its debt burden. Given the following capital structure information and an expected EBIT of $50 million (plus or minus 10 percent) next year, should FFF change their capital structure?

	CURRENT	PROPOSED
Total assets	$750 million	$750 million
Debt	450 million	300 million
Equity	300 million	450 million
Common stock price	$30	$30
Number of shares	10,000,000	15,000,000
Interest rate	12%	12%

5. Redo Problem 4, assuming that the less leveraged capital structure will result in a borrowing cost of 10% and a common stock price of $40.

6. A firm has sales of $10 million, variable costs of $4 million, fixed expenses of $1.5 million, interest costs of $2 million, and a 30 percent average tax rate.
    a. Compute its DOL, DFL, and DCL.
    b. What will be the expected level of EBIT and net income if next year's sales rise 10 percent?
    c. What will be the expected level of EBIT and net income if next year's sales fall 20 percent?

7. Here are the income statements for Genatron Manufacturing for 2010 and 2011:

INCOME STATEMENT	2010	2011
Net sales	$1,300,000	$1,500,000
Cost of goods sold	780,000	900,000
Gross profit	$520,000	$600,000
General and administrative	150,000	150,000
Marketing expenses	130,000	150,000
Depreciation	40,000	53,000
Interest	45,000	57,000
Earnings before taxes	$155,000	$190,000
Income taxes	62,000	76,000
Net income	$93,000	$114,000

Assuming one-half of the general and administrative expenses are fixed costs, estimate Genatron's degree of operating leverage, degree of financial leverage, and degree of combined leverage in 2010 and 2011.

8. The Nutrex Corporation wants to calculate its weighted average cost of capital. Its target capital structure weights are 40 percent long-term debt and 60 percent common equity. The before-tax cost of debt is estimated to be 10 percent and the company is in the 40 percent tax bracket. The current risk-free interest rate is 8 percent on Treasury bills. The expected return on the market is 13 percent and the firm's stock beta is 1.8.

   a. What is Nutrex's cost of debt?
   b. Estimate Nutrex's expected return on common equity using the security market line.
   c. Calculate the after-tax weighted average cost of capital.

9. The following are balance sheets for the Genatron Manufacturing Corporation for the years 2010 and 2011:

BALANCE SHEET	2010	2011
Cash	$50,000	$40,000
Accounts receivable	200,000	260,000
Inventory	450,000	500,000
Total current assets	700,000	800,000
Fixed assets (net)	300,000	400,000
Total assets	$1,000,000	$1,200,000
Bank loan, 10%	$90,000	$90,000
Accounts payable	130,000	170,000
Accruals	50,000	70,000
Total current liabilities	$270,000	$330,000
Long-term debt, 12%	300,000	400,000
Common stock, $10 par	300,000	300,000
Capital surplus	50,000	50,000
Retained earnings	80,000	120,000
Total liabilities and equity	$1,000,000	$1,200,000

   a. Calculate the weighted average cost of capital based on book value weights. Assume an after-tax cost of new debt of 8.63 percent and a cost of common equity of 16.5 percent.
   b. The current market value of Genatron's long-term debt is $350,000. The common stock price is $20 per share and there are 30,000 shares outstanding. Calculate the WACC using market value weights and the component capital costs in (a).
   c. Recalculate the WACC based on both book value and market value weights assuming that the before-tax cost of debt will be 18 percent, the company is in the 40 percent income tax bracket, and the after-tax cost of common equity capital is 21 percent.

10. The Basic Biotech Corporation wants to determine its weighted average cost of capital. Its target capital structure weights are 50 percent long-term debt and 50 percent common equity. The before-tax cost of debt is estimated to be 10 percent, and the company is in the 30 percent tax bracket. The current risk-free interest rate is 8 percent on Treasury bills. The after-tax cost of common equity capital is 14.5 percent. Calculate the after-tax weighted average cost of capital.

11. **Challenge Problem** Use various Internet resources and information contained in this text to estimate the cost of debt, cost of retained earnings, the cost of new equity, and the weighted average cost of capital for the following firms: Walgreens, Microsoft, and ExxonMobil. As an approximation, use current book value ratios as estimates of their target capital structure weights.

12. **Challenge Problem** Through library or Internet resources, find information regarding the sources of long-term financing for AT&T. What are the current market prices for their outstanding bonds and stock? Estimate their current market value weights. Estimate the cost of each financing source and, assuming the current market value weights equal AT&T's target capital structure, estimate its weighted average cost of capital.

13. Derive Equation 18.8 for the internal growth rate. Let S = last year's sales revenue; A = last year's total assets; D = last year's total liabilities; E = last year's stockholder's equity; NI/S = the firm's (presumably constant) profit margin, the ratio of net income to sales; g = the firm's expected sales growth rate; and RR = the firm's (presumably constant) retention ratio.

Using these symbols and relationships you are familiar with, find the following:

   a. What will this year's net income equal?
   b. How much will be added to stockholder's equity this year?
   c. What is this year's level of assets?
   d. What is the change in assets between last year and this year?
   e. The change in assets computed in (d) has to be financed.

Assuming only internal financing is available; compute the firm's internal growth rate. [Hint: Set your answers to (b) and (d) equal to each other, and solve for g, the growth rate.]

14. Using the same notation used in the previous problem, now assume that the firm will raise some funds externally in order to keep the firm's debt-to-equity (D/E) ratio constant.

   a. What will this year's net income equal?
   b. How much will be added to stockholder's equity this year?
   c. If the D/E ratio remains constant, how much external debt can the firm raise this year?
   d. What is this year's level of assets?
   e. What is the change in assets between this year and the last?
   f. The change in assets computed in (e) has to be financed.

Assuming a constant debt-to-equity ratio, compute the firm's sustainable growth rate. [Hint: Add your answers to (b) and (c) together and set them equal to the solution to (e) then solve for g.]

15. Below are items from recent financial statements from Moss and Mole Manufacturing:

2011 BALANCE SHEET (ALL NUMBERS ARE IN THOUSANDS)	
Total assets	$192,000
Stockholder's equity	$44,000
Total liabilities	$148,000

2011 INCOME STATEMENT	
Sales	$260,000
Net income	$37,500
Dividends paid	$18,750

a. Find M&MM's internal growth rate.
b. Find their sustainable growth rate.

16. The following information is from the financial statements of Bagle's Biscuits:

2011 BALANCE SHEET (ALL NUMBERS ARE IN MILLIONS)

Total assets	$134.9
Stockholder's equity	$51.7
Total liabilities	$83.2

2011 INCOME STATEMENT

Sales	$137.5
Net income	$8.0
Dividends paid	$3.2

a. Find Bagle's internal growth rate.
b. Compute Bagle's sustainable growth rate.

17. Income statements for Mount Lewis Copy Centers for 2010 and 2011 appear below. Data is in thousands of dollars.

	2010	2011
Sales	$20,000	$21,000
Cost of goods sold	10,000	10,500
Leases	2,500	3,000
Depreciation	2,000	2,100
EBIT	$5,500	$5,400
Interest	3,000	3,200
EBT	$2,500	$2,200
Taxes (30%)	750	660
Net income	$1,750	$1,540

a. Compute and interpret the degree of operating leverage, degree of financial leverage, and degree of combined leverage in 2010. Assume the components of the costs of goods sold are all variable costs.
b. Compute and interpret the degree of operating leverage, degree of financial leverage, and degree of combined leverage in 2011. Assume the components of the costs of goods sold are all variable costs.
c. Why did these numbers change between 2010 and 2011?

18. Using the income statements from the Mount Lewis Copy Centers for 2010 and 2011 in Problem 17, find the percentage change in sales, EBIT, and net income. Use them to compute the degree of operating leverage, financial leverage, and combined leverage.

19. Here's a recent income statement from TC1 Telecommunications Services, Inc. (numbers are in millions):

Sales	$53.7
Costs of goods sold	20.2
Depreciation	13.9
EBIT	$19.6
Interest expense	12.4
EBT	$7.2
Taxes (25%)	1.8
Net Income	$5.4

a. Compute TC1's degree of financial, operating, and combined leverage if one-half of the costs of good sold are variable costs and one-half are fixed costs.
b. Assume during the current year TC1's sales rise to $59.5 million. What is your estimate of TC1's net income this year?
c. Assume during the current year TC1's sales fall to $49.3 million. What is your revised estimate for TC1's net income?

20. **Challenge Problem** Company A1 intends to raise $3 million by either of two financing plans:

Plan A: Sell 100,000 shares of stock at $30 net to firm

Plan B: Issue $3 million in long-term bonds with a 10 percent coupon

The firm expects an EBIT of $1 million. Currently A1 has 50,000 shares outstanding and no debt in its capital structure. Its tax rate is 34 percent.

a. What EBIT indifference level is associated with these two proposals?
b. Draw an EBIT/eps graph showing the various levels of eps and EBIT including the expected EBIT. What should A1 do in this case?

21. **Challenge Problem** Big 10 + 1 Corp. intends to raise $5 million by one of two financing plans:

Plan A: Sell 1,250,000 shares at $4 per share net to the firm

Plan B: Issue $5 million in ten-year debentures with a 9 percent coupon rate

The firm expects an EBIT level of $800,000. Currently Big 10 + 1 has 100,000 shares outstanding and $2 million of debt with a 5 percent coupon in its capital structure. The tax rate is 34 percent.

a. Draw an EBIT/eps graph showing the various levels of eps and EBIT.
b. What is the EBIT indifference point?
c. When will eps be zero under either alternative?
d. What type of financing should the firm choose?
e. Suppose under the equity financing option at an EBIT level of $800,000, the firm's P/E ratio is 10; for the debt financing option, the P/E ratio is 7. What should the firm do?

22. **Challenge Problem** Champion Telecommunications is restructuring. Currently Champion has no debt outstanding. After it restructures, debt will be $5 million. The rate offered to bondholders is 10 percent. Champion currently has 700,000 shares outstanding at a market price of $40/share. Earnings per share are expected to rise.

a. What is the minimum level of EBIT that Champion is expecting? Ignore the consequences of taxes.
b. Calculate the minimum level of EBIT that Champion Telecommunications' managers are expecting, if the interest rate on debt is 5 percent.
c. Assume that Champion Telecommunications had EBIT of $2 million; was the leverage beneficial in (a)? In (b)?

• APPENDIX •

TABLE 1
Future Value of $1 (FVIF)

TABLE 2
Present Value of $1 (PVIF)

TABLE 3
Future Value of a $1 Ordinary Annuity (FVIFA)

TABLE 4
Present Value of a $1 Ordinary Annuity (PVIFA)

TABLE I
Future Value of $1 (FVIF)

YEAR	1%	2%	3%	4%	5%	6%	7%	8%	9%
1	1.010	1.020	1.030	1.040	1.050	1.060	1.070	1.080	1.090
2	1.020	1.040	1.061	1.082	1.102	1.124	1.145	1.166	1.188
3	1.030	1.061	1.093	1.125	1.158	1.191	1.225	1.260	1.295
4	1.041	1.082	1.126	1.170	1.216	1.262	1.311	1.360	1.412
5	1.051	1.104	1.159	1.217	1.276	1.338	1.403	1.469	1.539
6	1.062	1.126	1.194	1.265	1.340	1.419	1.501	1.587	1.677
7	1.072	1.149	1.230	1.316	1.407	1.504	1.606	1.714	1.828
8	1.083	1.172	1.267	1.369	1.477	1.594	1.718	1.851	1.993
9	1.094	1.195	1.305	1.423	1.551	1.689	1.838	1.999	2.172
10	1.105	1.219	1.344	1.480	1.629	1.791	1.967	2.159	2.367
11	1.116	1.243	1.384	1.539	1.710	1.898	2.105	2.332	2.580
12	1.127	1.268	1.426	1.601	1.796	2.012	2.252	2.518	2.813
13	1.138	1.294	1.469	1.665	1.886	2.113	2.410	2.720	3.066
14	1.149	1.319	1.513	1.732	1.980	2.261	2.579	2.937	3.342
15	1.161	1.346	1.558	1.801	2.079	2.397	2.759	3.172	3.642
16	1.173	1.373	1.605	1.873	2.183	2.540	2.952	3.426	3.970
17	1.184	1.400	1.653	1.948	2.292	2.693	3.159	3.700	4.328
18	1.196	1.428	1.702	2.026	2.407	2.854	3.380	3.996	4.717
19	1.208	1.457	1.754	2.107	2.527	3.026	3.617	4.316	5.142
20	1.220	1.486	1.806	2.191	2.653	3.207	3.870	4.661	5.604
25	1.282	1.641	2.094	2.666	3.386	4.292	5.427	6.848	8.623
30	1.348	1.811	2.427	3.243	4.322	5.743	7.612	10.063	13.268

(*Continues*)

Note: The basic equation for finding the future value interest factor (FVIF) is:

$$FVIF_{r,n} = (1 + r)^n$$

where r is the interest rate and n is the number of periods in years.

TABLE I
Future Value of $1 (FVIF) (*Continued*)

10%	12%	14%	15%	16%	18%	20%	25%	30%
1.100	1.120	1.140	1.150	1.160	1.180	1.200	1.250	1.300
1.210	1.254	1.300	1.322	1.346	1.392	1.440	1.563	1.690
1.331	1.405	1.482	1.521	1.561	1.643	1.728	1.953	2.197
1.464	1.574	1.689	1.749	1.811	1.939	2.074	2.441	2.856
1.611	1.762	1.925	2.011	2.100	2.288	2.488	3.052	3.713
1.772	1.974	2.195	2.313	2.436	2.700	2.986	3.815	4.827
1.949	2.211	2.502	2.660	2.826	3.185	3.583	4.768	6.276
2.144	2.476	2.853	3.059	3.278	3.759	4.300	5.960	8.157
2.358	2.773	3.252	3.518	3.803	4.435	5.160	7.451	10.604
2.594	3.106	3.707	4.046	4.411	5.234	6.192	9.313	13.786
2.853	3.479	4.226	4.652	5.117	6.176	7.430	11.642	17.922
3.138	3.896	4.818	5.350	5.936	7.288	8.916	14.552	23.298
3.452	4.363	5.492	6.153	6.886	8.599	10.699	18.190	30.288
3.797	4.887	6.261	7.076	7.988	10.147	12.839	22.737	39.374
4.177	5.474	7.138	8.137	9.266	11.974	15.407	28.422	51.186
4.595	6.130	8.137	9.358	10.748	14.129	18.488	35.527	66.542
5.054	6.866	9.276	10.761	12.468	16.672	22.186	44.409	86.504
5.560	7.690	10.575	12.375	14.463	19.673	26.623	55.511	112.460
6.116	8.613	12.056	14.232	16.777	23.214	31.948	69.389	146.190
6.728	9.646	13.743	16.367	19.461	27.393	38.338	86.736	190.050
10.835	17.000	26.462	32.919	40.874	62.669	95.396	264.700	705.640
17.449	29.960	50.950	66.212	85.850	143.371	237.376	807.790	2,620.000

APPENDIX • Present Value of $1 (PVIF)

TABLE 2
Present Value of $1 (PVIF)

YEAR	1%	2%	3%	4%	5%	6%	7%	8%	9%	10%
1	0.990	0.980	0.971	0.962	0.952	0.943	0.935	0.926	0.917	0.909
2	0.980	0.961	0.943	0.925	0.907	0.890	0.873	0.857	0.842	0.826
3	0.971	0.942	0.915	0.889	0.864	0.840	0.816	0.794	0.772	0.751
4	0.961	0.924	0.888	0.855	0.823	0.792	0.763	0.735	0.708	0.683
5	0.951	0.906	0.863	0.822	0.784	0.747	0.713	0.681	0.650	0.621
6	0.942	0.888	0.837	0.790	0.746	0.705	0.666	0.630	0.596	0.564
7	0.933	0.871	0.813	0.760	0.711	0.665	0.623	0.583	0.547	0.513
8	0.923	0.853	0.789	0.731	0.677	0.627	0.582	0.540	0.502	0.467
9	0.914	0.837	0.766	0.703	0.645	0.592	0.544	0.500	0.460	0.424
10	0.905	0.820	0.744	0.676	0.614	0.558	0.508	0.463	0.422	0.386
11	0.896	0.804	0.722	0.650	0.585	0.527	0.475	0.429	0.388	0.350
12	0.887	0.788	0.701	0.625	0.557	0.497	0.444	0.397	0.356	0.319
13	0.879	0.773	0.681	0.601	0.530	0.469	0.415	0.368	0.326	0.290
14	0.870	0.758	0.661	0.577	0.505	0.442	0.388	0.340	0.299	0.263
15	0.861	0.743	0.642	0.555	0.481	0.417	0.362	0.315	0.275	0.239
16	0.853	0.728	0.623	0.534	0.458	0.394	0.339	0.292	0.252	0.218
17	0.844	0.714	0.605	0.513	0.436	0.391	0.317	0.270	0.231	0.198
18	0.836	0.700	0.587	0.494	0.416	0.350	0.296	0.250	0.212	0.180
19	0.828	0.686	0.570	0.475	0.396	0.331	0.276	0.232	0.194	0.164
20	0.820	0.673	0.554	0.456	0.377	0.312	0.258	0.215	0.178	0.149
25	0.780	0.610	0.478	0.375	0.295	0.233	0.184	0.146	0.116	0.092
30	0.742	0.552	0.412	0.308	0.231	0.174	0.131	0.099	0.075	0.057

(*Continues*)

Note: The basic equation for finding the present value interest factor (PVIF) is:

$$PVIF_{r,n} = \frac{1}{(1 + r)^n}$$

where r is the interest or discount rate and n is the number of periods in years.

TABLE 2
Present Value of $1 (PVIF) (*Continued*)

12%	14%	15%	16%	18%	20%	25%	30%
0.893	0.877	0.870	0.862	0.847	0.833	0.800	0.769
0.797	0.769	0.756	0.743	0.718	0.694	0.640	0.592
0.712	0.675	0.658	0.641	0.609	0.579	0.512	0.455
0.636	0.592	0.572	0.552	0.516	0.482	0.410	0.350
0.567	0.519	0.497	0.476	0.437	0.402	0.328	0.269
0.507	0.456	0.432	0.410	0.370	0.335	0.262	0.207
0.452	0.400	0.376	0.354	0.314	0.279	0.210	0.159
0.404	0.351	0.327	0.305	0.266	0.233	0.168	0.123
0.361	0.308	0.284	0.263	0.225	0.194	0.134	0.094
0.322	0.270	0.247	0.227	0.191	0.162	0.107	0.073
0.287	0.237	0.215	0.195	0.162	0.135	0.086	0.056
0.257	0.208	0.187	0.168	0.137	0.112	0.069	0.043
0.229	0.182	0.163	0.145	0.116	0.093	0.055	0.033
0.205	0.160	0.141	0.125	0.099	0.078	0.044	0.025
0.183	0.140	0.123	0.108	0.084	0.065	0.035	0.020
0.163	0.123	0.107	0.093	0.071	0.054	0.028	0.015
0.146	0.108	0.093	0.080	0.060	0.045	0.023	0.012
0.130	0.095	0.081	0.069	0.051	0.038	0.018	0.009
0.116	0.083	0.070	0.060	0.043	0.031	0.014	0.007
0.104	0.073	0.061	0.051	0.037	0.026	0.012	0.005
0.059	0.038	0.030	0.024	0.016	0.010	0.004	0.001
0.033	0.020	0.015	0.012	0.007	0.004	0.001	0.000

TABLE 3
Future Value of a $1 Ordinary Annuity (FVIFA)

YEAR	1%	2%	3%	4%	5%	6%	7%	8%
1	1.000	1.000	1.000	1.000	1.000	1.000	1.000	1.000
2	2.010	2.020	2.030	2.040	2.050	2.060	2.070	2.080
3	3.030	3.060	3.091	3.122	3.152	3.184	3.215	3.246
4	4.060	4.122	4.184	4.246	4.310	4.375	4.440	4.506
5	5.101	5.204	5.309	5.416	5.526	5.637	5.751	5.867
6	6.152	6.308	6.468	6.633	6.802	6.975	7.153	7.336
7	7.214	7.434	7.662	7.898	8.142	8.394	8.654	8.923
8	8.286	8.583	8.892	9.214	9.549	9.897	10.260	10.637
9	9.369	9.755	10.159	10.583	11.027	11.491	11.978	12.488
10	10.462	10.950	11.464	12.006	12.578	13.181	13.816	14.487
11	11.567	12.169	12.808	13.486	14.207	14.972	15.784	16.645
12	12.683	13.412	14.192	15.026	15.917	16.870	17.888	18.977
13	13.809	14.680	15.618	16.627	17.713	18.882	20.141	21.495
14	14.947	15.974	17.086	18.292	19.599	21.015	22.550	24.215
15	16.097	17.293	18.599	20.024	21.579	23.276	25.129	27.152
16	17.258	18.639	20.157	21.825	23.657	25.673	27.888	30.324
17	18.430	20.012	21.762	23.698	25.840	28.213	30.840	33.750
18	19.615	21.412	23.414	25.645	28.132	30.906	33.999	37.450
19	20.811	22.841	25.117	27.671	30.539	33.760	37.379	41.466
20	22.019	24.297	26.870	29.778	33.066	36.786	40.995	45.762
25	28.243	32.030	36.459	41.646	47.727	54.865	63.249	73.106
30	34.785	40.568	47.575	56.805	66.439	79.058	94.461	113.283

(*Continues*)

Note: The basic equation for finding the future value interest factor of an ordinary annuity (FVIFA) is:

$$FVIFA_{r,n} = \sum_{t=1}^{n}(1+r)^{n-t} = \frac{(1+r)^n - 1}{r}$$

where r is the interest rate and n is the number of periods in years.

Future Value of a $1 Annuity Due (FVIFAD)
The future value interest factor of an annuity due (FVIFAD) may be found by using the following formula to convert FVIFA values found in Table 3:

$$FVIFAD_{r,n} = FVIFA_{r,n}(1+r)$$

where r is the interest rate and n is the number of periods in years.

TABLE 3
Future Value of a $1 Ordinary Annuity (FVIFA) (*Continued*)

9%	10%	12%	14%	16%	18%	20%	25%	30%
1.000	1.000	1.000	1.000	1.000	1.000	1.000	1.000	1.000
2.090	2.100	2.120	2.140	2.160	2.180	2.200	2.250	2.300
3.278	3.310	3.374	3.440	3.506	3.572	3.640	3.813	3.990
4.573	4.641	4.779	4.921	5.066	5.215	5.368	5.766	6.187
5.985	6.105	6.353	6.610	6.877	7.154	7.442	8.207	9.043
7.523	7.716	8.115	8.536	8.977	9.442	9.930	11.259	12.756
9.200	9.487	10.089	10.730	11.414	12.142	12.916	15.073	17.583
11.028	11.436	12.300	13.233	14.240	15.327	16.499	19.842	23.858
13.021	13.579	14.776	16.085	17.518	19.086	20.799	25.802	32.015
15.193	15.937	17.549	19.337	21.321	23.521	25.959	33.253	42.619
17.560	18.531	20.655	23.044	25.733	28.755	32.150	42.566	56.405
20.141	21.384	24.133	27.271	30.850	34.931	39.580	54.208	74.327
22.953	24.523	28.029	32.089	36.786	42.219	48.497	68.760	97.625
26.019	27.975	32.393	37.581	43.672	50.818	59.196	86.949	127.910
29.361	31.772	37.280	43.842	51.660	60.965	72.035	109.690	167.290
33.003	35.950	42.753	50.980	60.925	72.939	87.442	138.110	218.470
36.974	40.545	48.884	59.118	71.673	87.068	105.931	173.640	285.010
41.301	45.599	55.750	68.394	84.141	103.740	128.117	218.050	371.520
46.018	51.159	63.440	78.969	98.603	123.414	154.740	273.560	483.970
51.160	57.275	72.052	91.025	115.380	146.628	186.688	342.950	630.170
84.701	98.347	133.334	181.871	249.214	342.603	471.981	1,054.800	2,348.800
136.308	164.494	241.333	356.787	530.312	790.948	1,181.882	3,227.200	8,730.000

TABLE 4
Present Value of a $1 Ordinary Annuity (PVIFA)

YEAR	1%	2%	3%	4%	5%	6%	7%	8%	9%	10%
1	0.990	0.980	0.971	0.962	0.952	0.943	0.935	0.926	0.917	0.909
2	1.970	1.942	1.913	1.886	1.859	1.833	1.808	1.783	1.759	1.736
3	2.941	2.884	2.829	2.775	2.723	2.673	2.624	2.577	2.531	2.487
4	3.902	3.808	3.717	3.630	3.546	3.465	3.387	3.312	3.240	3.170
5	4.853	4.713	4.580	4.452	4.329	4.212	4.100	3.993	3.890	3.791
6	5.795	5.601	5.417	5.242	5.076	4.917	4.767	4.623	4.486	4.355
7	6.728	6.472	6.230	6.002	5.786	5.582	5.389	5.206	5.033	4.868
8	7.652	7.325	7.020	6.733	6.463	6.210	5.971	5.747	5.535	5.335
9	8.566	8.162	7.786	7.435	7.108	6.802	6.515	6.247	5.995	5.759
10	9.471	8.983	8.530	8.111	7.722	7.360	7.024	6.710	6.418	6.145
11	10.368	9.787	9.253	8.760	8.306	7.887	7.499	7.139	6.805	6.495
12	11.255	10.575	9.954	9.385	8.863	8.384	7.943	7.536	7.161	6.814
13	12.134	11.348	10.635	9.986	9.394	8.853	8.358	7.904	7.487	7.103
14	13.004	12.106	11.296	10.563	9.899	9.295	8.745	8.244	7.786	7.367
15	13.865	12.849	11.938	11.118	10.380	9.712	9.108	8.559	8.061	7.606
16	14.718	13.578	12.561	11.652	10.838	10.106	9.447	8.851	8.313	7.824
17	15.562	14.292	13.166	12.166	11.274	10.477	9.763	9.122	8.544	8.022
18	16.398	14.992	13.754	12.659	11.690	10.828	10.059	9.372	8.756	8.201
19	17.226	15.678	14.324	13.134	12.085	11.158	10.336	9.604	8.950	8.365
20	18.046	16.351	14.877	13.590	12.462	11.470	10.594	9.818	9.129	8.514
25	22.023	19.523	17.413	15.622	14.094	12.783	11.654	10.675	9.823	9.077
30	25.808	22.397	19.600	17.292	15.372	13.765	12.409	11.258	10.274	9.427

(*Continues*)

Note: The basic equation for finding the present value interest factor of an ordinary annuity (PVIFA) is:

$$FVIFA_{r,n} = \sum_{t=1}^{n} \frac{1}{(1+r)^t} = \frac{1 - \frac{1}{(1+r)^n}}{r}$$

where r is the interest or discount rate and n is the number of periods in years.

Present Value of a $1 Annuity Due (PVIFAD)
The present value interest factor of an annuity due (PVIFAD) may be found by using the following formula to convert PVIFA values found in Table 4:

$$PVIFAD_{r,n} = PVIFA_{r,n}(1+r)$$

where r is the interest or discount rate and n is the number of periods in years.

TABLE 4
Present Value of a $1 Ordinary Annuity (PVIFA) (*Continued*)

12%	14%	16%	18%	20%	25%	30%
0.893	0.877	0.862	0.847	0.833	0.800	0.769
1.690	1.647	1.605	1.566	1.528	1.440	1.361
2.402	2.322	2.246	2.174	2.106	1.952	1.816
3.037	2.914	2.798	2.690	2.589	2.362	2.166
3.605	3.433	3.274	3.127	2.991	2.689	2.436
4.111	3.889	3.685	3.498	3.326	2.951	2.643
4.564	4.288	4.039	3.812	3.605	3.161	2.802
4.968	4.639	4.344	4.078	3.837	3.329	2.925
5.328	4.946	4.607	4.303	4.031	3.463	3.019
5.650	5.216	4.833	4.494	4.193	3.571	3.092
5.938	5.453	5.029	4.656	4.327	3.656	3.147
6.194	5.660	5.197	4.793	4.439	3.725	3.190
6.424	5.842	5.342	4.910	4.533	3.780	3.223
6.628	6.002	5.468	5.008	4.611	3.824	3.249
6.811	6.142	5.575	5.092	4.675	3.859	3.268
6.974	6.265	5.668	5.162	4.730	3.887	3.283
7.120	5.373	5.749	4.222	4.775	3.910	3.295
7.250	6.467	5.818	5.273	4.812	3.928	3.304
7.366	6.550	5.877	5.316	4.843	3.942	3.311
7.469	6.623	5.929	5.353	4.870	3.954	3.316
7.843	6.873	6.097	5.467	4.948	3.985	3.329
8.055	7.003	6.177	5.517	4.979	3.995	3.332

GLOSSARY

A

acceptance receivable from the sale of merchandise on the basis of a draft or bill of exchange drawn against the buyer or the buyer's bank

accommodative function Fed efforts to meet credit needs of individuals and institutions, clearing checks, and supporting depository institutions

adjustable-rate mortgage (ARM) interest rate and periodic payments that vary with market interest rates over the real estate loan's life

administrative inflation the tendency of prices, aided by union-corporation contracts, to rise during economic expansion and to resist declines during recessions

advance factoring factor pays the firm for its receivables before the account due date

aftermarket period during which members of the syndicate may not sell the securities for less than the initial offering price

agency costs tangible and intangible expenses borne by shareholders because of the actual or potential self-serving actions of managers

agents hired by the principals to run the firm

American depository receipt (ADR) receipt that represents foreign shares to U.S. investors

amortized loan a loan repaid in equal payments over a specified time

annual percentage rate (APR) determined by multiplying the interest rate charged per period by the number of periods in a year

annual report contains descriptive information and numerical records on the operating and financial performance of a firm during the past year

annualize a return state the return as the annual return that would result in the observed percentage return

annuity a series of equal payments that occur over a number of time periods

annuity due exists when the equal payments occur at the beginning of each time period

arbitrage (1) buying commodities, securities, or bills of exchange in one market and immediately selling them in another to make a profit from price differences in the two markets; (2) operation that takes place if there is a mispricing between two different markets for the same asset that leads to a risk-free profit

ask price requested by the seller

asset management ratios indicate the extent to which assets are used to support sales

assets financial and physical items owned by a business

at-the-money an option's exercise price equals the current market price of the underlying asset

automatic stabilizers continuing federal programs that stabilize economic activity

automatic transfer service (ATS) accounts provide for direct deposits to, and payments from, checkable deposit accounts

average tax rate determined by dividing the taxes paid by the taxable income

B

balance of payment a summary of all economic transactions between one country and the rest of the world

balance of trade the net value of a country's exports of goods and services compared to its imports

balance sheet statement of a company's financial position as of a particular date

bank holding company company that holds voting power in two or more banks through stock ownership

bank liquidity   reflects ability to meet depositor withdrawals and to pay off other liabilities when due

bank reserves   vault cash and deposits held at Federal Reserve Banks

bank solvency   reflects ability to keep the value of a bank's assets greater than its liabilities

banker's acceptances   a promise of future payment issued by a firm and guaranteed by a bank

banking system   includes commercial banks, savings and loans, savings banks, and credit unions that operate in the U.S. financial system

bankruptcy costs   explicit and implicit costs associated with financial distress

barter   exchange of goods or services without using money

base case   firm's after-tax cash flows without the project

bearer bonds   have coupons that are literally "clipped" and presented, like a check, to the bank for payment; the bond issuer does not know who is receiving the interest payments

benefit/cost ratio (profitability index [PI])   ratio between the present values of the cash flows and the project's cost

best-effort agreement   agreement by the investment banker to sell securities to the issuing corporation; assumes no risk for the possible failure of the flotation

beta   measure of an asset's systematic risk

bid   price offered by a potential buyer

bimetallic standard   money standard based on two metals, usually silver and gold

blanket inventory lien   claim against a customer's inventory when the individual items are indistinguishable

blue-sky laws   protect the investor from fraudulent security offerings

bond rating   assesses both the collateral underlying the bonds as well as the ability of the issuer to make timely payments of interest and principal

branch banks   bank offices under a single bank charter

break-even analysis   used to estimate how many units of product must be sold for the firm to break even or have a zero profit

Bretton Woods system   international monetary system in which the U.S. dollar was valued in gold and other exchange rates were pegged to the dollar

broker   one who assists in the trading process by buying or selling securities in the market for an investor

brokerage firms   assist individuals to purchase new or existing securities issues or to sell previously purchased securities

budgetary deficit   occurs when expenditures are greater than revenues

budgets   financial plans indicating expected revenues, spending, and investment needs

business finance   study of financial planning, asset management, and fund-raising by businesses and financial institutions

business risk   measured by variability in EBIT over time

buying on margin   investor borrows money and invests it along with his own funds in securities

bylaws   rules established to govern the corporation; they deal with how the firm will be managed and the rights of the stockholder

C

call deferment period   specified period after the issue during which the bonds cannot be called

call option   contract for the purchase of a security within a specified time and at a specified price

call price   price paid to the investor for redemption prior to maturity, typically par value plus a call premium of one year's interest

call risk   risk of having a bond called away and reinvesting the proceeds at a lower interest rate

callable bonds   can be redeemed prior to maturity by the issuing firm

callable preferred stock   gives the corporation the right to retire the preferred stock at its option

cannibalization   situation in which a project robs cash flow from the firm's existing lines of business

capacity   ability to pay bills

capital   adequacy of owners' equity relative to existing liabilities

capital account balance   foreign government and private investment in the United States netted against similar U.S. investment in foreign countries

Capital Asset Pricing Model (CAPM)   states that expected return on an asset depends on its level of systematic risk

capital budgeting   process of identifying, evaluating, and implementing a firm's investment opportunities

capital consumption adjustment   estimates of the "using up," or depreciation, of plant and equipment assets for business purposes

capital formation   (1) process of constructing residential and nonresidential structures, manufacturing producers' durable equipment, and increasing business inventories; (2) the creation of productive facilities such as buildings, tools, and equipment

capital gains   gains or losses on capital assets held for more than one year

capital markets   where debt securities with maturities longer than one year and corporate stocks are issued or traded

capital market securities   debt securities with maturities longer than one year and corporate stocks

capital structure   firm's mix of debt and equity

cash budget   tool the treasurer uses to forecast future cash flows and estimate future short-term borrowing needs

cash conversion cycle time between a firm paying its suppliers for inventory and collecting cash from customers on a sale of the finished product

central bank a federal government agency that facilitates operation of the financial system and regulates money supply growth

central limit order book limit "book" in which the specialist keeps unexecuted limit orders

certificates of deposit (CDs) time deposits with a stated maturity

character ethical quality upon which one can base a judgment about a customer's willingness to pay bills

charter provides the corporate name, indicates the intended business activities, provides names and addresses of directors, and indicates how a firm will be capitalized with stock

chartists (technicians) study graphs of past price movements, volume, etc., to try to predict future prices

chief financial officer (CFO) responsible for the controller and the treasury functions of a firm

clean draft a draft that is not accompanied by any special documents

closed-end mortgage bond does not permit future bond issues to be secured by any of the assets pledged as security to it

coefficient of variation (CV) measures the risk per unit of return

collateral assets that are available to provide security for the potential credit

collateralized bonds pledge securities to protect the bondholders against loss in case of default

combined leverage effect on earnings produced by the operating and financial leverage

commercial bank accepts deposits, makes loans, and issues check-writing accounts

commercial finance company organization without a bank charter that advances funds to businesses

commercial letter of credit statement by a bank guaranteeing acceptance and payment of a draft up to a stated amount

commercial paper (1) short-term promissory note sold by high-credit-quality corporations; notes are backed solely by the credit quality of the issuer; (2) short-term unsecured promissory notes

commission (house) brokers act as agents to execute customers' orders for securities purchases and sales

common stock represents ownership shares in a corporation

common-size financial statement expresses balance sheet dollar figures as a percent of total assets and income statement numbers as a percent of total revenue to facilitate comparisons between different-size firms

compensating balance requirement that 10 to 20 percent of a loan be kept on deposit at the bank

compound interest interest earned on interest in addition to interest earned on the principal or investment

compounding an arithmetic process whereby an initial value increases at a compound interest rate over time to reach a future value

conditions current economic climate and state of the business cycle

constant payout ratio the declared dividends are a constant percentage of the firm's earnings

Consumer Credit Protection Act of 1968 act requiring clear explanation of consumer credit costs and prohibiting overly high-priced credit transactions

contractual savings savings accumulated on a regular schedule by prior agreement

contractual savings organizations collect premiums and contributions from participants and provide insurance against major financial losses and retirement benefits

contribution margin contribution of each unit sold that goes toward paying fixed costs

controller manages accounting, cost analysis, and tax planning

conversion ratio number of shares into which a convertible bond can be converted

conversion value stock price times the conversion ratio

convertible bond can be changed or converted, at the investor's option, into a specified number of shares of the issuer's common stock

convertible preferred stock has special provision that makes it possible to convert it to common stock of the corporation, generally at the stockholder's option

corporate bond debt instrument issued by a corporation to raise long-term funds

corporate equity capital financial capital supplied by the owners of a corporation

corporation legal entity created under state law with unending life that offers limited financial liability to its owners

correlation statistical concept that relates movements in one set of returns to movements in another set over time

cost of capital (1) project's required rate of return; (2) minimum acceptable rate of return to a firm on a project

cost-push inflation occurs when prices are raised to cover rising production costs, such as wages

cost-volume-profit analysis used by managers for financial planning to estimate the firm's operating profits at different levels of unit sales

coupon payments interest payments paid to the bondholders

covenants impose additional restrictions or duties on the firm

credit bureaus source of credit information about business firms and individuals

credit cards provide predetermined credit limits to consumers when the cards are issued

credit money money worth more than what it is made of

credit rating indicates the expected likelihood that a borrower will pay a debt according to the terms agreed to

credit risk (default risk) the chance of nonpayment or delayed payment of interest or principal

credit score a number that indicates the creditworthiness or likelihood that a borrower will make loan payments when due

credit union a cooperative nonprofit organization that exists primarily to provide member depositors with consumer credit

cross-sectional analysis different firms are compared at the same point in time

crowding out lack of funds for private borrowing caused by the sale of government obligations to cover large federal deficits

cumulative preferred stock requires that before dividends on common stock are paid, preferred dividends must be paid not only for the current period but also for all previous periods in which preferred dividends were missed

currency exchange rate value of one currency relative to another

currency exchange markets electronic markets where banks and institutional traders buy and sell various currencies on behalf of businesses and other clients

current account balance the flow of income into and out of the United Sates during a specified time period

current assets cash and all other assets that are expected to be converted into cash within one year

D

dealer satisfies the investor's trades by buying and selling securities from its own inventory

dealer system depends on a small group of dealers in government securities with an effective marketing network throughout the United States

debenture bonds unsecured obligations that depend on the general credit strength of the corporation for their security

debit cards provide for immediate direct transfer of deposit amounts

debt management various Treasury decisions connected with refunding debt issues

debt securities markets where money market securities, bonds, and mortgages are sold and traded

default risk risk that a borrower will not pay interest and/or principal on a loan when due

default risk premium compensation for the possibility of the borrower's failure to pay interest and/or principal when due

defensive activities Fed activities that offset unexpected monetary developments and contribute to the smooth everyday functioning of the economy

deficit economic unit generates less money that it spends resulting in a need for additional money

deficit financing how a government finances its needs when spending is greater than revenues

deficit reserves the amount that required reserves are greater than total reserves

degree of combined leverage (DCL) percentage change in earnings per share that results from a 1 percent change in sales volume

degree of financial leverage (DFL) measures the sensitivity of eps to changes in EBIT

degree of operating leverage (DOL) measures the sensitivity of operating income to changes in the level of output

demand-pull inflation occurs during economic expansions when demand for goods and services is greater than supply

depository institutions accept deposits from individuals and then lend pooled deposits to businesses, governments, and individuals

depreciation devaluing a physical asset over the period of its expected life

depreciation tax shield (1) tax reduction due to depreciation of fixed assets; equals the amount of the depreciation expense multiplied by the firm's tax rate; (2) tax reduction due to noncash depreciation expense, equals the depreciation expense multiplied by the tax rate

derivative deposit deposit of funds that were borrowed from the reserves of primary deposits

derivative security value determined by the value of another investment vehicle

derivative securities markets where financial contracts that derive their values from underlying debt and equity securities are originated and traded

designated market makers (DMM) assigned dealers who have the responsibility of making a market in an assigned security

development stage requires estimating relevant cash inflows and outflows

deviations computed as a periodic return minus the average return

direct financing involves use of securities that represent specific contracts between the savers and borrowers themselves

direct quotation method indicates the amount of a home country's currency necessary to purchase one unit of a foreign currency

dirty float intervention by central banks to control exchange rates in the foreign exchange market's flexible exchange system

discount bond bond that is selling below par value

discount rate interest rate that a bank must pay to borrow from its regional Federal Reserve Bank

discounted loan borrower receives the principal less the interest at the time the loan is made; the principal is repaid at maturity

discounting an arithmetic process whereby a future value decreases at a compound interest rate over time to reach a present value

disintermediation periods of significant decrease in funds moving through depository institutions to the credit markets

dissave to liquidate savings for consumption uses

diversification occurs when we invest in several different assets rather than just a single one

dividend payout ratio the proportion of each dollar of earnings that is paid to shareholders as a dividend; equals one minus the retention rate

dividend reinvestment plans (DRIPS) allow shareholders to easily purchase additional shares with their dividends

documentary draft draft that is accompanied by an order bill of lading and other documents

draft (bill of exchange) an unconditional order for the payment of money from one person to another

dual banking system allows commercial banks to obtain charters either from the federal government or a state government

Du Pont analysis technique of breaking down return on total assets and return on equity into their component parts

due diligence detailed study of a corporation

Dutch auction an offering process in which investors bid on prices and number of securities they wish to purchase; the securities are sold at the highest price that allows all the offered securities to be sold

dynamic actions Fed actions that stimulate or repress the level of prices or economic activity

E

EBIT/eps analysis allows managers to see how different capital structures affect the earnings and risk levels of their firms

economic risk risk associated with possible slow or negative economic growth, as well as with the likelihood of variability

effective annual rate (EAR) measures the true interest rate when compounding occurs more frequently than once a year

efficient market market in which prices adjust quickly after the arrival of new information and the price change reflects the economic value of the information, on average

electronic data interchange the use of communications and computer systems to convey ordering, invoice, and payment information between suppliers and customers

electronic funds transfer systems (EFTS) electronic method of receiving and disbursing funds

eligible paper short-term promissory notes eligible for discounting with Federal Reserve Banks

enhancement increase in the cash flows of the firm's other products that occur because of a new project

entrepreneurial finance study of how growth-driven, performance-focused, early-stage firms raise financial capital and manage operations and assets

equipment trust certificate gives the bondholder a claim to specific "rolling stock" (movable assets) such as railroad cars or airplanes

equity capital equity funds or stock investments made by the owners of a firm

equity funds supplied by the owners that represent their residual claim on the firm

Equity securities markets where ownership rights in the form of stocks are initially sold and traded

ethical behavior how an individual or organization treats others legally, fairly, and honestly

euro common currency that has replaced the individual currencies of twelve member countries of the European Union

Eurobond bond denominated in U.S. dollars that is sold to investors in a country outside the United States

Eurocurrencies all non-U.S. currencies held by banks outside their country of origin

Eurodollar bonds dollar denominated bonds sold outside the United States

Eurodollars U.S. dollars placed in foreign banks

European Central Bank (ECB) conducts monetary policy for the twelve European countries that adopted the euro as their common currency

European Monetary Union (EMU) organization of European countries that agreed to have a common overall monetary policy and the euro as common currency

European Union (EU) organization established to promote trade and economic development among European countries

ex-ante expected or forecasted

excess reserves the amount that total reserves are greater than required reserves

exchange rate value of one currency in terms of another

exchange rate risk fluctuating exchange rates lead to varying levels of U.S. dollar-denominated cash flows

exercise price (strike price) price at which an underlying asset can be traded

expectations theory states that shape of the yield curve indicates investor expectations about future inflation rates

Export-Import Bank bank established to aid in financing and facilitating trade between the United States and other countries

extendable notes have their coupons reset every two or three years to reflect the current interest rate environment and any changes in the firm's creditworthiness; the investor can accept the new coupon rate or put the bonds back to the firm

F

face value principal amount or par value that the issuer is obligated to repay at maturity

factor engages in accounts-receivable financing for business; purchases accounts outright and assumes all credit risks

Fed Board of Governors seven-member board of the Federal Reserve that sets monetary policy

Fed discount rate interest rate that a bank must pay to borrow from its regional Federal Reserve Bank

federal funds very short-term loans between depository institutions with excess funds and those with a need for funds

federal funds rate rate on overnight loans from banks with excess reserves to banks who have deficit reserves

Federal Reserve float temporary increase in bank reserves from checks credited to one bank's reserves and not yet debited to another's

Federal Reserve System (Fed) U.S. central bank that sets monetary policy and regulates banking system

federal statutory debt limits limits on the federal debt set by Congress

fiat money legal tender proclaimed to be money by law

field warehouse enterprise establishes a warehouse on the grounds of the borrowing business establishment

finance study of how individuals, institutions, governments, and businesses acquire, spend, and manage financial resources

finance companies provide loans directly to consumers and businesses or aid individuals in obtaining financing of durable goods and homes

finance firms provide loans directly to consumers and businesses and help borrowers obtain mortgage loans on real property

financial assets (1) claims against the income or assets of individuals, businesses, and governments; (2) claims against the income or assets of others; (3) claims in the form of obligations or liabilities issued by individuals, businesses, financial intermediaries, and governments

financial disintermediation reduction in the flow of savings through depository institutions and into the credit markets

financial environment financial system, institutions, markets, businesses, individuals, and global interactions that help the economy operate efficiently

financial institutions intermediaries that help the financial system operate efficiently and transfer funds from savers to individuals, businesses, and governments that seek to spend or invest the funds

financial intermediaries firms that bring about the flow of funds from savers to borrowers

financial intermediation process by which savings are accumulated in depository institutions and then lent or invested

financial leverage ratios indicate the extent to which borrowed funds are used to finance assets, as well as the ability of a firm to meet its debt payment obligations

financial management involves financial planning, asset management, and fund raising decisions to enhance the value of businesses

financial markets locations or electronic forums that facilitate the flow of funds among investors, businesses, and governments

financial risk variations in income before taxes over time because fixed interest expenses do not change when operating income rises or falls

financial system interaction of intermediaries, markets, instruments, policy makers, and regulations to aid the flow from savings to investments

first mortgage bonds backed or secured by specifically pledged property of a firm (real estate, buildings, and other assets classified as real property)

fiscal agent role of the Fed in collecting taxes, issuing checks, and other activities for the Treasury

fiscal policy government influence on economic activity through taxation and expenditure plans

fixed-rate mortgage fixed interest rate with a constant periodic payment over the real estate loan's life

flexible exchange rates a system in which international exchange rates are determined by supply and demand

float the delay in the payment system between when funds are sent by a payer and credited to the payee's bank account and deducted from the payer's bank account

floor brokers independent brokers who handle the commission brokers' overflow

flotation initial sale of newly issued debt or equity securities

flotation costs (1) comprised of direct costs, the spread, and underpricing; (2) costs of issuing stock; includes accounting, legal, and printing costs of offering shares to the public, as well as the commission earned by the investment bankers who market the new securities to investors

follow-up a stage in the capital budgeting process during which managers track, review, or audit a project's results

foreign bond bond issued by a corporation or government that is denominated in the currency of a foreign country where it is sold

foreign exchange markets electronic markets in which banks and institutional traders buy and sell various currencies on behalf of businesses and other clients

forward exchange rate rate for the purchase or sale of a currency where delivery will take place at a future date

fourth market large institutional investors arrange the purchase and sale of securities among themselves without the benefit of broker or dealer

fractional reserve system reserves held with the Fed that are equal to a certain percentage of bank deposits

full-bodied money coins that contain the same value in metal as their face value representative

future value value of a savings amount or investment at a specified time in the future

futures contract obligates the owner to purchase the underlying asset at a specified price on a specified day

G

generally accepted accounting principles (GAAP) set of guidelines as to the form and manner in which accounting information should be presented

Glass-Steagall Act provided for separation of commercial banking and investment banking activities in the United States

global bonds generally denominated in U.S. dollars and marketed globally

global depository receipt (GDR) listed on the London Stock Exchange; facilitates trading in foreign shares

gold standard currencies of countries are convertible into gold at fixed exchange rates

goodwill an intangible asset that equals reflects the value of a firm acquired in a purchase or merger that is not reflected in its assets and liabilities

Gordon Model (constant dividend growth model) a means of estimating common stock prices by assuming constant divided growth over time

government expenditures (GE) expenditures for goods and services plus gross investments by federal, state, and local governments

government purchases (GP) expenditures for goods and services by federal, state, and local governments

Gramm-Leach-Bliley Act of 1999 repealed the separation of commercial banking and investment banking activities provided for in the Glass-Steagall Act

greenbacks money issued by the U.S. government to help finance the Civil War

gross domestic product (GDP) measures the output of goods and services in an economy

gross private domestic investment (GPDI) investment in residential and nonresidential structures, producers' durable equipment, and business inventories

H

hedge reduce risk

high-yield or junk bonds bonds that have a relatively high probability of default

house (commission) brokers act as agents to execute customers' orders for securities purchases and sales

I

identification stage finding potential capital investment opportunities and identifying whether a project involves a replacement decision and/or revenue expansion

implementation stage executing accepted projects

income statement reports the revenues generated and expenses incurred by the firm over an accounting period

incremental cash flows represent the difference between the firm's after-tax cash flows with the project and the firm's after-tax cash flows without the project

independent brokers independent brokers who handle the commission brokers' overflow

independent projects projects not in direct competition with one another

indirect financing financing created by an intermediary that involves separate instruments with lenders and borrowers

indirect quotation method indicates the amount of a foreign currency necessary to purchase one unit of the home country's currency

individual net worth sum of an individual's money, real assets, and financial assets less the individual's debt obligations

industry comparative analysis compares a firm's ratios against average ratios for other companies in the industry

inflation (1) a rise in prices not offset by increases in quality; (2) occurs when an increase in the price of goods or services is not offset by an increase in quality

inflation premium average inflation rate expected over the life of the security

initial margin (1) initial equity percentage; (2) required deposit of funds for those who are purchasers and sellers of futures, usually 3–6% of the contract

initial public offering (IPO) initial sale of equity to the public

insurance companies provide financial protection to individuals and businesses for life, property, liability, and health uncertainties

interest rate price that equates the demand for and supply of loanable funds

interest rate parity (IRP) currency of a country with a relatively higher interest rate will depreciate relative to the currency of a country with a relatively lower interest rate

interest rate risk (1) fluctuating interest rates lead to varying asset prices—in the context of bonds, rising (falling) interest rates result in falling (rising) bond prices; (2) possible price fluctuations in fixed-rate debt instruments associated with changes in market interest rates

intermediation the accumulation and lending of savings by depository institutions

internal growth rate a measure of how quickly a firm can grow without needing additional outside financing

internal rate of return (IRR) method return that causes the net present value to be zero

international banking exists when banks operate in more than one country

International Monetary Fund (IMF) created to promote world trade through monitoring and maintaining fixed exchange rates and by making loans to countries with payments problems

international monetary system institutions and mechanisms to foster international trade, manage the flow of financial capital, and determine currency exchange rates

in-the-money option has a positive intrinsic value; for a call (put) option, the underlying asset price exceeds (is below) the stroke price

investment bank helps businesses sell their securities to raise financial capital

investment bankers (underwriters) assist corporations by raising money through the marketing of corporate securities

investment banking firms sell or market new securities issued by businesses to individual and institutional investors

investment companies sell shares in their firms to individuals and others and invest the pooled proceeds in corporate and government securities

investment grade bonds ratings of Baa or higher that meet financial institution investment standards

investments involves sale or marketing of securities, the analysis of securities, and the management of investment risk through portfolio diversification

J

junk bonds or high-yield bonds bonds with ratings that are below investment grade, that is, that are Ba1, BB+, or lower

L

legal tender money backed only by government credit

liabilities creditors' claims on a firm

limit order maximum buying price (limit buy) or the minimum selling price (limit sell) specified by the investor

limited branch banking allows additional banking offices within a geographically defined distance of a bank's main office

limited liability company (LLC) organizational form whose owners have limited liability; the firm can have an unlimited number of shareholders; income is taxed only once as personal income of the shareholders

limited partners face limited liability; their personal assets cannot be touched to settle the firm's debt

limited partnership has at least one general partner who has unlimited liability; the liability of the limited partners is limited to their investment

line of credit loan limit the bank establishes for each of its business customers

liquidity how easily an asset can be exchanged for money

liquidity preference theory states that investors are willing to accept lower interest rates on short-term debt securities, which provide greater liquidity and less interest rate risk

liquidity premium compensation for securities that cannot easily be converted to cash without major price discounts

liquidity ratios indicate the ability of the firm to meet short-term obligations as they come due

liquidity risk likelihood that a bank will be unable to meet depositor withdrawal demands and other liabilities when due

loan amortization schedule a schedule of the breakdown of each payment between interest and principal, as well as the remaining balance after each payment

loanable funds theory states that interest rates are a function of the supply of and demand for loanable funds

lockbox payments are sent to a P.O. box and processed by a bank to reduce collection float

M

M1 money supply consists of currency, traveler's checks, demand deposits, and other checkable deposits

M2 money supply M1 plus highly liquid financial assets including savings accounts, small time deposits, and retail money market mutual funds

M3 money supply M2 plus large time deposits and institutional money market mutual funds

macro finance study of how financial intermediaries, financial markets, and policy makers interact and operate within financial systems

maintenance margin minimum margin to which an investment may fall before a margin call will be placed

margin minimum percentage of the purchase price that must represent the investor's equity or unborrowed funds

margin call investor faces the option of either closing the position or investing additional cash to increase the position's equity or margin

marginal tax rate paid on the last dollar of income

market maker one who facilitates market transactions by selling (buying) when other investors wish to buy (sell)

market order open order of an immediate purchase or sale at the best possible price

market portfolio portfolio that contains all risky assets

market segmentation theory states that interest rates may differ because securities of different maturities are not perfect substitutes for each other

market stabilization intervention of the syndicate to repurchase securities in order to maintain their price at the offer price

market timing hypothesis firms try to time the market by selling common stock when their stock price is high and repurchasing shares when their stock price is low

market value added (MVA) measures the value created by the firm's managers

market value ratios indicates the value of a firm in the market place relative to financial statement values

marketable government securities securities that may be bought and sold through the usual market channels

maturity factoring firm selling its accounts receivable is paid on the normal collection date or net due date of the account

maturity matching approach financing strategy that attempts to match the maturities of assets with the maturities of the liabilities with which they are financed

maturity risk premium compensation expected by investors due to interest rate risk on debt instruments with longer maturities

medium of exchange the basic function of money

merchandise trade balance the net difference between a country's import and export of goods

mission statement statement of a firm's reason for being; sometimes called a vision statement

modified internal rate of return (MIRR) method a technique that finds the return that equates the present value of a project's outflows to the future value of its inflows

MOGS Mission, Objectives, Goals, and Strategies

monetary base banking system reserves plus currency held by the public

monetary policy formulated by the Fed to regulate money supply growth

monetizing the debt Fed increases the money supply to help offset the demand for increased funds to finance the deficit

money anything that is generally accepted as payment for goods, services, and debts

money market mutual funds (MMMFs) issue shares to customers and invest the proceeds in highly liquid, very short maturity, interest-bearing debt instruments

money markets where debt instruments of one year or less are issued or traded

money market securities debt securities with maturities of one year or less

money multiplier number of times the monetary base can be expanded or magnified to produce a given money supply level

mortgage loan backed by real property in the form of buildings and houses

mortgage-backed security debt security created by pooling together a group of mortgage loans

mortgage banking firms originate mortgage loans on homes and other real property by bringing together borrowers and institutional investors

mortgage bonds backed or secured by specifically pledged property of a firm (real estate, buildings, and other assets classified as real property)

mortgage markets where mortgage loans to purchase building and houses are originated and traded

multibank holding company (MBHC) permits a firm to own and control two or more banks

municipal bond long-term debt security issued by a state or local government

mutual fund open-end investment company that can issue an unlimited number of its shares to its investors and use the pooled proceeds to purchase corporate and government securities

mutually exclusive projects selecting one project precludes others from being undertaken

N

negative correlation two time series tend to move in opposite directions

negotiable certificates of deposit (negotiable CD) short-term debt instrument issued by depository institutions that can be traded in the secondary money markets

net exports (NE) exports of goods and services minus imports

net present value (NPV) present value of a project's cash flows minus its cost

net working capital dollar amount of a firm's current assets minus current liabilities

nominal interest rate interest rate that is observed in the marketplace

nonbank financial conglomerates large corporations that offer various financial services

noncumulative preferred stock makes no provision for the accumulation of past missed dividends

nonmarketable government securities issues that cannot be transferred between persons or institutions but must be redeemed with the U.S. government

NPV profile the graphical relationship between a project's NPV and cost of capital

O

odd lot sale or purchase of less than 100 shares

off-budget outlays funding for some government agencies that is not included in the federal budget

offer price price at which the security is sold to the investors

one-bank holding companies (OBHCs) permits a firm to own and control only one bank

open-end mortgage bond allows the same assets to be used as security in future issues

open-market operations buying and selling of securities by the Federal Reserve to alter the supply of money

operating cycle time between receiving raw materials and collecting cash from receivables

opportunity cost cost of passing up the next best alternative

optimum debt/equity mix proportionate use of debt and equity that minimizes the firm's cost of capital

option financial contract that gives the owner the option or choice of buying or selling a particular good at a specified price on or before a specified expiration date

option premium price paid for the option itself

option writer seller of option contracts

order bill of lading document given by a transportation company that lists goods to be transported and terms of the shipping agreement

ordinary annuity exists when the equal payments occur at the end of each time period (also referred to as a deferred annuity)

out-of-the-money option has a zero intrinsic value; for a call (put) option, the underlying asset price is below (exceeds) the strike price

P

par value stated value of a stock on the balance sheet; accounting and legal concept bearing no relationship to a firm's stock price or book value

participating preferred stock allows preferred shareholders to receive a larger dividend under certain conditions when common shareholder dividends increase

partnership form of business organization in which two or more people own a business operated for profit

payback period method determines the time in years it will take to recover, or pay back, the initial investment in fixed assets

pecking order hypothesis a theory that explains that managers prefer to use additions to retained earnings to finance the firm, then debt, and as a final resort new equity

pension funds receive contributions from employees and/or their employers and invest the proceeds on behalf of the employees for use during their retirement years

personal consumption expenditures (PCE) expenditures by individuals for durable goods, nondurable goods, and services

personal finance study of how individuals prepare for financial emergencies, protect against premature death and property losses, and accumulate wealth

personal saving savings of individuals equal to personal income less personal current taxes less personal outlays

pledge obtain a short-term loan by using accounts receivable as collateral

poison pills provisions in a corporate charter that make a corporate takeover more unattractive

political risk actions by a sovereign nation to interrupt or change the value of cash flows accruing to foreign investors

portfolio any combination of financial assets or investments

positive correlation two time series tend to move in conjunction with each other

precautionary motives holding funds to meet unexpected demands

pre-authorized checks regular, (typically) monthly deductions by a vendor from a customer's checking account

pre-emptive rights rights of existing shareholders to purchase any newly issued shares

preferred stock equity security that has preference, or a senior claim, to the firm's earnings and assets over common stock

premium bond bond that is selling in excess of its par value

present value value today of a savings amount or investment

primary deposit deposit that adds new reserves to a bank

primary market original issue market in which securities are initially sold

primary reserves vault cash and deposits held at other depository institutions and at Federal Reserve Banks

primary securities market involved in creating and issuing new securities, mortgages, and other claims to wealth

prime mortgage home loan made to a borrower with a relatively high credit score indicating the likelihood that loan payments will be made as agreed to

prime rate (1) interest rate on short-term unsecured loans to highest-quality business customers; (2) interest rate the bank charges its most creditworthy customers

principal-agent problem conflict of interest between the principals and agents

principals owners of the firm

private placement sale of securities to a small group of private investors

profitability index (PI) (benefit/cost ratio) ratio between the present values of the cash flows and the project's cost

profitability ratios indicate the firm's ability to generate returns on its sales, assets, and equity

program trading technique for trading stocks as a group rather than individually, defined as a minimum of at least fifteen different stocks with a minimum value of $1 million

progressive tax rate based on the concept that the higher the income the larger the percentage of income that should be paid in taxes

proprietorship business venture that is owned by a single individual who personally receives all profits and assumes all responsibility for the debts and losses of the business

prospectus document that details the issuer's operations and finances and must be provided to each buyer of a newly issued security

public offering sale of securities to the investing public

purchasing power parity (PPP) currency of a country with relatively higher inflation rate will depreciate relative to the currency of a country with a relatively lower inflation rate

purchasing power risk changes in inflation affect revenues, expenses, and profitability

put option contract for the sale of securities within a specified time period and at a specified price

572 GLOSSARY

putable bonds (retractable bonds) allow the investor to force the issuer to redeem the bonds prior to maturity

R

random walk prices appear to fluctuate randomly over time, driven by the random arrival of new information

ratio analysis financial technique that involves dividing various financial statement numbers into one another

real assets include the direct ownership of land, buildings or homes, equipment, inventories, durable goods, and precious metals

real rate of interest interest rate on a risk-free debt instrument when no inflation is expected

registered bonds the issuer knows the names of the bondholders and the interest payments are sent directly to the bondholder

registered traders buy and sell stocks for their own account

Regulation Z enacts Truth in Lending section of the Consumer Credit Protection Act with intent to make consumers able to compare costs of alternate forms of credit

reinvestment rate risk (rollover risk) fluctuating interest rates cause coupon or interest payments to be reinvested at different interest rates over time

remote capture scanning of paper checks to electronically gather and transmit the payment information

representative full-bodied money paper money fully backed by a precious metal

repurchase agreements short-term debt security where the seller agrees to repurchase the security at a specified price and date

required reserve ratio percentage of deposits that must be held as reserves

required reserves the minimum amount of total reserves that a depository institution must hold

residual dividend policy dividends vary over time based on the firm's excess funds

restricted stock shares of stock awarded to managers who vest, or become saleable, after a stated number of years

retention rate the proportion of each dollar of earnings that is kept by the firm

retractable bonds (putable bonds) allow the investor to force the issuer to redeem the bonds prior to maturity

revolving credit agreement legal obligation of the bank to provide up to the agreed-upon borrowing limit

risk-adjusted discount rate (RADR) adjusts the required rate of return at which the analyst discounts a project's cash flows; projects with higher (or lower) risk levels require higher (or lower) discount rates

risk-free rate of interest interest rate on a debt instrument with no default, maturity, or liquidity risks (Treasury securities are the closest example)

rollover risk (reinvestment rate risk) fluctuating interest rates cause coupon or interest payments to be reinvested at different interest rates over time

round lot sale or purchase of 100 shares

Rule of 72 used to approximate the time required for an investment to double in value

S

savings income that is not consumed but held in the form of cash and other financial assets

savings and loan association accepts individual savings and lends pooled savings to individual, primarily in the form of mortgage loans, and businesses

savings bank accepts the savings of individuals and lends pooled savings to individuals primarily in the form of mortgage loans

savings deficit occurs when investment in real assets exceeds current income

savings-investment process involves the direct or indirect transfer of individual savings to business firms in exchange for their securities

savings surplus occurs when current income exceeds investment in real assets

secondary market market in which securities are traded among investors

secondary reserves short-term securities held by banks that can be quickly converted into cash at little cost

secondary securities market market for transferring existing securities between investors

secured loan loan backed by collateral

securities firms accept and invest individual savings and also facilitate the sale and transfer of securities between investors

securities markets physical locations or electronic forums where debt and equity securities are sold and traded

securitization Process of pooling or packaging mortgage loans into debt securities

selection stage applying appropriate capital budgeting techniques to help make a final accept or reject decision

semi-strong-form efficient market market in which all public information, both current and past, is reflected in asset prices

settlement price determined by a special committee that determines the approximate closing price

shelf registration allows firms to register security issues (both debt and equity) with the SEC, and have them available to sell for two years

short sale sale of securities that the seller does not own

short-term investment policy statement guidelines for the types of securities and diversification requirements to use when investing funds

sight draft draft requiring immediate payment

simple interest interest earned only on the investment's principal

sinking fund requirement that the firm retire specific portions of the bond issue over time

sinking fund payments periodic bond principal repayments to a trustee

Special Drawing Rights (SDRs) reserve asset created by the IMF and consisting of a basket of currencies that could be used to make international payments

special dividend an extra dividend declared by the firm over and above its regular dividend payout

specialists assigned dealers who have the responsibility of making a market in an assigned security

speculative inflation caused by the expectation that prices will continue to rise, resulting in increased buying to avoid even higher future prices

speculative motives holding funds to take advantage of unusual cash discounts for needed materials

spot exchange rate rate being quoted for current delivery of the currency

spot market cash market for trading stocks, bonds, or other assets

spread difference between the offer price and the price paid by the investment bank

stand-alone principle analysis focuses on the project's own cash flows, uncontaminated by cash flows from the firm's other activities

standard deviation square root of the variance

standard of value a function of money that occurs when prices and debts are stated in terms of the monetary unit

statement of cash flows provides a summary of the cash inflows (sources) and cash outflows (uses) during a specified accounting period

statewide branch banking allows banks to operate offices throughout a state

static trade-off hypothesis a theory that states that firms attempt to balance the benefits of debt versus its disadvantages to determine an optimal capital structure

stock certificate certificate showing an ownership claim of a specific company

stock dividend a dividend in which investors receive shares of stock rather than cash

stock options allow managers to purchase a stated number of the firm's shares at a specified price

stock split the firms distributes additional shares for every share owned

stop-loss order order to sell stock at the market price when the price of the stock falls to a specified level

store of purchasing power when money is held as a liquid asset

store of value money held for some period of time before it is spent

street name (1) allows stock to be held in the name of the brokerage house; (2) an investor's securities are kept in the name of the brokerage house to facilitate record keeping, settlement, safety against loss or theft, and so on

strong-form efficient market market in which prices reflect all public and private knowledge, including past and current information

subchapter S corporation has fewer than thirty-five shareholders, none of which is another corporation; its income is taxed only once, as personal income of the shareholders

subordinated debenture claims of these bonds are subordinate or junior to the claims of the debenture holders

subprime mortgage home loan made to a borrower with a relatively low credit score indicating the likelihood that loan payments might be missed when due

sunk cost project-related expense not dependent on whether or not the project is undertaken

Supplemental Liquidity Provider (SLP) assigned dealers who have a responsibility of trading in an assigned security to increase liquidity on NYSE-listed stocks

surplus economic unit generates more money than it spends resulting in excess money

sustainable growth rate the estimate of how quickly a firm may grow by maintaining a constant mix of debt and equity

SWOT Analysis A review of a firm's internal strengths and weaknesses and its external opportunities and threats

syndicate group of several investment banking firms that participate in underwriting and distributing a security issue

systematic risk (market risk) risk that cannot be eliminated through diversification

T

target dividend payout policy the dividend payout ratio adjusts over time to a target level set by management

tax policy setting the level and structure of taxes to affect the economy

tax risk variations in a firm's tax rate and tax-related charges over time due to changing tax laws and regulations

technician (chartists) study graphs of past price movements, volume, etc., to try to predict future prices

term structure relationship between interest rates or yields and the time to maturity for debt instruments of comparable quality

third market market for large blocks of listed stocks that operates outside the confines of the organized exchanges

thrift institutions noncommercial bank depository institutions that accumulate individual savings and primarily make consumer and mortgage loans

time draft draft that is payable at a specified future date

time value of money the mathematics of finance whereby interest is earned over time by saving or investing money

token coins coins containing metal of less value than their stated value

tombstones announcements of securities offerings

total reserves deposits held in Federal Reserve Banks and cash in depository institutions

trade credit credit extended on purchases to a firm's customers

trade discounts provided to purchasers as an incentive for early or prompt payment of accounts

transactions motive demand for cash needed to conduct day-to-day operations

transfer payments government payments for which no current services are given in return

traveler's letter of credit issued by a bank to banks in other countries authorizing them to cash checks or purchase drafts presented by the bearer

treasurer oversees the traditional functions of financial analysis

Treasury bills federal obligations that bear the shortest original maturities

Treasury bonds long-term debt instrument issued by the U.S. federal government

Treasury notes federal obligations issued for maturities of two to ten years

trend or time series analysis used to evaluate a firm's performance over time

trust indenture contract that lists the various provisions and covenants of the loan arrangement

trust receipt (1) an instrument through which a bank retains title to goods until they are paid for; (2) lien against specific identifiable items in inventory

trustee individual or organization that represents the bondholders to ensure the indenture's provisions are respected by the bond issuer

U

underpricing represents the difference between the aftermarket stock price and the offering price

underwriting agreement contract in which the investment banker agrees to buy securities at a predetermined price and then resell them to the investors

undistributed profits proportion of after-tax profits retained by corporations

unit banking exists when a bank can have only one full-service office

universal bank can engage in both commercial banking and investment banking activities

unsecured loan loan that is a general claim against the borrower's assets

unsystematic risk risk that can be diversified away

usury the act of lending money at an excessively high interest rate

V

variance derived by summing the squared deviations and dividing by n – 1

velocity of money the rate of circulation of the money supply

voluntary savings savings held or set aside by choice for future use

W

warehouse receipt inventory is placed in a bonded warehouse for safekeeping; items are removed as they are paid for

weak-form efficient market market in which prices reflect all past information

weighted average cost of capital (WACC) represents the minimum required rate of return on a capital budgeting project; it is found by multiplying the marginal cost of each capital structure component by its appropriate weight, and summing the terms

working capital assets needed to carry out the normal operations of the business

World Bank International Bank for Reconstruction and Development created to help economic growth in developing countries

Y

Yankee bonds dollar denominated bonds issued in the United States by a foreign issuer

yield curve graphic presentation of the term structure of interest rates at a given point in time

yield to maturity (YTM) return on a bond if it is held to maturity

Z

zero-balance account an arrangement between a bank and firm to transfer sufficient funds to a disbursement account to cover the day's checks presented to the bank for payment

· INDEX ·

Note: Page numbers followed by an *f* indicate figures; those followed by *t* indicate tables.

A

acceptances
    bankers', 36*f*, 144*f*, 146, 434
    defined, 473
    in short-term financing, 473
accountants, 6
accounting principles, 359–361, 360*t*
accounts receivable financing, 468–471
    factoring, 468, 469–471, 471*t*
    pledging, 468–469, 471*t*
accounts receivable management, 439–442
    credit analysis, 439
    credit terms and collection efforts, 440–442
    credit-reporting agencies, 439–440
accounts receivable period, 421
activity ratios. *See* asset management ratios
adjustable-rate mortgages (ARMs), 16, 225
administrative inflation, 198
advance factoring, 469
advance refunding, 190
aftermarket, 287
agency
    costs, 372, 544–545
    problems, reducing, 372–374
agents, 371
aggressive financing strategy, 455
American depository receipts (ADRs), 301
amortization schedule, 224, 225*t*
amortized loans, 224
annual percentage rate (APR), 227–229
annual reports, 359
annualized rates of return, 278–279
annuities
    annual payments, determining, 223–225
    defined, 217

    future value, 217–219
    future value interest factor (FVIFA), 219
    loan amortization schedule, 224, 225*t*
    ordinary, 217–219
    periodic payments, 223–225
    present value, 220–221
    present value interest factor (PVIFA), 221
annuity due
    future value, 233–234
    interest rates for, 235–236
    present value, 234–235
    time requirements for, 235–236
appreciation, currency exchange rate, 137–138
arbitrage, 138–139
ask prices, 294
asset management, 69–70
asset management ratios, 392–394
    average collection period, 393–394
    defined, 392
    example, 395*f*
    fixed assets turnover, 393
    inventory turnover, 394
    total assets turnover, 393
assets
    balance sheet, 65–67, 362, 363–364
    capital pricing model, 336–339
    cash and balances due, 65
    current, 363, 430–438
    current versus total ratio, 419*f*
    defined, 362
    financial, 12, 13, 14, 29, 238
    financing policy and, 545
    fixed, 480
    historical returns and risks of, 327*t*, 327–328
    investment requirements, 405–406
    liquidity, 30
    loans, 66–67
    operating return on, 399

575

576 INDEX

assets (*Contd.*)
  real, 29
  securities, 65–66
  securitization, 245
  tangible/intangible mix, 547
  total, return on, 399
at-the-money options, 314
automatic stabilizers, 111
automatic transfer service (ATS) accounts, 35
average collection period, 393–394
average payment period, 391, 422

B

balance of payments
  accounts, 148–151
  defined, 148
  U.S., 149*t*
balance of trade, 148
balance sheets, 64–68, 362–365
  assets, 65–67, 362, 363–364
  commercial bank, 64*f*
  defined, 64, 362
  equation, 363
  example, 363*t*, 390*t*
  liabilities, 68, 363, 364–365
  owners' equity, 365
  ratio analysis of, 388–389
Bank Holding Company Act of 1956, 63
bank management, 68–73
  asset, 69–70
  capital, 70–72
  financial crisis (2007–09) and, 72–73
  liability, 70
  liquidity, 69–70
Bank of England (BOE), 99
Bank of Japan (BOJ), 99
bank reserves, 119*f*, 119–122
bankers' acceptances, 146
  in cash and marketable securities management, 434
  characteristics, 36*f*
  defined, 37, 146
  illustrated, 144*f*
  in international trade, 146
banking system
  check processing through, 56*f*
  defined, 55
  dual, 62
  functions, 55–56
  historical development, 57
  legislation, 54–55, 58–60
  loanable funds role, 184–185
  movement to central banking, 81–82
  overview, 53–56
  prior to Fed, 80–82
  regulation, 58–62
  weaknesses, 80–81
bankruptcy costs, 542–544
banks
  balance sheet, 64–68
  central, 81, 99
  commercial, 51, 54
  early chartered, 57
  first, U.S., 57

  functions, 55–56
  holding companies, 63–64
  investment, 54
  liquidity, 68
  liquidity and solvency trade-off, 69*f*
  merging, 461*t*
  savings, 51
  second, U.S., 57–58
  solvency, 68–69
  state, 58
  structure, 62–64
  universal, 55
barter, 29
base case, 498
bearer bonds, 241
benefit/cost ratio, 494
best-effort agreements, 283
beta, 337–339
  coefficient calculation, 348*t*
  defined, 337
  estimating, 346–349
  examples, 339*t*
  portfolio, 349
bid price determination, 517–519
  cash flow estimation, 518–519
  cash flow summary, 518*t*
  initial investment outlay, 517
  salvage value, 517
bid prices, 294
bimetallic standard, 30
blanket inventory liens, 471
blue-sky laws, 291
bond markets, 15, 248
bond valuation, 260–267
  credit risk, 264–265
  interest rate risk, 265–266
  political risk, 267
  present value determination, 260–263
  reinvestment rate risk, 266–267
  risk, 264–267
  yield to maturity calculation, 263–264
bonds
  bearer, 241
  bondholder security and, 244–246
  callable, 246
  closed-end mortgage, 245
  common elements, 241*t*
  conversion ratio, 246
  conversion value, 246
  convertible, 246
  corporate, 173*f*, 173, 199*t*, 201, 531*f*, 532*t*
  coupon rate, 250
  covenants, 242–243
  debenture, 245
  discount, 262
  Eurodollar, 248
  first mortgage, 245
  global, 248
  high-yield, 201, 244
  income from, 247–248
  investment grade, 199
  junk, 201, 244
  municipal, 172–173*f*

INDEX   577

open-end mortgage, 245
par value, 240
premium, 262–263
public offerings, 239t
putable, 246
quotation, 248f, 249f
quotes, reading, 248–250
ratings, 243t, 243–244
registered, 241
subordinate debenture, 245
Treasury, 172, 173f, 187–188
Yankee, 248
book value (BV), 512
borrowing-related cultural shift, 175
branch banking, 63
break-even analysis, 407
Bretton Woods system, 131
brokerage firms, 53
brokers, 291
budgetary deficit, 165
budgets, 405, 425–429
business angels, 291
business risk
  defined, 323, 538
  in financing strategy, 547
businesses. *See also* small business
  accounting principles, 359–361
  annual report, 359
  balance sheet, 362–365
  corporate governance, 371–374
  corporation, 357–359
  equity, 363
  ethics, 370–371
  financial goals and, 354
  financial statements, 367–368
  goal of, 368–371
  income statement, 361–362
  linking strategy and financial plans, 370
  mission statement, 353–354
  nonpublic, criterion, 370
  organization chart, 374–376, 375f
  organizational forms, 354–359, 355t
  owner's equity, 365
  proprietorship, 355–357
  shareholder wealth, 368–370
  starting, 353–354
  statement of cash flows, 365–367
buying on margin, 295–296

C

call deferment period, 246
call options, 311, 313f
call prices, 246
call risk, 246
callable bonds, 246
callable preferred stock, 253
cannibalization, 498
capacity, 439
capital
  bank management, 70–72
  corporate equity, 250–254
  cost of, 486, 522, 524–532

debt, 240–250
defined, 439
equity, 356
venture, 525
working, 363, 390, 417–449
capital account balance, 149
Capital Asset Pricing Model (CAPM), 336–339
  beta, 337–339, 346–349
  defined, 337
  security market line (SML), 347–349, 348f
capital budget projects
  cash flow estimation, 497–503, 511–519
  identifying, 480–482
  initial outlay, 511–512
  MOGS for, 481
  net present value, 480–481
  operating life, 512
  stages, 511–513
  SWOT analysis, 481
  termination, 512–513
capital budgeting
  analysis, 479–510
  defined, 480
  development stage, 482
  discounted cash flow technique conflicts, 494–495
  follow-up analysis, 483
  identification stage, 482
  implementation stage, 482–483
  internal rate of return (IRR) method, 488–491
  manager honesty, 503–505
  managerial flexibility and options, 497
  net present value (NPV) method, 485–488
  payback period, 495–496
  process, 482–485
  profitability index (PI), 494
  risk-related considerations, 505–506
  safety margin, 497
  selection stage, 482
  techniques, 485–492
  theory versus practice, 496–497
capital consumption adjustment, 169
capital management, 70–72
capital market securities, 172–173, 173f
capital markets, 14, 328–331
capital structure
  decisions, 532–533
  defined, 522
  EBIT/eps analysis, 536–538
  example, 536t, 537t
  insights from theory and practice, 542–547
  options, 523t
  reasons for choosing, 522–524
  scenario analysis, 537t
  unexpected growth effects, 535–536
  weights, 529
careers, 19–21
  business financial planning, 396
  contractual savings and real property organizations, 20
  depository financial institutions, 19
  financial management, 19
  in investments, 339–341

578 INDEX

careers (*Contd.*)
  opportunities, 20–21, 65, 121, 302, 327
  personal financial planning, 327
  securities markets and investment firms, 20–21
cash
  as bank asset, 65
  getting and keeping, 436–438
  inflows, 425–426, 426*t*
  management, 443
  minimum desired balance, 425
  monthly flows, 428*t*, 429*t*
  net monthly flows, 427*t*, 429*t*
  outflows, 426–427, 427*t*
cash and marketable securities management, 430–436. *See also* working capital
  bankers' acceptances, 434
  commercial paper, 433
  Eurodollars, 434
  federal funds, 432–433
  financial crisis and, 435–436
  municipal securities, 434
  negotiable certificates of deposit, 433
  precautionary motives, 430
  short-term investment policy statement, 434–435
  speculative motives, 430
  transactions motive, 430
  U.S. Treasury bills, 431–432
cash budgets, 425–429
  cash inflows, 425–426, 426*t*
  cash outflows, 426–427, 427*t*
  constructing, 427–428
  defined, 425
  minimum desired cash balance, 425
  monthly, 428*t*, 429*t*
  seasonal versus level production, 428–429
cash conversion cycle, 419–421
  defined, 420
  increases, 420
  length determination, 421–422
cash flow estimation, 497–499
  applications, 513–519
  approaches, 499–503
  bid price determination, 517–519
  for cost-saving project, 515–517
  example, 501–502
  from financing activities, 501
  incremental after-tax operating cash flows, 498–499, 513–514, 515–516
  initial outlay, 511–512, 513, 515, 517
  from investment activities, 501
  from operations, 499–501
  project operating life, 512
  project stages and, 511–513
  project termination, 512–513, 516–517
  for revenue expanding project, 513–515
  salvage value, 512–513, 514, 517
cash flows
  discounted technique conflicts, 494–495
  increment, 498
  irrelevant, 499
  isolating, 498–499
  patterns, 494
  project statement of, 500*t*

  relevant, 498–499
  sources, 365
  statement of, 365–367
  uses, 366
central banks, 81, 99
certificates of deposit (CDs), 36, 68, 70
chairs, Fed, 86–87
character, 439
chartists, 329
check processing, 56*f*
checkable deposit expansion, 114–118
checkable deposits, 113
checks
  clearance among Fed districts, 96–97
  clearance and collection, 95
  clearance through Fed branch banks, 97
  pre-authorized, 437
  processing method, 96*f*
  routing, 97–99
  traveler's, 147
chief financial officer (CFO), 374
clean drafts, 142
clearing float, 437
closed-end mortgage bonds, 245
coefficient of variation (CV), 322
coins, 30–32, 95
collateralized debt obligation (CDO), 72
collection efforts, 440–441
collection float, 436, 438*t*
co-maker loans, 473
combined leverage, 540
commercial banks
  balance sheet, 64*f*
  defined, 51, 54
  lines of credit, 460
  revolving credit agreements, 462–463
  for short-term financing, 460–463
  as small business credit providers, 83
commercial finance companies, 465–466
commercial letters of credit, 144, 145*f*
commercial paper
  in cash and marketable securities management, 433
  characteristics, 36*f*
  defined, 37, 466
  in financial crisis, 466
  issuance, 467
  for short-term financing, 466–468
  yield, 468
commissions, 299–300
common stock, 173, 251–252. *See also* stocks
  certificates, 250*f*
  cost of, 528
  defined, 251
  elements of, 251*t*
  groups, 252
  par value, 252
common-size financial statements, 367*f*, 367–368
compensating balance, 461
competitive bidding, 284–285
compound interest, 207
compounding
  defined, 207
  equation form, 207

frequent intervals, 226–227
in future values determination, 207–211
graph form, 210f
inflation implications, 211
conditions, 439
conservative financing strategy, 455
constant dividend growth model, 268–269
consumer credit
  APR, 227–229
  cost of, 227–230
  EAR, 227–229
  unethical lenders, 227
Consumer Credit Protection Act, 94
consumer price index (CPI), 195, 196f
contractual savings organizations, 50, 52f, 52
contribution margin, 409
controller, 374
convertible bonds, 246
convertible preferred stock, 253
corporate bonds, 173f, 173, 531f, 532t
corporate governance, 371–374
  agency problem reduction, 372–374
  principal–agent problem, 371–372
corporate savings, 168t–169
corporations
  bylaws, 358
  charter, 358
  defined, 357
  limited liability company (LLC), 358–359
  subchapter S, 358
correlation, 333
cost of capital, 525–528
  business use as, 530–532
  common equity, 527–528
  common stock, 528
  debt, 526
  defined, 486, 522
  in financial crisis, 532
  preferred stock, 526
  required rate of return and, 524–525
  retained earnings, 527–528
  weighted average, 528–532
cost-push inflation, 196
costs
  agency, 544–545
  bankruptcy, 542–544
  financing, 499
  fixed, 539–540
  opportunity, 498
  short-term financing, 473–475
  sunk, 499
cost-saving project, 515t, 515–517, 516t, 517t
cost-volume-profit analysis, 407–409
  break-even analysis, 407
  contribution margin, 409
  relationships, 408f
coupon rate, 250
credit
  analysis, 439
  consumer, cost of, 227–230
  lines of, 460–461
  policy change analysis, 442t

revolving, agreements, 462–463
terms, 440–442
trade, 440, 463–465
transfer of, 99
credit bureaus, 439
credit cards, 40
credit money, 35
credit rating, 16
credit risk, 70
  in bond valuation, 264–265
  defined, 264
  spreads, 265f
credit scores, 16–17
credit unions
  charters, 62
  defined, 51
  saving with, 59
credit-reporting agencies, 439–440
cross-sectional analysis, 389
crowding out, 112
cumulative preferred stock, 253
currency, 95, 119–120
currency exchange markets
  crossrates, 134t
  defined, 133
  risk management, 140–141
  selected, 134t
currency exchange rates
  appreciation, 137–138
  arbitrage and, 138–139
  defined, 43, 133
  depreciation, 137–138
  determination, 135f
  developments for U.S. dollar, 139–140
  direct quotation method, 133
  economic risk and, 137
  factors affecting, 135–137
  flexible, 132
  indirect quotation method, 133, 134
  interest rate parity (IRP), 137
  political risk and, 137
  purchasing power parity (PPP), 136–137
  supply and demand relationships, 135–136
current account balance, 149
current assets, 363
  defined, 363
  management of, 430–438
  total ratio versus, 419f

D

dealer system, 188
dealers, 291
debenture bonds, 245
debit cards, 36
debt
  corporate use trends, 523–524
  cost of, 526
  federal statutory, 165
  financing, 165
  long-term, 533f
  management, 112–113
  management attitude towards, 547

debt (Contd.)
  monetizing, 108
  stock market equity ratio, 524f
debt capital, 240–250
debt securities, 14
debt securities markets, 14–15
default risk premiums, 185, 198–201
  on corporate bonds, 199t, 200
  defined, 198
deficit
  budgetary, 165
  reserves, 119
  savings, 167
deficit economic unit, 26
deficit financing, 112
degree of combined leverage (DCL), 540–542
degree of financial leverage (DFL), 540
degree of operating leverage, 409–412, 540
  defined, 409
  fixed costs and, 412
  formula, 411
demand-pull inflation, 197
deposit money, 35–36
depository institutions
  cash and balances due from, 65
  defined, 50
  Fed transactions, 121
  loan to, 90
  types of, 51
Depository Institutions Deregulation and Monetary Control Act of 1980, 59–60, 89
deposits
  checkable, 113, 114–118
  contraction of, 118–119
  demand, 35
  derivative, 114
  expansion, 114–118
  primary, 114
depreciation
  basics, 384–385
  currency exchange rate, 137–138
  defined, 364
  in income statement, 361
  methods, 385
  tax shield, 502–503
derivative deposits, 114
derivative markets, 15
derivative securities, 173, 309–310
  defined, 15, 173
  existence of, 309–310
  hedge use, 310
  option contracts, 309
designated market markers (DMMs), 293, 298
deviations, 320–322
direct quotation method, 133
disbursement float, 436, 438t
discount bonds, 262
discount rate policy, 90–92
discounted cash flow techniques, 494–495
discounted loans, 462
discounting
  defined, 211
  equation form, 212

frequent intervals, 226–227
in present value determination, 211–214
distribution channel access, 482
distributions, 322t
diversification
  defined, 8–9, 332
  illustration, 334t
  risk and, 335f
  for small investor, 331
dividend growth model, 527–528
dividends, 254–257
  constant, 268
  payout ratio, 255, 534
  reinvestment plans (DRIPS), 254–255
  residual policy, 256
  share repurchases, 257
  special, 255–256
  stock, 256
  target payout policy, 255
documentary drafts, 142
domestic economic influences, 271
Dow Jones Industrial Average stocks, 300t
drafts
  bank assistance in collection, 142
  clean, 142
  defined, 141–142
  documentary, 142
  sight, 142
  time, 142
Du Pont analysis, 402–404
  defined, 403
  example, 403t
  illustrated, 404f
dual banking system, 62
dual-listed stocks, 292
due diligence, 282
Dutch auctions, 285

E

earnings before interest and taxes (EBIT), 361, 539
EBIT/eps analysis, 536–538
  defined, 536
  example, 537f
  indifference level, 536–538
  practical implications, 538
economic cycles, 170–171
economic expectations, 170
economic growth, 104–105
economic influences, 270–271
economic policy objectives, 104–106
economic risk, 137
economies of scale, 482
effective annual rate (EAR), 227–229
efficient markets, 328–331
electronic data interchange (EDI), 438, 443
electronic invoice presentment and payments system (EIPP), 445
employment, high, 105
enhancement, 498
entrepreneurial finance, 6
equipment trust certificates, 245
equity
  company, 363
  cost of, 527–528

owner's, 345
    return on, 399
equity capital, 356
equity multiplier ratio, 396–397
equity securities markets, 15
ethical behavior
    in bond rating determination, 265
    business, 370–371
    consumer credit lenders, 227
    defined, 10
    in government, 107–108
    international business, 141
    investments, 339–341
    money, 33–35
    S&L crisis, 60–61
    securities markets, 302–303
    working capital, 418
ethical standards, 341*t*
euro, 43, 132–133
Eurodollars
    bonds, 248
    defined, 434
European Central Bank (ECB), 99, 108
European Monetary Union (EMU), 108, 132
European Union (EU), 108, 132
ex ante, 324
excess reserves, 117
exchange rate risk, 267, 323
exchange rates. *See* currency exchange rates
exercise price (strike price), 310
expectations theory, 192
exporter financing, 141–144. *See also* international trade
    bank assistance in collection of drafts, 142
    sight and time drafts, 141–142
    through exporter's bank, 142–144
Export-Import Bank, 146–147
extendable notes, 246

F

factoring
    advance, 469
    defined, 468
    maturity, 469
    pledging comparison, 471*t*
    process, 469–471
    with/without recourse, 469
Fannie Mae, 17
Federal Deposit Insurance Corporation (FDIC), 61–62, 93
Federal Deposit Insurance Corporation Improvement Act of 1991 (FDICIA), 62
federal funds
    in cash and marketable securities management, 432–433
    characteristics, 36*f*
    defined, 37
    rate, 93
Federal Open Market Committee (FOMC), 85–86, 92
Federal Reserve Act, 59, 82
Federal Reserve Notes, 33, 34*f*
Federal Reserve System (Fed), 79–102
    actions after September 11, 2001 terrorist attacks, 43
    advisory committees, 86
    Board of Governors (BOG), 85
    branch banks, 85
    chair, 86–87
    components, 82
    consumer protection responsibilities, 95*f*
    defined, 82
    depository institution transactions, 121
    directors and officers, 84–85
    district banks, 84–85
    Federal Open Market Committee (FOMC), 85–86
    float, 121–122
    lending rate, 91*f*
    map illustration, 84*f*
    member banks, 82–83
    monetary policy, 87–93
    open-market operations, 120–121
    organization, 83*f*
    payments mechanism, 94–99
    regulatory responsibilities, 94
    service functions, 94–99
    structure, 82–87
    summary, 100
    supervisor responsibilities, 93–94
    transactions, 120–122
    transfer of credit, 99
    Treasury transactions, 122
Federal Savings and Loan Insurance Corporation (FSLIC), 61, 61–62
federal statutory debt, 165
fiat money, 32, 33*f*
field warehouses, 472
finance
    areas of study, 2, 3*f*
    careers, 19–21
    defined, 2, 5
    entrepreneurial, 6
    in organization chart, 374–376, 375*f*
    personal, 6
    reasons for studying, 6–7
finance firms, 51, 53
finance principles, 7–10
    defined, 7–8
    diversification of risk, 8–9
    financial markets are efficient, 9
    management versus owner objectives, 9–10
    reputation matters, 10
    risk versus return, 8
    time value of money, 8
Financial Accounting Standards Board (FASB), 359
financial assets
    defined, 29, 238
    in financial system, 12
    marketing, 13
    transferring, 14
financial calculators, 208, 212
financial crisis (2007–2009), 17–19, 72–73
    borrowing-related cultural shift, 175
    commercial paper in, 466
    cost of capital, 532
    early factors, 173–175
    effects, 18
    as perfect storm, 17, 18, 106
    short-term firm financing impact, 435–436
    U.S. dollar and, 140

financial crisis (*Contd.*)
    U.S. government response, 19
    U.S. Treasury activities, 112
    working capital and, 418
financial environment, 4–24, 5*f*
    defined, 5
    elements, 6
    valuation and, 270–271
financial institutions. *See also* banks
    careers, 19
    contractual savings organizations, 50, 52
    defined, 5
    depository, 50, 51
    examples, 2, 6
    finance firms, 51, 53
    as financial environment element, 6
    financial functions, 12*f*
    in financial system, 11–12
    operation, 3
    securities firms, 51, 53
    types, 50*f*–51
Financial Institutions Reform, Recovery, and Enforcement Act (FIRREA), 61
financial intermediation, 50
financial leverage ratios, 394–398
    defined, 394
    equity multiplier, 396–397
    example, 398*f*
    interest coverage, 397
    total debt to total assets, 394–396
financial management
    careers, 19
    defined, 2–3, 6
    as financial environment element, 6
financial managers, 6
financial markets
    capital, 4
    characteristics, 14
    debt securities, 14–15
    defined, 5
    derivative securities, 15
    efficiency, 9
    elements, 2
    equity securities, 15
    as financial environment element, 6
    financial functions, 12*f*
    in financial system, 12
    foreign exchange, 15
    information efficient, 9
    interest rate determination in, 181*f*
    money, 14
    primary, 14
    secondary, 14
    types, 14–15
financial planning
    careers, 396
    linking strategy and, 370
    long-term, 404–412
    personal, 13, 35, 165, 188, 215, 331
financial risk, 324
financial statements, 367–368
    analysis, 388
    balance sheets, 362–365, 363*t*
    common-size, 367*f*, 367–368
    income statement, 361–362
    statement of cash flow, 365–367, 366*t*
financial system
    characteristics and requirements, 11–12
    components and functions, 12*f*
    defined, 11
    elements, 2
    financial assets, 12
    financial institutions, 11–12
    financial markets, 12
    functions, 12–14
    graphic view, 11*f*
    monetary system, 11
    overview, 11–14
    policy makers, 11
financing
    accounts receivable, 468–471
    cash flow from, 501
    costs, 499
    debt, 165
    deficit, 112
    external, 407
    internally generated, 406
    international trade, 141–147
    long-term, 459
    short-term, 451–478
financing strategies. *See also* working capital
    aggressive approach, 455
    conservative approach, 455
    guidelines, 547
    illustrated, 454*f*
    maturity-matching approach, 453–454
first mortgage bonds, 245
fiscal policy, 109
fiscal policy makers, 164–165
fixed assets, 393, 480
fixed-rate mortgages, 15–16
flexible exchange rates, 132
float
    clearing, 437
    collection, 436, 438*t*
    defined, 436
    delivery, 437
    disbursement, 436, 438*t*
    Federal Reserve, 121–122
    managed, 151
floatation, 282, 289
Foreign Corrupt Practices Act (FCPA), 141
foreign exchange markets. *See* currency exchange markets
foreign securities, 301–302
foreign systems, 73
fourth market, 298
fractional reserve system, 114
full-bodied money, 31, 32
future value. *See also* time value of money
    annuity, 217–219
    annuity due, 233–234
    compounding for, 207–211
    defined, 206
    equating present value and, 214–215
    interest factor (FVIF), 209, 210*t*, 226
    interest factor of annuity (FVIFA), 219

interest rate and time period relationships, 210*f*
key, 208, 212
futures contracts, 310–311, 311*f*
futures exchanges, 310*t*

G

Garn-St. Germain Depository Institutions Act of 1982, 60
generally accepted accounting principles (GAAP), 359–361
Ginnie Mae, 17
Glass-Steagall Act of 1933, 54, 291
global bonds, 248
global depository receipts (GDRs), 301
gold standard, 130
goodwill, 364
Gordon model, 268
government
    budget, 163–164
    debt financing, 165
    ethical behavior in, 107–108
    financial crisis response, 19
    financing assistance for small business, 107
    fiscal policy, 109
    fiscal policy makers, 164–165
    fundraising, 108
    influence on economy, 108–109
    loanable funds role, 184–185
government expenditures (GE), 159
Gramm-Leach-Bliley Act of 1999, 55
gross domestic product (GDP), 40–41, 108
    calculation, 41
    components, 159–161
    defined, 40, 104
    government expenditures (GE), 159
    gross private domestic investment (GPDI), 160
    growth, 105
    net exports (NE), 160
    personal consumption expenditures (PCE), 159
    product consumption, investment, international components, 160*t*
gross private domestic investment (GPDI), 160
growth rates
    internal, 534
    planning, 533–536
    sustainable, 534–535
    unexpected effects, 535–536

H

hedge, 310
high-yield bonds, 201, 244
house brokers, 293
Humphrey-Hawkins Act, 104
hypertext markup language (HTML), 445

I

importer financing, 144–146
income
    from bonds, 247–248
    federal taxation, 382–384
    levels of, 169–170
income statements, 361–362
    defined, 361
    example, 362*t*, 391*t*
    leverage effects on, 541*t*
    project, 500*t*
    ratio analysis of, 388–389
incremental cash flows, 498
independent brokers, 293
independent projects, 480
indexes, market, 300–301
indirect quotation method, 133, 134
individual net worth, 30
industry comparative analysis, 389
inflation
    administrative, 198
    compounding and, 211
    cost-push, 196
    defined, 41, 105, 193
    demand-pull, 197
    premiums, 185, 193–198
    speculative, 197–198
    types of, 196–198
    U.S., 194–196
inflationary bias, 198
initial margin, 296, 311
initial public offerings (IPO)
    average initial returns, 288*f*
    defined, 282
    first-day returns, 290*f*
    floatation costs, 289
    number of, 290*f*
insurance companies, 52
interest
    compound, 207
    simple, 206
interest coverage ratio, 397
interest rate parity (IRP), 137
interest rate risk
    in bond valuation, 265–266
    defined, 71, 185, 266, 324
interest rates, 179–204
    annuities, 222–223
    annuity due, 235–236
    bond price relationship, 265*f*
    computing, 462
    defined, 180
    determination in financial markets, 181*f*
    levels, historical changes, 181–185
    loanable funds theory, 182–185
    market, determinants, 185–186
    nominal, 185
    risk-free, 186
    short-term, 431*f*
    solving for, 215–216, 222–223
    term structure, 190–193
internal growth rate, 534
internal rate of return (IRR), 488–492
    calculation, 489–490
    in capital budgeting, 488–491
    conflicts, 494–495
    defined, 488
    modified (MIRR), 492–494
    NPV and, 491–492
international banking, 73

584 INDEX

international finance
    conducting business in, 140–141
    development of, 130
    ethical issues, 141
International Monetary Fund (IMF), 131
international monetary system, 43–44
    defined, 130
    evolution, 130–132
international price movements, 194
international trade, 141–147
    balance, 147–151
    bankers' acceptances, 146
    exporter financing, 141–144
    Export-Import Bank, 146–147
    importer financing, 144–146
    traveler's checks, 147
    traveler's letter of credit, 147
international transaction balance, 105–106, 147–151
in-the-money options, 314
inventory
    loans, 471–472
    management, 442–443
    period, 421
    tracking, 445
    turnover ratio, 394
investment bankers (underwriters), 282–287
investment banking firms, 53, 54, 289
investment companies, 53
investment grade bonds, 199
investments
    career opportunities, 339–341
    cash flow from, 501
    defined, 6
    ethics, 339–341
    as financial environment element, 6
    savings link, 161–162
    savings transfer into, 26–27f
    in U.S., 162t

J

junk bonds, 201, 244
just-in-time (JIT) inventory management, 442

L

liabilities
    bank balance sheet, 68
    business balance sheet, 364–365
    defined, 363
    divided by total assets, 457f
liability management, 70
life insurance loans, 473
life stages, 171–172
limit orders, 294
limited branch banking, 63
limited liability companies (LLCs), 358–359
limited partners, 357
limited partnerships, 357
lines of credit, 460–461
liquidity, 30
    management, 69–70
    premium, 186
    ratios, 390, 392f

liquidity preference theory, 193
loanable funds. *See also* interest rates
    banking system role, 184–185
    demand, interest rate effects, 184
    expansion of deposits and, 184
    government role, 184–185
    international factors and, 185
    liquidity attitudes and, 184
    sources of, 182–183
    supply factors, 183–185
    theory, 182–185
    volume of savings and, 183–184
loans
    amortized, 224, 225t
    as bank asset, 66–67
    co-maker, 473
    discounted, 462
    inventory, 471–472
    life insurance, 473
    secured, 66
    secured by stocks and bonds, 472
    unsecured, 66
lockbox system, 437
long-term financial planning, 404–412
    cost-volume-profit analysis, 407–409
    degree of operating leverage, 409–412
    percentage of sales technique, 405–407
long-term financing
    external sources, 238–240
    patterns, 459f

M

M1 money supply, 37–39
M2 money supply, 39
M3 money supply, 39–40
maintenance margin, 296
managed floats, 151
management objectives, 9–10
margin
    calls, 296
    contribution, 409
    defined, 295
    initial, 296, 311
    maintenance, 296
    net profit, 398
    operating profit, 398
    price-variable cost, 539
marginal tax rate, 382
market orders, 294
market portfolio, 337
market segmentation theory, 193
market stabilization, 287
market timing hypothesis, 545–546
market value added (MVA), 369
market value ratios, 399–402
    defined, 399
    example, 401f
    P/E, 399–401
    price-to-book-value, 401
marketable debt securities, 190t, 190
marketable government securities, 187
marketable obligations, 187–188

Markets in Financial Instruments Directive (MiFID), 305
maturity factoring, 469
maturity-matching approach, 453–454
medium of exchange, 29
merchandise trade balance, 148
mission statements, 353–354
modified accelerated cost recovery system (MACRS), 384, 385
modified internal rate of return (MIRR), 492–494
   calculation process, 492
   decision rule, 494
   defined, 492
   example, 493*f*
MOGS (Mission, Objectives, Goals, and Strategies), 481
monetary base, 123
Monetary Control Act, 60
monetary policy, 87–93
   defensive activities, 88
   defined, 87
   dynamic actions, 87
   Fed discount rate, 90–92
   implementation of, 93
   open-market operations, 92–93
   reserve requirements, 88–89
monetary system
   accommodative function, 88
   defined, 11
   financial functions, 12*f*
   illustrated, 28*f*
   international, 43–44
   local, 35
   overview, 27–29
   participants, 28*f*
   summary, 44–45
monetizing the debt, 108
money
   coins, 30–32
   creation of, 12
   credit, 35
   defined, 29
   development in U.S., 30–36
   ethical issues, 33–35
   fiat, 32, 33*f*
   full-bodied, 31
   as medium of exchange, 29
   multiplier, 123
   paper currency, 32–35
   physical, 30–35
   representative full-bodied, 32, 33*f*
   as standard of value, 30
   as store of value, 29–30
   time value. *See* time value of money
   transfer of, 13
   velocity of, 40, 123
money market mutual funds (MMMFs), 39, 59
money market securities, 36*f*, 36–37
money markets, 14, 36
money supply
   changing, 113–119
   economic activity and, 40–43
   exclusions, 40
   M1, 37–39
   M2, 39

M3, 39–40
   measures, 37–40, 38*f*
mortgage banking firms, 53
mortgage bonds, 245
mortgage markets, 15, 17
mortgage-backed securities, 16, 17, 72
mortgages
   adjustable-rate (ARMs), 16, 225
   characteristics, 173*f*
   defined, 15, 172
   fixed-rate, 15–16
   prime, 17
   real loans with monthly payments, 225
   subprime, 17, 72
   types of, 15–16
multibank holding companies (MBHCs), 63
municipal bonds, 172–173, 173*f*
municipal securities, 434
mutual funds, 53
mutually exclusive projects, 480

N

NASDAQ, 292, 293, 294, 297, 298, 303
National Banking Acts, 58–59, 80
National Credit Union Administration (NCUA), 94
National Credit Union Share Insurance Fund (NCUSIF), 62
negative correlations, 333
negotiable certificates of deposit (negotiable CDs), 36*f*
   in cash and marketable securities management, 433
   defined, 36
   in liability management, 70
negotiable orders of withdrawal (NOW), 59
net exports (NE), 160
net present value (NPV), 480–481, 485–488
   calculation, 486*t*, 487
   in capital budgeting, 485–488
   conflicts, 494–495
   defined, 485–486
   discount rates relationship, 488
   IRR and, 491–492
   profile, 488
   spreadsheet functions, 487–488
net profit margin, 398
net working capital
   defined, 390, 452
   divided by total assets, 456*f*
   negative, 453*f*
   positive, 452*f*
net worth, 30
New York Stock Exchange (NYSE), 292–294
nominal interest rate, 185
noncumulative preferred stock, 253
nondebt tax shields, 542, 547
nonmarketable government securities, 189

O

odd lots, 296
offer price, 283
Office of the Comptroller of the Currency (OCC), 93–94
one-bank holding companies (OBHCs), 63
open-end mortgage bonds, 245
open-market operations, 92–93, 120–121

INDEX

operating cycle
   defined, 419
   illustrated, 420f
   length, 421–422
operating profit margin, 398
operating return on assets, 399
opportunity costs, 498
optimum debt/equity mix, 522
options, 311–312
   at-the-money, 314
   call, 311, 313f
   defined, 311
   in-the-money, 314
   out-of-the-money, 314
   payoff diagrams, 312–314, 313f
   premium, 312
   put, 311, 313f
   quotations, 312f
   stock, 372–373
   writer, 312
order bills of lading, 142, 143f
ordinary annuities
   217–219. See annuities
   defined, 217
   future value (FVA), 218
   future value interest factor (FVIFA), 219, 226
   present value (PVA), 220
organization charts, 374–376, 375f
out-of-the-money options, 314
over-the-counter (OTC) market, 297
owners' capital, 68
owners' equity, 365

P

paper currency, 32–35
par value, 240, 252
participating preferred stock, 253
partnerships, 356–357
payback period, 495–496
payoff diagrams, 312–314
pecking order hypothesis, 545
pension funds, 52
percentage of sales technique, 405–407. See also long-term financial planning
   asset investment requirements, 405–406
   example, 406t
   external financing requirements, 407
   internally generating financing, 406
personal consumption expenditures (PCE), 159
personal finance, 6
personal financial planning, 13, 35, 138, 165, 188, 215, 331
personal savings, 167t–168t
physical money, 30–35
pledging, 468–469, 471t
poison pills, 372
policy makers, 11
   economic policy objectives and, 107f
   ethical behavior and, 107–108
   in EU, 108
   fiscal, 164–165
   groups, 106–108
   principle responsibilities, 109

political risk, 137, 267
portfolios
   beta estimation, 349
   defined, 331
   diversification, 333–334
   expected return, 331–332
   market, 337
   number of investments, 334–335
   returns and risk, 331–336
   variance and standard deviation of return, 332–333
positive correlation, 333
pre-authorized checks, 437
precautionary motives, 430
preferred stock, 252–253, 526. See also stocks
premium bonds, 262–263
present value. See also time value of money
   annuity, 220–221
   annuity due, 234–235
   bond, 260–263
   defined, 206
   discounting to determine, 211–214
   equating future values and, 214–215
   interest factor (PVIF), 213, 214t
   interest factor of annuity (PVIFA), 221
   interest rate and time period relationships, 214f
   key, 208, 212
   net, 480, 485–488
   ordinary annuity (PVA), 220
price movements, international, 194
price stability, 105
price/earnings (P/E) ratio, 399–401
price-to-book-value ratio, 401
primary deposits, 114
primary markets, 14, 282–290
primary reserves, 69
prime mortgages, 17
prime rate, 66, 460
principal–agent problem, 371–372
   agency costs, 372
   agents, 371
   defined, 10, 371
   poison pills, 372
   principals, 371
principals, 371
private placement, 282
product differentiation, 482
profitability, 547
profitability index (PI), 494
profitability ratios, 398–399, 400f
profits, undistributed, 166
program trading, 297
projects. See capital budget projects; cash flow estimation
proprietorships
   defined, 355
   equity capital, 356
   limited partnership, 357
   partnership, 356–357
prospectus, 282
public debt securities, 189t, 189
public offerings, 282
purchase power risk, 324

purchasing power parity (PPP), 136–137
put options, 311, 313f
putable bonds, 246

Q

quick ratio, 391

R

radio frequency identification (RFID) tags, 445
random walk, 329
rates of return
    annualized, 278–279
    arithmetic average, 319–320
    cost of capital, 524–525
    holding period, 278
ratio analysis
    asset management, 392–394
    balance sheet, 388–389
    benefit/cost, 494
    cross-sectional, 389
    defined, 388
    Du Pont, 402–404
    financial leverage, 394–398
    income statement, 388–389
    industry comparative, 389
    market value, 399–402
    profitability, 398–399
    trend (time series), 389
    for Walgreens, 402
ratios
    asset management, 392–394
    dividend growth, 524
    financial leverage, 394–398
    liquidity, 390, 392f
    market value, 399–402
    profitability, 398–399, 400f
    quick, 391
    types of, 389–402
real assets, 29
real rate of interest, 185
recessions, 325
registered bonds, 241
registered brokers, 293
Regulation Z, 94
reinvestment rate risk, 266–267
remote capture, 438
representative full-bodied money, 32, 33f
repurchase agreements, 36f, 37
reputation, 10
reserves
    bank, 119–122
    deficit, 119
    excess, 117
    primary, 69
    required, 119
    required ratio, 117, 119
    secondary, 70
residual dividend policy, 256
Resolution Trust Corporation (RTC), 61
restricted stock, 373
retained earnings, 527–528
retractable bonds, 246

return and risk, 8
    ex ante, 324
    expected measures of, 324–326
    historical, 327t, 327–328
    portfolio, 331–336
    single financial asset, 318–322
returns
    comparison, 338f
    distribution of, 322t
    on equity, 399
    negative correlations, 333
    operating, 399
    portfolio, 331–333
    positive correlation, 333
    stock, 332f
    on total assets, 399
    Treasury bond, 332f
revenue expanding project, 513–515, 514t, 515t
revolving credit agreements, 462–463
rights offerings, 284
risk
    in bond valuation, 264–267
    business, 323, 538, 547
    call, 246
    categories example, 506t
    credit, 264–265
    default, 185, 198–201, 264
    diversification and, 8–9, 335f
    economic, 137
    examples, 336t
    exchange rate, 267, 323
    financial, 324
    interest-rate, 71, 265–266, 324
    management attitude towards, 547
    maturity, premium, 185
    political, 137, 267
    portfolio, 334–336
    purchasing power, 324
    reinvestment rate, 266–267
    short-term financing, 460
    sources, 323t, 323–324
    standard deviation as measure, 320–322
    in stock valuation, 269–270
    systematic, 336
    tax, 324
    unsystematic, 335–336
    variance as measure, 320
risk foreign exchange, 140–141
risk-adjusted discount rate (RADR), 505
risk-free rate of interest, 186
rollover risk. *See* reinvestment rate risk
round lots, 296
Rule of 72, 217

S

salvage value, 512–513, 514, 517
Sarbanes-Oxley Act of 2002 (SOX), 373–374
savings
    accumulation of, 13
    corporate, 168t–169
    creation of, 166–167

588 INDEX

savings (*Contd.*)
  deficit, 167
  defined, 166
  domestic supply of, 166
  economic cycles and, 170–171
  economic expectations and, 170
  factors affecting, 169–172
  foreign sources of, 166
  income levels and, 169–170
  investment link, 161–162
  investment of, 13
  lending, 13
  life stages and, 171–172
  major sources of, 167–169
  personal, 167*t*–168*t*
  surplus, 166
  in U.S., 162*t*
  volume of, 183–184
savings and loan associations
  charters, 62
  crisis, 60–61
  defined, 51
  ethical issues, 60
savings banks, 51
savings–investment process, 158–178
  defined, 26
  focus, 27
  illustrated, 27*f*
  indirect transfers, 26
  in U.S., 162*t*
secondary markets, 292–298
  defined, 14, 282
  mortgage, 17
secondary reserves, 70
secured loans, 66
securities
  as bank asset, 65–66
  capital market, 172–173
  corporate bond, 173*f*, 173
  corporate stock, 173*f*, 173
  cost of going public, 287–289
  derivative, 173, 309–310
  floatation, 282
  foreign, 301–302
  listing, 294
  marketable debt, 190*t*, 190
  marketable government, 187
  mortgage, 72, 172, 173*f*
  municipal, 172–173*f*, 434
  nonmarketable government, 189
  offering announcement, 286*f*
  originating, 282
  private placement, 282
  prospectus, 282
  public debt, 189*t*, 189
  public offering, 282
  risk-free, 186–190
  selling, 285–287
  trading, 292–298
  treasury bond, 172, 173*f*
  underwriting, 282, 283–285
Securities and Exchange Commission (SEC), 291

Securities Exchange Act of 1934, 291
securities firms, 51, 53
securities markets, 281–308
  careers, 20
  fourth, 298
  good, 298–299
  indexes, 300–301
  inside information and, 302–303
  over-the-counter, 297
  primary, 282–290
  role, 2
  secondary, 292–298
  structure, changes in, 303–305
  summary, 305
  third, 298
securitization, 16, 72, 245
security exchanges
  indexes, 299
  NASDAQ, 292, 293, 294, 297–298, 303
  NYSE, 292–294, 298
  organized, 292
security market line (SML), 347–349, 348*f*
security transactions, 294–298
  ask prices, 294
  bid prices, 294
  buying on margin, 295–296
  commissions, 299–300
  limit orders, 294
  market orders, 294
  odd lot, 296
  program trading, 297
  record keeping, 296–297
  round lot, 296
  short sales, 295
  spread, 294
  stop-loss orders, 294–295
semistrong-form efficient markets, 329
settlement price, 311
shareholder wealth, 368–370
shelf registration, 284
short sales, 295
short-term financing, 451–478. *See also* working capital
  accounts receivable, 468–471
  advantages, 459
  aggressive approach, 455
  commercial bank lending for, 460–463
  commercial finance companies for, 465–466
  commercial paper for, 466–468
  conservative approach, 455
  cost of, 473–475
  current/fixed asset mix and, 456
  cyclical variations and, 458
  factors affecting, 456–460
  firm size/age and, 457
  growth/profitability and, 457
  inventory loans, 471
  maturity-matching approach, 453–454
  operating characteristics and, 456–458
  patterns, 459*f*
  providers, 460–468
  risk, 460
  sales trends and, 458

seasonal variation and, 458
secured by stocks/bonds, 472
trade credit from suppliers for, 463–465
short-term investment policy statements, 434–435, 435t
sight drafts, 142
simple interest, 206
sinking fund payments, 397
sinking funds, 246–247
Small Business Administration (SBA), 7, 463
small businesses
   bank financing for, 464
   business angels, 291
   commercial banks as credit providers, 83
   credit types used by, 54
   family business, 183, 356
   finding foreign customers, 133
   government financing assistance for, 107
   importance in economy, 7
   life cycle patterns, 163
   rates of return calculation, 209
   reasons for failure, 402
   starting, 29
   start-up financing sources, 242
   success habits, 354
   venture capital as financing source, 525
   working capital management, 431
special dividends, 255–256
Special Drawing Rights (SDRs), 113, 131
speculative inflation, 197–198
spot market, 309
spreads, 283, 294
spreadsheet programs, 208–209, 213, 221
standard deviation, 320–322
   defined, 320
   portfolio return, 332–333
standard of value, 30
statement of cash flows, 365–367, 366t
statewide branch banking, 63
static trade-off hypothesis, 543f, 543
stock options, 372–373
stock valuation, 267–270
   with constant dividend growth rates, 268–269
   with constant dividends, 268
   determination principle, 267
   risk in, 269–270
stocks
   certificates, 250f–251
   common, 173, 250f, 251–252, 528
   corporate, 173
   dividends, 256
   Dow Jones Industrial Average, 300t
   dual-listed, 292
   net percentage of financing from, 240f
   preferred, 252–253, 526
   public offerings, 239t
   quotes, reading, 253–254
   restricted, 373
   share repurchases, 257
   splits, 257
   street name, 295
stop-loss orders, 294–295
store of value, 29–30

strong-form efficient markets, 329
subordinate debenture bonds, 245
subprime mortgages, 17, 72
sunk costs, 499
Supplemental Liquidity Providers (SLPs), 293
supply and demand, 135–136, 180
surplus economic unit, 26
sustainable growth rate, 524–525
SWOT analysis, 481
syndicates, 287
systematic risk, 336

T

tax policy, 112
tax rates, 382
tax risk, 324
tax shields
   depreciation, 502–503
   nondebt, 542, 547
tax status, 189
term structure
   defined, 190
   interest rates, 190–193
   theories, 192–193
   Treasury securities, 191t
terminal value, 492
third market, 298
thrift institutions, 51, 58
time drafts, 142
time periods
   annuities, 223
   annuity due problems, 235–236
   solving for, 216–217, 223
time value of money, 205–232
   concepts, 206–207
   defined, 8, 206
   future value, 206, 207–211, 217–219
   present value, 206, 211–214, 220–221
tombstones, 286f, 286
total assets turnover ratio, 393
total debt to total assets ratio, 394–396
trade credit, 463–465
   cost, 464–465
   defined, 440
   terms, 464
trade discounts, 464
transactions motive, 430
transfer payments, 111
traveler's checks, 147
traveler's letter of credit, 147
treasurer, 374
Treasury bills, 187
   in cash and marketable securities management, 431–432
   characteristics, 36f
   defined, 36, 187
   issuance, 187
Treasury bonds, 187–188
   characteristics, 173f
   defined, 172, 187
Treasury Inflation Protected Securities (TIPS), 247
Treasury notes, 187
trend (time series) analysis, 389

trust indenture, 242
trust receipts, 146, 471
trustees, 242

U

underpricing, 287
underwriting, 283–285
    agreement, 283
    best-effort agreement, 283
    competitive bidding, 284–285
    diagram, 283f
    rights offerings, 284
    shelf registration, 284
undistributed profits, 166
unethical behavior, 10
unit banking, 63
U.S. dollar, 30
    exchange, 15
    financial crisis and, 140
    value, 139f
U.S. Travel Act, 141
U.S. Treasury
    cash balance management, 109–110
    crisis-related activities, 112
    Fed transactions, 122
    policy instruments, 109–112
    receipts and outlays, 110
    tax and loan accounts, 110
universal banks, 55
unsecured loans, 66
unsystematic risk, 335–336
utilization ratios. *See* asset management ratios

V

valuation
    of bonds, 260–267
    domestic economic influences, 271
    financial environment and, 270–271
    global economic influences, 270
    industry/competition and, 271
    principles, 258–260
    of stocks, 267–270
variance
    computing, 320t
    defined, 320
    finding, 325
    portfolio return, 332–333
velocity of money, 40, 123
venture capital, 525

W

warehouse receipts, 471
weak-form efficient markets, 329–330
weighted average cost of capital (WACC), 528–532
    business use of cost of capital, 530–532
    capital structure weights, 529
    debt ratio versus, 543f
    defined, 528
    target weights measurement, 529–530
working capital
    accounts receivable, 439–442
    cash budgets, 425–429
    current assets, 430–438
    defined, 363, 452
    ethical issues, 418
    finance strategies, 452–455
    financial crisis and, 418
    inventory, 442–443
    managing, 417–449
    net, 390, 452–453
    requirements, 422–424
    for small businesses, 431
    technology and, 443–445
World Bank, 131

X

XML, 443–445

Y

Yankee bonds, 248
yield curves
    defined, 190
    examples, 432f
    relationship between economy, 191–192
    for Treasury securities, 192f
yield to maturity (YTM), 263–264

Z

zero-balance accounts, 437